LITURGICAL SERVICES

OF THE

REIGN OF QUEEN ELIZABETH.

The Parker Society.

Instituted A.D. M.DCCC.XL.

For the Publication of the Works of the Fathers and Early Writers of the Reformed English Church.

LITURGICAL SERVICES.

LITURGIES

AND

OCCASIONAL FORMS OF PRAYER

SET FORTH IN THE

REIGN OF QUEEN ELIZABETH.

EDITED FOR

The Parker Society,

BY THE

REV. WILLIAM KEATINGE CLAY, B.D.,
PERPETUAL CURATE OF THE HOLY TRINITY ELY.

Wipf & Stock
PUBLISHERS
Eugene, Oregon

Wipf and Stock Publishers
199 West 8th Avenue, Suite 3
Eugene, Oregon 97401

Liturgical Services, Liturgies and Occasional forms of Prayer set forth in the Reign of Queen Elizabeth
By Clay, William K
ISBN: 1-59244-552-7
Publication date 2/13/2004
Previously published by Cambridge, 1847

CONTENTS.

	PAGE
THE Preface	ix
The Litany and Suffrages. 1558.	1
The Litany used in the Queen's Majesty's Chapel. 1559.	9
The Book of Common Prayer and Administration of the Sacraments, and other Rites and Ceremonies in the Church of England. 1559.	23
Godly Prayers	246
Prayers	258
The Form and Manner of making and consecrating Bishops, Priests, and Deacons. 1559	272
Liber Precum Publicarum, seu ministerii Ecclesiasticæ administrationis Sacramentorum, aliorumque rituum et cæremoniarum in Ecclesia Anglicana. 1560	299
In Commendationibus Benefactorum	432
Celebratio Cœnæ Domini in Funebribus	433
The New Calendar. 1561	435
A List of Occasional Forms of Prayer and Services	457
A short Form and Order for seasonable weather, and good success of the Common affairs of the Realm. 1560	475
A Prayer for the present estate in the churches. 1562	476
A Form, and also an Order of public fast, to be used during this time of mortality, and other afflictions, wherewith the Realm at this present is visited. 1563	478
An Homily appointed to be read in the time of sickness	491
A Form of Meditation very meet to be daily used of householders in this dangerous and contagious time. 1563	503
Thanksgiving to God for withdrawing and ceasing the Plague. 1563	508
A short Form of Thanksgiving to God for ceasing the contagious sickness of the Plague. 1564	513
A Form to excite all godly people to pray unto God for the delivery of those Christians, that are now invaded by the Turk. 1565	519
A short Form of Thanksgiving to God for the delivery of the Isle of Malta, &c. 1565	524

[LITURG. QU. ELIZ.]

CONTENTS.

	PAGE
A Form to excite and stir all godly people to pray unto God for the preservation of those Christians and their Countries, that are now invaded by the Turk in Hungary, or elsewhere. 1566.	527
The Prayer on account of the rising in the North. 1569	536
A Thanksgiving for the suppression of the last rebellion. 1570	538
A Form of Common Prayer necessary for the present time and state. 1572	540
A Form of Prayer with Thanksgiving, to be used every year, the 17th of November, being the day of the Queen's Majesty's entry to her reign. 1576	548
Metrical Anthems. 1578	558
The Order of Prayer to avert and turn God's wrath from us threatened by the late terrible Earthquake. 1580	562
The Report of the Earthquake	567
A godly Admonition for the time present	567
A Prayer for the estate of Christ's Church. 1580	576
A Prayer for all Kings, Princes, Countries, and People, which do profess the Gospel: And especially for our Sovereign Lady Queen Elizabeth. 1585	580
A Prayer and Thanksgiving for the Queen. 1585	581
A Prayer used in the Parliament only. 1585	582
An Order of Prayer and Thanksgiving for the preservation of the Queen's Majesty's life and safety. 1585	583
A Prayer of Thanksgiving for the deliverance of her Majesty from the murderous intention of Dr Parry. 1585	587
An Order for public Prayers convenient for this present time. 1586	591
An Order of Prayer and Thanksgiving for the preservation of her Majesty and the Realm from the traitorous and bloody practices of the Pope, and his adherents. 1586	595
A Prayer and Thanksgiving fit for this present. 1587	604
A Form of Prayer necessary for the present time and state. 1588.	608
A Psalm and Collect of Thanksgiving not unmeet for this present time. 1588	619
A godly Prayer for the preservation of the Queen's Majesty, and for her Armies both by sea and land. 1588	624
A Form of Prayer thought fit to be daily used in the English army in France. 1589	626
A Form of Prayer necessary for the present time and state. 1590.	632
Certain Prayers for the good success of the French King. 1590	647
A Prayer for the prosperity of the French King and his Nobility. 1590	652

CONTENTS.

	PAGE
An Order for Prayer and Thanksgiving for the safety and preservation of her Majesty and this Realm. 1594	654
A Prayer for the prosperous success of her Majesty's Forces and Navy. 1596	665
A Prayer made by the Queen at the departure of the fleet. 1596	666
A Prayer of Thanksgiving and for continuance of good success to her Majesty's Forces. 1596	668
Certain Prayers for the prosperous success of her Majesty's Forces and Navy. 1597	671
An Order for Prayer and Thanksgiving for the safety and preservation of her Majesty and this Realm. 1598	679
Certain Prayers fit for the time. 1601	689

PREFACE.

THE present volume comprises two Litanies, the English Prayer Book of 1559, the Godly Prayers, the Ordinal of 1559, the Latin Prayer Book of 1560, the New Calendar of 1561, and many Occasional Forms of Prayer set forth, chiefly by public authority, in the latter portion of the sixteenth century.

1. The peculiarity of the first Litany is its having Elizabeth's name, as queen, conjointly with the entreaty for deliverance 'from the tyranny of the bishop of Rome, and all his detestable enormities.' See pp. 4, 12, 70. It was apparently an unauthorised publication of the Protestants, solicitous, after the death of Mary, to recover (if possible) their lost ground. For the petition 'Pitifully behold the dolour[1] of our hart,' and the collects which are appended, prove that the Litany was not taken, as on any other supposition it undoubtedly would have been taken, from either of Edward's Prayer Books; but, most probably, with due omissions, from his Primer of 1547, or from Henry's Primer of 1545. The following passage out of the Proclamation, prefixed in the king's name to the Order of the Communion, shews a similar desire of anticipating public measures respecting religion to have existed in Edward's time :—' Whiche thing wee (by the help of God) mooste ernestly entende to bryng to effecte : Willyng all our louing subiectes in the meanetyme, to stay and quyet them selfes wyth this our direction, as men content to followe aucthoritie (accordyng to the bounden duety of subiectes) and not enterprisyng to roune afore, and so by their rashenes become the greatest hynderers of such thynges, as they more arrogantly then godly wolde seme (by their awne privat aucthoritie) mooste hotly to set forwarde.'

---

[1] The Ordinal of March, 1549 [1550—Original Letters, p. 81], is the only one of our Formularies, wherein we discover this expression; which, after all, is nothing more than a literal translation of the ancient Latin. See p. 343.

The University library, Cambridge (A. 17. 30), possesses another copy of this Litany, resembling the one here reprinted in every minute particular, but not in having the petition against 'the bishop of Rome,' which is its important feature. They constitute, then, two editions of the same publication; and as both evidently preceded 'The Letanye vsed in the Quenes Maiesties Chappel,' they must be referred to the very commencement of Elizabeth's reign. Each copy is in small octavo, and collates A iv.: though perfect, however, it has neither title-page nor colophon. Monumenta Ritualia, Vol. II. p. 98, note 74.

2. Instead of interfering in religious matters, Elizabeth wished quietly to wait for the decision of a parliament thereupon; and this, from no lukewarmness[1], surely, about the progress of the reformed doctrines, which, early in 1559, she is described by Cook and Jewel as most zealously and openly favouring; but rather, on the contrary, through her intense fear of allowing innovations. There was also an additional reason, why she exhibited so much reluctance to act without the sanction of the law, namely, 'lest the matter should seem to have been accomplished, not so much by the judgment of discreet men, as in compliance with the impulse of a furious multitude.' Still, how cautious and prudent soever she was herself, she could not infuse the same feeling into either division of her people. 'Now did both the Evangelics and the Papalins bestir themselves for their Parties.' Strype's Annals, Vol. I. p. 41. Nor was this conduct very unnatural, inasmuch as each, of course, drew omens of success, and therefore arguments for boldness, from the continued silence of the queen. Zurich Letters, Second Edition, pp. 16, 19, 22, 29.

At length, either really (as the document intimated) to put a stop to the internal dissensions of the Protestant party, 'some declaring for Geneva, and some for Frankfort' (ibid. p. 17), or covertly to discourage and cripple the Papists, whose ministers were much more numerous, on December

---

[1] Nares, indeed, in his Memoirs of Burleigh (Vol. II. p. 43), declares, that her opinions were 'at first liable to *some* doubts;' and Ranke (History of the Popes, Book III. chap. 5,) draws the same unwarranted conclusion from the fact of her having caused her accession to be notified to the reigning Pope.

the 27th Elizabeth sent out a proclamation[2], addressed to the lord mayor of London, condemning 'unfruteful dispute in matters of religion.' Henceforth, and until the meeting of parliament, men were solely 'to gyve audience to the gospels and epistels, commonly called the gospel and epistel of the day, and to the ten commaundments, [but apart from the responses—see pp. 19, 20,] in the vulgar tongue, without exposition or addition of any maner sense or meaning to be applyed or added : or to use any other maner publick prayer, rite, or ceremony in the church, but that which is already used, and by law receaved : or the common letany used at this present in her majesty's own chappel : and the Lord's prayer, and the crede in English.' Ibid. p. 16, note 4. Thus, notwithstanding the prohibition against preaching, a concession was made in favour of both religious persuasions. The Roman catholics were still to enjoy, for a limited period, their breviaries, and the celebration of their mass with all its rites, the elevation of the host only excepted (Burnet, Vol. II. p. 378); whilst to the Protestants, 'who could not yet get the Churches,' was granted the privilege of having the public worship partly carried on in their own language. Collier, Vol. II. p. 411. And yet the Protestants, at least, were not entirely debarred from preaching. In open private houses they might, by connivance of the magistrates, exercise their gifts; and during Lent they were admitted three times a week to preach even before the court. Moreover, some of them, more zealous than the rest, did not hesitate, in defiance of the proclamation, to preach 'the gospel in certain parish-churches.' Zurich Letters, pp. 21, 57, 58. Others, again, went so far as to introduce into their churches the Prayer Book, that, we may presume, of 1552, the last edition which could then be extant. For Pilkington (p. 626.) asks in 1563,—' Did not many in the university, and abroad in the realm, use this service openly and commonly in their churches, afore it was received or enacted by parliament?'

Simultaneously with the above proclamation, (and perhaps earlier,) must also have appeared copies of the second Litany in this volume; since we learn from Fuller (Book IX. p. 51),

---

[2] Edward VI. under circumstances in every respect similar, had done the same thing on the 23rd of September, 1548. Wilkins' Concilia, Vol. IV. p. 30.

that it began to be used on Sunday the first[1] of January, 1559, and he calls it 'the best *new yeers gift* that ever was bestowed on *England*.' Who arranged it, we know not; yet we need scarcely doubt of their being the same persons that were employed about the Prayer Book, a commission having been issued in December, 1558, for its revisal. Strype's Annals, Vol. I. p. 52. Cardwell's History of Conferences, pp. 43—48. Besides the copy of the Litany used for the present publication, another exists in the library of Emmanuel College, Cambridge. Though bearing the date 1559, both are early editions, this date being according to the modern method of beginning the year in January, as Jugge alone is the printer, and, from February the 7th, he had Cawode for his partner. Herbert's Ames, p. 713.

3. The parliament met for business on the 25th of January, 1559, but April the 28th arrived ere the act of uniformity passed both houses. Cardwell, pp. 24, 30. By this act the Prayer Book, as a second time revised, was ordered to be taken again into regular use only 'from and after the feaste of the Natiuitie of sainct John Baptist,' whereas the queen, through the greatness of her zeal, caused it to be read in her chapel on Sunday the 12th of May, the very first Sunday after the dissolution of the parliament; and on the following Wednesday it was also read before 'a very august Assembly of the Court' at St Paul's cathedral. Strype's Grindal, p. 24. Zurich Letters, pp. 37, 38. The whole body of the clergy, it is well known, did not display equal zeal in the cause (see Strype's Annals, Vol. I. pp. 136, 137); nor, from the strength of their popish prepossessions, was it in any manner to be expected of them generally.

Few of the earlier Prayer Books of Elizabeth still remain in existence; and, notwithstanding the length of her reign, or, perhaps, in consequence of it, those put forth in later years are not very common. This may be deemed surprising; but it is much more surprising, that we know of no copy, natural though it was for such copies to be printed, answering in all points to the Book mentioned in the act. For it is there

---

[1] Elizabeth had herself openly made alterations in the religious services on the previous Christmas day. Ellis's Letters, Second Series, Vol. II. p. 262. And, at most, two days subsequently this Litany was read before her.

said to be 'the booke aucthorised by Parliament in the .v. and sixt yere of the raygne of king Edward the sixt, with one alteracion, or addition of certayn Lessons to be vsed on euery Sonday[2] in the yere, and the fourme of the Letanie altered and corrected, and two sentences only added in the deliuery of the Sacrament to the communicantes, and none other, or otherwyse.' To this description the copy, (believed to be the only one of its kind,) from which the present reprint has been made, comes nearest, a copy varying in another, and by no means an unimportant, point from its predecessor of 1552, as can be seen by comparing the second rubric on p. 53 in both editions. Cardwell, pp. 21, 36. It may be thought, too, to vary by not containing the protestation respecting kneeling at the reception of the elements, commanded, in October, 1552, to be placed at the end of the Communion service. That protestation, however, having been introduced by an express order of the privy council, nearly seven months subsequent to the date of the second act of uniformity, would seem rather to have been passed by unnoticed, as no integral part of Edward's Book, than intentionally omitted. But, though passed by, it lay neither forgotten nor neglected. Bishops Grindal and Horn, when writing, in 1567, to Bullinger and Gualter, assure them, that it continued to be 'most diligently declared, published, and impressed upon the people.' Zurich Letters, p. 277.

Of the next series of Prayer Books printed in 1559, (in folio, of course, the size exclusively designed for the public ministrations of the clergy,) there are four copies by Grafton extant, in the Bodleian, the library of Corpus Christi College, Oxford, the British Museum, and the University library, Cambridge. The British Museum, the Minster library, York, the Rev. W. Maskell, and the Rev. J. Mendham, have likewise copies by Jugge and Cawode[3], which may, possibly, all

---

[2] To twenty-four holidays, which in 1549 had collects, epistles, and gospels, and seven of them second lessons, proper first lessons, both for morning and evening, were now assigned: also, to two, a first lesson in the evening; and to one, a first lesson in the morning. Holidays, therefore, seem included by the act under the head of Sundays, whilst in the Prayer Book the reverse generally occurs.

[3] A copy of a very small size by the same printers, once the property of the duke of Sussex, is at present possessed by the earl of Ashburnham.

belong to this same year 1559; still they can scarcely be all of the same impression, notwithstanding their agreement in one very peculiar reading. See p. 56, note 2. This second series has been usually considered hitherto to constitute the first[1] and only edition of Elizabeth's revised Book; which opinion, moreover, appeared to derive confirmation from a list of differences between Edward's of 1552 and her own, drawn up by no less a personage than an archbishop of Canterbury, and given at length in Strype's Annals, Vol. I. p. 84. It is true, one error exists in the historian's account of this document, since he assigns to Whitgift, what the original (Bibl. Lans. 120. art. 4), which from his reference he surely had before him, assigns distinctly to Parker. Nevertheless, the weight of his name, whichever dignitary it was, cannot rightly be adduced in support of the common notion, inasmuch as he meant merely to point out the then state of the Prayer Book, without at all going into the question respecting the gradations whereby it arrived at that state, even did they at the time occur to him.

All the books now under consideration go yet farther from the act, than Mr Maskell's first-mentioned Jugge and Cawode; and, as in the case of the rubric about vestments, with that enjoining kneeling at the reception of the elements (see Strype's Annals, Vol. I. Appendix, pp. 37, 39), as also, in 1552, in the case of the protestation before alluded to, on the sole authority, no doubt, of the crown, or its advisers. The collects at the end of the Litany, wherein lie the chief variations, will be found in due course, printed as a note (see pp. 76, 77.) from the Cambridge Grafton, so that a comparison can be easily instituted. The collects belonging to the Litany used in the queen's chapel must similarly be examined, they being exactly the same, and placed in the same order, as the collects given in this second edition of Elizabeth's Prayer Book, in spite of their having been so arranged, and printed, before her act of uniformity was introduced into parliament, or, it may be, drawn up. The copies of the later series accurately correspond with one another in every

---

[1] In 1844 Mr Pickering reprinted Grafton's Book of 1559, and described it as 'Commonly called the first Book of queen Elizabeth.' The copies by Grafton did, however, most probably, precede the *later* copies of the same year by Jugge and Cawode.

main feature, but have nevertheless their discrepancies, sufficient to shew that, as Grafton did not follow Jugge and Cawode, nor, on the other hand, Jugge and Cawode follow him, so neither did he rigorously follow even himself. For the four existing copies printed by him, and upon which most attention has been bestowed, can be proved on a slight inspection, particularly, of the Calendar, not all to belong to the same impression: wherefore, had it been esteemed necessary, a list of various readings, which are remarkable neither for number nor importance, might have been exhibited in the notes.

The text of Elizabeth's Prayer Book, however, though at length apparently settled, was not so in reality. First, it again underwent alteration by the authorised (Strype's Whitgift, Appendix, p. 80.) substitution of the New Calendar; then, by a change of lessons (typographical errors perpetuated,) for the evenings on the fifth Sunday after Trinity, St. James's Day, and the 21st of May; also, by a modification of the collect for St Mark's Day; and, lastly, by means of some inconsiderable verbal additions, which, taken from a copy dated 1596, are printed, where requisite, at the foot of each page, yet whose introduction into the Prayer Book was certainly no later than 1572.

Besides the authority of the church and the crown, and of those persons, who may be presumed to have acted under their influence, there was equally exercised upon the Prayer Book[2], so far as they could make it go, the authority of the Puritans. The changes also, which they originated, consisting both in what was omitted and in what was substituted, were of serious moment, interfering materially (the doctrine alone being left untouched) with our church's established rites and regulations. The endeavours of this party thus to further their own views commenced somewhere about 1578; at least, that is the earliest year in which we find their innovations, in relation to the public services, duly matured and formally promulgated. Their Prayer Book of the above date varies from the authorised one in the following particulars. It commences with the Table of Proper Lessons, *For morning, For euening,* being put in the place of *Mattens,*

[2] That huge volume off ceremonies. Troubles at Frankfort, p. xli. Filled with many absurdities and silly superfluities. Zurich Letters, p. 270.

Euensong :—*Minister* (of the word and sacraments) is printed throughout for *Priest*, which designation the Puritans banished, as Aaronic, and connected with rites suggesting the idea of a Saviour yet to come; possibly, also, on the contrary, that they might not seem in any way to countenance the Romish doctrine of the sacrament of the Lord's supper being a propitiatory sacrifice:—from the Communion service the first four rubrics are left out; but then this may have arisen from a different cause than a wish to suppress them, inasmuch as the reader is expressly referred to *the great booke of Common prayer*. The private celebration of the sacraments was an object of intense dislike to the Puritans, who thought, indeed, that a sermon ought in either case to precede, according to the direction in Knox's Book of Common Order. Hence came, therefore, the phrase *great number*, instead of *good number*, in the second rubric at the end of the Communion service;—the omission, in the service for Public Baptism, of the introductory rubric, which concludes with allowing children, 'if necessity so require,' being at all times baptized at home; and of *Public* in the heading of each page:—hence came, too, the omission of the whole service for Private Baptism[1], with the retention of only one rubric, the third, in the Communion of the Sick. No notice is taken of the service for Confirmation (see Troubles at Frankfort, p. xxxii.), nor, consequently, of the rubrics pertaining to it, namely, that after Public Baptism; the Address preceding, as the rubrics following, the Catechism; and the latter portion of those subjoined to Confirmation, the former portion, which is allowed to remain, being transferred to the end of the Catechism:—the explanatory rubric, introducing the Catechism, is enlarged, by adding a part of the rubric, which with us terminates the service; still, though Confirmation is there alluded to, it is not said to whom the child must be brought for that purpose. The service for the Churching of Women will likewise be sought for in vain[2], since (ibid. p. xxxiiii.) it

---

[1] '*The sacraments are not ordained of God to be used in private corners, as charms or sorceries, but left to the congregation, and necessarily annexed to God's word as seals of the same.*' Knox's Book of Common Order. Original Letters, p. 123.

[2] Nor is it, any more than the Commination service, in Herman's *Simplex ac Pia Deliberatio.*

'is not only in all things almoste common withe the Papistes, but also with the Jewes, bycause they are commaunded in stede off a lambe or doue to offre monie.' See Zurich Letters, pp. 272, 417, 448. In addition to the above alterations, the Puritans compiled a Calendar of their own: this, however, they intended rather as an accessory to that of the church, than as a substitute for it, placing the section applicable to each month at the bottom of its appropriate page. This Calendar, which had been printed in 1576, and occurs again in 1583, (Lewis's History of Translations of the Bible, pp. 265, 272,) is very curious, and on many accounts worthy of attention.

The Prayer Book, thus abridged and modified by the Puritans, did not long continue as just described, in consequence, probably, of no uniform practice prevailing among the party. At length, after several changes, it was brought into a form much more nearly resembling the standard copy. For in 1589 we find the rubric at the end of Public Baptism, the service for Private Baptism, the service for the Churching of Women, and the Address before the Catechism, restored to their due places. In both the services thus restored the word *Priest* remained unchanged, which may perhaps be regarded as a silent, but intelligible, sign, that the use of the services themselves was meant to be discouraged.

Besides the two descriptions of Prayer Books above mentioned, there was also a later one sent out on the part of the Puritans. This edition is connected, as it appears, with the reign of Elizabeth's successor[3], rather than with the reign of Elizabeth herself, and differs from the authorised Book merely in the putting of *For Morning, For Euening*, and *Minister*, where previously were *Mattens, Euensong*, and *Priest*, the last word still being unaltered in the services for Private Baptism and the Churching of Women. Besides, in this shape we may suppose, that this Prayer Book continued to be printed until the year 1616, that is, as long as the Geneva version of the Bible itself, to which every scriptural quotation and reference had from the first been uniformly

---

[3] The others seem scarcely to have been known to L'Estrange, who, commenting on the rubric before the Absolution in the Morning service, mentions (Alliance of Divine Offices, p. 75.) ' the word *Priest* changed into *Minister* both here, and in divers other places by the Reformers under K. James.'

adjusted. Not that our Prayer Book ceased to be tampered with so early, though no systematic plan was any longer pursued. During the next five and twenty years we find copies of a small size, (and there may be others,) in which *Minister* very often stands for *Priest*, and, occasionally, wherein they are alternated in a most extraordinary manner.

What has just been said relative to all these Puritan modifications of the Prayer Book is very remarkable, and only the more so, from the circumstance of their being invariably printed, no doubt, as part of an exclusive privilege, by the same individuals, who possessed the monopoly of printing the authorised Prayer Book. Thus, a copy of the latter, dated 1596, by the Deputies of Christopher Barker, was collated, for the purpose both of proving, that the Service Book established by competent authority did not suffer from such tamperings, and to represent its exact condition towards the close of Elizabeth's reign.

The Prayer Books put forth with the corrections of the Puritans (for we cannot imagine them to have proceeded from the printer) were not ostensibly intended for public and general use in church, where, indeed, they could not be used without severe penalties being incurred; nevertheless, we can scarcely affirm, even from their size, that less than this was aimed at. They were rarely independent[1] publications. Just as some editions of the Bishops' Bible were accompanied by the unadulterated Prayer Book, so did these mostly accompany the Geneva Bible: moreover, as a natural consequence, they then gave only the first few words of the epistles and gospels. It is singular, however, that the folio edition of the Geneva Bible of 1578, like the folio editions of the Bishops' Bible of 1568 (the first edition) and 1572, has two Psalters in parallel columns—*The translation according to the Ebrewe;* and— *The translation vsed in common prayer.* Now the latter translation being duly divided into *Morning prayer,* and

---

[1] In 1585 Barker printed a small *independent* Prayer Book, seemingly, for the Puritans, though their Book of 1578 did not form its basis, nor were the epistles and gospels, which are given in full, extracted from the Geneva version. It has *Annunciation of Marie* (see p. 438): *Priest* is a few times changed into *Minister:* many rubrics are entirely omitted, and others curtailed or strangely altered: also, the services for Private Baptism and Confirmation are wanting.

Euening prayer, presents very much the aspect of a regular provision for the public service, had circumstances been favourable to the design; and therefore seems to impart the same character to the Prayer Book at the beginning of the volume, especially when we take into consideration the nature of its contents. That the Puritans did not conduct their ministrations strictly after the authorised Book, is evident from Neal's History of the Puritans, Vol. I. p. 312, and Strype's Whitgift, pp. 125, 140, particularly from the archbishop's Articles of May, 1584, which are given in the Appendix, p. 49: evident, too, is it (ibid. p. 116), that the Bishops' Bible was not the only Bible read in the church[2].

4. There are two series of prayers, which generally go under the title of Godly Prayers: those, which, commencing with Whitchurche's quarto Prayer Book of 1552, are expressly so styled; and those, which, headed 'Prayers' only, were chiefly appended from the first to Sternhold and Hopkins's Metrical Version of the Psalms, or to the early Geneva editions of parts of that Version. As regards the reign of Elizabeth, Strype (Parker, p. 84.) perceived the first series added to a quarto Prayer Book of 1560 by Jugge and Cawode: the small copy of 1559, now in the library of lord Ashburnham, also has it. The prayers of the second series, on the contrary, were not printed so early in the same volume with our church services; and, when at length this did take place, the different impressions of the Prayer Book had only a greater or less number of either series, no copy possessing one of them entire.

Whether the first series was at any time held to be an integral part of our Prayer Book, is a point which fairly admits of doubt; as well, because, neither by themselves,

[2] It is impossible to do more than refer in a note to that Book, altered and abridged from Calvin's Form of Common Prayer, which, during the primacy of Whitgift, the more violent Puritans under Cartwright and Travers vainly endeavoured to induce the parliament to substitute in the place of the Common Prayer Book of our church. Bancroft's Dangerous Positions, p. 68. Bancroft's Survey, p. 66. Strype's Whitgift, pp. 177, 247, 256. Copies of this 'newe forme of common praier' prescribed for England are extant, without a date, printed at London by Robert Waldegrave; whilst others, in consequence of the Star-Chamber's order of June the 23rd, 1585, restricting printing, came out in 1586, 1587, 1594, &c. at Middleburgh, where was a company of English merchants, to whom Cartwright had been sometime minister. Neal, Vol. I. p. 310.

nor afterwards, (on being partially mixed up with the second series,) were they placed, until late in Elizabeth's reign, any where but in immediate connexion with the Psalter, or the Metrical Version annexed to it; as because several years elapsed, before they even appeared at all in the folio copies. Perhaps, being designed solely for the people's use in private, the printer, following up what had already occurred with the Primers, both Latin and English, first subjoined them by the permission, or secret direction, rather than by the formal command, of the heads of our church; and then they were continued, omitted, restored, and added to, as a mere matter of course[1]. The second series manifestly could have no public authority, composed as it principally was by the Marian exiles abroad, and extracted both out of Knox's Book of Common Order, and from the end of such editions of the Metrical Psalms, as the Puritans published at Geneva. Nor need we hesitate to allow this, when we observe, that even *The Confession of a Christian Faith*, as it is in Waldegrave's book, where it is entitled 'A Confession of the Fayth of the Churches of England,' and which originally belonged to the Geneva Common Prayer Book (Phenix, Vol. II. p. 204), was in 1583 joined to the collection. And this Confession, let it be remarked, continued so joined down to 1676, if not later: yet nothing of the kind ought to have been then printed with the Prayer Book, even, as it were, by prescription, since at the last review such additions were silently discouraged, and instead thereof four prayers placed after the service for the Visitation of the Sick.

It is not intended to enter at length into the question of the origin of these Prayers, the notes which accompany them being deemed sufficient. But it may be mentioned, that as the first series, which alone has any claim to antiquity, is in a great measure to be met with in Henry the eighth's Primer of 1545; so, most likely, the whole, or nearly the whole, of it may be traced up to the private devotional publications, the Primers and Horæ, of a still earlier date. The Parker Society

---

[1] The only positive allusion to them in high quarters, that we know of, concerns the Scottish Prayer Book of 1637, to whose compilers archbishop Laud was directed to write: "His Majesty commands that these prayers following, or any other (for they are different in several editions) be all left out, and not printed in your Liturgy."

has already reprinted several of the prayers, either in Bull's Christian Prayers, or in Edward the sixth's second Primer.

5. The Ordinal of 1559[2] differs from that of 1552 merely in one particular: an entirely new form of oath is inserted, with a corresponding alteration in the rubric preceding and introducing it. Copies thereof by Jugge and Cawode exist in the libraries of the Rev. W. Maskell, and the Rev. J. Mendham, and at York: a copy by Grafton is in the library of Corpus Christi College, Oxford. Herbert (Ames, p. 717) was acquainted with this edition, yet he seems only to have seen an impression by Jugge alone.

Elizabeth's act of uniformity not having noticed her Ordinal, in 1563 a cavil was raised respecting it by Bonner, then 'lying in the *Marshalsea* in *Southwark*.' He contended, that, since the Ordinal was a perfectly separate Service-book, it ought to have been distinctly specified. Consequently, Mary having repealed the act of 1552, which established in express words the previous Ordinal, and the edition of 1559 being (as he affirmed) void of authority, he would not allow Horn, bishop of Winchester, to be lawfully consecrated, nor submit himself, as an ecclesiastic, to his jurisdiction, by taking at his hands the oath of the Queen's sovereignty, which the ninth section of the act of supremacy, passed in 1559, and renewed in January 1563, required him to do. (Zurich Letters, p. 44.) This perverseness of his occasioned much controversy and disturbance: wherefore, in December 1566, the question was obliged to be settled in parliament by means of 'An Acte declaringe the manner of makinge and consecratinge of the Archbushopes and Busshops of this Realme to be good lawful and parfecte.' Strype's Annals, Vol. I. pp. 339—343, 492—494.

6. The Latin[3] Prayer Book of Elizabeth, though most commonly deemed a mere version of her English Book, and so called in her letters patent, (convenientem cum Anglicano nostro Publicarum precum libro,) is, in fact, almost an independent publication. This discrepancy, however, between

---

[2] Where are the Elizabethan Ordinals of a later date?

[3] Three other religious works, but for private use, came forth under Elizabeth's authority:—in 1560 an English Primer, and an Orarium; and in 1564, (if the copy of that year is really the earliest edition,) the Preces Privatæ.

its actual and its described state being felt at the time, Whitaker, the well-known master of St John's College, Cambridge, endeavoured in 1569 to account for it, when dedicating to his uncle, dean Nowell, a little[1] work which he had just completed: 'Quamvis alicubi ab Anglicano libro Latinus, quem ego sum secutus, primo aspectu differre videatur, et aliud quiddam sonare, nihil tamen est aliud, quam quod alter altero aliquando contractior aut fusior sit, quodque ille paucis contineat, idem hic pluribus exprimat verbis.' How far he was successful in his mode of explanation, even if we take no account of several of the Occasional services, will appear hereafter.

Carte (Vol. III. p. 393), resting upon Heylin (Elizabeth, p. 131), says, that the queen's primary object in causing this translation to be made, was 'to give the foreign world a right notion of the primitive purity and edifying nature of the *English* service.' He also presumes on Pius IV. having seen it, before he offered the queen (covertly in his letter of May the 15th, 1560, but more explicitly through his secret agent, Vincentio Parpalia, Abbot of St. Saviour's,) 'to confirm it [the English Book[2]—Camden (Kennet's Collection), p. 384], and allow the communion in both kinds, if she would reconcile herself and people to the see of *Rome*.' Laying out of sight for the present the direct evidence to the contrary, the very circumstances of the case lead to a strong presumption, that Carte's representation cannot be correct. The English and Latin Books differ materially from each other, a point which every one may readily ascertain for himself. To put the latter forward, then, as an accurate translation of the former, would have been an imposition very easy of detection to the Roman catholic priesthood in England, and, on detection, a sure cause of blame and of obloquy to the queen, who by a stretch of her prerogative had sanctioned it, and to her advisers. We had better keep strictly to the view inculcated

---

[1] Liber Precum Publicarum Ecclesiæ Anglicanæ in juventutis Græcarum literarum studiosæ gratiam, Latine Græceque æditus. Like the small English *Prayer*-books of the period, briefly called Psalters, it contained only the Morning and Evening prayers, the Litany, the Catechism, and the Collects.

[2] Camden does not depend much on what he styles 'his suppos'd Offers,' though he gives the rumour of the day, which may have been merely a trick of the Romish priests to cause divisions. See Strype's Annals, Vol. I. p. 221, and his reference.

PREFACE. xxiii

upon us by Elizabeth's letters patent; and these in positive words declare the Latin Prayer Book to have been exclusively designed, agreeably to their own humble request, for the universities and the great public schools; or, as the document quoted on p. xxxiii. expresses it, 'for the vse and exercise of suche Students and others learned in the laten tunge.' Accordingly, it was likewise recommended to the clergy generally in their private daily devotions (see p. 302), at which the sixth section of Edward's first act of uniformity permitted them to use the ' Latten, or anye suche other tongue.' Clay's Prayer Book Illustrated, p. 192.

Being drawn up with this intention, it did not really need the addition of the Occasional services, except, indeed, such as relate to the Visitation of the Sick and the Burial of the Dead. All the remaining ones, however, (not the Commination service, for which, as having been unaccountably omitted, the volume now edited is indebted to Aless,) are reprinted from a unique copy of the work belonging to the Rev. W. Maskell, Broadleaze, Devizes, who kindly caused them to be transcribed for that purpose. It would seem that, in the first instance, the Book was published, or, at least, was ready for publication, with them[3]; and they were placed immediately after the service for Burial: hence the colophon which follows the *Purificatio Mulierum* (p. 429), and concludes the intended volume. Subsequently, when cancelled, fresh sheets were struck off, beginning as on p. 430, the signatures being likewise resumed: Services for the Commendation of Benefactors, and for the celebration of the Lord's Supper at Funerals[4], were subjoined instead, yet not as if a part of the

---

[3] See the answer to the question, Quæ sunt? on p. 417. Had the Book so prepared any connexion with the first act of uniformity passed by the Irish parliament in the previous January, the last clause of which sanctions 'the Latin tongue' in places, 'where the common minister or priest hath not the use or knowledge of the English tongue?' Mant's History of the Church of Ireland, Vol. I. pp. 260, 261.

[4] Wolf, it appears, put out by themselves, in 1560, (the date is three times given,) these two Services, with the queen's letters patent, which work Sparrow (Collections, pp. 199—205), and Wilkins (Concilia, Vol. IV. pp. 217, 218), reprinted, the latter leaving out the title-page. See also Strype's Annals, Vol. I. pp. 216—218. We have the Commendation of Benefactors, with a translation, in L'Estrange, pp. 304—306. In 1570, Elizabeth prescribed to the University of Cambridge a similar Form of

c 2

Prayer Book itself; and the colophon, as a matter of course, removed to the end of such services. Thus, we may consider there to have been two editions of the Latin Prayer Book closely succeeding each other; and Mr. Maskell's rare volume, which has been followed in all respects, comprises the peculiarities of both.

The date usually assigned to the Latin Prayer Book is 1560, and, in spite of Dibdin's assertion (Typ. Antiq. Vol. IV. p. 25), that this date is merely conjectural, the common opinion is undoubtedly correct. For not only were Elizabeth's letters patent issued on April the 6th in that year, but, in the account of the *Cyclus Solaris* (p. 324) we have the following expression, *annus hic præsens*, 1560. Herbert, indeed, (Ames, p. 1602,) mentions a Latin Prayer Book printed by Wolf in 1559, (which date has been *written* upon the first page of Mr. Maskell's copy:) still, if we may judge from his mode of quoting the title, he could hardly have seen the work he meant. Dibdin has omitted the notice.

'The pen and diligence of *Walter Haddon*,' whose excellent Ciceronian style was much commended in those days, ('as some suppose,') were employed by the queen in preparing this version. Heylin (Elizabeth, p. 131). Collier (Vol. II. p. 463) seems to affirm, that Haddon had coadjutors, though he does not give us their names. But neither historian, it is manifest, had very diligently inquired into the subject; for, otherwise, they would soon have discovered, how little claim to the actual authorship of the Latin Prayer Book was possessed even by Haddon, whose name they may rightly have put forward in the matter, and to whom, therefore, in the present volume its compilation has been uniformly referred. The credit of the work is really due to Aless, the Scotch divinity professor of Leipsic, him, whom Cromwell, meeting by the way, carried with him, in 1537, to 'the Convocation House, where all the Bishops were assembled together' at Henry's special appointment to debate about religion; and who, 'having the Liberty to declare his Opinion concerning the *Sacraments*, endeavour'd to prove, that only

commendation in *English*. Statuta, cap. 50. This last Form, which was to be used after sermon solely in the public or university church, must not be confounded with the earlier one appointed for the private chapel of each college.

Baptism and the holy Eucharist were of divine Institution[1].'
Foxe, edit. 1684, Vol. II. p. 424. Collier, Vol. II. p. 121.
Aless's translation[2] formed completely the basis of that of
1560. He then resided in a foreign land, and very naturally desired to make known the progress of the reformed
doctrines and practices 'pæne patriæ ipsius' among the
people, with whom for eleven years he had dwelt,—uel ad
exemplum, uel consolationem, uel etiam dolorem aliquorum.
Another[3] object also influenced him :—Hæc editio dicatur
ac liber peculiariter ad eos mittitur, quicunque tandem futuri
sunt participes deliberationum de re Ecclesiastica, cuius constituendæ gratia sunt qui serio tandem conuentum habitum
iri existiment, annitente, & agente negocium, Imperatore
Carolo V. Augusto, &c.

Entertaining these views, he ought to have been particularly careful to set forth an accurate version of the English
Book, one capable of bearing a comparison word for word with
the original. Besides, he makes a great parade of his fide-

[1] Burnet (Vol. I. p. 214), and Collier, who follows him, wrongly
suppose this disputation to have taken place in 1536, as part of the regular proceedings of convocation then sitting.

[2] Ordinatio Ecclesiæ, seu Ministerii Ecclesiastici, in florentissimo
Regno Angliæ, conscripta sermone patrio, & in Latinam linguam bona
fide conuersa, Et ad consolationem Ecclesiarum Christi, ubicunque locorum ac gentium, his tristissimis temporibus, edita ab Alexandro Alesio,
Scoto, Sacræ Theologiæ Doctore. Lipsiæ. M.D.LI. 4to.

[3] Aless, says Burnet (Vol. II. p. 155), on the authority of Heylin
(p. 79), made his Latin translation for Bucer's use. Had such been the
case, the circumstance would certainly have been mentioned by him here.
It is clear, too, from a comparison of dates, that Bucer could not consult
this translation, whilst writing his 'Censura super Libro Sacrorum, seu
Ordinationis Ecclesiæ atque Ministerii Ecclesiastici in Regno Angliæ.'
For his treatise is dated 'Nonis Januarii,' and he died 'pridie Calendas
Martias' (P. Martyris Loci Communes, &c. Lond. 1583, p. 1088), 1551, the
same year in which it was published. Doubtless Aless's work is printed
in Bucer's Scripta Anglicana immediately before the Censura; but, as
the marginal notes will shew, this was merely to enable the reader to
understand the nature of his remarks. He only tells us himself (p. 456)
'librum istum Sacrorum (the English Prayer Book of 1549) per interpretem, quantum potui, cognoui diligenter.' Thus, most probably, Bucer had
recourse to an *oral*, not a printed, translation, and yet one was in existence as early as July, 1549. See p. xxxi., note 3. Strype (Cranmer, Oxford edit. Vol. I. p. 579) commits the extraordinary blunder of representing Aless's Ordinatio, &c. as a Latin version of some German work by Bucer.

lity: on the title-page he has 'bona fide conuersa;' and in his preface the following passage: 'Bona spes est, omnes intelligentes comperturos esse, quod accurate et fideliter in Latinum sermonem traducta sint ea, quæ in Britanico libro extant, simplicem hunc quidem, ut decuit, et Ecclesiastica consuetudine tritum, & interpretantem verbis usitatis descriptionem Britanicam, & hoc opus secundum illa exprimentem, nullis pigmentis aut coloribus additis.' These words may have been seriously written; nevertheless Aless did not seriously act up to them. Not that the book is faulty on account of its being, on the whole, a wrong representation of the doctrines and discipline of our church; but because, by culpable negligence, it may be, rather than always by design, interpolations, omissions[1], and loose translations, so frequently occur.

Take the notice respecting Ceremonies. What are we to think of sentences like these? 'Therefore, no man ought,' &c.:— Nemo hanc autoritatem sibi sumere debet, ut constituat ordinem aliquem in Ecclesia, nisi sit ad hoc *diuinitus* uocatus, & habeat autoritatem publicam & consensum Ecclesiæ. 'And he [Augustine] counselled,' &c.:—Idem consulit ut hoc iugum, quantum fieri potest cum tempore & quiete Ecclesiæ, aboleatur. *Questi sunt etiam post illum Ioannes Gerson, Thomas, & alii.* Quid, inquiunt, Sancte Pater Augustine, diceres, si nunc viveres? Cum paucæ admodum fuerint cærimoniæ tuo tempore in Ecclesia, &c. To go on to the Litany. It begins thus,—2. Pater de cœlis Deus. 2. Fili redemtor mundi Deus. 2. Spiritus sancte Deus, ab utroque procedens. Sancta Trinitas unus Deus; whilst the Chorus replies only, Miserere nobis. The petition against the bishop of Rome takes no notice of 'and all his detestable enormities.' 'To give to all nations,' &c. is translated, Ut omnibus *Christianis* pacem et concordiam, &c.; and the last two petitions, not to mention others, go very wide of the original. The Communion service equally suffered. To pass by the fourth

[1] The leaving out of all that pertained to the anointing, which the Book of 1549 allowed (see Liturgies of K. Edward VI. pp. 139, 143), cannot be palliated; any more than the insertion, on his own authority, of the rubric, with which he terminates the office for the Visitation of the Sick, and which Haddon (p. 403) adopted. In the note on that rubric it would have been more correct to say, that the reference is to the ancient service for the Romish sacrament of extreme unction, whereof the thirteenth psalm formed a part. Monumenta Ritualia, Vol. I. p. 84.

rubric at the commencement, the second Exhortation has for 'the most comfortable sacrament,' &c.,—Sacramentum plenum consolationis, Hoc est, corpus et sanguinem Christi. After 'faith in God's mercy' is foisted in, Nobis propter Christum gratis oblatæ. So, besides insertions equally unauthorised, 'minister of God and the church' is rendered, Tanquam Dei et Ecclesiæ Domini nostri Iesu Christi ministris. The rubric directly following the Offertory is, Harum et *similium sententiarum ex Thobia, Prouerbiis, uel Psalmis*, una aut plures canantur, &c. The side-notes at the consecration of the elements are unnoticed: the forms at delivering the elements not quite accurately given, and part of the rubric before offering the cup left out. Moreover, from the fourth rubric at the end of the office the sentence, 'but in each of them the whole body of our Saviour Jesu Christ,' is passed by: the last is made to pertain to the cup, as well as to the bread, contrary to its obvious purport, and in defiance of the intention of our church; and, generally, these rubrics are translated in a way, which admits of no justification[2].

Such was the book, which Haddon, when employed about his Latin edition of 1560, took for a model and guide. Now, from what has been adduced, some persons may imagine, that this latter publication is of no real value, how curious soever it may be. But we must not decide so hastily. Haddon's work came forth with the express sanction of Elizabeth's letters patent, which clearly demonstrated its importance: it was enjoined by her authority upon the universities, the great public schools, and the clergy in their private devotions; and, from a document to be quoted hereafter (see p. xxxiii), had accordingly been adopted in many places. Of necessity, therefore, this Prayer Book assumed a character, which must render it an object of no common interest, and ever entitle it to much consideration.

Though, however, it is manifest, that Haddon can advance no claim, except in a few particulars, to the merit, whatever it be, of the version, he is not to be considered as blindly following Aless's track on every occasion. In far too many cases he did so; and hence the strong resemblance, which the Latin Book of 1560 bears, in substance no less than in wording, to its English predecessor of 1549. Still, he did not so

[2] See Crosthwaite's Communio Fidelium, pp. 59—67.

follow Aless, as to omit correcting some of his faults, and, occasionally, his Latinity. The introductory part about Ceremonies Haddon re-translated: that *De anno et partibus eius* must be his; and so also the collect for St. Stephen's day, which, after all, varies from the English; whilst, in other places, as in the beginning of the Morning service, and in portions of the Communion service, he was, from the nature of the case, obliged to rest solely on himself, in order to bring his work into some conformity to the English Prayer Book of 1559, of which it professed to be a translation.

A question arises here, which would be well worth settling, did we possess the materials for settling it:—how far the observances of 1549 were intended to be brought back, and recommended to the clergy under the authority of the temporal head of their church. (Collier, Vol. II. p. 259.) In the Communion of the Sick, (to go no further,) the reservation of a portion of the consecrated elements is ordered, and L'Estrange (p. 300) justifies this, because learned societies, the greater light they enjoyed, the less prone would they be to error and superstition; as he justifies (p. 304) the celebration of the Lord's supper at funerals, because the whole Book was compiled for 'Men of discerning Spirits.' But was this design, or the result of haste and inattention? Did Haddon mean (of course, in obedience to command) to prepare a book which should allow such reservation; or did he merely transcribe what Aless had previously, and correctly, given? Many reasons induce us to think, that, if Haddon was careless, (and he cannot be wholly excused,) he ever remembered what he was about, and still fulfilled his appointed task. To refer only to the rubrics on p. 385; as the first is an instance of want of accuracy, so is the second of want of fidelity, and that, from the corrections on Aless's wording bringing it nearer than before to the Prayer Book of 1549.

One of the most remarkable discrepancies between Elizabeth's English and Latin Book is furnished by the absolution in the Communion service. In the Book of 1560 Christ is said to have given to the Church his own power (suam potestatem, p. 393,) of absolving penitents; an expression for which there existed not the slightest ground. This absolution, however, is a transcript from Aless; but not without the transcriber being quite alive to what he was about, for he made additions at the end, sufficient to mark deliberation and design. The history of the Latin form of absolution is curious. It was taken, as just stated, out of that version upon which Haddon so much relied : nevertheless, Aless, by inserting it therein, went further than he was justified in doing, inasmuch as the Prayer Book of 1549, which he proposed to render, is, in this respect, like our own at the present day. Aless, if not to be styled dishonest, which some persons are ready to affirm, was not, it need scarcely be repeated, very remarkable for faithfulness[1]. He had before turned into Latin the Order[2] of the Communion (Maskell's Ancient Liturgy, p. xcvii. note), and, having this ready at hand, incorporated the whole of it into his work, (as he did the proper preface for Easter from the Salisbury Missal,) without caring at all, or very slightly, whether it properly coincided with the English. Now the form of absolution belonging to the Order of the Communion, derived, like so much of our Occasional services, where they do not follow those previously existing (Laurence's Bampton Lectures, pp. 443, 444. Original Letters, pp. 19, 266, 344), from a work[3], in the nature of an Interim, then recently drawn up by Melancthon and Bucer for the use of the archbishoprick of Cologne (fol. xcii), is almost verbally as Aless has trans-

---

[1] See p. 421, note 1. By putting 'peruenient in Chorum' as the Latin of 'shall tarye still in the quire,' he may have wished, in the character of an interpreter, to affix his own meaning to a somewhat obscure rubric. Maskell's Ancient Liturgy, p. lxxvii.

[2] Coverdale (Vol. II. p. 525.) also translated the same Order into Latin, for the use of Calvin, but does not seem to have printed it. This, we may presume, was a verbal translation, and not such 'a platt,' as Knox and others a few years later sent to him, ' off the whole booke off England.' Troubles at Frankfort, p. xxviii.

[3] Nostra Hermanni ex gratia Dei Archiepiscopi Coloniensis, et Principis Electoris, &c. Simplex ac Pia Deliberatio, qua ratione Christiana & in uerbo Dei fundata Reformatio Doctrinæ, Administrationis diuinorum Sacramentorum, Cæremoniarum, totiusque curæ animarum, et aliorum Ministeriorum Ecclesiasticorum, apud eos qui nostræ Pastorali curæ commendati sunt, tantisper instituenda sit, donec Dominus dederit constitui meliorem, uel per liberam & Christianam Synodum, siue Generalem siue Nationalem, uel per Ordines Imperii Nationis Germanicæ in Spiritu Sancto congregatos. *Bonnæ.* Anno. M.D.XXXXV. Fol.

John Daye published an English translation of this book 'in the yere of our Lorde .1547. The xxi. of October ;' and again, in 1548.

lated it, except that he both left out 'blessed,' and inserted on his own authority not only 'Jesus Christus,' but that very important word 'suam,' for which the Simplex ac pia Deliberatio has 'hanc.' So far, therefore, he was in some degree right: still what, with these limitations, suited well the Order of the Communion, did not necessarily suit a later and different publication.

Among the things, which the reader of the Latin Prayer Book will not find, is the addition of 1552 giving permission to men to say their private prayers 'in any language that they themselves do understand;'—the rubrics pertaining to the vestments, to the choice of position for the table at the communion time, and to the sacramental bread;—also, some of those at the end of the Communion service, and of the Communion of the Sick. But the first omission arose from the closing sentence of Elizabeth's letters patent (p. 302), recommending to the clergy for that purpose this very Book: after the issuing of Elizabeth's Injunctions in July 1559, the second was rendered absolutely necessary (Sparrow's Collections, pp. 77, 83. Zurich Letters, pp. 228, 272); and the third became a thing of course, in consequence of the Latin Prayer Book not having any connexion with parochial ministrations. If, however, there are things, which the reader will not find in Haddon's publication, so are there in it some things, besides those already mentioned, which he would not expect to find. For instance, the notation of the Psalms is declared to be after the Vulgate, instead of after 'the great Englyshe Bible;' whilst in leap year the intercalary day, the second time of its being mentioned (see p. 323), is changed from the twenty-fifth to the twenty-fourth of February. Haddon similarly takes upon himself the office of interpreter. The last sentence of the second rubric on p. 327 distinctly informs us, that the Evening service ought to begin like the Morning service, a point about which some persons, we may suppose, even then unnecessarily entertained doubts: in the first rubric at the Communion (p. 383), 'immediately after' is rendered, immediate post principium matutinarum precum: the phrase, stantem ad sacram Mensam, on p. 385, seems also intended to determine the priest's position at that time with reference to the communion-table, as turned to it, not from it: 'offerings' in the first rubric on p. 388 is explained to signify 'oblationes et decimas' (L'Estrange, p. 180); as, in the last rubric on p. 399, 'Ecclesiastical duties' are made to mean 'decimas, oblationes, ceteraque debita;' and the phrase 'when there is no Communion,' which occurs on p. 196, is left as Aless translated it,—quando non adsunt communicantes. See also pp. 399, 426.

The Latin Prayer Book was not received every where with equal favour and respect. Strype, under the year 1568 (Parker, p. 269), tells us, that 'most of the Colleges' in Cambridge would not tolerate it, as being '*the Popes Dreggs;*' and even, 'that some of the Fellowship of *Benet* College went contemptuously from the Latin Prayers, the Master being the Minister then that read the same.'

Elizabeth's Latin Prayer Book was never before reprinted[1]. Herbert (Ames, p. 607), doubtless, refers to copies in quarto and octavo put forth in 1562; these, however, Dibdin (Typ. Antiq. Vol. IV. pp. 19, 27) declares to have been no more than a reissue of a different work, one printed in 1553 with the same title that Whitaker adopted in 1569. Nevertheless, since Prayer Books in Latin published during her reign have been often confounded with her own, a short account of them appears indispensable. They bear the names of Wolf, Vautrollier, and Jackson, as the printers; and, in the case of the last two, 'per assignationem Francisci Floræ.' Wolf, in 1571, (or rather in 1572, for the Psalter has both dates,) sent out what we may rightly deem the earliest[2] version into Latin of the whole Prayer Book. Herbert's Ames, p. 611. This the other printers carefully followed, and the copies (octavo) more commonly met with, though still very rare, are one in 1574 by Vautrollier, and another in 1594 by Jackson. Wolf's edition (and likewise the others) came out 'Cum priuilegio regiæ maiestatis;' the act of uniformity is prefixed; the Occasional services are each

---

[1] With respect to the names in the Calendar of this reprint, no attempt at correction has been made beyond such typographical errors, as seemed peculiar to the original. See particularly those put against Sept. the 11th, and Oct. the 26th and 30th.

[2] This remark pertains only to the times of Elizabeth; for two translations, of which Aless's was one, were made in Edward's reign, and a third undertaken, but left imperfect. Cardwell's Two Liturgies of Edward VI. compared, p. xvi. Original Letters, p. 535.

duly incorporated; and to the end is annexed Munster's translation of the Psalms: moreover, all the really important peculiarities, which distinguish the Book of 1560, are omitted. It was intentionally, therefore, made to exhibit a close resemblance to the English Prayer Book of 1559, or (to speak more correctly) of 1561, being designed, in conformity with the act of 1549 before quoted, for the private use of any one, who wished to perfect, or keep up, his knowledge of Latin.

But the fault of taking previously existing materials without due care was still evidenced in two remarkable ways. Aless had inadvertently rendered 'ouer night' in the second rubric preceding the Communion of the Sick by 'postridie' (see p. 404); and consequently, we have this error, adopted by Haddon, perpetuated through the whole reign of Elizabeth. So, also, have we invariably the collect for St Andrew's day as the English Prayer Book of 1549 represented it, instead of that introduced in 1552, and never afterwards altered: of course, however, Haddon having thoughtlessly copied Aless, who in this particular was right, was himself as thoughtlessly followed. It is strange, that early in the next century we perceive these same blunders again repeated in the Latin version of the Prayer Book incorporated into the Doctrina et Politia[1] of Dr Mocket, Warden of All Souls', Oxford, and chaplain to archbishop Abbot; a work of considerable importance, and now of no ordinary rarity.

As has just been asserted, no second edition of Elizabeth's Latin Prayer Book was ever published, at least in subsequent years: nevertheless, in the year 1615, if not before, an abridgment of it appeared, entitled, Liber Precum Publicarum in usum Ecclesiæ Cathedralis Christi, Oxon. It contains merely the Morning service, the Athanasian creed, the Evening service, the Litany and its Collects, followed by the Psalter: then come four prayers, (Pro officio totius Ecclesiæ in communi, Pro Rege, Tempore pestilentiæ, Pro docilitate,) of which the last two were taken from the Preces Privatæ, two graces, a prayer for the sovereign and people, with one for their founder Henry. This, enlarged by the additional Col-

---

[1] Doctrina et Politia Ecclesiæ Anglicanæ, a beatissimæ memoriæ principibus Edouardo sexto, Regina Elizabetha stabilitæ, et a religiosissimo et potentissimo monarcha Jacobo Magnæ Britan. &c. rege continuatæ. Londini. 1617. 4to.

lects after the Litany, introduced in 1604 and 1662, is still daily used for short Latin prayers during term time.

7. The New Calendar was the result of a prescript dated at Westminster, the 22nd of January, 'the thirde yere of o^r Raigne' [1561]. By this document 'Matthue Archebishop of Canterburye, Edmonde Byshopp of London, Willm. Byll our Almoner, and Walter Haddon one of the Masters of o^r Requests' were required 'to peruse the order of the Lessons thoroughe out the whole yere,' and to substitute in the place of 'certen chapters for lessons.... other chapters or parcels of scripture, tendinge in the hering of the vnlearned, or laye people, more to their edificacion[2]. Parker MSS. Corpus Christi College, Cambridge. Strype's Parker, pp. 82—84. Grindal's Remains, p. 157.

It entered, likewise, into the province of these royal commissioners to revise the Calendar in other respects. Hence the occurrence therein of many names of saints, which we may presume to have been now re-introduced for the reason subsequently assigned to the reader by a notice in the Preces Privatæ:—ut certarum quarundam rerum, quarum stata tempora nosse plurimum refert, quarumque ignoratio nostris hominibus obesse possit, quasi notæ quædam sint atque indicia. See also Cardwell, pp. 306, 341.

The same prescript also required the commissioners to make some regulations respecting the Collegiate churches, in which the Latin Prayer Book had been allowed to be used, 'so that our good purpos in the saide translacion be not frustrated, nor be corruptlye abused, contrarye to theffect of our meanynge.' What that meaning was, may be gathered from Elizabeth's letters patent, p. 301.

8. Nothing need here be said in relation to the Occasional services and Prayers[3], since in the volume itself an

---

[2] It was not uncommon to take the old Calendar out of the early Elizabethan Prayer Books, and insert this new one.

[3] The practice of publishing such Forms is coeval with the reformation. 'Occasional Prayers and Suffrages to be used throughout all Churches began now to be more usual than formerly. For these common Devotions were twice this year [1544] appointed by Authority, as they had been once the last; which I look upon the Archbishop to be the great instrument in procuring: that he might by this means, by little and little, bring into use Prayers in the English Tongue, which he so much desired; and that the People, by understanding part of

ample account is prefixed of the circumstances, which individually gave rise to them. Only one regular list of these Forms has been discovered, and that where we should least have expected to discover it, viz. in Dr Williams's library, in Red-cross Street, London, a Dissenters' foundation of about 150 years standing. It occurs in a manuscript volume containing chiefly biographical notices, written, apparently, about the end of the seventeenth century and, it may be, by Dr Calamy, the eminent Nonconformist, and grandson of the no less eminent Presbyterian, divine. This list, which enters somewhat into detail as to a few of the Services, and notices a good portion of those now reprinted between 1563 and 1601, commences thus: " There were severall forms of Prayer and Thanksgiving set forth in Queene Elizabeths Reigne upon severall Speciall Occasions, here followeth a list of the times and occasions of divers of them, taken out of a Printed Booke in 4°." Could the said 'Printed Booke' be recovered, we should obtain copies of two Forms (XXI., XLIII.), which seem to be completely lost; but, though searched for diligently, it is still missing. At the end of the list we are told, that " before all or most of these dayes of Fasting upon severall occasions in Queene Eliz. Reigne, there had been a Severe Prosecution of the Nonconformable Ministers, and a vigerous endeavor to suppress them from Preaching. 1. In Anno 1563. The first fast was for the Plague. A little before that, in Anno 1559, the Queenes Injunctions were put forth. And also, in Anno 1562, the Booke of Orders[1], which were very hard upon the Noncon-

---

their Prayers, might be the more desirous to have their whole Service rendered intelligible.' Strype's Cranmer, Book i. chap. xxix. One of the two instances assigned to 1544 must, in the opinion of Dr Jenkyns (Remains of Cranmer, Vol. IV. p. 320), be referred to the following year. See Cranmer's Works, Parker Society edition, Vol. II. p. 154, note 2; and p. 188, note 1.

[1] Parker (Strype's Life, p. 92.) framed '*Resolutions and Orders*' in 1561 to serve for uniformity of ministration, and concord, in the church, until the meeting of a synod. But, surely, the writer has erred, and meant the Book of Orders sent by the archbishop to Grindal March the 28th, 1566, for distribution through the province of Canterbury. This was a re-publication, with amendments, of the Advertisements, which, though wanting the queen's sanction, he had caused to be printed about a year before. Ibid. p. 216.

formists, and had restrained many of them. 2. In Anno 1572 there was a Form of Prayer set forth to be used four[2] dayes in a weeke. About that time the Nonconformists had been cruelly troubled with the Three[3] Articles that Archb. Parker required them to subscribe to. Mr Field and Mr Wilcocks were imprisoned for writing the Admonition. [Neal, Vol. I. pp. 190, 191.] 3. In Anno 1580 the Fast for the great Earthquake was kept every weeke. Before that yeare there had been a very universall Check given to the spreading of the Gospell, and to the Nonconformable Preachers, by the suspension of Archb. Grindall, and the suppression of Prophesyings. 4. In Anno 1585, before Mr Bunney's Prayers and Exercises[4] were set out, or the necessary and godly Prayers by the Bp. of London, which were put forth in the same yeare, there had been a universall and severe Prosecution of the Nonconformists for refusing to subscribe to Archb. Whitgift's Articles. [Strype's life, pp. 115, 125. Neal, Vol. I. p. 308.] 5. In Anno 1593, Certain Prayers were put forth to be read four dayes in a weeke, for the Plague, by the Bp. of London. Before that there had been a most universall Prosecution of the Nonconformists: Mr Cartwright, Mr Egerton, and multitudes more of them had been, and some of them still were, in Prison."

Some libraries, of course, are richer in these Forms than others. Those, whence the greatest assistance was obtained, exist at Durham, Lambeth, Emmanuel College, Cambridge, and Colchester. Among the remains, indeed, of archbishop Harsnet's library, in the last-named place, is a volume in this department of literature invaluable, and whose preservation ought to be cared for most solicitously. An examination of the Privy Council Minutes for Orders respecting the observance of the Services, and of the records in the State Paper Office,

[2] Neither here, nor below (see p. 528), has the writer represented the matter accurately. The original passage runs, 'not onely on Sundayes and holy dayes, but also on Wednesdayes and Fridayes.'

[3] Namely, to acknowledge the queen's supremacy, to agree to the Prayer Book with the Ordinal, and to allow the thirty-nine Articles of 1562. Subscription to the same three Articles Whitgift afterwards enforced, and in obedience to the same act passed in 1571.

[4] For the seventeenth of November, queen Elizabeth's accession-day. See some remarks by Brand (Popular Antiquities, Vol. I. p. 318.) respecting the observance of this day even in very modern times.

as well as of the Registers at York, for the Services themselves, was instituted; of each of which, in this respect, a great expectation had been raised only to be disappointed. Some of the Forms, whose titles appear in the list, are not here reprinted: numbers XXII., XXVII., and XXXV., because there seemed to be good reason for their omission: the others, because copies thereof could no where be discovered. The source, which in every instance furnished the transcript, is indicated between crotchets at the end of the title.

Sincere thanks are due to the Rev. W. Maskell for the ready access which he granted to his well-stored library of rare and choice books; also to the Rev. S. R. Maitland, the Rev. J. C. Crosthwaite, and the Rev. T. Lathbury, for the assistance so kindly rendered by them to the present publication. The editor equally wishes to acknowledge his obligations to the following gentlemen: P. de Bary, Esq. of the Privy Council Office, the Rev. E. J. Raines, librarian of the Minster library, York, the Rev. W. Greenwell, sub-librarian of bishop Cosin's library, Durham, the Rev. A. Tate, tutor of Emmanuel College, Cambridge, and the late G. Stokes, Esq., of Cheltenham.

ERRATA.

p. 27, l. 24, *for* alterations, *read* alteration, and *omit* the note.
p. 301, l. 29, read *Etonæ*.
     l. 31, omit [*edi.*]

THE LITANY AND SUFFRAGES.
1558.

[The unique copy here reprinted is in the Library of the Rev.
W. Maskell, Broadleaze, near Devizes.]

[LITURG. QU. ELIZ.]

¶ The Litany and Suffrages.

O God, the Father of heaven : have mercy upon us miserable sinners.

O God the Father of heaven : have mercy upon us miserable sinners.

O God the Son, redeemer of the world : have mercy upon us miserable sinners.

O God the Son, redeemer of the world : have mercy upon us miserable sinners.

O God the Holy Ghost, proceeding from the Father and the Son : have mercy upon us miserable sinners.

O God the Holy Ghost, proceeding from the Father and the Son : have mercy upon us miserable sinners.

O holy, blessed, and glorious Trinity, three persons and one God : have mercy upon us miserable sinners.

O holy, blessed, and glorious Trinity, three persons and one God : have mercy upon us miserable sinners.

Remember not Lord our offences, nor the offences of our forefathers, neither take thou vengeance of our sins : spare us good Lord, spare thy people, whom thou hast redeemed with thy most precious blood, and be not angry with us for ever :

Spare us good Lord.

From all evil and mischief, from sin, from the crafts and assaults of the devil, from thy wrath, and from everlasting dampnation :

Good Lord deliver us.

From all blindness of heart, from pride, vainglory, and hypocrisy, from envy, hatred and malice, and all uncharitableness :

Good Lord deliver us.

From fornication, and all other deadly sin, and from all the deceits of the world, the flesh, and the devil :

Good Lord deliver us.

From lightnings and tempests, from plague, pestilence, and famine, from battle, and murder, and from sudden death :

Good Lord deliver us.

From all sedition and privy conspiracy, from the tyranny of the bishop of Rome, and all his detestable enormities, from all false doctrine and heresy, from hardness of heart, and contempt of thy word and commandment:
> Good Lord deliver us.

By the mystery of thy holy incarnation, by the[1] holy nativity and circumcision, by thy baptism, fasting and temptation:
> Good Lord deliver us.

By thine agony and bloody sweat, by thy cross and passion, by thy precious death and burial, by thy glorious resurrection and ascension, and by the coming of the Holy Ghost:
> Good Lord deliver us.

In all time of our tribulation, in all time of our wealth, in the hour of death, and in the day of judgment:
> Good Lord deliver us.

We sinners do beseech thee to hear us, O Lord God, and that it may please thee to rule and govern thy holy church universal in the right way:
> We beseech thee to hear us good Lord.

That it may please thee to keep Elizabeth thy servant, our Queen, and governour:
> We beseech thee to hear us good Lord.

That it may please thee to rule her heart in thy faith, fear and love, and that she may always have affiance in thee, and ever seek thy honour and glory:
> We beseech thee to hear us good Lord.

That it may please thee to be her defender and keeper, giving her the victory over all her enemies:
> We beseech thee to hear us good Lord.

That it may please thee to illuminate all bishops, pastors and ministers of the church, with true knowledge and understanding of thy word, and that both by their preaching and living they may set it forth and shew it accordingly:
> We beseech thee to hear us good Lord.

That it may please thee to endue the lords of the council, and all the nobility, with grace, wisdom, and understanding:
> We beseech thee to hear us good Lord.

[1] Most probably, a misprint for, thy.

That it may please thee to bless and keep the magistrates, giving them grace to execute justice, and to maintain truth:
>We beseech thee to hear us good Lord.

That it may please thee to bless and keep all thy people:
>We beseech thee to hear us good Lord.

That it may please thee to give to all nations unity, peace, and concord:
>We beseech thee to hear us good Lord.

That it may please thee to give us an heart to love and dread thee, and diligently to live after thy commandments:
>We beseech thee to hear us good Lord.

That it may please thee to give all thy people encrease of grace, to hear meekly thy word, and to receive it with pure affection, and to bring forth the fruits of the Spirit:
>We beseech thee to hear us good Lord.

That it may please thee to bring into the way of truth all such as have erred, and are deceived:
>We beseech thee to hear us good Lord.

That it may please thee to strengthen such as do stand, and comfort and help the weak-hearted, and to raise up them that fall, and finally to beat down Sathan under our feet:
>We beseech thee to hear us good Lord.

That it may please thee to succour, help, and comfort, all that be in danger, necessity and tribulation:
>We beseech thee to hear us good Lord.

That it may please thee to preserve all that travel by land or by water, all women labouring of child, all sick persons and young children, and to shew thy pity upon all prisoners and captives:
>We beseech thee to hear us good Lord.

That it may please thee to defend, and provide for the fatherless children and widows, and all that be desolate and oppressed:
>We beseech thee to hear us good Lord.

That it may please thee to have mercy upon all men:
>We beseech thee to hear us good Lord.

That it may please thee to forgive our enemies, persecutors and slanderers, and to turn their hearts:
> We beseech thee to hear us good Lord.

That it may please thee to give and preserve to our use the kindly fruits of the earth, so that in due time we may enjoy them:
> We beseech thee to hear us good Lord.

That it may please thee to give to us true repentance, to forgive us all our sins, negligences and ignorances, to and[1] endue us with the grace of thy holy Spirit, to amend our lives according to thy holy word:
> We beseech thee to hear us good Lord.

Son of God : we beseech thee to hear us.
> Son of God : we beseech thee to hear us.

O Lamb of God, that takest away the sins of the world:
> Grant us thy peace.

O Lamb of God, that takest away the sins of the world:
> Have mercy upon us.

O Christ hear us.
> O Christ hear us.

Lord have mercy upon us.
> Lord have mercy upon us.

Christ have mercy upon us.
> Christ have mercy upon us.

Lord have mercy upon us.
> Lord have mercy upon us.

Our Father which art in. &c.
And suffer us not to be led into temptation.
> But deliver us from evil. Amen.

Versicle.   O Lord deal not with us after our sins.
Answer.   Neither reward us after our iniquities.

Let us pray.

O God merciful Father, that despisest not the sighing of a contrite heart, nor the desire of such as be sorrowful, mercifully assist our prayers, that we make before thee in all our troubles and adversities, whensoever they oppress us:

[1 Misprint for, and to.]

and graciously hear us, that those evils, which the craft and subtlety of the devil or man worketh against us, be brought to nought, and by the providence of thy goodness they may be dispersed, that we thy servants, being hurt by no persecutions, may evermore give thanks unto thee in thy holy church: through Jesu Christ our Lord. Amen.

O Lord arise, help us, and deliver us for thy name's sake.

O God, we have heard with our ears, and our fathers have declared unto us the noble works, that thou didst in their days, and in the old time before them.

O Lord arise, help us, and deliver us for thine honour.

Glory be to the Father, and to the Son, and to the Holy Ghost.

As it was in the beginning, is now, and ever shall be, world without end. Amen.

From our enemies defend us, O Christ.

Graciously look upon our afflictions.

Pitifully behold the dolour of our heart.

Mercifully forgive the sins of thy people.

Favourably with mercy hear our prayers.

O Son of David, have mercy upon us.

Both now and ever vouchsafe to hear us, O Christ.

Graciously hear us, O Christ.

Graciously hear us, O Lord Christ.

Versicle. O Lord, let thy mercy be shewed upon us.
Answer. As we do put our trust in thee.

¶ Let us pray.

WE humbly beseech thee, O Father, mercifully to look upon our infirmities, and for the glory of thy name sake turn from us those evils that we most righteously have deserved. And grant that in all our troubles, we may put our whole trust and confidence in thy mercy, and evermore serve thee in holiness and pureness of living, to thy honor and glory: through our only mediator and advocate Jesus Christ, our Lord. Amen.

O GOD, whose nature and property is, ever to have mercy and to forgive, receive our humble petitions: and though we be tied and bound with the chain of our sins, yet let the pitifulness of thy great mercy loose us: for the honour of Jesus Christ's sake, our mediator and advocate.

ALMIGHTY and everlasting God, which only workest great marvels, send down upon our Bishops and curates, and all congregations committed to their charge, the healthful spirit of thy grace, and that they may truly please thee: Pour upon them the continual dew of thy blessing: grant this, O Lord, for the honour of our advocate and mediator Jesus Christ. Amen.

GRANT we beseech thee, O Almighty God, that we in our trouble put our whole confidence upon thy mercy, that we against all adversity be defended under thy protection: grant this, O Lord God, for our only mediator and advocate Jesus Christ's sake. Amen.

☞ A Prayer of Chrysostome.

ALMIGHTY God, which hast given us grace at this time with one accord, to make our common supplications unto thee, and dost promise that when two or three be gathered together in thy name, thou will grant their requests: fulfil now, O Lord, the desires and petitions of thy servants, as may be most expedient for them: granting us in this world, knowledge of thy truth, and in the world to come, life everlasting. Amen.

THE LITANY,

USED IN

THE QUEEN'S MAJESTY'S CHAPEL,

ACCORDING TO THE TENOR OF THE PROCLAMATION.

ANNO CHRISTI
1559.

The Le-
tanye, vsed in
the Quenes Maiesties
Chappel, according
to the tenor of
the Procla-
mation.

(∴)

Anno Christi
1559.

[The copy which has been followed is in archbishop Harsnet's Library, Colchester.]

A Confession.

ALMIGHTY God merciful Father, maker of all things, Judge of all men, I acknowledge and bewail my manifold sins and wickedness, which I from time to time most wickedly have committed, by thought word and deed, against thy divine majesty, provoking most justly thy wrath and indignation against me. I do earnestly repent, and am heartily sorry for these my misdoings; the remembrance of them is grievous unto me, the burden of them is too heavy for me: have mercy upon me, have mercy upon me: most merciful Father, for the Lord Jesus Christ's sake, forgive me all that is past, and grant that I may ever hereafter serve and please thee in newness of life, to the honour and glory of thy name, through Jesus Christ our Lord. Amen.

The Litany.

O God the Father of heaven : have mercy upon us miserable sinners.

O God the Father of heaven : have mercy upon us miserable sinners.

O God the Son redeemer of the world : have mercy upon us miserable sinners.

O God the Son redeemer of the world : have mercy upon us miserable sinners.

O God the Holy Ghost, proceeding from the Father and the Son : have mercy upon us miserable sinners.

O God the Holy Ghost, proceeding from the Father and the Son : have mercy upon us miserable sinners.

O holy blessed and glorious Trinity, three persons and one God : have mercy upon us miserable sinners.

O holy, blessed and glorious Trinity, three persons and one God : have mercy upon us miserable sinners.

Remember not Lord our offences, nor the offences of our forefathers, neither take thou vengeance of our sins :

Spare us good Lord, spare thy people whom thou hast redeemed with thy most precious blood, and be not angry with us for ever:
> Spare us good Lord.

From all evil and mischief, from sin, from the crafts and assaults of the devil, from thy wrath and from everlasting dampnation:
> Good Lord deliver us.

From all blindness of heart: from pride, vainglory, and hypocrisy, from envy, hatred and malice, and all uncharitableness:
> Good Lord deliver us.

From fornication, and all other deadly sin, and from all the deceits of the world, the flesh, and the devil:
> Good Lord deliver us.

From lightning and tempest, from plage, pestilence and famine, from battle, and murder, and from sudden death:
> Good Lord deliver us.

From all sedition and privy conspiracy, from all false doctrine and heresy, from hardness of heart, and contempt of thy word and commandment:
> Good Lord deliver us.

By the mystery of thy holy incarnation, by thy holy nativity and circumcision, by thy baptism, fasting and temptation:
> Good Lord deliver us.

By thine agony and bloody sweat, by thy Cross and passion, by thy precious death and burial, by thy glorious resurrection and ascension, and by the coming of the Holy Ghost:
> Good Lord deliver us.

In all time of our tribulation, in all time of our wealth, in the hour of death, and in the day of judgment:
> Good Lord deliver us.

We sinners do beseech thee to hear us O Lord God, and that it may please thee to rule and govern thy holy church universally in the right way:
> We beseech thee to hear us good Lord.

That it may please thee to keep and strengthen in the true worshipping of thee, in righteousness and holiness of life, thy servant Elizabeth, our most gracious Queen and governour:

> We beseech thee to hear us good Lord.

That it may please thee to rule her heart in thy faith, fear and love, and that she may evermore have affiance in thee, and ever seek thy honour and glory:

> We beseech thee to hear us good Lord.

That it may please thee to be her defender and keeper, giving her the victory over all her enemies:

> We beseech thee to hear us good Lord.

That it may please thee to illuminate all Bishops, pastors, and Ministers of the church, with true knowledge and understanding of thy word, and that both by their preaching and living they may set it forth and shew it accordingly:

> We beseech thee to hear us good Lord.

That it may please thee to endue the lords of the council, and all the Nobility, with grace, wisdom, and understanding:

> We beseech thee to hear us good Lord.

That it may please thee to bless and keep the magistrates, giving them grace to execute justice, and to maintain truth:

> We beseech thee to hear us good Lord.

That it may please thee to bless and keep all thy people:

> We beseech thee to hear us good Lord.

That it may please thee to give to all nations unity, peace and concord:

> We beseech thee to hear us good Lord.

That it may please thee to give us an heart to love and dread thee, and diligently to live after thy commandments:

> We beseech thee to hear us good Lord.

That it may please thee to give all thy people encrease of grace, to hear meekly thy word, and to receive it with pure affection, and to bring forth the fruits of the Spirit:

> We beseech thee to hear us good Lord.

That it may please thee to bring into the way of truth all such as have erred, and are deceived:

> We beseech thee to hear us good Lord.

That it may please thee to strengthen such as do stand,

and comfort and help the weak-hearted, and to raise up them that fall, and finally to beat down Sathan under our feet :
> We beseech thee to hear us good Lord.

That it may please thee to succour, help and comfort, all that be in danger, necessity and tribulation :
> We beseech thee to hear us good Lord.

That it may please thee to preserve all that travel by land or by water, all women labouring of child, all sick persons and young children, and to shew thy pity upon all prisoners and captives :
> We beseech thee to hear us good Lord.

That it may please thee to defend, and provide for the fatherless children and widows, and all that be desolate and oppressed :
> We beseech thee to hear us good Lord.

That it may please thee to have mercy upon all men :
> We beseech thee to hear us good Lord.

That it may please thee to forgive our enemies, persecutors and slanderers, and to turn their hearts :
> We beseech thee to hear us good Lord.

That it may please thee to give and preserve to our use the kindly fruits of the earth, so that in due time we may enjoy them :
> We beseech thee to hear us good Lord.

That it may please thee to give to us true repentance, to forgive us all our sins, negligences and ignorances, to endue us with the grace of thy holy Spirit, to amend our lives according to thy holy word :
> We beseech thee to hear us good Lord.

Son of God : we beseech thee to hear us.
> Son of God, we beseech thee to hear us.

O Lamb of God, that takest away the sins of the world :
> Grant us thy peace.

O Lamb of God, that takest away the sins of the world :
> Have mercy upon us.

O Christ hear us.
> O Christ hear us.

Lord have mercy upon us.
> Lord have mercy upon us.

Christ have mercy upon us.
> Christ have mercy upon us.

Lord have mercy upon us.
> Lord have mercy upon us.

Our Father, which art. &c.
And lead us not into temptation.
But deliver us from evil.
Versicle. O Lord, deal not with us after our sins.
Answer. Neither reward us after our iniquities.

Let us pray.

O God merciful Father, that despisest not the sighing of a contrite heart, nor the desire of such as be sorrowful, mercifully assist our Prayers that we make before thee in all our troubles and adversities, whensoever they oppress us: and graciously hear us, that those evils, which the craft and subtlety of the devil or man worketh against us, be brought to nought, and by the providence of thy goodness they may be dispersed, that we thy servants, being hurt by no persecution, may evermore give thanks unto thee in thy holy church: through Jesu Christ our Lord. Amen.

O Lord arise, help us, and deliver us for thy name's sake.

O God, we have heard with our ears, and our fathers have declared unto us the noble works, that thou diddest in their days, and in the old time before them.

O Lord arise, help us, and deliver us for thine honour.

Glory be to the Father. &c.
As it hath been from the beginning, is now and ever shall be world. &c. Amen.
From our enemies defend us O Christ.
> Graciously look upon our afflictions.

Pitifully behold the sorrows of our heart.
> Mercifully forgive the sins of thy people.

Favourably with mercy hear our prayers.
> O Son of David have mercy upon us.

Both now and ever vouchsafe to hear us, O Christ.

  Graciously hear us, O Christ.
  Graciously hear us, O Lord Christ.

¶ The Versicle. O Lord, let thy mercy be shewed upon us.
¶ The Answer. As we do put our trust in thee.

¶ Let us Pray.

WE humbly beseech thee, O Father, mercifully to look upon our infirmities, and for the glory of thy name's sake turn from us all those evils that we most righteously have deserved. And grant that in all our troubles we may put our whole trust and confidence in thy mercy, and evermore serve thee in holiness and pureness of living, to thy honour and glory: through our only mediator, and advocate Jesus Christ, our Lord.

A prayer for the Queen's Majesty.

O LORD our heavenly Father, high and &[1] mighty, King of kings, Lord of Lords, the only ruler of Princes, which doest from thy throne behold all the dwellers upon earth: most heartily we beseech thee with thy favour to behold our most gracious sovereign Lady Queen Elizabeth, and so replenish her with the grace of thy holy Spirit, that she may alway incline to thy will, and walk in thy way. Indue her plentifully with heavenly gifts: Grant her in health and wealth long to live, strength her that she may vanquish and overcome all her enemies; and finally after this life, she may attain everlasting joy and felicity: Through Jesus Christ our Lord. Amen.

ALMIGHTY and everlasting God, which only workest great marvels, send down upon our Bishops and Curates, and all congregations committed to their charge, the healthful spirit of thy grace, and that they may truly please thee. Pour upon them the continual dew of thy blessing: Grant this, O Lord, for the honour of our advocate and mediator Jesus Christ. Amen.

[[1] Misprint for, and.]

¶ A Prayer of Chrysostome.

ALMIGHTY God, which hast given us grace at this time with one accord, to make our common supplications unto thee, and dost promise that when two or three be gathered together in thy name, thou wilt grant their requests: fulfil now, O Lord, the desires and petitions of thy servants, as may be most expedient for them, granting us in this world knowledge of thy truth, and in the world to come life everlasting. Amen.

ii. Corinth. xiii.

THE grace of our Lord Jesus Christ, and the love of God, and the fellowship of the Holy Ghost, be with us all evermore. Amen.

Here endeth the Litany used in the Queen's Chapel.

For rain, if the time require.

O GOD, heavenly Father, which by thy Son Jesus Christ hast promised to all them that seek thy kingdom, and the righteousness thereof, all things necessary to their bodily sustenance: Send us, we beseech thee, in this our necessity, such moderate rain and showers, that we may receive the fruits of the earth, to our comfort, and to thy honour, through Jesus Christ our Lord. Amen.

For fair weather.

O LORD God, which for the sin of man didst once drown all the world except eight persons, and afterward of thy great mercy didst promise never to destroy it so again: we humbly beseech thee, that although we for our iniquities have worthily deserved this plague of rain and waters; yet upon our true repentance thou wilt send us such weather, whereby we may receive the fruits of the earth in due season, and learn both by thy punishment to amend our lives, and for thy clemency to give thee praise and glory, through Jesus Christ our Lord. Amen.

¶ In the time of dearth or famine.

O GOD, heavenly Father, whose gift it is that the rain doth fall, the earth is fruitful, beasts increase, and fishes do multiply: Behold, we beseech thee, the afflictions of thy people, and grant that the scarcity and dearth (which we do now most justly suffer for our iniquity) may through thy goodness be mercifully turned into cheapness and plenty, for the love of Jesu Christ our Lord, to whom, with thee and the Holy Ghost, be praise for ever. Amen.

¶ In the time of War.

O ALMIGHTY God, King of all Kings, and governour of all things, whose power no creature is able to resist, to whom it belongeth justly to punish sinners, and to be merciful unto them that truly repent: Save and deliver us (we humbly beseech thee) from the hands of our enemies; abate their pride, assuage their malice, and confound their devices; that we being armed with thy defence may be preserved evermore from all perils to glorify thee, which art the only giver of all victory, through the merits of thy only Son Jesus Christ our Lord. Amen.

¶ In the time of any common plague, or Sickness.

O ALMIGHTY God, which in thy wrath in the time of King David, didst slay with the plague of pestilence lxx. M. and yet, remembering thy mercy, didst save the rest; have pity upon us miserable sinners, that now are visited with great sickness and mortality; that like as thou didst then command thine angel to cease from punishing, so it may now please thee to withdraw from us this plague and grievous sickness, through Jesu Christ our Lord. Amen.

O GOD, whose nature and property is, ever to have mercy and to forgive, receive our humble petitions: and though we be tied and bound with the chain of our sins; yet let the pitifulness of thy great mercy loose us, for the honour of Jesus Christ's sake, our mediator and advocate. Amen.

¶ The Lord's prayer.

OUR Father which art in heaven, hallowed be thy name. Thy kingdom come. Thy will be done in earth, as it is in heaven. Give us this day our daily bread. And forgive us our trespasses, as we forgive them that trespass against us. And lead us not into temptation. But deliver us from evil. Amen.

¶ The Creed.

I BELIEVE in God the Father almighty, maker of heaven and earth: And in Jesus Christ his only Son our Lord: Which was conceived by the Holy Ghost, born of the Virgin Mary. Suffered under Ponce Pilate, was crucified, dead and buried, he descended into hell. The third day he rose again from the dead. He ascended into heaven, and sitteth on the right hand of God the Father almighty. From thence shall he come to judge the quick and the dead. I believe in the Holy Ghost. The holy catholic church. The communion of saints. The forgiveness of sins. The resurrection of the body. And the life everlasting. Amen.

¶ The .x. Commandments. Exodi. xx.

I am the Lord thy God, which have brought thee out of the land of Egypt, out of the house of bondage.

I. Thou shalt have none other Gods but me.

II. Thou shalt not make to thyself any graven Image, nor the likeness of any thing that is in heaven above, or in the earth beneath, nor in the water under the earth: thou shalt not bow down to them nor worship them.

For I, the Lord thy GOD, am a jealous God, and visit the sins of the fathers upon the children, unto the third and fourth generation of them that hate me, and shew mercy unto thousands in them that love me, and keep my commandments.

III. Thou shalt not take the name of the Lord thy God in vain:

For the Lord will not hold him guiltless that taketh his name in vain.

IV. Remember thou keep holy the saboth day.

Six days shalt thou labour, and do all that thou hast to do: but the seventh day is the Sabboth of the Lord thy God. In it thou shalt do no manner of work, thou and thy son, and thy daughter, thy man servant, and thy maid servant, thy cattle, and the stranger that is within thy gates: for in six days the Lord made heaven and earth, the sea, and all that in them is, and rested the seventh day; wherefore the Lord blessed the seventh day, and hallowed it.

V. Honour thy father and thy mother:

That thy days may be long in the land which the Lord thy God giveth thee.

VI. Thou shalt do no murther.
VII. Thou shalt not commit adultery.
VIII. Thou shalt not steal.
IX. Thou shalt not bear false witness against thy neighbour.
X. Thou shalt not covet thy neighbour's house, thou shalt not covet thy neighbour's wife, nor his servant, nor his maid, nor his ox, nor his ass, nor any thing that is his.

¶ Here follow certain Graces to be said, before and after meat.

THE eyes of all things do look up and trust in thee, O Lord: thou givest them meat in due season. Thou dost open thy hand, and fillest with thy blessing every living thing: good Lord, bless us and all these thy gifts, which we receive of thy bounteous liberality: Through Christ our Lord. Amen.

The King of eternal glory make us partakers of his heavenly table. Amen.

God is charity; and he that dwelleth in charity, dwelleth in God, and God in him: God grant us all to dwell in him. Amen.

¶ Grace after dinner.

THE God of peace and love vouchsafe alway to dwell with us. And thou Lord have mercy upon us.

Glory, honour, and praise be to thee, O God, which hast fed us from our tender age: and givest sustenance to every living thing: replenish our hearts with joy and gladness, that we may be rich and plentiful in all good works: Through our Lord Jesu Christ. Amen.

Grace before supper.

O LORD Jesu Christ, without whom nothing is sweet nor savoury, we beseech thee to bless us and our supper, and with thy blessed presence (O God) to cheer our hearts, that in all our meats and drinks we may taste and savour of thee, to thy honour and glory. Amen.

¶ Grace after supper.

BLESSED is God in all his ways: And holy in all his works. Our help is in the name of the Lord: Who hath made both heaven and earth. Blessed be the name of our Lord: From henceforth world without end. Amen.

Most mighty Lord and merciful Father, we yield thee hearty thanks for our bodily sustenance, requiring also most entirely thy gracious goodness, so to feed us with the food of thy heavenly grace, that we may worthily glorify thy holy name in this life, and after be partakers of the life everlasting: through our Lord Jesu Christ. Amen.

¶ Grace before meat.

WHETHER we eat or drink, or what thing else soever we do, let us do it to the laud, praise, and glory of God, who bless us and these his gifts, through our Lord Jesu Christ. Amen.

¶ Grace after meat.

Now we have well refreshed our bodies, let us remember the lamentable afflictions and miseries of many thousands our neighbours in Christ, visited by the hand of God, some with mortal plague and diseases, some with imprisonment, some with extreme poverty and necessity, that either they cannot, or they have not to feed as we have done; remember therefore how much and how deeply we here present are bound unto the goodness of Almighty God, for our health, wealth, and many other his benefits given unto us, through our most merciful Lord and Saviour Jesus Christ, to whom be praise, honour, and glory, world without end. Amen.

¶ GOD save the universal Church, and preserve our most gracious Queen Elizabeth, and the realm, and send us peace in our Lord Jesus, amen.

⁋ Imprinted at London,
by Rychard Jugge, Printer vnto
the Quenes Maiestie.
Cum priuilegio ad impri-
mendum solum.

THE

BOOK OF COMMON PRAYER,

AND

ADMINISTRATION OF THE SACRAMENTS

AND OTHER

RITES AND CEREMONIES

IN[1] THE

CHURCH OF ENGLAND.

Londini, in officina Richardi
Jugge, & Johannis
Cawode.

Cum privilegio Regiæ
Majestatis.

Anno. 1559.

[1 1596, of.]

The Booke of

common praier, and ad-

ministration of the

Sacramentes,

and other

rites

and Ceremonies in

the Churche of

Englande.

Londini, in officina Richardi
Jugge, & Iohannis
Cawode.

Cum priuilegio Regie
Maiestatis.

Anno. 1559.

[The copy, which has been reprinted, is in the Library of the Rev. W. Maskell, Broadleaze, near Devizes.]

¶ The Boke of

common praier, and administration of the

Sacramentes,

and other

rites

and Ceremonies in

the Churche of

Englande.

Londini[1], *in officina* Richardi Graftoni.

Cum priuilegio Regie
Maiestatis.

Anno. 1559.

[1 Over these words a printed label is pasted, bearing—*Londini, in officina Richardi Iugge, & Iohannis Cawode.*]

[The copy, which has been collated, is in the University Library, Cambridge.]

The contents
of this Book.

---

1. An act for the uniformity of Common prayer.
2. A Preface.
3. Of Ceremonies, why some be abolished, and some retained.
4. The order how the Psalter is appointed to be read.
5. The table for the order of the Psalms to be said at Morning and Evening prayer.
6. The order how the rest of holy Scripture is appointed to be read.
7. Proper Psalms and Lessons at Morning and Evening prayer, for sundays, and certain feasts and days.
8. An Almanack.
9. The table and Calendar for Psalms and Lessons, with necessary Rules, appertaining to the same.
10. The order for Morning prayer and Evening prayer, throughout the year.
11. The Litany.
12. The Collects, Epistles, and Gospels, to be used at the ministration of the holy Communion, throughout the year.
13. The order of the ministration of the holy Communion.
14. Baptism both public and private.
15. Confirmation, where also is a Catechism for children.
16. Matrimony.
17. Visitation of the sick.
18. The Communion of the sick.
19. Burial.
20. The thanksgiving of women after childbirth.
21. A Commination against sinners, with certain prayers to be used divers times in the year.

⁋ An Act for the uniformity of Common Prayer, and Service in the Church, and the administration of the Sacraments.

WHERE at the death of our late Sovereign lord King Edward the sixt, there remained one uniform order of common service and prayer, and of the administration of Sacraments, Rites, and Ceremonies, in the church of England, which was set forth in one book, entituled: The book of common prayer, and administration of Sacraments, and other Rites and ceremonies in the church of England, authorized by Act of Parliament, holden in the fift and sixt years of our said late Sovereign lord king Edward the sixth, entituled: An act for the uniformity of Common prayer, and administration of the Sacraments, the which was repealed and taken away by act of Parliament, in the first year of the reign of our late Sovereign Lady Queen Mary, to the great decay of the due honour of God, and discomfort to the professors of the truth of Christ's religion:

Be it therefore enacted by the authority of this present parliament, that the said statute[1] of repeal, and every thing therein contained, only concerning the said book, and the Service, administration of Sacraments, Rites, and Ceremonies, contained or appointed, in, or by the said book, shall be void and of none effect, from, and after the feast of the Nativity of S. John Baptist, next coming. And that the said book, with the order of service, and of the administration of Sacraments, Rites and Ceremonies, with the alterations[2], and additions, therein added and appointed by this estatute, shall stand, and be from and after the said feast of the nativity of Saint John Baptist, in full force and effect, according to the tenor and effect of this statute[1], any thing in the aforesaid estatute[3] of repeal, to the contrary notwithstanding.

And further be it enacted by the queen's highness, with the assent of the lords and commons, in this present Parliament assembled, and by authority of the same, that all and singular ministers, in any cathedral, or parish church, or other place within this realm of England, Wales, and the marches of the same, or other the queen's dominions, shall from, and after the feast of the Nativity of Saint John Baptist next coming, be bounden to say and use the Mattins, Evensong, celebration of the Lord's supper, and administration of each of the Sacraments, and all their Common and open prayer, in such order and form, as is mentioned in the said book, so authorized by Parliament in the said

[1 Grafton, estatute.]   [2 Grafton, alteracion.]
[3 Grafton, statute.]

.v. and .vi. year of the reign of king Edward the sixt, with one alteration or addition of certain lessons to be used on every Sunday in the year, and the form of the Litany altered and corrected, and two Sentences only added in the delivery of the Sacrament to the communicants, and none other, or other wise. And that if any manner of person[1], vicar, or other whatsoever minister that ought or should sing or say common prayer mentioned in the said book, or minister the Sacraments from and after the feast of the Nativity of Saint John Baptist next coming, refuse to use the said common prayers, or to minister the Sacraments in such Cathedral or parish Church, or other places, as he should use to minister the same, in such order and form, as they be mentioned and set forth in the said book : or shall wilfully, or obstinately standing in the same, use any other rite, ceremony, order, form, or manner of celebrating of the Lord's supper openly or privily, or Mattins, Evensong, administration of the Sacraments, or other open prayers than is mentioned and set forth in the said book [*Open prayer in and throughout this Act, is meant that prayer which is for other to come unto, or hear, either in Common Churches, or privy Chapels, or Oratories, commonly called the Service of the Church*] or shall preach, declare, or speak any thing in the derogation or depraving of the said book, or any thing therein contained, or of any part thereof, and shall be thereof lawfully convicted according to the laws of this realm, by verdict of .xii. men, or by his own confession, or by the notorious evidence of the fact : shall lose and forfeit to the Queen's highness, her heirs and successors, for his first offence, the profit of all his spiritual benefices or promotions, coming or arising in one whole year next after this conviction. And also that the person so convicted, shall for the same offence suffer imprisonment by the space of .vi. months, without bail or mainprise. And if any such person once convict of any offence, concerning the premises, shall after his first conviction eftsoons offend, and be thereof in form aforesaid lawfully convict : that then the same person shall for his second offence suffer imprisonment by the space of one whole year, and also shall therefore be deprived, *ipso facto*, of all his spiritual promotions. And that it shall be lawful to all patrons or donors of all and singular the same spiritual promotions, or of any of them, to present or collate to the same, as though the person and persons so offending were dead ; and that if any such person or persons, after he shall be twice convicted in form aforesaid, shall offend against any of the premises the third time, and shall be thereof in form aforesaid lawfully convicted : That then the person so offending, and convict[2] the third time, shall be deprived, *ipso facto*, of all his spiritual promotions, and also shall suffer imprisonment during his life.

AND if the person that shall offend, and be convict in form aforesaid, concerning any of the premises, shall not be beneficed, nor have any spiritual promotion : That then the same person so offending and convict, shall for the first offence suffer imprisonment during one whole

[[1] Person or parson : rector.]   [[2] Grafton, conuicted.]

year next after his said conviction, without bail or mainprise. And if any such person, not having any spiritual promotion, after his first conviction, shall eftsoons offend in any thing concerning the premises, and shall in form aforesaid be thereof lawfully convicted: That then the same person shall for his second offence, suffer imprisonment during his life.

AND it is ordained and enacted by the authority abovesaid, that if any person or persons whatsoever, after the said feast of the Nativity of Saint John Baptist next coming, shall in any Enterludes, Plays, Songs, Rhymes, or by other open words, declare or speak any thing in the derogation, depraving or despising of the same book, or of any thing therein contained, or any part thereof, or shall by open fact, deed, or by open threatenings, compel or cause, or otherwise procure or maintain any Parson, Vicar, or other Minister, in any Cathedral or parish Church, or in Chapel, or in any other place to sing or say any common and open prayer, or to minister any Sacrament otherwise, or in any other manner and form than is mentioned in the said book, or that by any of the said means shall unlawfully interrupt or let any parson, vicar, or other minister, in any Cathedral, or parish Church, Chapel, or any other place to sing or say common and open prayer, or to minister the Sacraments or any of them, in such manner and form, as is mentioned in the said book : That then every such parson[3] being thereof lawfully convicted in form above said, shall forfeit to the Queen our Sovereign Lady, her heirs and successors, for the first offence a hundreth marks. And if any parson or parsons, being once convict of any such offence eftsoons offend against any of the last recited offences, and shall in form aforesaid be thereof lawfully convict : That then the same parson so offending and convict, shall for the second offence forfeit to the Queen our Sovereign Lady, her heirs and successors, four hundreth marks. And if any parson after he, in form aforesaid, shall have been twice convict of any offence, concerning any of the last recited offences, shall offend the third time, and be thereof in form abovesaid lawfully convict: That then every parson so offending and convict, shall for his third offence, forfeit to our Sovereign Lady the Queen, all his goods and catelles, and shall suffer inprisonment during his life. And if any person or persons that for his first offence, concerning the premises, shall be convict in form aforesaid, do not pay the sum to be paid by virtue of his conviction, in such manner and form as the same ought to be paid, within .vi. weeks next after his conviction, that then every person so convict, and so not paying the same, shall for the same first offence, in stead of the said sum, suffer imprisonment by the space of .vi. months, without bail or mainprise. And if any person or persons, that for his second offence concerning the premises, shall be convict in form aforesaid, do not pay the said sum to be paid by virtue of his conviction, and this estatute, in such manner and form as the same ought to be paid, within .vi. weeks next after his said second conviction : that then every person so

[3 'Parson' often stands in this Act for *person*.]

convicted and not so[1] paying the same, shall for the same second offence, in the stead of the said sum, suffer imprisonment during .xii. months, without bail or mainprise. And that from and after the said feast of the Nativity of S. John Baptist next coming, all and every person and persons, inhabiting within this realm or any other the Queen's Majesty's dominions, shall diligently and faithfully, having no lawful or reasonable excuse to be absent, endeavour themselves to resort to their parish Church or Chapel accustomed, or upon reasonable let thereof, to some usual place where common Prayer, and such Service of God shall be used in such time of let upon every Sunday, and other days ordained and used to be kept as holy days. And then and there to abide orderly, and soberly during the time of the common prayer, preachings, or other service of God, there to be used and ministered, upon pain of punishment by the censures of the church. And also upon pain that every person so offending shall forfeit for every such offence .xii. d. to be levied by the Churchwardens of the parish, where such offence shall be done, to the use of the poor of the same parish, of the goods, lands, and tenements of such offender, by way of distress. And for due execution hereof, the Queen's most excellent Majesty, the lords Temporal, and all the commons in this present parliament assembled, doth in God's name earnestly require and charge all the Archbishops, Bishops, and other ordinaries, that they shall endeavour themselves to the uttermost of their knowledges, that the due and true execution hereof may be had throughout their diocese, and charges, as they will answer before God for such evils and plages, wherewith almighty God may justly punish his people for neglecting this good and wholesome law. And for their authority in this behalf, be it further enacted by the authority aforesaid, that all and singular the same archbishops, bishops, and all other their officers, exercising ecclesiastical jurisdiction, as well in place exempt as not exempt, within their diocese, shall have full power and authority by this act, to reform, correct, and punish by censures of the church, all and singular persons, which shall offend within any their[2] jurisdictions or diocese, after the said feast of the Nativity of Saint John Baptist next coming, against this act and statute. Any other law, statute, privilege, liberty, or provision heretofore made, had, or suffered to the contrary notwithstanding.

AND it is ordained and enacted by the authority aforesaid, that all and every justices of Oyer and determiner, or justices of Assize, shall have full power and authority in every of their open and general Sessions, to enquire, hear and determine all, and all manner of offences that shall be committed or done contrary to any article contained in this present act, within the limits of the commission to them directed, and to make process for the execution of the same, as they may do against any person being indicted before them of trespass, or lawfully convicted thereof.

[1] Misprint in both editions of 1559 for, so not.]
[2] Grafton, of their.]

PROVIDED always and be it enacted by the authority aforesaid, that all and every Archbishop and Bishop, shall or may at all time and times at his liberty and pleasure, join and associate himself, by virtue of this act, to the said justices of Oyer and determiner, or to the said justices of assize, at every of the said open and general Sessions, to be holden in any place within his diocese, for and to the enquiry, hearing and determining of the offences aforesaid.

PROVIDED also and be it enacted by the authority aforesaid, that the books concerning the said Services, shall at the costs and charges of the parishioners of every parish, and Cathedral Church, be attained and gotten before the said feast of the Nativity of Saint John Baptist next following, and that all such parishes and Cathedral Churches or other places, where the said books shall be attained and gotten before the said feast of the Nativity of Saint John Baptist, shall within three weeks next after the said books so attained and gotten, use the said service and put the same in ure[3] according to this act.

AND be it further enacted by the authority aforesaid, that no parson or parsons shall be at any time hereafter impeached or otherwise molested of or for any of the offences above mentioned, hereafter to be committed or done contrary to this act, unless he or they so offending, be thereof indicted at the next general Sessions, to be holden before any such justices of Oyer and determiner, or justices of assize, next after any offence committed or done contrary to the tenor of this act.

PROVIDED always and be it ordained and enacted by the authority aforesaid, that all and singular Lords of the Parliament for the third offence above mentioned, shall be tried by their peers.

PROVIDED also and be it ordained and enacted by the authority aforesaid, that the Major of London, and all other Majors, Bailiffs, and other head officers of all and singular Cities, Boroughs, and Towns Corporate within this realm, Wales, and the marches of the same, to the which justices of Assize do not commonly repair, shall have full power and authority by virtue of this act, to enquire, hear, and determine the offences abovesaid, and every of them yearly, within .xv. days after the feast of Easter, and S. Michael the archangel, in like manner and form as justices of Assize and Oyer and determiner may do.

PROVIDED always and be it ordained and enacted by the authority aforesaid, that all and singular Archbishops and Bishops, and every of their Chancellors, Commissaries, Archdeacons, and other ordinaries, having any peculiar ecclesiastical jurisdiction, shall have full power and authority by virtue of this act, as well to enquire in their visitation, synods, and elsewhere within their jurisdiction, at any other time and place, to take occasions[4] and informations of all and every the things above mentioned, done, committed, or perpetrated within the limits of their jurisdictions and authority, and to punish the same by admoni-

[3 Ure: use, practice.]
[4 Misprint in both editions of 1559 for, accusations. See the twelfth section of Edward's first Act, whence this is taken.]

tion, excommunication, sequestration, or deprivation and other censures and process in like form as heretofore hath been used in like cases by the Queen's ecclesiastical laws.

PROVIDED always and be it enacted, that whatsoever person offending in the premises, shall for the offence first receive punishment of the ordinary, having a testimonial thereof under the said ordinary's seal, shall not for the same offence eftsoons be convicted before the justices. And likewise receiving for the said first[1] offence punishment by the justices, he shall not for the same offence eftsoons receive punishment of the ordinary. Any thing contained in this act to the contrary notwithstanding.

PROVIDED always and be it enacted, that such ornaments of the Church, and of the ministers thereof, shall be retained and be in use as was in this Church of England, by authority of Parliament, in the second year of the reign of King Edward the vi. until other order shall be therein taken by the authority of the Queen's Majesty, with the advice of her Commissioners appointed and authorized under the great seal of England, for causes ecclesiastical, or of the Metropolitan of this realm. And also that if there shall happen any contempt or irreverence to be used in the ceremonies or rites of the Church, by the misusing of the orders appointed in this book: The Queen's Majesty may by the like advice of the said commissioners, or Metropolitan, ordain and publish such further ceremonies or rites as may be most for the advancement of God's glory, the edifying of his Church, and the due reverence of Christ's holy mysteries and Sacraments.

AND be it further enacted by the authority aforesaid, that all laws, statutes, and ordinances, wherein or whereby any other Service, administration of Sacraments, or Common prayer, is limited, established, or set forth to be used within this realm, or any other the Queen's dominions or countries, shall from henceforth be utterly void and of none effect.

[[1] Both editions of 1559 have the word 'fyrst' here misplaced. See the last section of Edward's Act, 1549.]

The Preface.

THERE was never any thing by the wit of man so well devised, or so sure established, which in continuance of time hath not been corrupted: as (among other things) it may plainly appear by the common prayers in the church, commonly called divine service. The first original and ground whereof if a man would search out by the ancient fathers, he shall find that the same was not ordained but of a good purpose, and for a great advancement of godliness. For they so ordered the matter, that all the whole bible (or the greatest part thereof) should be read over once in[2] the year: intending thereby, that the clergy, and specially such as were ministers of the congregation, should (by often reading and meditation of God's word) be stirred up to godliness themselves, and be more able to[3] exhort other by wholesome doctrine, and to confute them that were adversaries to the truth. And further, that the people (by daily hearing of holy scripture read in the church) should continually profit more and more in the knowledge of God, and be the more inflamed with the love of his true religion. But these many years passed, this godly and decent order of the ancient fathers hath been so altered, broken, and neglected, by planting in uncertain Stories, Legends, Responds, Verses, vain Repetitions, Commemorations, and Synodals, that commonly when any book of the bible was begun, before three or four chapters were read out, all the rest are[4] unread: and in this sort, the book of Esay was begun in Advent, and the book of Genesis in Septuagesima; but they were only begun, and never read through. After a like sort were other books of holy scripture used. And moreover, whereas S. Paul would have such language spoken to the people in the church, as they might understand, and have profit by hearing the same: the service in this church of England (these many years) hath been read in Latin to the people, which they understood not: so that they have heard with their ears only, and their hearts, spirit, and mind, have not been edified thereby. And furthermore, notwithstanding that the ancient fathers have divided the Psalms into seven portions, whereof every one was called a Nocturn: now of late time, a few of them have been daily said, and oft repeated, and the rest utterly omitted. Moreover, the number and hardness of the rules, called the Pie[5], and the manifold changings of the service, was the cause, that to turn the book

[2 1596, euery yeere.]   [3 Grafton, also to exhorte.]
[4 Grafton and 1596, were.]
[5 A table used anciently to find out the service belonging to each day. For the origin of the term, see a quotation from Nicholls in the notes to Mant's Book of Common Prayer. The other terms employed in this preface are there also explained.]

[LITURG. QU. ELIZ.]

only was so hard and intricate a matter, that many times there was more business to find out what should be read, than to read it when it was found out.

These inconveniences therefore considered, here is set forth such an order, whereby the same shall be redressed. And for a readiness in this matter, here is drawn out a kalendar for that purpose, which is plain and easy to be understanden[1], wherein (so much as may be) the reading of holy scriptures is so set forth, that all things shall be done in order, without breaking one piece thereof[2] from another. For this cause be cut off Anthems, Responds, Invitatories[3], and such like things, as did break the continual course of the reading of the scripture. Yet because there is no remedy, but that of necessity there must be some rules, therefore certain rules are here set forth, which as they be few in number, so they be plain and easy to be understanden[1]. So that here you have an order for prayer (as touching the reading of holy scripture) much agreeable to the mind and purpose of the old fathers, and a great deal more profitable and commodious, than that which of late was used. It is more profitable, because here are left out many things, whereof some be untrue, some uncertain, some vain and superstitious, and is ordained nothing to be read, but the very pure word of God, the holy scriptures, or that which is evidently grounded upon the same, and that in such a language and order, as is most easy and plain for the understanding both of the readers and heares[4]. It is also more commodious, both for the shortness thereof, and for the plainness of the order, and for that the rules be few and easy. Furthermore, by this order, the Curates shall need none other books for their public service, but this book and the bible: by the means whereof, the people shall not be at so great charge[5] for books, as in time past they have been.

And where[6] heretofore there hath been great diversity, in saying and singing in Churches within this realm, some following Salisbury use, some Hereford use, some the use of Bangor, some of York, and[7] some of Lincoln: Now from henceforth, all the whole realm shall have but one use. And if any would[8] judge this way more painful, because that all things must be read upon the book, whereas before, by the reason of so often repetition, they could say many things by heart: if those men will weigh their labour, with the profit and knowledge which daily they shall obtain by reading upon the book, they will not refuse the pain, in consideration of the great profit that shall ensue thereof.

And for as much as nothing can almost be so plainly set forth, but doubts may rise in the use and practising of the same: To appease

[1 1596, understanded.]   [2 1596 omits, thereof.]
[3 A scriptural sentence, generally adapted to the day, was not only prefixed to the ninety-fifth psalm, but repeated in part, or entirely, after each verse of it. Palmer's Origines Liturgicæ, Vol. I. p. 222.]
[4 Misprint for, hearers.]   [5 1596, charges.]
[6 where : whereas.]   [7 1596 omits, and.]
[8 1596, will.]

all such diversity (if any arise) and for the resolution of all doubts concerning the manner how to understand do and execute the things contained in this Book, the parties that so doubt, or diversely take any thing, shall alway resort to the Bishop of the diocese, who by his discretion shall take order for the quieting and appeasing of the same, so that the same order be not contrary to any thing contained in this Book. And if the Bishop of the Diocese be in[9] any doubt, then may he send for the resolution thereof unto the Archbishop.

> Though it be appointed in the afore written Preface, that all things shall be read and sung in the Church, in the English tongue, to the end that the congregation may be thereby edified: yet it is not meant, but when men say Morning and Evening prayer privately, they may say the same in any language that they themselves do understand[10].
>
> And all Priests and Deacons shall be bound to say daily the Morning and Evening prayer, either privately or openly, except they be letted[11] by preaching, studying of divinity, or by some other urgent cause.
>
> And the Curate that ministereth in every parish Church or Chapel, being at home, and not being otherwise reasonably letted, shall say the same in the Parish Church or Chapel where he ministereth, and shall toll a bell thereto a convenient time before he begin, that such as be disposed may come to hear God's word, and to pray with him.

[9 1596, in doubt.]

[10 See Elizabeth's Letters patent prefixed to her Latin Prayer Book, at the end.]

[11 1596, let.]

¶ Of Ceremonies

why some be abolished, and some retained.

Of such Ceremonies as be used in the church, and have had their beginning by the institution of man: some at the first were of godly entent and purpose devised, and yet at length turned to vanity and superstition: some entered into the church by undiscreet devotion, and such a zeal as was without knowledge; and forbecause they were winked at in the beginning, they grew daily to more and more abuses: which, not only for their unprofitableness, but also because they have much blinded the people, and obscured the glory of God, are worthy to be cut away and clean rejected. Other there be, which although they have been devised by man, yet it is thought good to reserve them still, as well for a decent order in the church (for the which they were first devised) as because they pertain to edification: whereunto all things done in the church (as the Apostles[1] teacheth) ought to be referred. And although the keeping or omitting of a Ceremony (in itself considered) is but a small thing: yet the wilful and contemptuous transgression and breaking of a common order and discipline is no small offence before God.

Let all things be done among you (saith S. Paul) in a seemly and due order. The appointment of the which order pertaineth not to private men: therefore no man ought to take in hand, nor[2] presume to appoint or alter any public or common order in Christ's church, except he be lawfully called and authorized thereunto.

And whereas in this our time the minds of men are so diverse, that some think it a great matter of conscience to depart from a piece of the least of their Ceremonies (they be so addicted to their old customs;) and again, on the other side, some be so new fangled, that they would innovate all thing, and so[3] do despise the old, that nothing can like

[1 Misprint for, Apostle.]   [2 Grafton, or.]
[3 1596, so despise.]

them, but that is new; it was thought expedient, not so much to have respect how to please and satisfy either of these parties, as how to please God, and profit them both. And yet, lest any man should be offended (whom good reason might satisfy) here be certain causes rendered, why some of the accustomed Ceremonies be put away, and some retained and kept still.

Some are put away, because the great excess and multitude of them hath so increased in these latter days, that the burthen of them was intolerable; whereof S. Augustine in his time complained, that they were grown to such a number, that the state of Christian people was in worse case (concerning that matter) than were the Jews. And he counselled that such yoke and burthen should be taken away, as time would serve quietly to do it.

Bue[1] what would S. Augustine have said, if he had seen the ceremonies of late days used among us: whereunto the multitude used in his time was not to be compared? This our excessive multitude of Ceremonies was so great, and many of them so dark; that they did more confound, and darken, than declare and set forth Christ's benefits unto us.

And besides this, Christ's gospel is not a Ceremonial law (as much of Moses' law was), but it is a religion to serve God, not in bondage of the figure or shadow, but in the freedom of spirit, being content only with those Ceremonies, which do serve to a decent order and godly discipline, and such as be apt to stir up the dull mind of man to the remembrance of his duty to God, by some notable and special signification, whereby he might be edified.

Furthermore, the most weighty cause of the abolishment of certain Ceremonies was, that they were so far abused, partly by the superstitious blindness of the rude and unlearned, and partly by the unsatiable avarice of such as sought more their own lucre, than the glory of God: that the abuses could not well be taken away, the thing remaining still. But now as concerning those persons, which peradventure will be offended, for that some of the old ceremonies are retained still: if they consider that without some Ceremonies it is not possible to keep any order or quiet discipline in the church, they shall easily perceive just cause to reform their judgments. And if

[1 Misprint for, But.]

they think much, that any of the old do remain, and would rather have all devised anew: Then such men granting some ceremonies convenient to be had, surely where the old may be[1] well used, there they cannot reasonably reprove the old, only for their age, without bewraying of their own folly. For in such a case, they ought rather to have reverence unto them for their antiquity, if they will declare themselves to be more studious of unity and concord, than of innovations and new fangleness, which (as much as may be with the true setting forth of Christ's religion) is always to be eschewed. Furthermore, such shall have no just cause with the Ceremonies reserved to be offended. For as those be taken away, which were most abused, and did burthen men's consciences without any cause: so the other that remain, are retained for a discipline and order, which (upon just causes) may be altered and changed, and therefore are not to be esteemed equal with God's law. And moreover, they be neither dark nor dumb ceremonies: but are so set forth, that every man may understand what they do mean, and to what use they do serve. So that it is not like that they in time to come should be abused as the other have been. And in these our doings we condemn no other nations, nor prescribe any thing but to our own people only. For we think it convenient that every country should use such ceremonies, as they shall think best to the setting forth of God's honour or[2] glory, and to the reducing of the people to a most perfect and godly living, without error or superstition; and that they should put away other things which from time to time they perceive to be most abused, as in men's ordinances it often chanceth diversly in divers countries.

[1 Grafton, well be.]   [2 1596, and.]

1559.]   39

The Table and kalendar expressing the Order of the
    Psalms and Lessons to be said at[3] Morning and
        Evening Prayer throughout the year,
            except certain proper feasts, as
                the rules following more
                    plainly declare.

¶ The order how the Psalter is appointed to be read.

THE Psalter shall be read through once every Month. And, because that some months be longer than some other be, it is thought good to make them even, by this means.

To every Month, shall be appointed (as concerning this purpose) just .xxx. days.

And because January and March hath[4] one day above the said number, and February which is placed between them both, hath only .xxviii. days: February shall borrow of either of the months (of January and March) one day. And so the Psalter which shall be read in February, must begin the[5] last day of January, and end the first day of March.

And whereas May, July, August, October, and December, have[6] .xxxi. days apiece: it is ordered that the same Psalms shall be read the last day of the said Months, which were read the day before. So that the Psalter may begin again the first day of the next Months[7] ensuing.

Now to know what Psalms shall be read every day, look in the kalendar the number that is appointed for the Psalms, and then find the same number in this table, and upon that number shall you see what Psalms shall be said at Morning and Evening Prayer.

And where the .cxix. Psalm is divided into .xxii. portions, and is over long to be read at one time: it is so ordered, that at one time shall not be read above four or five of the said portions, as you shall perceive to be noted in this table following.

And here is also to be noted, that in this table, and in all other parts of the service, where any Psalms are appointed, the number is expressed after the great English Bible, which from the .ix. Psalm unto the .cxlviii. Psalm (following the division of the Hebrews) doth vary in numbers from the common Latin translation.

[3 Grafton, at the.]   [4 1596, haue.]
[5 1596, at the last.]   [6 Grafton, hath.]
[7 Grafton and 1596, monethe.]

The[1] Table for the Order of the Psalms, to be said at Morning and Evening Prayer.

Days[2] of the Month.	Psalms[3] for Morning prayer.	Psalms[3] for Evening prayer.
i.[4]	1, 2, 3, 4, 5.	6, 7, 8.
ii.	9, 10, 11.	12, 13, 14.
iii.	15, 16, 17.	18.
iv.	19, 20, 21.	22, 23.
v.	24, 25, 26.	27, 28, 29.
vi.	30, 31.	32, 33, 34.
vii.	35, 36.	37.
viii.	38, 39, 40.	41, 42, 43.
ix.	44, 45, 46.	47, 48, 49.
x.	50, 51, 52.	53, 54, 55.
xi.	56, 57, 58.	59, 60, 61.
xii.	62, 63, 64.	65, 66, 67.
xiii.	68.	69, 70.
xiv.	71, 72.	73, 74.
xv.	75, 76[5], 77.	78.
xvi.	79, 80, 81.	82, 83, 84, 85.
xvii.	86, 87, 88.	89.
xviii.	90, 91, 92.	93, 94.
xix.	96[6], 97.	98, 99, 100, 101.
xx.	102, 103.	104.
xxi.	105.	106.
xxii.	107.	108, 109.
xxiii.	110, 111, 112, 113.	114, 115.
xxiv.	116, 117, 118.	119. Inde. 4.
xxv.	Inde. 5.	Inde. 4.
xxvi.	Inde. 5.	Inde. 4.
xxvii.	120, 121, 122, 123, 124, 125.	126, 127, 128, 129, 130, 131.
xxviii.	132, 133, 134, 135.	136, 137, 138.
xxix.	139, 140, 141.	142, 143.
xxx.	144, 145, 146.	147, 148, 149, 150.

[[1] 1596 has this immediately before the calendar.]
[[2] Not in Grafton.]
[[3] Psalms for, not in Grafton.] [[4] Grafton omits, i.]
[[5] Grafton, lxvi. lxvii.]
[[6] Grafton and 1596 insert, xcv.]

⁋ The Order how the rest of holy scripture (beside the Psalter) is appointed to be read.

The old Testament is appointed for the first lessons, at Morning and Evening prayer, and shall be read through, every year once, except certain books and Chapters, which be least edifying, and might best be spared, and therefore be left unread.

The new Testament is appointed for the second Lessons, at Morning and Evening prayer, and shall be read over orderly every year thrice, beside the Epistles and Gospels: except the Apocalypse, out of the which there be only certain Lessons appointed, upon diverse proper feasts.

And to know what Lessons shall be read every day: find the day of the month in the Kalendar following, and there ye shall perceive the books and Chapters that shall be read for the Lessons, both at Morning and Evening prayer.

And here is to be noted, that whensoever there be any proper Psalms or Lessons appointed for the Sundays or for any feast moveable or unmoveable: then the Psalms and Lessons, appointed in the kalendar, shall be omitted for that time.

Ye must note also that the Collect, Epistle and Gospel, appointed for the Sunday, shall serve all the week after, except there fall some feast that hath his proper.

This is also to be noted, concerning the Leap years, that the .xxv. day of February, which in Leap year is counted for two days, shall in those two days alter neither Psalm nor Lesson: but the same Psalms and Lessons, which be said the first day, shall also serve for the second day.

Also, wheresoever the beginning of any Lesson, Epistle or Gospel is not expressed: there ye must begin at the beginning of the Chapter.

And wheresoever is not expressed how far shall be read, there shall you read to the end of the Chapter.

⁋ Proper lessons to be read for the first lessons, both at morning prayer and evening prayer, on the Sundays throughout the Year, and for some also the second Lessons.

	Mattins.	Evensong.		Mattins.	Evensong.
Sundays of Advent.			Sunday after Ascension day.	Deut. 12	Deut. 13
The first	Esa. 1	Esa. 2	Whitsunday.		
2	5	24	1 Lesson	Deut. 17	Deut. 18
3	25	26	2 Lesson	Acte. 10.	Acte. 19.
4	30	32		Then Peter opened his. &c.	It fortuned whenApollo went to Corinth. &c. unto After these things.
Sundays after Christmas.	Mattins.	Evensong.			
The first	37	38			
2	41	43			
Sundays after the Epiphany.			Trinity Sunday.		
The first	44	46	1 Lesson	Gen. 18	Josue 1
2	51	53	2 Lesson	Math. 3	
3	55	56	Sundays after the Trinity.		
4	57	58			
5	59	64			
			The first	Josue 10	Josue 23
Septuage.	Gen. 1	Gen. 2	2	Judic. 4	Judic. 5
			3	1 King 2	1 King 3
Sexagesi.	3	6	4	12	13
			5	15	16[1]
Quinqua.	9	12	6	2 Kyng 12	2 Kyng 21
Lent.			7	22	24
			8	3 King 13	3 King 17
1 Sunday	19	22	9	18	19
2	27	34	10	21	22
3	39	42	11	4 King 5	4 King 19[2]
4	43	45	12	10	18
5	Exod. 3	Exod. 5	13	19	23
6	9	10	14	Jerem. 5	Jerem. 22
Easter day.	Mattins.	Evensong.	15	35	36
1 Lesson	12	14	16	Ezech. 2	Ezech. 14
2 Lesson	Rom. 6	Act. 2	17	16	18
			18	20	24
Sundays after Easter.			19	Daniel 3	Daniel 6
			20	Joel 2	Miche 6
The first	Nume. 16	Nume. 22	21	Abac. 2	Prov. 1
2	23	25	22	Prov. 2	3[3]
3	Deut. 4	Deut. 5	23	11	12
4	6	7	24	13	14
5	8	9	25	15	16
			26	17	19

[1 Grafton, xv.] [2 Misprint for, ix.] [3 Grafton, ii.]

Lessons proper for holy days.

	Mattins.	Evensong.		Mattins.	Evensong.
S. Andrew.	Prov. 20	Prov. 21	Annunciation of our Lady.	Eccle. 2	Eccle. 3
S. Thomas the Apostle.	23	24	Wednesday afore Easter.	Osee 13	Osee 14
Nativity of Christ. 1 Lesson	Esay 9	Esay 7. God spake once again to Achas. &c.	Thursday before Easter.	Dan. 9	Jerem. 31
2 Lesson	Luke 2, *unto* and unto men of good will.	Titus 3. The kindness and love. &c.	Good Friday.	Gen. 22	Esay 53
			Easter Even.	Zach. 9	Exod. 13
S. Stephen.			Monday in Easter week.		
1 Lesson	Prov. 28	Eccles. 4	1 Lesson	Exod. 16	17
2 Lesson	Acte 6 & 7. Stephen full of faith and power. &c., *unto* And when .xl. years. &c.	Acte 7. And when .xl. years were expired, there appeared unto Moses. &c. *unto* Stephen full of the Holy. &c.	2 Lesson	Math. 28	Acte 3
			Tuesday in Easter[5].		
			1 Lesson	Exod. 20	Exod. 32
			2 Lesson	Luke 24. *unto* And behold .ii. of them.	1 Cor. 15
S. John.			S. Mark.	Eccle. 4	Eccle. 5
1 Lesson	Eccles. 5	Eccles. 6	Philip & Jacob.	7	9
2 Lesson	Apoc. 1	Apoc. 22	Ascension Day.	Deut. 10	Deut. 11
Innocents.	Jerem. 31, *unto* Moreover I heard Ephraim.	Wisd. 1	Monday in Whitsun week.	30	31
Circumcision day.			Tuesday in Whitsun week.	32	34[6]
1 Lesson	Gen. 17	Deut. 10. and now Israel. &c.	S. Barnabe.		
2 Lesson	Rom. 2	Coloss. 2	1 Lesson	Eccle. 10	Eccle. 12
Epiphany day.			2 Lesson	Act. 14	Act. 15. *unto,* After certain days.
1 Lesson	Esay 60	Esay 49	S. John Baptist.		
2 Lesson	Luke 3. and it fortuned. &c.	John 2. after this he went to Capernaum.	1 Lesson	Malach. 3	Malach. 4
			2 Lesson	Math. 3	Math. 14. *unto,* When Jesus heard.
Conversion of S. Paul.			S. Peter.		
1 Lesson	Wisd. 5	Wisd. 6	1 Lesson	Eccle. 15	Eccle. 19
2 Lesson	Act. 22. *unto* they heard him.	Act. 2[4]	2 Lesson	Act. 3	Act. 4
			S. James.	Eccle. 21	23
Purification of the Virgin Mary.	Wisd. 9	Wisd. 12	S. Bartholomew.	25	29
S. Mathie.	Wisdom 19	Eccle. 1	S. Mathew.	35	38

[[4] Misprint in both editions of 1559 for, xxvi. See Calendar.]
[[5] week, omitted in both editions.]   [[6] Grafton, xxiiii.]

Lessons proper for holy days.

	Mattins.	Evensong.		Mattins.	Evensong.
S. Michael.	Eccle. 39	Eccle. 44	All Saints.		
S. Luke.	51	Job 1	1 Lesson	Wisd. 3. *unto* blessed is rather the barren.	Wisd. 5. *unto* his jealousy also.
S. Simon & Jude.					
1 Lesson	24	42	2 Lesson	Heb. 11, 12. Saints by faith *unto* If you endure chastening.	Apoc. 19. *unto* And I saw an angel stand.
2 Lesson	25[1]				

Proper Psalms on certain days.

	Mattins.	Evensong.		Mattins.	Evensong.
Christmas day.	Psal. 19 45 85	Psal. 89 110 132	Ascension day.	Psal. 8 15 21	Psal. 24 68 108
Easter day.	2 57 111	113 114 118	Whitsunday.	45[2] 67	104 145

[[1] Both chapters should have been assigned for the first lesson. See New Calendar.]

[[2] Probably, a mere misprint. See Clay's Prayer Book Illustrated, p. 11, note c. Grafton, xlviii.]

¶ A[3] brief declaration
when every Term beginneth
and endeth.

BE it known that Easter Term beginneth always, the .xviii. day after Easter, reckoning Easter day for one. And endeth the Monday next after the Ascension day.

Trinity Term beginneth alway, the Friday next after Trinity Sunday, and endeth the .xxviii. day of June.

Michaelmas Term, beginneth the ninth or tenth day of October, and endeth the .xxviii. or .xxix. day of November.

Hilary Term beginneth the .xxiii. or .xxiv. day of January, and endeth the .xii. or .xiii. day of February.

In Easter Term, on the Ascension day. In Trinity Term, on the Nativity of Saint John Baptist. In Michaelmas Term, on the feast of All Saints. In Hilary Term, on the feast of the Purification of our Lady. The Queen's Judges of Westminster do not use to sit in Judgment, nor upon any Sundays.

[3 Not in Grafton.]

¶ An Almanack for .xxx. Years.

¶ The years of our Lord.	¶ The Golden Number.	The Epacta.	¶ The Cycle of the Sun.	Dominical letter.	Easter day.
1559	2	22	28	A.	26 March.
1560	3	3	1	G. F.	14 April.
1561	4	14	2	E.	6 April.
1562	5	25	3	D.	29 March.
1563	6	6	4	C.	11 April.
1564	7	17	5	B. A.	2 April.
1565	8	28	6	G.	22 April.
1566	9	9	7	F.	14 April.
1567	10	20	8	C.[2]	30 March.
1568	11	1	9	D. C.	18 April.
1569	12	12	10	B.	10 April.
1570	13	23	11	A.	26 March.
1571	14	4	12	G.	15 April.
1572	15	15	13	F. E.	6 April.
1573	16	26	14	D.	22 March.
1574	17	7	15	C.	11 April.
1575	18	18	16	B.	3 April.
1576	19	119[1]	17	A. G.	22 April.
1577	1	11	18	F.	7 April.
1578	2	22	19	E.	30 March.
1579	3	3	20	D.	29 April.
1580	4	14	21	C. B.	3 April.
1581	5	25	22	A.	26 March.
1582	6	6	23	G.	15 April.
1583	7	17	24	F.	31 March.
1584	8	28	25	E. D.	19 April.
1585	9	9	26	C.	11 April.
1586	10	20	27	B.	3 April.
1587	11	1	28	A.	16 April.
1588	12	12	1	G.[3]	7 April.

[1 Grafton, 0.]   [2 Misprint for, E.]
[3 F, omitted in Jugge and Cawode.]

[1559.]   47

¶ January hath xxxi. days.

			Psalms 1 Less.	Morning prayer. 2 Less.	Evening prayer. 1 Less.	2 Less.
2¹	A	Kalend. Circumcision.²	1	Gen. 17	Rom. 2	Deut. 10	Coloss. 2
	b	4 No. Ortus³ solis.	2	Gen. 1	Math. 1	Gen. 2	Rom. 1
11	c	3 No. Ho. 8. Mi. 3.	3	3	2	4	2
	d	Prid. No. Occasus Ho.	4	5	3	6	3
9	e	Nonæ.⁴ 3. Mi. 57.	5	7	4	8	4
8	f	8 Id. *Epiphanie*.	6	Esai. 60	Luke 3	Esai. 49	Jhon 2
	g	7 Idus.	7⁶	Gen. 9	Math. 5	Gen. 11	Rom. 5
6	A	6 Idus.	8	12	6	13	6
5	b	5 Idus.	9	14	7	15	7
	c	4 Idus.	10	16	8	17	8
13	d	3 Idus. Sol in Aquario.	11	18	9	19	9
2	e	Prid. Id.	12	20	10	21	10
	f	Idus.	13	22	11	23	11
10	g	19 kal. Februarii.	13⁷	24	12	25	12
	A	18 kal.	15	26	13	27	13
17	b	17 kal. Term⁸ beginneth	16	28	14	29	14
7	c	16 kal.	17	30	15	31	15
	d	15 kal.	18	32	16	33	16
15	e	14 kal.	19	34	17	35	1 Cor. 1
4	f	13 kal.	20	36	18	37	2
	g	12 kal.	21	39	19	39	3
12	A	11 kal.	22	40	20	41	4
1	b	10 kal.	23	42	21	63¹⁰	5
	c	9 kal.	24	44	22	45	Act. 26
9	d	8 kal. *Convers. Pauli*.	25	46	Act. 22	47	1 Cor. 7
	e	7 kal.	26⁶	48	Mat. 13⁹	49	8
17	f	9⁵ kal.	26	50	24	Exod. 1	9
6	g	5 kal.	28	Exod. 2	25	3	10
	A	4 kal.	29	4	26	5	11
14	b	3 kal.	30	6	27	7	12
3	c	Pridie kal.	1	8	28	9	

¹ Grafton has no Golden numbers. The numbers appointed for the Psalms come here, though their heading remains, as in Jugge and Cawode. These printers afterwards adopted Grafton's arrangement.
² Red letter days are shewn by italics.   ³ Not in Grafton.
⁴ Grafton, Nonas. And so in the other months.   ⁵ Misprint for, 6.
⁶ Misprint for, 8.   ⁷ Misprint for, 14.   ⁸ Misprint for, 27.
⁹ Misprint for, xxiii.   ¹⁰ Misprint for, xliii.

¶ February hath xxviii. days.

			Psalms 1 Less.	Morning prayer. 2 Less.	Evening prayer. 1 Less.	2 Less.
	d	Kalend.	2	Exod. 10	Mark 1	Exod. 11	1 Cor. 13
11	e	4 No.¹¹ *Puri. Mary.*	3	12	2	13	14
19	f	3 No. Ortus solis Ho. 7.	4	14	3	15	15
	g	Prid. No. Mi.14. Occas.	5	16	4	17	16
8	A	Nonæ. Ho. 4. Mi. 46.	6	18	5	19	2 Cor. 1
16	b	8 Idus.	7	20	6	21	2
5	c	7 Idus.	8	22	7	22¹³	3
	d	6 Idus.	9	24	8	32	4
13	e	5 Idus.	10	33	9	34	5
2	f	4 Idus. Sol. in Piscibus.	11	35	10	40	6
	A	3 Idus.	12	Lev. 18	11	Lev. 19	7
10	b	Prid. Id.	13	20	12	Num. 10	8
	b	Idus.	14	Num. 11	13	12	9
18	c	16 kal. Martii.	15	13	14	14	10
7	d	15 kal.	16	15	15	16	11
	e	14 kal.	17	17	16	18	12
15	f	13 kal.	18	19	Lu.¹² 1	20	13
4	g	12 kal.	19	21	di. 1	22	Galat. 1
12	A	11 kal.	20	23	2	24	2
1	b	10 kal.	21	25	3	26	3
	c	9 kal.	22	27	4	28	4
9	d	8 kal.	23	29	5	30	5
	e	7 kal.	24	31	6	32	6
17	f	6 kal. *S. Mathias*.	25	33	7	34	Ephes. 1
6	g	5 kal.	26	35	8	36	2
	A	4 kal.	27	Deut. 1	9	Deut. 2	3
14	b	3 kal.	28	3	10	4	4
3	c	Prid. kl.	29	5	11	6	5

¹¹ No, omitted in Grafton.
¹² Grafton inserts, di.
¹³ Misprint for, xxiii.

[1559.

❧ March hath xxxi. days.

			Morning prayer.		Evening prayer.	
			Psalms 1 Less.	2 Less.	1 Less.	2 Less.
3	d	Kalend.	30	Deut. 7	Deut. 8	Ephes. 6
	e	6 No.	1	9	10	Philip. 1
11	f	5 No. Ortus solis.	2	11	12	2
	g	4 No. Ho. 6. Mi. 18.	3	13	14	3
19	A	3 No. Occasus.	4	15	16	4
8	b	Prid. No. Ho. 5. Mi. 42.	5	17	18	Colos. 1
	c	Nonae.	6	19	20	2
16	d	8 Idus.	7	21	22	3
5	e	7 Idus.	8	23	24	4
	f	6 Idus.	9	25	26	1 Thes. 1
13	g	5 Idus.	10	27	28	2
2	A	4 Idus Sol in Ariete	11	29	30	3
	b	3 Id. Equinoctium.[1]	12	31	32	4
10	c	Prid. No.[2]	13	33	34	5
	d	Idus.	14	Josue 1	Josue 2	2 Thes. 1
18	e	17 kl.	15	3	4	2
7	f	16 kl. Aprilis.	16	4	5	3
	g	15 kl.	17	5	6	1 Tim. 1
15	A	14 kl. Easter term	18	6	7	2, 3
4	b	13 kl. beginneth	19	7	8	4
	c	12 kl. the xvii.	20	8	9	5
12	d	11 kl. day after	21	9	10	6
1	e	10 kl. Easter day.	22	10	11	2 Tim. 1
	f	9 kl.	23	12	20	2
9	g	8 kl.	24	21	22	3
	A	7 kl. Annun. of Ma.	25	23	24	4
17	b	9[3] kl.	26	Judic. 1	Judic. 2	Titus 1
6	c	5 kal.	27	3	4	2, 3
	d	4 kal.	28	5	6	Phil. 1
14	e	3 kal.	29	7	8	Heb. 1
3	f	Prid. kl.	30	10[4]	10	2

[1] Grafton has, Equinoctium, two days higher; and also, Annunciatio, as Aprilis, one day higher.
[2] Misprint for, Id.
[3] Misprint for, 6.
[4] Grafton, ix.

❧ April hath xxx. days.

			Morning prayer.		Evening prayer.	
			Psalms 1 Less.	2 Less.	1 Less.	2 Less.
11	g	Kalend.	1	Judic. 11	John 19	Judic. 12	Heb. 3
	A	4 No. Ortus solis Ho. 6.	2	13	20	14	4
19	b	3 No. Mi. 17. Occasus.	3	15	21	16	5
8	c	Prid. No. Ho. 6. Mi. 43.	4	17	Acts 1	18	6
	d	Nonae.	5	19	2	20	7
16	e	8 Idus.	6	21	3	Ruth 1	9
5	f	7 Idus.	7	Ruth 2	4	3	10
	A	6 Idus.	8	4	5	1 Reg. 1	11
13	g	5 Idus.	9	1 Reg. 2	6	3	12
2	b	4 Idus. Sol[5] in Tauro.	10	4	7	5	13
	c	3 Idus.	11	6	8	7	Jac. 1
10	d	Prid. Id.	12	8	9	9	2
	e	Idus.	13	10	10	11	3
18	f	18 kal. Maii.	14	12	11	13	4
7	g	17 kal.	15	14	12	15	5
	A	16 kal.	16	16	13	17	1 Pet. 1
15	b	15 kal.	17	18	14	19	2
4	c	14 kal.	18	20	15	21	3
	d	13 kal.	19	22	16	23	4
12	e	12 kal.	20	24	17	25	5
1	f	11 kal.	21	26	18	27	2 Pet. 1
	g	10 kal.	22	18[6]	19	29	2
9	A	9 kal. S. George.	23	30	20	31	3
	b	8 kal.	24	2 Reg. 1	21	2 Reg. 2	1 John 1
17	c	7 kal. Mark Evan.	25	3	22	4	2
6	d	6 kal.	26	5	23	6	3
	e	5 kal.	27	7	24	8	4
14	f	4 kal.	28	9	25	10	5
3	g	3 kal.	29	11	26	12	2, 3. Joh.
	A	Prid. kl.	30	13	27	14	

[5] Grafton has this two days lower.
[6] Misprint for, xxviii.

[1559.]   49

¶ May hath xxxi. days.

				Psalms	Morning prayer 1 Less.	Morning prayer 2 Less.	Evening prayer 1 Less.	Evening prayer 2 Less.
11	b	Kalend. *Phil. et Ja.*[1]	1	2	2 Reg. 15	Act 8	2 Reg. 16	Judas. 1
	c	6 No. Ortus solis		2	17[3]	23	18	Rom. 1
19	d	5 No. Ho. 4. Mi. 23.		3	19	Math. 1	20	2
8	e	4 No. Occasus.		4	21	2	22.[?]	3
	f	3 No. Ho. 7. Mi. 17.		5	23	3	24	4
16	g	Prid. No.		6	3 Reg. 1	4	3 Reg. 1	5
5	A	Nonæ.		7	2	5	2	6
	b	8 Idus.		8	3	6	4	7
13	c	7 Idus.		9	5	7	9	8
2	d	6 Idus.		10	9	8	10	9
	e	5 Idus. Sol. in Gem.		11	11	9	12	10
10	f	4 Idus.		12	13	10	14	11
	g	3 Idus.		13	15	11	16	12
18	A	Prid. Id.		14	17	12	18	13
7	b	Idus.		15	19	13	20	14
	c	17 kal. Junii.		16	21	14[3]	22	15
15	d	16 kal. Term endeth		17	4 Reg. 1	15	4 Reg. 2	16
4	e	15 kal. the monday		18	3	16	4[4]	1 Cor. 1
	f	14 kal. after Ascen-		19	5	17	6	2
12	g	13 kal. sion day.		20	7	18	8	3
1	A	12 kal.		21	9	19	10	4
	b	11 kal.		22	11	20	12	5
9	c	10 kal.		23	13	21	14	6
	d	9 kal.		24	15	22	16	7
17	e	8 kal.		25	17	23	18	8
6	f	7 kal.		26	29[4]	24	20	9
	g	6 kal.		27	21	25	22	10
14	A	5 kal.		28	23	26	24	11
3	b	4 kal.		29	25	27	25[7]	12
	c	3 kal.		30[2]	1 Esd. 1	28	1 Esd. 3	13
11	d	Prid. kl.			3	Mark 1	4	14

[1] Grafton has black letters.
[2] Grafton has 31 in the case of every month, except December. [6] Grafton, iii.
[3] Grafton, vii. [4] Misprint for, xix. [5] Grafton, xxiiii.
[7] Grafton, i Esd. i. The other lessons are ii, iii, iiii, v.

¶ June hath xxx. days.

				Psalms	Morning prayer 1 Less.	Morning prayer 2 Less.	Evening prayer 1 Less.	Evening prayer 2 Less.
	e	Kalend.		1	1 Esd. 5[5]	Mark 2	6 Esd. 6[7]	1 Cor. 15
19	f	4 No. Ortus solis Ho. 3.		2	7	3	8	16
8	g	3 No. Mi. 48. Occasus.		3	9	4	10	2 Cor. 1
16	A	Prid. No. Ho. 8. Mi. 12.		4	2 Esd. 1	5	2 Esd. 2	2
5	b	Nonæ. Trinity Term be-		5		6	4	3
	c	8 Idus. ginneth .xii.		6	5	7	6	4
13	d	7 Idus. days after		7	7	8	8	5
2	e	6 Idus. Whitsunday		8	9	9	10	6
	f	5 Idus. & continueth		9	11	10	13	7
10	g	4 Idus. xix days.		10	Hester 1	11	Hester 2	
	A	3 Idus. *Barnab. Ap.*		11	3	Act 14	4	Act 15
18	b	Prid. Id. Sol. in Can.[1]		12	5	Mark 12	6	2 Cor. 9
7	c	Idus.[2] Solstitium Æsti-		13	7	13	8	10
	d	vum.[3]		14	9	14	Job 1	11
15	e	18 kal.		15	Job 2	15	3	12
4	f	17 kal.		16	4	16	5	13
	g	16 kal.		17	6	Luke 1	7	Galat. 1
12	A	15 kal.[4]		18	8	2	9	2
1	b	14 kal.		19	10	3	11	3
	c	13 kal.		20	12	4	13	4
9	d	12 kal.		21	14	5	15	5
	e	11 kal.		22	16	6	17. 18	6
17	f	10 kal.		23	19	7	20	Ephes. 1
6	g	9 kal.		24	Mal. 3	Math. 3	Mal. 4	Math. 14
	A	8 kal. *Joan Bapt.*		25	Job 21	Luke 8	Job 22	Ephes. 2
14	b	7 kal.		26	23	9	24. 25	3
3	c	6 kal.		27	26, 27	10	28	4
	d	5 kal.		28	29	11	30	5
11	e	4 kal.		29	31	Act 3	32	Act 4
	f	3 kal. *S. Peter Ap.*		30	33	Luke 12	34	Ephes. 6

[1] Grafton has this one day lower.   [2] Julii, omitted.   [3] Not in Grafton.
[4] Grafton, Terme begun.
[5] The lessons in Grafton are vi, viii, x, ii. Esd. ii, iiii, vi, viii, x, xii.
[6] i, omitted.
[7] The lessons in Grafton are vii, ix, ii. Esd. i, iii, v, vii, ix, xi, xiii.

[LITURG. QU. ELIZ.]   4

50   [1559.

¶ August hath xxxi. days.

			Psalms	Morning prayer. 1 Less.	2 Less.	Evening prayer. 1 Less.	2 Less.
8	c	Kalend Lammas.	1	Jer. 12	John 20	Jer. 13	Heb. 4
16	d	4 No.	2	14	21	15	5
5	e	3 No. Ortus solis.	3	16	Act 1	17	6
	f	Prid. No. Hora. 4. Mi.	4	18	2	19	7
13	g	Nonæ. 37. Occasus.	5	20	3	21	8
2	A	8 Idus. Ho. 7. Mi. 23.	6	22	4	23[4]	9
	b	7 Idus.	7	24	5	25	10
10	c	6 Idus.	8	26	6	27	11
	d	5 Idus.	9	28	7	29[5]	12
18	e	4 Idus. S. Laurence.[1]	10	30	8	31	13
7	f	3 Idus.	11	32	9	33	Jac. 1
15	g	Prid Id.	12	34	10	35	2
	A	Idus.	13	36	11	37	3
4	b	9 1[2] kal. Septembris.	14	38	12	39	4
	c	18 kal. Sol in Virgine.	15	40	13	41	5
12	d	71 kal. [end [3]	16	42	14	43	1 Pet. 1
1	e	16 kal. The dog days	17	44	15	45. 46	2
	f	14 kal.	18	47	16	48	3
9	g	15 kal.	19	49	17		4
	A	13 kal.	20	51	18	52	5
17	b	12 kal.	21	Lam. 1	19	Lam. 2	2 Pet. 1
6	c	11 kal.	22	3	20	4	2
	d	10 kal.	23	5	21	Ezech. 2	3
14	e	9 kal. Bartho. Ap.	24	Ezech. 3	22	6	1 Joh. 1
3	f	8 kal.	25	7	23	13	2
11	A	7 kal.	26	14	24	18	3
	b	6 kal.	27	33	25	34	4
19	c	5 kal.	28	Dan. 1	26	Dan. 2	5
8	d	4 kal.	29	3	27	4	2, 3 Joh.
	e	3 kal.	30	5	28	6	Judas 1
		Prid. kl.		7	Math. 1	8	Rom. 1

[1] Grafton has red letters.   [3] Not in Grafton.   See Sep. 5.
[2] Four misprints occur close together.   [6] 1. omitted.
[4] Grafton, ix.   [5] Grafton, xxii.

¶ July hath xxxi. days.

			Psalms	Morning prayer. 1 Less.	2 Less.	Evening prayer. 1 Less.	2 Less.
19	g	Kalend.	1	Job 35	Luke 13	Job 36	Philip. 1
8	A	6 No. Ortus solis Ho. 3.	2	37	14	38	2
	b	5 No. Mi. 53. Occasus.	3	39	15	40	3
16	c	4 No. Ho. 8. Mi. 7.	4	41	16	42	4
5	d	3 No.	5	Prov. 1	17	Prov. 2	Coloss. 1
	e	Prid. No.[1]	6	3	18	4	2
13	f	Nonæ. Dog days begin.[2]	7	5	19	6	3
2	g	8 Idus.	8	7	20	8	4
	A	7 Idus.	9	9	21	10	1 Tes. 1
10	b	6 Idus.	10	11	22	12	2
	c	5 Idus.	11	13	23	14	3
18	d	4 Idus.	12	15	24	16	4
7	e	3 Idus.	13	17	John 1	18	5
	f	Prid. Id. Sol in Leone.	14	19	2	20	2 Tes. 1
15	g	Idus.	15	21	3	22	2
4	A	17 kal. Augusti.	16	23	4	24	3
	b	16 kal.	17	25	5	26	1 Tim. 1
12	c	15 kal.	18	27	6	28	2. 3
1	d	14 kal.	19	29	7	30	4
	e	13 kal.	20	31	8	Eccle. 1	5
9	f	21[3] kal.	21	Eccle. 2	9	3	6
	g	11 kal.	22	4	10	5	2 Tim. 1
17	A	10 kal.	23	6	11	7	2
6	b	9 kal. James Apo.	24	8	12	9	3
	c	8 kal.	25	10	13	11	4
14	d	7 kal.	26	12	14	Jere. 1	Titus 1
3	e	6 kal.	27	Jere. 2	15	3	2. 3
	f	5 kal.	28	4	16	5	Phile. 1
11	g	4 kal.	29	6	17	7	Hebr. 1
	A	3 kal.	30	8	18	9	2
19	b	Prid. kl.		10	19	11	3

[1] Grafton, Terme ende.   [2] Grafton omits, begin.
[3] Misprint for, 12.

[1559.]   51

¶ September hath .xxx. days.

					Morning prayer.		Evening prayer.	
				Psalms	1 Less.	2 Less.	1 Less.	2 Less.
16	f	Kalend.		1	Dan. 9	Math. 2	Dan. 10	Rom. 2
5	g	4 No. Ortus solis Ho. 5.		2	11	3	12	3
	A	[1] 3 No. Mi. 36. Occasus.		3	13	4	14	4
13	b	Prid. No. Ho. 6. Mi. 24.		4	Oze 1	5	Oze 2. 5, 6	5
2	c	Nonæ. Dog days end.		5	4	6	8	6
	d	8 Idus.		6	7	7	10	7
10	e	7 Idus.		7	9	8	12	8
	f	6 Idus.		8	11	9	14	9
18	g	5 Idus.		9	13	10	Joel 2	10
7	A	[1] 4 Idus.		10	Joel 1	11	Amos 1	11
	b	3 Idus.		11	3	12	3	12
15	c	Prid. Id.		12	Amos 2	13	5	13
4	d	Idus. Sol [2] in Libra.		13	4	14	7	14
	e	18 kal. Octobris.		14	6	15	9	15
12	f	17 kal. Æquinoctium		15	8	16	Jonas 1	16
1	g	16 kal. [autumnale.[3]	16	Abd. 1	17	4	1 Cor. 1
	A	15 kal.		17	Jon. 2. 3	18	Miche 2	2
9	b	14 kal.		18	Miche 1	19	4	3
	c	13 kal.		19	3	20	6	4
17	d	12 kal.		20	5	21	Naum 1	5
6	e	11 kal. S. Mathew.		21	7	22 [5]	3	6
	f	10 kal.		22	Naum 2	23	Abac. 2	7
14	g	9 kal.		23	Abac. 1	24	Soph. 1	8
3	A	8 kal.		24	3	25	3	9
	b	7 kal.		25	Soph. 2	26	Agge. 2	10
11	c	6 kal.		26	Agge. 1	27	Zach.2.3	11
	d	5 kal.		27	Zach. 1	28	6	12
19	e	4 kal.		28	4, 5	Mark 1	8	13
8	f	3 kal. S.[4] Michael.		29	7	2	8	14
	g	Prid. kl.		30	9	3	10	15

[1] Omitted in Grafton.   [2] Grafton has this two days lower.
[3] Not in Grafton.   [4] Grafton omits, S.
[5] Grafton, xii.

¶ October hath .xxxi. days.

					Morning prayer.		Evening prayer.	
				Psalms	1 Less.	2 Less.	1 Less.	2 Less.
16	A	Kalend.		1	Zach. 11	Mark 4	Zach. 12	1 Cor. 16
5	b	6 No. Ortus solis.		2	13	5	14	2 Cor. 1
13	c	5 No. Hora. 6. Mi. 35.		3	Mal. 1	6	Mal. 2	2
2	d	4 No. Occasus.		4	3	7	4	3
	e	3 No. Ho. 5. Mi. 25.		5	Toby 1	8	Toby 2	4
10	f	Prid. No.		6	3	9	4	5
	g	Nonæ.		7	5	10	6	6
18	A	8 Idus.		8	7	11	8	7
7	b	7 Idus. Term begin.		9	9	12	10	8
	c	6 Idus.		10	11	13	12	9
15	d	5 Idus.		11	13	14	14	10
4	e	4 Idus.		12	Judit 1	15	Judit 2	11
	f	3 Idus.		13	3	16	4	12
12	g	Prid. Id. Sol. in Scor-	14	5	Luk.di.1	6	13
1	A	Idus. [pione.		15	7	di. 1	8	Galat.1
	b	17 kal. Novembris.		16	9	2	10	2
9	c	16 kal.		17	11	3	12	3
	d	15 kal. Luke Evan.		18	13	4	14	4
17	e	14 kal.		19	15	5	16	5
6	f	13 kal.		20	Sap. 1	6	Sap. 2	6
	g	12 kal.		21	3	7	4	Ephes. 1
14	A	11 kal.		22	5	8	6	2
3	b	10 kal.		23	7	9	8	3
	c	9 kal.		24	9	10	10	4
11	d	8 kal.		25	11	11	12	5
	e	7 kal.		26	13	12	14	6
19	f	6 kal.		27	15	13	16	Philip. 1
8	A	5 kal. Sim. and Jude.	28	17	14	18	2
	b	4 kal.		29	19	15	Eccle. 1	3
16	c	3 kal.		30	Eccle. 2	16	3	4
5		Prid. kl.			4	17	5	Colos. 1

4—2

52   [1559.

¶ November hath xxx. days.

			Psalms	Morning prayer. 1 Less.	2 Less.	Evening prayer. 1 Less.	2 Less.
13	d	Kalend. *All Saints.*	1	Sap. 3	11, 12	Sap. 5	Apoc. 19
1	e	¹ No. Ortus solis Ho. 7.	2	Eccle. 6	Luke 18	Eccle. 7	Coloss. 2
	f	¹ No Mi. 34. Occasus.	3	8	19	9	3
10	g	Prid. No. Ho. 4. Mi. 26.	4	10	20	11	4
	A	Nonæ.	5	12	21	13	1 Thes. 1
18	b	8 Idus.	6	14	22	15	2
7	c	7 Idus.	7	16	23	17	3
	d	6 Idus.	8	18	24	19	4
15	e	5 Idus.	9	20	John 1	21	5
4	f	4 Idus.	10	22	2	23	2 Thes. 1
	g	3 Idus.	11	24	3	25	2
12	A	Prid. Id.	12	26	4	27	3
1	b	Idus. Sol in Sagitario.	13	28	5	29	1 Tim. 1
	c	18 kal. Decembris.	14	30	6	31	2. 3
9	d	17 kal.	15	32	7	33	4
	e	16 kal.	16	34	8	35	5
17	f	15 kal.	17	36	9	37	6
6	g	14 kal.	18	38	10	39	2 Tim. 1
	A	13 kal.	19	40	11	41	2
14	b	12 kal.	20	42	12	43	3
3	c	11 kal.	21	44	13	45	4
	d	10 kal.	22	46	14	47	Titus 1
11	e	9 kal.²	23	48	15	49	2. 3
	f	8 kal.	24	50	16	51	Phil. 1
19	g	7 kal.	25	Baruc. 3	17	Baruc. 2	Heb. 1
8	A	6 kal.	26	3	18	4	2
	b	5 kal.	27	5	19	6	3
16	c	4 kal. Term end.	28	Esay 1	20	Esay 2	4
5	d	3 kal.	29	3	21	4	5
	e	Prid. kl.³ *Andr. Ap.*	30	5	Act 1	6	6

¹ iiii. iii. omitted.
² Grafton has, S. Clement, against this day. Jugge and Cawode also insert his name.
³ Grafton omits, kl.

Subsequent impressions by

¶ December hath xxxi. days.

			Psalms	Morning prayer. 1 Less.	2 Less.	Evening prayer. 1 Less.	2 Less.
14	f	1 Kalend.	1	Esay 7	Act 2	Esay 8	Heb. 7
2	g	1 No. Sol oritur Ho. 8. Mi. 12.	2	9	3	10	8
10	A	3 No.	3	11	4	12	9
	b	Prid. No. Occ. Ho. 3. Mi. 48.	4	13	5	14	10
	c	Nonæ.	5	15	6	16	11
18	d	8 Idus.	6	17	di. 7	18	12
7	e	7 Idus.	7	19	di. 7	20, 21	13
	f	² Idus.	8	22	8	23	James 1
15	g	5 Idus.	9	24	9	25	2
4	A	4 Idus.	10	26	10	27	3
	b	3 Idus.	11	28	11	29	4
12	c	Prid. Id. Sol in Capri-	12	30	12	31	5
1	d	Idus. [corno.	13	32	13	33	1 Pet. 1
	e	19 kal. Januarii.	14	34	14	35	2
9	f	18 kal.	15	36	15	37	3
	g	17 kal.	16	38	16	39	4
17	A	16 kal.	17	40	17	41	5
6	b	15 kal.	18	42	18	43	2 Pet. 1
	c	14 kal.	19	44	19	45	2
14	d	13 kal. *Thomas Apo.*	20	46	20	47	3
	e	12 kal.	21	48	21	49	1 John 1
11	f	11 kal.	22	50	22	51	2
	g	10 kal.	23	52	23	53	3
	A	9 kal.	24	54	24	55	4
19	b	8 kal. *Christmas.*	25	Esay 9	Luke 22	Esay 7	Titus 3
8	c	7 kal. *S. Stephen.*	26	56	Act 6, 7	57	Act 7
	d	6 kal. *S. John.*³	27	58	Apoc. 1	59	Apoc. 22
16	e	5 kal. *Innocents.*	28	Jer. 31	Act 25	60	1 John 5
5	f	4 kal.	29	Esay 61	26	62	2 John 1
	g	⁴ kal.	30	63	27	64	3 John 1
13	A	Prid. kl.	30	65	18⁵	66⁶	Judas 1

¹ f, g, omitted.   ² vi. omitted.   ³ Grafton adds, euan.
⁴ iii. omitted.   ⁵ Misprint for, xxviii.   ⁶ Grafton, lxv.

THE[1] ORDER

WHERE

Morning and Evening prayer

shall be used and said.

The morning and evening prayer shall be used in the accustomed place of the church, chapel, or Chancel, except it shall be otherwise determined by the ordinary of the place: and the chancels shall remain, as they have done in times past.

And here is to be noted, that the minister at the time of the communion, and at all other times in his ministration, shall use such ornaments in the church as were in use by authority of parliament in the second year of the reign of king Edward the .VI. according to the act of parliament set in the beginning of this book.

¶ AN ORDER

for Morning prayer

daily throughout the year.

At the beginning both of Morning prayer, and likewise of Evening prayer, the minister shall read, with a loud voice, some one of these sentences of the scriptures that follow. And then he shall say that, which is written after the said sentences.

AT what time soever a sinner doth repent him of his sin Eze. xviii. from the bottom of his heart: I will put all his wickedness out of my remembrance, saith the Lord.

I do know mine own wickedness, and my sin is alway[2] Psal. li. against me.

Turn thy face away from our sins, O Lord, and blot Psal. li. out all our offences.

A sorrowful spirit is a Sacrifice to God: despise not, O Psal. li. Lord, humble and contrite hearts.

[1 Grafton has, *Mornyng prayer*, for a head line. 1578, The booke of Common prayer, and administration of the Sacramentes.]

[2 Grafton, alwaies.]

Joel ii.   Rend your hearts, and not your garments, and turn to the Lord, your God: because he is gentle and merciful, he is patient and of much mercy, and such a one that is sorry for your afflictions.

Dan. ix.   To thee, O Lord God, belongeth mercy and forgiveness; for we have gone away from thee, and have not hearkened to thy voice, whereby we might walk in thy laws which thou hast appointed for us.

Jer. ii.[1]   Correct us, O Lord, and yet in thy judgment; not in thy fury, lest we should be consumed and brought to nothing.

Math. iii.   Amend your lives, for the kingdom of God is at hand.

Luke xv.   I will go to my father, and say to him: Father I have sinned against heaven and against thee, I am no more worthy to be called thy son.

Psal. cxlii.[2]   Enter not into judgment with thy servants, O Lord, for no flesh is righteous in thy sight.

1 John i.   If we say that we have no sin, we deceive ourselves, and there is no truth in us.

DEARLY beloved brethren, the scripture moveth us in sundry places to acknowledge and confess our manifold sins and wickedness: and that we should not dissemble nor cloke them before the face of Almighty God our heavenly Father, but confess them with an humble, lowly, penitent, and obedient heart: to the end that we may obtain forgiveness of the same by his infinite goodness and mercy. And although we ought at all times humbly to knowledge[3] our sins before God: yet ought we most chiefly so to do, when we assemble and meet together to render thanks for the great benefits that we have received at his hands, to set forth his most worthy praise, to hear his most holy word, and to ask those things which be requisite and necessary, as well for the body as the soul. Wherefore I pray and beseech you, as many as be here present, to accompany me with a pure heart and humble voice, unto the throne of the heavenly grace, saying after me:

[[1] Misprint in both editions of 1559 for, x.]
[[2] Grafton, clxiii. 1596, cxliii. This last is right according to the notation pointed out in p. 39.]
[[3] 1596, acknowledge.]

¶ A general confession, to be said of the whole congregation after the minister, kneeling.

ALMIGHTY and most merciful Father, We have erred, and strayed from thy ways, like lost sheep. We have followed too much the devices and desires of our own hearts. We have offended against thy holy laws. We have left undone those things which we ought to have done, and we have done those things which we ought not to have done, and there is no health in us: but thou, O Lord, have mercy upon us miserable offenders. Spare thou them, O God, which confess their faults. Restore thou them that be penitent, according to thy promises declared unto mankind, in Christ Jesu our Lord. And grant, O most merciful Father, for his sake, that we may hereafter live a godly, righteous, and sober life, to the glory of thy holy name[4].

The absolution, to be pronounced by the Minister alone.

ALMIGHTY God, the Father of our Lord Jesus Christ, which desireth not the death of a sinner, but rather that he may turn from his wickedness, and live: and hath given power and commandment to his ministers, to declare and pronounce to his people, being penitent, the absolution and remission of their sins: he pardoneth and absolveth all them which truly repent, and unfeignedly believe his holy gospel: Wherefore we beseech him to grant us true repentance and his holy Spirit, that those things may please him, which we do at this present, and that the rest of our life hereafter may be pure, and holy: so that at the last we may come to his eternal joy, through Jesus Christ our Lord[5].

The people shall answer, Amen.

Then shall the minister begin the Lord's prayer with a loud voice.

OUR Father which art in heaven, Hallowed be thy name. Thy kingdom come. Thy will be done in earth as it is in heaven. Give us this day our daily bread. And forgive us our trespasses, as we forgive them that trespass against us. And lead us not into temptation. But deliver us from evil. Amen.

[4 Grafton and 1596, Amen.]   [5 Grafton, Amen.]

Then likewise he shall say.

O Lord open thou our lips.

Answer. And our mouth shall shew forth thy praise.

Priest.[1] O God make[2] speed to save us.

Answer. O Lord make haste to help us.

Priest.[1] Glory[3] be to the Father. &c.

As it was in the beginning. &c.

Praise ye the Lord.

Then shall be said or sung this Psalm following:

Venite[4]
exultemus:
Domino.
xcv.

O COME, let us sing unto the Lord : let us heartily rejoice in the strength of our salvation.

Let us come before his presence with thanksgiving : and shew ourself glad in him with Psalms.

For the Lord is a great God : and a great king above all gods.

In his hand are all the corners of the earth : and the strength of the hills is his also.

The sea is his, and he made it, and his hands prepared the dry land.

O come, let us worship, and fall down : and kneel before the Lord our maker.

For he is the Lord our God : and we are the people of his pasture, and the sheep of his hands.

To day if ye will hear his voice, harden not your hearts : as in the Provocation, and as in the day of Temptation in the wilderness;

When your fathers tempted me, proved me, and saw my works.

Forty years[5] long was I grieved with this generation, and said : It is a people that do err in their hearts, for they have not known my ways.

Unto whom I sware in my wrath : that they should not enter into my rest.

Glory be to the Father[6]. &c.

[1 1578, *Minister.*]

[2 Later copies by Jugge and Cawode, yet apparently of the same year, have, make haste to spede us.]

[3 Grafton has all this in full.]

[4 Not in Grafton, nor in 1596.] [5 Grafton, yere.]

[6 Grafton, and to the sonne. &c. As it was in the beginning, is now. &c. 1596 has the *Gloria Patri* in full.]

Then shall follow certain Psalms in order, as they be appointed in a Table made for that purpose: except there be proper Psalms appointed for that day. And at the end of every Psalm throughout the year, and likewise in the end of *Benedictus, Benedicite, Magnificat,* and *Nunc Dimittis,* shall be repeated:

Glory be to the Father[8]. &c.

Then shall be read two Lessons distinctly with a loud voice, that the people may hear. The first of the old Testament, the second of the new, like as they be appointed by[9] the Kalendar, except there be proper lessons assigned for that day: the minister that readeth the lesson, standing and turning him so, as he may best be heard of all such as be present. And before every lesson, the minister shall say thus. The first, second, third, or fourth Chapter of Genesis, or Exodus, Mathew, Mark, or other like, as is appointed in the Kalendar. And in the end of every chapter, he shall say,

Here endeth such a Chapter, of such a Book.

And (to the end the people may the better hear) in such places where they do sing, there shall the lessons be sung in a plain tune, after the manner of distinct reading: and likewise the Epistle and Gospel.

After the first lesson shall follow *Te Deum laudamus,* in English daily through[10] the whole year.

Te Deum laudamus.

We praise thee, O God : we knowledge thee to be the Lord.

All the earth doth worship thee, the Father everlasting.

To thee all Angels cry aloud : the heavens and all the powers therein.

To thee Cherubin and Seraphin, continually do cry.

Holy, holy, holy Lord God of Sabaoth.

Heaven and earth are full of the Majesty of thy glory.

The glorious company of the Apostles, praise thee.

The goodly fellowship of the Prophets, praise thee.

The noble army of Martyrs, praise thee.

The holy Church throughout all the world, doth knowledge thee :

The Father of an infinite Majesty ;

Thy[11] honourable, true, and only Son ;

[7 Grafton, bene.]
[8 Grafton, and to the sonne. &c. The variations in this particular will not be again noticed.]
[9 1596, in.]
[10 1596, throughout.]
[11 1596, Thine.]

Also the Holy Ghost, the Comforter.

Thou art the king of glory, O Christ.

Thou art the everlasting Son of the Father.

When thou tookest upon thee to deliver man, thou didst not abhor the virgin's womb.

When thou hadst overcomed[1] the sharpness of death, thou didst open the Kingdom of heaven to all believers.

Thou sittest on[2] the right hand of God, in the glory of the Father.

We believe that thou shalt come to be our judge.

We therefore pray thee, help thy servants, whom thou hast redeemed with thy precious blood.

Make them to be numbered with thy Saints, in glory everlasting.

O Lord save thy people : and bless thine heritage.

Govern them and lift them up for ever.

Day by day we magnify thee.

And we worship thy name, ever world without end.

Vouchsafe, O Lord, to keep us this day without sin.

O Lord have mercy upon us : have mercy upon us.

O Lord, let thy mercy lighten upon us : as our trust is in thee.

O Lord, in thee have I trusted : let me never be confounded.

Or this Canticle, *Benedicite omnia opera Domini Domino.*

Benedicite.   O ALL the[3] Works of the Lord, bless ye the Lord : praise him and magnify him for ever.

O ye Angels of the Lord, bless ye the Lord : praise ye[4] him and magnify him for ever.

O ye heavens, bless ye the Lord : praise him, and magnify him for ever.

O ye waters that be above the firmament, bless ye the Lord : praise him and magnify him for ever.

O all ye powers of the Lord, bless ye the Lord : praise him and magnify him for ever.

O ye sun and moon, bless ye the Lord : praise him and magnify him for ever.

[[1] Grafton and 1596, ouercome.]   [[2] 1596, at.]
[[3] Grafton and 1596, ye.]   [[4] 1596, praise him.]

O ye stars of heaven, bless ye the Lord : praise him and magnify him for ever.

O ye showers and dew, bless ye the Lord : praise him and magnify him for ever.

O ye winds of God, bless ye the Lord : praise him and magnify him for ever.

O ye fire and heat, bless ye the Lord : praise him and magnify him for ever.

O ye winter and summer, bless ye the Lord : praise him and magnify him for ever.

O ye dews and frosts, bless ye the Lord : praise him and magnify him for ever.

O ye frost and cold, bless ye the Lord : praise him and magnify him for ever.

O ye ice and snow, bless ye the Lord : praise him and magnify him for ever.

O ye nights and days, bless ye the Lord : praise him and magnify him for ever.

O ye light and darkness, bless ye the Lord : praise him and magnify him for ever.

O ye lightnings and clouds, bless ye the Lord : praise him and magnify him for ever.

O let the earth bless the Lord : yea, let it praise him and magnify him for ever.

O ye mountains and hills, bless ye the Lord : praise him and magnify him for ever.

O all ye green things upon the earth, bless ye the Lord : praise him and magnify him for ever.

O ye wells, bless ye the Lord : praise him and magnify him for ever.

O ye seas and floods, bless ye the Lord : praise him and magnify him for ever.

O ye whales and all that move in the waters, bless ye the Lord : praise him and magnify him for ever.

O all ye fowls of the air, bless ye the Lord : praise him and magnify him for ever.

O all ye beasts and cattle, bless ye the Lord : praise him and magnify him for ever.

O ye children of men, bless ye the Lord : praise him and magnify him for ever.

O let Israel bless the Lord : praise him and magnify him for ever.

O ye Priests of the Lord, bless ye the Lord : praise him and magnify him for ever.

O ye servants of the Lord, bless ye the Lord : praise him and magnify him for ever.

O ye spirits and souls of the righteous, bless ye the Lord : praise him and magnify him for ever.

O ye holy and humble men of heart, bless ye the Lord : praise him and magnify him for ever.

O Ananias, Azarias, and Misael, bless ye the Lord : praise him and magnify him for ever.

Glory be to the Father, and to the Son. &c.

¶ And after the second lesson shall be used and said *Benedictus*, in English, as followeth :

Benedictus.   Blessed be the Lord God of Israel : for he hath visited and redeemed his people.

And hath raised up a mighty salvation for us : in the house of his servant David.

As he spake by the mouth of his holy Prophets : which have been since the world began;

That we should be saved from our enemies : and from the hands of all that hate us.

To perform thy[1] mercy promised to our forefathers : and to remember his holy covenant;

To perform the oath which he sware to our forefather Abraham : that he would give us.

That we being delivered out of the hands of our enemies : might serve him without fear,

In holiness and righteousness before him : all the days of our life.

And thou Child shalt be called the Prophet of the Highest : for thou shalt go before the face of the Lord, to prepare his ways.

To give knowledge of salvation unto his people : for the remission of their sins.

Through the tender mercy of our God : whereby the day-spring from an[2] high hath visited us.

[1 Misprint for, the.]   [2 Grafton, on.]

To give light to them that sit in darkness, and in the shadow of death : and to guide our feet into the way of peace.

Glory be to the Father, and to the Son : and to the Holy Ghost :

As it was in the beginning, is now, and ever shall be : world without end. Amen.

Or[3] else this Psalm.

O be joyful in the Lord (all ye lands :) serve the Lord with gladness, and come before his presence with a song. *Jubilate deo. Psal. c.*

Be ye sure that the Lord he is God : it is he that hath made us, and not we ourselves; we are his people, and the sheep of his pasture.

O go your way into his gates with thanksgiving, and into his courts with praise : be thankful unto him, and speak good of his Name.

For the Lord is gracious, his mercy is everlasting : and his truth endureth from generation to generation.

Glory be to the Father, and to the Son. &c. As it was in the beginning, is now, and ever shall be, world without end. Amen.

¶ Then shall be said the Creed, by the minister and the people standing.

I BELIEVE in God the Father Almighty, maker of heaven and earth. And in Jesus Christ his only Son our Lord. Which was conceived by the Holy Ghost, Born of the virgin Mary. Suffered under Ponce Pilate, was crucified, dead and buried, He descended into hell. The third day he rose[4] again from the dead. He ascended into heaven, and sitteth on the right hand of God the Father Almighty. From thence shall he[5] come to judge the quick and the dead. I believe in the Holy Ghost. The holy Catholic Church. The communion of Saints. The forgiveness of sins. The resurrection of the body. And the life everlasting. Amen.

[[3] Grafton, Or the .c. Psalme. *Jubilate.* Grafton has nothing in the margin here : it is uncertain whether he has elsewhere, as the book is slightly damaged. 1596, *Or this C. Psalme. Jubilate Deo. Jubilate Deo,* also in the margin.]

[[4] Grafton, arose.]   [[5] Grafton and 1596, he shall.]

And after that, these prayers following, as well at Evening prayer as at Morning prayer: all devoutly kneeling.

The Minister first pronouncing with a loud voice.

The Lord be with you.

Answer. And with thy spirit.

The[1] Minister. Let us pray.

Lord have mercy upon us.

Christ have mercy upon us.

Lord have mercy upon us.

Then the Minister, Clerks and people, shall say the Lord's prayer, in English, with a loud voice.

¶ Our Father which art[2]. &c.

Then the Minister standing up, shall say.

O Lord shew thy mercy upon us:

Answer. And grant us thy salvation.

Priest[3]. O Lord save the Queen:

Answer. And mercifully hear us, when we call upon thee.

Priest. Endue thy ministers with righteousness:

Answer. And make thy chosen people joyful.

Priest. O Lord save thy people:

Answer. And bless thine inheritance.

Priest. Give peace in our time O Lord:

Answer. Because there is none other that fighteth for us, but only thou O God.

Priest. O God make clean our hearts within us:

Answer. And take not thine[4] holy Spirit from us.

Then shall follow three Collects, The first of the day, which shall be the same that is appointed at the Communion. The second for peace. The third for grace to live well. And the two last Collects shall never alter, but daily be said at Morning prayer throughout all the year, as followeth.

The Second Collect for Peace.

O GOD, which art author of peace, and lover of concord, in knowledge of whom standeth our eternal life, whose service is perfect freedom: defend us thy humble servants in all assaults of our enemies, that we, surely trusting in thy defence,

[1 Grafton has not, The.]
[2 art, not in Grafton. And so elsewhere.]
[3 1578, *Minister*. So, also, in the next four instances.]
[4 Grafton, thy.]

may not fear the power of any adversaries: through the might of Jesu[5] Christ our Lord. Amen.

The third Collect for grace.

O LORD our heavenly Father, Almighty and everlasting God, which hast safely brought us to the beginning of this day: defend us in the same with thy mighty power, and grant that this day we fall into no sin, neither run into any kind of danger; but that all our doings may be ordered by thy governance, to do always that is righteous in thy sight: through Jesus Christ our Lord. Amen.

¶ AN Order
for Evening prayer

throughout the year.

The Priest[6] shall say.

¶ Our Father which art. &c.

Then likewise he shall say.

O Lord open thou our lips:
Answer. And our mouth shall shew forth thy praise.
Priest.[6] O God make speed to save us:
Answer. Lord[7] make haste to help us.
Priest.[6] Glory be to the Father, and to the Son: and to the Holy Ghost.
As it was in the beginning, is now, and ever shall be: world without end. Amen.
Praise ye the Lord.

Then Psalms[8], in order as they be appointed in the Table for Psalms, except there be proper Psalms appointed for that day. Then a lesson of the old Testament as is appointed likewise in the Kalendar, except there be proper lessons appointed for that day. After that, *Magnificat*, in English, as followeth.

My soul doth magnify the Lord. *Magnificat.[9]* Luc. i.

[5] 1596, Jesus.]   [6] 1578, Minister.]   [7] 1596, O Lord.]
[8] 1596, the Psalmes.]   [9] Not in Grafton.]

And my spirit hath rejoiced in God my Saviour.

For he hath regarded the lowliness of his handmaiden.

For behold, from henceforth all generations shall call me blessed.

For he that is mighty hath magnified me : and holy is his name.

And his mercy is on them that fear him : throughout all generations.

He hath shewed strength with his arm : he hath scattered the proud in the imagination of their hearts.

He hath put down the mighty from their seat : and hath exalted the humble and meek.

He hath filled the hungry with good things : and the rich he hath sent empty away.

He, remembering his mercy, hath holpen his servant Israel : as he promised to our forefathers, Abraham and his seed for ever.

Glory be to the Father, and to the Son. &c.

As it was in the beginning, is now, and ever. &c.

¶ Or[1] else this Psalm.

Cantate Domino.
Psal. xcviii.

O SING unto the Lord a new song : for he hath done marvellous things.

With his own right hand, and with his holy arm : hath he gotten himself the[2] victory.

The Lord declared his salvation : his righteousness hath he openly shewed in the sight of the heathen.

He hath remembered his mercy and truth toward the house of Israel : and all the ends of the world have seen the salvation of our God.

Shew yourselves joyful unto the Lord all ye lands : sing, rejoice and give thanks.

Praise the Lord upon the harp : sing to the harp with a Psalm of thanksgiving.

With trumpets also and shawms : O shew yourselves joyful before the Lord the king.

Let the sea make a noise and all that therein is : the round world, and they that dwell therein.

[[1] Grafton, Or the .xcviii Psalme, *Cantate Domino Canticum novum.*]
[[2] the, not in Grafton.]

Let the floods clap their hands, and let the hills be joyful together before the Lord : for he is come to judge the earth.

With righteousness shall he judge the world : and the people with equity.

Glory be to the Father. &c.

As it was in the. &c.

Then a Lesson of the New Testament. And after that, (*Nunc dimittis*) in English, as followeth.

LORD, now lettest thou thy servant depart in peace : according to thy word.

For mine eyes have seen : thy salvation.

Which thou hast prepared : before the face of all people.

To be a light to lighten the Gentiles : and to be the glory of thy people Israel.

Glory be to the Father, and to the Son, and. &c.

As it was in the beginning, and is now. &c. Amen.

Or[3] else this Psalm.

GOD be merciful unto us, and bless us : and shew us the light of his countenance, and be merciful unto us. *Deus misereatur.* Psal. lxvii.

That thy way may be known upon earth : thy saving health among all nations.

Let the people praise thee O God : yea, let all the people praise thee.

O let the nations rejoice and be glad : for thou shalt judge the[4] folk righteously, and govern the nations upon earth.

Let the people praise thee, O God : let all the people praise thee.

Then shall the earth bring forth her increase : and God, even our own God, shall give us his blessing.

God shall bless us : and all the ends of the world shall fear him.

Glory be to the Father. &c.

As it was in the beginning. &c.

Then shall follow the Creed, with other prayers, as is before appointed at Morning prayer, after *Benedictus*; and with three[5] Collects :

[3 Grafton, Or this Psalm, *Deus misereatur nostri*, in English.]
[4 Grafton, thy.]   [5 Grafton, the.]

[LITURG. QU. ELIZ.]

First of the day: the second of peace. third[1] for aid against all perils. as hereafter followeth. Which two last Collects shall be daily said at Evening prayer without alteration.

¶ The second Collect at Evening prayer.

O GOD, from whom all holy desires, all good counsels, and all just works do proceed: give unto thy servants that peace, which the world cannot give: that both our hearts may be set to obey thy commandments, and also that by thee we being defended from the fear of our enemies, may pass our time in rest and quietness, through the merits of Jesus Christ our Saviour. Amen.

The third Collect, for aid against all perils.

LIGHTEN our darkness, we beseech thee, O Lord, and by thy great mercy defend us from all perils and dangers of this night, for the love of thy only Son our Saviour Jesus Christ. Amen.

¶ In the feasts of Christmas, the Epiphany, Saint Mathie, Easter, the Ascension, Pentecost, Saint John Baptist, Saint James, Saint Bartholomew, Saint Mathew, Saint Simon and Jude, Saint Andrew, and Trinity Sunday, shall be sung or said, immediately after *Benedictus*, this confession of our Christian faith.

Quicunque vult[2].

WHOSOEVER will be saved: before all things it is necessary that he hold the catholic faith.

Which faith except every one do keep holy and undefiled: without doubt he shall perish everlastingly.

And the catholic faith is this: that we worship one God in Trinity, and Trinity in Unity;

Neither confounding the persons: nor dividing the substance.

For there is one person of the Father, another of the Son: and another of the Holy Ghost.

But the Godhead of the Father, of the Son, and of the Holy Ghost is all one: the glory equal, the majesty coeternal.

Such as the Father is, such is the Son: and such is the Holy Ghost.

The Father uncreate, the Son uncreate: and the Holy Ghost uncreate.

[[1] Grafton, thyrde the for. 1596, *The third for.*]
[[2] Not in Grafton.]

The Father incomprehensible, the Son incomprehensible : and the Holy Ghost incomprehensible.

The Father eternal, the Son eternal : and the Holy Ghost eternal.

And yet they are not three eternals : but one eternal.

As also there be not three incomprehensibles, nor three uncreated : but one uncreated, and one incomprehensible.

So likewise the Father is almighty, the Son almighty : and the Holy Ghost almighty.

And yet they[3] are not three almighties : but one almighty.

So the Father is God, the Son is God : and the Holy Ghost is God.

And yet are[4] they not three Gods : but one God.

So likewise the Father is Lord, the Son Lord : and the Holy Ghost Lord.

And yet not three Lords : but one Lord.

For like as we be compelled by the Christian verity : to acknowledge every person by himself to be God and Lord ;

So are we forbidden by the catholic religion : to say, there be three Gods, or three Lords.

The Father is made of none : neither created nor begotten.

The Son is of the Father alone : not made nor created, but begotten.

The Holy Ghost is of the Father and of the Son : neither made, nor created, nor begotten, but proceeding.

So there is one Father, not three Fathers, one Son, not three Sons : one Holy Ghost, not three Holy Ghosts.

And in this Trinity, none is afore or after other : none is greater, nor[5] less than an[6] other.

But the whole three persons : be coeternal together and coequal.

So that in all things, as is aforesaid : the Unity in Trinity, and the Trinity in Unity is to be worshipped.

He therefore that will be saved : must thus think of the Trinity.

Furthermore, it is necessary to everlasting salvation : that he also believe rightly in the Incarnation of our Lord Jesu Christ.

[3 Grafton, are not there. 1596, are they not.]
[4 1596, they are not.]
[5 1596, or.]
[6 an, not in Grafton.]

For the right faith is, that we believe and confess : that our Lord Jesus Christ, the Son of God, is God and man.

God of the substance of the Father, begotten before the worlds : and man of the substance of his mother, born in the world.

Perfect God, and perfect man of a reasonable soul : and human flesh subsisting.

Equal to the Father, as touching his Godhead : and inferior to the Father, touching his manhood.

Who although he be God and man : yet he is not two, but one Christ.

One, not by conversion of the Godhead into flesh : but by taking of the manhood into God.

One altogether, not by confusion of substance : but by unity of person.

For as the reasonable soul and flesh is[1] one man : so God and man is[1] one Christ.

Who suffered for our salvation : descended into hell, rose again the third day from the dead.

He ascended into heaven, he sitteth on the right hand of the Father, God Almighty : from whence he shall come to judge the quick and the dead.

At whose coming all men shall rise again with their bodies : and shall give account for their own works.

And they that have done good, shall go into life everlasting : and they that have done evil, into everlasting fire.

This is the Catholic faith : which except a man believe faithfully, he cannot be saved.

Glory be to the Father, and to the Son : and to the Holy Ghost.

As it was in the beginning, is now, and ever shall be : world without end. Amen.

Thus endeth the order of Morning and Evening prayer, through[2] the whole year.

[[1] Grafton, is but.]   [[2] 1596, throughout.]

Here followeth the Litany to be used upon Sundays, Wednesdays, and Fridays, and at other times, when it shall be commanded by the Ordinary.

O GOD the Father of heaven : have mercy upon us miserable sinners.

O[3] God the Father of heaven : have mercy upon us miserable sinners.

O God the Son, redeemer of the world : have mercy upon us miserable sinners.

O God the Son, redeemer of the world : have mercy upon us miserable sinners.

O God the Holy Ghost, proceeding from the Father and the Son : have mercy upon us miserable sinners.

O God the Holy Ghost, proceeding from the Father and the Son : have mercy upon us miserable sinners.

O holy, blessed, and glorious Trinity, three Persons and one God : have mercy upon us miserable sinners.

O holy, blessed, and glorious Trinity, three Persons and one God : have mercy upon us miserable sinners.

Remember not, Lord, our offences, nor the offences of our forefathers, neither take thou vengeance of our sins : spare us, good Lord, spare thy people whom thou hast redeemed with thy most precious blood, and be not angry with us for ever.

Spare us, good Lord.

From all evil and mischief, from sin, from the crafts and assaults of the devil, from thy wrath, and from everlasting damnation.

Good Lord deliver us.

From all blindness of heart, from pride, vain glory, and hypocrisy, from envy, hatred and malice, and all uncharitableness.

Good Lord deliver us.

[[3] Grafton abbreviates the first four responses.]

From fornication and all other deadly sin, and from all the deceits of the world, the flesh and the devil.

Good Lord deliver us.

From lightning[2] and tempest, from plague, pestilence and famine, from battle and murther, and from sudden death.

Good Lord deliver us.

From all sedition and privy conspiracy, from all false doctrine and heresy, from hardness of heart, and contempt of thy word and commandment.

Good Lord deliver us.

By the mystery of thy holy Incarnation, by thy holy Nativity and Circumcision, by thy baptism, fasting and temptation.

Good Lord deliver us.

By thine agony and bloody sweat, by thy cross and passion, by thy precious death and burial, by thy glorious resurrection and ascension, and by the coming of the Holy Ghost.

Good Lord deliver us.

In all our[3] time of tribulation, in all time of our wealth, in the hour of death, and in the day of Judgment.

Good Lord deliver us.

We sinners do beseech thee to hear us (O Lord God,) and that it may please thee to rule and govern thy holy church universally in the right way.

We beseech thee to hear us good Lord.

That it may please thee to keep and strengthen in the true worshipping of thee, in righteousness and holiness of life, thy Servant Elizabeth our most gracious Queen and governour.

We beseech thee to hear us good Lord.

That it may please thee to rule her heart in thy faith, fear and love, and[4] that she may evermore have affiance in thee, and ever seek thy honour and glory.

We beseech thee to hear us good Lord.

That it may please thee to be her defender and keeper, giving her the victory over all her enemies.

We beseech thee to hear us good Lord.

[[1] Grafton, *Euening prayer.*]
[[2] Grafton, lightninges and tempestes.]
[[3] Grafton and 1596, time of our.]   [[4] and, not in Grafton.]

That it may please thee to illuminate all Bishops, Pastors, and Ministers of the Church, with true knowledge and understanding of thy word: and that both by their preaching and living they may set it forth and shew it accordingly.

We beseech thee to hear us good Lord.

That it may please thee to endue the Lords of the council, and all the nobility, with grace, wisdom, and understanding.

We beseech thee to hear us good Lord.

That it may please thee to bless and keep the Magistrates, giving them grace to execute justice, and to maintain truth.

We beseech thee to hear us good Lord.

That it may please thee to bless and keep all thy people.

We beseech thee to hear us good Lord.

That it may please thee to give to all nations unity, peace and concord.

We beseech thee to hear us good Lord.

That it may please thee to give us an heart to love and dread thee, and diligently to live after thy commandments.

We beseech thee to hear us good Lord.

That it may please thee to give all[5] thy people increase of grace, to hear meekly thy word, and to receive it with pure affection, and to bring forth the fruits of the Spirit.

We beseech thee to hear us good Lord.

That it may please thee to bring into the way of truth, all such as have erred and are deceived.

We beseech thee to hear us good Lord.

That it may please thee to strengthen such as do stand, and to comfort and help the weak-hearted, and to raise them[6] up that fall, and finally to beat down Satan under our feet.

We beseech thee to hear us good Lord.

That it may please thee to succour, help and comfort, all that be in danger, necessity, and tribulation.

We beseech thee to hear us good Lord.

That it may please thee to preserve all that travel by land or by water, all women labouring of child, all sick persons and young children, and to shew thy pity upon all prisoners and captives.

We beseech thee to hear us good Lord.

[5 1596, to all.]   [6 1596, up them.]

That it may please thee to defend and provide for the fatherless children and widows, and all that be desolate and oppressed.

 We beseech thee to hear us good Lord.

That it may please thee to have mercy upon all men.

 We beseech thee to hear us good Lord.

That it may please thee to forgive our enemies, persecutors and slanderers, and to turn their hearts.

 We beseech thee to hear us good Lord.

That it may please thee to give and preserve to our use the kindly fruits of the earth, so as in due time we may enjoy them.

 We beseech thee to hear us good Lord.

That it may please thee to give us true repentance, to forgive us all our sins, negligences, and ignorances, and to endue us with the grace of thy holy Spirit to amend our lives according to thy holy word.

 We beseech thee to hear us good Lord.

Son of God : we beseech thee to hear us.

 Son of God : we beseech thee to hear us.

O Lamb of God that takest away the sins of the world :

 Grant us thy peace.

O Lamb of God that takest away the sins of the world :

 Have mercy upon us.

O Christ hear us.

 O Christ hear us.

Lord have mercy upon us.

 Lord have mercy upon us.

Christ have mercy upon us.

 Christ have mercy upon us.

Lord have mercy upon us.

 Lord have mercy upon us.

Our[1] Father, which art in heaven. &c.

---

[1] This mode of arranging the Lord's Prayer occurs six times, and may be explained from a rubric in the Salisbury Breviary:—*Notandum est, quod nunquam in ecclesia Sarisburiensi incipitur* Pater noster *a sacerdote in audientia ad aliquod servitium, nisi ad missam tantum. Et postea dicat sacerdos in audientia,* Et ne nos. *Chorus,* Sed libera. Dominica

And lead us not into temptation.
But deliver us from evil [2].

The Versicle.   O Lord deal not with us after our sins.
The Answer.   Neither reward us after our iniquities.

Let us pray.

O GOD merciful Father, that despisest not the sighing of a contrite heart, nor the desire of such as be sorrowful: mercifully assist our prayers that we make before thee, in all our troubles and adversities whensoever they oppress us. And graciously hear us, that those evils, which the craft and subtilty of the devil or man worketh against us, be brought to nought, and by the providence of thy goodness they may be dispersed, that we thy servants, being hurt by no persecutions, may evermore give thanks unto[3] thee in thy holy church, through Jesu[4] Christ our Lord.

O Lord arise, help us, and deliver us for thy name's sake.

O GOD we have heard with our ears, and our fathers have declared unto us, the noble works that thou didst in their days, and in the old time before them.

O Lord arise, help us, and deliver us, for thine honour.

Glory be to the Father, and to the Son, and to the Holy Ghost: as it was in the beginning, is now, and ever shall be: world without end. Amen.

From our enemies defend us, O Christ.
Graciously look upon our afflictions.
Pitifully behold the sorrows of our heart[5].
Mercifully forgive the sins of thy people.
Favourably with mercy hear our prayers.
O Son of David have mercy upon us.
Both now and ever vouchsafe to hear us, O Christ.
Graciously hear us, O Christ, Graciously hear us, O Lord Christ.

The Versicle.   O Lord let thy mercy be shewed upon us.
The Answer.   As we do put our trust in thee.

Prima Adventus, Ad Matutinas, Noct. I. See L'Estrange's Alliance, p. 327.]
[2 Grafton and 1596, Amen.]   [3 Grafton, to.]
[4 Grafton and 1596, Jesus.]   [5 1596, hearts.]

Let us pray.

WE humbly beseech thee, O Father, mercifully to look upon our infirmities, and for the glory of thy name's sake, turn from us all those evils that we most righteously have deserved: and grant that in all our troubles we may put our whole trust and confidence in thy mercy, and evermore serve thee in holiness and pureness of living, to thy honour and glory: through our only mediator and advocate Jesus Christ our Lord. Amen.

For[1] rain, if the time require.

O GOD heavenly Father, which by thy Son Jesu Christ hast promised to all them that seek thy kingdom and the righteousness thereof, all things necessary to their bodily sustenance: send us we beseech thee, in this our necessity, such moderate rain and showers, that we may receive the fruits of the earth to our comfort, and to thy honour: through Jesus Christ our Lord. Amen.

For fair weather.

O LORD God, which for the sin of man didst once drown all the world, except eight persons, and afterward of thy great mercy didst promise never to destroy it so again: we humbly beseech thee, that although we for our iniquities have worthily deserved this plague of rain and waters, yet upon our true repentance thou wilt send us such weather, whereby we may receive the fruits of the earth in due season, and learn both by thy punishment to amend our lives, and for thy clemency to give thee praise and glory: through Jesus Christ our Lord. Amen.

In the time of dearth and famine.

O GOD heavenly Father, whose gift it is that the rain doth fall, the earth is fruitful, beasts increase, and fishes do multiply: behold, we beseech thee, the afflictions of thy people, and grant that the scarcity and dearth (which we do now most justly suffer for our iniquity) may through thy goodness be mercifully turned into cheapness and plenty, for the love of Jesu Christ our Lord: to whom with thee and the Holy Ghost. &c.

[[1] The later impressions by Jugge and Cawode follow Grafton in all respects, as regards these collects. See pp. 76, 77.]

¶ Or thus.

O God merciful Father, which, in the time of Heliscus the prophet, didst suddenly turn in Samaria great scarcity and dearth into plenty and cheapness, and extreme famine into abundance of victual: Have pity upon us, that now be punished for our sins with like adversity; increase the fruits of the earth by thy heavenly benediction; and grant, that we, receiving thy bountiful liberality, may use the same to thy glory, our comfort, and relief of our needy neighbours: through Jesu Christ our Lord. Amen.

In the time of war.

O Almighty God, King of all kings, and governour of all things, whose power no creature is able to resist, to whom it belongeth justly to punish sinners, and to be merciful to them that truly repent: save and deliver us (we humbly beseech thee) from the hands of our enemies: abate their pride, assuage their malice, and confound their devices; that we, being armed with thy defence, may be preserved evermore from all perils to glorify thee, which art the only giver of all victory, through the merits of thy only Son Jesu Christ our Lord.

In the time of any common plague or sickness.

O Almighty God: which in thy wrath in the time of king David didst slay with the plague of pestilence sixty and ten thousand, and yet remembering thy mercy didst save the rest: have pity upon us miserable sinners, that now are visited with great sickness and mortality; that like as thou didst then command thy Angel to cease from punishing, so it may now please thee to withdraw from us this plague and grievous sickness, through Jesu Christ our Lord.

¶ And the Litany shall ever end with this Collect following.

Almighty God, which hast given us grace at this time with one accord to make our common supplications unto thee, and dost promise that when two or three be gathered in thy name, thou wilt grant their requests: fulfil now, O Lord, the desires and petitions of thy servants, as may be most expedient for them, granting us in this world knowledge of thy truth, and in the world to come, life everlasting. Amen.

[A Prayer of[1] the Queen's Majesty.

O LORD our heavenly Father, high and mighty King of kings, Lord of lords, the only ruler of princes, which dost from thy throne behold all the dwellers upon earth, most heartily we beseech thee with thy favour to behold our most gracious sovereign Lady Queen Elizabeth, and so replenish her with the grace of thy Holy Spirit, that she may alway incline to thy will, and walk in thy way: Indue her plentifully[2] with heavenly gifts: Grant her in health and wealth long to live: strength[3] her that she may vanquish and overcome all her enemies: And finally after this life she may attain everlasting joy and felicity, through Jesus Christ our Lord. Amen.

ALMIGHTY and everlasting God, which only workest great marvels, send down upon our Bishops and Curates, and all congregations committed to their charge, the healthful spirit of thy grace, and that they may truly please thee, pour upon them the continual dew of thy blessing: Grant this, O Lord, for the honour of our advocate and mediator, Jesus Christ. Amen.

¶ A Prayer of Chrysostome.

ALMIGHTY God, which hast given us grace at this time with one accord to make our common supplications unto thee, and dost promise that when two or three be gathered together in thy name thou wilt grant their requests: fulfil now, O Lord, the desires and petitions of thy servants, as may be most expedient for them, granting us in this world knowledge of thy truth, and in the world to come life everlasting. Amen[4].

¶ ii. Corin. xiii.

THE grace of our Lord Jesus Christ, and the love of God, and the fellowship of the Holy Ghost, be with us all evermore. Amen.

¶ For rain, if the time require.

O GOD heavenly Father, which by thy Son Jesus Christ hast promised to all them that seek thy kingdom, and the righteousness thereof, all things necessary to their bodily sustenance: Send us, we beseech thee, in this our necessity, such moderate rain and showers, that we may receive the fruits of the earth to our comfort and to thy honour, through Jesus Christ our Lord. Amen.

¶ For fair weather.

O LORD God, which for the sin of man didst once drown all the world, except eight persons, and afterward of thy great mercy didst promise never to destroy it so again: we humbly beseech thee, that although we for our iniquities have worthily deserved this plague of rain and

[1] 1596, for.]
[3] 1596, strengthen.]
[2] 1596, plenteously.]
[4] Not in 1596.]

waters, yet upon our true repentance thou wilt send us such weather, whereby we may receive the fruits of the earth in due season, and learn both by thy punishment to amend our lives, and for thy clemency to give thee praise and glory, through Jesus Christ our Lord. Amen.

¶ In the time of dearth and famine.

O GOD heavenly Father, whose gift it is that the rain doth fall, the earth is fruitful, beasts increase, and fishes do multiply: Behold, we beseech thee, the afflictions of thy people, and grant that the scarcity and dearth (which we do now most justly suffer for our iniquity) may through thy goodness be mercifully turned into cheapness and plenty, for the love of Jesu[5] Christ our Lord, to whom with thee and the Holy Ghost be[6] praise for ever. Amen.

¶ In the time of War.

O ALMIGHTY God, King of all kings, and governour of all things, whose power no creature is able to resist, to whom it belongeth justly to punish sinners, and to be merciful unto them that truly repent: Save and deliver us (we humbly beseech thee) from the hands of our enemies; abate their pride, assuage their malice, and confound their devices; that we, being armed with thy defence, may be preserved evermore from all perils to glorify thee, which art the only giver of all victory, through the merits of thy only son Jesus Christ our Lord. Amen[7].

¶ In the time of any common plague or sickness.

O ALMIGHTY God, which in thy wrath in the time of king David didst slay with the plague of pestilence three score and ten thousand, and yet remembering thy mercy, didst save the rest: have pity upon us miserable sinners, that now are visited with great sickness, and mortality; that like as thou didst then command thine angel to cease from punishing, so it may now please thee to withdraw from us this plague, and grievous sickness, through Jesus Christ our Lord. Amen.

O GOD, whose nature and property is ever to have mercy, and to
forgive, receive our humble petitions: and though we be
tied and bound with the chain of our sins, yet
let the pitifulness of thy great mercy
loose us, for the honour of Jesus
Christ's sake, our mediator
and advocate.
Amen.]

[5 1596, Jesus.]   [6 1596, be all honour. &c.]
[7 Not in 1596.]

¶ The[1] Collects, Epistles and Gospels,

to be used at the celebration of the Lord's supper and holy Communion, through the year.

The first Sunday of[2] Advent.

The Collect.

ALMIGHTY God, give us grace that we may cast away the works of darkness, and put upon us the armour of light, now in the time of this mortal life (in the which thy Son Jesus Christ came to visit us in great humility;) that in the last day, when he shall come again in[3] glorious majesty to judge both the quick and the dead, we may rise to the life immortal through him: who liveth and reigneth with thee and the Holy Ghost, now and ever. Amen.

The Epistle.

Rom. xiii.

OWE nothing to any man, but this, that ye love one another. For he that loveth another, fulfilleth the law. For these commandments: Thou shalt not commit adultery: Thou shalt not kill: Thou shalt not steal: Thou shalt bear no false witness: Thou shalt not lust: and so forth, (if there be any other commandment,) it is all comprehended in this saying: namely, Love thy neighbour as thyself. Love hurteth not his neighbour: therefore is love the fulfilling of the Law. This also, we know the season, how that it is time, that we should now awake out of sleep; for now is our salvation nearer, than when we believed. The night is passed, the day is come nigh: let us therefore cast away the deeds of darkness, and let us put on the armour of light. Let us walk honestly, as it were in the day light: not in eating and drinking, neither in chambering and wantonness, neither in strife and envying: but put ye on the Lord Jesus Christ, and make not provision for the flesh, to fulfil the lusts of it.

The Gospel.

Math. xxi.

AND when they drew nigh to Jerusalem, and were come to Bethphage unto mount Olivet: then sent Jesus two of his disciples, saying unto them: Go into the town that lieth over against you, and anon you[4] shall find an Ass bound, and a colt with her; loose them, and bring them unto me. And if any man say ought unto you, say ye, The Lord hath

---

[[1] 1578, *The Collectes, with the order how to finde the beginning and ende of the* Epistles and Gospels in the newe Testament, by the Chapter and the verse, as it is appoynted in the booke of Common prayer.]

[[2] 1596, in.]   [[3] Grafton and 1596, in his.]

[[4] Grafton, ye.]

need of them: and straightway he will let them go. All this was done, that it might be fulfilled, which was spoken by the Prophet, saying: Tell ye the daughter of Sion: behold, thy king cometh unto thee, meek, sitting upon an Ass, and a colt, the foal of the Ass used to the yoke. The Disciples went, and did as Jesus commanded them, and brought the Ass, and the colt, and put on them their clothes, and set him thereon. And many of the people spread their garments in the way. Other cut down branches from the trees, and strawed them in the way. Moreover, the people that went before, and they that came after cried, saying: *Hosanna*, to the son of David: Blessed is he that cometh in the name of the Lord: *Hosanna* in the highest. And when he was come to Jerusalem, all the city was moved, saying, Who is this? And the people said: This is Jesus the Prophet of Nazareth, a city of Galilee. And Jesus went into the temple of God, and cast out all them that sold and bought in the temple, and overthrew the tables of the money changers, and the seats of them that sold doves, and said unto them, It is written: My house shall be called the house of prayer, but ye have made it a den of thieves.

The second Sunday[5].

The Collect.

BLESSED Lord, which hast caused all holy scriptures to be written for our learning: Grant us that we may in such wise hear them, read, mark, learn, and inwardly digest them: that by patience and comfort of thy holy word, we may embrace and ever hold fast the blessed hope of everlasting life, which thou hast given us in our Saviour Jesus Christ[6].

The Epistle.

WHATSOEVER things are written aforetime, they are written for our learning, that we through patience, and comfort of the scriptures, might have hope. The God of patience and consolation grant you to be like-minded one towards another, after the ensample of Christ Jesu: that ye all agreeing together, may with one mouth praise God, the Father of our Lord Jesu[7] Christ. Wherefore receive ye one another, as Christ received us, to the praise of GOD. And this I say: that Jesus Christ was a minister of the Circumcision for[8] the truth of GOD, to confirm the promises made unto the fathers: and that the Gentiles might praise GOD for his mercy, as it is written: For this cause I will praise thee among the Gentiles, and sing unto thy name. And again he saith: Rejoice ye gentiles with his people. And again: Praise the Lord all ye Gentiles, and laud him all ye nations together. And again Esay saith: There shall be the root of Jesse, and he that shall rise to reign over the Gentiles, in him shall the Gentiles trust. The God of hope fill you with all joy and peace in believing, that ye may be rich in hope, through the power of the Holy Ghost. Rom. xv.

[5 1596, in Aduent.]   [6 Grafton, Amen.]
[7 Grafton, Jesus.]   [8 Grafton, of.]

The Gospel.

Luke xxi. THERE shall be signs in the sun and in the moon, and in the stars: and in the earth the people shall be at their wits' end, through despair. The sea and the water shall roar, and men's hearts shall fail them for fear, and for looking after those things, which shall come on the earth. For the powers of heaven shall move. And then shall they see the Son of man come in a cloud, with power and great glory. When these things begin to come to pass, then look up, and lift up your heads; for your redemption draweth nigh. And he shewed them a similitude: Behold the Fig tree, and all other trees: when they shoot forth their buds, ye see and know of your own selves, that Summer is then nigh at hand. So likewise ye also (when ye see these things come to pass) be sure that the kingdom of God is nigh. Verily I say unto you: this generation shall not pass, till all be fulfilled. Heaven and earth shall pass, but my words shall not pass.

¶ The third Sunday [1].

The Collect.

LORD, we beseech thee, give ear to our prayers, and by thy gracious visitation lighten the darkness of our heart, by our Lord Jesus Christ[2].

The Epistle.

1 Cor. iv. LET a man this wise esteem us, even as the ministers of Christ, and stewards of the secrets of God. Furthermore, it is required of the stewards, that a man be found faithful. With me it is but a very small thing, that I should be judged of you, either of man's judgment: no, I judge not mine own self; for I know nought by myself, yet am I[3] not thereby justified. It is the Lord that judgeth me. Therefore, judge nothing before the time, until the Lord come, which will lighten things that are hid in darkness, and open the counsels of the hearts: and then shall every man have praise of God.

The Gospel.

Math. xi. WHEN John, being in prison, heard the works of Christ, he sent two of his Disciples, and said unto him: Art thou he that shall come, or do we look for another? Jesus answered, and said unto them: Go, and shew John again, what ye have heard and seen. The blind receive their sight, the lame walk, the lepers are cleansed, and the deaf hear, the dead are raised up, and the poor receive the glad tidings of the gospel: and happy is he that is not offended by me. And as they departed, Jesus began to say unto the people, concerning John: What went ye out into the wilderness to see? A reed that is shaken with the wind? Or what went ye out to[4] see? A man clothed in soft raiment? Behold, they that wear soft clothing, are in kings' houses. But what went ye out for to see? A

[1 1596, in Aduent.] [2 Grafton, Amen.]
[3 Grafton, not I.] [4 Grafton, for to see.]

prophet? Verily I say unto you, and more than a prophet. For this is he of whom it is written: Behold, I send my messenger before thy face, which shall prepare thy way before thee.

The fourth Sunday [5].

The Collect.

LORD, raise up (we pray thee) thy power, and come among us, and with great might succour us; that whereas (through our sins and wickedness) we be sore let and hindered, thy bountiful grace and mercy (through the satisfaction of thy Son our Lord) may speedily deliver us: to whom with thee and the Holy Ghost be honour and glory world without end [6].

The Epistle.

REJOICE in the Lord alway, and again I say, rejoice. Let your soft- Philip. iv. ness be known to all men: the Lord is even at hand. Be careful for nothing, but in all prayer and supplication let your petitions be manifest unto GOD, with giving of thanks. And the peace of God (which passeth all understanding), keep your hearts and minds, through Christ Jesu.

The Gospel.

THIS is the record of John, when the Jews sent priests and levites John i.[7] from Jerusalem, to ask him, What art thou? And he confessed, and denied not, and said plainly: I am not Christ. And they asked him: What then? art thou Helias? And he saith: I am not. Art thou the Prophet? And he answered, no. Then said they unto him: What art thou? that we may give an answer unto them that sent us: What sayest thou of thyself? He said: I am the voice of a crier in the wilderness: make straight the way of the Lord, as said the Prophet Esay. And they which were sent, were of the Pharisees: and they asked him, and said unto him: Why baptizest thou then, if thou be not Christ, nor Helias, neither that Prophet? John answered them, saying: I baptize with water, but there standeth one among you, whom ye know not: he it is, which though he came after me, was before me, whose shoe latchet I am not worthy to unloose. These things were done at Bethabara, beyond Jordan, where John did baptize.

Christmas [8] day.

The Collect.

ALMIGHTY God, which hast given us thy only begotten Son to take our nature upon him, and this day to be born of a pure virgin: Grant that we, being regenerate and made thy children by adoption and grace,

[5 1596, in Aduent.]   [6 Grafton, Amen.]
[7 Grafton, i. John i. A misprint.]   [8 Grafton prefixes, On.]

[LITURG. QU. ELIZ.]

may daily be renewed by thy Holy Spirit, through the same our Lord Jesus Christ: who liveth and reigneth[1] with. &c. Amen.

The Epistle.

Heb. i. GOD in times past, diversely and many ways spake unto the fathers by Prophets: but in these last days, he hath spoken to us by his own Son, whom he hath made heir of all things, by whom also he made the world. Which (son) being the brightness of his glory, and the very Image of his substance, ruling all things with the word of his power, hath by his own person purged our sins, and sitteth on the right hand of the majesty on high: being so much more excellent than the Angels, as he hath by inheritance obtained a more excellent name than they. For unto which of the Angels said he at any time: Thou art my son, this day have I begotten thee? And again: I will be his father, and he shall be my son? And again, when he bringeth in the first begotten Son into the world, he saith: And let all the Angels of God worship him. And unto the Angels he saith, He maketh his Angels spirits, and his ministers a flame of fire. But unto the Son he saith: Thy seat (O God) shall be for ever and ever. The sceptre of thy kingdom is a right sceptre. Thou hast loved righteousness, and hated iniquity: wherefore, God, even thy God hath anointed thee with oil[2] of gladness, above thy fellows. And thou Lord in the beginning hast laid the foundation of the earth: and the heavens are the works of thy hands. They shall perish, but thou endurest: But they all shall wax old as doth a garment, and as a vesture shalt thou change them, and they shall be changed. But thou art even the same, and thy years shall not fail.

The Gospel.

John i. IN the beginning was the word, and the word was with God, and God was the word. The same was in the beginning with God. All things were made by it, and without it was made nothing that was made. In it was life, and the life was the light of men: and the light shineth in the darkness, and the darkness comprehended it not. There was sent from God a man, whose name was John. The same came as a witness, to bear witness of the light, that all men through him might believe. He was not that light, but was sent to bear witness of the light. That light was the true light, which lighteth[3] every man that cometh into the world. He was in the world, and the world was made by him, and the world knew him not. He came among his own, and his own received him not. But as many as received him, to them gave he power to be made sons of God; even them that believed on his name, which were born, not of blood, nor of the will of the flesh, nor yet of the will of man, but of God. And the same word became flesh, and dwelt among us: and we saw the glory of it, as the glory of the only begotten Son of the Father, full of grace and truth.

[1 Grafton, with thee and the Holy Ghost, now and euer. Amen.]
[2 Grafton, the oyle.]   [3 Grafton, lighteneth.]

S. Stephen's day.

The Collect.

GRANT us, O Lord, to learn to love our enemies by the example of thy martyr Saint Stephen, who prayed for his persecutors to thee: which livest[4]. &c.

¶ Then shall follow a[5] Collect of the Nativity, which shall be said continually unto[6] New[7] year's day.

[8]

AND Stephen, being full of the Holy Ghost, looked up steadfastly with Act. vii. his eyes into heaven, and saw the glory of God, and Jesus standing on the right hand of God, and said: Behold, I see the heavens open, and the Son of man standing on the right hand of God. Then they gave a shout with a loud voice, and stopped their ears, and ran upon him all at once, and cast him out of the city, and stoned him. And the witnesses laid down their clothes at a young man's feet, whose name was Saul. And they stoned Stephen, calling on and saying: Lord Jesu receive my spirit. And he kneeled down, and cried with a loud voice: Lord, lay not this sin to their charge. And when he had thus spoken, he fell asleep.

The Gospel.

BEHOLD, I send unto you prophets, and wise men, and Scribes, and Math. xxiii. some of them ye shall kill, and crucify: and some of them shall ye scourge in your synagogues, and persecute them from city to city, that upon you may come all the righteous blood, which hath been shed upon the earth, from the blood of righteous Abel, unto the blood of Zacharias, the son of Barachias, whom ye slew between the temple and the altar. Verily I say unto you: all these things shall come upon this generation. O Jerusalem, Jerusalem, thou that killest the Prophets, and stonest them which are sent unto thee: how often would I have gathered thy children together, even as the hen gathereth her chickens under her wings, and ye would not! Behold, your house is left unto you desolate. For I say unto you: ye shall not see me henceforth, till that ye say: Blessed is he that cometh in the name of the Lord.

Saint John Evangelist's day.

The Collect.

MERCIFUL Lord, we beseech thee to cast thy bright beams of light upon thy Church: that it being lightened by the doctrine of thy blessed Apostle and Evangelist John, may attain to thy everlasting gifts. Through Jesus Christ our Lord. Amen.

[[4] Grafton, and reignest. &c.]   [[5] Grafton and 1596, the.]
[[6] 1578, vntill.]   [[7] Grafton, Newes.]   [[8] The Epistle, omitted.]

The Epistle.

i. John i.

THAT which was from the beginning, which we have heard, which we have seen with our eyes, which we have looked upon, and our hands have handled of the word of life: And the life appeared, and we have seen and bear witness, and shew unto you that eternal life, which was with the Father, and appeared unto us: that which we have seen, and heard, declare we unto you, that ye also may have fellowship with us, and that our fellowship may be with the Father, and his Son Jesus Christ. And this we write unto you, that ye may rejoice, and that your joy may be full. And this is the tidings, which we have heard of him, and declare unto you, that God is light, and in him is no darkness at all. If we say, we have fellowship with him, and walk in darkness, we lie, and do not the truth. But and if we walk in light, even as he is in light, then have we fellowship with him, and the blood of Jesus Christ his Son cleanseth us from all sin. If we say, we have no sin, we deceive ourselves, and the truth is not in us. If we knowledge our sins, he is faithful and just, to forgive us our sins, and to cleanse us from all unrighteousness. If we say, we have not sinned, we make him a liar, and his word is not in us.

The Gospel.

John xxi.

JESUS said unto Peter: Follow thou me. Peter turned about, and saw the disciple, whom Jesus loved, following (which also leaned on his breast at supper and said: Lord, which is he that betrayeth thee?) when Peter therefore saw him, he said to Jesus: Lord, what shall he here do? Jesus said unto him: If I will have him to tarry till I come, what is that to thee? Follow thou me. Then went this saying abroad among the brethren, that that disciple should not die. Yet Jesus said not to him, he shall not die: but if I will that he tarry till I come, what is that to thee? The same disciple is he, which testifieth of these things, and wrote these things: and we know that his testimony is true. There are also many other things which Jesus did, the which if they should be written every one, I suppose the world could not contain the books that should be written.

¶ The[1] Innocents' day.

The Collect.

ALMIGHTY God, whose praise this day the young Innocents thy witnesses hath[2] confessed and shewed forth, not in speaking but in dying: mortify and kill all vices in us, that in our conversation our life may express thy faith, which with our tongues we do confess: through Jesus Christ our Lord.

The Epistle.

Apoc. xiv.

I LOOKED, and lo, a lamb stood on the mount Sion, and with him an .c. and .xliiii. thousand, having his name, and his Father's name

[[1] The, not in 1596.] [[2] Grafton and 1596, haue.]

written in their foreheads. And I heard a voice from heaven, as the sound of many waters, and as the voice of a great thunder. And I heard the voice of harpers, harping with their harps. And they sung as it were a new song before the seat, and before the .iiii. beasts, and the elders; and no man could learn the song, but the hundred[3] forty and four thousand, which were redeemed from the earth. These are they, which were not defiled with women, for they are virgins. These follow[4] the Lamb, wheresoever he goeth. These were redeemed from men, being the firstfruits unto God, and to the Lamb; and in their mouths was found no guile: for they are without spot before the throne of God.

The Gospel.

THE Angel of the Lord appeared to Joseph in a sleep, saying: Arise, Math. ii. and take the child and his mother, and flee[5] into Egypt, and be thou there till I bring thee word. For it will come to pass, that Herod shall seek the child to destroy him. So when he awoke, he took the child and his mother by night, and departed into Egypt, and was there unto the death of Herod; that it might be fulfilled, which was spoken of the Lord by the prophet, saying: Out of Egypt have I called my Son. Then Herod, when he saw that he was mocked of the Wise men, he was exceeding wroth, and sent forth men of war, and slew all the children, that were in Bethlehem, and in all the coasts (as many as were two years[6] old or under) according to the time, which he had diligently known out of the Wise men. Then was fulfilled that, which was spoken by the Prophet Jeremy, where as he said: In Rama was there a voice heard, lamentation, weeping, and great mourning: Rachel weeping for her children, and would not be comforted, because they were not.

The Sunday after Christmas day.

The Collect.

ALMIGHTY God, which hast given. &c.[7] *As upon Christmas day.*

The Epistle.

AND I say, that the heir (as long as he is a child) differeth not from Gal. iv. a servant, though he be Lord of all; but is under tutors and governors, until the time that the father hath appointed. Even so we also, when we were children, were in bondage under the ordinances of the world. But when the time was full come, God sent his Son, made of a woman, and made bond unto the law, to redeem them, which were bond unto the law; that we through election might receive the inheritance, that belongeth unto the natural sons. Because ye are sons, God hath sent the spirit of his Son into our hearts, which crieth Abba Father. Wherefore now, thou art not a servant, but a son. If thou be a son, thou art also an heir of God through Christ.

[3 Grafton, c. and .xliiii.]   [4 Grafton, folowed.]   [5 Grafton, flie.]
[6 Grafton, yeare.]   [7 Grafton prints the Collect at length.]

The Gospel.

Math. i. THIS is the book of the generation of Jesus Christ, the son of David, the son of Abraham: Abraham begat Isaac: Isaac begat Jacob: Jacob begat Judas, and his brethren: Judas begat Phares, and Zaram of Thamar: Phares begat Esrom: Esrom begat Aram: Aram begat Aminadab: Aminadab begat Naasson: Naasson begat Salmon: Salmon begat Boos of Rahab: Boos begat Obed of Ruth: Obed begat Jesse: Jesse begat David the king: David the king begat Salomon, of her that was the wife of Urie: Salomon begat Roboam: Roboam begat Abia: Abia begat Asa: Asa begat Josaphat: Josaphat begat Joram: Joram begat Osias: Osias begat Joatham: Joatham begat Achas: Achas begat Ezechias: Ezechias begat Manasses: Manasses begat Amon: Amon begat Josias: Josias begat Jechonias and his brethren, about the time that they were carried away to Babylon: And after they were brought to Babylon, Jechonias begat Salathiel: Salathiel begat Zorobabel: Zorobabel begat Abiud: Abiud begat Eliachim: Eliachim begat Azor: Azor begat Sadoc: Sadoc begat Achin: Achin begat Eliud: Eliud begat Eleasar: Eleasar begat Matthan: Matthan begat Jacob: Jacob begat Joseph, the husband of Mary; of whom was born Jesus, even he that is called Christ. And so all the generations, from Abraham to David, are .xiiii. generations. And from David, unto the captivity of Babylon, are .xiiii. generations. And from the captivity of Babylon unto Christ, are .xiiii. generations.

The birth of Jesus Christ was on this wise: when his mother Mary was married to Joseph (before they came to dwell together) she was found with child by the Holy Ghost. Then Joseph her husband (because he was a righteous man, and would not put her to shame) was minded privily to depart from her. But while he thus thought, behold, the Angel of the Lord appeared unto him in sleep, saying: Joseph thou son of David, fear not to take unto thee Mary thy wife: for that which is conceived in her, cometh of the Holy Ghost. She shall bring forth a son, and thou shalt call his name Jesus: for he shall save his people from their sins.

All this was done, that it might be fulfilled, which was spoken of the Lord by the Prophet, saying: Behold, a maid shall be with child, and shall bring forth a son, and they shall call his name Emanuell: which if a man interpret, is as much to say, as God with us. And Joseph, as soon as he awoke out of sleep, did as the Angel of the Lord had bidden him: and he took his wife unto him, and knew her not, till she had brought forth her[1] first begotten son, and called his name Jesus.

The Circumcision of Christ.

The Collect.

ALMIGHTY God, which madest thy blessed Son to be circumcised and obedient to the law for man: grant us the true circumcision of the

[[1] Grafton, the.]

spirit, that our hearts and all our[2] members being mortified from all worldly and carnal lusts, may in all things obey thy blessed will: through the same thy Son Jesus Christ our Lord.

The Epistle.

BLESSED is that man, to whom the Lord will not impute sin. Came this blessedness then upon the uncircumcision, or upon the circumcision also? For we say, that faith was reckoned to Abraham for righteousness. How was it then reckoned? When he was in the circumcision, or when he was in the uncircumcision? Not in time of circumcision, but when he was yet uncircumcised. And he received the sign of circumcision, as a seal of the righteousness of faith, which he had yet being uncircumcised; that he should be the father of all them that believe, though they be not circumcised, that righteousness might be imputed to them also; and that he might be the father of circumcision, not unto them only which came of the circumcised, but unto them also that walk in the steps of the faith, that was in our father Abraham before the time of circumcision. For the promise (that he should be heir of the world) happened not to Abraham, or to his seed, through the law, but through the righteousness of faith. For if they which are of the law, be heirs, then is faith but vain, and the promise of none effect. Rom. iv.

The Gospel.

AND it fortuned, as soon as the Angels were gone away from the shepherds into heaven, they said one to another: Let us go now even unto Bethleem, and see this thing, that[3] we hear say is happened, which the Lord hath shewed unto us. And they came with haste, and found Mary and Joseph, and the babe, laid in a manger. And when they had seen it, they published abroad the saying, that was told them of that child. And all they that heard it, wondered at those things, which were told them of the shepherds; but Mary kept all those sayings, and pondered them in her heart. And the shepherds returned, praising and lauding God, for all the things that they had heard, and seen, even as it was told unto them. And when the eight day was come that the child should be circumcised, his name was called Jesus, which was named of the Angel, before he was conceived in the womb. Luke ii.

¶ If there be a Sunday between the Epiphany and the Circumcision, then shall be used the same Collect, Epistle and Gospel at the Communion, which was used upon the day of Circumcision.

¶ The Epiphany.

The Collect.

O GOD, which by the leading of a star didst manifest thy only-begotten Son to the Gentiles: mercifully grant, that we which know thee now by faith, may after this life have the fruition of thy glorious Godhead, through Christ our Lord[4].

[2 Grafton omits, our.]   [3 Grafton, whiche.]   [4 1596, Amen.]

The Epistle.

Ephe. iii.

For this cause I Paul am a prisoner of Jesus Christ, for you Heathen, if ye have heard of the ministration of the grace of God, which is given me to youward. For by revelation shewed he the mystery unto me, as I wrote afore in few words: whereby when ye read, ye may understand my knowledge in the mystery of Christ: which mystery in times past was not opened unto the sons of men, as it is now declared unto his holy Apostles and Prophets by the Spirit; that the Gentiles should be inheritors also, and of the same body, and partakers of his promise of Christ, by the means of the gospel, whereof I am made a minister, according to the gift of the grace of God, which is given unto me, after the working of his power. Unto me the least of all saints, is this grace given, that I should preach among the Gentiles the unsearchable riches of Christ, and to make all men see, what the fellowship of the mystery is, which from the beginning of the world, hath been hid in God, which made all things, through Jesus Christ: to the intent that now unto the rulers and powers in heavenly things, might be known by the congregation the manifold wisdom of God, according to the eternal purpose, which he wrought in Christ Jesu our Lord, by whom we have boldness and entrance with the confidence which is by the faith of him.

The Gospel.

Math. ii.

When Jesus was born in Bethleem a city of Jewry, in the time of Herod the king: Behold, there came wise men from the East to Jerusalem, saying: Where is he that is born King of the Jews? For we have seen his star in the East, and are come to worship him. When Herod the king had heard these things, he was troubled, and all the city of Jerusalem with him. And when he had gathered all the chief priests, and Scribes of the people together, he demanded of them, where Christ should be born. And they said unto him, At Bethleem in Jewry. For thus it is written by the Prophet: And thou, Bethleem in the land of Jewry, art not the least among the princes of Juda: for out of thee there shall come unto me the captain that shall govern my people Israel. Then Herod (when he had privily called the wise men) he inquired of them diligently, what time the star appeared; and he bade them go to Bethleem, and said: Go your way thither, and search diligently for the child: and when ye have found him, bring me word again, that I may come and worship him also. When they had heard the king, they departed: and lo, the star which they saw in the East, went before them, till it came and stood over the place, wherein the child was. When they saw the star, they were exceeding glad, and went into the house, and found the child with Mary his mother, and fell down flat and worshipped him, and opened their treasures, and offered unto him gifts: Gold, Frankincense, and Myrrh. And after they were warned of God in sleep that they should not go again to Herod, they returned into their own country another way.

The first Sunday after the Epiphany.
The Collect.

LORD, we beseech thee mercifully to receive the prayers of thy people which call upon thee: and grant that they may both perceive and know what things they ought to do, and also have grace and power faithfully to fulfil the same, through Jesus Christ our Lord[1].

The Epistle.

I BESEECH you therefore, brethren, by the mercifulness of God, that Rom. xii. ye make your bodies a quick sacrifice, holy, and acceptable unto God, which is your reasonable serving of God; and fashion not your selves, like unto this world: but be ye changed in your shape, by the renewing of your mind, that ye may prove what thing that good and acceptable and perfect will of God is. For I say (through the grace that unto me given is[2]) to every man among you, that no man stand high in his own conceit, more than it becometh him to esteem of him self: but so judge of him self, that he be gentle and sober, according as God hath dealt to every man the measure of faith. For as we have many members in one body, and all members have not one office, so we, being many, are one body in Christ, and every man among our selves one another's members.

The Gospel.

THE father and mother of Jesus went to Jerusalem after the custom Luke ii. of the feast day. And when they had fulfilled the days, as they returned home, the child Jesus abode still in Jerusalem, and his father and mother knew not of it: but they, supposing him to have been in the company, came a day's journey, and sought him among their kinsfolk and acquaintance. And when they found him not, they went back again to Jerusalem, and sought him. And it fortuned that after three days they found him in the temple, sitting in the midst of the Doctors, hearing them, and posing them. And all that heard him, were astonied at his understanding and answers. And when they saw him, they marvelled, and his mother said unto him: Son, why hast thou thus dealt with us? Behold, thy father and I have sought thee, sorrowing. And he said unto them: How happened[3] that ye sought me? wist you[4] not that I must go about my Father's business? And they understood not that saying, which he spake unto them. And he went down with them, and came to Nazareth, and was obedient unto them: but his mother kept all these sayings together in her heart. And Jesus prospered in wisdom and age, and in favour with God and men.

The second Sunday after the Epiphany.
The Collect.

ALMIGHTY and everlasting God, which dost govern all things in heaven and earth: mercifully hear the supplications of thy people, and grant us thy peace all the days of our life.

[1 Grafton and 1596, Amen.]   [2 Grafton, is gyuen.]
[3 Grafton, happened it.]   [4 Grafton, ye.]

90   THE SECOND SUNDAY AFTER THE EPIPHANY.   [1559.

The Epistle.

Rom. xii.

SEEING that we have diverse gifts, according to the grace that is given unto us: if a man have the gift of prophecy, let him have it, that it be agreeing to the faith. Let him that hath an office, wait on his office. Let him that teacheth, take heed to his doctrine. Let him that exhorteth, give attendance to his exhortation. If any man give, let him do it with singleness. Let him that ruleth do it with diligence. If any man shew mercy, let him do it with cheerfulness. Let love be without dissimulation. Hate that which is evil, and cleave to[1] that which is good. Be kind one to another, with brotherly love. In giving honour, go one before another. Be not slothful in the business which you[2] have in hand. Be fervent in spirit. Apply your selves to the time. Rejoice in hope. Be patient in tribulation. Continue in prayer. Distribute unto the necessity of the saints. Be ready to harbour. Bless them which persecute you: bless, I say, and curse not. Be merry with them that are merry, weep with them that weep: be of like affection one towards another. Be not high minded, but make your selves equal to them of the lower sort.

The Gospel.

John ii.

AND the third day was there a marriage in Cana, a city of Galilee, and the mother of Jesus was there. And Jesus was called (and his disciples) unto the marriage. And when the wine failed, the mother of Jesus said unto him: They have no wine. Jesus said unto her: Woman, what have I to do with thee? Mine hour is not yet come. His mother said unto the ministers: Whatsoever he saith unto you, do it. And there were standing there .vi. waterpots of stone, after the manner of purifying of the Jews, containing .ii. or .iii. firkins apiece. Jesus said unto them: Fill the waterpots with water. And they filled them up to the brim. And he said unto them: Draw out now, and bear unto the governour of the feast. And they bare it. When the ruler of the feast had tasted the water turned into wine, and knew not whence it was (but the ministers, which drew the water, knew), he called the bridegroom, and said unto him: Every man at the beginning doth set forth good wine, and when men be drunk[3], then that which is worse: but thou hast kept the good wine until now. This beginning of miracles did Jesus, in Cana of Galilee, and shewed his glory, and his disciples believed on him.

The third Sunday[4].

The Collect.

ALMIGHTY and everlasting God, mercifully look upon our infirmities: and in all our dangers and necessities, stretch forth thy right hand to help and defend us, through Christ our Lord.

The Epistle.

Rom. xii.

BE not wise in your own opinions. Recompense to no man evil for evil. Provide aforehand things honest, not only before God, but also in

[1 Grafton, vnto.]   [2 Grafton, ye.]
[3 Grafton, drunken.] [4 1596, after *the Epiphanie.*]

THE THIRD SUNDAY AFTER THE EPIPHANY

the sight of all men. If it be possible (as much as is in you) live peaceably with all men. Dearly beloved, avenge not your selves, but rather give place unto wrath. For it is written: Vengeance is mine, I will reward, saith the Lord. Therefore, if thine enemy hunger, feed him: if he thirst, give him drink. For in so doing, thou shalt heap coals of fire on his head. Be not overcome of evil, but overcome evil with goodness.

The Gospel.

WHEN he was come down from the mountain, much people followed him. And behold, there came a Leper, and worshipped him saying: Master, if thou wilt, thou canst make me clean. And Jesus put forth his hand, and touched him, saying: I will, be thou clean: and immediately his leprosy was cleansed. And Jesus said unto him: Tell no man, but go and shew thyself to the Priest, and offer the gift (that Moses commanded to be offered) for a witness unto them. And when Jesus was entered into Capernaum, there came unto him a Centurion, and besought him, saying: Master, my servant lieth at home sick of the Palsy, and is grievously pained. And Jesus said: When I come unto him, I will heal him. The Centurion answered, and said: Sir, I am not worthy, that thou shouldest come under my roof: but speak the word only, and my servant shall be healed. For I also am a man subject to the authority of another, and have soldiers under me: and I say to this man, go, and he goeth: and to another man, come, and he cometh: and to my servant, do this, and he doeth it. When Jesus heard these words, he marvelled, and said to them that followed him: Verily I say unto you, I have not found so great faith in Israel. I say unto you, that many shall come from the East, and West, and shall rest with Abraham, Isaac, and Jacob, in the kingdom of heaven: but the children of the kingdom shall be cast out into utter darkness; there shall be weeping and gnashing with[5] teeth. And Jesus said unto the Centurion: Go thy way, and as thou believest, so be it unto thee: and his servant was healed in the self same hour. *Math. viii.*

The fourth Sunday[6].

The Collect.

GOD, which knowest us to be set in the midst of so many and great dangers, that for man's frailness we cannot always stand uprightly: Grant to us the health of body and soul, that all those things which we suffer for sin, by thy help we may well pass and overcome: through Christ our Lord.

The Epistle.

LET every soul submit him self unto the authority of the higher powers: for there is no power but of God. The powers that be, are ordained of God. Whosoever therefore resisteth power, resisteth the ordinance of God: but they that resist, shall receive to them selves damnation. For rulers are not fearful to them that do good, but to them that *Rom. xiii.*

[5 Grafton, of.]   [6 1596, after *the Epiphanie.*]

do evil. Wilt thou be without fear of the power? do well then, and so shalt thou be praised of the same: for he is the minister of God for thy wealth. But and if thou do that, which is evil, then fear, for he beareth not the sword for nought: for he is the minister of God, to take vengeance on them that do evil. Wherefore, ye must needs obey, not only for fear of vengeance, but also because of conscience. And even for this cause, pay ye tribute: for they are God's ministers, serving for that purpose. Give to every man therefore his duty: tribute, to whom tribute belongeth: custom, to whom custom is due: fear, to whom fear belongeth: honour, to whom honour pertaineth.

The Gospel.

Math. viii.
AND when he entered into a ship, his disciples followed him. And behold, there arose a great tempest in the sea, in so much as the ship was covered with waves; but he was asleep. And his disciples came to him, and awoke him, saying: Master, save us, we perish. And he said unto them: Why are ye fearful, O ye of little faith? Then he arose, and rebuked the winds and the sea, and there followed a great calm. But the men marvelled, saying: What manner of man is this, that both winds and sea obey him? And when he was come to the other side into[1] the country of the Gergesites, there met with him .ii. possessed of devils, which came out of the graves, and were out of measure fierce, so that no man might go by that way. And behold, they cried out saying: O Jesu, thou Son of God, what have we to do with thee? art thou come hither to torment us before the time? And there was a good way off from them a herd of swine, feeding. So the devils besought him, saying: If thou cast us out, suffer us to go into the herd of swine. And he said unto them: Go your ways. Then went they out, and departed into the herd of swine. And behold, the whole herd of swine was carried headlong into the sea, and perished in the waters. Then they that kept them, fled, and went their ways into the city, and told every thing, and what had happened unto the possessed of the devils. And behold, the whole city came out to meet Jesus: and when they saw him, they besought him, that he would depart out of their coasts.

The fifth Sunday[2].

The Collect.

LORD, we beseech thee to keep thy Church and household continually in thy true religion: that they which do lean only upon hope of thy heavenly grace, may evermore be defended by thy mighty power: Through Christ[3] our Lord.

The Epistle.

Phil. ii.[4]
PUT upon you, as the elect of God, tender mercy, kindness, humbleness of mind, meekness, longsuffering, forbearing one another, and forgiv-

---

[1 Grafton, in.]   [2 1596, after *the Epiphanie*.]
[3 1596, Jesus Christ.]   [4 Misprint for, *Col.* iii.]

ing one another, if any man have a quarrel against another: as Christ forgave you, even so do ye. Above all these things, put on love, which is the bond of perfectness. And the peace of God rule your hearts, to the which peace ye are called in one body: And see that ye be thankful. Let the word of Christ dwell in you plenteously, with all wisdom: Teach and exhort your own selves in psalms, and hymns, and spiritual songs, singing with grace in your hearts to the Lord. And whatsoever ye do, in word, or deed, do all in the name of the Lord Jesu, giving thanks to God the Father by him.

The Gospel.

THE kingdom of heaven is like unto a man, which sowed good Math. xiii. seed in his field: but while men slept, his enemy came, and sowed tares among the wheat, and went his way. But when the blade was sprung up, and had brought forth fruit, then appeared the tares also. So the servants of the housholder came, and said unto him: Sir, didst not thou sow good seed in thy field? from whence then hath it tares? He said unto them: The envious man hath done this. The servant said unto him: Wilt thou then that we go and weed them up? But he said: Nay, lest while ye gather up the tares, ye pluck up also the wheat with them: let both grow together until the harvest: and in the time of harvest I will say to the reapers: Gather ye first the tares, and bind them together in sheaves, to be brent; but gather the wheat into my barn.

The .vi. Sunday (if there be so many) shall have the same Collect, Epistle and Gospel, that was upon the fift Sunday.

The Sunday called Septuagesima.

The Collect.

O LORD, we beseech thee favourably to hear the prayers of thy people, that we which are justly punished for our offences, may be mercifully delivered by thy goodness, for the glory of thy Name, through Jesu[5] Christ our Saviour, who liveth and reigneth[6], world without end[7].

The Epistle.

PERCEIVE ye not, how that they, which run in a course, run all, i. Cor. ix. but one receiveth the reward? So run, that ye may obtain. Every man that proveth masteries, abstaineth from all things. And they do it to obtain a crown that shall perish, but we to obtain an everlasting crown. I therefore so run, not as at an uncertain thing. So fight I, not as one that beateth the air: but I tame my body, and bring it into subjection, lest by any means it come to pass, that when I have preached to other, I myself should be a cast away.

[[5] Grafton and 1596, Jesus.]   [[6] Grafton, reygneth. &c.]
[[7] 1596, Amen.]

The Gospel.

Math. xx.

THE kingdom of heaven is like unto a man that is an housholder, which went out early in the morning, to hire labourers into his vineyard. And when the agreement was made with the labourers, for a penny a day, he sent them into his vineyard. And he went out about the third hour, and saw other standing idle in the marketplace, and said unto them: Go ye also into the vineyard, and whatsoever is right, I will give you. And they went their way. Again, he went out about the .vi. and .ix. hour, and did likewise. And about the .xi. hour, he went out, and found other standing idle, and said unto them: Why stand ye here all the day idle? They said unto him: Because no man hath hired us. He saith unto them: Go ye also into the vineyard, and whatsoever is right, that shall ye receive. So when even was come, the Lord of the vineyard said unto his steward: Call the labourers, and give them their hire, beginning at the last, until the first. And when they did come, that came about the .xi. hour, they received every man a penny. But when the first came also, they supposed that they should have received more, and they likewise received every man a penny. And when they had received it, they murmured against the good man of the house, saying: These last have wrought but one hour, and thou hast made them equal with us, which have borne the burthen and heat of the day. But he answered unto one of them, and said: Friend, I do thee no wrong: didst not thou agree with me for a penny? Take that thine is, and go thy way: I will give unto this last, even as unto thee. Is it not lawful for me to do as me lusteth with mine own goods? Is thine eye evil, because I am good? So the last shall be first, and the first shall be last. For many be called, but few be chosen.

The Sunday called Sexagesima.

The Collect.

LORD God, which seest that we put not our trust in any thing that we do: mercifully grant, that by thy power we may be defended against all adversity, through Jesus Christ our Lord.

The Epistle.

ii. Cor. xi.

YE suffer fools gladly, seeing yourselves are wise. For ye suffer, if a man bring you into bondage: if a man devour: if a man take: if a man exalt him self: if a man smite you on the face. I speak as concerning rebuke, as though we had been weak in this behalf. Howbeit, whereinsoever any man dare be bold, (I speak foolishly), I dare be bold also. They are Hebrews, even so am I. They are Israelites, even so am I. They are the seed of Abraham, even so am I. They are the ministers of Christ (I speak like a fool), I am more: In labours more abundant: In stripes above measure: In prison more plenteously: In death oft. Of the Jews .v. times received I .xl. stripes save one: Thrice was I beaten with rods: I was once stoned: I suffered thrice shipwreck: Night and day have I been in the deep sea. In journeying often: in perils of waters: in perils of robbers: in jeopardies of mine own nation: in jeopardies among the Heathen: in perils in the city: in perils in wilderness: in perils in the sea: in perils among false brethren: in labour and travail: in watchings often: in hunger and thirst: in fastings often: in cold and nakedness: beside the things, which outwardly happen[1] unto me, I am cumbered daily, and do care for all congregations. Who is weak, and I am not weak? Who is offended, and I burn not? If I must needs boast, I will boast of the things that concern mine infirmities. The God and Father of our Lord Jesus Christ, which is blessed for evermore, knoweth that I lie not.

The Gospel.

WHEN much people were gathered together, and were come to him out of all cities, he spake by a similitude. The sower went out to sow his seed: and as he sowed, some fell by the way side, and it was trodden down, and the fowls of the air devoured it up. And some fell on stones, and as soon as it was sprung up, it withered away, because it lacked moistness. And some fell among thorns, and the thorns sprang up with it, and choked it. And some fell on good ground, and sprang up, and bare fruit an hundredfold. And as he said these things, he cried: He that hath ears to hear, let him hear. And his disciples asked him, saying: What manner of similitude is this? And he said: Unto you it is given to know the secrets of the kingdom of God, but to other by parables: that when they see, they should not see; and when they hear, they should not understand. The parable is this: The seed is the word of God: those that are beside the way, are they that hear: then cometh the devil, and taketh away the word out of their hearts, lest they should believe, and be saved. They on the stones are they, which when they hear, receive the word with joy; and these have no roots, which for a while believe, and in time of temptation go away. And that which fell among thorns, are they, which when they have heard, go forth, and are choked with cares and riches, and voluptuous living, and bring forth no fruit. That which fell in the good ground are they, which with a pure and good heart hear the word and keep it, and bring forth fruit through patience. Luke viii.

The Sunday called Quinquagesima.

The Collect.

O LORD which dost teach us, that all our doings without charity are nothing worth, send thy Holy Ghost, and pour in[2] our hearts that most excellent gift of charity, the very bond of peace and all virtues, without the which whosoever liveth, is counted dead before thee: Grant this for thy[3] only Son Jesus Christ's sake.

[1] Grafton, happened.] [2] Grafton and 1596, into.]
[3] 1596, thine.]

The Sunday called Quinquagesima. [1559.

The Epistle.

i. Cor. xiii.

Though I speak with tongues of men and of Angels, and have no love, I am even as sounding brass, or as a tinkling cymbal. And though I could prophesy, and understand all secrets, and all knowledge; yea, if I have all faith, so that I could move mountains out of their places, and yet have no love, I am nothing. And though I bestow all my goods to feed the poor, and though I gave my body, even that I burned, and yet have no love, it profiteth me nothing. Love suffereth long, and is courteous, love envieth not, love doth not frowardly, swelleth not, dealeth not dishonestly, seeketh not her own, is not provoked to anger, thinketh none evil, rejoiceth not in iniquity. But rejoiceth in the truth: suffereth all things, believeth all things, hopeth all things, endureth all things. Though that prophesying fail, either tongues cease, or knowledge vanish away, yet love falleth never away. For our knowledge is unperfect, and our prophesying is unperfect: But when that which is perfect is come, then that which is unperfect shall be done away. When I was a child, I spake as a child, I understood as a child, I imagined as a child. But as soon as I was a man, I put away childishness. Now we see in a glass, even in a dark speaking: but then shall we see face to face. Now I know unperfectly, but then shall I know, even as I am known. Now abideth faith, hope, and love, even these three: but the chief of these is love.

The Gospel.

Luke xvii.[1]

Jesus took unto him the .xii. and said unto them: Behold, we go up to Jerusalem, and all shall be fulfilled that are written by the Prophets of the son of man. For he shall be delivered unto the Gentiles, and shall be mocked, and despitefully entreated, and spitted on. And when they have scourged him, they will put him to death, and the third day he shall rise again. And they understood none of these things. And this saying was hid from them, so that they perceived not the things which were spoken. And it came to pass, that as he was come nigh to[2] Hiericho, a certain blind man sat by the highway side begging. And when he heard the people pass by, he asked what it meant. And they said unto him, that Jesus of Nazareth passed by. And he cried, saying: Jesu[3] thou son of David, have mercy on me. And they which went before, rebuked him, that he should hold his peace. But he cried so much the more: Thou son of David, have mercy on me. And Jesus stood still, and commanded him to be brought unto him. And when he was come near, he asked him, saying: What wilt thou that I do unto thee? And he said: Lord, that I might receive my sight. And Jesus said unto him: Receive thy sight, thy faith hath saved thee. And immediately he received his sight, and followed him, praising God. And all the people, when they saw it, gave praise unto God.

[1 Misprint for, xviii.]
[3 Grafton, Jesus.]
[2 Grafton, vnto.]

The first day of Lent.
The Collect.
ALMIGHTY and everlasting God, which hatest nothing that thou hast made, and dost forgive the sins of all them that be penitent: Create and make in us new and contrite hearts, that we worthily lamenting our sins, and knowledging our wretchedness, may obtain of thee, the God of all mercy, perfect remission and forgiveness, through Jesus Christ.

The Epistle.
TURN you unto me with all your hearts, with fasting, weeping and mourning: rent your hearts and not your clothes. Turn you unto the Lord your God; for he is gracious and merciful, longsuffering, and of great compassion, and ready to pardon wickedness. Then (no doubt) he also shall turn and forgive: and after his chastening, he shall let your increase remain for meat and drink offerings unto the Lord your God. Blow out with the trumpet in Sion, proclaim a fasting, call the congregation, and gather the people together: warn the congregation, gather the elders, bring the children and sucklings together. Let the bridegroom go forth of his chamber, and the bride out of her closet. Let the priests serve the Lord between the porch and the altar, weeping and saying: Be favourable, O Lord, be favourable unto thy people: let not thine heritage be brought to such confusion, lest the heathen be Lords thereof: Wherefore should they say among the heathen: Where is now their God? *Joel ii.*

The Gospel.
WHEN ye fast, be not sad as the hypocrites are: for they disfigure their faces, that it may appear unto men how that they fast. Verily I say unto you, they have their reward. But thou, when thou fastest, anoint thine head, and wash thy face, that it appear not unto men how[4] thou fastest, but unto thy Father which is in secret: and thy Father which seeth in secret, shall reward thee openly. Lay not up for your selves treasure upon earth, where the rust and moth doth corrupt, and where thieves break through and steal. But lay up for you treasures in heaven, where neither rust nor moth doth corrupt, and where thieves do not break through, nor steal. For where your treasure is, there will your hearts be also. *Math. vi.*

The first Sunday in Lent.
The Collect.
O LORD, which for our sake didst fast forty days and forty nights: Give us grace to use such abstinence, that our flesh being subdued to the spirit, we may ever obey thy godly motions, in righteousness and true holiness, to thy honour and glory: which livest and reignest. &c.

The Epistle.
WE as helpers exhort you, that ye receive not the grace of God in vain. For he saith: I have heard thee in a time accepted, and in *ii Cor. vi.*

[4 Grafton, how that thou.]

the day of salvation have I succoured thee. Behold, now is that accepted time: behold, now is that day of salvation. Let us give none occasion of evil, that in our office be found no fault: but in all things let us behave ourselves as the ministers of God: in much patience, in afflictions, in necessities, in anguishes[1], in stripes, in prisonments, in strifes[2], in labours, in watchings, in fastings, in pureness, in knowledge, in longsuffering, in kindness, in the Holy Ghost, in love unfeigned, in the word of truth, in the power of God: by the armour of righteousness of the right hand and of the left: by honour and dishonour: by evil report and good report: as deceivers, and yet true: as unknown, and yet known: as dying, and behold we live: as chastened, and not killed: as sorrowing, and yet alway merry: as poor, and yet make many rich: as having nothing, and yet possessing all things.

The Gospel.

Math. iv.

THEN was Jesus led away of the spirit into wilderness, to be tempted of the devil. And when he had fasted forty days and forty nights, he was at the last an hungered. And when the tempter came to him, he said: If thou be the Son of God, command that these stones be made bread. But he answered and said: It is written, man shall not live by bread only, but by every word that proceedeth out of the mouth of God. Then the devil taketh him up into the holy city, and setteth him on a pinnacle of the temple, and saith unto him: If thou be the Son of God, cast thy self down headlong. For it is written, he shall give his Angels charge over thee, and with their hands they shall hold thee up, lest at any time thou dash thy foot against a stone. And Jesus said unto him: It is written again: Thou shalt not tempt the Lord thy God. Again the dyvil taketh him up into an exceeding high mountain, and shewed him all the kingdoms of the world, and the glory of them, and saith unto him: All these will I give thee, if thou wilt fall down and worship me. Then saith Jesus unto him: Avoid Sathan, for it is written: Thou shalt worship the Lord thy God, and him only shalt thou serve. Then the devil leaveth him: and behold, Angels came and ministered unto him.

The second Sunday[3].

The Collect.

ALMIGHTY God, which dost see that we have no power of our selves to help our selves: keep thou us both outwardly in our bodies, and inwardly in our souls, that we may be defended from all adversities which may happen to the body, and from all evil thoughts which may assault and hurt the soul: through Jesus Christ. &c.

The Epistle.

1 Thess. iv.

WE beseech you brethren, and exhort you by the Lord Jesus, that ye increase more and more, even as ye have received of us, how ye ought to

[1 Grafton, anguish.]   [2 Grafton, striues.]
[3 1596, in Lent.]

walk, and[4] to please God. For ye know what commandments we gave you by our Lord Jesus Christ. For this is the will of God, even your holiness: that ye should abstain from fornication, and that every one of you should know how to keep his vessel in holiness and honour, and not in the lust of concupiscence, as do the heathen, which know not God: that no man oppress and defraud his brother in bargaining, because that the Lord is the avenger of all such things, as we told you before, and testified. For God hath not called us unto uncleanness, but unto holiness. He therefore that despiseth, despiseth not man, but God which hath sent his Holy Spirit among you.

The Gospel.

JESUS went thence, and departed into the coasts of Tyre and Sidon: Math. xv. and behold, a woman of Canaan (which came out of the same coasts) cried unto him, saying: Have mercy on me, O Lord, thou son of David. My daughter is piteously vexed with a devil. But he answered her nothing at all. And his disciples came and besought him, saying: Send her away, for she crieth after us. But he answered, and said: I am not sent but to the lost sheep of the house of Israel. Then came she and worshipped him, saying: Lord help me. He answered and said: It is not meet to take the children's bread, and cast it to dogs. She answered and said: Truth Lord, for the dogs eat of the crumbs which fall from their master's table. Then Jesus answered and said unto her: O woman, great is thy faith: be it unto thee, even as thou wilt. And her daughter was made whole, even the same time.

The third Sunday[5].

The Collect.

WE beseech thee almighty God, look upon the hearty desires of thy humble servants: and stretch forth the right hand of thy majesty, to be our defence against all our enemies: through Jesus Christ our Lord.

The Epistle.

BE you the followers of God as dear children, and walk in love even Ephe. v. as Christ loved us and gave him self for us an offering and a sacrifice of a sweet savour to God. As for fornication, and all uncleanness, or covetousness, let it not be once named among you, as it becometh saints; or filthiness, or foolish talking, or jesting, which are not comely, but rather giving of thanks. For this ye know, that no whoremonger, either unclean person, or covetous person (which is a worshipper of images) hath any inheritance in the kingdom of Christ and of God. Let no man deceive you with vain words: For because of such things cometh the wrath of God upon the children of disobedience. Be not ye therefore companions of them. Ye were sometimes[6] darkness, but now are ye light in the Lord: walk as children of light; for the fruit of the Spirit consisteth in all good-

[[4] Grafton, and please.]   [[5] 1596, in Lent.]
[[6] Grafton, sometime.]

ness, and righteousness, and truth. Accept that which is pleasing unto the Lord, and have no fellowship with the unfruitful works of darkness, but rather rebuke them. For it is a shame even to name those things, which are done of them in secret: but all things when they are brought forth by the light, are manifest. For whatsoever is manifest, the same is light: wherefore he saith: Awake thou that sleepest, and stand up from death, and Christ shall give thee light.

The Gospel.

Luke xii. [1]

JESUS was casting out a devil that was dumb. And when he had cast out the devil, the dumb spake, and the people wondered. But some of them said: He casteth out devils through Beelzebub the chief of the devils. And other tempted him, and required of him a sign from heaven. But he knowing their thoughts, said unto them: Every kingdom divided against itself, is desolate: and one house doth fall upon another. If Sathan also be divided against himself, how shall his kingdom endure? Because ye say I cast out devils through Beelzebub. If I by the help of Beelzebub cast out devils, by whose help do your children cast them out? Therefore shall they be your judges. But if I with the finger of God cast out devils, no doubt the kingdom of God is come upon you. When a strong man armed watcheth his house, the things that he possesseth are in peace. But when a stronger than he cometh upon him, and overcometh him; he taketh from him all his harness (wherein he trusted) and divideth his goods. He that is not with me, is against me. And he that gathereth not with me, scattereth abroad. When the unclean spirit is gone out of a man, he walketh through dry places seeking rest. And when he findeth none, he saith: I will return again into my house whence I came out. And when he cometh, he findeth it swept and garnished. Then goeth he and taketh to him seven other spirits worse than himself, and they enter in and dwell there. And the end of that man is worse than the beginning. And it fortuned that as he spake these things, a certain woman for[2] the company lift up her voice, and said unto him: Happy is the womb that bare thee, and the paps which gave thee suck. But he said: Yea, happy are they that hear the word of God and keep it.

The fourth Sunday[3].

The Collect.

GRANT, we beseech thee, almighty God, that we which for our evil deeds are worthily punished, by the comfort of thy grace may mercifully be relieved: through our Lord Jesus Christ.

The Epistle.

Gala. iv.

TELL me (ye that desire to be under the law) do ye not hear of the law? for it is written that Abraham had two sons: the one by a

[[1] Misprint for, xi.]   [[2] Grafton, of.]
[[3] Grafton and 1596, in Lent.]

bond maid, the other by a free woman. Yea, and he which was born of the bond woman, was born after the flesh; but he which was born of the free woman, was born by promise: which things are spoken by an allegory. For these are two Testaments, the one from the mount Sina, which gendereth[4] unto bondage, which is Agar: For mount Sina is Agar in Arabia, and bordereth upon the city, which is now called Jerusalem, and is in bondage with her children. But Jerusalem, which is above, is free, which is the mother of us all. For it is written: Rejoice thou barren that bearest no children: break forth and cry, thou that travailest not: for the desolate hath many mo children than she which hath an husband. Brethren, we are after Isaac the children of promise. But as then he that was born after the flesh, persecuted him that was born after the spirit; even so is it now. Nevertheless, what saith the scripture? Put away the bond woman and her son. For the son of the bond woman shall not be heir with the son of the free woman. So then brethren, we are not children of the bond woman, but of the free woman.

The Gospel.

JESUS departed over the sea of Galilee, which is the Sea of Tiberias; and a great multitude followed him, because they saw his miracles which he did on them that were diseased. And Jesus went up into a mountain, and there he sat with his disciples. And Easter, a feast of the Jews, was nigh. When Jesus then lift up his eyes, and saw a great company come unto him, he said unto Philip: Whence shall we buy bread that these may eat? This he said to prove him, for he[5] himself knew what he would do. Philip answered him: Two hundred pennyworth of bread are not sufficient for them, that every man may take a little. One of his disciples, Andrew, (Simon Peter's brother) saith unto him: There is a lad which hath five barley loaves, and two fishes; but what are they among so many? And Jesus said, Make the people sit down. There was much grass in the place: so the men sat down, in number about five M. And Jesus took the bread, and when he had given thanks, he gave to the disciples, and the disciples to them that were set down, and likewise of the fishes as much as they would. When they had eaten enough, he said unto his disciples: Gather up the broken meat which remaineth, that nothing be lost. And they gathered it together, and filled .xii. baskets with the broken meat of the five barley loaves: which broken meat remained unto them that had eaten. Then those men (when they had seen the miracle that Jesus did) said: This is of a truth the same Prophet that should come into the world.

[4 Grafton, engendereth.]   [5 Grafton, for himself.]

The fifth Sunday[1].

The Collect.

WE beseech thee, almighty God, mercifully to look upon thy people: that by thy great goodness they may be governed and preserved evermore both in body and soul: through Jesus Christ our Lord.

The Epistle.

Heb. ix.

CHRIST being an high Priest of good things to come, came by a greater and a more perfect tabernacle, not made with hands, that is to say, not of this building, neither by the blood of goats and calves, but by his own blood he entered in once into the holy place, and found eternal redemption. For if the blood of oxen and of goats, and the ashes of a young cow, when it was sprinkled, purifieth the unclean as touching the purifying of the flesh: how much more shall the blood of Christ (which through the eternal Spirit offered himself without spot to God) purge your conscience from dead works, for to serve the living God? And for this cause he is the Mediator of the new testament, that through death, which chanced for the redemption of those transgressions that were under the first testament, they which are called might receive the promise of eternal inheritance.

The Gospel.

John viii.

WHICH of you can rebuke me of sin? If I say the truth, why do ye not believe me? He that is of God, heareth God's words: Ye therefore hear them not, because ye are not of God. Then answered the Jews, and said unto him: Say we not well that thou art a Samaritan and hast the devil? Jesus answered: I have not the devil: but I honour my Father, and ye have dishonoured me. I seek not mine own praise: there is one that seeketh and judgeth. Verily, verily, I say unto you, if a man keep my saying, he shall never see death. Then said the Jews unto him: Now know we that thou hast the devil. Abraham is dead, and the Prophets, and thou sayest: If a man keep my saying he shall never taste of death. Art thou greater than our father Abraham, which is dead? And the Prophets are dead: whom makest thou thyself? Jesus answered: If I honour myself, mine honour is nothing: it is my Father that honoureth me, which ye[2] say is your GOD, and yet ye[2] have not known him; but I know him: and if I say I know him not, I shall be a liar like unto you. But I know him and keep his saying. Your father Abraham was glad to see my day: and he saw it and rejoiced. Then said the Jews unto him: Thou art not yet fifty year old, and hast thou seen Abraham? Jesus said unto them: Verily, verily I say unto you: ere Abraham was born, I am. Then took they up stones to cast at him: but Jesus hid himself, and went out of the temple.

[1 Grafton and 1596, in Lent.]   [2 Grafton, you.]

The Sunday next before Easter.

The Collect.

ALMIGHTY and everlasting God, which of thy tender love toward[3] man, hast sent our Saviour Jesus Christ to take upon him our flesh, and to suffer death upon the Cross, that all mankind should follow the example of his great humility: mercifully grant, that we both follow the example of his patience, and be made partakers of his resurrection: through the same Jesus Christ our Lord[4].

The Epistle.

LET the same mind be in you, that was also in Christ Jesu: which when Col. iii.[5] he was in the shape of God, thought it no robbery to be equal with God: nevertheless he made himself of no reputation, taking on him the shape of a servant, and became like unto man[6], and was found in his apparel as a man. He humbled himself, and became obedient to the death, even the death of the cross. Wherefore God hath also exalted him on high, and given him a name which is above all names: that in the name of Jesus every knee should bow, both of things in heaven, and things in earth, and things under the earth: and that all tongues should confess, that Jesus Christ is the Lord, unto the praise of God the Father.

The Gospel.

AND it came to pass, when Jesus had finished all these sayings, he Mat. xxvi. said unto his disciples, Ye know that after two days shall be Easter, and the son of man shall be delivered over to be crucified. Then assembled together the chief Priests, and the Scribes, and the Elders of the people, unto the palace of the high Priest (which was called Caiphas), and held a council that they might take Jesus by subtilty, and kill him. But they said: Not on the holy day, lest there be an uproar among the people. When Jesus was in Bethany in the house of Simon the Leper, there came unto him a woman having an alabaster box of precious ointment, and poured it on his head, as he sat at the board. But when his disciples saw it, they had indignation, saying: Whereto serveth this waste? This ointment might have been well sold, and given to the poor. When Jesus understood that, he said unto them: Why trouble ye the woman? for she hath wrought a good work upon me. For ye have the poor always with you, but me ye shall not have always. And in that she hath cast this ointment on my body, she did it to bury me. Verily I say unto you: Wheresoever this gospel shall be preached in all the world, there shall also this be told that she hath done for a memorial of her. Then one of the twelve (which was called Judas Iscarioth) went unto the chief Priests, and said unto them: What will ye give me, and I will deliver him unto you? And they appointed unto him .xxx. pieces of silver. And from that time forth, he sought opportunity to betray him. The first

[3 Grafton and 1596, towardes.] [4 Grafton, Amen.]
[5 Misprint for, *Philip.* ii. See p. 92.] [6 Grafton, men.]

day of sweet bread, the disciples came to Jesus, saying to him: Where wilt thou that we prepare for thee, to eat the Passover? And he said: Go into the city to such a man, and say unto him: The Master saith, my time is at hand, I will keep my Easter by thee with my disciples. And the disciples did as Jesus had appointed them, and they made ready the Passover. When the even was come, he sat down with the .xii. And as they did eat, he said: Verily I say unto you, that one of you shall betray me. And they were exceeding sorrowful, and began every one of them to say unto him: Lord, is it I? He answered and said: He that dippeth his hand with me in the dish, the same shall betray me. The son of man truly goeth, as it is written of him: but woe unto that man by whom the son of man is betrayed. It had been good for that man, if he had not been born. Then Judas, which betrayed him, answered and said: Master, is it I? He said unto him: Thou hast said. And when they were eating, Jesus took bread, and when he had given thanks, he brake it and gave it to the disciples, and said: Take, eat, this is my body. And he took the cup, and thanked, and gave[1] it to them, saying: Drink ye all of this: For this is my blood (which is of the new Testament) that is shed for many, for the remission of sins. But I say unto you: I will not drink henceforth of this fruit of the vine tree, until the day when I shall drink it new with you in my Father's kingdom. And when they had said grace, they went out unto mount Olivete. Then said Jesus unto them: All ye shall be offended because of me this night. For it is written: I will smite the shepherd, and the sheep of the flock shall be scattered[2] abroad: but after I am risen again, I will go before you into Galile. Peter answered, and said unto him: Though all men be offended because of thee, yet will I not be offended. Jesus said unto him: Verily I say unto thee, that in this same night, before the cock crow, thou shalt deny me thrice. Peter said unto him: Yea, though I should die with thee, yet will I not deny thee. Likewise also said all the disciples. Then came Jesus with them unto a farm place (which is called Gethsemane) and said unto the disciples: Sit ye here while I go and pray yonder. And he took with him Peter, and the two sons of Zebede, and began to wax sorrowful and heavy. Then said Jesus unto them: My soul is heavy even unto the death. Tarry ye here and watch with me. And he went a little farther, and fell flat on his face, and prayed, saying: O my Father, if it be possible, let this cup pass from me: nevertheless, not as I will, but as thou wilt. And he came unto the disciples, and found them asleep, and said unto Peter: What, could ye not watch with me one hour? Watch and pray that ye enter not into temptation: the spirit is willing, but the flesh is weak. He went away once again and prayed, saying: O my Father, if this cup may not pass away from me except I drink of it, thy will be fulfilled. And he came and found them asleep again, for their eyes were heavy. And he left them, and went again and prayed the third time, saying the same words. Then cometh he to his disciples, and said unto them: Sleep on now and take your rest. Behold, the hour is at hand,

[1 Grafton, gaue it them.]   [2 Grafton omits a whole line.]

and the son of man is betrayed into the hands of sinners. Rise, let us be going: behold, he is at hand that doth betray me. While he yet spake, lo, Judas one of the number of the .xii. came and with him a great multitude with swords and staves, sent from the chief Priests and Elders of the people. But he that betrayed him, gave them a token, saying: Whomsoever I kiss, the same is he, hold him fast. And forthwith he came to Jesus, and said, Hail Master, and kissed him. And Jesus said unto him: Friend, wherefore art thou come? Then came they and laid hands on Jesus, and took him. And behold, one of them that were with Jesus, stretched out his hand and drew his sword, and stroke a servant of the high Priest, and smote off his ear. Then said Jesus unto him: Put up thy sword into the sheath, for all they that take the sword, shall perish with the sword. Thinkest thou that I cannot now pray to my Father, and he shall give me, even now, more than .xii. legions of Angels? But how then shall the scriptures be fulfilled? For thus must it be. In that same hour said Jesus to the multitude: Ye be come out as it were to a thief with swords and staves, for to take me. I sat daily with you teaching in the temple, and ye took me not. But all this is done that the scriptures of the prophets might be fulfilled. Then all the disciples forsook him and fled. And they took Jesus and led him to Cayphas the high priest, where the Scribes and the Elders were assembled. But Peter followed him afar off unto the high priest's palace, and went in, and sat with the servants to see the end. The chief priests and elders[3], and all the council, sought false witness against Jesus (for to put him to death) but found none: yea, when many false witnesses came, yet found they none. At the last came .ii. false witnesses, and said: This fellow said: I am able to destroy the temple of God, and to build it again in .iii. days. And the chief priest arose, and said unto him: Answerest thou nothing? Why do these bear witness against thee? But Jesus held his peace. And the chief priest answered, and said unto him: I charge thee by the living God, that thou tell us, whether thou be Christ the son of God. Jesus said unto him: Thou hast said: Nevertheless I say unto you, hereafter shall ye see the son of man sitting on the right hand of power, and coming in the clouds of the sky. Then the high priest rent his clothes, saying: He hath spoken blasphemy, what need we of any more witnesses? Behold, now ye have heard his blasphemy, what think ye? They answered, and said, He is worthy to die. Then did they spit in his face, and buffeted him with fists. And other smote him on the face with the palm of their hands, saying: Tell us, thou Christ, who is he that smote thee? Peter sat without in the court, and a damsel came to him, saying: Thou also wast[4] with Jesus of Galile. But he denied before them all, saying: I wot not what thou sayest. When he was gone out into the porch, another wench saw him, and said unto them that were there: This fellow was also with Jesus of Nazareth. And again he denied with an oath, saying: I do not know the man. After a while came unto him they that stood by, and said unto Peter: Surely thou art even one of

[3 Grafton, the elders.]   [4 Grafton, wert.]

them, for thy speech bewrayeth thee. Then began he to curse and to swear, that he knew not the man. And immediately the cock crew: and Peter remembered the word of Jesu, which said unto him: Before the cock crow, thou shalt deny me thrice: and he went out and wept bitterly. When the morning was come, all the chief priests and elders of the people held a counsel against Jesus, to put him to death, and brought him bound, and delivered him unto Poncius Pilate the deputy. Then Judas (which had betrayed him) seeing that he was condemned, repented himself, and brought again the .xxx. plates of silver to the chief priests and Elders, saying: I have sinned betraying the innocent blood. And they said: What is that to us? See thou to that. And he cast down the silver plates in the temple, and departed, and went and hanged himself. And the chief priests took the silver plates, and said: It is not lawful for to put them into the treasury, because it is the price of blood. And they took counsel, and bought with them a potter's field to bury strangers in. Wherefore the field is called[1] Acheldema, that is, the field of blood, until this day. Then was fulfilled that which was spoken by Jeremy the Prophet, saying: And they took .xxx. silver plates, the price of him that was valued, whom they bought of the children of Israel, and gave them for the potter's field, as the Lord appointed me. Jesus stood before the deputy, and the deputy asked him, saying: Art thou the king of the Jews? Jesus said unto him: Thou sayest. And when he was accused of the chief Priests and Elders, he answered nothing. Then said Pilate unto him: Hearest thou not how many witnesses they lay against thee? And he answered him to never a word: insomuch that the deputy marvelled greatly. At that feast the deputy was wont to deliver unto the people a prisoner whom they would desire. He had then a notable prisoner called Barrabas. Therefore when they were gathered together, Pilate said: Whether will ye that I give loose unto you Barrabas, or Jesus which is called Christ? For he knew that for envy they had delivered him. When he was set down to give judgment, his wife sent unto him, saying: Have thou nothing to do with that just man: For I have suffered this day many things in my sleep, because of him. But the chief priests and elders persuaded the people that they should ask Barrabas, and destroy Jesus. The deputy answered, and said unto them: Whether of the twain will ye that I let loose unto you? They said, Barrabas. Pilate said unto them: What shall I do then with Jesus, which is called Christ? They all said unto him: Let him be crucified. The deputy said: What evil hath he done? but they cried more saying: Let him be crucified. When Pilate saw that he could prevail nothing, but that more business was made, he took water, and washed his hands before the people, saying, I am innocent of the blood of this just person, see[2] ye. Then answered all the people, and said, His blood be on us and on our children. Then let he Barrabas loose unto them, and scourged Jesus, and delivered him to be crucified. Then the soldiers of the deputy took Jesus into the common hall, and gathered unto him all the company:

[1 Grafton, called the fielde of.]   [2 Grafton, ye shall se.]

and they stripped him, and put on him a purple robe, and platted a crown of thorns, and put it upon his head, and a reed in his right hand, and bowed the knee before him, and mocked him, saying: Hail king of the Jews: and when they had spit upon him, they took the reed and smote him on the head. And after that they had mocked him, they took the robe off him again, and put his own raiment on him, and led him away to crucify him. And as they came out, they found a man of Cirene (named Simon) him they compelled to bear his cross. And they came unto the place which is called Golgotha, that is to say (a place of dead men's skulls) and gave him vinegar mingled with gall to drink: and when he had tasted thereof, he would not drink. When they had crucified him, they parted his garments, and did cast lots, that it might be fulfilled which was spoken by the Prophet: They parted my garments among them, and upon my vesture did they cast lots. And they sat and watched him there, and set up over his head the cause of his death written: This is Jesus the king of the Jews. Then were there two thieves crucified with him, one on the right hand, and another on the left. They that passed by, reviled him, wagging their heads, and saying: Thou that destroyedst the temple of God, and didst build it in .iii. days, save thyself. If thou be the son of God, come down from the cross. Likewise also the high Priests mocking him with the Scribes and elders, said: He saved other, himself he cannot save. If he be the king of Israel, let him now come down from the cross, and we will believe him. He trusted in God, let him deliver him now, if he will have him: for he said, I am the son of God. The thieves also which were crucified with him, cast the same in his teeth. From the sixth hour was there darkness over all the land, until the ninth hour. And about the ninth hour, Jesus cried with a loud voice, saying, Ely, Ely, lama sabathanye? that is to say: My God, my God, why hast thou forsaken me? Some of them that stood there, when they heard that, said: This man calleth for Helias. And straightway one of them ran and took a sponge, and when he had filled it full of vinegar, he put it on a reed, and gave him to drink. Other said: Let be, let us see whether Helias will come and deliver him. Jesus when he had cried again with a loud voice, yielded up the ghost. And behold, the vail of the temple did rent in .ii. parts, from the top to the bottom, and the earth did quake and the stones rent, and graves did open and many bodies of saints, which slept, arose and went out of the graves after his resurrection, and came into the holy city, and appeared unto many. When the Centurion, and they that were with him watching Jesus, saw the earthquake, and those things which happened, they feared greatly, saying: Truly this was the son of God. And many women were there (beholding him afar off) which followed Jesus from Galile, ministering unto him: among which was Mary Magdalene, and Mary the mother of James and Joses, and the mother of Zebede's children.

Monday before Easter.

The Epistle.

Esa. lxiii.   WHAT is he this that cometh from Edom, with red coloured clothes of Bosra (which is so costly cloth) and cometh in so mightily with all his strength? I am he that teacheth righteousness, and am of power to help. Wherefore then is thy clothing red, and thy raiment like his that treadeth in the wine press? I have trodden the press myself alone, and of all people there is not one with me. Thus will I tread down mine enemies in my wrath, and set my feet upon them in mine indignation: and their blood shall bespring my clothes, and so will I stain all my raiment. For the day of vengeance is assigned in my heart, and the year when my people shall be delivered is come. I looked about me, and there was no man to shew me any help. I marvelled that no man held me up. Then I held me by mine own arm, and my ferventness sustained me. And thus will I tread down the people in my wrath, and bathe them in my displeasure, and upon the earth will I lay their strength. I will declare the goodness of the Lord, yea and the praise of the Lord for all that he hath given us, for the great good that he hath done for Israel, which he hath given them of his own favour, and according to the multitude of his loving kindness: For he said, These no doubt are my people, and no shrinking children; and so he was their saviour. In their troubles he was also troubled with them, and the Angel that went forth from his presence, delivered them. Of very love and kindness that he had unto them, he redeemed them. He hath borne them and carried them up, ever since the world began. But after they provoked him to wrath and vexed his holy mind, he was their enemy and fought against them himself. Yet remembered Israel the old time of Moses, and his people, saying: Where is he that brought them from the water of the sea: with them that feed his sheep? where is he that hath given his Holy Spirit among them? He led them by the right hand of Moses, with his glorious arm: dividing the water before them (whereby he gat himself an everlasting name:) he led them in the deep as an horse is led in the plain, that they should not stumble, as a tame beast goeth in the field: and the breath given of God giveth him rest. Thus, (O God) hast thou led thy people, to make thyself a glorious name withal. Look down then from heaven, and behold the dwellingplace of thy sanctuary, and thy glory. How is it that thy jealousy, thy strength, the multitude of thy mercies, and thy loving kindness, will not be intreated of us? yet art thou our Father. For Abraham knoweth us not, neither is Israel acquainted with us: But thou Lord art our Father and Redeemer, and thy name is everlasting. O Lord, wherefore hast thou led us out of thy way? wherefore hast thou hardened our hearts that we fear thee not? Be at one with us again for thy servant's sake, and for the generation of thine heritage. Thy people have had but a little of thy Sanctuary in possession: for our enemies have trodden down the holy place. And we were thine from the beginning, when thou wast[1] not their Lord, for they have not called upon thy name.

The Gospel.

AFTER two days was Easter, and the days of sweet bread. And the high Priests and the Scribes sought how they might take him by craft, and put him to death. But they said: Not in the feast day, lest any business arise among the people. And when he was in Bethany in the house of Simon the leper, even as he sat at meat, there came a woman having an alabaster box of ointment, called Nard, that was pure and costly: and she brake the box and poured it upon his head. And there were some that were not content within themselves, and said: What needed[2] this waste of ointment? for it might have been sold for more than three hundred pence, and have been given unto the poor. And they grudged against her. And Jesus said: Let her alone, why trouble ye her? She hath done a good work on me; for ye have poor with you always, and whensoever ye will ye may do them good: but me have ye not always. She hath done that she could, she came aforehand to anoint my body to the burying. Verily I say unto you, wheresoever this gospel shall be preached throughout the whole world, this also that she hath done, shall be rehearsed in[3] remembrance of her. And Judas Iscarioth one of the twelve went away unto the high priests to betray him unto them. When they heard that, they were glad, and promised that they would give him money. And he sought how he might conveniently betray him. And the first day of sweet bread (when they offered the Passover) his disciples said unto him: Where wilt thou that we go and prepare that thou mayest eat the Passover? And he sent forth two of his disciples, and said unto them: Go ye unto[4] the city, and there shall meet you a man bearing a pitcher of water, follow him. And whithersoever he goeth in, say ye unto the goodman of the house, The master saith, Where is the guest chamber, where I shall eat the Passover with my disciples? And he will shew you a great parlour paved and prepared; there make ready for us. And his disciples went forth, and came into the city, and found as he had said unto them: and they made ready the Passover. And when it was now eventide, he came with the twelve. And as they sat at board and did eat, Jesus, said: Verily I say unto you, one of you (that eateth with me) shall betray me. And they began to be sorry, and to say to him one by one: Is it I? and another said: Is i I? He answered and said unto them: It is one of the .xii. even he that dippeth with me in the platter. The son of man truly goeth as it is written of him, but woe unto that man by whom the son of man is betrayed: good were it for that man, if he had never been born. And as they did eat, Jesus took bread, and when he had given thanks, he brake it, and gave to them, and said: Take, eat, this is my body. And he took the cup, and when he had given thanks, he took it to them, and they all drank of it. And he said unto them: This is my blood of the new

Mar. xiv.

[1 Grafton, wart.]   [2 Grafton, needeth.]
[3 Grafton, in the.] [4 Grafton, into.]

testament, which is shed for many. Verily I say unto you: I will drink no more of the fruit of the vine, until that day that I drink it new in the kingdom of God. And when they had said grace, they went out to the mount Olivete. And Jesus saith unto them: All ye shall be offended because of me this night. For it is written: I will smite the shepherd, and the sheep shall be scattered: but after that I am risen again I will go into Galile before you. Peter said unto him: And though all men be offended, yet will not I. And Jesus saith unto him: Verily I say unto thee, that this day even in this night, before the cock crow twice thou shalt deny me three times. But he spake more vehemently: No, if I should die with thee, I will not deny thee. Likewise also said they all. And they came into a place which was named Gethsemany, and he said to his disciples: Sit ye here while I go aside and pray. And he taketh with him Peter, and James, and John, and began to wax abashed and to be in an agony, and said unto them: My soul is heavy even unto the death: tarry ye here and watch. And he went forth a little, and fell down flat on the ground and prayed, that if it were possible, the hour might pass from him. And he said: Abba Father, all things are possible unto thee; take away this cup from me: nevertheless, not as I will, but that thou wilt be done. And he came and found them sleeping, and saith to Peter: Simon, sleepest thou? Couldst not thou watch one hour? watch ye and pray, lest ye enter into temptation: the spirit truly is ready, but the flesh is weak. And again he went aside and prayed, and spake the same words. And he returned and found them asleep again, for their eyes were heavy, neither wist they what to answer him. And he came the third time, and said unto them: Sleep henceforth and take your ease, it is enough. The hour is come: behold the son of man is betrayed into the hands of sinners. Rise up, let us go: Lo, he that betrayeth me is at hand. And immediately while he yet spake, cometh Judas (which was one of the twelve) and with him a great number of people with swords and staves from the high priests and scribes, and elders. And he that betrayed him, had given them a general token, saying: Whosoever I do kiss, the same is he; take and lead him away warily. And as soon as he was come, he goeth straightway to him, and saith unto him: Master, Master, and kissed him: and they laid their hands on him, and took him. And one of them that stood by, drew out a sword, and smote a servant of the high priest's, and cut off his ear. And Jesus answered, and said unto them: Ye be come out as unto a thief with swords and staves, for to take me: I was daily with you in the temple teaching, and ye took me not: but these things come to pass that the scripture should be fulfilled. And they all forsook him and ran away. And there followed him a certain young man clothed in linen upon the bare, and the young men caught him, and he left his linen garment, and fled from them naked. And they led Jesus away to the high priest of all, and with him came all the high priests and the elders and the scribes. And Peter followed him a great way off (even till he was come into the palace of the high priest) and he sat with the servants, and warmed himself at the fire. And the high priests and all the council sought for witness against Jesu to put him to death, and found none: for many bare false witness against him, but their witnesses agreed not together. And there arose certain and brought false witness against him, saying: We heard him say, I will destroy this temple that is made with hands, and within three days I will build another made without hands. But yet their witnesses agreed not together. And the high priest stood up among them, and asked Jesus, saying: Answerest thou nothing? How is it that these bear witness against thee? But he held his peace, and answered nothing. Again the high priest asked him and said unto him: Art thou Christ the son of the Blessed? And Jesus said: I am. And ye shall see the son of man sitting on the right hand of power, and coming in the clouds of heaven. Then the high priest rent his clothes, and said: What need we any further of witnesses? ye have heard blasphemy, what think ye? And they all condemned him to be worthy of death. And some began to spit at him, and to cover his face, and to beat him with fists, and to say unto him, Aread[1]: and the servants buffeted him on the face. And as Peter was beneath in the palace, there came one of the wenches of the highest priest; and when she saw Peter warming himself, she looked on him, and said: Wast not thou also with Jesus of Nazareth? And he denied, saying: I know him not, neither wot I what thou sayest. And he went out into the porch, and the cock crew. And a damsel (when she saw him) began again to say to them that stood by: This is one of them. And he denied it again. And anon after they that stood by said again unto Peter: Surely thou art one of them, for thou are of Galile, and thy speech agreeth thereto. But he began to curse and to swear saying: I know not this man of whom ye speak. And again the cock crew, and Peter remembered the word that Jesus had said unto him: Before the cock crow twice, thou shalt deny me three times. And he began to weep.

Tuesday before Easter.

The Epistle.

THE Lord God hath opened mine ear; therefore can I not say nay, Esai. L neither withdraw myself: but I offer my back unto the smiters, and my cheeks to the nippers. I turn not my face from shame and spitting, and the Lord God shall help me: Therefore shall I not be confounded. I have hardened my face like a flint-stone, for I am sure that I shall not come to confusion. He is at hand that justifieth me; who will then go to law with me? Let us stand one against another: if there be any that will reason with me, let him come hereforth to[2] me. Behold, the Lord God standeth by me; what is he then that can condemn me? lo, they shall be like as an old cloth, the moth shall eat them up. Therefore, whoso feareth the Lord among you, let him hear the voice of his servant. Whoso walketh in darkness, and no light shineth upon him, let him put his trust in the name of the Lord, and hold him up by his God But

[1 Aread: declare, explain.]   [2 Grafton, vnto.]

take heed, ye all kindle a fire of the wrath of God, and stir up the coals: walk on in the glistering of your own fire, and in the coals that ye have kindled. This cometh unto you from my hand, namely that ye shall sleep in sorrow.

The Gospel.

Mar. xv.

AND anon in the dawning, the high priests held a council with the Elders and the Scribes, and the whole congregation, and bound Jesus and led him away, and delivered him to Pilate. And Pilate asked him: Art thou the king of the Jews? And he answered, and said to him: Thou sayest it. And the high Priests accused him of many things. So Pilate asked him again, saying: Answerest thou nothing? Behold how many things they lay to thy charge. Jesus answered yet nothing, so that Pilate marvelled. At that feast Pilate did deliver unto them a prisoner, whomsoever they would desire. And there was one that was named Barrabas, which lay bound with them that made insurrection: he had committed murther. And the people called unto him, and began to desire him, that he would do according as he had ever done unto them. Pilate answered them, saying: Will ye that I let loose unto you the king of the Jews? for he knew that the high Priests had delivered him of envy. But the high priests moved the people that he should rather deliver Barrabas unto them. Pilate answered again, and said unto them: What will ye that I then do unto him, whom ye call the king of the Jews? And they cried again, Crucify him. Pilate said unto them: What evil hath he done? And they cried the more fervently, Crucify him. And so Pilate, willing to content the people, let loose Barrabas unto them, and delivered up Jesus (when he had scourged him) for to be crucified. And the soldiers led him away into the common hall, and called together the whole multitude; and they clothed him with purple, and they platted a crown of thorns, and crowned him withal, and began to salute him: Hail king of the Jews. And they smote him on the head with a reed, and did spit upon him, and bowed their knees and worshipped him. And when they had mocked him, they took the purple off him, and put his own clothes on him, and led him out to crucify him. And they compelled one that passed by, called Simon of Sirene (the father of Alexander and Rufus,) which came out of the field, to bear his cross. And they brought him to a place named Golgotha (which if a man interpret, is the place of dead men's skulls:) and they gave him to drink wine mingled with myrrh, but he received it not. And when they had crucified him, they parted his garments, casting lots upon them what every man should take. And it was about the third hour, and they crucified him. And the title of his cause was written, The king of the Jews. And they crucified with him two thieves; the one on his right hand, and the other on his left. And the Scripture was fulfilled, which saith: He was counted among the wicked. And they that went by railed on him, wagging their heads, and saying: A wretch, thou that destroyest the temple, and buildest it again in three days, save thyself and come down from the cross. Likewise also mocked him the high Priests among themselves with the Scribes, and said: He saved other men, himself he cannot save. Let Christ the king of Israel descend now from the cross, that we may see and believe. And they that were crucified with him checked him also. And when the sixth hour was come, darkness arose over all the earth, until the ninth hour. And at the ninth hour Jesus cried with a loud voice, saying: Eloy, Eloy, lama sabathany: which is, if one interpret it, My God, my God, why hast thou forsaken me? And some of them that stood by, when they heard that, said: Behold, he calleth for Helias. And one ran and filled a spunge full of vinegar, and put it on a reed, and gave him to drink, saying: Let him alone, let us see whether Helias will come and take him down. But Jesus cried with a loud voice and gave up the ghost. And the vail of the temple rent in two pieces from the top to the bottom. And when the Centurion (which stood before him) saw that he so cried, and gave up the ghost, he said: Truly this man was the son of God. There were also women a good way off, beholding him: among whom was Mary Magdalene, and Mary the mother of James the little, and of Joses, and Mary Salome (which also when he was in Galile had followed him, and ministered unto him) and many other women, which came up with him to Jerusalem. And now when the even was come, (because it was the day of preparing that goeth before the Sabboth,) Joseph of the city of Arimathia, a noble counsellor, which also looked for the kingdom of God, came and went in boldly into Pilate, and begged of him the body of Jesu. And Pilate marvelled that he was already dead, and called unto him the Centurion, and asked of him whether he had been any while dead. And when he knew the truth of the Centurion, he gave the body to Joseph; and he bought a linen cloth, and took him down, and wrapped him in the linen cloth, and laid him in a sepulchre that was hewn out of a rock, and rolled a stone before the door of the sepulchre. And Mary Magdalene and Mary Joses beheld where he was laid.

Wednesday before Easter.

The Epistle.

WHERE as is a testament, there must also (of necessity) be the death Heb. ix. of him that maketh the testament. For the testament taketh authority when men are dead: for it is yet of no value as long as he that maketh the testament is alive: for which cause also neither the first testament was ordained without blood. For when Moses had declared all the commandment to all the people, according to the law, he took the blood of calves and of goats, with water and purple wool, and yssop, and sprinkled both the book and all the people, saying: This is the blood of the testament, which God hath appointed unto you. Moreover he sprinkled the tabernacle with blood also, and all the ministering vessels. And almost all things are by the law purged with blood, and without shedding of blood is no remission. It is need then, that the similitudes of heavenly things be purified with such things; but that the heavenly things themselves, be purified with better sacrifices than are those. For

Christ is not entered into the holy places that are made with hands (which are similitudes of true things), but is entered into very heaven, for to appear now in the sight of God for us: not to offer himself often, as the high Priest entereth into the holy place every year with strange blood; for then must he have often suffered since the world began. But now in the end of the world hath he appeared once, to put sin to flight by the offering up of himself. And as it is appointed unto all men that they shall once die, and then cometh the judgment: Even so Christ was once offered to take away the sins of many; and unto them that look for him, shall he appear again without sin, unto salvation.

The Gospel.

Luke xxii.

THE feast of sweet bread drew nigh, which is called Easter: and the high Priests and Scribes sought how they might kill him; for they feared the people. Then entered Satan into Judas, whose sirname was Iscariothe (which was of the number of the .xii.) and he went his way and commoned with the high Priests and officers, how he might betray him unto them. And they were glad, and promised to give him money. And he consented, and sought opportunity to betray him unto them, when the people were away. Then came the day of sweet bread, when of necessity the passover must be offered. And he sent Peter and John, saying: Go and prepare us the passover, that we may eat. They said unto him: Where wilt thou that we prepare? And he said unto them: Behold, when ye enter into the city, there shall a man meet you bearing a pitcher of water: him follow into the same house that he entereth in, and ye shall say unto the good man of the house: The master saith unto thee, Where is the guest chamber where I shall eat the passover with my disciples? And he shall shew you a great parlour paved, there make ready. And they went and found as he had said unto them, and they made ready the passover. And when the hour was come, he sat down and the .xii. Apostles with him. And he said unto them: I have inwardly desired to eat this passover with you before that I suffer. For I say unto you, henceforth will I not eat of it any more, until it be fulfilled in the kingdom of God. And he took the cup, and gave thanks, and said: Take this, and divide it among you. For I say unto you: I will not drink of the fruit of this vine, until the kingdom of God come. And he took bread, and when he had given thanks, he brake it, and gave unto them, saying: This is my body which is given for you: This do in the remembrance of me. Likewise also when he had supped, he took the cup, saying: This cup is the new testament in my blood, which is shed for you. Yet behold the hand of him that betrayeth me, is with me on the table. And truly the Son of man goeth as it is appointed; but woe unto that man, by whom he is betrayed. And they began to enquire among themselves, which of them it was that should do it. And there was a strife among them, which of them should seem to be the greatest. And he said unto them: The kings of nations reign over them, and they that have authority upon them, are called gracious: but ye shall not so be. But he that is greatest among you, shall be as the younger; and he that is chief, shall be as he that doth minister. For whether is greater, he that sitteth at meat, or he that serveth? Is it not he that sitteth at meat? But I am among you as he that ministereth. Ye are they which have bidden with me in my temptations. And I appoint unto you a kingdom, as my Father hath appointed to me, that ye may eat and drink at my table in my kingdom, and sit on seats, judging the .xii. tribes of Israel. And the Lord said: Simon, Simon, behold, Satan hath desired to sift you, as it were wheat: But I have prayed for thee, that thy faith fail not. And when thou art converted, strength thy brethren. And he said unto him: Lord, I am ready to go with thee into prison, and to death. And he said: I tell thee Peter, the cock shall not crow this day, till thou have denied[1] me thrice that thou knewest me. And he said unto them: When I sent you without wallet, and scrip, and shoes, lacked ye any thing? And they said, No. Then said he unto them: But now he that hath a wallet, let him take it up, and likewise his scrip: and he that hath no sword, let him sell his coat and buy one. For I say unto you, that yet the same which is written must be performed in me: Even among the wicked was he reputed: For those things which are written of me have an end. And they said: Lord, behold, here are two swords: and he said unto them: It is enough. And he came out, and went (as he was wont) to Mount Olivet. And the disciples followed him. And when he came to the place, he said unto them, Pray, lest ye fall into temptation. And he gat himself from them about a stone's cast, and kneeled down and prayed, saying: Father, if thou wilt, remove this cup from me: Nevertheless, not my will, but thine be fulfilled. And there appeared an angel unto him from heaven, comforting him. And he was in an agony, and prayed the longer: and his sweat was like drops of blood, trickling down to the ground. And when he arose[2] from prayer, and was come to his disciples, he found them sleeping for heaviness, and he said unto them: Why sleep ye? Rise and pray, lest ye fall into temptation. While he yet spake, behold, there came a company, and he that was called Judas, one of the twelve, went before them, and pressed nigh to Jesus, to kiss him. But Jesus said unto him: Judas, betrayest thou the son of man with a kiss? When they which were about him saw what would follow, they said unto him: Lord, shall we smite with the sword? And one of them smote a servant of the high priest's, and stroke off his right ear. Jesus answered and said: Suffer ye thus far forth. And when he touched his ear, he healed him. Then Jesus said unto the high priests, and rulers of the temple, and the elders, which were come to him: Ye be come out as unto a thief, with swords and staves. When I was daily with you in the temple, ye stretched forth no hands against me: but this is even your very hour, and the power of darkness. Then took they him and led him, and brought him to the high priest's house. But Peter followed afar off. And when they had kindled a fire in the midst of the palace, and were set down together,

[1 Grafton, denyed thryse that thou knowest me.]
[2 Grafton, rose.]

Peter also sat down among them. But when one of the wenches beheld him, as he sat by the fire, (and looked upon him) she said: This same fellow was also with him. And he denied him, saying: Woman, I know him not. And after a little while, another saw him, and said: Thou art also of them. And Peter said, Man, I am not. And about the space of an hour after, another affirmed, saying: Verily this fellow was with him also, for he is of Galile. And Peter said: Man, I wot not what thou sayest. And immediately while he yet spake, the cock crew. And the Lord turned back and looked upon Peter. And Peter remembered the word of the Lord, how he had said unto him: Before the cock crow, thou shalt deny me thrice: and Peter went out and wept bitterly. And the men that took Jesus mocked him, and smote him: and when they had blindfolded him, they stroke him on the face, and asked him saying: Aread, who is he that smote thee? And many other things despitefully said they against him. And as soon as it was day, the elders of the people, and the high Priests and Scribes, came together, and led him into their council, saying: Art thou very Christ? tell us. And he said unto them: If I tell you, ye will not believe me: and if I ask you, you will not answer, nor let me go: hereafter shall the son of man sit on the right hand of the power of God. Then said they all: Art thou then the son of God? He said: Ye say that I am. And they said: What need we of any further witness? For we ourselves have heard of his own mouth.

Thursday before[1] Easter.

The Epistle.

1 Cor. xi.[2] THIS I warn you of, and commend not, that ye come not together after a better manner, but after a worse. For first of all, when ye come together in the congregation, I hear that there is dissension among you, and I partly believe it. For there must be sects among you, that they which are perfect among you may be known. When ye come together therefore into one place, the Lord's supper cannot be eaten; for every man beginneth afore to eat his own supper. And one is hungry, and another is drunken. Have ye not houses to eat and drink in? despise ye the congregation of God, and shame them that have not? what shall I say unto you? shall I praise you? In this I praise you not. That which I delivered unto you, I received of the Lord. For the Lord Jesus[3], the same night in which he was betrayed, took bread, and when he had given thanks, he brake it, and said: Take ye and eat, this is my body which is broken for you. This do ye in the remembrance of me. After the same manner also, he took the cup when supper was done, saying: This cup is the new Testament in my blood. This do, as oft as ye drink it, in remembrance of me. For as often as ye shall eat this bread, and drink of this cup, ye shall shew the Lord's death till he come. Wherefore, whosoever shall eat of this bread, and drink

[1 Grafton, next before.]   [2 Grafton omits the reference.]
[3 Grafton, Jesu.]

of this cup of the Lord unworthily, shall be guilty of the body and blood of the Lord. But let a man examine himself, and so let him eat of the bread, and drink of the cup. For he that eateth and drinketh unworthily eateth and drinketh his own damnation, because he maketh no difference of the Lord's body. For this cause many are weak and sick among you, and many sleep. For if we had judged ourselves, we should not have been judged. But when we are judged of the Lord, we are chastened, that we should not be damned with the world. Wherefore, my brethren, when ye come together to eat, tarry one for another. If any man hunger, let him eat at home, that ye come not together unto condemnation. Other things will I set in order when I come.

The Gospel.

THE whole multitude of them arose, and led him unto Pilate. And Luk. xxii.[4] they began to accuse him saying: We found this fellow perverting the people, and forbidding to pay tribute to Cesar, saying that he is Christ a king. And Pilate apposed him saying: Art thou the king of the Jews? He answered him, and said: Thou sayest it. Then said Pilate to the high priests and to the people: I find no fault in this man. And they were the more fierce, saying: He moveth the people, teaching throughout all Jury, and began at Galile, even to this place. When Pilate heard mention of Galile, he asked whether the man were of Galile. And as soon as he knew that he belonged unto Herode's jurisdiction, he sent him to Herode, which was also at Jerusalem at that time. And when Herode saw Jesus, he was exceeding glad; for he was desirous to see him of a long season, because he had heard many things of him, and he trusted to have seen some miracles done by him. Then he questioned with him many words. But he answered him nothing. The high priests and Scribes stood forth and accused him straitly. And Herode with his men of war despised him. And when he had mocked him, he arrayed him in white clothing, and sent him again to Pilate. And the same day Pilate and Herode were made friends together: for before they were at variance. And Pilate called together the high priests, and the rulers, and the people, and said unto them: Ye have brought this man unto me, as one that perverteth the people: and behold, I examine him before you, and find no fault in this man of those things whereof ye accuse him; no, nor yet Herod. For I sent you unto him, and lo, nothing worthy of death is done unto him: I will therefore chasten him, and let him loose. For of necessity he must have let one loose to them at that feast. And all the people cried at once, saying: Away with him, and deliver us Barrabas: which for a certain insurrection made in the city, and for a murther, was cast into prison. Pilate spake again unto them, willing to let Jesus loose. But they cried, saying: Crucify him, crucify him. He said unto them the third time: What evil hath he done? I find no cause of death in him:

[[4] Misprint for, xxiii.]

I will therefore chasten him, and let him go. And they cried with loud voices, requiring that he might be crucified. And the voices of them and of the high priests prevailed. And Pilate gave sentence that it should be as they required; and he let loose unto them him that for insurrection and murther was cast into prison, whom they had desired: and he delivered to them Jesus, to do with him what they would. And as they led him away, they caught one Simon of Cyrene coming out of the field: and on him laid they the cross, that he might bear it after Jesus. And there followed him a great company of people, and of women, which bewailed and lamented him. But Jesus turned back unto them, and said: Ye daughters of Jerusalem, weep not for me: but weep for yourselves, and for your children. For behold the days will come, in the which they shall say: Happy are the barren, and the wombs that never bare, and the paps which never gave suck. Then shall they begin to say to the mountains, Fall on us: and to the hills, Cover us. For if they do this in a green tree, what shall be done in the dry? And there were two evil doers led with him to be slain. And after that they were come to the place (which is called Calvarie), there they crucified him and the evil doers: one on the right hand, and the other on the left. Then said Jesus: Father, forgive them, for they wot not what they do. And they parted his raiment, and cast lots. And the people stood and beheld. And the rulers mocked him with them, saying: He saved other men, let him save himself if he be very Christ the chosen of God. The soldiers also mocked him, and came and offered him vinegar, and said: If thou be the king of Jews, save thyself. And a superscription was written over him, with letters of Greek, and Latin, and Hebrew: This is the King of the Jews. And one of the evil doers, which were hanged, railed on him, saying: If thou be Christ, save thyself and us. But the other answered and rebuked him, saying: Fearest thou not God, seeing thou art in the same damnation? We are righteously punished, for we receive according to our deeds: but this man hath done nothing amiss. And he said unto Jesus: Lord, remember me when thou comest into thy kingdom. And Jesus said unto him: Verily I say unto thee; to day shalt thou be with me in Paradise. And it was about the sixth hour: and there was a darkness over all the earth, until the ninth hour, and the sun was darkened. And the vail of the temple did rent, even through the midst. And when Jesus had cried with a loud voice, he said: Father, into thy hands I commend my spirit. And when he thus had[1] said, he gave up the ghost. When the Centurion saw what had happened, he glorified GOD, saying: Verily this was a righteous man. And all the people that came together to that sight, and saw the things which had happened, smote their breasts and returned. And all his acquaintance, and the women that followed him from Galile, stood afar off beholding these things. And behold, there was a man named Joseph, a counsellor, and he was a good man and a just: the same had not consented to the counsel and

[1 Grafton, had thus.]

deed of them; which was of Arimathia, a city of the Jews, which same also waiteth[2] for the kingdom of God: he went unto Pilate and begged the body of Jesus; and took it down, and wrapped it in a linen cloth, and laid it in a sepulchre that was hewn in stone, wherein never man before had been laid. And that day was the preparing of the Sabboth, and the Sabboth drew on. The women that followed after, which had come with him from Galile, beheld the sepulchre, and how his body was laid. And they returned, and prepared sweet odours and ointments; but rested on the Sabboth day, according to the commandments.

¶ On Good Friday.

The Collects.

ALMIGHTY God, we beseech thee graciously to behold this thy family, for the which our Lord Jesus Christ was contented to be betrayed and given up into the hands of wicked men, and to suffer death upon the cross: who liveth and reigneth[3]. &c.

ALMIGHTY and everlasting God, by whose spirit the whole body of the church is governed and sanctified: receive our supplications and prayers, which we offer before thee for all estates of men in thy holy congregation, that every member of the same in his vocation and ministry may truly and godly serve thee: through our Lord Jesus Christ.

MERCIFUL God, who hast made all men, and hatest nothing that thou hast made, nor wouldest the death of a sinner, but rather that he should be converted and live: have mercy upon all Jews, Turks, Infidels, and Heretics, and take from them all ignorance, hardness of heart, and contempt of thy word. And so fetch them home, blessed Lord, to thy flock, that they may be saved among the remnant of the true Israelites, and be made one fold under one shepherd Jesus Christ our Lord: who liveth[4] and reigneth. &c.

The Epistle.

THE law (which hath but a shadow of good things to come, and Heb. x. not the very fashion of things themselves) can never with those sacrifices, which they offer year by year continually, make the comers thereunto perfect. For would not then those sacrifices have ceased to have been offered, because that the offerers once purged should have had no more conscience of sins: Nevertheless, in those sacrifices is there mention made of sins every year. For the blood of oxen and goats can not take away sins. Wherefore, when he cometh into the world, he saith: Sacrifice and offering thou wouldest not have, but a body hast thou ordained me. Burnt offerings also for sin hast thou not allowed. Then

[2 Grafton, wayted.]
[3 Grafton, with thee, and the holy ghoste nowe and ever &c.]
[4 Grafton, who liveth. &c.]

said I: Lo, I am here. In the beginning of the book it is written of me, that I should do thy will, O God. Above, when he saith: Sacrifice and offering, and burnt sacrifices, and sin offerings thou wouldest not have, neither hast thou allowed them (which yet are offered by the law), then said he: Lo, I am here to do thy will, O God: he taketh away the first to establish the latter, by the which will we are made holy, even by the offering of the body of Jesu Christ once for all. And every priest is ready daily ministering and offering oftentimes one manner of oblation, which can never take away sins. But this man, after he hath offered one sacrifice for sins, is set down for ever on the right hand of God, and from henceforth tarrieth till his foes be made his foot stool. For with one offering hath he made perfect for ever them that are sanctified. The holy ghost himself also beareth us record, even when he told before: This is the testament that I will make unto them. After those days (saith the Lord) I will put my laws in their hearts, and in their minds will I write them, and their sins and iniquities will I remember no more. And where remission of these things is, there is no more offering for sins. Seeing therefore, brethren, that by the means of the blood of Jesu we have liberty to enter into the holy place, by the new and living way, which he hath prepared for us, through the vail (that is to say by his flesh:) And seeing also that we have an high priest which is ruler over the house of God, let us draw nigh with a true heart in a sure faith, sprinkled in our hearts from an evil conscience, and washed in our bodies with pure water: let us keep the profession of our hope, without wavering (for he is faithful that promised); and let us consider one another, to the intent that we may provoke unto love, and to good works, not forsaking the fellowship that we have among ourselves, as the manner of some is: but let us exhort one another, and that so much the more, because ye see that the day draweth nigh.

The Gospel.

Joh. xviii.

WHEN Jesus had spoken these words, he went forth with his disciples over the brook Cedron, where was a garden, into the which he then entered with his disciples. Judas which also[1] betrayed him, knew the place: for Jesus ofttimes resorted thither with his disciples. Judas then after he had received a bonde[2] of men (and ministers of the high priests and Pharisees) came thither with lanterns, and firebrands, and weapons. And Jesus knowing all things that should come on him went forth and said unto them: Whom seek ye? They answered him: Jesus of Nazareth. Jesus said unto them: I am he. Judas also which betrayed him, stood with them. As soon then as he had said unto them: I am he, they went backward, and fell to the ground. Then asked he them again: Whom seek ye? They said, Jesus of Nazareth. Jesus answered: I have told you that I am he. If ye seek me therefore, let these go their way; that the saying might be fulfilled which he spake: Of them which

[1 Grafton, also which.]   [2 Grafton, band.]

thou gavest me, have I not lost one. Then Simon Peter having a sword, drew it, and smote the high Priest's servant, and cut off his right ear. The servant's name was Malchus. Therefore saith Jesus unto Peter, Put up thy sword into thy[3] sheath: shall I not drink of the cup which my Father hath given me? Then the company, and the captain, and the ministers of the Jews took Jesus, and bound him, and led him away to Annas first; for he was father-in-law to Caiphas, which was the high Priest the same year. Caiphas was he that gave counsel to the Jews, that it was expedient that one man should die for the people. And Simon Peter followed Jesus, and so did another disciple: that disciple was known to the high Priest, and went in with Jesus unto the palace of the high Priest. But Peter stood at the door without. Then went out that other disciple (which was known to the high priest) and spake to the damsel that kept the door, and brought in Peter. Then said the damsel that kept the door unto Peter: Art not thou also one of this man's disciples? He said: I am not. The servants and ministers stood there, which had made a fire of coals: for it was cold, and they warmed themselves. Peter also stood among them and warmed himself. The high priest then asked Jesus of his disciples, and of his doctrine. Jesus answered him: I spake openly in the world: I ever taught in the synagogue, and in the temple whither all the Jews have resorted, and in secret have I said nothing. Why askest thou me? Ask them which heard me, what I said unto them. Behold, they can tell what I said. When he had thus spoken, one of the ministers, which stood by, smote Jesus on the face, saying: Answerest thou the high priest so? Jesus answered him: If I have evil spoken, bear witness of the evil: But if I have well spoken, why smitest thou me? And Annas sent him bound unto Caiphas the high priest. Simon Peter stood and warmed himself. Then said they unto him: Art not thou also one of his disciples? He denied it, and said, I am not. One of the servants of the high priest's (his cousin, whose ear Peter smote off) said unto him: Did not I see thee in the garden with him? Peter therefore denied again: and immediately the cock crew. Then led they Jesus from Caiphas into the hall of judgment. It was in the morning, and they themselves went not into the judgment hall, lest they should be defiled, but that they might eat the Passover. Pilate then went out to them, and said: What accusation bring you against this man? They answered, and said unto him: If he were not an evil doer, we would not have delivered him unto thee. Then said Pilate unto them: Take ye him and judge him after your own law. The Jews therefore said unto him: It is not lawful for us to put any man to death: that the words of Jesus might be fulfilled, which he spake signifying what death he should die. Then Pilate entered into the judgment hall again, and called Jesus, and said unto him: Art thou the king of the Jews? Jesus answered: Sayest thou that of thyself, or did other tell it thee of me? Pilate answered: Am I a Jew? Thine own nation and high Priests have delivered thee unto me: what hast thou done?

[3 Grafton, the.]

Jesus answered: My kingdom is not of this world: if my kingdom were of this world, then would my ministers surely fight, that I should not be delivered to the Jews: but now is my kingdom not from hence. Pilate therefore said unto him: Art thou a King then? Jesus answered: Thou sayest that I am a king. For this cause was I born, and for this cause came into the world, that I should bear witness unto the truth. And all that are of the truth, hear my voice. Pilate said unto him: What thing is truth? And when he had said this, he went out again unto the Jews, and saith unto them: I find in him no cause at all: Ye have a custom that I should deliver you one loose at Easter: will ye that I loose unto you the king of the Jews? Then cried they all again, saying: Not him, but Barrabas. The same Barrabas was a murtherer. Then Pilate took Jesus therefore, and scourged him. And the soldiers wound a crown of thorns, and put it on his head. And they did on him a purple garment, and came unto him and said: Hail king of the Jews: and they smote him on the face. Pilate went forth again, and said unto them: Behold, I bring him forth to you that ye may know that I find no fault in him. Then came Jesus forth, wearing a crown of thorn, and a robe of purple. And he saith unto them: Behold the man. When the Priests therefore and[1] the ministers saw him, they cried, Crucify him, crucify him. Pilate saith unto them: Take ye him and crucify him; for I find no cause in him. The Jews answered him: We have a law, and by our law he ought to die, because he made himself the Son of God. When Pilate heard that saying, he was the more afraid, and went again into the judgment hall, and said[2] unto Jesus: Whence art thou? But Jesus gave him none[3] answer. Then said Pilate unto him: Speakest thou not unto me? knowest thou not that I have power to crucify thee, and have power to loose thee? Jesus answered: Thou couldest have no power at all against me, except it were given thee from above: Therefore he that delivered me unto thee, hath the more sin. And from thenceforth sought Pilate means to loose him: but the Jews cried, saying: If thou let him go, thou art not Cesar's friend: for whosoever maketh himself a king, is against Cesar. When Pilate heard that saying, he brought Jesus forth, and sat down to give sentence in a place that is called the pavement, but in the Hebrew tongue, Gabbatha. It was the preparing day of Easter, about the sixth hour. And he saith unto the Jews: Behold your king. They cried, saying: Away with him, away with him, crucify him. Pilate saith unto them: Shall I crucify your king? The high priests answered: We have no king but Cesar. Then delivered he him to them to be crucified. And they took Jesus and led him away; and he bare his cross, and went forth into a place which is called the place of dead men's skulls, but in Hebrew, Golgotha: where they crucified him, and two other with him, on either side one, and Jesus in the midst. And Pilate wrote a title and put it upon the cross. The writing was, Jesus of Nazareth king of the Jews. This title read

[1 Grafton omits, and the ministers.]
[2 Grafton, sayeth.]   [3 Grafton, no.]

many of the Jews: for the place where Jesus was crucified was near to the city. And it was written in Hebrew, Greek, and Latin. Then said the high priests of the Jews to Pilate: Write not, King of the Jews, but that he said, I am king of the Jews. Pilate answered: What I have written that I have written. Then the soldiers, when they had crucified Jesus, took his garments, and made four parts, to every soldier a part, and also his coat. The coat was without seam, wrought upon throughout. They said therefore among themselves: Let us not divide it, but cast lots for it who shall have it: that the scripture might be fulfilled, saying: They have parted my raiment among them, and for my coat did they cast lots. And the soldiers did such things in deed. There stood by the cross of Jesus his mother, and his mother's sister, Mary the wife of Cleophas, and Mary Magdalene. When Jesus therefore saw his mother, and the disciple, whom he loved, standing, he saith unto his mother: Woman, behold thy son. Then said he to the disciple: Behold thy mother. And from that hour the disciple took her for his own.

After these things, Jesus knowing that all things were now performed, that the scripture might be fulfilled, he saith: I thirst. So there stood a vessel by, full of vinegar: therefore they filled a spunge with vinegar, and wound it about with ysope, and put it to his mouth. As soon as Jesus then received of the vinegar, he said: It is finished; and bowed his head, and gave up the ghost. The Jews therefore, because it was the preparing of the Sabboth, that the bodies should not remain upon the Cross on the Sabboth day (for that Sabboth day was an high day), besought Pilate that their legs might be broken, and that they might be taken down. Then came the soldiers and brake the legs of the first, and of the other which was crucified with him. But when they came to Jesus, and saw that he was dead already, they brake not his legs: but one of the soldiers with a spear thrust him into the side, and forthwith there came out blood and water. And he that saw it bare record, and his record is true. And he knoweth that he saith true, that ye might believe also. For these things were done, that the scripture should be fulfilled: Ye shall not break a bone of him. And again another scripture saith: They shall look upon him whom they have pierced. After this, Joseph of Aramathia (which was a disciple of Jesus, but secretly for fear of the Jews) besought Pilate that he might take down the body of Jesus. And Pilate gave him license: He came therefore and took the body of Jesus. And there came also Nicodemus (which at the beginning came to Jesus by night) and brought of myrrh and aloes mingled together, about an hundred pound weight. Then took they the body of Jesus, and wound it in linen clothes with the odours, as the manner of the Jews is to bury. And in the place where he was crucified, there was a garden, and in the garden a new sepulchre, wherein was never man laid: There laid they Jesus therefore because of the preparing of the Sabboth of the Jews; for the sepulchre was nigh at hand.

Easter even.

The Epistle.

1 Peter iii.   IT is better (if the will of God be so) that ye suffer for well doing than for evil doing. Forasmuch as Christ hath once suffered for sins, the just for the unjust, to bring us to God: and was killed as pertaining to the flesh, but was quickened in the Spirit. In which Spirit he also went and preached to the spirits that were in prison, which sometime had been disobedient, when the long suffering of God was once looked for, in the days of Noe, while the ark was a preparing; wherein a few, that is to say, eight souls were saved by the water: like as Baptism also now saveth us: not the putting away of the filth of the flesh, but in that a good conscience consenteth to God by the resurrection of Jesus Christ, which is on the right hand of God, and is gone into heaven, angels, powers, and might, subdued unto him.

The Gospel.

Mat. xxvii.   WHEN the even was come, there came a rich man of Aramathia, named Joseph, which also was Jesus' disciple. He went unto Pilate and begged the body of Jesus. Then Pilate commanded the body to be delivered. And when Joseph had taken the body, he wrapped it in a clean linen cloth, and laid it in his new tomb, which he had hewn out, even in the rock, and rolled a great stone to the door of the sepulchre, and departed. And there was Mary Magdalene, and the other Mary sitting over against the sepulchre. The next day that followeth the day of preparing, the high Priests and Pharisees came together unto Pilate, saying: Sir, we remember that this deceiver said while he was yet alive, After three days I will rise again. Command therefore that the sepulchre be made sure until the third day, lest his disciples come and steal him away, and say unto the people, he is risen from the dead: and the last error shall be worse than the first. Pilate said unto them: Ye have a watch, go your way, make it as sure as ye can. So they went and made the sepulchre sure with the watch men, and sealed the stone.

Easter day.

At morning prayer, instead of the Psalm, O come let us, &c. these anthems shall be sung or said.

CHRIST rising again from the dead, now dieth not. Death from henceforth hath no power upon him. For in that he died, he died but once to put away sin: but in that he liveth, he liveth unto God. And so likewise, count[1] yourselves dead unto sin, but living unto God in Christ Jesus our Lord[2].

CHRIST is risen again the firstfruits of them that sleep: for seeing that by man came death, by man also cometh the resurrection of the

[¹ Grafton, accompt.]   [² Grafton, Amen.]

EASTER DAY.

dead. For as by Adam all men do die, so by Christ, all men shall be restored to life.

The Collect.

ALMIGHTY God, which through thy only begotten Son, Jesus Christ, hast overcome death, and opened unto us the gate of everlasting life: we humbly beseech thee, that as by thy special grace preventing us thou dost put in our minds good desires; so by thy continual help we may bring the same to good effect, through Jesus Christ our Lord: who[3] liveth and reigneth. &c.

The Epistle.

IF ye be risen again with Christ, seek those things which are above, Coll. iii. where Christ sitteth on the right hand of God. Set your affection on heavenly things, and not on earthly things. For ye are dead, and your life is hid with Christ in God. Whensoever Christ (which is our life) shall shew himself, then shall ye also appear with him in glory. Mortify therefore your earthly members, fornication, uncleanness, unnatural lust, evil concupiscence, and covetousness, which is worshipping of Idols: for which things' sake, the wrath of God useth to come on the children of unbelief, among whom ye walked sometime when ye lived in them.

The Gospel.

THE first day of the Sabboths, came Mary Magdalene early (when it John xx. was yet dark) unto the sepulchre, and saw the stone taken away from the grave. Then she ran and came to Simon Peter, and to the other disciple whom Jesus loved, and saith unto them: They have taken away the Lord out of the grave, and we cannot tell where they have laid him. Peter therefore went forth, and that other disciple, and came unto the sepulchre. They ran both together, and that other disciple did out run Peter, and came first to the sepulchre. And when he had stooped down, he saw the linen clothes lying, yet went he not in. Then came Symon Peter following him, and went into the sepulchre, and saw the linen clothes lie, and the napkin that was about his head, not lying with the linen clothes, but wrapped together in a place by itself. Then went in also that other disciple which came first to the sepulchre, and he saw and believed. For as yet they knew not the scripture that he should rise again from death. Then the disciples went away again to their own home[4].

Monday in Easter week.

The Collect.

ALMIGHTY God, which through thy only begotten Son, Jesus Christ, hath[5] overcome death and opened unto us the gate of everlasting life: We humbly beseech thee, that as by thy special grace preventing us thou dost put in our minds good desires: so by thy continual help we

[3 Grafton, who. &c.]   [4 Grafton, house.]
[5 Grafton and 1596, hast.]

may bring the same to good effect, through Jesus Christ our Lord: who[1] liveth and reigneth. &c.

The Epistle.

Act. x.

PETER opened his mouth, and said: Of a truth I perceive that there is no respect of persons with God: but in all people, he that feareth him and worketh righteousness, is accepted with him. Ye know the preaching that God sent unto the children of Israel, preaching peace by Jesus Christ which is Lord over all things: which preaching was published throughout all Jewry (and began in Galile, after the Baptism which John preached) how GOD anointed Jesus of Nazareth with the Holy Ghost, and with power. Which Jesus went about doing good and healing all that were oppressed of the devil; for GOD was with him. And we are witnesses of all things which he did in the land of the Jews, and at Iherusalem; whom they slew and hanged on tree. Him God raised up the third day, and shewed him openly, not to all the people, but to us witnesses (chosen before of God for the same intent), which did eat and drink with him after he arose from death. And he commanded us to preach unto the people, and to testify that it is he which was ordained of GOD to be the judge of the quick and the dead. To him give all the prophets witness, that through his name, whosoever believeth in him, shall receive remission of sins.

The Gospel.

Lu. xxiii.[2]

BEHOLD, two of the Disciples went that same day to a town called Emaus, which was from Jerusalem about .lx.[3] furlongs: and they talked together of all the things that had happened. And it chanced, while they commoned together and reasoned, Jesus himself drew near, and went with them. But their eyes were holden that they should not know him. And he said unto them: What manner of communications are these that ye have one to another as ye walk, and are sad? And the one of them (whose name was Cleophas) answered and said unto him: Art thou only a stranger in Jerusalem, and hast not known the things which have chanced there in these days? He said unto them: What things? And they said unto him: Of Jesus of Nazareth, which was a Prophet, mighty in deed and word before God and all the people: and how the high priests and our rulers delivered him to be condemned to death, and have crucified him. But we trusted that it had been he, which should have redeemed Israel. And as touching all these things, to-day is even the third day that they were done: yea, and certain women also of our company made us astonied, which came early unto the sepulchre, and found not his body, and came, saying that they had seen a vision of Angels, which said that he was alive. And certain of them which were with us went to the sepulchre, and found it even so as the women had said, but him they saw not. And he said unto them:

[1 Grafton, who. &c.]   [2 Misprint for, xxiiii.]
[3 Grafton, thre score.]

O fools and slow of heart to believe all that the Prophets have spoken. Ought not Christ to have suffered these things, and to enter into his glory? And he began at Moses and all the Prophets, and interpreted unto them in all scriptures which were written of him. And they drew nigh unto the town, which they went unto. And he made as though he would have gone further. And they constrained him, saying: Abide with us, for it draweth towards night, and the day is far passed. And he went in to tarry with them. And it came to pass as he sat at meat with them, he took bread and blessed it, and brake, and gave to them. And their eyes were opened, and they knew him, and he vanished out of their sight. And they said between themselves: Did not our hearts burn within us while he talked with us by the way, and opened to us the scriptures? And they rose up the same hour, and returned to Jerusalem, and found the eleven gathered together, and them that were with them, saying: The Lord is risen in deed, and hath appeared to Simon. And they told what things were done in the way, and how they knew him in breaking of bread.

Tuesday in Easter week.

The Collect.

ALMIGHTY Father, which hast given thy only Son to die for our sins, and to rise again for our justification: Grant us so to put away the leaven of malice and wickedness, that we may alway serve thee in pureness of living and truth: through Jesus Christ our Lord.

The Epistle.

YE men and brethren, children of the generation of Abraham, and whosoever among you feareth GOD: to you is this word of salvation sent. For the inhabitants of Jerusalem and their rulers, because they knew him not, nor yet the voices of the Prophets, which are read every Sabboth day, they have fulfilled them in condemning him. And when they found no cause of death in him, yet desired they Pilate to kill him. And when they had fulfilled all that were written of him, they took him down from the tree, and put him in a sepulchre. But GOD raised him again from death the third day, and he was seen many days of them which went with him from Galile to Jerusalem, which are witnesses unto the people. And we declare unto you, how that the promise (which was made unto the fathers) God hath fulfilled unto their children, (even unto us) in that he raised up Jesus again. Even as it is written in the second Psalm: Thou art my Son, this day have I begotten thee. As concerning that he raised him up from death, now no more to return to corruption, he said on this wise: The holy promises made to David will I give faithfully unto you. Wherefore he saith also in another place: Thou shalt not suffer thine holy to see corruption. For David (after that he had in his time fulfilled the will of God) fell on sleep, and was laid unto his fathers, and saw corruption. But he whom God raised again, saw no corruption. Be it known unto you therefore,

Act. xiii.

(ye men and brethren) that through this man is preached unto you forgiveness of sins, and that by him all that believe are justified from all things, from which ye could not be justified by the law of Moses. Beware therefore, lest that fall on you which is spoken of in the Prophets: Behold, ye despisers, and wonder, and perish ye: for I do a work in your days, which ye shall not believe though a man declare it unto you.

The Gospel.

Lu. xxiv.
JESUS stood in the midst of his disciples, and said unto them: Peace be unto you: It is I, fear not. But they were abashed and afraid, and supposed that they had seen a spirit: And he said unto them: Why are ye troubled, and why do thoughts arise in your hearts? Behold my hands and my feet, that it is even I myself. Handle me and see, for a spirit hath no[1] flesh and bones, as ye see me have. And when he had thus spoken, he shewed them his hands and his feet. And while they yet believed not for joy, and wondered, he said unto them: Have ye here any meat? And they offered him a piece of broiled fish, and of an honey comb. And he took it, and did eat before them. And he said unto them: These are the words which I spake unto you, while I was yet with you: That all must needs be fulfilled, which were written of me in the law of Moyses, and in the prophets, and in the Psalms. Then opened he their wits that they might understand the scriptures, and said unto them: Thus it is written, and thus it behoved Christ to suffer, and to rise again from death the third day, and that repentance and remission of sins should be preached in his name among all nations, and must begin at Jerusalem. And ye are witnesses of these things.

The first Sunday after Easter.

The Collect.

ALMIGHTY God. &c. *As*[2] *at the Communion on Easter day.*

The Epistle.

i John v.
ALL that is born of God, overcometh the world. And this is the victory that overcometh the world, even our faith. Who is he that overcometh the world, but he that believeth that Jesus is the Son of God? This Jesus Christ is he that came by water and blood, not by water only, but by water and blood. And it is the spirit that beareth witness, because the spirit is truth. For there are three which bear record in heaven: the Father, the Word, and the Holy Ghost, and these three are one. And there are three which bear record in earth, the spirit, and water, and blood: and these three are one. If we receive the witness of men, the witness of God is greater. For this is the witness of GOD that is greater, which he testified of his Son. He that believeth on the Son of God, hath the witness in himself. He that believeth not God, hath made him a liar, because he believeth not the record that God gave his[3] Son. And this is

[[1] Grafton, not.]   [[2] 1578, *As upon Easter day.*]
[[3] Grafton, of his.]

the record, how that God hath given unto us eternal life, and this life is in his Son. He that hath the Son, hath life: and he that hath not the Son of God, hath not life.

The Gospel.

THE same day at night, which was the first day of the Sabboths, when the doors were shut, (where the disciples were assembled together for fear of the Jews,) came Jesus, and stood in the midst, and said unto them: Peace be unto you. And when he had so said, he shewed unto them his hands, and his side. Then were the disciples glad, when they saw the Lord. Then said Jesus to them again: Peace be unto you. As my Father sent me, even so send I you also. And when he had said these words, he breathed on them, and said unto them: Receive ye the Holy Ghost. Whosoever's sins ye remit, they are remitted unto them. And whosoever's sins ye retain, they are retained. *John xx.*

The second Sunday after[4] Easter.

The Collect.

ALMIGHTY God, which hast given thy holy[5] Son to be unto us both a sacrifice for sin, and also an example[6] of godly life: give us the grace that we may always most thankfully receive that his inestimable benefit, and also daily endeavour ourselves to follow the blessed steps of his most holy life.

The Epistle.

THIS is thank worthy, if a man for conscience toward GOD endure grief, and suffer wrong undeserved. For what praise is it, if when ye be buffeted for your faults, ye take it patiently? But and if when ye do well, ye suffer wrong, and take it patiently, then is there thank with God. For hereunto verily were ye called. For Christ also suffered for us, leaving us an ensample, that ye should follow his steps, which did no sin, neither was there guile found in his mouth: which when he was reviled, reviled not again: when he suffered, he threatened not: but committed the vengeance to him that judgeth righteously: which his own self bare our sins in his body on the tree, that we being delivered from sin, should live unto righteousness: by whose stripes ye were healed. For ye were as sheep going astray, but are now turned unto the shepherd, and bishop of your souls. *1 Pet. ii.*

The Gospel.

CHRIST said unto his disciples: I am the good shepherd: a good shepherd giveth his life for the sheep. An hired servant, and he which is not the shepherd (neither the sheep are his own) seeth the wolf coming, and leaveth the sheep, and fleeth[7], and the wolf catcheth, and scattereth the sheep. The hired servant fleeth[7], because he is an hired servant, and *John x.*

[4 Grafton has not, after Easter.]   [5 1596, thine only.]
[6 Grafton and 1596, ensample.]   [7 Grafton, flieth.]

[LITURG. QU. ELIZ.]

careth not for the sheep. I am the good shepherd, and know my sheep, and am known of mine. As my Father knoweth me, even so know I also my Father. And I give my life for the sheep: and other sheep I have, which are not of this fold: Them also must I bring, and they shall hear my voice, and there shall be one fold and one shepherd.

¶ The third Sunday[1].

The Collect.

ALMIGHTY God, which sheweth[2] to all men that be in error the light of thy truth, to the intent that they may return into the way of righteousness: grant unto all them that be admitted into the fellowship of Christ's religion, that they may eschew those things that be contrary to their profession, and follow all such things as be agreeable to the same: through our Lord Jesus Christ.

The Epistle.

i. Peter ii.

DEARLY beloved, I beseech you as strangers and pilgrims, abstain from fleshly lusts, which fight against the soul: and see that ye have honest conversation among the Gentiles, that whereas they backbite you as evil doers, they may see your good works, and praise God in the day of visitation. Submit yourselves therefore to every[3] man for the Lord's sake; whether it be unto the king, as unto the chief head: either unto rulers, as unto them that are sent of him, for the punishment of evil doers, but for the laud of them that do well. For so is the will of GOD, that with well doing ye may stop the mouths of foolish and ignorant men: as free, and not as having the liberty for a cloak of maliciousness, but even as the servants of God. Honour all men, love brotherly fellowship, fear God, honour the king.

The Gospel.

John xvi.

JESUS said to his disciples: After a while ye shall not see me: and again after a while ye shall see me: for I go to the Father. Then said some of his disciples between themselves: What is this that he saith unto us: after a while ye shall not see me, and again after a while ye shall see me, and that I go to the Father? They said therefore: What is this that he saith, after a while? We cannot tell what he saith. Jesus perceived that they would ask him, and said unto them: Ye enquire of this between yourselves, because I said: After a while ye shall not see me, and again after a while ye shall see me. Verily, verily I say unto you: ye shall weep and lament, but contrariwise the world shall rejoice. Ye shall sorrow, but your sorrow shall be turned to joy. A woman, when she travaileth, hath sorrow because her hour is come. But as soon as she is delivered of the child, she remembereth no more the anguish, for joy that a man is born into the world. And ye now therefore have sorrow: but I will see you again, and your hearts shall rejoice, and your joy shall no man take from you.

[[1] 1596, after Easter.] [[2] Grafton, shewest.] [[3] Grafton, all maner of men.]

The fourth Sunday[4].

The Collect.

ALMIGHTY God, which dost make the minds of all faithful men to be of one will: grant unto thy people, that they may love the thing which thou commandest, and desire that which thou dost promise: that among the sundry and manifold changes of the world, our hearts may surely there be fixed, where as true joys are to be found: through Christ[5] our Lord.

The Epistle.

EVERY good gift, and every perfect gift, is from above, and cometh down from the father of lights, with[6] whom is no variableness, neither shadow of change. Of his own will begat he us, with the word of truth, that we should be the firstfruits of his creatures. Wherefore (dear brethren) let every man be swift to hear, slow to speak, slow to wrath. For the wrath of man worketh not that which is righteous before GOD. Wherefore lay apart all filthiness, and superfluity of maliciousness, and receive with meekness the word that is graffed in you, which is able to save your souls. *James i.*

The Gospel.

JESUS said unto his disciples: Now I go my way to him that sent me, and none of you asketh me whether I go. But, because I have said such things unto you, your hearts are full of sorrow. Nevertheless, I tell you the truth, it is expedient for you, that I go away. For if I go not away, that comforter will not come unto you. But if I depart, I will send him unto you. And when he is come, he will rebuke the world of sin, and of righteousness, and of judgment. Of sin, because they believe not on me. Of righteousness, because I go to my Father, and ye shall see me no more. Of judgment, because the prince of this world is judged already. I have yet many things to say unto you, but ye cannot bear them away now: howbeit, when he is come (which is the Spirit of truth) he will lead you into all truth. He shall not speak of himself, but whatsoever he shall hear, that shall he speak: and he will shew you things to come. He shall glorify me, for he shall receive of mine, and shall shew unto you. All things that the Father hath, are mine: therefore said I unto you, that he shall take of mine, and shew unto you. *John xvi.*

The fifth Sunday[4].

The Collect.

LORD, from whom all good things do come: grant us thy humble servants, that by thy holy inspiration we may think those things that be good, and by thy merciful guiding may perform the same, through our Lord Jesus Christ[7].

[4 1596, after Easter.]   [5 Grafton, Christ. &c.]
[6 Grafton, in.]   [7 Grafton, Amen.]

The Epistle.

James i.

SEE that ye be doers of the word, and not hearers only, deceiving your own selves. For if any man hear the word, and declareth not the same by his works, he is like unto a man beholding his bodily face in a glass. For as soon as he hath looked on himself, he goeth his way, and forgetteth immediately, what his fashion was. But whoso looketh in the perfect law of liberty, and continueth therein (if he be not a forgetful hearer, but a doer of the work) the same shall be happy in his deed. If any man among you seem to be devout, and refraineth not his tongue, but deceiveth his own heart, this man's devotion is in vain. Pure devotion, and undefiled before God the Father, is this: to visit the fatherless and widows in their adversity, and to keep himself unspotted of the world.

The Gospel.

John xvi.

VERILY, verily, I say unto you: whatsoever ye ask the Father in my name, he will give it you. Hitherto have ye asked nothing in my name. Ask and ye shall receive, that your joy may be full. These things have I spoken unto you by proverbs. The time will come when I shall no more speak unto you by proverbs: but I shall shew you plainly from my Father. At that day shall ye ask in my name: and I say not unto you, that I will speak unto my Father for you. For the Father himself loveth you, because ye have loved me, and have believed that I came out from God. I went out from the Father, and came into the world. Again, I leave the world, and go to the Father.

His disciples said unto him: Lo, now thou talkest plainly, and speakest no proverb. Now are we sure, that thou knowest all things, and needest not that any man should ask thee any question; therefore believe we, that thou camest from God. Jesus answered them: Now ye do believe. Behold, the hour draweth nigh, and is already come, that ye shall be scattered every man to his own, and shall leave me alone: and yet am I not alone, for the Father is with me. These words have I spoken unto you, that in me ye might have peace, for in the world shall ye have tribulation: but be of good cheer, I have overcome the world.

¶ The[1] Ascension day.

The Collect.

GRANT we beseech thee, almighty God, that like as we do believe thy only begotten Son our Lord to have ascended into the heavens: so we may also in heart and mind thither ascend, and with him continually dwell.

The Epistle.

Acts i.

IN the former treatise (dear Theophilus) we have spoken of all that Jesus began to do, and teach, until the day in which he was taken up, after that he through the Holy Ghost had given commandments unto

[[1] The, not in Grafton.]

the Apostles, whom he had chosen; to whom also he shewed himself alive after his Passion (and that by many tokens) appearing unto them forty days, and speaking of the Kingdom of God, and gathered them together, and commanded them, that they should not depart from Ierusalem, but to wait for the promise of the Father, whereof (saith he) ye have heard of me. For John truly baptized with water, but ye shall be baptized with the Holy Ghost after these few days. When they therefore were come together, they asked of him, saying: Lord, wilt thou at this time restore again the kingdom of Israel? And he said unto them: It is not for you to know the times, or the seasons, which the Father hath put in his own power. But ye shall receive power, after the Holy Ghost is come upon you. And ye shall be witnesses unto me, not only in Ierusalem, but also in all Jewry, and in all Samaria, and even unto the world's end. And when he had spoken these things, while they beheld, he was taken up on high, and a cloud received him up out of their sight. And while they looked stedfastly up toward heaven as he went, behold, two men stood by them in white apparel, which also said: Ye men of Galile, why stand ye gazing up into heaven? This same Jesus, which is taken up from you into heaven, shall so come, even as ye have seen him go into heaven.

The Gospel.

JESUS appeared unto the .xi. as they sat at meat: and cast in their Mar. xvi. teeth their unbelief, and hardness of heart, because they believed not them, which had seen that he was risen again from the dead: and he said unto them: Go ye into all the world, and preach the gospel to all creatures: he that believeth, and is baptized, shall be saved. But he that believeth not, shall be damned. And these tokens shall follow them that believe. In my name they shall cast out devils, they shall speak with new tongues, they shall drive away serpents. And if they drink any deadly thing, it shall not hurt them. They shall lay their hand [2] on the sick, and they shall recover. So then, when the Lord had spoken unto them, he was received into heaven, and is on the right hand of God. And they went forth, and preached every where, the Lord working with them, and confirming the word with miracles following.

The [3] Sunday after the ascension day.

The Collect.

O GOD, the king of glory, which hast exalted thine only Son Jesus Christ with great triumph unto thy kingdom in heaven: we beseech thee leave us not comfortless, but send to us thine Holy Ghost to comfort us, and exalt us unto [4] the same place, whither our Saviour Christ is gone before: who liveth and reigneth. &c.

[[2] Grafton, handes.]   [[3] The, not in 1596.]   [[4] Grafton, to.]

The Sunday after the Ascension.

The Epistle.

i. Pete. iv.

THE end of all things is at hand: be ye therefore sober, and watch unto prayer. But above all things, have fervent love among yourselves, for love shall cover the multitude of sins. Be ye herberous[1] one to another without grudging. As every man hath received the gift, even so minister the same one to another, as good ministers of the manifold graces[2] of GOD. If any man speak, let him talk as the words of GOD. If any man minister, let him do it as of the ability, which GOD ministereth to him, that God in all things may be glorified, through Jesus Christ: to whom be praise and dominion for ever and ever. Amen.

The Gospel.

John xv.

WHEN the Comforter is come, whom will I send unto you from the Father (even the Spirit of truth, which proceedeth of the Father) he shall testify of me. And ye shall bear witness also, because ye have been with me from the beginning. These things have I said unto you, because ye[3] should not be offended. They shall excommunicate you: yea, the time shall come, that whosoever killeth you, will think that he doth God service. And such things will they do unto you, because they have not known the Father, neither yet me. But these things I have told you, that when the time is come, ye may remember then that I told you.

Whitsunday.

The Collect.

GOD, which as upon this day hast taught the hearts of thy faithful people, by the sending to them the light of thy Holy Spirit: grant us by[4] the same Spirit to have a right judgment in all things, and evermore to rejoice in his holy Comfort, through the merits of Christ Jesu our Saviour: who liveth and reigneth with thee in the unity of the same Spirit, one God world without end[5].

The Epistle.

Acts ii.

WHEN the fifty days were come to an end, they were all with one accord together in one place. And suddenly there came a sound from heaven, as it had been the coming of a mighty wind, and it filled all the house where they sat. And there appeared unto them cloven tongues, like as they had been of fire, and it sat upon each one of them: and they were all filled with the Holy Ghost, and began to speak with other tongues, even as the same Spirit gave them utterance. Then were dwelling at Ierusalem Jews, devout men, out of every nation of them, that are under heaven. When this was noised about, the multitude came together, and were astonied, because that every man heard them speak with his own language.

[1 Herberous, or harborous: hospitable.] [2 Grafton, grace.]
[3 Grafton, you.] [4 Grafton omits, by.]
[5 Grafton and 1596, Amen.]

They wondered all, and marvelled, saying among themselves: Behold, are not all these which speak of Galile? And how hear we every man his own tongue, wherein we were born? Parthians and Medes, and Elamites, and the inhabiters of Mesopotamia, and of Jewry, and of Capadocia, of Pontus, and Asia, Phrygia, and Pamphylia, of Egypt, and of the parties of Lybia, which is beside Syren, and strangers of Rome, Jews, and Proselytes, Greeks, and Arabians, we have heard them speak in our own tongues, the great works of God.

The Gospel.

JESUS said unto his Disciples: If ye love me, keep my commandments, and I will pray the Father, and he shall give you another Comforter, that he may abide with you for ever: even the Spirit of truth, whom the world cannot receive, because the world seeth him not neither knoweth him. But ye know him, for he dwelleth with you, and shall be in you. I will not leave you comfortless, but will come to you. Yet a little while, and the world seeth me no more; but ye see me. For I live, and ye shall live. That day shall ye know, that I am in my Father, and you in me, and I in you. He that hath my commandments, and keepeth them, the same is he that loveth me. And he that loveth me, shall be loved of my Father, and I will love him, and will shew mine own self unto him. Judas saith unto him (not Judas Iscariath) Lord, what is done that thou wilt shew thyself unto us, and not unto the world? Jesus answered, and said unto them[7]: If a man love me, he will keep my sayings, and my Father will love him: and we[8] will come unto him, and dwell with him. He that loveth me not, keepeth not my sayings. And the word which ye hear, is not mine, but the Father's, which sent me. These things have I spoken unto you, being yet present with you. But the Comforter, which is the Holy Ghost, whom my[9] Father will send in my name, he shall teach you all things, and bring all things to your remembrance, whatsoever I have said unto you. Peace I leave with you: my peace I give unto you. Not as the world giveth, give I unto you. Let not your hearts be grieved, neither fear. Ye have heard how I said unto you: I go and come again unto you. If ye loved me, ye would verily rejoice, because I said, I go unto the Father. For the Father is greater than I. And now have I shewed you before it come, that, when it is come to pass, ye might believe. Hereafter will I not talk many words unto you. For the prince of this world cometh, and hath nought in me. But that the world may know, that I love the Father. And as the Father gave me commandment, even so do I.

Joh. xiii.[6]

[6 Misprint for, xiiii.]
[8 Grafton, he.]
[7 Grafton, him.]
[9 Grafton, the.]

¶ Monday in Whitsun week

The Collect.

GOD[1] which. &c. (As upon Whitsunday.)

The Epistle.

Acts x.[2]

THEN Peter opened his mouth, and said: Of a truth, I perceive that there is no respect of persons with God: but in all people, he that feareth him, and worketh righteousness, is accepted with him. Ye know the preaching that God sent unto the children of Israel, preaching peace by Jesus Christ, which is Lord over all things: which preaching was published throughout all Jewry, (and began in Galile, after the baptism, which John preached) how God anointed Jesus of Nazareth with the Holy Ghost, and with power. Which Jesus went about doing good, and healing all that were oppressed of the devil. For God was with him. And we are witnesses of all things, which he did in the land of the Jews, and at Ierusalem; whom they slew, and hanged on a tree: Him God raised up the third day, and shewed him openly, not to all the people, but unto us witnesses (chosen before of God, for the same intent) which did eat and drink with him, after he arose from death. And he commanded us to preach unto the people, and to testify that it is he, which was ordained of God, to be the judge of quick and dead. To him give all the Prophets witness, that through his name, whosoever believeth in him, shall receive remission of sins. While Peter yet spake these words, the Holy Ghost fell on all them, which heard the preaching. And they of the circumcision, which believed, were astonied, as many as came with Peter, because that on the Gentiles also was shed out the gift of the Holy Ghost. For they heard them speak with tongues, and magnify God. Then answered Peter: Can any man forbid water, that these should not be baptized, which have received the Holy Ghost as well as we? And he commanded them to be baptized in the name of the Lord. Then prayed they him to tarry a few days.

The Gospel.

John iii.

So God loved the world, that he gave his only begotten Son, that whosoever believeth in him should not perish, but have everlasting life. For God sent not his Son into the world, to condemn the world, but that the world through him might be saved. But he that believeth on him, is not condemned. But he that believeth not, is condemned already, because he hath not believed in the name of the only begotten Son of God. And this is the condemnation: that light is come into the world, and men loved darkness more than light, because their deeds were evil. For every one that evil doeth, hateth the light, neither cometh to the light,

[1] Grafton, God, which hast given. &c. 1596, God, which as upon this day hast taught the heartes of thy faithfull. &c.]

[2] Grafton, iiii. A misprint.]

1559.]   THE TUESDAY AFTER WHITSUNDAY.   137

lest his deeds should be reproved. But he that doth the truth, cometh to the light, that his deeds may be known, how that they are wrought in God.

The³ Tuesday after Whitsunday.

The Collect.

¶ God⁴ which. &c. (As upon Whitsunday.)

The Epistle.

WHEN the Apostles, which were at Ierusalem, heard say, that Sama- Acts viii. ria had received the word of God: they sent unto them Peter and John. Which when they were come down, prayed for them, that they might receive the Holy Ghost. For as yet he was come on none of them, but they were baptized only in the name of Christ Jesu. Then laid they their hands on them, and they received the Holy Ghost.

The Gospel.

VERILY, verily, I say unto you: he that entereth not in by the door John x. into the sheepfold, but climbeth up some other way, the same is a thief and a murtherer. But he that entereth in⁵ by the door, is the shepherd of the sheep: To him the porter openeth, and the sheep hear his voice, and he calleth his own sheep by name, and leadeth them out. And when he hath sent forth his own sheep, he goeth before them, and the sheep follow him: for they know his voice. A stranger will they not follow, but will flee⁶ from him, for they know not the voice of strangers. This proverb spake Jesus unto them, but they understood not, what things they were, which he spake unto them. Then said Jesus unto them again: Verily, verily I say unto you: I am the door of the sheep. All (even as many as came before me) are thieves and murtherers, but the sheep did not hear them. I am the door: by me if any enter in, he shall be safe, and shall go in and out, and find pasture. A thief cometh not, but for to steal, kill, and destroy. I am come that they might have life, and that they might have it more abundantly.

Trinity Sunday.

The Collect.

ALMIGHTY and everlasting God, which hast given unto us thy servants grace by the confession of a true faith to acknowledge the glory of the eternal Trinity, and in the power of the divine majesty to worship the unity: we beseech thee, that through the stedfastness of this faith we may evermore be defended from all adversity, which livest and reignest one God, world without end. Amen.

[³ 1596, Tuesday in Whitsunweeke.]

[⁴ Grafton, God, which hast given. &c. 1596, God, which as upon this day hast taught the heartes of thy faithful people. &c.]

[⁵ Grafton has not, in.]   [⁶ Grafton, flye.]

The Epistle.

Apoc. iv.

AFTER this I looked, and behold, a door was open in heaven, and the first voice which I heard, was as it were of a trumpet, talking with me, which said: Come up hither, and I will shew thee things, which must be fulfilled hereafter. And immediately I was in the spirit. And behold, a seat was set in heaven, and one sat on the seat. And he that sat was to look upon like unto a jasper stone, and a sardine stone. And there was a rainbow about the seat, in sight like unto an emerald.' And about the seat were .xxiiii. seats. And upon the seats .xxiiii. elders sitting, clothed in white raiment, and had on their heads crowns of gold. And out of the seat proceeded lightnings, and thunderings, and voices: and there were seven lamps of fire burning before the seat, which are the seven spirits of God. And before the seat, there was a sea of glass, like unto crystal, and in the midst of the seat, and round about the seat, were four beasts full of eyes, before and behind. And the first beast was like a lion, and the second beast like a calf, and the third beast had a face as a man, and the fourth beast was like a flying eagle. And the four beasts had each of them six wings about him, and they were full of eyes within. And they did not rest day neither night, saying: Holy, holy, holy, Lord God almighty, which was, and is, and is to come. And when those beasts gave glory, and honour, and thanks to him that sat on the seat (which liveth for ever and ever) the .xxiiii. elders fell down before on[1], that sat on the throne, and worshipped him that liveth for ever, and cast their crowns before the throne, saying: Thou art worthy, O Lord, (our God) to receive glory, and honour, and power: for thou hast created all things, and for thy will's sake they are, and were created.

The Gospel.

John iii.

THERE was a man of the Pharisees, named Nichodemus, a Ruler of the Jews. The same came to Jesus by night, and said unto him: Rabbi, we know, that thou art a teacher, come from God, for no man could do such miracles, as thou doest, except God were with him. Jesus answered, and said unto him: Verily, verily I say unto thee, except a man be born from above, he cannot see the kingdom of God. Nichodemus said unto him: How can a man be born, when he is old? Can he enter into his mother's womb, and be born again? Jesus answered: Verily, verily I say unto thee, except a man be born of water, and of the spirit, he cannot enter into the kingdom of God. That which is born of the flesh, is flesh: and that which is born of the spirit, is spirit. Marvel not thou that I said to thee, ye must be born from above. The wind bloweth where it lusteth, and thou hearest the sound thereof, but thou canst not tell, whence it cometh, nor whether he[2] goeth: So is every one that is born of the spirit. Nichodemus answered, and said unto him: How can these things be? Jesus answered, and said unto him: Art thou a master in Israel, and knowest not these things? Verily, verily, I say unto thee: we speak that we know, and testify that we have seen: and

[1 Misprint for, him.]   [2 Grafton, or whether it.]

ye receive not our witness. If I have told you earthly things, and ye believe not; how shall ye believe, if I tell you of heavenly things? And no man ascendeth up to heaven, but he that came down from heaven, even the son of man, which is in heaven. And as Moyses lift up the serpent in the wilderness, even so must the son of man be lift up: that whosoever believeth in him, perish not, but have everlasting life.

¶ The first Sunday after Trinity Sunday[3].

The Collect.

GOD the strength of all them that trust in thee, mercifully accept our prayers. And because the weakness of our mortal nature can do no good thing without thee : grant us the help of thy grace, that in keeping of thy commandments we may please thee both in will and deed, through Jesus Christ our Lord.

The Epistle.

DEARLY beloved, let us love one another: for love cometh of God. And every one that loveth, is born of God, and knoweth God. He that loveth not, knoweth not God. For God is love. In this appeareth the love of God to us ward, because that God sent his only begotten Son into the world, that we might live through him. Herein is love, not that we loved God, but that he loved us, and sent his Son to be the agreement for our sins. Dearly beloved, if God so loved us, we ought also one to love another. No man hath seen God at any time. If we love one another, God dwelleth in us, and his love is perfect in us. Hereby know we, that we dwell in him, and he in us, because he hath given us of his spirit. And we have seen, and do testify, that the Father sent the Son to be the saviour of the world : whosoever confesseth, that Jesus is the Son of God, in him dwelleth God, and he in God. And we have known and believed the love that God hath to us. God is love, and he that dwelleth in love, dwelleth in God, and God in him. Herein is the love perfect in us, that we should trust in the day of judgment. For as he is, even so are we in this world. There is no fear in love, but perfect love casteth out fear, for fear hath painfulness. He that feareth is not perfect in love. We love him, for he loved us first. If a man say : I love God, and yet hate his brother, he is a liar. For how can he that loveth not his brother, whom he hath seen, love God whom he hath not seen? And this commandment have we of him, that he which loveth God should love his brother also. *i. John iv.*

The Gospel.

THERE was a certain rich man, which was clothed in purple, and fine white, and fared deliciously every day. And there was a certain beggar named Lazarus, which lay at his gate full of sores, desiring to be refreshed with the crumbs which fell from the rich man's board, and no man gave unto him. The dogs came also and licked his sores. And it *Luke xvi.*

[[3] The second 'Sunday' not in 1596.]

fortuned that the beggar died, and was carried by the angels into Abraham's bosom. The rich man also died, and was buried. And being in hell in torments, he lift up his eyes and saw Abraham afar off, and Lazarus in his bosom, and he cried and said : Father Abraham, have mercy on me, and send Lazarus, that he may dip the tip of his finger in water, and cool my tongue, for I am tormented in this flame. But Abraham said : Son, remember that thou in thy life-time receivedst thy pleasure, and contrariwise Lazarus received pain. But now he is comforted, and thou art punished. Beyond all this, between us and you there is a great space set, so that they which would go from hence to you cannot, neither may come from thence to us. Then he said : I pray thee therefore, father, send him to my father's house (for I have five brethren) for to warn them, lest they come also into this place of torment. Abraham said unto him : They have Moyses and the Prophets, let them hear them. And he said, Nay, father Abraham, but if one come unto them from the dead, they will repent. He said unto him : If they hear not Moyses and the Prophets, neither will they believe though one rose from death again.

The second Sunday [1].

The Collect.

LORD, make us to have a perpetual fear and love of thy holy name; for thou never failest to help and govern them, whom thou dost bring up in thy stedfast love. Grant this. &c.

The Epistle.

1. John iii.   MARVEL not my brethren, though the world hate you. We know that we are translated from death unto life, because we love the brethren. He that loveth not his brother, abideth in death. Whosoever hateth his brother is a manslayer. And ye know that no manslayer hath eternal life abiding in him. Hereby perceive we love, because he gave his life for us, and we ought to give our lives for the brethren. But whoso hath this world's good, and seeth his brother have need, and shutteth up his compassion from him, how dwelleth the love of God in him? My babes, let us not love in word, neither in tongue: but in deed, and in verity. Hereby we know that we are of the verity, and can quiet our hearts before him. For if our heart condemn us, God is greater than our heart, and knoweth all things. Dearly beloved, if our heart condemn us not, then have we trust to God ward ; and whatsoever we ask, we receive of him, because we keep his commandments, and do those things which are pleasant in his sight. And this is *his* commandment, that we believe on the name of his Son Jesus Christ, and love one another, as he gave commandment. And he that keepeth his commandments, dwelleth in him, and he in him : and hereby we know that he abideth in us, even by the spirit which he hath given us.

[[1] 1596, after Trinitie. And so throughout.]

The Gospel.

A CERTAIN man ordained a great supper, and bade many, and sent his servant at supper time to say to them that were bidden: Come, for all things are now ready. And they all at once began to make excuse. The first said unto him: I have bought a farm, and I must needs go, and see it; I pray thee have me excused. And another said : I have bought yoke of oxen, and I go to prove them ; I pray thee have me excused. And another said, I have married a wife, and therefore I cannot come. And the servant returned, and brought his Master word again thereof. Then was the good man of the house displeased, and said unto his servant, Go out quickly into the streets, and quarters of the city, and bring in hither the poor, and feeble, and the halt and blind. And the servant said: Lord, it is done as thou hast commanded, and yet there is room. And the Lord said unto the servant: Go out unto the highways and hedges, and compel them to come in, that my house may be filled. For I say unto you, that none of these men which were bidden, shall taste of my supper. Luk. xiv.

The third Sunday.

The Collect.

LORD, we beseech thee mercifully to hear us, and unto whom thou hast given an[2] hearty desire to pray : grant that by thy mighty aid we may be defended, through Jesus Christ our Lord.

The Epistle.

SUBMIT yourselves every man one to another, knit yourselves together in lowliness of mind. For God resisteth the proud, and giveth grace to the humble. Submit yourselves therefore under the mighty hand of God, that he may exalt you, when the time is come. Cast all your care upon him, for he careth for you. Be sober, and watch : for your adversary the devil, as a roaring lion, walketh about, seeking whom he may devour, whom resist stedfast in the faith : knowing that the same afflictions are appointed unto your brethren that are in the world. But the God of all grace, which hath called us unto his eternal glory by Christ Jesu, shall his own self (after that ye have suffered a little affliction) make you perfect, settle, strength, and stablish you. To him be glory and dominion for ever and ever. Amen. i. Peter v.[3]

The Gospel.

THEN resorted unto him all the Publicans and sinners for to hear him. And the Pharisees and Scribes murmured, saying : He receiveth sinners, and eateth with them. But he put forth this parable unto them, saying : What man among you, having an .c. sheep (if he lose one of them) doth not leave ninety and nine in the wilderness, and goeth after that which is lost, until he find it? And when he hath found it, he layeth Luke xv.

[2 Grafton omits, an.]   [3 Grafton, Rom. viii. A misprint.]

it on his shoulders with joy. And as soon as he cometh home, he calleth together his lovers and neighbours, saying unto them: Rejoice with me, for I have found my sheep, which was lost. I say unto you, that likewise joy shall be in heaven over one sinner that repenteth, more than over ninety and nine just persons, which need no repentance. Either what woman having .x. groats, (if she lose one) doth not light a candle, and sweep the house, and seek diligently till she find it? And when she hath found it, she calleth her lovers and her neighbours together, saying: Rejoice with me, for I have found the groat which I lost. Likewise I say unto you, shall there be joy in the presence of the Angels of God over one sinner that repenteth.

The fourth Sunday.

The Collect.

GOD the protector of all that trust in thee, without whom nothing is strong, nothing is holy, increase and multiply upon us thy mercy, that thou being our ruler and guide, we may so pass through things temporal, that we finally lose not the things eternal: grant this, heavenly Father, for Jesus[1] Christ's sake our Lord.

The Epistle.

Rom. viii.

I SUPPOSE that the afflictions of this life are not worthy of the glory, which shall be shewed upon us. For the fervent desire of the creature abideth, looking when the sons of God shall appear, because the creature is subdued to vanity against the will thereof, but for his will, which hath subdued the same in hope. For the same creature shall be delivered from the bondage of corruption, into the glorious liberty of the sons of God. For we know that every creature groaneth with us also, and travaileth in pain, even unto this time: not only it, but we also which have the first fruits of the Spirit, mourn in ourselves also, and wait for the adoption (of the children of God) even the deliverance of our bodies.

The Gospel.

Luke vi.

BE ye merciful as your father also is merciful. Judge not, and ye shall not be judged: condemn not, and ye shall not be condemned. Forgive, and ye shall be forgiven. Give, and it shall be given unto you, good measure, and pressed down, and shaken together, and running over, shall men give into your bosoms. For with the same measure, that ye mete withal, shall other men mete to you again. And he put forth a similitude unto them. Can the blind lead the blind? Do they not both fall into the ditch? The disciple is not above his master: Every man shall be perfect, even as his master is. Why seest thou a mote in thy brother's eye[2], but considerest not the beam that is in thine own eye? Either how canst thou say to thy brother: Brother, let me pull out the mote that is in thine eye, when thou seest not the beam that is in thine

[[1] Grafton, Jesu.]   [[2] Grafton omits a line.]

own eye? First, thou hypocrite, cast out the beam out of thine own eye, then shalt thou see perfectly, to pull out the mote, that is in thy brother's eye.

The fifth Sunday.

The Collect.

GRANT, Lord, we beseech thee, that the course of this world may be so peaceably ordered by thy governance, that thy congregation may joyfully serve thee in all godly quietness: through Jesus Christ our Lord.

The Epistle.

BE you all of one mind, and of one heart, love as brethren, be pitiful, i. Pet. iii. be courteous (meek) not rendering evil for evil, or rebuke for rebuke: but contrariwise, bless, knowing that ye are thereunto called, even that ye should be heirs of the blessing. For he that doth long after life, and loveth to see good days, let him refrain his tongue from evil, and his lips that they speak no guile. Let him eschew evil, and do good, let him seek peace, and ensue it. For the eyes of the Lord are over the righteous, and his ears are open unto their prayers. Again, the face of the Lord is over them that do evil. Moreover, who is he that will harm you, if ye follow that which is good? yea, happy are ye, if any trouble happen unto you for righteousness' sake. Be not ye afraid for any terror of them, neither be ye troubled, but sanctify the Lord God in your hearts.

The Gospel.

IT came to pass, that (when the people pressed upon him, to hear the Luke v.3 word of God) he stood by the lake of Genazareth, and saw two ships stand by the lake's side, but the fisher men were gone out of them, and were washing their nets. And he entered into one of the ships (which pertained to Simon) and prayed him, that he would thrust out a little from the land. And he sat down, and taught the people out of the ship. When he had left speaking, he said unto Simon: Launch out into the deep, and let slip your nets to make a draught. And Simon answered, and said unto him: Master, we have laboured all night, and have taken nothing. Nevertheless, at thy commandment, I will loose forth the net. And when they[5] had so done, they inclosed a great multitude of fishes. But their net brake, and they beckoned to their fellows (which were in the other ship) that they should come and help them. And they came and filled both ships, that they sunk again. When Simon Peter saw this, he fell down at Jesus' knees, saying: Lord, go from me, for I am a sinful man. For he was astonied, and all that were with him, at the draught of fishes which they had taken: and so was also James and John, the sons of Zebede, which were partners with Simon. And Jesus said unto Simon: Fear not, from henceforth thou shalt catch men. And they brought the ships to land, and forsook all and followed him.

[3 Grafton, i. A misprint.]   [4 Grafton, he had thus done.]

The sixth Sunday.

The Collect.

God, which hast prepared to them that love thee such good things as pass all man's understanding: pour into our hearts such love toward thee, that we loving thee in all things, may obtain thy promises, which exceed all that we can desire, through Jesus Christ our Lord.

The Epistle.

Roma. vi.

Know ye not, that all we which are baptized in Jesus Christ, are baptized to die with him? We are buried then with him by baptism, for to die, that likewise as Christ was raised from death, by the glory of the Father, even so we also should walk in a new life. For if we be graft[1] in death like unto him, even so shall we be partakers of the holy resurrection. Knowing this that your old man is crucified with him also, that the body of sin might utterly be destroyed, that henceforth we should not be servants unto sin. For he that is dead, is justified from sin. Wherefore if we be dead with Christ, we believe that we shall also live with him, knowing that Christ being raised from death, dieth no more. Death hath no more power over him. For as touching that he died, he died concerning sin once: and as touching that he liveth, he liveth unto God. Likewise consider ye also, that ye are dead as touching sin, but are alive unto God, through Jesus Christ our Lord.

The Gospel.

Math. v.

Jesus said unto his disciples: Except your righteousness exceed the righteousness of the Scribes, and Pharisees, ye cannot enter into the kingdom of heaven. Ye have heard that it was said unto them of old time, Thou shalt not kill, whosoever killeth shall be in danger of judgment. But I say unto you: that who so ever is angry with his brother (unadvisedly) shall be in danger of judgment. And who so ever say unto his brother, Racha, shall be in danger of a counsel. But who so ever saith, Thou fool, shall be in danger of hell fire. Therefore, if thou offerest thy gift at the altar, and there rememberest that thy brother hath ought against thee, leave there thine offering before the altar, and go thy way first, and be reconciled to thy brother, and then come and offer thy gift. Agree with thine adversary quickly, whiles thou art in the way with him, lest at any time the adversary deliver thee to the judge, and the judge deliver thee to the minister, and then thou be cast into prison. Verily I say unto thee: thou shalt not come out thence, till thou have paid the uttermost farthing.

The .vii. Sunday.

The Collect.

Lord of all power and might, which art the author and giver of all good things: graff in our hearts the love of thy name, increase in us

[1 Grafton, graffed.]

true religion, nourish us with all goodness, and of thy great mercy keep us in the same: Through Jesus Christ our Lord.

The Epistle.

I SPEAK grossly, because of the infirmity of your flesh. As ye have Roma. vi. given your members servants to uncleanness, and to iniquity, (from one iniquity to another) even so now give over your members servants unto righteousness, that ye may be sanctified. For when ye were servants of sin, ye were void of righteousness. What fruit had you [2] then in those things whereof ye are now ashamed? For the end of those things are [3] death. But now are ye delivered from sin, and made the servants of God, and have your fruit to be sanctified, and the end everlasting life. For the reward of sin is death: but eternal life is the gift of GOD, through Jesus Christ our Lord.

The Gospel.

IN those days, when there was a very great company, and had nothing Math. [4] viii. to eat, Jesus called his disciples unto him, and said unto them: I have compassion on the people, because they have been now with me three days, and have nothing to eat: and if I send them away fasting, to their own houses, they shall faint by the way: for divers of them came from far. And his disciples answered him: Where should a man have bread here in the wilderness, to satisfy these? And he asked them: How many loaves have ye? They said, Seven. And he commanded the people to sit down on the ground. And he took the seven loaves: And when he had given thanks, he brake, and gave to his disciples, to set before them. And they did set them before the people. And they had a few small fishes. And when he had blessed, he commanded them also to be set before them. And they did eat, and were sufficed. And they took up of the broken meat that was left seven baskets full. And they that did eat were above four thousand. And he sent them away.

The .viii. Sunday.

The Collect.

GOD, whose providence is never deceived: we humbly beseech thee, that thou wilt put away from us all hurtful things, and give [5] those things which be profitable for us: through Jesus Christ our Lord.

The Epistle.

BRETHREN, we are debtors, not to the flesh, to live after the flesh. Rom. viii.[6] For if ye live after the flesh, ye shall die. But if ye through the spirit do mortify the deeds of the body, ye shall live. For as many as are led by the spirit of God, they are the sons of God. For ye have not received

[2 Grafton, ye.]   [3 Grafton, is.]
[4 Misprint for, Mark.]   [5 Grafton, geve to us.]
[6 Grafton, i. Peter v. A misprint: see p. 141, note 3.]

[LITURG. QU. ELIZ.]

the spirit of bondage, to fear any more, but ye have received the spirit of adoption, whereby ye cry: Abba, Father. The same spirit certifieth our spirit, that we are the sons of God. If we be sons, then are we also heirs: the heirs I mean of God, and heirs annexed with Christ; if so be that we suffer with him, that we may be also glorified together with him.

The Gospel.

Math. vii. BEWARE of false Prophets, which come to you in sheep's clothing, but inwardly they are ravening wolves. Ye shall know them by their fruits. Do men gather grapes of thorns? Or figs of thistles? Even so every good tree bringeth forth good fruits. But a corrupt tree bringeth forth evil fruits. A good tree cannot bring forth bad fruits, neither can a bad tree bring forth good fruits. Every tree that bringeth not forth good fruit, is hewn down and cast into the fire. Wherefore by their fruits ye shall know them. Not every one that saith unto me Lord, Lord, shall enter into the kingdom of heaven: but he that doth the will of my Father which is in heaven, he shall enter into the kingdom of heaven.

The .ix. Sunday.

The Collect.

GRANT to us, Lord, we beseech thee, the spirit to think and do always such things as be rightful; that we which cannot be without thee, may by thee be able to live according to thy will. Through Jesu Christ our Lord.

The Epistle.

i. Cor. x. BRETHREN, I would not that ye should be ignorant, how that our fathers were all under the cloud, and all passed through the sea, and were all baptized under Moyses in the cloud, and in the sea, and did all eat of one spiritual meat, and did all drink of one spiritual drink. And they drank of the spiritual Rock that followed them, which Rock was Christ. But in many of them had God no delight. For they were overthrown in the wilderness. These are ensamples to us, that we should not lust after evil things, as they lusted. And that ye should not be worshippers of images, as were some of them, according as it is written: The people sat down to eat and drink, and rose up to play. Neither let us be defiled with fornication, as some of them were defiled with fornication, and fell in one day .xxiii. M. Neither let us tempt Christ, as some of them tempted, and were destroyed of serpents. Neither murmur ye, as some of them murmured, and were destroyed of the destroyer. All these things happened unto them for ensamples: but are written to put us in remembrance, whom the ends of the world are come upon. Wherefore, let him that thinketh he standeth, take heed lest he fall. There hath none other temptation taken you, but such as followed the nature of man. But God is faithful, which shall not suffer you to be tempted above your strength: but shall in the midst of temptation make a way, that ye may be able to bear it.

The Gospel.

JESUS said to his disciples: There was a certain rich man which had Luke xvi. a steward, and the same was accused unto him, that he had wasted his goods. And he called him and said unto him: How is it, that I hear this of thee? Give accounts of thy stewardship, for thou mayest be no longer steward. The steward said within himself: What shall I do? For my master taketh away from me the stewardship. I cannot dig, and to beg I am ashamed. I wot what to do, that when I am put out of the stewardship, they may receive me into their houses. So when he had called all his master's debtors together, he said unto the first: How much owest thou unto my master? And he said: An hundred tons of oil. And he said unto him: Take thy bill, and sit down quickly, and write fifty. Then said he to another: How much owest thou? And he said: An hundred quarters of wheat. He said unto him: Take thy bill, and write fourscore. And the Lord commended the unjust steward, because he had done wisely. For the children of this world are in their nation wiser than the children of light. And I say unto you: Make you friends of the unrighteous Mammon, that when ye shall have need, they may receive you into everlasting habitations.

The tenth Sunday.
The Collect.

LET thy merciful ears, O Lord, be open to the prayers of thy humble servants: and that they may obtain their petitions, make them to ask such things as shall please thee: through Jesus Christ our Lord.

The Epistle.

CONCERNING spiritual things (brethren) I would not have you igno- i. Cor. xii. rant. Ye know that ye were Gentiles, and went your ways unto dumb images, even as ye were led. Wherefore I declare unto you, that no man speaking by the spirit of God, defieth Jesus. Also no man can say, that Jesus is the Lord, but by the Holy Ghost. There are diversities of gifts, yet but one Spirit. And there are differences of administrations, and yet but one Lord. And there are divers manners of operations, and yet but one God, which worketh all in all. The gift of the Spirit is given to every man to edify withal. For to one is given, through the Spirit, the utterance of wisdom: To another is given the utterance of knowledge, by the same Spirit. To another is given faith, by the same Spirit. To another the gift of healing, by the same Spirit. To another power to do miracles. To another to prophecy. To another judgment to discern spirits. To another divers tongues. To another the interpretation of tongues: But these all worketh the self same Spirit, dividing to every man a several gift, even as he will.

The Gospel.

AND when he was come near to Hierusalem, he beheld the city, and Luk. xix. wept on it, saying: If thou hadst known those things, which belong[1]

[[1] Grafton, belongeth.]

unto thy peace, even in this thy day, thou wouldest take heed. But now are they hid from thine eyes: For the days shall come unto thee, that thy enemies shall cast a bank about thee, and compass thee round, and keep thee in on every side, and make thee even with the ground, and the[1] children which are in thee. And they shall not leave in thee one stone upon another, because thou knowest not the time of thy visitation. And he went into the temple, and began to cast out them that sold therein, and them that bought, saying unto them: It is written, my house is the house of prayer; but ye have made it a den of thieves. And he taught daily in the temple.

The .xi. Sunday.

The Collect.

GOD, which declarest thy almighty power, most chiefly in shewing mercy and pity: give unto us abundantly thy grace, that we running to thy promises, may be[2] partakers of thy heavenly treasure: through Jesus Christ our Lord.

The Epistle.

i. Cor. xv.

BRETHREN, as pertaining to the Gospel, which I preached unto you, which ye have also accepted, and in the which ye continue, by the which ye are also saved: I do you to wit after what manner I preached unto you, if ye keep it, except ye have believed in vain. For first of all, I delivered unto you that which I received, how that Christ died for our sins, agreeing to the scriptures: and that he was buried, and that he rose again the third day, according to the scriptures: and that he was seen of Cephas, then of the .xii. After that, he was seen of mo than .v. c. brethren at once, of which many remain unto this day, and many are fallen asleep. After that appeared he to James, then to all the Apostles. And last of all he was seen of me, as of one that was born out of due time. For I am the least of the Apostles, which am not worthy to be called an Apostle, because I have persecuted the congregation of God. But by the grace of God I am that I am: and his grace which is in me, was not in vain. But I laboured more abundantly than they all: yet not I, but the grace of God, which is with me. Therefore, whether it were I or they, so we preached, and so ye have believed.

The Gospel.

Luc. xviii.

CHRIST told this parable unto certain, which trusted in themselves, that they were perfect, and despised other. Two men went up into the temple to pray, the one a Pharisee, and the other a Publican. The Pharisee stood, and prayed thus with himself: God, I thank thee that I am not as other men are, extortioners, unjust, adulterers, or as this publican. I fast twice in the week: I give tithe of all that I possess. And the Publican, standing afar off, would not lift up his eyes to heaven, but smote his breast, saying: God be merciful to me a sinner. I tell you this man

[[1] Grafton, thy.]   [[2] Grafton, be made.]

departed home to his house justified more than the other. For every man that exalteth himself, shall be brought low: and he that humbleth himself shall be exalted.

The .xii. Sunday.

The Collect.

ALMIGHTY and everlasting God, which art always more ready to hear than we to pray: and art wont to give more than either we desire or deserve: Pour down upon us the abundance of thy mercy, forgiving us those things whereof our conscience is afraid, and giving unto us that, that our prayer dare not presume to ask: through Jesus Christ our Lord.

The Epistle.

SUCH trust have we through Christ to Godward, not that we are sufficient of ourselves to think any thing, as of ourselves; but if we be able unto any thing, the same cometh of God, which hath made us able to minister the new Testament, not of the letter, but of the spirit. For the letter killeth, but the spirit giveth life: If the ministration of death through the letters figured in stones was glorious, so that the children of Israel could not behold the face of Moses, for the glory of his countenance (which glory is done away) why shall not the ministration of the spirit be much more glorious? For if the ministration of condemnation be glorious, much more doth the ministration of righteousness exceed in glory. ii. Cor. iii.

The Gospel.

JESUS departed from the coasts of Tyre and Sidon, and came unto the sea of Galile, through the mids of the coasts of the .x. cities. And they brought unto him one that was deaf, and had an impediment in his speech, and they prayed him to put his hand upon him. And when he had taken him aside from the people, he put his fingers into his ears, and did spit, and touched his tongue, and looked up to heaven, and sighed and said unto him: Ephata, that is to say: Be opened. And straightway his ears were opened, and the string of his tongue was loosed, and he spake plain. And he commanded them, that they should tell no man. But the more he forbade them, so much the more a great deal they published, saying: He hath done all things well, he hath made both the deaf to hear, and the dumb to speak. Mark vii.

The .xiii. Sunday.

The Collect.

ALMIGHTY and merciful God, of whose only gift it cometh, that thy faithful people do unto thee true and laudable service: grant, we beseech thee, that we may so run to thy heavenly promises, that we fail not finally to attain the same: Through Jesus Christ our Lord.

The Epistle.

Gala. iii.

To Abraham and his seed were the promises made. He saith not, in his seeds, as many: but in thy seed, as of one, which is Christ. This I say, that the law which began afterward, beyond .iiii. c. xxx. years, doth not disannul the Testament that was confirmed afore of God unto Christward, to make the promise of none effect. For if the inheritance come of the law, it cometh not now of promise. But God gave it to Abraham by promise. Wherefore then serveth the law? The law was added because of transgression (till the seed came, to whom the promise was made) and it was ordained by Angels, in the hand of a mediator. A mediator is not a mediator of one : but God is one. Is the law then against the promise of God? God forbid. For if there had been a law given, which could have given life, then no doubt righteousness should have come by the law. But the scripture concludeth all things under sin, that the promise by the faith of Jesus Christ should be given to them that believe.

The Gospel.

Luk. x.

Happy are the eyes which see the things that ye see. For I tell you, that many Prophets and Kings have desired to see those things which ye see, and have not seen them; and to hear those things which ye hear, and have not heard them. And behold, a certain lawyer stood up, and tempted him, saying: Master, what shall I do to inherit eternal life? He said unto him: What is written in the law? How readest thou? And he answered and said: Love the Lord thy God with all thy heart, and with all thy soul, and with all thy strength, and with all thy mind: and thy neighbour as thyself. And he said unto him: Thou hast answered right. This do, and thou shalt live. But he, willing to justify himself, said unto Jesus: And who is my neighbour? Jesus answered, and said: A certain man descended from Ierusalem to Hiericho, and fell among thieves, which robbed him of his raiment, and wounded him, and departed, leaving him half dead. And it chanced that there came down a certain Priest that same way, and when he saw him, he passed by. And likewise a Levite, when he went nigh to the place, came and looked on him, and passed by. But a certain Samaritan, as he journeyed, came unto him: and when he saw him, he had compassion on him, and went to and bound up his wounds, and poured in oil and wine, and set him on his own beast, and brought him to a common inn, and made provision for him. And on the morrow, when he departed, he took out two pence, and gave them to the host, and said unto him: Take cure of him, and whatsoever thou spendest more, when I come again, I will recompense thee. Which now of these three thinkest thou, was neighbour unto him, that fell among the thieves? And he said unto him: He that shewed mercy on him. Then said Jesus to him: Go and do thou likewise.

1559.] THE FOURTEENTH SUNDAY AFTER TRINITY. 151

The .xiiii. Sunday.

The Collect.

ALMIGHTY and everlasting God, give unto us the increase of faith, hope and charity, and that we may obtain that which thou dost promise, make us to love that which thou dost command, through Jesus[1] Christ our Lord.

The Epistle.

I SAY, walk in the spirit, and fulfil not the lust of the flesh. For the flesh lusteth contrary to the spirit, and the spirit contrary to the flesh. These are contrary one to an[2] other, so that ye can not do whatsoever ye would. But and if ye be led of the Spirit, then are ye not under the law. The deeds of the flesh are manifest, which are these: adultery, fornication, uncleanness, wantonness, worshipping of Images, witchcraft, hatred, variance, zeal, wrath, strife, seditions, sects, envying, murder, drunkenness, gluttony, and such like. Of the which I tell you before, as I have told you in times past, that they which commit such things, shall not be inheritors of the kingdom of God. Contrarily, the fruit of the Spirit is love, joy, peace, longsuffering, gentleness, goodness, faithfulness, meekness, temperance. Against such there is no law. They truly that are Christ's, have crucified the flesh with the affections and lusts. *Gala. v.*

The Gospel.

AND it chanced, as Jesus went to Ierusalem, that he passed through Samaria and Galile. And as he entered into a certain town, there met him ten men that were lepers, which stood afar off, and put forth their voices, and said: Jesus Master, have mercy upon us. When he saw them, he said unto them: Go shew yourselves unto the Priests. And it came to pass that as they went, they were cleansed. And one of them, when he saw that he was cleansed, turned back again, and with a loud voice praised God, and fell down on his face at his feet, and gave him thanks. And the same was a Samaritan. And Jesus answered, and said: Are there not ten cleansed? but where are those nine? There are not found that returned again to give God praise, save only this stranger. And he said unto him: Arise, go thy way, thy faith hath made thee whole. *Luk. xvii.*

The .xv. Sunday.

The Collect.

KEEP we beseech thee, O Lord, the[3] Church with thy perpetual mercy: and because the frailty of man, without thee, cannot but fall; keep us ever by thy help, and lead us to all things profitable to our salvation, through Jesus Christ our Lord. Amen[4].

[1 Grafton, Jesu.]   [2 Grafton, the.]
[3 Grafton, thy.]   [4 Amen, not in 1596.]

The Epistle.

Gala. vi.

YE see how large a letter I have written to you with mine own hand. As many as desire with outward appearance to please carnally, the same constrain you to be circumcised, only lest they should suffer persecution for the cross of Christ. For they themselves which are circumcised, keep not the law, but desire to have you circumcised, that they might rejoice in your flesh. God forbid that I should rejoice, but in the Cross of our Lord Jesu Christ, whereby the world is crucified unto me, and I unto the world. For in Christ Jesu, neither circumcision availeth any thing at all, nor uncircumcision: but a new creature. And as many as walk according unto this rule, peace be on them, and mercy, and upon Israel that pertaineth to God. From henceforth, let no man put me to business: for I bear in my body the marks of the Lord Jesu. Brethren, the grace of our Lord Jesu Christ be with your spirit. Amen.

The Gospel.

Math. vi.

No man can serve two Masters: for either he shall hate the one, and love the other, or else lean to the one, and despise the other: ye cannot serve God and Mammon. Therefore I say unto you: be not careful for your life, what ye shall eat, or drink; or[1] yet for your body, what raiment you[2] shall put on. Is not the life more worth than meat? and the body more of value than raiment? Behold the fowls of the air; for they sow not, neither do they reap, nor carry into the barns: and your heavenly Father feedeth them. Are ye not much better than they? Which of you (by taking careful thought) can add one cubit unto his stature? And why care ye for raiment? Consider the lilies of the field, how they grow: They labour not, neither do they spin. And yet I say unto you, that even Salomon in all his royalty was not clothed like one of these. Wherefore, if GOD so clothe the grass of the field (which though it stand to day, is to morrow cast into the furnace) shall he not much more do the same for you, O ye of little faith? Therefore take no thought, saying: What shall we eat, or what shall we drink, or wherewith shall we be clothed? After all these things do the Gentiles seek. For your heavenly Father knoweth that ye have need of all these things. But rather seek ye first the kingdom of GOD, and the righteousness thereof, and all these things shall be ministered unto you. Care not then for to[3] morrow, for to morrow day shall care for itself: sufficient unto the day is the travail thereof.

The .xvi. Sunday.

The Collect.

LORD, we beseech thee, let thy continual pity cleanse and defend thy congregation: and because it can not continue in safety without thy succour, preserve it evermore by thy help and goodness: through Jesus Christ our Lord.

[1 Grafton, nor.]   [2 Grafton, ye.]   [3 Grafton, the.]

The Epistle.

I DESIRE that you faint not, because of my tribulations that I suffer for your sakes, which is your praise. For this cause I bow my knees unto the Father of our Lord Jesus Christ, which is Father of all, that is called Father in heaven and in earth, that he would grant you according to the riches of his glory, that ye may be strengthed with might by his Spirit in the inner man, that Christ may dwell in your hearts by faith, that ye being rooted and grounded in love, might be able to comprehend with all saints, what is the breadth, length, depth, and height, and to know the excellent love of the knowledge of Christ, that ye might be fulfilled with all fulness, which cometh of God. Unto him that is able to do exceeding abundantly, above all that we ask, or think, according to the power that worketh in us, be praise in the congregation by Christ Jesus, throughout all generations from time to time. Amen. *Ephe. iii.*

The Gospel.

AND it fortuned that Jesus went into a city called Naim, and many of his disciples went with him, and much people. When he came nigh to the gate of the city, behold, there was a dead man carried out, which was the only son of his mother, and she was a widow; and much people of the city was with her. And when the Lord saw her, he had compassion on her, and said unto her: Weep not. And he came nigh, and touched the coffin, and they that bare him stood still. And he said: Young man, I say unto thee, arise. And he that was dead, sat up, and began to speak. And he delivered him to his mother. And there came a fear on them all. And they gave the glory unto God, saying: A great Prophet is risen up among us, and God hath visited his people. And this rumour of him went forth throughout all Jewry, and throughout all the regions, which lie round about. *Luke vii.*

The .xvii. Sunday.

The Collect.

LORD, we pray thee that thy grace may always prevent and follow us, and make us continually to be given to all good works: through Jesu Christ our Lord.

The Epistle.

I (which am a prisoner of the Lord's) exhort you, that ye walk worthy of the vocation wherewith ye are called, with all lowliness and meekness, with humbleness of mind, forbearing one another, through love, and be diligent to keep the unity of the spirit, through the bond of peace, being one body, and one spirit, even as ye are called in one hope of your calling. Let there be but one Lord, one faith, one baptism, one God and Father of all, which is above all, and through all, and in you all. *Ephe. iv.*

154 THE SEVENTEENTH SUNDAY AFTER TRINITY. [1559.

The Gospel.

Luk. xiv. IT chanced that Jesus went into the house of one of the chief Pharisees to eat bread on the sabboth day, and they watched him. And behold, there was a certain man before him, which had the dropsy. And Jesus answered and spake unto the Lawyers and Pharisees, saying: Is it lawful to heal on the sabboth day? And they held their peace. And he took him, and healed him, and let him go: and answered them, saying: Which of you shall have an ass or an ox fallen into a pit, and will not straightway pull him out on the sabboth day? And they could not answer him again to these things. He put forth also a similitude to the guests, when he marked how they pressed to be in the highest rooms, and said unto them: When thou art bidden to a wedding of any man: sit not down in the highest room, lest a more honourable man than thou be bidden of him, and he (that bade him and thee) come and say to thee: Give this man room, and thou begin with shame to take the lowest room. But rather when thou art bidden, go and sit in the lowest room, that when he that bade thee cometh, he may say unto thee, Friend, sit up higher. Then shalt thou have worship in the presence of them that sit at meat with thee. For whosoever exalteth himself shall be brought low, and he that humbleth himself shall be exalted.

The .xviii. Sunday.

The Collect.

LORD, we beseech thee, grant thy people grace to avoid the infections of the devil, and with pure heart and mind to follow thee, the only God: through Jesus Christ our Lord.

The Epistle.

i. Cor. i.[1] I THANK my God always on your behalf, for the grace of God, which is given you by Jesus Christ, that in all things ye are made rich by him, in all utterance, and in all knowledge: by the which things the testimony of Jesus Christ was confirmed in you: so that ye are behind in no gift, waiting for the appearing of our Lord Jesus Christ, which shall also strength you to the end, that you may be blameless in the day of the coming of our Lord Jesus Christ.

The Gospel.

Mat. xxi.[2] WHEN the Pharisees had heard that Jesus did put the Sadducees to silence, they came together: and one of them (which was a Doctor of Law) asked him a question, tempting him, and saying: Master, which is the greatest commandment in the Law? Jesus said unto him: Thou shalt love the Lord thy God, with all thy heart, and with all thy soul, and with all thy mind. This is the first and greatest commandment. And the second is like unto it: Thou shalt love thy neighbour as thyself. In these two commandments hang all the law, and the Pro-

[[1] Grafton omits the reference.] [[2] Misprint for, xxii.]

phets. While the Pharisees were gathered together, Jesus asked them, saying: What think ye of Christ? Whose son is he? They said unto him: The son of David. He said unto them: How then doth David in spirit call him Lord, saying: The Lord said unto my Lord, sit thou on my right hand, till I make thine enemies thy footstool? If David then call him Lord, how is he then his son? And no man was able to answer him any thing, neither durst any man (from that day forth) ask him any mo questions.

The .xix. Sunday.

The Collect.

O GOD, forasmuch as without thee we are not able to please thee: Grant that the working of thy mercy may in all things direct and rule our hearts: through Jesus Christ our Lord.

The Epistle.

THIS I say, and testify through the Lord, that ye henceforth walk Ephe. iv. not as other Gentiles walk, in vanity of their mind, while they are blinded in their understanding, being far from a Godly life, by the means of the ignorance that is in them, and because of the blindness of their hearts, which, being past repentance, have given themselves over unto wantonness, to work all manner of uncleanness even with greediness. But ye have not so learned Christ: if so be that ye have heard of him, and have been taught in him, as the truth is in Jesu (as concerning the conversation in times past) to lay from you the old man, which is corrupt, according to the deceivable lusts; to be renewed also in the spirit of your mind, and to put on that new man, which after God is shapen in righteousness, and true holiness. Wherefore put away lying, and speak every man truth unto his neighbour, forasmuch as we are members one of another. Be angry, and sin not. Let not the sun go down upon your wrath, neither give place to the backbiter. Let him that stole, steal no more, but let him rather labour with his hands the thing, which is good, that he may give him[3] that needeth. Let not[4] filthy communication proceed out of your mouth; but that which is good, to edify withal, as oft as need is, that it may minister grace unto the hearers. And grieve not the Holy Spirit of God, by whom ye are sealed unto the day of redemption. Let all bitterness, and fierceness, and wrath, and roaring, and cursed speaking, be put away from you, with all maliciousness. Be ye courteous one to another, merciful, forgiving one another, even as God for Christ's sake hath forgiven you.

The Gospel.

JESUS entered into a ship, and passed over, and came into his own Math. ix. city: And behold, they brought to him a man sick of the palsy, lying in a bed. And when Jesus saw the faith of them, he said to the sick of

[3 Grafton, vnto him.]   [4 Grafton, no.]

the palsy: Son, be of good cheer, thy sins be forgiven thee. And behold, certain of the Scribes said within themselves: This man blasphemeth. And when Jesus saw their thoughts, he said: Wherefore think ye evil in your hearts? Whether is it easier to say, thy sins be forgiven thee, or to say, arise, and walk? But that ye may know, that the son of man hath power to forgive sins in earth; then saith he to the sick of the palsy: Arise, take up thy bed, and go unto thine house. And he arose, and departed to his house. But the people that saw it marvelled, and glorified God, which had given such power unto men.

The .xx. Sunday.

The Collect.

ALMIGHTY and merciful God, of thy bountiful goodness keep us from all things that may hurt us: that we being ready both in body and soul, may with free hearts accomplish those things that thou wouldest have done: Through Jesus Christ our Lord.

The Epistle.

Ephe. v.

TAKE heed therefore, how ye walk circumspectly, not as unwise, but as wise men, redeeming the time, because the days are evil: wherefore be[1] ye not unwise, but understand what the will of the Lord is, and be not drunken with wine, wherein is excess. But be filled with the spirit, speaking unto yourselves in psalms, and hymns, and spiritual songs, singing and making melody to the Lord in your hearts, giving thanks always for all things unto God the Father, in the name of our Lord Jesus Christ: submitting yourselves one to another in the fear of God.

The Gospel.

Math. xx.[2]

JESUS said to his disciples: The kingdom of heaven is like unto a man that was a king, which made a marriage for his son, and sent forth his servants, to call them that were bidden to the wedding, and they would not come. Again he sent forth other servants, saying: Tell them which are bidden, Behold, I have prepared my dinner, mine oxen and my fatlings are killed, and all things are ready, come unto the marriage. But they made light of it, and went their ways, one to his farm place, another to his merchandise, and the remnant took his servants, and entreated them shamefully, and slew them. But when the king heard thereof, he was wroth, and sent forth his men of war, and destroyed those murtherers, and brent up their city. Then said he to his servants, The marriage indeed is prepared, but they which were bidden were not worthy. Go ye therefore out into the highways, and as many as ye find, bid them to the marriage. And the servants went forth into the highways, and gathered together all, as many as they could find, both good, and bad, and the wedding was furnished with guests. Then the king came in, to see the guests, and when he spied there a man which had not

[1 Grafton, be not.]   [2 Misprint for, xxii.]

on a wedding garment, he said unto him, Friend, how camest thou in hither, not having a wedding garment? And he was even speechless. Then said the king to the ministers: Take and bind him hand and foot, and cast him into utter[3] darkness; there shall be weeping, and gnashing of teeth. For many be called, but few are chosen.

The .xxi. Sunday.

The Collect.

GRANT, we beseech thee, merciful Lord, to thy faithful people pardon and peace, that they may be cleansed from all their sins, and serve thee with a quiet mind, Through Jesus Christ our Lord.

The Epistle.

My brethren, be strong through the Lord, and through the power of Ephe. vi. his might. Put on all the armour of God, that ye may stand against all the assaults of the devil: for we wrestle not against blood, and flesh, but against rule, against power, against worldly rulers, even governors of the darkness of this world, against spiritual craftiness in heavenly things. Wherefore take unto you the whole armour of God, that ye may be able to resist in the evil day, and stand perfect in all things. Stand therefore, and your loins gird with the truth, having on the breastplate of righteousness, and having shoes on your feet, that ye may be prepared for the gospel of peace. Above all, take to you the shield of faith, wherewith ye may quench all the fiery darts of the wicked. And take the helmet of salvation, and the sword of the Spirit, which is the word of God. And pray always with all manner of prayer, and supplication in the Spirit, and watch thereunto with all instance and supplication, for all saints: and for me, that utterance may be given unto me, that I may open my mouth freely, to utter the secrets of my gospel, (whereof I am a messenger in bonds,) that therein I may speak freely, as I ought to speak.

The Gospel.

THERE was a certain ruler, whose son was sick at[4] Capernaum. As John iv. soon as the same heard that Jesus was come out of Jewry into Galile, he went unto him, and besought him, that he would come down and heal his son. For he was even at the point of death. Then said Jesus unto him: Except ye see signs, and wonders, ye will not believe. The ruler said unto him: Sir, come down, or ever that my son die. Jesus saith unto him: Go thy way, thy son liveth. The man believed the word that Jesus had spoken unto him. And he went his way. And as he was going down, the servants met him, and told him, saying: Thy son liveth. Then inquired he of them the hour when he began to amend. And they said unto him: Yesterday at the seventh hour the fever left him. So the father knew that it was the same hour, in the which Jesus said unto

[3 Grafton, outter.]   [4 Grafton, in.]

158 THE TWENTY-SECOND SUNDAY AFTER TRINITY. [1559.

him, Thy son liveth, and he believed, and all his household. This is again the second miracle that Jesus did, when he was come out of Jewry into Galile.

The .xxii. Sunday.

The Collect.

LORD, we beseech thee to keep thy household, the church, in continual godliness: that through thy protection it may be free from all adversities, and devoutly given to serve thee in good works, to the glory of thy name. Through Jesus Christ our Lord[1].

The Epistle.

Philip. i.

I THANK my God with all remembrance of you, always in all my prayers for you, and pray with gladness: Because ye are come into the fellowship of the gospel, from the first day until now. And am surely certified of this, that he which hath begun a good work in you, shall perform it until the day of Jesus Christ: as it becometh me, that I should so judge of you all, because I have you in my heart, forasmuch as ye are all companions of grace with me, even in my bonds, and in the defending and establishing[2] of the gospel. For God is my record, how greatly I long after you all, from the very heart root in Jesus Christ. And this I pray, that your love may increase yet more and more in knowledge, and in all understanding, that ye may accept the things that are most excellent, that ye may be pure, and such as offend no man, until the day of Christ, being filled with the fruit of righteousness, which cometh by Jesus Christ, unto the glory, and praise of God.

The Gospel.

Math. xviii.

PETER said unto Jesus: Lord, how oft shall I forgive my brother, if he sin against me? till seven times? Jesus said[3] unto him: I say not unto thee, until seven times: but seventy times seven times. Therefore is the kingdom of heaven likened unto a certain man, that was a king, which would take accounts of his servants. And when he had begun to reckon, one was brought unto him, which ought[4] him ιx.M. talents; but forasmuch as he was not able to pay, his Lord commanded him to be sold, and his wife and children, and all that he had, and payment to be made. The servant fell down, and besought him, saying: Sir, have patience with me, and I will pay thee all. Then had the Lord pity on that servant, and loosed him, and forgave him the debt. So the same servant went out, and found one of his fellows, which ought him an hundred pence, and he laid hands on him, and took him by the throat, saying: Pay that thou owest. And his fellow fell down, and besought him, saying: Have patience with me, and I will pay thee all. And he would not, but went and cast him into prison, till he should pay the debt. So when his fel-

[1 Grafton, Amen.] [2 Grafton, stablishing.]
[3 Grafton, saythe.] [4 Grafton, owed.]

lows saw what was done, they were very sorry, and came and told unto their lord all that had happened. Then his lord called him, and said unto him: O thou ungracious servant, I forgave thee all that debt, when thou desiredst me: shouldest not thou also have had compassion on thy fellow, even as I had pity on thee? And his Lord was wroth, and delivered him to the jailors, till he should pay all that was due unto him. So likewise shall my heavenly Father do also unto you, if ye from your hearts forgive not (every one his brother) their trespasses.

The .xxiii. Sunday.

The Collect.

GOD our refuge and strength, which art the author of all Godliness, be ready to hear the devout prayers of the[5] Church: and grant that those things which we ask faithfully, we may obtain effectually: Through Jesu[6] Christ our Lord[7].

The Epistle.

BRETHREN, be followers together of me, and look on them which walk even so, as ye have us for an ensample[8]. For many walk (of whom I have told you often, and now tell you weeping) that they are the enemies of the Cross of Christ; whose end is damnation, whose belly is their god, and glory to their shame, which are worldly minded. But our conversation is in heaven, from whence we look for the Saviour, even the Lord Jesus Christ, which shall change our vile body, that he may make it like unto his glorious body, according to the working, whereby he is able also to subdue all things unto himself.

Philip. iii.

The Gospel.

THEN the Pharisees went out, and took counsel, how they might tangle him in his words. And they sent out unto him their disciples, with Herod's servants, saying: Master, we know that thou art true, and teachest the way of God truly, neither carest thou for any man: for thou regardest not the outward appearance of men. Tell us therefore, how thinkest thou? Is it lawful that tribute be given unto Cæsar or not? But Jesus perceiving their wickedness, said: Why tempt ye me, ye hypocrites? shew me the tribute money. And they took him a penny. And he said unto them: Whose is this image and superscription? They said unto him, Cesar's. Then said he unto them: Give therefore unto Ceasar, the things which are Ceasar's: and unto God those things, which are God's. When they heard these words, they marvelled, and left him, and went their way.

Mat. xxii.

[5 Grafton, thy.]
[7 Grafton, Amen.]
[6 1596, Jesus.]
[8 Grafton, example.]

The .xxiv. Sunday.

The Collect.

LORD, we beseech thee, assoil[1] thy people from their offences: that through thy bountiful goodness, we may be delivered from the bands of all those sins, which by our frailty we have committed: Grant this. &c.[2]

The Epistle.

Collos. i.

WE give thanks to God, the Father of our Lord Jesus Christ, always for you in our prayers: for we have heard of your faith in Christ Jesu, and of the love, which ye bear to all saints, for the hope's sake which is laid up in store for you in heaven: of which hope ye heard before, by the true word of the Gospel, which is come unto you even as it is, fruitful, and groweth as it is also among you, from the day in the which ye heard of it, and had experience in the grace of God through the truth; as ye learned of Epaphras, our dear fellow servant, which is for you a faithful minister of Christ; which also declared unto us your love, which ye have in the spirit. For this cause we also, ever since the day we heard of it, have not ceased to pray for you, and to desire that ye might be fulfilled with the knowledge of his will, in all wisdom and spiritual understanding, that ye might walk worthy of the Lord, that in all things ye may please, being fruitful in all good works, and increasing in the knowledge of God, strengthed with all might, through his glorious power, unto all patience and long suffering, with joyfulness, giving thanks unto the Father, which hath made us meet to be partakers of the inheritance of saints in light.

The Gospel.

Math. ix.

WHILE[3] Jesus spake unto the people: behold, there came a certain ruler, and worshipped him, saying: My daughter is even now deceased, but come and lay thy hand upon her, and she shall live. And Jesus arose, and followed him, and so did his disciples. And behold, a woman which was diseased with an issue of blood twelve years, came behind him, and touched the hem of his vesture: for she said within herself: If I may touch but even his vesture only, I shall be safe. But Jesus turned him about, and when he saw her, he said: Daughter, be of good comfort, thy faith hath made thee safe. And the woman was made whole, even the same time. And when Jesus came into the ruler's house, and saw the minstrels, and people making a noise, he said unto them: Get you hence, for the maid is not dead but sleepeth. And they laughed him to scorn. But when the people were put forth, he went in, and took her by the hand, and said: Damsel, arise. And the damsel arose. And this noise was abroad in all that land.

[1 Assoil: absolve.]   [2 Grafton, Amen.]
[3 Grafton, Whilest.]

1559.] THE TWENTY-FIFTH SUNDAY AFTER TRINITY.

The .xxv. Sunday.

The Collect.

STIR up, we beseech thee, O Lord, the wills of thy faithful people: that they plenteously bringing forth the fruit of good works, may of thee be plenteously rewarded: through Jesus Christ our Lord[4].

The Epistle.

BEHOLD, the time cometh, saith the Lord, that I will raise up the righteous branch he[5] David, which King shall bear rule, and of[6] shall prosper with wisdom, and shall set up equity and righteousness again in earth. In his time shall Juda be saved, and Israel shall dwell without fear: And this is the name, that they shall call him, even the Lord our Righteousness. And therefore behold, the time cometh, saith the Lord, that it shall be no more said, The Lord liveth, which brought the children of Israel out of the land of Egypt: but, The Lord liveth, which brought forth, and led the seed of the house of Israel out of the North land, and from all countries where I have scattered them: and they shall dwell in their own land again.

The Gospel.

WHEN Jesus lift up his eyes, and saw a great company come unto him: he saith unto Philip, Whence shall we buy bread, that these may eat? This he said to prove him, for he himself knew what he would do. Philip answered him: Two .c. penny worth of bread are not sufficient for them, that every man may take a little. One of his Disciples (Andrew Simon Peter's brother) said unto him: There is a lad here, which hath five barley loaves, and two fishes: but what are they among so many? And Jesus said: Make the people sit down. There was much grass in the place. So the men sat down, in number about five thousand. And Jesus took the bread, and when he had given thanks, he gave to the disciples, and the disciples to them that were set down. And likewise of the fishes, as much as they would. When they had eaten enough, he saith unto his disciples: Gather up the broken meat which remaineth, that nothing be lost. And they gathered it together, and filled .xii. baskets with the broken meat of the five barley loaves, which broken meat remained unto them that had eaten. Then those men (when they had seen the miracle that Jesus did) said: This is of a truth the same Prophet that should come into the world. John vi.

¶ If there be any mo Sundays before Advent Sunday, to supply the same shall be taken the[7] service of some of those Sundays, that were omitted between the Epiphany and Septuagesima.

[4 Grafton and 1596, Amen.]
[5 The reference is omitted. Grafton, Jer. xxiii.]
[6 These words have been transposed.]
[7 1578, the Collect, Epistle and Gospel.]

Saint Andrew's day.

The Collect.

ALMIGHTY God, which didst give such grace unto thy holy apostle saint Andrew, that he readily obeyed the calling of thy Son Jesus Christ, and followed him without delay: Grant unto us all, that we being called by thy holy word, may forthwith give over our selves, obediently to follow thy holy commandments: through the same Jesus Christ our Lord[1].

The Epistle.

Rom. x.

IF thou knowledge with thy mouth, that Jesus is the Lord, and believe in thy heart that God raised him up from death, thou shalt be safe. For to believe with the heart justifieth, and to knowledge with the mouth maketh a man safe. For the Scripture saith: Whosoever believeth on him, shall not be confounded. There is no difference between the Jew and the Gentile. For one is Lord of all, which is rich unto all that call upon him. For whosoever doth call on the name of the Lord, shall be safe. How then shall they call on him, on whom they have not believed? How shall they believe on him, on whom they have not heard? How shall they hear without a preacher? And how shall they preach, without they be sent? As it is written: How beautiful are the feet of them, which bring tidings of peace, and bring tidings of good things. But they have not all obeyed to the gospel. For Esay saith: Lord, who hath believed our sayings? So then faith cometh by hearing, and hearing cometh by the word of God. But I ask, have they not heard? No doubt their sound went out into all lands, and their words into the ends of the world. But I demand, whether Israel did know or not? First Moses saith, I will provoke you to envy by them that are no people, by a foolish nation I will anger you. Esay after that is bold, and saith: I am found of them that sought me not: I am manifest unto them that asked not after me. But against Israel he saith: All day long have I stretched forth my hands unto a people that believeth not, but speaketh against me.

The Gospel.

Math. iv.

As Jesus walked by the sea of Galile, he saw two brethren, Simon, which was[2] called Peter, and Andrew his brother, casting a net into the sea, (for they were fishers) and he saith unto them: Follow me, and I will make you to become fishers of men. And they straightway left their nets, and followed him. And when he was gone forth from thence, he saw other two brethren, James the son of Zebede, and John his brother, in the ship, with Zebede their father, mending their nets, and he called them, and they immediately left the ship, and their father, and followed him.

[1 Grafton, Amen.]   [2 Grafton, is.]

¶ Saint Thomas the Apostle.

The Collect.

ALMIGHTY everliving[3] God, which for the more confirmation of the faith, didst suffer thy holy Apostle Thomas to be doubtful in thy Son's resurrection: grant us so perfectly, and without all doubt to believe in thy Son Jesus Christ, that our faith in thy sight never[4] be reproved: hear us, O Lord, through the same Jesus Christ: to whom with thee and the Holy Ghost be all honour. &c.

The Epistle.

Now are ye not strangers, nor foreigners, but citizens with the saints, Ephe. ii. and of the household of God: and are built upon the foundation of the Apostles, and Prophets, Jesus Christ himself being the head corner stone: in whom what building soever is coupled together, it groweth unto an holy temple of the Lord: in whom also ye are built together, to be an habitation of God through the Holy Ghost.

The Gospel.

THOMAS one of the twelve, which is[5] called Didimus, was not with John xx. them, when Jesus came. The other disciples therefore said unto him: We have seen the Lord. But he said unto them: Except I see in his hands the print of the nails, and put my finger into the print of the nails, and thrust my hand into his side, I will not believe. And after eight days, again his disciples were within, and Thomas with them. Then came Jesus, when the doors were shut, and stood in the midst, and said: Peace be unto you. And after that he said to Thomas: Bring thy finger hither, and see my hands, and reach hither thy hand, and thrust it into my side, and be not faithless, but believing. Thomas answered, and said unto him: My Lord, and my God. Jesus said unto him: Thomas, because thou hast seen me, thou hast believed: blessed are they that have not seen, and yet have believed. And many other signs truly did Jesus, in the presence of his disciples, which are not written in this book. These are written, that ye might believe that Jesus Christ is the Son of God, and that (in believing) ye might have life through his name.

The Conversion of Saint Paul.

The Collect.

GOD, which hast taught all the world through the preaching of thy blessed Apostle saint Paul: grant we beseech thee, that we which have his wonderful conversion in remembrance, may follow and fulfil thy holy doctrine that he taught: through Jesu Christ our Lord[6].

[3 1596, & euerliuing.]   [4 1596, may neuer.]
[5 Grafton, was.]   [6 Grafton, Amen.]

The Epistle.

Acts ix.[1]

AND Saul yet breathing out threatenings and slaughter against the Disciples of the Lord, went unto the high Priest, and desired of him letters, to carry to Damasco to the Synagogues: that if he found any of this way (were they men, or women,) he might bring them bound to Jerusalem. And when he journeyed, it fortuned that as he was come nigh to Damasco, suddenly there shined round about him a light from heaven, and he fell to the earth, and heard a voice, saying to him: Saul, Saul, why persecutest thou me? And he said: What art thou Lord? And the Lord said: I am Jesus whom thou persecutest: It is hard for thee to kick against the prick. And he, both trembling and astonied, said: LORD, what wilt thou have me to do? And the Lord said unto him: Arise, and go into the city, and it shall be told thee what thou must do. The men which journeyed with him, stood amazed, hearing a voice, but seeing no man. And Saul arose from the earth, and when he opened his eyes, he saw no man. But they led him by the hand, and brought him into Damasco. And he was .iii. days without sight, and neither did eat nor drink. And there was a certain disciple at Damasco, named Ananias, and to him said the Lord in a vision: Ananias: and he said: Behold, I am here, Lord. And the Lord said unto him: Arise, and go into the street (which is called straight) and seek in the house of Judas, after one called Saul of Tharsus. For behold, he prayeth, and hath seen in a vision a man named Ananias, coming in to him, and putting his hands on him, that he might receive his right. Then Ananias answered: Lord, I have heard by many of this man, how much evil he hath done to thy saints at Jerusalem. And here he hath authority of the high priests, to bind all that call on thy name. The Lord said unto him: Go thy way, for he is a chosen vessel unto me, to bear my name before the Gentiles, and kings, and the children of Israel. For I will shew him how great things he must suffer for my name's sake. And Ananias went his way, and entered into the house, and put his hands on him, and said: Brother Saul, the Lord that appeared unto thee in the way as thou camest, hath sent me, that thou mightest receive thy sight, and be filled with the Holy Ghost. And immediately there fell from his eyes, as it had been scales, and he received sight, and arose, and was baptized, and received meat, and was comforted. Then was Saul a certain days with the disciples, which were at Damasco. And straightway he preached Christ in the Synagogues, how that he was the Son of God. But all that heard him were amazed, and said, Is not this he that spoiled them which called on this name in Jerusalem, and came hither for that intent, that he might bring them bound unto the high priests? But Saul increased the more in strength, and confounded the Jews which dwelt at Damasco, affirming that this was very Christ.

The Gospel.

Math. xix.

PETER answered, and said unto Jesus: Behold we have forsaken all,

[1 Grafton, i. A misprint.]

and followed thee, what shall we have therefore? Jesus said unto them: Verily I say unto you, that when the Son of man shall sit in the seat of his majesty, ye that have followed me in the regeneration, shall sit also upon twelve[2] seats, and judge the twelve Tribes of Israel. And every one that forsaketh house, or brethren, or sisters, or father, or mother, or wife, or children, or lands, for my name's sake, shall receive an hundred fold, and shall inherit everlasting life: but many that are first shall be last, and the last shall be first.

¶ The Purification of saint Mary the Virgin.

The Collect.

ALMIGHTY and everlasting God, we humbly beseech thy Majesty, that as thy only begotten Son was this day presented in the Temple in substance of our flesh: so grant that we may be presented unto thee with pure and clear minds. By Jesus Christ our Lord.

The Epistle.

¶ The [3]same that is appointed for the Sunday.

The Gospel.

WHEN the time of their Purification (after the law of Moses) was Luke ii. come, they brought him to Jerusalem, to present him to the Lord (as it is written in the law of the Lord: Every man child that first openeth the matrix, shall be called holy to the Lord,) and to offer (as it is said in the law of the Lord) a pair of turtle doves, or two young pigeons. And behold, there was a man in Jerusalem, whose name was Symeon. And the same man was just and godly, and looked for the consolation of Israel, and the Holy Ghost was in him. And an answer had he received of the Holy Ghost, that he should not see death, except he first saw the Lord Christ. And he came by inspiration into the temple.

¶ S. Mathie's day.

The Collect.

ALMIGHTY God, which in the place of the traitor Judas didst choose thy faithful servant Mathie to be of the number of thy twelve Apostles: Grant that thy church being alway preserved from false Apostles, may be ordered and guided by faithful and true pastors: Through Jesus Christ our Lord.

The Epistle.

IN those days Peter stood up, in the mids of the Disciples and said: Acts i. the number of names that were together, were about an .c.xx. Ye men and brethren, this scripture must needs have been fulfilled, which the

[2 Grafton, the twelve.]
[3 1578, The same Epistle appoynted ye Sunday before.]

Holy Ghost, through the mouth of David, spake before of Judas, which was guide to them that took Jesus. For he was numbered with us, and had obtained fellowship in[1] his administration. And the same hath now possessed a plat of ground with the reward of iniquity, and when he was hanged, burst asunder[2] in the midst, and all his bowels gushed out. And it was known unto all the inhabiters of Jerusalem: insomuch that the same field is called in their mother tongue Acheldama, that is to say, the bloody field. For it is written in the book of Psalms: His habitation be void, and no man be dwelling therein, and his Bishoprick let another take. Wherefore, of these men, which have companied with us (all the time that the Lord Jesus had all his conversation among us, beginning at the baptism of John, unto that same day, that he was taken up from us) must one be ordained, to be a witness with us of his resurrection. And they appointed two, Joseph which is called Barsabas (whose sirename was Justus) and Mathias. And when they prayed, they said: Thou, Lord, which knowest the hearts of all men, shew whether of these two thou hast chosen, that he may take the room of this ministration and Apostleship, from which Judas by transgression fell, that he might go to his own place. And they gave forth their lots, and the lot fell on Mathias, and he was counted with the eleven Apostles.

The Gospel.

Math. xi.[3]

IN that time Jesus answered and said: I thank thee (O Father) Lord of heaven and earth, because thou hast hid these things from the wise and prudent, and hast shewed them unto babes: verily, Father, even so was it thy good pleasure. All things are given unto me of my Father. And no man knoweth the Son, but the Father: neither knoweth any man the Father, save the Son, and he to whomsoever the Son will open him. Come unto me all ye that labour and are laden, and I will ease you. Take my yoke upon you, and learn of me, for I am meek and lowly in heart, and ye shall find rest unto your souls: for my yoke is easy, and my burden is light.

The[4] Annunciation of the Virgin Mary.

The Collect.

WE beseech thee Lord, pour thy grace into our hearts, that, as we have known Christ thy Son's incarnation, by the message of an angel, so by his cross and passion, we may be brought unto the glory of his resurrection: through the same Christ our Lord.

The Epistle.

Esai. vii.

GOD spake once again unto Ahaz, saying: Require a token of the Lord thy God, whether it be toward the depth beneath, or toward the height above. Then said Ahaz: I will require none, neither will I tempt the

[[1] Grafton, in this ministracion.]   [[2] Grafton, in sonder.]
[[3] Grafton, ix. A misprint.]   [[4] The, not in 1596.]

Lord. And he said: Hearken to, ye of the house of David: is it not enough for you, that ye be grievous unto men, but ye must grieve my God also? And therefore the Lord shall give you a token: behold, a Virgin shall conceive and bear a son, and thou his mother shall call his name Emanuel: Butter and honey shall he eat, that he may know to refuse the evil, and choose the good.

The Gospel.

AND in the sixth month, the Angel Gabriel was sent from God, unto a city of Galilee named Nazareth, to a Virgin, spoused to a man, whose name was Joseph, of the house of David, and the Virgin's name was Mary. And the Angel went in unto her, and said: Hail full of grace, the Lord is with thee: Blessed art thou among women. When she saw him, she was abashed at his saying: and cast in her mind, what manner of salutation that should be. And the Angel said unto her: Fear not Mary, for thou hast found grace with God. Behold, thou shalt conceive in thy womb, and bear a son, and shalt call his name Jesus. He shall be great, and shall be called the Son of the highest. And the Lord God shall give unto him the seat of his father David, and he shall reign over the house of Jacob for ever, and of his kingdom there shall be none end. Then said Mary to the Angel: How shall this be, seeing I know not a man? And the Angel answered and said unto her: The Holy Ghost shall come upon thee, and the power of the highest shall overshadow thee. Therefore also that holy thing, which shall be born, shall be called the Son of God. And behold, thy cousin Elizabeth, she hath also conceived a son in her age. And this is the sixth month to her, which was called barren: for with God nothing shall be unpossible. And Mary said: Behold the handmaid of the Lord, be it unto me, according to thy word. And the Angel departed from her. *Luke i.*

S. Mark's day.

The Collect.

ALMIGHTY God, which hast instructed thy holy Church with the heavenly doctrine of thy Evangelist Saint Mark, give us grace so[5] to be established by thy holy gospel that we be not, like children, carried away with every blast of vain doctrine: Through Jesus Christ our Lord.

The Epistle.

UNTO every one of us is given grace, according to the measure of the gift of Christ. Wherefore he saith: When he went up on high he led captivity captive, and gave gifts unto men. That he ascended, what *Ephes. iv.*

[5 1578, 1596, that we be not like children carried away with euery blast of vaine doctrine, but firmely to be established in the trueth of thy holy Gospel.—This modification of the Collect was introduced very early in Elizabeth's reign. We find it first in a folio Prayer Book by Jugge and Cawode, without date, but whose Psalter has the date 1564.]

meaneth it, but that he also descended first, into the lowest parts of the earth? He that descended, is even the same also that ascended up above all heavens, to fulfil all things. And the very same made some Apostles, some Prophets, some Evangelists, some shepherd and teachers: to the edifying of the saints, to the work and administration, even to the edifying of the body of Christ, till we all come to the unity of the faith, and knowledge of the Son of God, unto a perfect man, unto the measure of the full perfect age of Christ. That we henceforth should be no more children, wavering and carried about with every wind of doctrine, by the wiliness of men, through craftiness, whereby they lay await for us, to deceive us. But let us follow the truth in love, and in all things grow in him, which is the head, even Christ, in whom if all the body be coupled and knit together, throughout every joint, wherewith one ministereth to another (according to the operation, as every part hath his measure) he increaseth the body, unto the edifying of itself through love.

The Gospel.

John xv.   I AM the true vine, and my Father is a husbandman. Every branch that beareth not fruit in me, he will take away. And every branch that beareth fruit, will he purge, that it may bring forth more fruit. Now are ye clean through the words which I have spoken unto you. Bide in me, and I in you. As the branch cannot bear fruit of itself, except it bide in the vine: no more can ye, except ye abide in me. I am the Vine, ye are the branches. He that abideth in me, and I in him, the same bringeth forth much fruit. For without me can ye do nothing. If a man bide not in me, he is cast forth as a branch, and is withered: and men gather them, and cast them into the fire, and they burn. If ye abide in me, and my words abide in you, ask what ye will, and it shall be done for you. Herein is my Father glorified, that ye bear much fruit, and be come my disciples. As the Father hath loved me, even so also have I loved you. Continue you in my love. If ye keep my commandments, ye shall bide in my love, even as I have kept my Father's commandments, and abide in his love. These things have I spoken unto you, that my joy might remain in you, and that your joy might be full.

S. Philip and James[1].

The Collect.

ALMIGHTY God, whom truly to know is everlasting life: grant us perfectly to know thy Son Jesus Christ, to be the way, the truth and the life, as thou hast taught Saint Philip, and other the Apostles, Through Jesus Christ our Lord.

The Epistle.

James i.   JAMES the servant of God, and of the Lord Jesus Christ, sendeth greeting to the twelve tribes, which are scattered abroad. My brethren, count it for an exceding joy, when ye fall into diverse temptations: knowing

[1 1596, day.]

this, that the trying of your faith gendereth patience: and let patience have her perfect work, that ye may be perfect and sound, lacking nothing. If any of you lack wisdom, let him ask of him that giveth it, even God, which giveth to all men indifferently, and casteth no man in the teeth, and it shall be given him. But let him ask in faith, and waver not: for he that doubteth, is like a wave on[2] the sea which is tost of the winds, and carried with violence. Neither let that man think, that he shall receive any thing of the Lord. A wavering minded man is unstable in all his ways. Let the brother, which is of low degree, rejoice when he is exalted. Again, let him that is rich, rejoice when he is made low. For even as the flower of the grass, shall he pass away. For as the sun riseth with heat, and the grass withereth, and his flower falleth away, and the beauty of the fashion of it perisheth: even so shall the rich man perish in his ways. Happy is the man that endureth temptation: For when he is tried, he shall receive the crown of life, which the Lord hath promised to them that love him.

The Gospel.

AND Jesus said unto his disciples: Let not your hearts be troubled, John xiv. Ye believe in God, believe also in me. In my Father's house are many mansions. If it were not so, I would have told you. I go to prepare a place for you. And if I go to prepare a place for you, I will come again, and receive you even unto myself: that where I am, there may ye be also. And whither I go, you[3] know, and the way ye know. Thomas saith unto him: Lord, we know not whither thou goest. And how is it possible for us to know the way? Jesus saith unto him: I am the way, and the truth, and the life. No man cometh to the Father but by me: if ye had known me, ye had known my Father also. And now ye know him, and have seen him. Philip saith unto him: Lord, shew us the Father, and it sufficeth us. Jesus saith unto him: Have I been so long time with you, and yet hast thou not known me? Philip, he that hath seen me, hath seen my Father: and how sayest thou then, shew us the Father? Believest not thou, that I am in the Father, and the Father in me? The words that I spake[4] unto you, I spake[4] not of myself: But the Father that dwelleth in me, is he that doeth the works. Believe me that I am in the Father, and the Father in me. Or else believe me for the works' sake. Verily, verily I say unto you: he that believeth on me, the works that I do, the same shall he do also, and greater works than these shall he do, because I go unto my Father. And whatsoever ye ask in my name, that will I do, that the Father may be glorified by the Son. If ye shall ask any thing in my name, I will do it.

[2 Grafton, of.]   [3 Grafton, ye.]
[4 Grafton, speake.]

S. Barnabie, Apostle.

The Collect.

LORD Almighty, which hast endued thy holy Apostle Barnabas with singular gifts of thy[1] Holy Ghost: let us not be destitute of thy manifold gifts, nor yet of grace to use them alway to thy honour and glory: Through Jesus Christ our Lord.

The Epistle.

Acts xi.

TIDINGS of these things came unto the ears of the congregation, which was in Jerusalem. And they sent forth Barnabas, that he should go unto Antioche, which when he came and had seen the grace of God, was glad, and exhorted them all, that with purpose of heart they would continually cleave unto the Lord. For he was a good man, and full of the Holy Ghost, and of faith, and much people was added unto the Lord. Then departed Barnabas to Tharsus, to seek Saul. And when he had found him, he brought him unto Antioche. And it chanced, that a whole year they had their conversation with the congregation there, and taught much people: insomuch that the disciples of Antioche were the first that were called Christen[2]. In those days came Prophets from the city of Jerusalem unto Antioche. And there stood up one of them, named Agabus, and signified by the Spirit, that there should be great dearth throughout all the world, which came to pass in the Emperor Claudius' days. Then the Disciples, every man according to his ability, purposed to send succour unto the brethren, which dwelt in Jurie: which thing they also did, and sent it to the Elders by the hands of Barnabas and Saul.

The Gospel.

John xv.

THIS is my commandment, that ye love together as I have loved you. Greater love hath no man, than this: that a man bestow his life for his friends. Ye are my friends, if ye do whatsoever I command you. Henceforth call I not you servants, for the servant knoweth not what his Lord doeth. But you have I called friends: for all things that I have heard of my Father, have I opened to you: ye have not chosen me, but I have chosen you, and ordained you to go and bring forth fruit, and that your fruit should remain: that whatsoever ye ask of the Father in my name, he may give it you.

S. John Baptist.

The Collect.

ALMIGHTY God, by whose providence thy servant John Baptist was wonderfully born, and sent to prepare the way of thy Son our Saviour, by preaching of penance: Make us so to follow his doctrine and holy life, that we may truly repent according to his preaching: and after his

[1 1596, the.]   [2 Grafton, christian.]

example constantly speak[3] the truth, boldly rebuke vice, and patiently suffer for the truth's sake: through Jesus Christ our Lord.

The Epistle.

BE of good cheer, my people, O ye prophets, comfort my people, saith your God, comfort Jerusalem at the heart, and tell her, that her travail is at an end, that her offence is pardoned, that she hath received at the Lord's hand sufficient correction for all her sins. A voice cried in wilderness, prepare the way of the Lord in the wilderness, make straight the path for our God in the desert. Let all valleys be exalted, and every mountain and hill be laid low; whatso is crooked, let it be made straight, and let the rough be made plain fields. For the glory of the Lord shall appear, and all flesh shall at once see it: for why, the mouth of the Lord hath spoken it. The same voice spake. Now cry. And the prophet answered: What shall I cry? That all flesh is grass, and that all the goodliness thereof is as the flower of the field. The grass is withered, the flower falleth away. Even so is the people as grass, when the breath of the Lord bloweth upon them. Nevertheless, whether the grass wither, or that the flower fade away, yet the word of our God endureth for ever. Go up unto the high hill (O Syon) thou that bringest good tidings, lift up thy voice with power, O thou preacher Jerusalem: Lift it up without fear, and say unto the cities of Juda. Behold your God, behold, the Lord God shall come with power, and bear rule with his arm. Behold, he bringeth his treasure with him, and his works go before him. He shall feed his flock like an herdman. He shall gather the Lambs together with his arm, and carry them in his bosom, and shall kindly entreat those that bear young. *Esay. xl.*

The Gospel.

ELIZABETH's time came that she should be delivered, and she brought forth a Son. And her neighbours and her cousins heard how the Lord had shewed great mercy upon her, and rejoiced with her. And it fortuned, that in the eight day they came to circumcise the child, and called his name Zachary, after the name of his father. And his mother answered, and said: Not so, but his name shall be called John. And they said unto her: There is none in thy kindred that is named with this name. And they made signs to his father, how he would have him called. And he asked for writing tables, and wrote, saying: His name is John. And they marvelled all. And his mouth was opened immediately, and his tongue also, and he spake, and praised God. And fear came on all them that dwelt nigh unto him. And all these sayings was[4] noised abroad throughout all the high country of Jewry, and they that heard them laid them up in their hearts, saying: What manner of child shall this be? And the hand of the Lord was with him. And his father Zacharias was filled with the Holy Ghost, and prophesied, saying: Praised be the Lord God of Israel, for he hath visited and redeemed his people. And hath raised up an horn of salvation unto us, in the house of his servant David. *Luke i.*

[[3] Grafton, to speake.]   [[4] Grafton, were.]

Even as he promised by the mouth of his holy Prophets, which were since the world began. That we should be saved from our enemies, and from the hand of all that hate us. That he would deal mercifully with our fathers, and remember his holy covenant. And he would perform the oath which he sware to our father Abraham for to forgive us. That we being delivered out of the hands of our enemies, might serve him without fear all the days of our life, in such holiness and righteousness as are acceptable for[1] him. And thou child shalt be called the Prophet of the Highest: for thou shalt go before the face of the Lord, to prepare his ways. To give knowledge of salvation unto his people, for the remission of sins. Through the tender mercy of our God, whereby the day spring from an high hath visited us. To give light to them that sat in darkness, and in the shadow of death, to guide our feet into the way of peace. And the child grew, and waxed strong in spirit, and was in wilderness till the day came, when he should shew himself unto the Israelites.

Saint Peter's day.

The Collect.

ALMIGHTY God, which by thy Son Jesus Christ hast given to thy Apostle saint Peter many excellent gifts, and commandest[2] him earnestly to feed thy flock: make, we beseech thee, all bishops and Pastors diligently to preach thy holy word, and the people obediently to follow the same, that they may receive the crown of everlasting glory: through Jesus Christ our Lord.

The Epistle.

AT the same time Herode the king stretched forth his hands to vex certain of the congregation. And he killed James the brother of John with the sword. And because he saw it[4] pleased the Jews, he proceeded further, and took Peter also. Then were the days of sweet bread. And when he had caught him, he put him in prison also, and delivered him to four quaternions of soldiers, to be kept: intending after Easter to bring him forth to the people. And Peter was kept in prison, but prayer was made without ceasing of the congregation unto God for him. And when Herode would have brought him out unto the people, the same night slept Peter between two soldiers, bound with two chains: and the keepers before the door kept the prison. And behold, the Angel of the Lord was there present, and a light shined in the habitation. And he smote Peter on the side, and stirred him up, saying: Arise up quickly. And his chains fell from his hands. And the Angel said unto him: Gird thyself, and bind on thy sandals. And he so did. And he saith unto him: Cast thy garment about thee, and follow me. And he came out, and followed

[1 Grafton, before.]   [2 Grafton and 1596, commaundedste.]
[3 The reference is omitted. Grafton, Actes. xii. 1596, Acts 12. 1.]
[4 Grafton, that it pleased.]

him, and wist not that it was truth, which was done by the Angel, but thought he had seen a vision. When they were past the first and second watch, they came unto the iron gate, that leadeth unto the city, which opened to them by the own accord, and they went out and passed through one street, and forthwith the Angel departed from him. And when Peter was come to himself, he said: Now I know of a surety, that the Lord hath sent his Angel, and hath delivered me out of the hand of Herode, and from all waiting[5] of the people of the Jews.

The Gospel.

WHEN Jesus came into the coasts of the city, which is called Cesarea Math. xv.[6] Philippi, he asked his disciples, saying: Whom do men say, that I the son of man am? They said: Some say that thou art John Baptist, some Helias, some Jeremias, or one of the Prophets. He saith unto them: But whom say ye that I am? Symon Peter answered and said: Thou art Christ, the Son of the living God. And Jesus answered, and said unto him: Happy art thou, Simon, the son of Jonas, for flesh and blood hath not opened that unto thee, but my Father which is in heaven. And I say unto thee, that thou art Peter: and upon this rock I will build my congregation. And the gates of hell shall not prevail against it. And I will give unto thee the keys of the kingdom of heaven, and whatsoever thou bindest in earth, shall be bound in heaven: and whatsoever thou loosest in earth, shall be loosed in heaven.

¶ Saint James the Apostle.

The Collect.

GRANT, O merciful God, that as thine[7] holy apostle saint[8] James, leaving his father and all that he had, without delay, was obedient unto the calling of thy Son Jesus Christ, and followed him: so we, forsaking all worldly and carnal affections, may be[9] evermore ready to follow thy commandments through Jesu Christ our Lord[10].

The Epistle.

IN those days came Prophets from the city of Jerusalem unto Anti- Acts xi. oche. And there stood up one of them, named Agabus, and signified by the spirit, that there should be great dearth throughout all the world, which came to pass in the Emperor Claudius' days. Then the Disciples, every man according to his ability, purposed to send succour unto the brethren, which dwelt in Jewry: which thing they also did, and sent it to the Elders by the hands of Barnabas and Saul. At the same time Acts xii. Herode the King stretched forth his hands, to vex certain of the congregation. And he killed James the brother of John with the sword. And, because he saw it pleased the Jews, he proceeded farther, and took Peter also.

[5 Grafton, the waityng.]
[7 Grafton, thy.]
[9 Grafton, euermore be.]
[6 Misprint for, xvi.]
[8 1596 has not, saint.]
[10 Grafton, Amen.]

The Gospel.

Mat. xx.

THEN came to him the mother of Zebedee's children, with her sons, worshipping him, and desiring a certain thing of him: And he said unto her: What wilt thou? She said unto him: Grant that these my two sons may sit, the one on thy right hand, and the other on thy left, in thy kingdom. But Jesus answered, and said: Ye wot not what ye ask. Are ye able to drink of the cup, that I shall drink of, and to be baptized with the baptism that I am baptized with? They said unto him: We are. He said unto them: Ye shall drink in deed of my cup, and be baptized with the baptism, that I am baptized with: but to sit on my right hand, and on my left, is not mine to give, but it shall chance unto them, that it is prepared for of my Father. And when the ten heard this, they disdained at the two brethren. But Jesus called them unto him, and said: Ye know that the princes of the nations have dominion over them, and they that are great men, exercise authority upon them. It shall not be so among you. But whosoever will be great among you, let him be your minister: and whosoever will be chief among you, let him be your servant. Even as the Son of man came not to be ministered unto, but to minister, and to give his life a redemption for many.

¶ S. Bartholomew[1].

The Collect.

O ALMIGHTY and everlasting God, which hast given grace to thy[2] Apostle Bartholomew truly to believe, and to preach thy word: grant we beseech thee unto thy church, both to love that he believed, and to preach that he taught: through Christ our Lord.

The Epistle.

BY the hands of the apostles were many signs and wonders shewed among the people. And they were all together with one accord in Salomon's porch. And of other durst no man join himself to them: nevertheless the people magnified them. The number of them that believed in the Lord, both of men and women, grew more and more: insomuch that they brought the sick into the streets, and laid them on beds and couches, that at the least way, the shadow of Peter, when he came by, might shadow some of them. There came also a multitude out of the cities round about unto Jerusalem, bringing sick folks, and them which were vexed with unclean spirits: and they were healed every one.

The Gospel.

Luk. xxii.

AND there was a strife among them, which of them should seem to be the greatest. And he said unto them: The kings of nations reign over them, and they that have authority upon them, are called gracious Lords. But ye shall not so be. But he that is greatest among you, shall be as the

[1 1596, Apostle.]   [2 Grafton and 1596, thine.]
[3 The reference is omitted. Grafton, Actes. v. 1596, Act. 5. 12.]

younger: and he that is chief, shall be as he that doth minister. For whether is greater, he that sitteth at meat, or he that serveth? Is not he, that sitteth at meat? But I am among you as he that ministereth. Ye are they which have bidden with me in my temptations. And I appoint unto you a Kingdom, as my Father hath appointed unto me, that ye may eat and drink at my table in my kingdom, and sit on seats judging the .xii. Tribes of Israel.

Saint Mathew[4].

The Collect.

ALMIGHTY God, which by thy blessed Son didst call Mathew from the receipt of custom to be an Apostle and Evangelist: Grant us grace to forsake all covetous desires, and inordinate love of riches, and to follow thy said Son Jesus Christ: who liveth and reigneth. &c.

The Epistle.

SEEING that we have such an office, even as God hath had mercy on ii. Cor. iv. us, we go not out of kind, but have cast from us the clokes of unhonesty, and walk not in craftiness, neither handle we the word of God deceitfully, but open the truth, and report ourselves to every man's conscience in the sight of God. If our Gospel be yet hid, it is hid among them that are lost, in whom the God of this world hath blinded the minds of them, which believe not, lest the light of the Gospel of the glory of Christ (which is the Image of God) should shine unto them. For we preach not ourselves, but Christ Jesus to be the Lord, and ourselves your servants for Jesus' sake. For it is God, that commandeth the light to shine out of darkness, which hath shined in our hearts, for to give the light of the knowledge of the glory of God in the face of Jesus Christ.

The Gospel.

AND as Jesus passed forth from thence, he saw a man (named Mathew) Math. ix. sitting at the receipt of custom, and he said unto him: Follow me. And he arose, and followed him. And it came to pass, as Jesus sat at meat in his house: behold, many Publicans also and sinners that came, sat down with Jesus and his disciples. And when the Pharisees saw it, they said unto his disciples: Why eateth your master with Publicans and sinners? But when Jesus heard that, he said unto them: They that be strong need not the Physician, but they that are sick. Go ye rather and learn what that meaneth: I will have mercy, and not sacrifice: for I am not come to call the righteous, but sinners to repentance.

¶ S. Michael and all Angels.

The Collect.

EVERLASTING God, which hast ordained and constituted the services of all Angels and men in a wonderful order: mercifully grant, that they

[4 1596, Apostle.]

176   S. MICHAEL AND ALL ANGELS DAY.   [1559.

which alway do thee service in heaven, may by thy appointment succour, and defend us in earth: through Jesus Christ our Lord. &c.[1]

The Epistle.

Apo. xii. THERE was a great battle in heaven: Michael and his Angels fought with the Dragon, and the Dragon fought with his angels, and prevailed not, neither was there place found any more in heaven. And the great Dragon, that old Serpent called the devil, and Sathanas, was cast out, which deceiveth all the world. And he was cast into the earth, and his Angels were cast out also with him. And I heard a loud voice, saying: In heaven is now made salvation and strength, and the Kingdom of our God, and the power of his Christ. For the accuser of our brethren is cast down, which accused them before God day and night. And they overcame him by the blood of the lamb, and by the word of their testimony, and they loved not their lives unto the death. Therefore rejoice heavens, and ye that dwell in them. Woe unto the inhabiters of the earth, and of the sea: for the devil is come down unto you, which hath great wrath, because he knoweth that he hath but a short time.

The Gospel.

Mat. xviii. AT the same time came the disciples unto Jesus saying: Who is the greatest in the kingdom of heaven? Jesus called a child unto him, and set him in the midst of them, and said: Verily, I say unto you, except ye turn and become as children, ye shall not enter into the kingdom of heaven. Whosoever therefore humbleth himself as this child, that same is the greatest in the kingdom of heaven. And whosoever receiveth such a child in my name, receiveth me. But whoso doth offend one of these little ones which believe in me, it were better for him, that a mill stone were hanged about his neck, and that he were drowned in the depth of the sea. Woe unto the world because of offences: necessary it is, that offences come: But woe unto the man by whom the offence cometh. Wherefore, if thy hand, or thy foot hinder thee, cut him off, and cast it from thee. It is better for thee to enter into life halt, or maimed, rather than thou shouldest (having two hands or two feet) be cast into everlasting fire. And if thine eye offend thee, pluck it out, and cast it from thee. It is better for thee to enter into life with one eye, rather than (having two eyes) to be cast into hell fire. Take heed that ye despise not one of these little ones: For I say unto you: that in heaven their Angels do always behold the face of my Father, which is in heaven.

Saint Luke the Evangelist.

The Collect.

ALMIGHTY God, which calledst Luke the physician, whose praise is in the gospel, to be a physician of the soul: it may please thee by the wholesome medicines of his doctrine to heal all the diseases of our souls through thy Son Jesu[2] Christ our Lord.

[[1] Grafton, Amen.]   [[2] 1596, Jesus.]

The Epistle.

WATCH thou in all things, suffer afflictions, do the work throughly ii. Tim. iii. [3]
of an Evangelist, fulfil thine office unto the uttermost: be sober. For I
am now ready to be offered, and the time of my departing is at hand. I
have fought a good fight, I have fulfilled my course, I have kept the
faith. From henceforth there is laid up for me a crown of righteousness,
which the Lord (that is a righteous judge,) shall give me at that day: not
to me only, but to [4] all them, that love his coming. Do thy diligence,
that thou mayest come shortly unto me. For Demas hath forsaken me,
and loveth this present world, and is departed unto Thessalonica, Cres-
cens is gone to Galacia, Titus unto Dalmacia; only Lucas is with me.
Take Mark, and bring him with thee, for he is profitable unto me for
the ministration: And Tichicus have I sent to Ephesus. The cloke
that I left at Troada with Carpus, when thou comest, bring with thee,
and the books, but specially the parchment. Alexander the copper
smith did me much evil: the Lord reward him according to his deeds:
of whom be thou ware also; for he hath greatly withstand our words.

The Gospel.

THE Lord appointed other seventy (and two) also, and sent them two Luk. x.
and two before him, into every city and place, whither he himself would
come. Therefore he said unto them: The harvest is great, but the
labourers are few. Pray ye therefore the Lord of the harvest, to send
forth labourers into the harvest. Go your ways: behold, I send you forth
as lambs among wolves. Bear no wallet, neither scrip, nor shoes, and
salute no man by the way. Into whatsoever house ye enter, first say:
Peace be to this house. And if the son of peace be there, your peace
shall rest upon him: if not, it shall return to you again. And in the same
house tarry still, eating and drinking such as they give. For the labourer
is worthy of his reward.

Simon and Jude, Apostles.

The Collect.

ALMIGHTY God, which hast builded thy congregation upon the foundation of the Apostles and Prophets, Jesu [3] Christ himself being the head
corner stone: grant us so to be joined together in unity of spirit by their
doctrine, that we may be made an holy temple acceptable to thee:
through Jesu [5] Christ our Lord [6].

The Epistle.

JUDAS the servant of Jesu Christ, the brother of James: to them which Judas i.
are called, and sanctified in God the Father, and preserved in Jesu Christ:
Mercy unto you, and peace, and love be multiplied. Beloved, when I
gave all diligence to write unto you of the common salvation, it was need-

[3 A misprint for, iiii.]   [4 Grafton, vnto.]
[5 1596, Jesus.]   [6 Grafton, Amen.]

[LITURG. QU. ELIZ.]

ful for me to write unto you, to exhort you that ye should continually labour in the faith, which was once given unto the saints. For there are certain ungodly men craftily crept in, of which it was written aforetime unto such judgment. They turn the grace of our God unto wantonness, and deny God (which is the only Lord) and our Lord Jesu Christ. My mind is therefore to put you in remembrance, forasmuch as ye once know this, how that the Lord (after that he had delivered the people out of Egypt) destroyed them which after believed not. The Angels also, which kept not their first state [1], but left their own habitation, he hath reserved in everlasting chains, under darkness, unto the judgment of the great day: even as Sodome and Gomor, and the cities about them, which in like manner defiled themselves with fornication, and followed strange flesh, are set forth for an example, and suffer the pain of eternal fire: likewise these being deceived by dreams, defile the flesh, despise rulers, and speak evil of them that are in authority.

The Gospel.

John xv.

THIS command I you, that ye love together. If the world hate you, ye know, it hated me before it hated you. If ye were of the world, the world would love his own: howbeit, because ye are not of the world, but I have chosen you out of the world, therefore the world hateth you. Remember the word that I say unto you : The servant is not greater than the lord. If they have persecuted me, they will also persecute you. If they have kept my saying, they will keep yours also. But all these things will they do unto you for my name's sake, because they have not known him that sent me. If I had not come and spoken unto them, they should have had no sin: but now have they [2] nothing to cloke their sin withal. He that hateth me, hateth my Father also. If I had not done among them the works, which none other man did, they should have had no sin. But now have they both seen and hated not only me, but also my Father. But this happeneth that the saying might be fulfilled that is written in their law: They hated me without a cause. But when the Comforter is come, whom I will send unto you from the Father, even the Spirit of truth (which proceedeth of the Father) he shall testify of me. And ye shall bear witness also, because ye have been with me from the beginning.

¶ All Saints.

The Collect.

ALMIGHTY God, which hast knit together thy [3] elect in one Communion and fellowship, in the mystical body of thy Son Christ our Lord: grant us grace so to follow thy holy saints in all virtues [4], and godly living, that we may come to those unspeakable [5] joys, which thou hast prepared for them that unfeignedly love thee : through Jesus Christ our Lord. [6]

[1 Grafton, estate.] [2 Grafton, they have.]
[3 Grafton, thy thy.] [4 1596, vertuous.]
[5 Grafton, inspeakeable.] [6 Grafton and 1596, Amen.]

The Epistle.

BEHOLD, I John saw another Angel ascend from the rising of the Sun, which had the seal of the living God, and he cried with a loud voice to the four Angels (to whom power was given to hurt the earth and the sea) saying: Hurt not the earth, neither the sea, neither the trees, till we have sealed the servants of our God in their foreheads. And I heard the number of them which were sealed: and there were sealed an .c. & .xliiii. M. of all the tribes of the children of Israel. Apo. vii.
 Of the tribe of Juda were sealed .xii. M.
 Of the tribe of Ruben were sealed .xii. M.
 Of the tribe of Gad were sealed .xii. M.
 Of the tribe of Aser were sealed .xii. M.
 Of the tribe of Neptalim were sealed .xii. M.
 Of the tribe of Manasses were sealed .xii. M.
 Of the tribe of Simeon were sealed .xii. M.
 Of the tribe of Levi were sealed .xii. M.
 Of the tribe of Isachar were sealed .xii. M.
 Of the tribe of Zabulon were sealed .xii. M.
 Of the tribe of Joseph were sealed .xii. M.
 Of the tribe of Ben Jamin were sealed .xii. M.

After this I beheld: and lo, a great multitude (which no man can number) of all nations, and people, and tongues, stood before the seat, and before the Lamb, clothed with long white garments, and Palms in their hands, and cried with a loud voice, saying: Salvation be ascribed to him that sitteth upon the seat of our God, and unto the Lamb. And all the Angels stood in the compass of the seat, and of the elders, and the .iiii. beasts, and fell before the seat on their faces, and worshipped God, saying: Amen. Blessing, and glory, and wisdom, and thank, and honour, and power, and might, be unto our God for evermore. Amen.

The Gospel.

JESUS seeing the people, went up into the mountain: and when he was set, his Disciples came to him, and after that he had opened his mouth, he taught them, saying: Blessed are the poor in spirit, for theirs is the kingdom of heaven. Blessed are they that mourn, for they shall receive comfort. Blessed are the meek, for they shall receive the inheritance of the earth. Blessed are they which hunger and thirst after righteousness, for they shall be satisfied. Blessed are the merciful, for they shall obtain mercy. Blessed are the pure in heart, for they shall see God. Blessed are the peacemakers, for they shall be called the Children of God. Blessed are they which suffer persecution for righteousness' sake, for theirs is the kingdom of heaven. Blessed are ye, when men revile you, and persecute you, and shall falsely say all manner of evil sayings against you for my sake: rejoice, and be glad, for great is your reward in heaven. For so persecuted they the Prophets, which were before you. Math. v.

☙ THE ORDER
for the
Administration of the Lord's Supper,
or
Holy Communion.

So[1] many as do intend[2] to be partakers of the holy Communion, shall signify their names to the Curate over night, or else in the morning, afore the beginning of morning prayer or immediately after.

And if any of those be an open and notorious evil liver, so that the congregation by him is offended, or have done any wrong to his neighbours by word or deed: The Curate having knowledge thereof, shall call him, and advertise him, in any wise not to presume to the Lord's Table, until he have openly declared himself to have truly repented and amended his former naughty life, that the congregation may thereby be satisfied, which afore were offended; and that he have recompensed the parties, whom he hath done wrong unto, or at the least declare himself to be in full purpose so to do, as soon as he conveniently may.

¶ The same order shall the Curate use with those, betwixt whom he perceiveth malice and hatred to reign, not suffering them to be partakers of the Lord's Table, until he know them to be reconciled. And if one of the parties so at variance be content to forgive from the bottom of his heart all that the other hath trespassed against him, and to make amends for that he himself hath offended, and the other party will not be persuaded to a godly unity, but remain still in his frowardness and malice: The Minister in that case ought to admit the penitent person to the holy Communion, and not him that is obstinate.

¶ The Table having at the Communion time a fair white linen cloth upon it, shall stand in the body of the Church, or in the Chancel, where Morning prayer and Evening prayer be appointed to be said. And the Priest, standing at the northside of the Table, shall say the Lord's prayer with this collect following.

ALMIGHTY God, unto whom all hearts be open, all desires known, and from whom no secrets are hid: cleanse the

[[1] 1578, So many as intend to be partakers of the holy Communion, &c. *And so forth, as in the great book of Common prayer.*
Our Father, which art in heaven, &c.
Then follows the Collect for purity in full.]
[[2] Grafton, as entend.]

thoughts of our hearts by the inspiration of thy Holy Spirit, that we may perfectly love thee, and worthily magnify thy holy name: through Christ our Lord. Amen.

¶ Then shall the [3] Priest rehearse distinctly all the .x. Commandments: and the people kneeling, shall after every Commandment ask God's mercy for their transgression of the same, after this sort.

Minister. God spake these words, and said: I am the Lord thy God, Thou shalt have none other Gods but me.

People. Lord have mercy upon us, and incline our hearts to keep this law.

Minister. Thou shalt not make to thyself any graven image, nor the likeness of any thing that is in heaven above, or in the earth beneath, nor [4] in the water under the earth. Thou shalt not now [5] bow down to them, nor worship them: for I the Lord thy God am a jealous God, and visit the sin of the fathers upon the children, unto the third and .iiii. generation of them that hate me, and shew mercy unto thousands in them that love me, and keep my commandments.

People. Lord have mercy upon us, and incline our hearts to keep this law.

Minister. Thou shalt not take the name of the Lord thy God in vain: for the Lord will not hold him guiltless that taketh his name in vain.

People. Lord have mercy upon us, and incline our hearts to keep this law.

Minister. Remember that thou keep holy the Sabboth day: six days shalt thou labour and do all that thou hast to do, but the .vii. day is the Sabboth of the Lord thy God. In it thou shalt do no manner of work, thou and thy son and thy daughter, thy man servant, and thy maid servant, thy cattle, and the stranger that is within thy gates: For in .vi. days the Lord made heaven and earth, the sea, and all that in them is, and rested the seventh day: wherefore the Lord blessed the seventh day and hallowed it.

People. Lord have mercy upon us, and incline our. &c.

Minister. Honour thy Father and thy Mother, that thy

[3] 1578, *the Minister.*]   [4] Grafton and 1596, or.]
[5] Grafton and 1596, not bow down.]

days may be long in the land which the Lord thy God giveth thee.

People. Lord have mercy upon us, and incline our. &c.

Minister.[1] Thou shalt do[2] no murther.

People. Lord have mercy upon us, and incline our. &c.

Minister. Thou shalt not commit adultery.

People. Lord have mercy upon us, and incline our. &c.

Minister. Thou shalt not steal.

People. Lord have mercy upon us, and incline our. &c.

Minister. Thou shalt not bear false witness against thy neighbour.

People. Lord have mercy upon us, and incline our hearts to keep this law.

Minister. Thou shalt not covet thy neighbour's house. Thou shalt not covet thy neighbour's wife, nor his servant, nor his maid, nor his ox, nor his ass, nor any thing that is his.

People. Lord have mercy upon us, and write all these thy laws in our hearts, we beseech thee.

¶ Then shall follow the Collect of the day with one of these two Collects following for the Queen: the Priest[3] standing up and saying.

¶ Let us pray. Priest[3].

ALMIGHTY God, whose kingdom is everlasting, and power infinite: have mercy upon the whole congregation, and so rule the heart of thy chosen servant Elizabeth, our Queen and Governour, that she (knowing whose minister she is) may above all things seek thy honour and glory: and that we her subjects, (duly considering whose authority she hath) may faithfully serve, honour, and humbly obey her, in thee, and for thee, according to thy blessed word and ordinance: Through Jesus Christ our Lord: who with thee and the Holy Ghost liveth and reigneth ever one God, world without end. Amen.

ALMIGHTY and everlasting God, we be taught by thy holy word, that the hearts of kings[4] are in thy rule and governance, and that thou dost dispose and turn them, as it seemeth best to thy godly wisdom: we humbly beseech

[1 Grafton, The Minister.] [2 Grafton, not do.]
[3 1578, *Minister.*] [4 Grafton, Princes.]

thee, so to dispose and govern the heart of Elizabeth, thy servant, our Queen and Governour, that in all her thoughts, words, and works, she may ever seek thy honour and glory, and study to preserve thy people committed to her charge, in wealth, peace, and godliness. Grant this, O merciful Father, for thy dear Son's sake Jesus Christ our Lord Amen.

¶ Immediately after the Collects, the Priest [5] shall read the Epistle beginning thus:

¶ The Epistle written in the. Chapter of.

And the Epistle ended, he shall say the Gospel, beginning thus.

The Gospel, written in the. Chapter of.

And the Epistle and Gospel being ended, shall be said the Creed.

I BELIEVE in one God, the Father almighty, maker of heaven and earth, and of all things visible and invisible. And in one Lord Jesu Christ, the only begotten Son of GOD, begotten of his Father before all worlds: God of God, light of light, very God of very God: begotten[6], not made, being of one substance with the Father, by whom all things were made: who for us men and for our salvation came down from heaven, and was incarnate by the Holy Ghost of the virgin Mary, and was made man: and was crucified also for us, under Poncius Pilate. He suffered and was buried. And the third day he rose again according to the scriptures: and ascended into heaven, and sitteth at the right hand of the Father. And he shall come again with glory, to judge both the quick and the dead: Whose kingdom shall have none end.

And I believe in the Holy Ghost, The Lord and giver of life, who proceedeth from the Father and the Son, who with the Father and the Son together is worshipped and glorified, who spake by the Prophets. And I believe one Catholic and Apostolic church. I acknowledge one Baptism, for the remission of sins. And I look for the resurrection of the dead, and the life of the world to come. Amen.

¶ After the Creed, if there be no sermon, shall follow one of the homilies already set forth, or hereafter to be set forth by common authority.

[5 1578, *the Minister.*]   [6 Grafton, gotten.]

¶ After such sermon, homily, or exhortation, the Curate shall declare unto the people whether there be any holy days or fasting days the week following: and earnestly exhort them to remember the poor, saying one or mo of these sentences following, as he thinketh most convenient by his discretion.

Math. v.   LET your light so shine before men, that they may see your good works, and glorify your Father which is in heaven.

Math. vi.   Lay not up for[1] yourselves treasure upon the earth, where the rust and moth doth corrupt, and where thieves break through and steal. But lay up for yourselves treasures in heaven, where neither rust nor moth doth corrupt, and where thieves do not break through and steal.

Math. vii. Whatsoever you[2] would that men should do unto you, even so do unto them: for this is the law and the Prophets.

Math. vii. Not every one that saith unto me, Lord, Lord, shall enter into the kingdom of heaven: but he that doeth the will of my Father which is in heaven.

Luke xix.   Zache stood forth, and said unto the Lord: Behold Lord, the half of my goods I give to the poor, and if I have done any wrong to any man, I restore four fold.

i. Cor. ix. Who goeth a warfare at any time of his own cost? who planteth a vineyard, and eateth not of the fruit thereof? or who feedeth a flock, and eateth not of the milk of the flock?

i. Cor. ix. If we have sown unto you spiritual things, is it a great matter, if we shall reap your worldly things?

i. Cor. ix. Do ye not know, that they which minister about holy things, live of the sacrifice? They[3] which wait of the altar, are partakers with the altar. Even so hath the Lord also ordained, that they which preach the gospel, should live of the gospel.

i.[5] Cor. ix. He which soweth little, shall reap little: and he that soweth plenteously, shall reap plenteously. Let every man do according as he is disposed in his heart, not grudging[4], or of necessity: for God loveth a cheerful giver.

Gala. vi.   Let him that is taught in the word, minister unto him that teacheth, in all good things. Be not deceived, God is not mocked: for whatsoever a man soweth, that shall he reap.

[1 Grafton omits, for.]
[3 1596, and they.]
[5 Misprint for, ii.]

[2 1596, ye.]
[4 Grafton, grudgynglye.]

While we have time, let us do good unto all men, and Gala. vi. specially unto them, which are of the household of faith.

Godliness is great riches, if a man be contented[6] with i. Tim. vi. that he hath: for we brought nothing into the world, neither may we carry any thing out.

Charge them which are rich in this world, that they be i. Tim. vi. ready to give, and glad to distribute: laying up in store for themselves a good foundation against the time to come, that they may attain eternal life.

God is not unrighteous, that he will forget your works Heb. vi. and labour that proceedeth of love: which love ye have shewed for his name's sake, which have ministered unto saints, and yet do minister.

To do good, and to distribute, forget not: for with such Heb. xiii. sacrifices God is pleased.

Whoso hath this world's good, and seeth his brother have i. John iii. need, and shutteth up his compassion from him, how dwelleth the love of God in him?

Give almose of thy goods, and turn never thy face from Toby iv. any poor man, and then the face of the Lord shall not be turned away from thee.

Be merciful after thy power. If thou hast much, give Toby iv. plenteously: If thou hast little, do thy diligence gladly to give of that little: for so gatherest thou thyself a good reward in the day of necessity.

He that hath pity upon the poor, lendeth unto the Lord: Prov. xix. and look what he layeth out, it shall be paid him again.

Blessed be the man that provideth for the sick and needy, Psal. xli.[7] the Lord shall deliver him in the time of trouble.

¶ Then shall the Churchwardens, or some other by them appointed, gather the devotion of the people, and put the same into the poor men's box: and upon the offering[8] days appointed, every man and woman shall pay to the Curate the due and accustomed offerings[9]: after which done, the Priest[10] shall say.

[[6] Grafton and 1596, content.]
[[7] Grafton and 1596, lxi. A misprint.]
[[8] These had originally been Christmas, Easter, Whitsuntide, and the feast of the dedication of the parish church: but in 1536 Henry VIII. commanded the feast of the nativity of Saint John the Baptist, and that of Saint Michael, to be substituted for the last two. Wilkins' Concilia, Vol. III. p. 824. Gibson's Codex, p. 739.]
[[9] See the Latin Prayer Book.] [[10] 1578, the Minister.]

Let us pray for the whole state[1] of Christ's Church militant here in earth.

If there be none[2] alms given unto the poor, then shall the words of accepting our alms be left out unsaid.

ALMIGHTY and everliving God, which by thy holy Apostle hast taught us to make prayers and supplications, and to give thanks for all men: we humbly beseech thee most mercifully to accept our almose and to receive these our prayers which we offer unto thy divine Majesty: beseeching thee to inspire continually the universal Church with the spirit of truth, unity and concord: And grant that all they that do confess thy holy name, may agree in the truth of thy holy word, and live in unity and godly love. We beseech thee also to save and defend all Christian Kings, Princes, and Governours, and specially thy servant Elizabeth our Queen, that under her we may be godly and quietly governed: and grant unto her whole council, and to all that be put in authority under her, that they may truly and indifferently minister justice, to the punishment of wickedness and vice, and to the maintenance of God's true religion and virtue. Give grace (O heavenly Father) to all Bishops, pastors and Curates, that they may both by their life and doctrine set forth thy true[3] and lively word, and rightly and duly administer thy holy Sacraments: and to all thy people give thy heavenly grace, and especially to this congregation here present, that with meek heart and due reverence they may hear and receive thy holy word, truly serving thee in holiness and righteousness all the days of their life. And we most humbly beseech thee of thy goodness (O Lord) to comfort and succour all them which in this transitory life be in trouble, sorrow, need, sickness, or any other adversity: Grant this, O Father, for Jesus Christ's sake our only mediator and advocate. Amen.

¶ Then shall follow this exhortation, at certain times when the Curate shall see the people negligent to come to the holy Communion.

WE[4] be come together at this time, dearly beloved brethren, to feed at the Lord's supper, unto the which in God's behalf I bid you all that be here present, and beseech you for

[[1] Grafton, estate.]   [[2] Grafton and 1596, no.]
[[3] Grafton, true liuely.]
[[4] This exhortation appears to be translated from Peter Martyr's *Adhortatio ad Cœnam Domini Mysticam.* See his *Loci Communes,* &c. p. 1067. Lond. 1583.]

the Lord Jesus Christ's sake, that ye will not refuse to come thereto, being so lovingly called and bidden of God himself. Ye know how grievous and unkind a thing it is, when a man hath prepared a rich feast, decked his table with all kind of provision, so that there lacketh nothing but the guests to sit down: and yet they which be called without any cause most unthankfully refuse to come. Which of you in such a case would not be moved? Who would not think a great injury and wrong done unto him? Wherefore, most dearly beloved in Christ, take ye good heed lest ye, withdrawing yourselves from this holy supper, provoke God's indignation against you. It is an easy matter for a man to say, I will not Communicate, because I am otherwise letted with worldly business: but such excuses be not so easily accepted and allowed before God. If any man say, I am a grievous sinner, and therefore am afraid to come: wherefore then do you[5] not repent and amend? When God calleth you, be you not ashamed to say you[5] will not come? When you should return to God, will you excuse yourself and say that you be not ready? Consider earnestly with yourselves how little such feigned excuses shall avail before God. They that refused the feast in the Gospel, because they had bought a farm, or would try their yokes of oxen, or because they were married, were not so excused, but counted unworthy of the heavenly feast: I for my part am here present, and according unto[6] mine office, I bid you in the name of God, I call you in Christ's behalf, I exhort you, as you love your own salvation, that ye will be partakers of this holy Communion. And as the Son of God did vouchsafe to yield up his soul by death upon the Cross for your health: even so it is your duty to receive the Communion together in the remembrance of his death, as he himself commanded. Now, if you will in no wise thus do, consider with yourselves how great injury you[5] do unto God, and how sore punishment hangeth over your heads for the same. And whereas you[5] offend God so sore in refusing this holy banquet, I admonish, exhort, and beseech you, that unto this unkindness ye will not add any more. Which thing ye shall do, if ye stand by as gazers and lookers on[7] them that do Communicate, and be no

[5 Grafton, ye.] [6 Grafton, to.]
[7 Grafton, of.]

partakers of the same yourselves. For what thing can this be accounted else, than a further contempt and unkindness unto God? Truly it is a great unthankfulness to say nay when ye be called: but the fault is much greater when men stand by, and yet will neither eat nor drink this holy Communion with other. I pray you what can this be else, but even to have the Mysteries of Christ in derision? It is said unto all: Take ye and eat. Take and drink ye all of this: do this in remembrance of me. With what face then, or with what countenance shall ye hear these words? What will this be else but a neglecting, a despising, and mocking of the Testament of Christ? Wherefore rather than you should so do, depart you hence, and give place to them that be godly disposed. But when you depart, I beseech you ponder with yourselves from whom you depart: ye depart from the Lord's Table, ye depart from your brethren, and from the banquet of most heavenly food. These things if ye earnestly consider, ye shall by God's grace return to a better mind; for the obtaining whereof we shall make our humble petitions, while we shall receive the holy Communion.

¶ And some time shall be said this also at the discretion of the Curate.

DEARLY beloved, forasmuch as our duty is to render to Almighty God our heavenly Father most hearty thanks, for that he hath given his Son our Saviour Jesus Christ, not only to die for us, but also to be our spiritual food and sustenance, as it is declared unto us, as well by God's word, as by the holy Sacraments[1] of his blessed body and blood; the which being so comfortable a thing to them which receive it worthily, and so dangerous to them that will presume to receive it unworthily: My duty is to exhort you to consider the dignity of the holy mystery, and the great peril of the unworthy receiving thereof, and so to search and examine your own consciences, as you should come holy and clean to a most godly and heavenly feast: so that in no wise you come but in the marriage garment, required of God in holy scripture; and so come and be received as worthy partakers of such a heavenly table. The way and means thereto is: First to examine your lives and conversation by the rule of God's commandments,

[1 Sacraments: sacramental signs or representations. See Cranmer's Answer to Gardiner, Preface, p. 3. Parker Society.]

and whereinsoever ye shall perceive yourselves to have offended, either by will, word, or deed, there bewail your own sinful lives, confess yourselves to Almighty God, with full purpose of amendment of life. And if ye shall perceive your offences to be such, as be not only against God, but also against your neighbours: then ye shall reconcile yourselves unto them, ready to make restitution and satisfaction according to the uttermost of your powers, for all injuries and wrongs done by you to any other: and likewise being ready to forgive other that have offended you, as you would have forgiveness of your offences at God's hand: for otherwise the receiving of the holy Communion doth nothing else but increase your damnation. And because it is requisite that no man should come to the holy Communion but with a full trust in God's mercy, and with a quiet conscience: therefore if there be any of you which by the means aforesaid can not quiet his own conscience, but requireth further comfort, or counsel; then let him come to me, or some other discreet and learned Minister of God's word, and open his grief, that he may receive such ghostly counsel, advice, and comfort, as his conscience may be relieved, and that by the ministry of God's word he may receive comfort and the benefit of absolution, to the quieting of his conscience, and avoiding[2] of all scruple and doubtfulness.

¶ Then shall the Priest[3] say this exhortation.

DEARLY beloved in the Lord: ye that mind to come to the holy Communion of the body and blood of our Saviour Christ, must consider what S. Paul writeth to[4] the Corinthians, how he exhorteth all persons diligently to try and examine themselves, before they presume to eat of that bread, and drink of that cup: for as the benefit is great, if with a truly penitent heart and lively faith we receive that holy sacrament (for then we spiritually eat the flesh of Christ, and drink his blood, then we dwell in Christ and Christ in us, we be one with Christ, and Christ with us:) so is the danger great, if we receive the same unworthily. For then we be guilty of the body and blood of Christ our Saviour. We eat and drink our own damnation, not considering the Lord's body. We

[[2] Grafton, aduoiding.] [[3] 1578, *the Minister.*]
[[4] Grafton, vnto.]

kindle God's wrath against us, we provoke him to plague us with divers diseases, and sundry kinds of death. Therefore, if any of you be a blasphemer of God, an hinderer or slanderer of his word, an adulterer, or be in malice or envy, or in any other grievous crime, bewail your sins, and come not to this holy Table, lest, after the taking of that holy Sacrament, the devil enter into you, as he entered into Judas, and fill you full of all iniquities, and bring you to destruction, both of body and soul. Judge therefore yourselves (brethren) that ye be not judged of the Lord. Repent you truly for your sins past, have a lively and stedfast faith in Christ our Saviour. Amend your lives, and be in perfect charity with all men, so shall ye be meet partakers of those holy mysteries. And above all things ye must give most humble and hearty thanks to God the Father, the Son, and the Holy Ghost, for the redemption of the world by the death and passion of our Saviour Christ both God and man, who did humble himself, even to the death upon the Cross for us miserable sinners, which lay in darkness and shadow of death, that he might make us the children of God, and exalt us to everlasting life. And to the end that we should alway remember the exceeding great love of our Master and only Saviour Jesu Christ, thus dying for us, and the innumerable benefits (which by his precious bloodshedding) he hath obtained to us, he hath instituted and ordained holy mysteries, as pledges of his love, and continual remembrance of his death, to our great and endless comfort. To him therefore, with the Father and the Holy Ghost, let us give (as we are most bounden) continual thanks: submitting ourselves wholly to his holy will and pleasure, and studying to serve him in true holiness and righteousness all the days of our life. Amen.

¶ Then shall the Priest[1] say to them that come to receive the holy Communion.

You that do truly and earnestly repent you of your sins, and be in love and charity with your neighbours, and intend to lead a new life, following the commandments of God, and walking from henceforth in his holy ways: Draw near, and take this holy Sacrament to your comfort: make your humble confession to Almighty God, before this congre-

[[1] 1578, *the Minister.*]

gation here gathered together in his holy name, meekly kneeling upon your knees.

¶ Then shall this general confession be made, in the name of all those that are minded to receive the [2] holy Communion, either by one of them, or else by [3] one of the ministers, or by the Priest himself, all kneeling humbly upon their knees.

ALMIGHTY God, Father of our Lord Jesus Christ, maker of all things, judge of all men : we knowledge [4] and bewail our manifold sins and wickedness, which we from time to time most grievously have committed, by thought, word and deed, against thy divine majesty ; provoking most justly thy wrath and indignation against us : we do earnestly repent, and be heartily sorry for these our misdoings : the remembrance of them is grievous unto us, the burthen of them is intolerable : have mercy upon us, have mercy upon us, most merciful Father, for thy Son our Lord Jesus Christ's sake : forgive us all that is past, and grant that we may ever hereafter serve and please thee, in newness of life, to the honour and glory of thy name : through Jesus Christ our Lord. Amen.

¶ Then shall the Priest [5] or the bishop, being present, stand up, and turning himself to the people, say [6] thus.

ALMIGHTY God our heavenly Father, who of his great mercy hath promised forgiveness of sins to all them, which with hearty repentance and true faith turn unto [7] him : have mercy upon you, pardon and deliver you from all your sins, confirm and strength [8] you in all goodness, and bring you to everlasting life : through Jesus Christ our Lord. Amen.

¶ Then shall the priest also say.

Hear what comfortable words our Saviour Christ saith to all [9] that truly turn to him.

COME unto me all that travail and be heavy laden, and I shall [10] refresh you. So God loved the world, that he gave

[2 Grafton, this.]   [3 1578, *by the Minister himselfe, all.*]
[4 Grafton, acknowledge.]
[5 1578, *the Minister.* And so in the next four cases.]
[6 Grafton, shall say.]   [7 Grafton, to.]
[8 Grafton, strengthen.]   [9 Grafton, all them.]
[10 1596, will.]

his only begotten Son, to the end that all that believe in him, should not perish but have life everlasting.

Hear also what saint Paul saith.

This is a true saying, and worthy of all men to be received, that Jesus Christ came into the world to save sinners.

Hear also what Saint John saith.

If any man sin, we have an advocate with the Father, Jesus Christ the righteous, and he is the propitiation for our sins.

¶ After the which, the priest shall proceed, saying.

Lift up your hearts.
Answer. We lift them up unto the Lord.
Priest. Let us give thanks unto our Lord God.
Answer. It is meet and right so to do.
Priest. It is very meet, right, and our bounden duty that we should at all times, and in all places, give thanks unto[1] thee, O Lord holy Father, almighty everlasting God.

☞ Here shall follow the proper Preface[2], according to the time, if there be any specially appointed, or else immediately shall follow: Therefore with Angels. &c.

¶ Proper prefaces.

¶ Upon Christmas day and seven days after.

BECAUSE thou didst give Jesus Christ, thine only Son, to be born as this day for us, who by the operation of the Holy Ghost, was made very man of the substance of the virgin Mary his mother, and that without spot of sin, to make us clean from all sin. Therefore. &c.[3]

Upon Easter day, and seven days after.

BUT chiefly are we bound to praise thee, for the glorious resurrection of thy Son Jesus Christ our Lord: for he is the very Paschal Lamb, which was offered for us, and hath taken away the sin of the world, who by his death hath destroyed death, and by his rising to life again hath restored to us everlasting life. Therefore with. &c.

[[1] Grafton, to.]   [[2] Grafton, prefaces.]
[[3] Grafton, with Aungels. &c. And so in every other case but the last.]

Upon the Ascension day, and seven days after.

THROUGH thy most dear beloved Son, Jesus Christ our Lord: who after his most glorious resurrection manifestly appeared to all his Apostles, and in their sight ascended up into heaven, to prepare a place for us, that where he is, thither might we also ascend, and reign with him in glory. Therefore with. &c.

Upon Whitsunday, and six days after.

THROUGH Jesus[4] Christ our Lord, according to whose most true promise, the Holy Ghost came down this day from heaven, with a sudden great sound, as it had been a mighty wind, in the likeness of fiery tongues, lighting upon the Apostles, to teach them, and to lead them to all truth, giving them both the gift of divers languages, and also boldness with fervent zeal, constantly to preach the Gospel unto all nations, whereby we are brought out of darkness and error into the clear light and true knowledge of thee, and of thy Son Jesus Christ. Therefore with. &c.

Upon the Feast of Trinity only.

IT is very meet, right, and our bounden duty, that we should at all times, and in all places, give thanks to thee, O Lord, almighty and everlasting God, which art one God, one Lord, not one only person, but three persons in one substance: for that which we believe of the glory of the Father, the same we believe of the Son, and of the Holy Ghost, without any difference or inequality. Therefore with. &c.

After which preface, shall follow immediately.

¶ THEREFORE with Angels and Archangels, and with all the company of heaven, we laud and magnify thy glorious name, evermore praising thee, and saying: Holy, holy, holy, Lord God of hosts: heaven and earth are full of thy glory; glory be to thee, O Lord most high.

Then shall the Priest[5] kneeling down at God's board, say in the name of all them that shall receive the Communion, this prayer following:

WE do not presume to[6] this thy Table (O merciful Lord) trusting in our own righteousness, but in thy manifold and

[4 Grafton, Jesu.]   [5 1578, *the Minister.*]
[6 Grafton, 1578, 1596, to come to this.]

[LITURG. QU. ELIZ.]

great mercies: we be not worthy so much as to gather[1] the crumbs under thy table: but thou art the same Lord, whose property is always to have mercy: grant us therefore (gracious Lord) so to eat the flesh of thy dear Son Jesus Christ, and to drink his blood, that our sinful bodies may be made clean by his body, and our souls washed through his most precious blood; and that we may evermore dwell in him, and he in us. Amen[2].

Then the Priest[3] standing up, shall say as followeth:

ALMIGHTY God our heavenly Father, which of thy tender mercy didst give thine only Son Jesus Christ, to suffer death upon the cross for our redemption, who made there (by his one[4] oblation of himself once offered) a full, perfect and sufficient Sacrifice, Oblation, and Satisfaction for the sins of the whole world: and did[5] institute, and in his holy Gospel command us to continue, a perpetual memory of that his precious death, until his coming again. Hear us, O merciful Father, we beseech thee: and grant that we receiving these thy creatures of bread and wine, according to thy Son our Saviour Jesu Christ's holy Institution, in remembrance of his death and Passion, may be partakers of his most blessed body and blood: who, in the same night that he was betrayed, took bread, and, when he had given thanks, he brake it, and gave it to his Disciples, saying: Take, eat, this is my body which is given for you. Do this in remembrance of me. Likewise after supper he took the cup, and when he had given thanks, he gave it to them, saying: Drink ye all of this, for this is my blood of the New Testament, which is shed for you and for many, for remission of sins: do this as oft as ye shall drink it in remembrance of me.

¶ Then shall the minister first receive the Communion in both kinds himself, and next deliver it to other ministers, if any be there present (that they may help the chief minister,) and after to the

[1 Grafton and 1596, gather vp.]   [2 Grafton omits, Amen.]
[3 1578, *the Minister*.]

[4 In 1597 we find 'own,' which reading existed, though by no means uniformly, for many years. Whether this was really an error, cannot easily be determined, since even in the earliest edition of the Prayer Book (Grafton, March, 1549) the passage runs 'his awne oblacion.']

[5 Grafton, diddest.]

people in their hands kneeling. And when he delivereth the **bread**, he shall say,

THE body of our Lord Jesus[6] Christ, which was given for thee, preserve thy body and soul into everlasting life: and take and eat this in remembrance that Christ died for thee, and[7] feed on him in thine heart by faith, with thanksgiving.

And the minister that delivereth the cup, shall say,

THE blood of our Lord Jesus[6] Christ, which was shed for thee, preserve thy body and soul into everlasting life: and drink this in remembrance that Christ's blood was shed for thee, and be thankful.

Then shall the Priest[8] say the Lord's prayer, the people repeating after him every petition.

¶ After shall be said as followeth.

O LORD and heavenly Father, we thy humble servants entirely desire thy fatherly goodness, mercifully to accept this our Sacrifice of praise and thanksgiving: most humbly beseeching thee to grant, that by the merits and death of thy Son Jesus Christ, and through faith in his blood, we and all thy whole church, may obtain remission of our sins, and all other benefits of his passion. And here we offer and present unto thee, O Lord, our selves, our souls, and bodies, to be a reasonable, holy, and lively Sacrifice unto thee, humbly beseeching thee, that all we which be partakers of this holy Communion, may be fulfilled with thy grace, and heavenly benediction. And although we be unworthy, through our manifold sins, to offer unto thee any sacrifice: yet we beseech thee to accept this our bounden duty and service, not weighing our merits, but pardoning our offences, through Jesus Christ our Lord: by whom and with whom, in the unity of the Holy Ghost, all honour and glory be unto thee, O Father Almighty, world without end. Amen.

Or this,

ALMIGHTY and everliving[9] God, we most heartily thank thee, for that thou dost vouchsafe to feed us, which have duly received these holy mysteries, with the spiritual food of the most precious body and blood of thy Son our Saviour

[6 Grafton, Jesu.] [7 Grafton omits, and.]
[8 1578, *the Minister*.] [9 Grafton, euerlastinge.]

Jesus Christ: and dost assure us thereby of thy favour and goodness toward us, and that we be very members incorporate in thy mystical body, which is the blessed company of all faithful people, and be also heirs through hope of thy everlasting kingdom, by the merits of the most precious death and passion of thy dear Son: we now most humbly beseech thee, O heavenly Father, so to assist us with thy grace, that we may continue in that holy fellowship, and do all such good works as thou hast prepared for us to walk in, through Jesus Christ our Lord: to whom, with thee and the Holy Ghost, be all honour and glory, world without end. Amen.

Then shall be said or sung.

GLORY be to God on high. And in earth peace, good will towards men. We praise thee, we bless thee, we worship thee, we glorify thee, we give thanks to thee, for thy great glory. O Lord God, heavenly King, God the Father Almighty. O Lord, the only begotten Son Jesu Christ: O Lord God, Lamb of God, Son of the Father, that takest away the sins of the world, have mercy upon us: thou that takest away the sins of the world, have mercy upon us. Thou that takest away the sins of the world, receive our prayer. Thou that sittest at the right hand of God the Father, have mercy upon us. For thou only art holy: thou only art the Lord: thou only, (O Christ,) with the Holy Ghost, art most high in the glory of God the Father. Amen.

Then the Priest[1] or the Bishop, if he be present, shall let them depart with this blessing.

THE peace of God which passeth all understanding keep your hearts and minds in the knowledge and love of God, and of his Son Jesu Christ our Lord: and the blessing of God Almighty, the Father, the Son, and the Holy Ghost, be amongst[2] you, and remain with you always. Amen.

¶ Collects to be said after the Offertory, when there is no Communion: every such day one. And the same may be said also as often as occasion shall serve after the Collects, either of Morning and Evening Prayer, Communion, or Litany, by the discretion of the minister.

ASSIST us mercifully, O Lord, in these our supplications and prayers, and dispose the way of thy servants toward

[1 1578, *the Minister.*]   [2 Grafton, among.]

the attainment of everlasting salvation: that among all the changes and chances of this mortal life, they may ever be defended by thy most gracious and ready help: through Christ our Lord. Amen.

O ALMIGHTY Lord and everliving God, vouchsafe, we beseech thee, to direct, sanctify and govern both our hearts and bodies, in the ways of thy laws, and in the works of thy commandments: that through thy most mighty protection, both here and ever, we may be preserved in body and soul: through our Lord and Saviour Jesus Christ. Amen.

GRANT, we beseech thee, Almighty God, that the words which we have heard this day with our outward ears, may through thy grace be so grafted[3] inwardly in our hearts, that they may bring forth in us the fruit of good living, to the honour and praise of thy name: through Jesus Christ our Lord. Amen.

PREVENT us, O Lord, in all our doings, with thy most gracious favour, and further us with thy continual help, that in all our works begun, continued, and ended in thee, we may glorify thy holy name, and finally by thy mercy obtain everlasting life: through Jesus Christ our Lord. Amen.

ALMIGHTY God, the fountain of all wisdom, which knowest our necessities before we ask, and our ignorance in asking: we beseech thee to have compassion upon our infirmities, and those things which for our unworthiness we dare not, and for our blindness we cannot ask, vouchsafe to give us for the worthiness of thy Son Jesus Christ our Lord. Amen.

ALMIGHTY God, which hast promised to hear the petitions of them that ask in thy Son's name: we beseech thee mercifully to incline thine ears to us, that have made now our prayers and supplications unto thee: and grant that those things which we have faithfully asked according to thy will, may effectually be obtained, to the relief of our necessity, and to the setting forth of thy glory, through Jesus Christ our Lord. Amen.

[3 Grafton and 1596, graffed.]

¶ Upon the holy days, if there be no Communion, shall be said all that is appointed at the Communion, until the end of the Homily, concluding with the general prayer, for the whole state[1] of Christ's church militant here in earth: and one or mo of these Collects before rehearsed, as occasion shall serve.

¶ And there shall be no celebration of the Lord's Supper except there be a[2] good number to communicate with the priest[3], according to his discretion.

¶ And if there be not above twenty persons in the Parish of discretion to receive the communion: yet there shall be no Communion, except four, or three at the least communicate with the priest[3]. And in Cathedral and[4] Collegiate churches, where be many Priests[5] and Deacons, they shall all receive the Communion with the Minister every Sunday at the least, except they have a reasonable cause to the contrary.

¶ And to take away the superstition which any person hath, or might have, in the bread and wine, it shall suffice that the bread be such, as is usual to be eaten at the Table with other meats, but the best and purest wheat bread, that conveniently may be gotten. And if any of the bread or wine remain, the Curate shall have it to his own use.

¶ The bread and wine for the Communion shall be provided by the Curate, and the Churchwardens, at the charges of the parish, and the parish shall be discharged of such sums of money, or other duties, which hitherto they have paid for the same, by order of their houses every Sunday[6].

¶ And note, that every Parishioner shall communicate at the least three times in the year: of which Easter to be one: and shall also receive the Sacraments, and other rites, according to 'the order in[7] this book appointed. And yearly, at Easter, every Parishioner shall reckon with his Parson, Vicar or Curate, or his, or their deputy or deputies, and pay to them or him all Ecclesiastical duties, accustomably due, then and at that time to be paid.

[1 Grafton, estate.]

[2 1578, *a great number*. This alteration first appears in a quarto Prayer Book of 1576 by Jugge, prefixed to a copy of the Bishops' Bible. Afterwards, as in 1617, it crept also into some of the authorised folios.]

[3 1578, *the Minister.*]   [4 1578, *or.*]

[5 1578, *Ministers.*]

[6 See 'Liturgies of K. Edward VI.', Parker Society, p. 98.]

[7 Grafton, of.]

¶ The Ministration of

Baptism.

to be used in the Church.

It[8] appeareth by ancient writers, that the sacrament of Baptism in the old time was not commonly ministered, but at two times in the year: at Easter, and Whitsuntide. At which times[9] it was openly ministered, in the presence of all the congregation: which custom (now being grown out of use,) although it cannot for many considerations be well restored again, yet it is thought good to follow the same as near as conveniently may be: wherefore the people are to be admonished, that it is most convenient that Baptism should not be ministered but upon Sundays and other holy days, when the most number of people may come together, as well for that the congregation there present may testify the receiving of them that be newly Baptized into the number of Christ's Church, as also because in the Baptism of Infants every man present may be put in remembrance of his own profession made to God in his Baptism. For which cause also, it is expedient that Baptism be ministered in the English tongue. Nevertheless (if necessity so require) children may at all times be baptized at home.

Publick[10] Baptism.

¶ When there are children to be baptized upon the Sunday, or holy day, the Parents shall give knowledge over night, or in the morning, afore the beginning of Morning prayer, to the Curate. And then the Godfathers, Godmothers, and people with the children, must be ready at the Font, either immediately after the last Lesson at Morning Prayer, or else immediately after the last Lesson at Evening Prayer, as the Curate by his discretion shall appoint. And then standing there, the Priest[11] shall ask whether the children be Baptized or no. If they answer, no: Then shall the Priest[11] say thus.

DEARLY beloved, forasmuch as all men be conceived and born in sin, and that our Saviour Christ saith, none can enter into the kingdom of God (except he be regenerate, and born

[8 1578 omits this rubric.] [9 Grafton, tyme.]
[10 Not in Grafton, nor in 1578.]
[11 1578, *the Minister.*]

anew of water and the Holy Ghost:) I beseech you to call upon God the Father, through our Lord Jesus Christ, that of his bounteous mercy, he will grant to these children, that thing which by nature they cannot have, that they may be Baptized with water and the Holy Ghost, and received into Christ's holy church, and be made lively members of the same.

Then the Priest[1] shall say.

Let us pray.

ALMIGHTY and everlasting God, which of thy great mercy didst save Noe and his family in the Ark, from perishing by water: and also didst safely lead the children of Israel thy people through the Red Sea: figuring thereby thy holy Baptism; and by the Baptism of thy wellbeloved Son Jesus Christ, didst sanctify the flood Jordan and all other waters to the mystical washing away of sin: We beseech thee, for thy[2] infinite mercies, that thou wilt mercifully look upon these children, sanctify them and wash them with thy Holy Ghost: that they, being delivered from thy wrath, may be received into the Ark of Christ's Church; and being stedfast in faith, joyful through hope, and rooted in charity, may so pass the waves of this troublesome world, that finally they may come to the land of everlasting life, there to reign with thee, world without end, through Jesus Christ our Lord. Amen.

ALMIGHTY and immortal God, the aid of all that need, the helper of all that flee[3] to thee for succour, the life of them that believe, and the resurrection of the dead: we call upon thee for these infants, that they, coming to thy holy Baptism, may receive remission of their sins by spiritual regeneration. Receive them, (O Lord) as thou hast promised by thy wellbeloved Son, saying, Ask and you shall have, seek and you shall find, knock and it shall be opened unto you. So give now unto us that ask. Let us that seek find. Open thy[4] gate to us that knock, that these infants may enjoy the everlasting benediction of thy heavenly washing, and may come to the eternal Kingdom, which thou hast promised by Christ our Lord. Amen.

[1 1578, *the Minister.*] [2 Grafton and 1596, thine.]
[3 Grafton, fly.] [4 1596, the gate.]

¶ Then shall the Priest[6] say: Hear the words of the Gospel written by Saint Mark in the tenth Chapter.

AT a certain time they brought children to Christ that he should touch them, and his disciples rebuked those that brought them. But when Jesus saw it, he was displeased, and said unto them: Suffer little children to come unto me, and forbid them not, for to such belongeth the kingdom of God. Verily I say unto you, whosoever doth not receive the kingdom of God, as a little child, he shall not enter therein. And when he had taken them up in his arms, he put his hands upon them and blessed them. Mar. x.

¶ After the Gospel is read, the minister shall make this brief exhortation upon the words of the Gospel.

FRIENDS, you[7] hear in this Gospel the words of our Saviour Christ, that he commanded the children to be brought unto him: how he blamed those that would have kept them from him: how he exhorteth[8] all men to follow their innocency. You[7] perceive how by his outward gesture and deed he declared his good will toward them. For he embraced them in his arms, he laid his hands upon them, and blessed them. Doubt not ye[9] therefore, but earnestly believe, that he will likewise favourably receive these present infants, that he will embrace them with the arms of his mercy, that he will give unto them the blessing of eternal life, and make them partakers of his everlasting kingdom. Wherefore we being thus persuaded of the good will of our heavenly Father, toward these infants declared by his Son Jesus Christ, and nothing doubting but that he favourably alloweth this charitable work of ours, in bringing these children to his holy Baptism: Let us faithfully and devoutly give thanks unto him, and say,

ALMIGHTY and everlasting God, heavenly Father, we give thee humble thanks, that thou hast vouchsafed[10] to call us to the knowledge of thy grace and faith in thee: increase this knowledge, and confirm this faith in us evermore: Give thy holy Spirit to these infants, that they may be born again, and be made heirs of everlasting salvation, through our Lord

[5 1578 uniformly omits, Public.] [6 1578, *the Minister.*]
[7 Grafton, ye.] [8 Grafton, exhorted.]
[9 Grafton, you.] [10 Grafton, vouchedsaufe.]

Jesus Christ; who liveth and reigneth with thee and the holy Spirit, now and for ever. Amen.

Then the Priest[1] shall speak unto the Godfathers and Godmothers on this wise:

WELLBELOVED friends, ye have brought these children here to be Baptized: ye have prayed that our Lord Jesus Christ would vouchsafe to receive them, to lay his hands upon them, to bless them, to release them of their sins, to give them the kingdom of heaven, and everlasting life. Ye have heard also that our Lord Jesus Christ hath promised in his Gospel to grant all these things that ye have prayed for: which promise he for his part will most surely keep and perform. Wherefore, after this promise made by Christ, these infants must also faithfully for their part promise by you that be their sureties, that they will forsake the devil and all his works, and constantly believe God's holy word, and obediently keep his commandments.

Then shall the Priest[1] demand of the Godfathers and Godmothers these questions following[2].

DOST thou forsake the devil and all his works, the vain pomp, and glory of the world, with all covetous[3] desires of the same, the[4] carnal desires of the flesh, so that thou wilt not follow, nor be led by them?

Answer. I forsake them all.

Minister[5]. Dost thou believe in God the Father Almighty maker of heaven and earth? And in Jesus Christ his only begotten Son our Lord, and that he was conceived by the Holy Ghost, born of the virgin Mary: that he suffered under Pontius Pilate, was crucified dead and buried, that he went down into hell, and also did rise again the third day: that he ascended into heaven, and sitteth at the right hand of God the Father Almighty, and from thence shall come again at the end of the world, to judge the quick and the dead?

And dost thou believe in the Holy Ghost, the holy Catholic Church, the Communion of saints, the remission of

---

[1] 1578, *the Minister.*]
[2] Grafton omits, following.]
[3] Grafton, al the couetous.]
[4] Grafton, and the.]
[5] Grafton, The Minister.]

sins, the resurrection of the flesh, and everlasting life after death?

Answer. All this I stedfastly believe.
Minister. Wilt thou be baptized in this faith?
Answer. That is my desire.

¶ Then shall the Priest[6] say.

O MERCIFUL God, grant that the old Adam in these children may be so buried, that the new man may be raised up in them. Amen.

Grant that all carnal affections may die in them, and that all things belonging to the spirit may live and grow in them. Amen.

Grant that they may have power and strength to have victory, and to triumph against the devil, the world and the flesh. Amen.

Grant that whosoever is here dedicated to thee by our office and ministry, may also be endued with heavenly virtues, and everlastingly rewarded through thy mercy, O blessed Lord God, who dost live and govern all things world without end. Amen.

ALMIGHTY everliving God, whose most dearly beloved Son Jesus Christ, for the forgiveness of our sins, did shed out[7] of his most precious side both water and bould[8], and gave commandment to his disciples that they should go teach all nations, and baptize them in the name of the Father, the Son, and of the Holy Ghost: Regard, we beseech thee, the supplications of thy congregation, and grant that all thy servants which shall be baptized in this water, may receive the fulness of thy grace, and ever remain in the number of thy faithful and elect children, through Jesus Christ our Lord[9].

Then the Priest shall take the child in his hands, and ask the name: and naming the child, shall dip it in the water, so it be discreetly and warily done, saying,

N. I Baptize thee in the name of the Father, and of the Son, and of the Holy Ghost. Amen.

[[6] 1578, *the Minister*. And so in the next five instances.]
[[7] Grafton, out his.]   [[8] Misprint for, bloud, *or* blood.]
[[9] Grafton and 1596 add, Amen.]

And if the child be weak, it shall suffice to pour water upon it, saying the foresaid words.

N. I Baptize thee in the name of the Father, and of the Son, and of the Holy Ghost. Amen.

¶ Then the Priest shall make a cross upon the child's forehead, saying.

WE receive this child into the congregation of Christ's flock, and do sign him with the sign of the cross, in token that hereafter he shall not be ashamed to confess the faith of Christ crucified, and manfully to fight under his banner against sin, the world, and the devil; and to continue Christ's faithful soldier and servant unto his lives end. Amen.

¶ Then shall the Priest say,

SEEING now, dearly beloved brethren, that these children be regenerate and grafted[1] into the body of Christ's congregation: let us give thanks unto God for these benefits, and with one accord make our prayers unto Almighty God, that they may lead the rest of their life according to this beginning.

¶ Then shall be said.

Our Father, which art in heaven. &c.

¶ Then shall the Priest say,

WE yield thee hearty thanks, most merciful Father, that it hath pleased thee to regenerate this infant with thy holy Spirit, to receive him for thine own child by adoption, and to incorporate him into thy holy congregation. And humbly we beseech thee to grant that he being dead unto sin, and living unto righteousness, and being buried with Christ in his death, may crucify the old man, and utterly abolish the whole body of sin, that as he is made partaker of the death of thy Son, so he may be partaker of his resurrection. So that finally, with the residue of thy holy congregation, he may be inheritor of thine everlasting kingdom: through Christ our Lord. Amen.

¶ At the last end, the Priest calling the Godfathers and Godmothers together, shall say this[2] short exhortation following.

FORASMUCH as these children have promised by you to forsake the devil and all his works, to believe in God, and to

[1 Grafton, graffed.]   [2 1578, 1596, this exhortation.]

serve him: you must remember that it is your parts and duties to see that these infants be taught, so soon as they shall be able to learn, what a solemn vow, promise and profession they have made by you. And that they may know these things the better, ye shall call upon them to hear sermons. And chiefly ye[3] shall provide that they may learn the Creed, the Lord's prayer, and the ten Commandments in the English tongue, and all other things which a Christian man ought to know and believe to his soul's health: and that these children may be virtuously brought up, to lead a godly and[4] a Christian life, remembering alway[5] that Baptism doth represent unto us our profession, which is to follow the example of our Saviour Christ, and to be made like unto him: that as he died and rose again for us, so should we which are baptized die from sin, and rise again unto righteousness: continually mortifying all our evil and corrupt affections, and daily proceeding in all virtue and godliness of living.

¶ The[6] Minister shall command that the Children be brought to the Bishop to be confirmed of him, so soon as they can say in their vulgar tongue the Articles of the faith, the Lord's prayer, and the x. commandments: and be further instructed in the Catechism set forth for that purpose, accordingly as it is there expressed.

[3 Grafton and 1596, you.] [4 Grafton, and christian.]
[5 Grafton and 1596, alwaies.] [6 This rubric is not in 1578.]

Of[1] them that be Baptized in private houses, in time of necessity.

¶ The Pastors and Curates shall oft[2] admonish the people that they defer not the Baptism of infants any longer than the Sunday, or other holy day next after the child be born, unless upon a great and reasonable cause declared to the Curate, and by him approved.

And also they shall warn them, that without great cause and necessity, they baptize not children at home in their houses. And when great need shall compel them so to do, that then they minister it[3] on this fashion.

First, let them that be present call upon God for his grace and say the Lord's prayer, if the time will suffer. And then one of them shall name the child, and dip him in the water, or pour water upon him, saying these words:

N. I Baptize thee in the name of the Father, and of the Son, and of the Holy Ghost. Amen.

And let them not doubt, but that the child so Baptized, is lawfully and sufficiently Baptized, and ought not to be baptized again in the Church. But yet nevertheless, if the child, which is after this sort Baptized, do afterward live: it is expedient that he be brought into the church, to the intent the priest may examine and try, whether the child be lawfully baptized or no. And if those that bring any child to the church do answer that he is already baptized, then shall the Priest examine them further.

By whom the child was baptized?

Who was present when the child was Baptized?

Whether they called upon God for grace and succour in that necessity?

With what thing, or what matter they did Baptize the child?

With what words the child was Baptized?

Whether they think the child to be lawfully and perfectly Baptized?

[1 1578 has not this Service.]   [2 1596, *often*.]
[3 Grafton omits, it.]

¶ And if the Minister shall prove by the answers of such as brought the child, that all things were done as they ought to be: Then shall not he christen the child again, but shall receive him as one of the flock of the true Christian people, saying thus.

I CERTIFY you, that in this case ye have done well and according unto due order concerning the baptizing of this child, which being born in original sin and in the wrath of God, is now, by the laver of regeneration in Baptism, received into the number of the children of God, and heirs of everlasting life: for our Lord Jesus Christ doth not deny his grace and mercy unto such infants, but most lovingly doth call them unto him, as the holy gospel doth witness to our comfort on this wise.

AT a certain time they brought children unto Christ, that he should touch them, and his disciples rebuked those that brought them. But when Jesus saw it, he was displeased, and said unto them: Suffer little children to come unto me, and forbid them not, for to such belongeth the kingdom of God. Verily I say unto you, whosoever doth not receive the kingdom of God as a little child, he shall not enter therein. And when he had taken them up in his arms, he put his hands upon them and blessed them.

¶ After the Gospel is read, the minister shall make this[6] brief exhortation upon the words of the Gospel.

FRIENDS, you[7] hear in this Gospel the words of our Saviour Christ, that he commanded the Children to be brought unto him: how he blamed those that would have kept them from him: how he exhorted all men to follow their innocency. Ye perceive how by his outward gesture and[8] deed he declared his good will toward them. For he embraced them in his arms, he laid his hands upon them, and blessed them: doubt ye[9] not therefore, but earnestly believe, that he hath likewise favourably received this present infant, that he hath embraced him with the arms of his mercy, that he hath given unto him the blessing of eternal life, and made him partaker of his everlasting kingdom. Wherefore we being

[4 Grafton, The Gospell.]   [5 Grafton, *Marke* x.]
[6 Grafton and 1596, this exhortacion.]
[7 Grafton, ye.]   [8 Grafton, in dede.]
[9 Grafton, you.]

thus persuaded of the good will of our heavenly Father, declared by his Son Jesus Christ, towards this infant: Let us faithfully and devoutly give thanks unto him, and say the prayer which the Lord himself taught, and in declaration of our faith let us recite the articles contained in our Creed.

¶ Here the Minister with the Godfathers and Godmothers shall say.

¶ OUR Father which art in heaven. &c.

¶ Then shall the Priest[1] demand the name of the child, which being by the Godfathers and Godmothers pronounced, the Minister shall say,

DOST thou in the name of this child forsake the Devil, and all his works, the vain pomp and glory of the world, with all the covetous desires of the same, the carnal desires of the flesh, and not to follow and be led by them?

Answer. I forsake them all.

Minister[2]. Dost thou in the name of this child profess this faith, to believe in God the Father almighty, maker of heaven and earth? And in Jesus Christ his only begotten Son our Lord: and that he was conceived by the Holy Ghost, born of the virgin Mary: that he suffered under Poncius[3] Pilate, was crucified, dead and buried: that he went down into hell, and also did rise again the third day: that he ascended into heaven, and sitteth at the right hand of God the Father almighty: and from thence he shall come again at the end of the world to judge the quick and the dead?

And do you in his name believe in the Holy Ghost. The holy Catholic Church. The communion of saints. The remission of sins. Resurrection[4], and everlasting life after death?

Answer. All this I stedfastly believe.

Let us pray.

ALMIGHTY and everlasting God heavenly Father, we give thee humble thanks, for that thou hast vouchsafed[5] to call us to the knowledge of thy grace and faith in thee: increase this knowledge, and confirm this faith in us evermore: Give thy holy Spirit to this infant, that he being born again, and being made heir of everlasting salvation, through our Lord

[1 Grafton, the Priest shal.]
[2 Grafton, The Minister.]
[3 Grafton, Ponce.]
[4 Grafton adds, of the fleshe.]
[5 Grafton, vouchedsafed.]

Jesus Christ, may continue thy servant, and attain thy promise, through the same our Lord Jesus Christ thy Son: who liveth and reigneth with thee in the unity of the same holy Spirit everlastingly[6]. Amen.

Then shall the Minister make this exhortation, to the Godfathers and Godmothers.

FORASMUCH as this child hath promised by you to forsake the Devil and all his works, to believe in God, and to serve him: you must remember that it is your part and duty to see that this infant be taught so soon as he shall be able to learn, what a solemn vow, promise, and profession he hath made by you. And that he may know these things the better, ye shall call upon him to hear sermons: and chiefly ye shall provide that he may learn the Creed, the Lord's prayer, and the ten Commandments in the English tongue, and all other things, which a Christian man ought to know and believe to his soul's health: and that this child may be virtuously brought up to lead a godly and a christian life: Remembering alway that baptism doth represent unto us our profession, which is to follow the example of our Saviour Christ, and be made like unto him: that as he died and rose again for us; so should we which are baptized, die from sin, and rise again unto righteousness, continually mortifying all our evil and corrupt affections, and daily proceeding in all virtue, and godliness of living[7].

¶ *And so forth as in Public Baptism.*

¶ *But if they which bring the infants to the Church, do make an uncertain answer to the Priest's questions, and say that they cannot tell what they thought, did, or said, in that great fear and trouble of mind (as oftentimes it chanceth) then let the Priest Baptize him in form above written, concerning Public Baptism, saving that at the dipping of the Child in the Font he shall use this form of words.*

IF thou be not baptized already. *N.* I baptize thee in the name of the Father, and of the Son, and of the holy Ghost. Amen.

[6 Grafton, euerlasting.]
[7 Grafton, liuing, &c.: consequently, he omits the next three words.]

⁋ Confirmation[1],

wherein is contained

a Catechism for Children.

To the end that Confirmation may be ministered to the more edifying of such as shall receive it (according unto S. Paul's doctrine, who teacheth that all things should be done in the Church to the edification of the same) it is thought good that none hereafter shall be confirmed, but such as can say in their mother tongue the articles of the faith, the Lord's prayer, and the ten commandments: and can also answer to such questions of this short Catechism, as the Bishop (or such as he shall appoint) shall by his discretion appose them in: and this order is most convenient to be observed for divers considerations.

First, because that when children come to the years of discretion, and have learned what their godfathers and godmothers promised for them in Baptism, they may then themselves with their own mouth, and with their own consent, openly before the church, ratify and confirm the same: and also promise that, by the grace of God, they will[2] evermore endeavour themselves faithfully to observe and keep such things, as they by their own mouth and confession have assènted unto.

Secondly, forasmuch as Confirmation is ministered to them that be Baptized, that by imposition of hands and prayer they may receive strength, and defence against all temptations to sin, and the assaults of the world, and the Devil: it is most meet to be ministered when children come to that age, that partly by the frailty of their own flesh, partly by the assaults of the world and the Devil, they begin to be in danger to fall into sundry kinds of sin.

Thirdly, for that it is agreeable with the usage of the Church in times past, whereby it was ordained that Confirmation should be ministered to them that were of perfect age, that they, being instructed in Christ's religion, should openly profess their own faith, and promise to be obedient unto the will of God.

And that no man shall think that any detriment shall come to children by deferring of their Confirmation, he shall know for truth that it is certain by God's word, that children, being baptized, have all things necessary for their salvation, and be undoubtedly saved.

[1 1578 omits this whole page.]   [2 Grafton, shall.]

✠ A Catechism, that is to say, an instruction to be learned of every child before he be[3] brought to be Confirmed of the Bishop.

Question. WHAT is your name?
Answer. *N.* or *M.*
Question. Who gave you this name?
Answer. My Godfathers and Godmothers in my Baptism, wherein I was made a member of Christ, the child of God, and an inheritor of the kingdom of heaven.
Question. What did your Godfathers and Godmothers then for you?
Answer. They did promise and vow three things in my name. First, that I should forsake the devil and all his works and pomps, the vanities of the wicked world, and all the sinful lusts of the flesh. Secondly, that I should believe all the articles of the Christian faith. And thirdly, that I should keep God's holy will and commandments, and walk in the same all the days of my life.
Question. Dost thou not think that thou art bound to believe and to do as they have promised for thee?
Answer. Yes, verily. And by God's help so I will. And I heartily thank our heavenly Father, that he hath[4] called me to this state of salvation, through Jesus Christ our Saviour. And I pray God to give me his grace, that I may continue in the same unto my lives end.
Question. Rehearse the articles of thy belief.
Answer. I believe in God the Father Almighty, Maker of heaven and[5] of earth. And in Jesus Christ his only Son our Lord. Which was conceived of[6] the Holy Ghost, born of the virgin Mary. Suffered under Ponce Pilate, was crucified, dead and buried, he descended into hell. The third day he rose again from the dead. He ascended into heaven, and sitteth at[7] the right hand of God the Father Almighty. From thence he shall come to judge the quick and the dead. I believe in the Holy Ghost. The holy Catholic Church.

[3 1578, *be confirmed, or admitted to receaue the holy Communion.*]
[4 Grafton, *hath he that.*]   [5 1596, *and earth.*]
[6 1596, *by.*]   [7 1596, *on.*]

The communion of Saints. The forgiveness of sins. The resurrection of the body. And the life everlasting. Amen.

Question. What dost thou chiefly learn in these articles of thy belief?

Answer. First, I learn to believe in God the Father, who hath made me and all the world.

Secondly, in God the Son, who hath redeemed me and all mankind.

Thirdly, in God the Holy Ghost, who sanctifieth me and all the elect people of God.

Question. You said that your Godfathers and Godmothers did promise for you, that you should keep God's commandments. Tell me how many there be?

Answer. Ten.

Question. Which be they?

Answer. The same which God spake in the .xx. Chapter of Exodus, saying: I am the Lord thy God, which have brought thee out of the land of Egypt, out of the house of bondage.

I. Thou shalt have none other Gods but me.

II. Thou shalt not make to thyself any graven image, nor the likeness of any thing that is in heaven above, or in the earth beneath, nor in the water under the earth: thou shalt not bow down to them nor worship them. For I the Lord thy God am a jealous God, and visit the sins of the fathers upon the children, unto the third and fourth generation of them that hate me, and shew mercy unto thousands in them that love me, and keep my commandments.

III. Thou shalt not take the name of the Lord thy God in vain: for the Lord will not hold him guiltless that taketh his name in vain.

IV. Remember that[1] thou keep holy the Sabboth day. Six days shalt thou labour and do all that thou hast to do: but the seventh day is the Sabboth of the Lord thy God. In it thou shalt do no manner of work, thou, and thy son and thy daughter, thy manservant, and thy maidservant, thy cattle, and the stranger that is within thy gates: for in six days the Lord made heaven and earth, the sea, and all that in them is, and rested the seventh day. Wherefore the Lord blessed the seventh day, and hallowed it.

[1 Grafton omits, that.]

V. Honour thy father and thy mother, that thy days may be long in the land which the Lord thy God giveth thee.

VI. Thou shalt do no murder.

VII. Thou shalt not commit adultery.

VIII. Thou shalt not steal.

IX. Thou shalt not bear false witness against thy neighbour.

X. Thou shalt not covet thy neighbour's house, thou shalt not covet thy neighbour's wife, nor his servant, nor his maid, nor his ox, nor his ass, nor any thing that is his.

Question. What dost thou chiefly learn by these commandments?

Answer. I learn two things. My duty towards God, and my duty towards my neighbour.

Question. What is thy duty towards God?

Answer. My duty towards God is, to believe in him, to fear him, and to love him with all my heart, with all my mind, with all my soul, and with all my strength. To worship him. To give him thanks. To put my whole trust in him. To call upon him. To honour his holy name and his word, and to serve him truly all the days of my life.

Question. What is thy duty towards[2] thy neighbour?

Answer. My duty towards my neighbour is, to love him as myself. And to do to all men as I would they should do unto me. To love, honour and succour my father and mother. To honour and obey the king[3] and his ministers. To submit myself to all my governors, teachers, spiritual Pastors and masters. To order myself lowly and reverently to all my betters. To hurt nobody by word nor deed. To be true and just in all my dealing. To bear no malice nor hatred in my heart. To keep my hands from picking and stealing, and my tongue from evil speaking, lying and slandering. To keep my body in temperance, soberness, and chastity. Not to covet nor desire other men's goods. But learn and labour truly to get mine own living, and to do my duty in that state of life, unto which it shall please God to call me.

Question. My good child know this, that thou art not able to do these things of thyself, nor to walk in the com-

[2 Grafton, toward.]

[3 Both editions of 1559 have this manifest misprint for, queen and her.]

mandments of God, and to serve him, without his special grace, which thou must learn at all times to call for by diligent prayer. Let me hear therefore, if thou canst say the Lord's prayer.

Answer. Our Father, which art in heaven, hallowed be thy name. Thy kingdom come. Thy will be done in earth as it is in heaven. Give us this day our daily bread. And forgive us our trespasses, as we forgive them that trespass against us. And lead us not into temptation. But deliver us from evil. Amen.

Question. What desirest thou of God in this prayer?

Answer. I desire my Lord God our heavenly Father, who is the giver of all goodness, to send his grace unto me and to all people, that we may worship him, serve him, and obey him as we ought to do. And I pray unto God, that he will send us all things that be needful both for our souls and bodies. And that he will be merciful unto us, and forgive us our sins: and that it will please him to save and defend us in all dangers ghostly and bodily: And that he will keep us from all sin and wickedness, and from our ghostly enemy, and from everlasting death. And this[1] I trust he will do of his mercy and goodness, through our Lord Jesu[2] Christ. And therefore I say. Amen. So be it[3].

So soon as the children can say in their mother tongue the articles of the faith, the Lord's prayer, and[4] the .x. Commandments: and also can answer to such questions of this short Catechism, as the Bishop (or such as he shall appoint) shall by his discretion appose them in: then shall they be brought to the Bishop by one that shall be his Godfather or Godmother, that every child may have a witness of his confirmation.

¶ And the Bishop shall confirm them on this wise.

Confirmation.

Our help is in the name of the Lord.

Answer. Which hath made both[5] heaven and earth.

[1 Grafton, thus.]   [2 1596, Jesus.]
[3 1578 places here the first rubric on p. 216 and part of the second, down to 'appointed for them to learn'. The Confirmation service itself with the other rubrics are omitted.]
[4 Grafton and 1596 omit, and.]   [5 1596 omits, both.]

1559.] CONFIRMATION. 215

Minister. Blessed is[6] the name of the Lord.
Answer. Henceforth world without end.
Minister. Lord hear our prayer.
Answer. And let our cry come to thee.

¶ Let us pray.

ALMIGHTY and everliving God, who[7] hast vouchsafed to regenerate these thy servants by water and the Holy Ghost, and hast given unto them forgiveness of all their sins: strengthen them we beseech thee (O Lord) with the Holy Ghost the comforter, and daily increase in them thy manifold gifts of grace: the spirit of wisdom and understanding, the spirit of counsel and ghostly strength, the spirit of knowledge and true godliness, and fulfil them (O Lord) with the spirit of thy holy fear. Amen.

Then the Bishop shall lay his hand upon every child severally, saying,

DEFEND, O Lord, this child with thy heavenly grace, that he may continue thine for ever, and daily increase in thy Holy Spirit more and more, until he come unto thy everlasting kingdom. Amen.

¶ Then shall the Bishop say[8].

ALMIGHTY everliving[9] God, which makest us both to will and to do those things that be good and acceptable unto thy Majesty: We make our humble supplications unto thee for these children, upon whom (after the example of thy holy Apostles) we have laid our hands, to certify them (by this sign) of thy favour, and gracious goodness toward them: let thy fatherly hand, we beseech thee, ever be over them: let thy Holy Spirit ever be with them; and so lead them in the knowledge and obedience of thy word, that in the end they may obtain the everlasting life, through our Lord Jesus Christ: who with thee and the Holy Ghost liveth and reigneth one God, world without end. Amen.

Then the Bishop shall bless the children, thus saying.

THE blessing of God Almighty, the Father, the Son, and the Holy Ghost, be upon you, and remain with you for ever. Amen.

[[6] 1596, be.] [[7] Grafton, which hast vouchedsafe.]
[[8] Grafton and 1596 add, Let vs praie.]
[[9] 1596, and euerliuing.]

¶ The Curate of every parish, or some other at his appointment, shall diligently upon Sundays and holydays, half an hour before Evensong[1], openly in the Church instruct and examine so many children of his parish sent unto him, as the time will serve, and as he shall think convenient, in some part of this Catechism.

¶ And all Fathers, and[2] Mothers, Masters and Dames, shall cause their children, servants, and prentices (which have not learned their Catechism) to come to the Church at the time appointed, and obediently to hear, and be ordered by the Curate, until such time as they have learned all that is here appointed for them to learn. And whensoever the Bishop shall give knowledge for children to be brought afore him to any convenient place, for their confirmation: Then shall the Curate of every parish either bring or send in writing the names of all those children of his Parish, which can say the Articles of their faith, the Lord's prayer, and the ten commandments: and also how many of them can answer to the other questions contained in this Catechism.

¶ And there shall none be admitted to the holy Communion, until such time as he can say the Catechism, and be confirmed.

[1 Grafton and 1578, Euenyng prayer.]
[2 Grafton and 1596 have not, and.]

The Form of
Solemnization of Matrimony.

¶ First the banns must be asked three several sundays or holydays, in the time of service, the people being present after the accustomed manner.

¶ And if the persons that would be married dwell in divers parishes, the banns must be asked in both parishes, and, the curate of the one parish shall not solemnize Matrimony betwixt them, without a certificate of the banns being thrice asked from the Curate of the other parish. At the day appointed for solemnization of Matrimony, the persons to be married shall come into the body of the church with their friends and neighbours. And there the Priest[3] shall thus say.

DEARLY beloved friends, we are gathered together here in the sight of God, and in the face of his congregation, to join together this man and this woman in holy matrimony, which is an honourable estate[4], instituted of GOD in paradise, in the time of man's innocency: signifying unto us the mystical union, that is betwixt Christ and his church: which holy estate[4] Christ adorned and beautified with his presence and first miracle that he wrought in Cana of Galilee, and is commended of Saint Paul to be honourable among all men, and therefore is not to be enterprised, nor taken in hand unadvisedly, lightly or wantonly, to satisfy men's carnal lusts and appetites, like brute beasts that have no understanding; but reverently, discreetly, advisedly, soberly, and in the fear of God: duly considering the causes for the which matrimony was ordained. One was, the procreation of children, to be brought up in the fear and nurture of the Lord, and praise of God. Secondly, it was ordained for a remedy against sin, and to avoid fornication, that such persons as have not the gift of continency, might marry, and keep themselves undefiled members of Christ's body. Thirdly, for the mutual society, help and comfort, that the one ought to have of the other, both in prosperity and adversity: into the which holy estate[4] these two persons

[3 1578, *the Minister.*]   [4 Grafton, state.]

present come now to be joined. Therefore if any man can shew any just cause, why they may not lawfully be joined together, let him now speak: or else hereafter for ever hold his peace.

And also speaking to the persons that shall be married, he shall say.

I REQUIRE and charge you (as you will answer at the dreadful day of judgment, when the secrets of all hearts shall be disclosed) that if either of you do know any impediment why ye may not be lawfully joined together in Matrimony, that ye confess it. For be ye well assured, that so many as be coupled together otherwise than God's word doth allow, are not joined together by God, neither is their Matrimony lawful.

At which day of marriage, if any man do allege and declare any impediment why they may not be coupled together in Matrimony by God's law or the laws of this Realm: and will be bound, and sufficient sureties with him, to the parties, or else put in a caution to the full value of such charges as the persons to be married doth[1] sustain to prove his allegation: then the solemnization must be deferred unto such time as the truth be tried. If no impediment be alleged, then shall the Curate say unto the man,

N. WILT thou have this woman to thy wedded wife, to live together after God's ordinance in the holy estate of Matrimony? Wilt thou love her, comfort her, honour and keep her, in sickness, and in health? And forsaking all other, keep thee only to her, so long as you both shall live?

The man shall answer,
I will.

Then shall the Priest[2] say to the woman,

N. WILT thou have this man to thy wedded husband, to live together after God's ordinance in the holy estate of Matrimony? Wilt thou obey him and serve him, love, honour, and keep him, in sickness and in health, and forsaking all other, keep thee only unto[3] him, so long as you both shall live?

The woman shall answer,
I will.

Then shall the Minister say,

Who giveth this woman to be married unto this man?

[[1] Grafton and 1596, do.]   [[2] 1578, *the Minister.*]
[[3] Grafton, to.]

And the Minister receiving the woman at her father or friend's hands, shall cause the man to take the woman by the right hand, and so either to give their troth to other. The man first saying.

I. N. take thee. N. to my wedded wife, to have and to hold from this day forward, for better, for worse, for richer, for poorer, in sickness, and in health, to love and to cherish, till death us depart, according to God's holy ordinance: and thereto I plight thee my troth.

Then shall they loose their hands, and the woman taking again the man by the right hand shall say.

I. N. take thee. N. to my wedded husband, to have and to hold from this day forward, for better, for worse, for richer, for poorer, in sickness, and in health, to love, cherish, and to obey, till death us depart, according to God's holy ordinance: and thereto I give thee my troth.

Then shall they again loose their hands, and the man shall give unto the woman a ring, laying the same upon the book with the accustomed duty to the priest[4] and Clerk. And the Priest taking the ring, shall deliver it unto the man, to put it upon the fourth finger of the woman's left hand. And the man taught by the priest shall say.

WITH this ring I thee wed: with my body I thee worship: and with all my worldly goods I thee endow. In the name of the Father, and of the Son, and of the Holy Ghost. Amen.

Then the man leaving the ring upon the fourth finger of the woman's left hand, the Minister shall say[5].

O ETERNAL God, creator and preserver of all mankind, giver of all spiritual grace, the author of everlasting life: Send thy blessing upon these thy servants, this man and this woman, whom we bless in thy name; that as Isaac and Rebecca lived faithfully together, so these persons may surely perform and keep the vow and covenant betwixt them made, whereof this ring given and received is a token and pledge, and may ever remain in perfect love and peace together, and live according unto thy laws: through Jesus Christ our Lord. Amen.

¶ Then shall the Priest[4] join their[6] right hands together, and say.

Those whom God hath joined together, let no man put asunder.

[4 1578, *the Minister*. And so throughout the rubric.]
[5 Grafton and 1596 add, Let us praye.]   [6 1596, *their hands*.]

Then shall the Minister speak unto the people.

FORASMUCH as .N. and .N. have consented together in holy wedlock, and have witnessed the same before God and this company, and thereto have given and pledged their troth, either to other, and have declared the same by giving and receiving of a Ring, and by joining of hands: I pronounce that they be man and wife together. In the name of the Father, and[1] of the Son, and of the Holy Ghost. Amen.

And the Minister shall add this blessing.

GOD the Father, God the Son, God the Holy Ghost, bless, preserve, and keep you: the Lord mercifully with his favour look upon you, and so fill you with all spiritual benediction and grace, that you may so live together in this life, that in the world to come you may have life everlasting. Amen.

Then the Ministers[2] or Clerks going to the Lord's table, shall say or sing, this Psalm following.

Beati omnes. Psal. cxxviii.

BLESSED are all they that fear the Lord, and walk in his ways.

For thou shalt eat the labour of thy hands : O well is thee, and happy shalt thou be.

Thy wife shall be as the fruitful vine : upon the walls of thy house.

Thy children like the olive branches : round about thy table.

Lo, thus shall the man be blessed : that feareth the Lord.

The Lord from out of Sion shall bless[3] thee : that thou shalt see Jerusalem in prosperity, all thy life long :

Yea, that thou shalt see thy children's[4] children : and peace upon Israel.

Glory be to the Father. &c.

As it was in the. &c.

Or[5] else this Psalm following.

Deus misereatur. Psal. lxvii.[6]

GOD be merciful unto us and bless us : and shew us the light of his countenance, and be merciful unto us.

That thy way may be known upon the earth : thy saving health among all nations.

[1 Grafton and 1596 omit, and.]
[2 A misprint in both editions of 1559. 1578, 1596, *Minister*.]
[3 1596, so blesse.] [4 Grafton, childres.]
[5 1596, *Or this Psalme*.] [6 Grafton, li. A misprint.]

Let the people praise thee (O God): yea let all the people praise thee.

O let the nations rejoice and be glad: for thou shalt judge the flock[7] righteously, and govern the nations upon the earth.

Let the people praise thee (O God): let all the people praise thee.

Then shall the earth bring forth her increase: and God, even our[8] God, shall give us his blessing.

God shall bless us, and all the ends of the world shall fear him.

Glory be to the Father. &c.

As it was in the. &c.

¶ The Psalm ended, and the man and the woman kneeling afore the Lord's table: the priest[9] standing at the table, and turning his face toward them, shall say,

Lord have mercy upon us.
Answer. Christ have mercy upon us.
Minister. Lord have mercy upon us.

OUR Father which art in heaven. &c.
And lead us not into temptation.
Answer. But deliver us from evil. Amen.
Minister. O Lord save thy servant, and thy handmaid.
Answer. Which put their trust in thee.
Minister. O Lord send them help from thy holy place.
Answer. And evermore defend them.
Minister. Be unto them a tower of strength.
Answer. From the face of their enemy.
Minister. O Lord, hear our prayer.
Answer. And let our cry come unto thee.

The[10] Minister.

O GOD of Abraham, God of Isaac, God of Jacob, bless these thy servants, and sow the seed of eternal life in their minds, that whatsoever in thy holy word they shall profitably learn, they may in deed fulfil the same. Look, O Lord, mercifully upon them from heaven, and bless them. And as thou didst send thy blessing upon Abraham and

[7 A misprint for, folk.] [8 1596, our owne.]
[9 1578, *the Minister.*] [10 1596, *Minister.*]

Sara to their great comfort: so vouchsafe to send thy blessing upon these thy servants, that they obeying thy will, and alway being in safety under thy protection, may abide in thy love unto their lives end: through Jesu[1] Christ our Lord. Amen.

¶ This prayer next following shall be omitted, where the woman is past child birth.

O MERCIFUL Lord and heavenly Father, by whose gracious gift mankind is increased: we beseech thee assist with thy blessing these two persons, that they may both be fruitful in procreation of children, and also live together so long in godly love and honesty, that they may see their children's[2] children, unto the third and fourth generation, unto thy praise and honour: through Jesus Christ our Lord. Amen.

O GOD, which by thy mighty power hast made all things of nought; which also, after other things set in order, didst appoint that out of man (created after thine own image and similitude) woman should take her beginning: and knitting them together, didst teach that it should never be lawful to put asunder those, whom thou by matrimony hadst made one: O God which hast consecrated the state of matrimony to such an excellent mystery, that in it is signified and represented the spiritual marriage and unity betwixt Christ and his church: Look mercifully upon these thy servants, that both this man may love his wife, according to thy word (as Christ did love his spouse the Church, who gave himself for it, loving and cherishing it even as his own flesh:) And also that this woman may be loving and amiable to her husband as Rachel, wise as Rebecca, faithful and obedient as Sara, and in all quietness, sobriety, and peace be a follower[3] of holy and godly matrons: O Lord, bless them both, and grant them to inherit thy everlasting kingdom: through Jesus Christ our Lord. Amen.

¶ Then shall the Priest[4] say,

ALMIGHTY God, which at the beginning did create our first parents Adam and Eve, and did sanctify and join them together in marriage: pour upon you the riches of his grace,

[1 1596, Jesus.]
[2 Grafton, childers.]
[3 Grafton, flower.]
[4 1578, *the Minister*.]

sanctify and bless you, that ye may please him both in body and soul, and live together in holy love, unto your lives end. Amen.

Then shall begin the Communion, and after the Gospel shall be said a sermon, wherein ordinarily (so oft as there is any marriage) the office of a man and wife shall be declared, according to holy scripture: or if there be no sermon, the Minister shall read this that followeth.

ALL ye which be married, or which intend to take the holy estate of matrimony upon you: hear what holy scripture doth say, as touching the duty of husbands toward their wives, and wives toward their husbands. Saint Paul (in his Epistle to the Ephesians, the fifth Chapter) doth give this commandment to all married men.

Ye husbands love your wives, even as Christ loved the church, and hath given himself for it, to sanctify it purging it in the fountain of water, through thy[5] word, that he might make it unto himself a glorious congregation, not having spot or wrinkle, or any such thing, but that it should be holy and blameless. So men are bound to love their own wives as their own bodies. He that loveth his own wife, loveth himself: for never did any man hate his own flesh, but nourisheth and cherisheth it, even as the Lord doth the congregation: for we are members of his body, of his flesh and of his bones.

For this cause shall a man leave father and mother, and shall be joined unto his wife, and they two shall be one flesh. This mystery is great: but I speak of Christ and of the congregation. Nevertheless, let every one of you so love his own wife, even as himself.

Likewise the same saint Paul (writing to the Colossians) Col. iii.[6] speaketh thus to all men that be married. Ye men, love your wives, and be not bitter unto them.

Hear also what Saint Peter the apostle of Christ, which i. Pet. iii. was himself a married man, saith unto all men that are married. Ye husbands, dwell with your wives according to knowledge: Giving honour unto the wife as unto the weaker vessel, and as heirs together of the grace of life, so that your prayers be not hindered.

[5] Grafton and 1596, the.]
[6] Grafton, iiii. The same misprint occurs on the next page.]

Hitherto ye have heard the duty of the husband toward the wife. Now likewise, ye wives, hear and learn your duty toward your husbands, even as it is plainly set forth in holy scripture.

Eph. v.

Saint Paul (in the forenamed Epistle to the Ephesians, fifth chapter[1]) teacheth you thus: Ye women, submit yourselves unto your own husbands as unto the Lord: for the husband is the wives head, even as Christ is the head of the Church. And he is also the Saviour of the whole body. Therefore as the church or congregation is subject unto Christ, so likewise let the wives also be in subjection unto their own husbands in all things. And again he saith: Let the wife reverence her husband. And (in his Epistle to the Colossians) Saint Paul giveth you this short lesson. Ye wives, submit yourselves unto your own husbands, as it is convenient in the Lord.

Col. iii.

i. Pet. iii.

Saint Peter also doth instruct you very godly, thus saying: Let wives be subject to their own husbands, so that if any obey not the word, they may be won without the word by the conversation of the wives, while they behold your chaste conversation coupled with fear: whose apparel let it not be outward, with braided[2] hair and trimming about with gold, either in putting on of gorgeous apparel: but let the hid man which is in the heart, be without all corruption, so that the spirit be mild and quiet, which is a precious thing in the sight of God. For after this manner (in the old time) did the holy women which trusted in God apparel themselves, being subject to their own husbands: as Sara obeyed Abraham, calling him lord; whose daughters ye are made, doing well, and being not dismayed with any fear.

The new married persons (the same day of their marriage) must receive the holy Communion.

[1 Grafton and 1596 omit these two words.]
[2 Grafton, broided.]

… The Order for the

Visitation of the Sick.

The Priest[3] entering into the sick person's house, shall say,

Peace be in this house, and to all that dwell in it.

When he cometh into the sick man's presence, he shall say, kneeling down,

REMEMBER not Lord our iniquities, nor the iniquities of our forefathers. Spare us good Lord, spare thy people, whom thou hast redeemed with thy most precious blood, and be not angry with us for ever.

Lord have mercy upon us.
Christ have mercy upon us.
Lord have mercy upon us.
Our Father, which art in heaven. &c.
And lead us not into temptation.
Answer. But deliver us from evil. Amen.
Minister. O Lord, save thy servant.
Answer. Which putteth his trust in thee.
Minister. Send him help from thy holy place.
Answer. And evermore mightily defend him.
Minister. Let the enemy have none advantage of him.
Answer. Nor the wicked approach to hurt him.
Minister. Be unto him, O Lord, a strong tower.
Answer. From the face of his enemy.
Minister. Lord hear our prayers.
Answer. And let our cry come unto thee.

The[4] Minister.

O LORD look down from heaven, behold, visit and relieve this thy servant. Look upon him with the eyes of thy mercy, give him comfort and sure confidence in thee: Defend him from the danger of the enemy, and keep him in perpetual peace and safety: through Jesus Christ our Lord. Amen.

[3 1578, *The Minister.*]   [4 Grafton and 1596, Minister.]

HEAR us, almighty and most merciful God, and Saviour: Extend thy accustomed goodness to this thy servant, which is grieved with sickness: Visit him, O Lord, as thou didst visit Peter's wife's mother, and the captain's servant. So visit and restore unto this sick person his former health (if it be thy will) or else give him grace so to take thy visitation, that after this painful life ended, he may dwell with thee in life everlasting. Amen.

¶ Then shall the Minister exhort the sick person after this form or other like.

DEARLY beloved know this: that Almighty God is the Lord of life and death, and over all things to them pertaining, as youth, strength, health, age, weakness, and sickness: wherefore, whatsoever your sickness is, know you certainly, that it is God's visitation.

And for what cause soever this sickness is sent unto you, whether it be to try your patience for the example of other, and that your faith may be found in the day of the Lord laudable, glorious, and honourable, to the increase of glory and endless felicity; or else it be sent unto you to correct and amend in you, whatsoever doth offend the eyes of our[1] heavenly Father: know you certainly, that if you truly repent you of your sins, and bear your sickness patiently, trusting in God's mercy for his dear Son Jesus Christ's sake, and render unto him humble thanks for his fatherly visitation, submitting yourself wholly to his will; it shall turn to your profit, and help you forward in the right way that leadeth unto everlasting life.

¶ If[2] the person visited be very sick, then the Curate may end his exhortation in this place.

¶ TAKE therefore in good worth the chastement of the Lord: For whom the Lord loveth, he chastiseth. Yea (as Saint Paul saith) he scourgeth every son which he receiveth: if you endure chastisement, he offereth him self unto you, as unto his own children. What son is he that the father chastiseth not? If ye be not under correction, (whereof all true children are partakers) then are ye bastards and not children. Therefore, seeing that when our carnal fathers do correct us, we reverently obey them: shall we not now much

[[1] 1596, your.] [[2] Grafton puts this in the margin.]

rather be obedient to our spiritual Father, and so live? And they for a few days do chastise[3] us after their own pleasure, but he doth chastise us for our profit: to the intent he may make us partakers of his holiness. These words, good brother, are God's words, and written in holy Scripture for our comfort and instruction, that we should patiently, and with thanksgiving, bear our heavenly Father's correction, when soever by any manner of adversity it shall please his gracious goodness to visit us. And there should[4] be no greater comfort to Christian persons, than to be made like unto Christ, by suffering patiently adversities, troubles, and sicknesses. For he him self went not up to joy, but first he suffered pain: he entered not into his glory before he was crucified. So truly our way to eternal joy is to suffer here with Christ, and our door to enter into eternal life is gladly to die with Christ, that we may rise again from death, and dwell with him in everlasting life. Now therefore, taking your sickness, which is thus profitable for you, patiently, I exhort you, in the name of God, to remember the profession which you made unto GOD in your Baptism. And forasmuch as after this life there is a count[5] to be given unto the righteous Judge, of whom all must be judged without respect of persons: I require you to examine your self and your state, both toward God and man: so that accusing and condemning yourself for your own faults, you may find mercy at our heavenly Father's hand for Christ's sake, and not be accused and condemned in that fearful judgment. Therefore I shall shortly rehearse the articles of our faith, that ye[6] may know whether you do believe, as a Christian man should, or no.

¶ Here the minister shall rehearse the articles of the faith, saying thus.

DOST thou believe in God the Father Almighty.

¶ And so forth, as it is in Baptism.

¶ Then shall the Minister examine whether he be in charity with all the world: Exhorting him to forgive, from the bottom of his heart, all persons that have offended him: and if he have offended other, to ask them forgiveness: And where he hath done injury or wrong to any man, that he make amends to the uttermost of his power. And if he have not afore disposed his goods, let him then make his will[7].

[[3] Grafton, chasten.]   [[4] Grafton, would.]
[[5] Grafton, an accompte.]   [[6] 1596, you.]
[[7] 1578, 1596, *make his will, and also declare......of his executors. But men, &c.* See the Latin Prayer Book.]

But men must be oft admonished that they set an order for their temporal goods and lands, when they be in health. And also declare his debts, what he oweth, and what is owing unto him, for discharging of his conscience, and quietness of his executors.

¶ These[1] words before rehearsed, may be said before the Minister begin his prayer, as he shall see cause.

¶ The Minister may not forget, nor omit to move the sick person, (and that most earnestly) to liberality toward the poor.

¶ Here shall the sick person make a special confession, if he feel his conscience troubled with any weighty matter. After which confession, the Priest[2] shall absolve him after this sort.

OUR Lord Jesus Christ, who hath left power to his church to absolve all sinners, which truly repent and believe in him, of his great mercy forgive thee thine offences: and by his authority committed to me, I absolve thee from all thy sins, in the name of the Father, and of the Son[3], and of the Holy Ghost. Amen.

¶ And then the Priest[2] shall say the Collect following.

¶ Let us pray.

O MOST merciful God, which, according to the multitude of thy mercies, dost so put away the sins of those which truly repent, that thou rememberest them no more: open thy eye of mercy upon this thy servant, who most earnestly desireth pardon and forgiveness. Renew in him, most loving Father, whatsoever hath been decayed by the fraud and malice of the devil, or by his own carnal will and frailness: preserve and continue this sick member in the unity of thy[4] church: consider his contrition, accept his tears, assuage his pain, as shall be seen to thee most expedient for him. And forasmuch as he putteth his full trust only in thy mercy, impute not unto him his former sins, but take him unto[5] thy favour: through the merits of thy most dearly beloved Son Jesus Christ. Amen.

¶ Then the Minister shall say this Psalm.

In te, Domine, speravi. Psal. xxi.[7]

IN[6] thee, O Lord, have I put my trust, let me never be put to confusion: but rid me, and deliver me into thy righteousness, incline thine ear unto me, and save me.

[1 Grafton, who places this direction at the side, commences it thus:—This may bee done before the minister begin his prayers, as, &c.]
[2 1578, *the Minister.*]   [3 Grafton, Sonne. &c. Amen.]
[4 1578, 1596, the.]   [5 Grafton, to.]   [6 Grafton, In the Lorde.]
[7 A misprint for, lxxi. in both editions of 1559.]

Be thou my strong hold (whereunto I may alway resort :) thou hast promised to help me, for thou art my house of defence, and my castle.

Deliver me (O my God) out of the hand of the ungodly : out of the hand of the unrighteous and cruel man.

For thou (O Lord God) art the thing that I long for : thou art my hope, even from my youth.

Through thee have I been holden up ever since I was born : thou art he that took me out of my mother's womb, my praise shall alway be of thee.

I am become as it were a monster unto many : but my sure trust is in thee.

O let my mouth be filled with thy praise : that I may sing of thy glory and honour all the day long.

Cast me not away in the time of age : forsake me not when my strength faileth me.

For mine enemies speak against me, and they that lay wait for my soul, take their counsel together, saying : God hath forsaken him, persecute him, and take him, for there is none to deliver him.

Go not far from me, O God : my God, haste thee to help me.

Let them be confounded and perish, that are against my soul : let them be covered with shame and dishonour that seek to do me evil.

As for me, I will patiently abide alway : and will praise thee more and more.

My mouth shall daily speak of thy righteousness and salvation : for I know no end thereof.

I will go forth in the strength of the Lord God : and will make mention of thy righteousness only.

Thou (O God) hast taught me from my youth up until now : therefore I will tell of thy wondrous works.

Forsake me not (O God) in mine old age, when I am gray headed : until I have shewed thy strength unto this generation, and thy power to all them that are yet for to come.

Thy righteousness (O God) is very high, and great things are they that thou hast done : O God, who is like unto thee?

O what great troubles and adversities hast thou shewed

me! and yet didst thou turn and refresh me : yea, and broughtest me from the deep of the earth again.

Thou hast brought me to great honour : and comforted me on every side.

Therefore will I praise thee and thy faithfulness, (O God) playing upon an instrument of music : unto thee will I sing upon the harp, O thou holy one of Israel.

My lips will be fain when I sing unto thee : and so will my soul, whom thou hast delivered.

My tongue also shall talk of thy righteousness all the day long : for they are confounded and brought unto shame, that seek to do me evil.

Glory be to the Father, and to the Son : and to the. &c.

As it was in the beginning, is now, and ever shall be : world without end. Amen.

¶ *Adding this.*

O SAVIOUR of the world, save us, which by thy cross and precious blood hast redeemed us, help us, we beseech thee, O God.

¶ *Then shall the Minister say,*

THE Almighty Lord, which is a most strong tower to all them that put their trust in him, to whom all things in heaven, in earth, and under earth[1], do bow and obey : be now and evermore thy defence : and make thee know and feel, that there is no other name under heaven given to man, in whom, and through whom, thou mayest receive health and salvation, but only the name of our Lord Jesus Christ. Amen.

[1 Grafton and 1596, the earth.]

¶ The Communion of the Sick.

FORASMUCH as all mortal men be subject to many sudden perils, diseases, and sicknesses, and ever uncertain what time they shall depart out of this life: Therefore, to the intent they may be always in a readiness to die, whensoever it shall please Almighty God to call them, the Curates shall diligently from time to time, but specially in the plague time, exhort their parishioners to the oft receiving in the church of the holy communion of the body and blood of our Saviour Christ. Which if they do, they shall have no cause in their sudden visitation to be unquieted for lack of the same: but if the sick person be not able to come to the church, and yet is desirous to receive the communion in his house, then he[2] must give knowledge over night, or else early in the morning, to the Curate, signifying also how many be appointed to communicate with him. And having a convenient place in the sick man's house, where the Curate may reverently minister, and a good number to receive the communion with the sick person, with all things necessary for the same, he shall there minister the holy communion[3].

The Collects[4].

ALMIGHTY everliving God, Maker of mankind, which dost correct those whom thou dost love, and chastisest every one whom thou dost receive: we beseech thee to have mercy upon this thy servant visited with thy hand, and to grant that he may take his sickness patiently, and recover his bodily health (if it be thy gracious will), and whensoever his soul shall depart from the body, it may be without spot presented unto thee: through Jesus Christ our Lord. Amen[5].

The Epistle.

MY son, despise not the correction of the Lord, neither faint when thou art rebuked of him. For whom the Lord   Hebr. ii.

[2 Grafton, yee.] [3 1578 omits this rubric.]
[4 A misprint for, Collect.]
[5 Grafton omits, Amen; and also, The Epistle.]

loveth, him he correcteth: yea, and he scourgeth every son whom he receiveth.

The Gospel.

John v. VERILY, verily I say unto you, he that heareth my word, and believeth on him that sent me, hath everlasting life, and shall not come unto damnation, but he passeth from death unto life.

> At the time of the distribution of the holy Sacrament, the Priest shall first receive the Communion himself, and after minister unto them that be appointed to communicate with the sick.

> But if any man, either by reason of extremity of sickness, or for lack of warning in due time to the Curate, or for lack of company to receive with him, or by any other just impediment, do not receive the Sacrament of Christ's body and blood: then the Curate shall instruct him, that if he do truly repent him of his sins, and stedfastly believe that Jesus Christ hath suffered death upon the cross for him, and shed his blood for his redemption, earnestly remembering the benefits he hath thereby, and giving him hearty thanks therefore, he doth eat and drink the body and blood of our Saviour Christ profitably to his soul's health, although he do not receive the Sacrament with his mouth.

> ¶ When[1] the sick person is visited, and receiveth the holy communion all at one time, then the priest[2], for more expedition, shall cut off the form of the visitation at the Psalm, *In thee, O Lord, have I put my trust*, and go straight to the communion.

> ¶ In the time of plague, sweat, or such other like contagious times of sicknesses or diseases, when none of the parish[3] or neighbours can be gotten to communicate with the sick in their houses, for fear of the infection, upon special request of the diseased, the Minister may alonely communicate with him.

[1 1578 has only this rubric.]   [2 1578, *the Minister*.]
[3 Grafton, Paroche.]

The Order for
the Burial of the Dead.

The priest[4] meeting the corpse at the church stile, shall say: Or else the priests[5] and clerks shall sing, and so go either unto the church, or towards the grave.

I AM the resurrection and the life (saith the Lord): he that believeth in me, yea, though he were dead, yet shall he live. And whosoever liveth and believeth in me, shall not die for ever. *John xi.*

I KNOW that my Redeemer liveth, and that I shall rise out of the earth in the last day, and shall be covered again with my skin, and shall see God in my flesh: yea, and I my self shall behold him, not with other, but with these[6] same eyes. *Job xix.*

WE brought nothing into this world, neither may we carry any thing out of this world. The Lord giveth, and the Lord taketh away. Even as it hath pleased the Lord, so cometh things to pass: blessed be the name of the Lord. *i. Tim. vi.* *Job i.*

When they come at[7] the grave, whiles the corpse is made ready to be laid into the earth, the[4] priest shall say, or the priest[8] and clerks shall sing.

MAN that is born of a woman hath but a short time to live, and is full of misery: he cometh up, and is cut down like a flower; he flieth as it were a shadow, and never continueth in one stay. In the midst of life we be in death: of whom may we seek for succour, but of thee, O Lord, which *Job xi.*[9]

[[4] 1578, *The Minister.*]
[[5] Misprint in both editions of 1559, and in 1596. 1578, *Ministers.*]
[[6] Grafton, the.]   [[7] Grafton and 1596, to.]
[[8] Grafton, priestes. 1578, *Ministers.* A misprint.]
[[9] Grafton, *Job* ix. 1596, Job 14. The last reference is the right.]

for our sins justly are displeased? Yet, O Lord God most holy, O Lord most mighty, O holy and most merciful Saviour, deliver us not into the bitter pains of eternal death. Thou knowest, Lord, the secrets of our hearts, shut not up thy merciful eyes to our prayers: But spare us, Lord most holy, O God most mighty, O holy and merciful Saviour, thou most worthy judge eternal, suffer us not at our last hour for any pains of death to fall from thee.

Then while the earth shall be cast upon the body by some standing by, the priest[1] shall say.

FORASMUCH as it hath pleased almighty God of his great mercy to take unto himself the soul of our dear brother here departed: we therefore commit his body to the ground, earth to earth, ashes to ashes, dust to dust, in sure and certain hope of resurrection to eternal life, through our Lord Jesus Christ: who shall change our vile body that it may be like to his glorious body, according to the mighty working, whereby he is able to subdue all things to himself.

Then shall be said, or sung,

I HEARD a voice from heaven saying unto me: Write from henceforth blessed are the dead which die in the Lord. Even so saith the Spirit, that they rest from their labours.

Then shall follow this lesson, taken out of the .xv. Chapter to the Corinthians, the first Epistle.

CHRIST is risen from the dead, and become the first-fruits of them that slept[2]. For by a man came death, and by a man came the resurrection of the dead. For as by Adam all die, even so by Christ shall all be made alive: but every man in his own order. The first is Christ, then they that are Christ's at his coming. Then cometh the end, when he hath delivered up the kingdom to God the Father, when he hath put down all rule and all authority and power. For he must reign till he have put all[3] his enemies under his feet. The last enemy that shall be destroyed, is death. For he hath put all things under his feet. But when he saith, all things are put under him, it is manifest that he is excepted, which did put all things under him. When all things are subdued unto him, then shall the Son also him self be subject unto him that put all things under him, that God may be all in all. Else what do they which are Baptized over the dead, if the dead rise not at all? Why are they then Baptized over them? yea, and why stand we alway then in jeopardy? By our rejoicing which I have in Christ Jesu our Lord, I die daily. That I have fought with beasts at Ephesus, after the manner

[[1] 1578, *the Minister.*] [[2] Grafton, slepe.] [[3] Grafton omits, all.]

of men, what avantageth it me, if the dead rise not again? Let us eat and drink, for to morrow we shall die. Be not ye deceived, evil words corrupt good manners. Awake truly out of sleep, and sin not. For some have not the knowledge of God. I speak this to your shame. But some man will say: How arise the dead? with what body shall they come? Thou fool, that which thou sowest is not quickened except it die. And what sowest thou? thou sowest not that body that shall be, but bare corn, as of wheat or some other: but God giveth it a body at his pleasure, to every seed his own body. All flesh is not one manner of flesh: but there is one manner of flesh of men, and other[4] manner of flesh of beasts, and other[4] of fishes, another of birds. There are also celestial bodies, and there are bodies terrestrial. But the glory of the celestial is one, and the glory of the terrestrial is another. There is one manner glory of the Sun, and another glory of the Moon, and another glory of the stars. For one star differeth from another in glory. So is the resurrection of the dead. It is sown in corruption, it riseth again in incorruption. It is sown in dishonour, it riseth again in honour. It is sown in weakness, it riseth again in power. It is sown a natural body, it riseth again a spiritual body. There is a natural body, and there is a spiritual body, as it is also written: the first man Adam was made a living soul, and the last Adam was made a quickening spirit. Howbeit, that is not first which is spiritual, but that which is natural, and then that which is spiritual. The first man is of the earth, earthy. The second man is the Lord from heaven, heavenly. As is the earthy, such are they that be earthy. And as is the heavenly, such are they that are heavenly. And as we have borne the Image of the earthy, so shall we bear the Image of the heavenly. This say I, brethren, that flesh and blood cannot inherit the kingdom of God, neither doth corruption inherit uncorruption[5]. Behold, I shew you a mystery. We shall not all sleep: but we shall all be changed, and that in a moment, in the twinkling of an eye by the last trump. For the trump shall blow, and the dead shall rise incorruptible, and we shall be changed. For this corruptible must put on incorruption, and this mortal must put on immortality. When this corruptible hath put on incorruption, and this mortal hath put on immortality: then shall be brought to pass the saying that is written, Death is swallowed up in victory. Death, where is thy sting? Hell, where is thy victory? The sting of death is sin, and the strength of sin is the law. But thanks be unto God, which hath given us victory, through our Lord Jesus Christ. Therefore, my dear brethren, be ye stedfast and unmovable, always rich in the work of the Lord, forasmuch as ye know how that your labour is not in vain in the Lord.

The Lesson ended, the Priest[6] shall say,

Lord, have mercy upon us.
Christ, have mercy upon us.

[4 Grafton, another.]   [5 Grafton, incorruption.]
[6 1578, the Minister.]

Lord, have mercy upon us.
¶ Our Father which art in heaven. &c.
And lead us not into temptation.
Answer. But deliver us from evil. Amen.

The Priest[1].

ALMIGHTY God, with whom do live the spirits of them that depart hence in the Lord, and in whom the souls of them that be elected, after they be delivered from the burden of the flesh, be in joy and felicity: We give thee hearty thanks, for that it hath pleased thee to deliver this .N. our brother, out of the miseries of this sinful world: beseeching thee, that it may please thee of thy gracious goodness, shortly to accomplish the number of thine elect, and to haste thy kingdom, that we with this our brother, and all other departed in the true faith of thy holy name, may have our perfect consummation and bliss, both in body and soul, in thy eternal and everlasting glory. Amen.

¶ The Collect.

O MERCIFUL God, the Father of our Lord Jesus Christ, who is the resurrection and the life, in whom whosoever believeth shall live, though he die, and whosoever liveth, and believeth in him, shall not die eternally: who also taught us (by his holy apostle Paul) not to be sorry, as men without hope, for them that sleep in him: We meekly beseech thee (O Father) to raise us from the death of sin unto the life of righteousness, that, when we shall depart this life, we may rest in him, as our hope is this our brother doth: and that at the general resurrection in the last day, we may be found acceptable in thy sight, and receive that blessing which thy wellbeloved Son shall then pronounce to all that love and fear thee, saying, Come ye blessed children of my Father, receive the kingdom prepared for you from the beginning of the world. Grant this, we beseech thee, O merciful Father, through Jesus Christ, our mediator and redeemer. Amen.

[1 1578, *Minister.*]

¶ The[2] thanks giving of women after child birth,

commonly called

the Churching of Women.

The woman shall come into the church, and there shall kneel down in some convenient place, nigh unto the place where the table standeth, and the priest standing by her shall say these words, or such like as the case shall require.

FORASMUCH as it hath pleased almighty[3] God of his goodness to give you safe deliverance, and hath preserved you in the great danger of childbirth : ye shall therefore give hearty thanks unto God and pray.

¶ Then shall the priest say this Psalm.

I have lifted[4] up mine eyes unto the hills : from whence cometh my help.

My help cometh even from the Lord : which hath made heaven and earth.

He will not suffer thy foot to be moved : and he that keepeth thee will not sleep.

Behold, he that keepeth Israel : shall neither slumber nor sleep.

The Lord him self is thy keeper : the Lord is thy defence upon thy right hand.

So that the sun shall not burn thee by day : neither[5] the moon by night.

The Lord shall preserve thee from all evil : yea, it is even he that shall keep thy soul.

The Lord shall preserve thy going out, and thy coming in : from this time forth for evermore.

Glory be to the Father, and to the Son, and to. &c.

As it was in the beginning, is now, and ever. &c.

Lord, have mercy upon us.

Christ, have mercy upon us.

Lord, have mercy upon us.

[2 1578 omits this Service.]   [3 Grafton, the almyghtye.]
[4 Grafton, lyfte.]   [5 1596, nor.]

¶ Our Father which. &c.
And lead us not into temptation.
Answer. But deliver us from evil. Amen.
Priest. O Lord, save this woman thy servant.
Answer. Which putteth her trust in thee.
Priest. Be thou to her a strong tower.
Answer. From the face of her enemy.
Priest. Lord, hear our prayer.
Answer. And let my[1] cry come unto thee.

Priest.

Let us pray.

O ALMIGHTY God, which hast delivered this woman thy servant from the great pain and peril of child birth: Grant we beseech thee (most merciful Father) that she, through thy help, may both faithfully live and walk in her vocation, according to thy will, in this life present; and also may be partaker of everlasting glory in the life to come: through Jesus Christ our Lord. Amen.

The woman that cometh to give her thanks, must offer accustomed offerings: and if there be a Communion, it is convenient that she receive the holy Communion.

[[1] Grafton and 1596, our.]

A Commination

against sinners, with certain prayers, to be used divers[2] times in the year.

¶ After Morning prayer, the people being called together by the ringing of a bell, and assembled in the Church, the English Litany shall be said, after the accustomed manner: which ended, the Priest[3] shall go into the pulpit and say thus.

BRETHREN, in the primitive church there was a godly discipline, that, at the beginning of Lent, such persons as were notorious sinners, were put to open penance, and punished in this world, that their souls might be saved in the day of the Lord; and that others[4] admonished by their example might be more afraid to offend. In the stead whereof, until the said discipline may be restored again (which thing is much to be wished) it is thought good, that at this time (in your presence) should be read the general sentences of God's cursing against impenitent sinners, gathered out of the .xxvii. Chapter of Deuteronomy, and other places of scripture; and that ye should answer to every sentence, Amen. To the intent that you, being admonished of the great indignation of God against sinners, may the rather be called to earnest and true repentance, and may walk more warily in these dangerous days, fleeing[5] from such vices, for the which ye affirm with your own mouths the curse of God to be due.

[[2] Though these 'times' have not been fixed by any precise rule of our church, archbishop Grindal (Remains, p. 158.) inquired, in 1576, of the churchwardens, whether, throughout the province of Canterbury, the Commination service was read 'three times at least in the year, that is to say, for order sake, yearly upon one of the three Sundays next before Easter, for the first time; upon one of the two Sundays next before the feast of Pentecost for the second time; and for the third time, upon one of the two Sundays next before the feast of the birth of our Lord, over and besides the accustomed reading thereof upon the first day of Lent.']

[[3] 1578, *the Minister.*]   [[4] 1596, other.]
[[5] Grafton, flieng.]

CURSED is the man that maketh any carved or molten Image, an abomination to the Lord, the work of the hands of the craftsman, and putteth it in a secret place to worship it.

And the people shall answer and say.

Amen.

Minister. Cursed is he that curseth his father and[1] mother.

Answer. Amen.

Minister. Cursed is he that removeth away the mark of his neighbour's land.

Answer. Amen.

Minister. Cursed is he that maketh the blind to go out of his way.

Answer. Amen.

Minister. Cursed is he that letteth in judgment the right of the stranger, of them that be fatherless, and of widows.

Answer. Amen.

Minister. Cursed is he that smiteth his neighbour secretly.

Answer. Amen.

Minister. Cursed is he that lieth with his neighbour's wife.

Answer. Amen.

Minister. Cursed is he that taketh reward to slay the soul of innocent blood.

Answer. Amen.

Minister. Curseth is he that putteth his trust in man, and taketh man for his defence; and in his heart goeth from the Lord.

Answer. Amen.

Minister. Cursed are the unmerciful, the fornicators, and adulterers, and the covetous persons, the worshippers of images, slanderers, drunkards, and extortioners.

Answer. Amen.

The Minister[2].

Psa. cxviii.[3] Now seeing that all they be accursed (as the Prophet David beareth witness) which do err and go astray from the commandments of God: let us (remembering the dreadful judgment hanging over our heads, and being always[4] at

---

[1 Grafton, or.]   [2 Grafton and 1596, Minister.]
[3 This reference is according to 'the common Latin translation', which ought not to have been the case. See p. 39. The same thing occurs on the next page.]   [4 Grafton, alway.]

hand) return unto our Lord God, with all contrition and meekness of heart, bewailing and lamenting our sinful life, knowledging and confessing our offences, and seeking to bring forth worthy fruits of penance. For now is the axe put unto the root of the trees, so that every tree which bringeth not forth good fruit, is hewn down and cast into the fire. It is a fearful thing to fall into the hands of the living God: he shall pour down rain upon the sinners, snares, fire, and brimstone, storm and tempest: this shall be their portion to drink. For lo, the Lord is comen out of his place, to visit the wickedness of such as dwell upon the earth. But who may abide the day of his coming? who shall be able to endure when he appeareth? His fan is in his hand, and he will purge his floor, and gather his wheat into the barn: but he will burn the chaff with unquenchable fire. The day of the Lord cometh as a thief upon the night; and when men shall say peace, and all things are safe, then shall suddenly destruction come upon them, as sorrow cometh upon a woman travailing with child, and they shall not escape: then shall appear the wrath of God in the day of vengeance, which obstinate sinners, through the stubbornness of their heart, have heaped unto them self, which despised the goodness, patience, and long sufferance of God, when he called them continually to repentance. Then shall they call upon me, saith the Lord, but I will not hear: they shall seek me early, but they shall not find me; and that, because they hated knowledge, and received not the fear of the Lord, but abhorred my counsel, and despised my correction: then shall it be too late to knock, when the door shall be shut, and too late to cry for mercy, when it is the time of justice. O terrible voice of most just judgment, which shall be pronounced upon them, when it shall be said unto them: Go, ye cursed, into the fire everlasting, which is prepared for the devil and his angels. Therefore, brethren, take we heed betime[5], while the day of salvation lasteth, for the night cometh when none can work: but let us, while we have the light, believe in the light, and walk as the children of the light, that we be not cast into the utter darkness, where is weeping and gnashing of teeth. Let us not abuse the goodness of God, which calleth us mercifully to

[5 Grafton, bytime.]

amendment, and of his endless pity promiseth[1] us forgiveness of that which is past, if (with a whole mind and true heart) we return unto him: for though our sins be red as scarlet, they shall be as white as snow: and though they be like purple, yet shall they be as white as wool. Turn you clean (saith the Lord) from all your wickedness, and your sin shall not be your destruction. Cast away from you all your ungodliness that ye have done, make you new hearts, and a new spirit: wherefore will ye die, O ye house of Israel? Seeing that I have no pleasure in the death of him that dieth (saith the Lord God.) Turn you then and you shall live. Although we have sinned, yet have we an Advocate with the Father, Jesus Christ the righteous: and he it is that obtaineth grace for our sins; for he was wounded for our offences, and smitten for our wickedness. Let us therefore return unto him, who is the merciful receiver of all true penitent sinners: assuring our self that he is ready to receive us, and most willing to pardon us, if we come to him with faithful repentance: if we will submit our selves unto him, and from henceforth walk in his ways; if we will take his easy yoke and light burden upon us, to follow him, in lowliness, patience, and charity, and be ordered by the governance of his Holy Spirit, seeking always his glory, and serving him duly in our vocation with thanks giving. This if we do, Christ will deliver us from the curse of the law, and from the extreme malediction, which light upon them that shall be set on the left hand: and he will set us on his right hand, and give us the blessed benediction of his Father, commanding us to take possession of his glorious kingdom; unto the which he vouchsafe to bring us all, for his infinite mercy. Amen[5].

Esai. i.
Ezechiel xxviii.[2]
i. John. ii.[3]
Esai. liii.
Math. xi.
Math. xxv.[4]

Then shall they all kneel upon their knees: and the Priests[6] and Clerks kneeling (where they are accustomed to say the Litany,) shall say this Psalm.

Miserere mei. Psal. li.

HAVE mercy upon me (O God) after thy great goodness: according to the multitude of thy mercies, do away mine offences.

[[1] Grafton, promised.]   [[2] Misprint for, xviii.]
[[3] Grafton has not this reference, and puts i for liii in the next.]
[[4] Grafton, xiii.]   [[5] Not in Grafton.]
[[6] A misprint in both editions of 1559. 1578, *the Minister*. 1596, *the Priest*.]

Wash me throughly from my wickedness : and cleanse me from my sin.

For I knowledge[7] my faults : and my sin is ever before me.

Against thee only have I sinned, and done this evil in thy sight : that thou mightest be justified in thy saying, and clear when thou art judged.

Behold, I was shapen in wickedness : and in sin hath my mother conceived me.

But lo, thou requirest truth in[8] inward parts : and shalt make me to understand wisdom secretly.

Thou shalt purge me with Isope, and I shall be clean : thou shalt wash me, and I shall be whiter than snow.

Thou shalt make me hear of joy and gladness : that the bones which thou hast broken may rejoice.

Turn thy face from my sins : and put out all my misdeeds.

Make me a clean heart (O God) : and renew a right spirit within me.

Cast me not away from thy presence : and take not thy Holy Spirit from me.

O give me the comfort of thy help again : and stablish me with thy free spirit.

Then shall I teach thy ways unto the wicked : and sinners shall be converted unto thee.

Deliver me from bloodguiltiness (O God) thou that art the God of my health : and my tongue shall sing of thy righteousness.

Thou shalt open my lips (O Lord :) my mouth shall shew thy praise.

For thou desirest no sacrifice, else would I give it thee : but thou delightest not in burnt offering.

The sacrifice of God is a troubled spirit : a broken and a contrite heart (O God) shalt thou not despise.

O be favourable and gracious unto Sion : build thou the walls of Hierusalem.

Then shalt thou be pleased with the sacrifice of righteousness, with the burnt offerings and oblations : then shall they offer young bullocks upon thine altar.

[7 Grafton, acknowledge.]   [8 1596, in the inward.]

Glory be to the Father, and to the Son. &c.
As it was in the beginning, and is now. &c.   Amen.
Lord, have mercy upon us.
Christ, have mercy upon us.
Lord, have mercy upon us.
¶ Our Father, which art in heaven. &c.
And lead us not into temptation.
Answer. But deliver us from evil.   Amen.
Minister. O Lord, save thy servants.
Answer. Which put their trust in thee.
Minister. Send unto them help from above.
Answer. And evermore mightily defend them.
Minister. Help us, O God our Saviour.
Answer. And for the glory of thy name's sake deliver us; be merciful unto us sinners, for thy name's sake.
Minister[1]. Lord, hear my prayers.
Answer. And let my cry come unto thee.

Let us pray.

O LORD, we beseech thee, mercifully hear our prayers, and spare all those which confess their sins to thee: that they (whose consciences by sin are accused) by thy merciful pardon may be absolved: Through Christ our Lord.   Amen.

O MOST mighty God and merciful Father, which hast compassion of all men, and hatest nothing that thou hast made: which wouldest not the death of a sinner, but that he should rather turn from sin, and be saved: mercifully forgive us our trespasses, receive[2] and comfort us, which be grieved and wearied with the burden of our sin. Thy property is to have mercy, to thee only it appertaineth to forgive sins: spare us therefore, good Lord, spare thy people whom thou hast redeemed. Enter not into judgment with thy servants, which be vile earth, and miserable sinners: but so turn thy[3] ire from us, which meekly knowledge our vileness, and truly repent us of our faults; so make haste to help us in this world, that we may ever live with thee in the world to come: through Jesus Christ our Lord.   Amen.

[1] Grafton and 1596, The Minister. O Lorde heare our praiers. They have also 'our' in the next suffrage. See p. 238.]

[2] Grafton omits, receive.]   [3] Grafton and 1596, thyne.]

¶ Then shall the people say this that followeth, after the Minister.

TURN thou us, O good Lord, and so shall we be turned: be favourable (O Lord) be favourable to thy people, which turn to thee in weeping, fasting, and praying; for thou art a merciful God, full of compassion, longsuffering, and of a great pity. Thou sparest when we deserve punishment, and in thy wrath thinkest upon mercy. Spare thy people, good Lord, spare them, and let not thy[4] heritage be brought to confusion: hear us (O Lord) for thy mercy is great, and after the multitude of thy mercies look upon us[5].

[4 1596, thine.]
[5 Later impressions of the Prayer Book by Jugge and Cawode have on the reverse of the last leaf:

This boke of praiers is to be solde as foloweth, and not aboue.

In Queers vnbounde.	ii. s. iiii. d.
In parchement bounde.	iii. s.
In Paste, or Borde bounde.	iii. s. viii. d.]

GODLY PRAYERS[1].

¶ Certain godly prayers to be used for sundry purposes.

A general confession of sins, to be said every morning.

O ALMIGHTY God, our heavenly Father, I confess and knowledge, that I am a miserable and a wretched sinner, and have manifold ways most grievously transgressed thy most godly commandments, through wicked thoughts, ungodly lusts, sinful words and deeds, and in my whole life. In sin am I born and conceived, and there is no goodness in me; inasmuch as if thou shouldest enter into thy narrow judgment with me, judging me according unto the same, I were never able to suffer or abide it, but must needs perish and be damned for ever: so little help, comfort, or succour is there either in me, or in any other creature. Only this is my comfort (O heavenly Father), that thou didst not spare thy only dear beloved Son, but didst give him up unto the most bitter, and most vile and slanderous death of the cross for me, that he might so pay the ransom for my sins, satisfy thy judgment, still and pacify thy wrath, reconcile me again unto thee, and purchase me thy grace and favour, and everlasting life. Wherefore, through the merit of his most bitter death and passion, and through his innocent bloodshedding, I beseech thee, O heavenly Father, that thou wilt vouchsafe to be gracious and merciful unto me, to forgive and pardon me all my sins, to lighten my heart with thy holy Spirit, to renew, confirm, and strengthen me with a right and a perfect faith, and to inflame me in love toward thee and my neighbour, that I may henceforth with a willing and a glad heart walk as it becometh me, in thy most godly commandments, and so glorify and praise thee everlasting[2]. And also that I may with a free conscience and quiet heart, in all manner of temptations,

[[1] We first find these Godly Prayers at the end of the Psalter belonging to the quarto Prayer Book of 1552, by Whitchurche: having however been similarly appended to the earlier Elizabethan Prayer Books, they are here reprinted from a copy of 1567, in the possession of the Rev. T. Lathbury of Bath.]

[[2] 1552, everlastingly.]

afflictions, or necessities, and even in the very pangs of death, cry boldly and merrily unto thee, and say : I believe in God the Father Almighty, maker of heaven and earth, and in Jesus Christ. &c. But, O Lord God, heavenly Father, to comfort myself in affliction and temptation with these articles of the Christian faith, it is not in my power; for faith is thy gift: and forasmuch as thou wilt be prayed unto, and called upon for it, I come unto thee, to pray and beseech thee, both for that and for all my other necessities, even as thy dear beloved Son our Saviour Christ Jesus hath himself taught us. And from the very bottom of my heart I cry, and say : O our Father, which art in heaven. &c.

¶ Prayers to be said in the morning.

O MERCIFUL Lord God, heavenly Father, I render most high lauds, praise, and thanks unto thee, that thou hast preserved me both this night, and all the time and days of my life hitherto, under thy protection, and hast suffered me to live until this present hour. And I beseech thee heartily, that[3] thou wilt vouchsafe to receive me this day, and the residue of my whole life from henceforth into thy tuition, ruling and governing me with thy holy Spirit, that all manner of darkness, of misbelief, infidelity, and of carnal lusts and affections, may be utterly chased and driven out of my heart, and that I may be justified and saved both body and soul through a right and a perfect faith, and so walk in the light of thy most godly truth, to thy glory and praise, and to the profit and furtherance of my neighbour, through Jesus Christ our Lord and Saviour. Amen.

ALL possible thanks that we are able we render unto thee, O Lord Jesus Christ, for that thou hast willed this night past to be prosperous unto us; and we beseech thee likewise to prosper all this same day unto us for thy glory, and for the health of our soul : and that thou which art the true light, not knowing any going down, and which art the Sun eternal, giving life, food, and gladness unto all things, vouchsafe to shine into our minds, that we may not any where stumble to fall into any sin, but may through thy good guiding and conducting come to the life everlasting. Amen.

[3 That, wanting in 1552.]

[1] O Lord Jesus Christ, which art the true Sun of the world, evermore arising, and never going down, which by thy most wholesome appearing and sight dost bring forth, preserve, nourish, and refresh all things, as well that are in heaven, as also that are on earth: we beseech thee mercifully and favourably to shine into our hearts, that the night and darkness of sins, and the mists of errors on every side driven away, thou brightly shining within our hearts, we may all our life space go without any stumbling or offence, and may decently and seemly walk, (as in the day time,) being pure and clean from the works of darkness, and abounding in all good works which God hath prepared for us to walk in: which with the Father and with the Holy Ghost livest and reignest for ever and ever. Amen.

O God and Lord Jesus Christ, thou knowest, yea, and hast also taught us, how great the infirmity and weakness of man is, and how certain a thing it is that it can nothing do without thy godly help. If man trust to himself, it cannot be avoided, but that he must headlong run and fall into a thousand undoings and mischiefs. O our Father, have thou pity and compassion upon the weakness of us thy children, be thou prest and ready to help us, always shewing thy mercy upon us, and prospering whatsoever we godly go about: so that, thou giving us light, we may see what things are truly good in deed; thou encouraging us, we may have an earnest desire to the same; and thou being our guide, we may come where to obtain them: for we having nothing but mistrust in our selves, do yield and commit our selves full and whole unto thee alone, which workest all things in all creatures, to thy honour and glory. So be it.

A prayer against temptation.

O Lord Jesus Christ, the only stay and fence of our mortal state, our only hope, our only salvation, our glory, and our triumph, who in the flesh (which thou hadst for our only cause taken upon thee) didst suffer thy self to be tempted of Sathan, and who only and alone of all men didst utterly overcome and vanquish sin, death, the world, the devil, and all the kingdom of hell: and whatsoever thou hast so overcomed, for our behoof it is that thou hast overcomed it: neither hath it been thy will to have any of thy servants keep battle or

[1 This Prayer is in the Primer of 1545.]

fight with any of the foresaid evils, but of purpose to reward us with a crown of the more glory for it, and to the intent that thou mightest likewise overthrow Sathan in thy members, as thou hadst afore done in thine own person. Give thou (we beseech thee) unto us thy soldiers (O Lion most victorious of the tribe of Judah) strength against the roaring Lion, which continually wandereth to and fro, seeking whom he may devour. Thou being that same serpent, the true giver of health and life, that were nailed on high upon a tree, give unto us, thy little seely ones, wiliness against the deceitful awaiting[2] of the most subtle serpent. Thou being a Lamb as white as snow, the vanquisher of Satan's tyranny, give unto us thy little sheep the strength and virtue of thy Spirit, that being in our own selves weak and feeble, and in thee strong and valiant, we may withstand and overcome all assaults of the devil, so that our ghostly enemy may not glory on us, but being conquered[3] through thee, we may give thanks to thy mercy, which never leaveth them destitute that put their trust in thee: who livest and reignest God for ever without end. Amen.

A prayer[4] for the obtaining of wisdom.

O GOD of our fathers, and Lord of mercy, thou that hast made all things with thy word, and ordained man through thy wisdom, that he should have dominion[5] over the creatures[6] which thou hast made, that he should order the world according to equity and righteousness, and execute judgment with a true heart: give me wisdom, which is ever about thy seat, and put me not out from among thy children: for I thy servant and son of thy handmaid am a feeble person, of a short time, and too young to the understanding of thy judgment and laws: yea, though a man be never so perfect among the children of men, yet if thy wisdom be not with him, he shall be nothing worth. O send thy wisdom out of thy holy heavens, and from the throne of thy majesty, that she may be with me and labour with me, that I may know what is

Sapien. ix.

[2 Awaiting: lying in wait.]   [3 conquerors, 1552.]
[4 'This Prayer is also set at the beginning of the Bishops' Bible, put forth by Archbishop Parker; who, we may conclude, ordered the setting of that Prayer there as proper to be used before the reading of any portions of the holy scripture.' Strype's Parker, p. 84. It is likewise in the Primer of 1545.]
[5 domination, 1552.]   [6 creature, 1552.]

acceptable in thy sight; for she knoweth and understandeth all things, and she shall conduct me right soberly in thy[1] works, and preserve me in her power: so shall my works be acceptable. Amen.

[2] A prayer against worldly carefulness.

O MOST dear and tender Father, our defender and nourisher, endue us with thy grace, that we may cast off the great blindness of our minds, and carefulness of worldly things, and may put our whole study and care in keeping of thy holy law; and that we may labour and travail for our necessities in this life, like the birds of the air, and the lilies of the field, without care. For thou hast promised to be careful for us, and hast commanded that upon thee we should cast all our care: which livest and reignest, world without end. Amen.

A prayer necessary for all persons.

O MERCIFUL God, I a wretched sinner reknowledge myself bound to keep thy holy commandments, but yet unable to perform them, and to be accepted for just without the righteousness of Jesu Christ thy only Son, who hath perfectly fulfilled thy law, to justify all men that believe and trust in him. Therefore grant me grace, I beseech thee, to be occupied in doing of good works, which thou commandest in holy scripture, all the days of my life, to thy glory; and yet to trust only in thy mercy, and in Christ's merits, to be purged from my sins, and not in my good works, be they never so many. [3] Give me grace to love thy holy word fervently, to search the scriptures diligently, to read them humbly, to understand them truly, to live after them effectually. Order my life so, O Lord, that it be alway acceptable unto thee. Give me grace not to rejoice in any thing that displeaseth thee, but evermore to delight in those things that please thee, be they never so contrary to my desires. Teach me so to pray, that my petitions may be graciously heard of thee. Keep me upright among diversity of opinions and judgments

[1] my, 1552.]   [2] In the Primer of 1545.]
[3] Commencing from this point, the present prayer is based completely upon one given in the Primer of 1545 (see Burton's Three Primers, p. 519), the latter, except at the end, being a version out of Aquinas made 'by the moste exselent Prynces, Mary. In the yere of oure lorde god M.cccc xxvii: And the xi. yere of here age.' Her prayer in its original state may be seen in the Monumenta Ritualia, Vol. II. pp. 266, 267.]

in the world, that I never swarve from thy truth taught in holy scripture. In prosperity, O Lord, save me, that I wax not proud. In adversity help me, that I neither despair nor blaspheme thy holy name, but taking it patiently, to give thee thanks, and trust to be delivered after thy pleasure. When I happen to fall into sin through frailty, I beseech thee to work true repentance in my heart, that I may be sorry without desperation, trust in thy mercy without presumption, that I may amend my life, and become truly religious without hypocrisy, lowly in heart without feigning, faithful and trusty without deceit, merry without lightness, sad without mistrust, sober without slothfulness, content with mine own without covetousness. To tell my neighbour his faults charitably without dissimulation. To instruct my household in thy laws truly. To obey our king[4] and all governours under him unfeignedly. To receive all laws and common ordinances (which disagreeth not from thy holy word) obediently. To pay every man that which I owe unto him truly. To backbite no man, nor slander my neighbour secretly, and to abhor all vice, loving all goodness earnestly. O Lord, grant me thus to do, for the glory of thy holy name. Amen.

A prayer[5] necessary to be said at all times.

O BOUNTIFUL Jesu, O sweet Saviour, O Christ the Son of God, have pity upon me, mercifully hear me, and despise not my prayer[6]. Thou hast created me of nothing, thou hast redeemed me from the bondage of sin, death, and hell, neither with gold nor silver, but with thy most precious body once offered upon the cross, and thine own blood shed once for all, for my ransom: therefore cast me not away, whom thou by thy great wisdom hast made: despise me not, whom thou hast redeemed with such a precious treasure; nor let my wickedness destroy that which thy goodness hath builded. Now whiles I live, O Jesu, have mercy on me; for if I die out of thy favour, it will be too late afterward to call for thy mercy: whiles I have time to repent, look upon me with thy merciful eyes, as thou didst vouchsafe to look upon Peter thine Apostle, that I may bewail my sinful life, and obtain thy favour, and die therein. I reknowledge, that if thou shouldest

[4 So it stands even in the edition of 1567.]
[5 An adaptation of 'a deuoute prayer of Saynte Bernardyn,' which, translated into English, is in Burton's Three Primers, pp. 166, 368.]
[6 prayers, 1552.]

deal with me according to very justice, I have deserved everlasting death. Therefore I appeal to thy high throne of mercy, trusting to obtain God's favour, not for my merits, but for thy merits, O Jesu, who hast given thy self an acceptable sacrifice to the[1] Father, to appease his wrath, and to bring all sinners (truly repenting and amending their evil life) into his favour again. Accept me, O Lord, among the number of them that shall be saved, forgive me[2] my sins, give me grace to lead a godly and innocent life, grant me thy heavenly wisdom, inspire my heart with faith, hope, and charity; give me grace to be humble in prosperity, patient in adversity, obedient to my rulers, faithful unto them that trust me, dealing truly with all men, to live chastely in wedlock, to abhor adultery, fornication, and all uncleanness, to do good after my power unto all men, to hurt no man; that thy name may be glorified in me during this present life, and that I afterward may obtain everlasting life, through thy mercy and the merits of thy passion. Amen.

¶ Certain[3] prayers, taken out of the service daily used in the queen's house.

Monday. ALMIGHTY God, the Father of mercy, and God of all comfort, the which only forgivest sin, forgive unto us our sins, good Lord, forgive unto us our sins; that by the multitude of thy mercies they may be covered, and not imputed unto us, and by the operation of the Holy Ghost we may have power and strength hereafter to resist sin: by our Saviour and Lord Jesu Christ. Amen.

Tuesday. O LORD God, which despisest not a contrite heart, and forgettest the sins and wickedness of a sinner, in what hour soever he doth mourn and lament his old manner of living: grant unto us, O Lord, true contrition of heart, that we may vehemently despise our sinful life past, and wholly be converted unto thee, by our Saviour and Lord Jesus Christ. Amen.

Wednesday. O MERCIFUL Father, by whose power and strength we may overcome our enemies both bodily and ghostly: grant

[1 thy, 1552.] [2 me, wanting in 1552.]
[3 Such was the title in 1552: some years later it ran,—Certaine godly prayers for sundry dayes.—The queen meant could be no other than Catherine Par, though she died in 1548, four years earlier than the date of the publication.]

unto us, O Lord, that, according to our promise made in baptism, we may overcome the chief enemies of our soul, that is, the desires of the world, the pleasures of the flesh, and the suggestions of the wicked spirit; and so after lead our lives in holiness and righteousness, that we may serve thee in spirit and in truth, and that by our Saviour and Lord Jesus Christ. Amen.

O ALMIGHTY and everlasting God, which not only givest *Thursday.* every good and perfite gift, but also increasest those gifts that thou hast given: we most humbly beseech thee, merciful God, to increase in us the gift of faith, that we may truly believe in thee, and in thy promises made unto us, and that neither by our negligence, nor infirmity of the flesh, nor by the[4] grievousness of temptation, neither by the subtle crafts and assaults of the devil, we be driven from faith in the blood of our Saviour and Lord Jesu Christ. Amen.

GRANT unto us, O merciful God, we most heartily be- *Friday.* seech thee, knowledge and true understanding of thy word, that all ignorance expelled, we may know what thy will and pleasure is in all things, and how to do our duties, and truly to walk in our vocation, and that also we may express in our living those things that we do know; that we be not only knowers of thy word, good Lord, but also be workers of the same: by our Saviour and Lord Jesu Christ. Amen.

O ALMIGHTY God, which hast prepared everlasting life to *Saturday.* all those that be thy faithful servants: grant unto us, Lord, sure hope of the life everlasting, that we, being in this miserable world, may have some taste and feeling of it in our hearts; and that not by our deserving, but by the merits and deserving of our Saviour and Lord Jesu Christ. Amen.

O MERCIFUL God, our only aid, succour and strength at all times, grant unto us, O Lord, that in the time of prosperity we be not proud, and so forget thee, but that with our whole power and strength we may cleave unto thee; and in the time of adversity, that we fall not to infidelity and desperation, but that always with a constant faith we may call for help unto thee: Grant this, O Lord, for our Advocate sake and Saviour Jesu Christ. Amen.

[[4] the, wanting in 1552.]

Sunday.

O ALMIGHTY and merciful Lord, which givest unto thy elect people the Holy Ghost, as a sure pledge of thy heavenly kingdom: Grant unto us, O Lord, thy[1] holy Spirit, that he may bear witness with our spirit, that we be thy children and heirs of thy kingdom, and that by the operation of this Spirit we may kill all carnal lusts, unlawful pleasures, concupiscence, evil affections, contrary unto thy will, by our Saviour and Lord Jesu Christ. Amen.

[2]A prayer for trust in God.

THE beginning of the fall of man was trust in himself. The beginning of the restoring of man was distrust in himself, and trust in God. O most gracious and most wise guide, our Saviour Christ, which dost lead them the right way to immortal blessedness, which truly and unfeignedly trusting in thee, commit themself to thee: Grant us, that like as we be blind and feeble in deed, so we may take and repute our selves, that we presume not of ourselves[3], to see to ourselves[3], but so far to see, that alway we may have thee before our eyes, to follow thee, being our guide, to be ready at thy call most obediently, and to commit our selves wholly unto thee; that thou, which only knowest the way, mayest lead us the same way unto our heavenly desires. To thee with the Father and the Holy Ghost be glory for ever. Amen.

A prayer for the concord of Christ's church.

ARISE, Lord, let thine enemies be scattered, thy haters put to flight, the righteous and Christ's disciples make pleasant and merry; let them sing praises and pleasant songs unto thee, let them blow abroad thy magnificence, let them most highly advance thy majesty; let thy glory grow, let the kingdom of Christ from heaven among the chosen be enlarged: be thou the father of the fatherless, the judge of the widows, and the protector of them namely[4] whom the world forsaketh, whose consciences be troubled, whom the world pursueth for Christ's sake, which be needy and wrapped full of misery. In thy house, O Lord, let us dwell in peace and concord; give us all one heart, one mind, one true interpretation upon thy word. Pluck off the bands, as well from the consciences as from the bodies of the miserable captives, and of them also

[¹ this, 1552.]   [² In the Primer of 1545.]
[³ our selfes, 1552.]   [⁴ Namely: especially.]

which [5] as yet be hedged in within the lists of death, and unadvisedly strive against grace. How dry, Lord, is the flock of thine heritage! I pray thee, pour down largely the showers of thy graces, let a more plenteous fruitfulness chance, let thy people be strengthened with thy Spirit: Grant us, Lord, thy word abundantly, so that there may be many preachers of thy gospel, which may within themselves holily conspire and agree. Let the church, the spouse of Christ, deal large spoils of the conquered Sathan. All that believe in thee by Christ, O Lord God of health, mought[6] lift thee up with praises, might renown thee and extol thee. We be entered into the voyage of salvation. Conduct us luckily unto the port, that being delivered by thee from the very death, we may escape and come to the very life. Finish the thing that thou hast begun in us, make us to increase from faith to faith, leave us not to our own will and choice, for it is slippery and ready to fall. To the thunderbolts of thy word put violence, that we may give the glory to thee alonely. Give to thy people courage and power to withstand sin, and to obey thy word in all things: O Lord God, most glorious and excellent over all.

<small>A prayer against the enemies of Christ's truth.</small>

DELIVER me, O Lord, from the ungodly and stiffnecked persons; for thou seest how in their hearts they imagine mischief, and have great pleasure to pick quarrels, their tongues be more sharp than any adder's sting, and under their lips lurketh poison of adders. But, O merciful Lord, let me not fall into their hands, that they handle not me after their own lusts. Thou only art my God, thou must hear my piteous plaint. Lord, that rulest altogether, that art the strength and power of my defence, be thou as a sallet[7] on my head whensoever the ungodly shall assault me: neither suffer thou not the wicked thus to prosper in their matters. Suffer not their crooked and malicious stomachs[8] to increase and spite-

[5] Qui adhuc funibus mortis sunt circumdati. Orarium, 1546. Ps. xviii. 5.]

[6] Te laudibus evehant, honorent te. Orarium, 1546. 'Maught' stands for, might; and that again for, may.]

[7] Sallet: a kind of helmet.]

[8] Stomachs: animos. Orarium, 1546. Ps. ci. 7.]

fully revile thee. Look upon thy poor wretch's cause, and rid me out of these daily grievances; then shall I with a upright[1] heart and pleasant countenance extol and magnify thy holy name. Amen.

[2] A prayer for patience in trouble.

How hast thou, O Lord, humbled and plucked me down! I dare now unnethes[3] make my prayers unto thee, for thou art angry with me, but not without my deserving. Certainly I have sinned, Lord, I confess it, I will not deny it. But, O my God, pardon my trespasses, release my debts, render now thy grace again unto me, stop my wounds, for I am all[4] to plagued and beaten: yet, Lord, this notwithstanding I abide patiently, and give mine attendance on thee, continually waiting for relief at thy hand, and that not without skill; for I have received a token of thy favour and grace towards me, I mean thy word of promise concerning Christ, who for me was offered on the cross for a ransom, a sacrifice and price for my sins: wherefore, according to that thy promise, defend me, Lord, by thy right hand, and give a gracious ear to my requests, for all man's stays are but vain. Beat down therefore mine enemies thine own self with thy power, which art mine only aider and protector, O Lord God Almighty. Amen.

A prayer to be said at night going to bed.

O MERCIFUL Lord God, heavenly Father, whether we sleep or wake, live or die, we are always thine. Wherefore I beseech thee heartily, that thou wilt vouchsafe to take care and charge of me, and not to suffer me to perish in the works of darkness, but to kindle the light of thy countenance in my heart, that thy godly knowledge may daily increase in me, through a right and pure faith, and that I may always be found to walk and live after thy will and pleasure, through Jesus Christ our Lord and Saviour. Amen.

¶ [2] A prayer to be said at the hour of death.

O LORD Jesu, which art the only health of all men living, and the everlasting life of them which die in faith: I wretched sinner give and submit my self wholly unto thy most blessed

[[1] a right up, 1552.]   [[2] In the Primer of 1545.]
[[3] Unnethes: scarcely, hardly.]   [[4] All to: completely.]

will. And I being sure that the thing cannot perish which is committed unto thy mercy, willingly now I leave this frail and wicked flesh, in hope of the resurrection, which in better wise shall restore it to me again. I beseech thee, most merciful Lord Jesus Christ, that thou wilt by thy grace make strong my soul against all temptations, and that thou wilt cover and defend me with the buckler of thy mercy against all the assaults of the devil. I see and knowledge, that there is in myself no help of salvation, but all my confidence, hope, and trust, is in thy most merciful goodness. I have no merits, nor good works, which I may allege before thee. Of sins and evil works (alas!) I see a great heap; but through thy mercy, I trust to be in the number of them, to whom thou wilt not impute their sins, but take and accept me for righteous and just, and to be the inheritor of everlasting life. Thou, merciful Lord, wert born for my sake, thou didst suffer both hunger and thirst for my sake, thou didst preach and teach, thou didst pray and fast for my sake, thou didst all good works and deeds for my sake, thou sufferedst most grievous pains and torments for my sake; and finally, thou gavest thy most precious body to die, and thy blood to be shed on the cross for my sake. Now, most merciful Saviour, let all these things profit me, which thou freely hast given me, that hast given thy self for me. Let thy blood cleanse and wash away the spots and foulness of my sins. Let thy righteousness hide and cover my unrighteousness. Let the merits of thy passion and blood be the satisfaction for my sins. Give me, Lord, thy grace, that my faith and salvation in thy blood waver not in me, but ever be firm and constant, that the hope of thy mercy and life everlasting never decay in me, that charity wax not cold in me: finally, that the weakness of my flesh be not overcome with the fear of death. Grant me, merciful Saviour, that when death hath shut up the eyes of my body, yet that the eyes of my soul may still behold and look upon thee: that when death hath taken away the use of my tongue and speech, yet that my heart may cry and say unto thee, *In manus tuas, Domine, commendo spiritum meum;* that is to say, O Lord, into thy hands I give and commit my soul. *Domine Jesu, accipe spiritum meum.* Lord Jesu, receive my soul unto thee. Amen.

[LITURG. QU. ELIZ.]

Prayers[1].

A form of prayer to be used in private houses every morning and evening.

☞ Morning prayer.

ALMIGHTY God and most merciful Father, we do not present our selves here before thy majesty, trusting in our own merits and worthiness, but in thy manifold mercies, which hast promised to hear our prayers, and grant our requests, which we shall make to thee in the name of thy beloved Son Jesus Christ our Lord: who hath also commanded us to assemble our selves together in his name with full assurance that he will not only be among us, but also be our mediator and advocate towards thy majesty, that we may obtain all things which shall seem expedient to thy blessed will for our necessities: therefore we beseech thee, most merciful Father, to turn thy loving countenance towards us, and impute not unto us our manifold sins and offences, whereby we justly deserve thy wrath and sharp punishment, but rather receive us to thy mercy for Jesus Christ's sake, accepting his death and passion as a just recompence for all our offences, in whom only thou art pleased, and through whom thou canst not be offended with us. And seeing that of thy great mercies we have quietly passed this night, grant, O heavenly Father, that we may bestow this day wholly in thy service, so that all our thoughts, words, and deeds, may redound to the glory of thy name, and good ensample to all men, who, seeing our good works, may glorify thee our heavenly Father. And forasmuch as of thy mere favour and love thou hast not only created us to thine own similitude and likeness, but also hast chosen us to be heirs with thy dear Son Jesus Christ of that immortal kingdom which thou preparedst for us before the beginning of the world; we beseech thee to increase our faith and knowledge, and to lighten our hearts with thy holy Spirit, that we may in the mean time live in godly conversation and integrity of life, knowing that idolaters, adulterers, covetous men, con-

[1 These Prayers were taken from the end of an edition of Sternhold and Hopkins's Psalms by John Day, 1566, in the Library of the Rev. T. Lathbury, Bath.]

tentious persons, drunkards, gluttons, and such like, shall not inherit the kingdom of God.

And because thou hast commanded us to pray one for another, we do not only make request (O Lord) for our selves, and them that thou hast already called to the true understanding of thy heavenly will; but for all people and nations of the world, who as they know by thy wonderful works, that thou art God over all, so they may be instructed by thy holy Spirit, to believe in thee their only Saviour and Redeemer. But forasmuch as they cannot believe except they hear, nor cannot hear but by preaching: and none can preach except they be sent: Therefore (O Lord) raise up faithful distributors of thy mysteries, who, setting apart all worldly respects, may both in their life and doctrine only seek thy glory. Contrarily confound Sathan, Antichrist, with all hirelings, whom thou hast already cast off into a reprobate sense; that they may not by sects, schisms, heresies, and errors disquiet thy little flock. And because (O Lord) we be fallen into the latter days and dangerous times, wherein ignorance hath gotten the upper hand, and Sathan by his ministers seek by all means to quench the light of thy Gospel; we beseech thee to maintain thy cause against those ravening wolves, and strengthen all thy servants, whom they keep in prison and bondage. Let not thy long suffering be an occasion, either to increase their tyranny, or to discourage thy children, neither yet let our sins and wickedness be a hindrance to thy mercies, but with speed (O Lord) consider these great miseries. For thy people Israel many times by their sins provoked thine anger, and thou punishedst them by thy just judgment; yet though their sins were never so grievous, if they once returned from their iniquity, thou receivedst them to mercy. We therefore, most wretched sinners, bewail our manifold sins, and earnestly repent us for our former wickedness and ungodly behaviour towards thee; and whereas we cannot of our selves purchase thy pardon, yet we humbly beseech thee for Jesus Christ's sake, to shew thy mercies upon us, and receive us again to thy favour. Grant us, dear Father, these our requests and all other things necessary for us, and thy whole church, according to thy promise in Jesus Christ our Lord. In whose name we beseech thee, as he hath taught us, saying. Our Father. &c.

A prayer to be said before meals.

ALL things depend upon thy providence (O Lord) to receive at thy hands due sustenance in time convenient. Thou givest to them and they gather it; thou openest thy hand, and they are satisfied with all good things: O heavenly Father, which art the fountain and full treasure of all goodness, we beseech thee to shew thy mercies upon us thy children, and sanctify these gifts which we receive of thy merciful liberality: grant us grace to use them soberly and purely according to thy blessed will, so that hereby we may acknowledge thee to be the author and giver of all good things, and above all, that we may remember continually to seek the spiritual food of thy word, wherewith our souls may be nourished everlastingly, through our Saviour Christ; who is the true bread of life, which came down from heaven, of whom whosoever eateth shall live for ever, and reign with him in glory, world without end. So be it.

A thanksgiving after meals.

LET all nations magnify the Lord, let all people rejoice in praising and extolling his great mercies. For his fatherly kindness is plentifully shewed forth upon us, and the truth of his promise endureth for ever.

We render thanks unto thee (O Lord God) for the manifold benefits which we continually receive at thy bountiful hand, not only for that it hath pleased thee to feed us in this present life, giving unto us all things necessary for the same, but especially because thou hast of thy free mercies fashioned us anew into an assured hope of a far better life, the which thou hast declared unto us by thy holy gospel. Therefore we humbly beseech thee (O heavenly Father) that thou wilt not suffer our affections to be so entangled, or rooted in these earthly and corruptible things; but that we may always have our minds directed to thee on high, continually watching for the coming of our Lord and Saviour Christ, what time he shall appear for our full redemption. To whom, with thee and the Holy Ghost, be all honour and glory, for ever and ever. So be it.

Another thanksgiving before meat.

ETERNAL and everliving God, Father of our Lord Jesus Christ, who of thy most singular love, which thou bearest to mankind, hast appointed to his sustenance, not only the fruits of the earth, but also the fowls of the air, the beasts of the field, and fishes of the sea, and hast commanded thy benefits to be received as from thy hands with thanksgiving, assuring thy children by the mouth of thy Apostle, that to the clean all things are clean, as the creatures which be sanctified by thy word and by prayer; grant unto us so moderately to use these thy gifts present, that, the bodies being refreshed, the souls may be more able to proceed in all good works, to the praise of thy holy name, through Jesus Christ our Lord. So be it.

Our Father, which art in. &c.

Another.

THE[1] eyes of all things do look up and trust in thee (O Lord:) thou givest them meat in due season, thou openest thy hand, and fillest with thy blessing every living creature: good Lord, bless us and all thy gifts which we receive of thy large liberality, through Jesus Christ our Lord. So be it.

Our Father. &c.

Another thanksgiving after meat.

GLORY, praise, and honour be unto thee, most merciful and omnipotent Father, who of thine infinite goodness hast created man to thine own image and similitude: who also hast fed, and daily feedest of thy most bountiful hand all living creatures: grant unto us, that as thou hast nourished these our mortal bodies with corporal food, so thou wouldest replenish our souls with the perfect knowledge of the lively word of thy beloved Son Jesus, to whom be praise, glory, and honour for ever. So be it.

GOD save the Church universal: our Queen and realm. God comfort all them that be comfortless. Lord, increase our faith. O Lord, for Christ thy Son's sake, be merciful to the common wealth, where thy Gospel is truly preached, an harbour granted to the afflicted members of Christ's body: and illuminate according to thy good pleasure all nations with the brightness of thy word. So be it.

[[1] See p. 20.]

¶ Another.

THE God of glory and peace, who hath created, redeemed, and presently fed us, be blessed for ever and ever. So be it.

THE God of all power, who hath called from death that great pastor of the sheep, our Lord Jesus, comfort and defend the flock, which he hath redeemed by the blood of the eternal testament; increase the number of true preachers, repress the rage of obstinate tyrants, mitigate and lighten the hearts of the ignorant, relieve the pains of such as be afflicted, but especially of those that suffer for the testimony of his truth; and finally confound Sathan by the power of our Lord Jesus Christ. Amen.

Evening[1] prayer.

O LORD God, Father everlasting, and full of pity, we acknowledge and confess, that we be not worthy to lift up our eyes to heaven, much less to present ourselves before thy majesty with confidence that thou wilt hear our prayers, and grant our requests, if we consider our own deservings. For our consciences do accuse us, and our sins witness against us, and we know that thou art an upright Judge, which doest not justify the sinners and wicked men, but punishest the faults of all such as transgress thy commandments. Yet, most merciful Father, since it hath pleased thee to command us to call on thee in all our troubles and adversities, promising even then to help us, when we feel ourselves (as it were) swallowed up of death and desperation, we utterly renounce all worldly confidence, and flee to thy sovereign bounty, as our only stay and refuge: beseeching thee not to call to remembrance our manifold sins and wickedness, whereby we continually provoke thy wrath and indignation against us, neither our negligence and unkindness, which have neither worthily esteemed nor in our lives sufficiently expressed the

[[1] Late in the reign of Elizabeth this Prayer is sometimes found without its corresponding morning one, and slightly altered at the beginning. Both are in a collection of Prayers for domestic use, afterwards added to the Book of Common Order; but, together with the first two Graces, they were originally subjoined to a Geneva edition, in 1556, of a portion of the metrical Psalms.]

sweet comfort of thy gospel revealed unto us; but rather to accept the obedience and death of thy Son Jesus Christ, who by offering up his body in sacrifice once for all, hath made a sufficient recompence for all our sins. Have mercy therefore upon us, (O Lord) and forgive us our offences. Teach us by thy holy Spirit, that we may rightly weigh them, and earnestly repent for the same. And so much the rather, (O Lord) because that the reprobate, and such as thou hast forsaken, cannot praise thee, nor call upon thy name; but the repenting heart, the sorrowful mind, the conscience oppressed, hungering and thirsting for thy grace, shall ever set forth thy praise and glory. And albeit we be but worms and dust, yet thou art our creator, and we be the work of thy hands: yea, thou art our Shepherd[2] and we thy children, thou art our Father[2] and we thy flock; thou art our Redeemer, and we the people whom thou hast bought; thou art our God, and we thine inheritance. Correct us not therefore in thine anger (O Lord) neither according to our deserts punish us, but mercifully chastise us with a fatherly affection, that all the world may know that at what time soever a sinner doth repent him of his sin from the bottom of his heart, thou wilt put away his wickedness out of thy remembrance, as thou hast promised by thy holy prophet[3].

Finally, forasmuch as it hath pleased thee to make the night for man to rest in, as thou hast ordained him the day to travail, grant (O dear Father) that we may so take our bodily rest, that our souls may continually watch for the time that our Lord Jesus Christ shall appear for our deliverance out of this mortal life, and in the mean season, that we (not overcomen by any fantasies, dreams, or other temptations) may fully set our minds upon thee, love thee, fear thee, and rest in thee: furthermore, that our sleep be not excessive or overmuch after the insatiable desires of our flesh, but only sufficient to content our weak nature, that we may be better disposed to live in all godly conversation, to the glory of thy holy name, and profit of our brethren. So be it.

[[2] 'Shepherd' and 'Father' have been interchanged.]

[[3] Down to this point, the Prayer bears a very strong resemblance to a much longer one in the Book of Common Order, entitled 'A godly Prayer,' and '*used to be said before the sermon, on the day which is appointed for common prayer.*']

¶ A[1] godly prayer to be said at all times.

HONOUR and praise be given to thee O Lord God Almighty, most dear Father of heaven, for all thy mercies and loving kindness shewed unto us, in that it hath pleased thy gracious goodness freely and of thine own accord, to elect and choose us to salvation before the beginning of the world; and even like continual thanks be given to thee for creating us after thine own image, for redeeming us with the precious blood of thy dear Son, when we were utterly lost, for sanctifying us with thy holy Spirit, in the revelation of thy holy word, for helping and succouring us in all our needs and necessities, for saving us from all dangers of body and soul, for comforting us so fatherly in all our tribulations and persecutions, for sparing us so long, and giving us so large a time for repentance. These benefits, O most merciful Father, like as we knowledge to have received them of thy only goodness, even so we beseech thee, for thy dear Son Jesus Christ's sake, to grant us always thy holy Spirit, whereby we may continually grow in thankfulness towards thee, to be led into all truth, and comforted in all our adversities. O Lord, strengthen our faith, kindle it more in ferventness and love towards thee, and our neighbours for thy sake. Suffer us not, most dear Father, to receive thy word any more in vain: but grant us always the assistance of thy grace and holy Spirit, that in heart, word, and deed we may sanctify and do worship to thy name. Help to amplify and increase thy kingdom, and whatsoever thou sendest, we may be heartily well content with thy good pleasure and will: Let us not lack the thing (O Father) without the which we can not serve thee, but bless thou so all the works of our hands that we may have sufficient, and not to be chargeable, but rather helpful unto others: be merciful (O Lord) to our offences, and seeing our debt is great, which thou hast forgiven us in Jesus Christ, make us to love thee and our neighbours so much the more. Be thou our Father, our captain, and defender in all temptations, hold thou us by thy merciful hand, that we may be delivered from all inconveniences, and end our lives in the sanctifying and honour[ing] of thy holy name, through Jesu Christ our Lord and only Saviour. So be it.

[1 See the Family Prayers in the Book of Common Order.]

LET thy mighty hand and outstretched arm (O Lord) be still our defence, thy mercy and loving kindness in Jesu Christ thy dear Son our salvation, thy true and holy word our instruction, thy grace and holy Spirit our comfort and consolation unto the end, and in the end. So be it.

O Lord, increase our faith.

A[2] confession of [for] all estates and times.

O ETERNAL God and most merciful Father, we confess and acknowledge here before thy divine majesty, that we are miserable sinners, conceived and born in sin and iniquity, so that in us there is no goodness. For the flesh evermore rebelleth against the Spirit, whereby we continually transgress thy holy precepts and commandments, and so purchase to ourselves through thy just judgment death and damnation. Notwithstanding (O heavenly Father) forasmuch as we are displeased with ourselves for the sins that we have committed against thee, and do unfeignedly repent us of the same: we most humbly beseech thee, for Jesus Christ's sake, to shew thy mercy on us, to forgive us all our sins, and to increase thy holy Spirit in us: that we, acknowledging from the bottom of our hearts our own unrighteousness, may from henceforth not only mortify our sinful lusts and affections, but also bring forth such fruits, as may be agreeable to thy most blessed will, not for the worthiness thereof, but for the merits of thy dearly beloved Son Jesus Christ our only Saviour, whom thou hast already given an oblation and offering for our sins; and for whose sake, we are certainly persuaded, that thou wilt deny us nothing that we shall ask in his name, according to thy will. For thy Spirit doth assure our consciences that thou art our merciful Father, and lovest us thy children through him, that nothing is able to remove thy heavenly grace and favour from us. To thee therefore (O Father) with the Son, and the Holy Ghost, be all honour and glory, world without end. So be it.

A prayer to be said before a man begin his work.

O LORD God, most merciful Father and Saviour, seeing it hath pleased thee to command us to travail, that we may

[[2] Under the title of 'The Confession of our Sins', we have this Prayer at the very commencement of the Book of Common Order, to be used by the Minister, '*When the congregation is assembled at the hour appointed.*']

relieve our need, we beseech thee of thy grace so to bless our labour, that thy blessing may extend unto us, without the which we are not able to continue; and that this great favour may be a witness unto us of thy bountifulness and assistance, so that thereby we may know the fatherly care that thou hast over us.

Moreover, O Lord, we beseech thee, that thou wouldest strengthen us with thy holy Spirit, that we may faithfully travail in our estate and vocation without fraud or deceit; and that we may endeavour our selves to follow thine holy ordinance, rather than to seek to satisfy our greedy affections or desire to gain. And if it please thee, O Lord, to prosper our labour, give us a mind also to help them that have need, according to that ability that thou of thy mercy shalt give us: and knowing that all good things come of thee, grant that we may humble our selves to our neighbours, and not by any means lift our selves up above them, which have not received so liberal a portion as of thy mercy thou hast given unto us. And if it please thee to try and exercise us by greater poverty and need, than our flesh would desire, that thou wouldest yet (O Lord) grant us grace to know that thou wilt nourish us continually through thy bountiful liberality, that we be not so tempted that we fall into distrust: but that we may patiently wait till thou fill us not only with corporal graces and benefits, but chiefly with thine heavenly and spiritual treasures, to the intent that we may always have more ample occasion to give thee thanks, and so wholly to rest upon thy mercy: hear us, O Lord of mercy, through Jesus Christ thy Son our Lord. Amen.

A[1] prayer for the whole state of Christ's church.

ALMIGHTY God, and most merciful Father, we humbly submit ourselves, and fall down before thy majesty, beseeching thee from the bottom of our hearts, that this seed of thy word now sown amongst us may take such deep root, that neither the burning heat of persecution cause it to wither, neither the thorny cares of this life choke it, but that, as seed sown in good ground, it may bring forth thirty, sixty, and an hundreth fold, as thy heavenly wisdom hath appointed: and because we have need continually to crave many things at thy

[[1] The Book of Common Order commands the Minister to use, 'after the sermon, this prayer following, or such like.']

hands, we humbly beseech thee (O heavenly Father) to grant us thy holy Spirit to direct our petitions, that they may proceed from such a fervent mind, as may be agreeable to thy most blessed will. And seeing that our infirmity is able to do nothing without thy help, and that thou art not ignorant with how many and great temptations we poor wretches are on every side inclosed and compassed: Let thy strength, O Lord, sustain our weakness, that we being defended with the force of thy grace, may be safely preserved against all assaults of Sathan, who goeth about continually like a roaring lion, seeking to devour us. Increase our faith, O merciful Father, that we do not swarve at any time from thy heavenly word, but augment in us hope and love, with a careful keeping of all thy commandments: that no hardness of heart, no hypocrisy, no concupiscence of the eyes, nor enticements of the world, do draw us away from thy obedience. And seeing we live now in these most perilous times, let thy fatherly providence defend us against the violence of our enemies, which do seek by all means to oppress thy truth. Furthermore, forasmuch as by thy holy apostle we be taught to make our prayers and supplications for all men: We pray not only for our selves here present, but beseech thee also to reduce all such as be yet ignorant, from the miserable captivity of blindness and errors, to the pure understanding and knowledge of thy heavenly truth, that we all with one consent and unity of minds, may worship thee our only God and Saviour: And that all pastors, shepherds, and ministers, to whom thou hast committed the dispensation of thy holy word, and charge of thy chosen people, may both in their life and doctrine be found faithful, setting only before their eyes thy glory, and that by them all poor sheep, which wander and go astray, may be gathered and brought home to thy fold.

Moreover, because the hearts of rulers are in thy hands: we beseech thee to direct and govern the hearts of all kings, princes, and magistrates, to whom thou hast committed the sword: especially (O Lord), according to our bounden duty, we beseech thee to maintain and increase the honourable estate of the queen's majesty, and all her most noble counsellors, and magistrates, and all the whole body of this common weal. Let thy fatherly favour so preserve them, and thy holy Spirit so govern their hearts, that they may in such sort execute their office, that thy religion may be purely maintained, manners reformed, and sin punished, according to the precise rule of thy holy word. And for that we be all members of the mystical body of Jesus Christ, we make our requests unto thee (O heavenly Father) for all such as are afflicted with any kind of cross or tribulation, as war, plague, famine, sickness, poverty, imprisonment, persecution, banishment, or any other kind of thy rods, whether it be calamity of body, or vexation of mind: that it would please thee to give them patience and constancy, till thou send them full deliverance of all their troubles. Root out from hence, O Lord, all ravening wolves, which to fill their bellies seek to destroy thy flock. And shew thy great mercies upon those our brethren in other countries, which are persecuted, cast into prison, and daily condemned for the testimony of thy truth. And though they be utterly destitute of all man's aid, yet let thy sweet comfort never depart from them; but so inflame their hearts with thy holy Spirit, that they may boldly and cheerfully abide such trial as thy godly wisdom shall appoint: so that at the length, as well by their death as by their life, the kingdom of thy dear Son Jesus Christ may increase and shine through all the world. In whose name we make our humble petitions to thee as he hath taught us. Our Father, which art. &c.

Another[1] prayer for the Morning.

O ALMIGHTY and most gracious GOD, we heartily thank thee for the sweet sleep and comfortable rest which thou hast given us this night: and forasmuch as thou hast commanded by thy holy word that no man should be idle, but all occupied in godly and virtuous exercises, every man according to his calling; we most humbly beseech thee, that thine eyes may attend upon us, daily defend us, cherish, comfort, and govern us, and all our counsels, studies, and labours, in such wise, that we may spend and bestow this day according to thy most holy will, without the hurting of our neighbours, and that we may diligently and warily eschew and avoid all things that should displease thee, set thee always before our eyes, live in

[1 This and the next two Prayers are found appended only to the later Prayer Books of Elizabeth's reign. The present one exists, however, in the English Salisbury Primer of 1556.]

thy fear, working that which may be found acceptable before thy divine majesty, through Christ our Lord. Amen.

A[2] prayer containing the duty of every true Christian.

O MOST mighty God, merciful and loving Father, I wretched sinner come unto thee in the name of thy dearly beloved Son Jesus Christ, my only Saviour and Redeemer: and most humbly beseech thee for his sake to be merciful unto me, and to cast all my sins out of thy sight and remembrance, through the merits of his bloody death and passion.

Pour upon me (O Lord) thy holy Spirit of wisdom and grace: Govern and lead me by thy holy word, that it may be a lantern unto my feet, and a light unto my steps. Shew thy mercy upon me, and so lighten the natural blindness and darkness of my heart through thy grace, that I may daily be renewed by the same Spirit and grace: by the which (O Lord) purge the grossness of my hearing and understanding, that I may profitably read, hear, and understand thy word and heavenly will, believe and practise the same in my life and conversation, and evermore hold fast that blessed hope of everlasting life.

Mortify and kill all vice in me, that my life may express my faith in thee: mercifully hear the humble suit of thy servant, and grant me thy peace all my days. Graciously pardon mine infirmities, and defend me in all dangers of body, goods and name: but most chiefly my soul against all assaults, temptations, accusations, subtle baits and sleights of that old enemy of mankind, Satan, that roaring lion, ever seeking whom he may devour.

And here (O Lord) I, prostrate with most humble mind, crave of thy divine majesty to be merciful unto the universal Church of thy Son Christ: and especially, according to my bounden duty, beseech thee for his sake to bless, save, and defend the principal member thereof, thy servant our most dear and sovereign Lady Queen Elizabeth: increase in her Royal heart true faith, godly zeal, and love of the same; and grant her victory over all her enemies, a long, prosperous, and honourable life upon earth, a blessed end, and life everlasting.

[[2] The prayer, of which this is an enlargement, has been reprinted by the Parker Society in Bull's Christian Prayers (p. 191): thus its date cannot really be later than 1566.]

Moreover, O Lord, grant unto her Majesty's most honourable counsellors, and every other member of this thy Church of England, that they and we in our several callings may truly and godly serve thee: Plant in our hearts true fear and honour of thy name, obedience to our Prince, and love to our neighbours: Increase in us true faith, and religion: Replenish our minds with all goodness, and of thy great mercy keep us in the same till the end of our lives: Give unto us a godly zeal in prayer, true humility in prosperity, perfect patience in adversity, and continual joy in the Holy Ghost.

And lastly, I commend unto thy Fatherly protection all that thou hast given me, as wife, children and servants. Aid me, O Lord, that I may govern, nourish, and bring them up in thy fear and service. And forasmuch as in this world I must always be at war and strife, not with one sort of enemies, but with an infinite number, not only with flesh and blood, but with the devil which is the prince of darkness, and with wicked men, executors of his most damnable will: Grant me therefore thy grace, that being armed with thy defence, I may stand in this battle with an invincible constancy against all corruption, which I am compassed with on every side, until such time as I having ended the combat, which during this life I must sustain, in the end I may attain to thy heavenly rest, which is prepared for me and all thine elect, through Christ our Lord and only Saviour. Amen.

The prayer of Manasseh, King of the Jews.

[Apocrypha.] O LORD Almighty, God of our fathers Abraham, Isaac, and Jacob, and of their righteous seed, which hast made heaven and earth with all their ornament, which hast bound the sea by the word of thy commandment, which hast shut up the deep and sealed it by thy terrible and glorious name, whom all do fear, and tremble before thy power: for the majesty of thy glory can not be borne, and thine angry threatening toward sinners is importable; but thy merciful promise is unmeasurable and unsearchable. For thou art the most high Lord, of great compassion, long suffering, and most merciful, and repentest for man's miseries. Thou, O Lord, according to thy great goodness hast promised[a] repentance and forgiveness to them that sin against thee, and for thine infinite mercies hast appointed repentance unto sinners, that

[a] Thou hast promised that repentance shall be the way for them to return to thee.

they may be saved. Thou therefore, O Lord, that art the God of the just, hast not appointed repentance to the just, as to Abraham, and Isaac and Jacob, which have not[a] sinned against thee; but thou hast appointed repentance unto me that am a sinner: for I have sinned above the number of the sand of the sea. My transgressions, O Lord, are multiplied: my transgressions are exceeding many: and I am not worthy to behold and see the height of the heavens for the multitude of mine unrighteousness. I am bowed down with many iron bands, that I cannot lift up mine head, neither have any release. For I have provoked thy wrath and done evil before thee. I did not thy will, neither kept I thy commandments. I have set up abominations and have multiplied offences. Now therefore I bow the knee of mine heart, beseeching thee of grace. I have sinned, O Lord, I have sinned, and I acknowledge my transgressions: but I humbly beseech thee, forgive me: O Lord, forgive me, and destroy me not with my transgressions. Be not angry with me for ever by reserving evil for me, neither condemn me into the lower parts of the earth. For thou art the God, even the God of them that repent: and in me thou wilt shew all thy goodness: for thou wilt save me that am unworthy, according to thy great mercy: therefore I will praise thee for ever all the days of my life. For all the power of the heavens praise thee, and thine is the glory for ever and ever. Amen.

[a] He speaketh this in comparison of himself and those holy fathers which have their commendation in the scriptures, so that in respect of himself he calleth their sins nothing, but attributeth unto them righteousness.

¶ The fourme

and maner of making

and consecratyng,

bisshops, prie-

stes, and

dea-

cons.

Anno domini.

1559.

[The copy, which has been followed, is in the Library of the Rev. W. Maskell.]

THE

FORM AND MANNER

OF

MAKING AND CONSECRATING

BISHOPS, PRIESTS, AND DEACONS.

ANNO DOMINI 1559.

[LITURG. QU. ELIZ.]

¶ The Preface.

It is evident unto all men, diligently reading holy Scripture, and ancient authors, that from the Apostles' time there hath been these orders of Ministers in Christ's Church: Bishops, Priests, and Deacons: which officers[1] were evermore had in such reverent estimation, that no man, by his own private authority, might presume to execute any of them, except he were first called, tried, examined, and known to have such qualities as were requisite for the same; and also by public prayer, with imposition of hands, approved and admitted thereunto. And therefore, to the intent these orders should be continued, and reverently used and esteemed in this Church of England: it is requisite, that no man (not being at this present Bishop, Priest, nor Deacon) shall execute any of them, except he be called, tried, examined, and admitted, according to the form hereafter following. And none shall be admitted a Deacon, except he be .xxi. years of age at the least. And every man, which is to be admitted a Priest, shall be full .xxiiii. years old. And every man, which is to be consecrated a Bishop, shall be fully thirty years of age. And the Bishop, knowing, either by him self or by sufficient testimony, any person to be a man of virtuous conversation, and without crime, and after examination and trial, finding him learned in the Latin tongue, and sufficiently instructed in holy Scripture, may, upon a Sunday or holy day, in the face of the Church, admit him a Deacon, in such manner and form, as hereafter followeth.

¶ The form and manner of ordering of Deacons.

First, when the day appointed by the Bishop is come, there shall be an exhortation, declaring the duty and office of such as come to be admitted Ministers, how necessary such orders are in the church of Christ, and also how the people ought to esteem them in their vocation.

¶ After the exhortation ended, the archdeacon, or his deputy, shall present such as come to the Bishop to be admitted, saying these words.

Reverend father in God, I present unto you these persons present, to be admitted Deacons.

The Bishop. Take heed that the persons whom ye present unto us, be apt and meet, for their learning and godly con-

[[1] Misprint for, offices.]

versation, to exercise their ministry duly, to the honour of God, and edifying of his church.

The Archdeacon shall answer.

I have inquired of them, and also examined them, and think them so to be.

¶ And then the Bishop shall say unto the people.

BRETHREN, if there be any of you, who knoweth any impediment, or notable crime, in any of these persons presented to be ordered Deacons, for the which he ought not to be admitted to the same, let him come forth in the name of GOD, and shew what the crime or impediment is.

¶ And if any great crime or impediment be objected, the Bishop shall surcease from ordering that person, until such time as the party accused shall try him self clear of that crime.

¶ Then the Bishop, commending such as shall be found meet to be ordered to the prayers of the congregation, with the Clerks and people present, shall say or sing the Litany as followeth, with the prayers.

The Litany and Suffrages.

O GOD the Father, of heaven : have mercy upon us miserable sinners.

O God the Father, of heaven : have mercy upon us miserable sinners.

O God the Son, Redeemer of the world : have mercy upon us miserable sinners.

O God the Son, Redeemer of the world : have mercy upon us miserable sinners.

O God the Holy Ghost, proceeding from the Father and the Son : have mercy upon us miserable sinners.

O God the Holy Ghost, proceeding from the Father and the Son : have mercy upon us miserable sinners.

O holy, blessed, and glorious Trinity, three persons and one God : have mercy upon us miserable sinners.

O holy, blessed, and glorious Trinity, three persons and one God : have mercy upon us miserable sinners.

Remember not, Lord, our offences, nor the offences of our forefathers, neither take thou vengeance of our sins. Spare us, good Lord, spare thy people whom thou hast redeemed with thy most precious blood, and be not angry with us for ever.

Spare us good Lord.

From all evil and mischief, from sin, from the crafts and assaults of the devil, from thy wrath, and from everlasting damnation:

Good Lord deliver us.

From all blindness of heart: from pride, vain glory, and hypocrisy, from envy, hatred, and malice, and all uncharitableness:

Good Lord deliver us.

From fornication, and all other deadly sin, and from all the deceits of the world, the flesh, and the devil:

Good Lord deliver us.

From lightning and tempest, from plage, pestilence, and famine, from battle, and murther, and from sudden death:

Good Lord deliver us.

From all sedition and privy conspiracy, from all false doctrine and heresy, from hardness of heart, and contempt of thy word and commandment:

Good Lord deliver us.

By the mystery of thy holy incarnation, by thy holy nativity and circumcision, by thy baptism, fasting, and temptation:

Good Lord deliver us.

By thine agony and bloody sweat, by thy cross and passion, by thy precious death and burial, by thy glorious resurrection and ascension, and by the coming of the Holy Ghost:

Good Lord deliver us.

In all time of our tribulation, in all time of our wealth, in the hour of death, and in the day of judgment:

Good Lord deliver us.

We sinners do beseech thee to hear us (O Lord God), and that it may please thee to rule and govern thy holy Church universally in the right way.

We beseech thee to hear us good Lord.

That it may please thee to keep and strengthen in the true worshipping of thee, in righteousness, and holiness of

life, thy servant Elizabeth, our most gracious Queen and governour:
> We beseech thee to hear us good Lord.

That it may please thee to rule her heart in thy faith, fear, and love, that she may always have affiance in thee, and ever seek thy honour and glory:
> We beseech thee to hear us good Lord.

That it may please thee to be her defender and keeper, giving her the victory over all her enemies:
> We beseech thee to hear us good Lord.

That it may please thee to illuminate all bishops, pastors, and Ministers of the Church, with true knowledge and understanding of thy word, and that both by their preaching and living they may set it forth, and shew it accordingly:
> We beseech thee to hear us good Lord.

That[1] it may please thee to endue the lords of the council, and all the Nobility, with grace, wisdom, and understanding:
> We beseech thee to hear us good Lord.

That it may please thee to bless and keep the Magistrates, giving them grace to execute justice, and to maintain truth:
> We beseech thee to hear us good Lord.

That it may please thee to bless and keep all thy people:
> We beseech thee to hear us good Lord.

That it may please thee to give to all nations unity, peace, and concord:
> We beseech thee to hear us good Lord.

That it may please thee to give us an heart to love and dread thee, and diligently to live after thy commandments:
> We beseech thee to hear us good Lord.

That it may please thee to give all thy people increase of grace, to hear meekly thy word, and to receive it with pure affection, and to bring forth the fruits of the Spirit:
> We beseech thee to hear us good Lord.

That it may please thee to bring into the way of truth all such as have erred and are deceived:
> We beseech thee to hear us good Lord.

[[1] This petition is printed twice, the one for the Candidates, which precedes it in both the Ordinals of king Edward, being omitted.]

That it may please thee to strengthen such as do stand, and to comfort and help the weak-hearted, and to raise them up that fall, and finally to beat down Sathan under our feet:
> We beseech thee to hear us good Lord.

That it may please thee to succour, help, and comfort all that be in danger, necessity, and tribulation:
> We beseech thee to hear us good Lord.

That it may please thee to preserve all that travel by land or by water, all women labouring of child, all sick persons and young children, and to shew thy pity upon all prisoners and captives:
> We beseech thee to hear us good Lord.

That it may please thee to defend and provide for the fatherless children and widows, and all that be desolate and oppressed:
> We beseech thee to hear us good Lord.

That it may please thee to have mercy upon all men:
> We beseech thee to hear us good Lord.

That it may please thee to forgive our enemies, persecutors and slanderers, and to turn their hearts:
> We beseech thee to hear us good Lord.

That it may please thee to give and preserve to our use the kindly fruits of the earth, so as in due time we may enjoy them:
> We beseech thee to hear us good Lord.

That it may please thee to give us true repentance, to forgive us all our sins, negligences and ignorances, and to endue us with the grace of thy holy Spirit, to amend our lives according to thy holy word:
> We beseech thee to hear us good Lord.

Son of God, we beseech thee to hear us.
> Son of God: we beseech thee to hear us.

O Lamb of God, that takest away the sins of the world.
> Grant us thy peace.

O Lamb of God, that takest away the sins of the world.
> Have mercy upon us.

O Christ hear us.
> O Christ hear us.

Lord have mercy upon us.
> Lord have mercy upon us.

Christ have mercy upon us.
> Christ have mercy upon us.

Lord have mercy upon us.
> Lord have mercy upon us.

¶ Our Father, which art in heaven. &c.
> And lead us not into temptation.

But deliver us from evil.

The Versicle. O Lord deal not with us after our sins.

The Answer. Neither reward us after our iniquities.

¶ Let us pray.

O GOD, merciful Father, that despisest not the sighing of a contrite heart, nor the desire of such as be sorrowful, mercifully assist our prayers, that we make before thee, in all our troubles and adversities, whensoever they oppress us; and graciously hear us, that those evils, which the craft and subtilty of the devil or man worketh against us, be brought to nought, and by the providence of thy goodness they may be dispersed, that we thy servants, being hurt by no persecutions, may evermore give thanks unto thee in thy holy church: through Jesu Christ our Lord.

O Lord, arise, help us, and deliver us, for thy name's sake.

O GOD, we have heard with our ears, and our fathers have declared unto us the noble works that thou didst in their days, and in the old time before them.

O Lord, arise, help us, and deliver us, for thine honour.

Glory be to the Father, and to the Son, and to the Holy Ghost: As it was in the beginning, is now, and ever shall be: world without end. Amen.

From our enemies defend us, O Christ.
> Graciously look upon our afflictions.

Pitifully behold the sorrows of our heart.
> Mercifully forgive the sins of thy people.

Favourably with mercy hear our prayers.
> O Son of David, have mercy upon us.

Both now and ever vouchsafe to hear us, O Christ.

Graciously hear us, O Christ: Graciously hear us, O Lord Christ.

¶ The Versicle.   O Lord let thy mercy be shewed upon us.
The Answer.   As we do put our trust in thee.

¶ Let us pray.

WE humbly beseech thee, O Father, mercifully to look upon our infirmities, and for the glory of thy name's sake turn from us all those evils, that we most righteously have deserved: And grant that in all our troubles we may put our whole trust and confidence in thy mercy, and evermore serve thee in holiness and pureness of living, to thy honour and glory: through our only mediator and advocate Jesus Christ our Lord. Amen.

ALMIGHTY God, which hast given us grace at this time with one accord, to make our common supplications unto thee, and dost promise that when two or three be gathered in thy name, thou wilt grant their requests: fulfil now, O Lord, the desires and petitions of thy servants, as may be most expedient for them, granting us in this world knowledge of thy truth, and in the world to come life everlasting. Amen.

Then shall be said also this that followeth.

ALMIGHTY God, which by the[1] divine providence hast appointed diverse orders of ministers in the church: and didst inspire thine holy Apostles to choose unto this order of Deacons the first martyr S. Stephin, with other: mercifully behold these thy servants, now called to the like office and administration: replenish them so with the truth of thy doctrine, and innocency of life, that both by word and good example they may faithfully serve thee in this office, to the glory of thy name, and profit of the congregation, through the merits of our Saviour Jesu Christ: who liveth and reigneth with thee, and the Holy Ghost, now and ever. Amen.

Then shall be sung or said the Communion of the day, saving the Epistle shall be read out of Timothe, as followeth:

LIKEWISE must the Ministers be honest, not double tongued, not given unto much wine, neither greedy of filthy lucre, but holding the mystery of the faith with a pure conscience. And let them first be proved, and then let them minister, so that no man be able to reprove them. Even so must their wives be honest, not evil speakers, but sober and faithful in

[1 Misprint for, thy.]

all things. Let the Deacons be the husbands of one wife, and such as rule their children well, and their own households. For they that minister well, get them selves a good degree, and a great liberty in the faith, which is in Christ Jesu.

These things write I unto thee, trusting to come shortly unto thee: but and if I tarry long, that then thou mayest yet have knowledge, how thou oughtest to behave thy self in the house of God, which is the congregation of the living God, the pillar and ground of truth. And without doubt, great is that mystery of godliness. God was shewed in the flesh, was justified in the spirit, was seen among the Angels, was preached unto the Gentiles, was believed on in the world, and received up in glory.

Or else this out of the sixt of the Acts.

THEN the twelve called the multitude of the disciples together, and said, It is not meet that we should leave the word of God, and serve tables. Wherefore, brethren, look ye out among you seven men of honest report, and full of the Holy Ghost, and wisdom, to whom we may commit this business: but we will give our selves continually to prayer, and to the administration of the word. And that saying pleased the whole multitude. And they chose Stephin, a man full of faith, and full of the Holy Ghost, and Philip, and Procorus, and Nicanor, and Timon, and Permenas, and Nicholas, a convert of Antioch. These they set before the Apostles, and when they had prayed, they laid their hands on them. And the word of God increased, and the number of the disciples multiplied in Jerusalem greatly, and a great company of the priests were obedient unto the faith.

¶ And before the Gospel, the Bishop, sitting in a chair, shall cause the Oath of the Queen's supremacy, and against the power and authority of all foreign potentates, to be ministered unto every of them that are to be ordered. -

¶ The Oath of the Queen's Sovereignty.

I *A. B.* do utterly testify and declare in my conscience that the queen's highness is the only supreme governour of this realm, and of all other her highness' dominions and countries, as well in all spiritual or ecclesiastical things or causes, as temporal; and that no foreign prince, person, prelate, state, or potentate, hath or ought to have any jurisdiction, power, superiority, pre-eminence or authority, ecclesiastical or spiritual, within this realm: and therefore I do utterly renounce and forsake all foreign jurisdictions, powers, superiorities and authorities, and do promise that from henceforth I shall bear faith and true allegiance to the Queen's highness, her heirs and lawful successors, and to my power shall assist and defend all jurisdictions, privileges, pre-eminences, and authorities granted or belonging to the Queen's highness, her heirs and successors, or united and annexed to the imperial crown of this realm, so help me God, and the contents of this book.

¶ Then shall the Bishop examine every one of them that are to be ordered, in the presence of the people, after this manner following.

Do you trust that you are inwardly moved by the Holy Ghost, to take upon you this office and ministration, to serve God, for the promoting of his glory, and the edifying of his people?

Answer. I trust so.

The Bishop. Do ye think that ye truly be called, according to the will of our Lord Jesus Christ, and the due order of this realm, to the ministry of the Church?

Answer. I think so.

The Bishop. Do ye unfeignedly believe all the Canonical scriptures of the old and new Testament?

Answer. I do believe.

The Bishop. Will you diligently read the same unto the people assembled in the church, where you shall be appointed to serve?

Answer. I will.

The Bishop. It pertaineth to the office of a Deacon in the church where he shall be appointed, to assist the Priest in divine service, and specially when he ministereth the holy communion, and to help him in distribution thereof, and to read holy scriptures and Homilies in the congregation, and to instruct the youth in the Catechism, to Baptize and to preach, if he be admitted thereto by the Bishop. And furthermore, it is his office, where provision is so made, to search for the sick, poor, and impotent people of the parish, and to intimate their estates, names, and places where they dwell, to the curate, that by his exhortation they may be relieved by the parish, or other convenient alms: will you do this gladly and willingly?

Answer. I will so do by the help of God.

The Bishop. Will you apply all your diligence to frame and fashion your own lives, and the lives of all your family, according to the doctrine of Christ, and to make both your selves and them, as much as in you lieth, wholesome examples of the flock of Christ?

Answer. I will so do, the Lord being my helper.

The Bishop. Will you reverently obey your ordinary, and other chief Ministers of the church, and them to whom the government and charge is committed over you, following with a glad mind and will their godly admonitions?

Answer. I will thus endeavour my self, the Lord being my helper.

Then the Bishop, laying his hands severally upon the head of every of them, shall say.

Take thou authority to execute the office of a Deacon in the church of God committed unto thee: in the name of the Father, the Son, and the Holy Ghost. Amen.

Then shall the Bishop deliver to every one of them the new Testament, saying.

Take thou authority to read the gospel in the church of God, and to preach the same, if thou be thereunto ordinarily[1] commanded.

Then one of them appointed by the Bishop shall read the gospel of that day.
Then shall the Bishop proceed to the Communion, and all that be ordered shall tarry and receive the holy Communion the same day with the Bishop.
The Communion ended, after the last Collect, and immediately before benediction, shall be said this Collect following.

ALMIGHTY God giver of all good things, which of thy great goodness hast vouchsafed to accept and take these thy servants unto the office of Deacons in thy church: make them we beseech thee (O LORD) to be modest, humble, and constant in their ministration, to have a ready will to observe all spiritual discipline, that they having always the testimony of a good conscience, and continuing ever stable, and strong in thy Son Christ, may so well use them selves in this inferior office, that they may be found worthy to be called unto the higher ministries in thy church, through the same thy Son our Saviour Christ: to whom be glory and honour, world without end. Amen.

And here it must be shewed unto the Deacon, that he must continue in that office of a Deacon the space of a whole year at the least (except for reasonable causes it be otherwise seen to his ordinary) to the intent he may be perfect, and well expert in the things appertaining to the Ecclesiastical administration: in executing whereof if he be found faithful and diligent, he may be admitted by his Diocesan to the order of Priesthood.

[[1] In 1662 this was changed into, licensed by the Bishop himself.]

The form of ordering Priests.

When the exhortation is ended, then shall follow the Communion. And for the Epistle shall be read out of the twenty Chapter of the Acts of the Apostles, as followeth:

Acts xx.

From Mileto Paul sent messengers to Ephesus, and called the Elders of the congregation: which when they were come to him, he said unto them. Ye know that from the first day that I came into Asia, after what manner I have been with you at all seasons, serving the Lord with all humbleness of mind, and with many tears and temptations, which happened unto me by the layings await of the Jews, because I would keep back nothing that was profitable unto you, but to shew you and teach you openly throughout every house: witnessing both to the Jews, and also to the Greeks, the repentance that is toward God, and the faith which is toward our Lord Jesus. And now behold, I go bound in the spirit unto Hierusalem, not knowing the things that shall come on me there, but that the Holy Ghost witnesseth in every city, saying, that bands and trouble abide me. But none of these things move me, neither is my life dear unto my self, that I might fulfil my course with joy and the ministration of the word, which I have received of the Lord Jesu, to testify the Gospel of the grace of God. And now behold, I am sure that henceforth ye all (through whom I have gone preaching the Kingdom of God) shall see my face no more. Wherefore I take you to record this day, that I am pure from the blood of all men. For I have spared no labour, but have shewed you all the counsel of God. Take heed therefore unto your selves, and to all the flock: among whom the Holy Ghost hath made you overseers, to rule the congregation of God, which he hath purchased with his blood. For I am sure of this, that after my departing shall grievous wolves enter in among you, not sparing the flock. Moreover of your own selves shall men arise, speaking perverse things, to draw disciples after them. Therefore awake, and remember that by the space of three years I ceased not to warn every one of you night and day, with tears.

And now brethren, I commend you to God, and to the word of his grace, which is able to build further, and to give you an inheritance among all them which are sanctified. I have desired no man's silver, gold or vesture. Yea, you know your selves, that these hands have ministered unto my necessities, and to them that were with me. I have shewed you all things, how that so labouring, ye ought to receive the weak, and to remember the words of the Lord Jesu, how that he said, it is more blessed to give, than to receive.

Or else this third Chapter of the first Epistle to Timothe.

I. Tim. iii.

This is a true saying: If any man desire the office of a Bishop, he desireth an honest work. A Bishop therefore must be blameless, the husband of one wife, diligent, sober, discreet, a keeper of hospitality, apt to teach, not given to overmuch wine, no fighter, not greedy of filthy lucre, but gentle, abhorring fighting, abhorring covetousness, one that ruleth well his own house, one that hath children in subjection with all reverence. For if a man cannot rule his own house, how shall he care for the congregation of God? he may not be a young scholar, lest he swell, and fall into the judgment of the evil speaker. He must also have a good report of them which are without, lest he fall into rebuke, and snare of the evil speaker.

Likewise must the Ministers be honest, not oubletongued, not given unto much wine, neither greedy of filthy lucre; but holding the mystery of the faith, with a pure conscience: and let them first be proved, and then let them minister so, that no man be able to reprove them.

Even so must their wives be honest, not evilspeakers: but sober and faithful in all things. Let the Deacons be the husbands of one wife, and such as rule their children well, and their own households. For they that minister well get them selves a good degree, and great liberty in the faith which is in Christ Jesu. These things write I unto thee, trusting to come shortly unto thee: but and if I tarry long, that then thou mayest have yet knowledge, how thou oughtest to behave thy self in the house of God, which is the congregation of the living God, the pillar and ground of truth.

And without doubt, great is that mystery of godliness: God was shewed in the flesh, was justified in the spirit, was seen among the Angels, was preached unto the Gentiles, was believed on in the world, and received up in glory.

After this shall be read for the gospel a piece of the last Chapter of Mathew, as followeth.

JESUS came and spake unto them, saying: All power is given unto me in heaven and in earth. Go ye therefore and teach all nations, baptizing them in the name of the Father, and of the Son, and of the Holy Ghost: teaching them to observe all things, whatsoever I have commanded you. And lo, I am with you alway, even until the end of the world.

Or else this that followeth out of the tenth chapter of John.

VERILY, verily, I say unto you: He that entereth not in by the door into the sheepfold, but climbeth up some other way, the same is a thief and a murtherer. But he that entereth in by the door, is the shepherd of the sheep: to him the porter openeth, and the sheep heareth his voice, and he calleth his own sheep by name and leadeth them out. And when he hath sent forth his own sheep, he goeth before them, and the sheep follow him, for they know his voice. A stranger will they not follow, but will flee from him, for they know not the voice of strangers. This Proverb spake Jesus unto them, but they understood not what things they were, which he spake unto them. Then said Jesus unto them again: Verily verily, I say unto you, I am the door of the sheep. All (even as many as come before me) are thieves and murtherers: but the sheep did not hear them. I am the door: by me if any man enter in, he shall be safe, and go in and out, and find pasture. A thief cometh not but for to steal, kill and to destroy. I am come that they might have life, and that they might have it more abundantly. I am the good shepherd: a good shepherd giveth his life for the sheep. An hired servant, and he which is not the shepherd (neither the sheep are his own) seeth the wolf coming, and leaveth the sheep and fleeth, and the wolf catcheth and scattereth the sheep. The hired servant fleeth, because he is an hired servant, and careth not for the sheep. I am the good shepherd, and know my sheep, and am known of mine. As my Father knoweth me, even so know I also my Father. And I give my life for the sheep: and other sheep I have, which are not of this fold. Them also must I bring, and they shall hear my voice, and there shall be one fold, and one shepherd.

Or else this of the .xx. Chapter of John.

THE same day at night, which was the first day of the Sabboths, when the doors were shut (where the disciples were assembled together, for fear of the Jews) came Jesus and stood in the mids, and said unto them: Peace be unto you. And when he had so said, he shewed unto them his hands and his side. Then were the disciples glad, when they saw the Lord. Then said Jesus unto them again: Peace be unto you. As my Father sent me, even so send I you also. And when he had said those words, he breathed on them, and said unto them: Receive ye the Holy Ghost. Whosoever[1] sins ye remit, they are remitted unto them: and whosoever's sins ye retain, they are retained.

When the Gospel is ended, then shall be said or sung.

COME, Holy Ghost, eternal God, proceeding from above:
Both from the Father and the Son, the God of peace and love.
Visit our minds, and into us thy heavenly grace inspire:
That in all truth and godliness, we may have true desire.
Thou art the very Comforter, in all woe and distress:
The heavenly gift of God most high, which no tongue can express:
The fountain and the lively spring of joy celestial:
The fire so bright, the love so clear, and Unction spiritual.
Thou in thy gifts art manifold, whereby Christ's Church doth stand:
In faithful hearts writing thy law, the finger of God's hand.
According to thy promise made, thou givest speech of grace:
That through thy help, the praise of God may sound in every place.
O Holy Ghost, into our wits send down thine heavenly light.
Kindle our hearts with fervent love, to serve God day and night.
Strength and stablish all our weakness, so feeble and so frail.
That neither flesh, the world nor devil, against us do prevail.
Put back our enemy far from us, and grant us to obtain:
Peace in our hearts with God and man, without grudge or disdain.

[1 Misprint for, whosoever's.]

And grant O Lord, that thou being our Leader and our Guide:
We may eschew the snares of sin, and from thee never slide.
To us such plenty of thy grace, good Lord grant, we thee pray:
That thou mayest be our comforter, at the last dreadful day.
Of all strife and dissension, O Lord, dissolve the bands:
And make the knots of peace and love, throughout all Christian lands.
Grant us O Lord, through thee to know the Father most of might:
That of his dear beloved Son we may attain the sight.
And that with perfect faith also, we may acknowledge thee:
The Spirit of them both alway, one God in persons three.
Laud and praise be to the Father, and to the Son equal:
And to the Holy Spirit also, one God coeternal.
And pray we that the only Son vouchsafe his Spirit to send:
To all that do profess his name, unto the worldes end. Amen.

And then the Archdeacon shall present unto the Bishop all them that shall receive the order of Priesthood that day. The Archdeacon saying.

REVEREND father in God, I present unto you these persons present, to be admitted to the Order of Priesthood.

Cum interrogatione et responsione, ut in Ordine Diaconatus.

And then the Bishop shall say to the people.

GOOD people, these be they whom we purpose, God willing, to receive this day unto the holy office of Priesthood. For after due examination, we find not the contrary but that they be lawfully called to their function and ministry, and that they be persons meet for the same: but yet if there be any of you which knoweth any impediment, or notable crime in any of them, for the which he ought not to be received into this holy ministry; now in the name of God declare the same.

And if any great crime or impediment be objected. &c.

Ut supra in Ordine Diaconatus usque ad finem Litanie cum hac Collecta.

ALMIGHTY GOD, giver of all good things, which by thy Holy Spirit hast appointed diverse orders of Ministers in thy church, mercifully behold these thy servants, now called to the office of Priesthood, and replenish them so with the truth of thy doctrine, and innocency of life, that both by word, and good example, they may faithfully serve thee in this office, to the glory of thy name, and profit of thy congregation, through the merits of our Saviour Jesu Christ: who liveth and reigneth with thee, and the Holy Ghost, world without end. Amen.

Then the Bishop shall minister unto every one of them the oath concerning the Queen's supremacy, as it is set out in the order of Deacons. And that done, he shall say unto them which are appointed to receive the said Office, as hereafter followeth.

You have heard, brethren, as well in your private examination, as in the exhortation, and in the holy lessons taken out of the Gospel, and of the writings of the Apostles, of what dignity, and of how great importance this office is (whereunto ye be called). And now we exhort you, in the name of our Lord Jesus Christ, to have in remembrance, into how high a dignity, and to how chargeable an office ye be called, that is to say, to be the messengers, the watchmen, the Pastors, and the stewards of the Lord: to teach, to premonish, to feed, and provide for the Lord's family: to seek for Christ's sheep that be dispersed abroad, and for his children which be in the midst of this naughty world, to be saved through Christ for ever. Have always therefore printed in your remembrance, how great a treasure is committed to your charge: for they be the sheep of Christ, which be bought with his death, and for whom he shed his blood. The church and congregation whom you must serve, is his spouse and his body. And if it shall chance the same church or any member thereof to take any hurt or hinderance, by reason of your negligence, ye know the greatness of the fault, and also of the horrible punishment which will ensue. Wherefore consider with your selves the end of your ministry, towards the children of God, toward the spouse and body of Christ, and see that you never cease your labour, your care and diligence, until you have done all that lieth in you, according to your bounden duty, to bring all such as are, or shall be committed to your charge, unto that agreement in faith, and knowledge of God, and to that ripeness and perfectness of age in Christ, that there be no place left among you[1], either for error in religion, or for viciousness in life.

Then, forasmuch as your office is both of so great excellency, and of so great difficulty, ye see with how great care and study ye ought to apply your selves, as well that you may shew your selves kind to that LORD, who hath placed you in so high a dignity, as also to beware that neither you your selves offend, neither be occasion that other offend. Howbeit,

[[1] Misprint for, them.]

ye can not have a mind and a will thereto of your selves, for that power and ability is given of God alone. Therefore ye see how ye ought and have need earnestly to pray for his Holy Spirit. And seeing that you can not by any other means compass the doing of so weighty a work pertaining to the salvation of man, but with doctrine and exhortation taken out of holy Scripture, and with a life agreeable unto the same; ye perceive how studious ye ought to be in reading and in learning the Scriptures, and in framing the manners, both of your selves, and of them that specially pertain unto you, according to the rule of the same Scriptures. And for this self same cause, ye see how you ought to forsake and set aside (as much as you may) all worldly cares and studies.

We have good hope, that you have well weighed and pondered these things with your selves long before this time, and that you have clearly determined, by God's grace, to give your selves wholly to this vocation, whereunto it hath pleased God to call you, so that (as much as lieth in you) you apply your selves wholly to this one thing, and draw all your cares and studies this way and to this end: and that you will continually pray for the heavenly assistance of the Holy Ghost from God the Father, by the meditation[2] of our only mediator and Saviour Jesus Christ, that by daily reading and weighing of the Scriptures ye may wax riper and stronger in your ministry; and that ye may so endeavour your selves from time to time to sanctify the lives of you and yours, and to fashion them after the rule and doctrine of Christ; and that ye may be wholesome and Godly examples and patterns for the rest of the congregation to follow. And that this present congregation of Christ here assembled may also understand your minds and wills in these things: and that this your promise shall more move you to do your duties, ye shall answer plainly to these things, which we, in the name of the congregation, shall demand of you, touching the same.

Do you think in your heart that you be truly called according to the will of our Lord Jesus Christ, and the order of this Church of England, to the ministry of Priesthood?

Answer. I think it.

The Bishop. Be you persuaded that the holy Scriptures contain sufficiently all doctrine required of necessity for eternal

[2 A misprint for, mediation.]

salvation, through faith in Jesu Christ: And are you determined with the said scriptures to instruct the people committed to your charge, and to teach nothing (as required of necessity to eternal salvation) but that you shall be persuaded may be concluded and proved by the scripture?

Answer. I am so persuaded, and have so determined by God's grace.

The Bishop. Will you then give your faithful diligence always, so to minister the doctrine and Sacraments, and the discipline of Christ, as the Lord hath commanded, and as this realm hath received the same, according to the commandments of God, so that you may teach the people committed to your cure and charge with all diligence to keep and observe the same?

Answer. I will so do, by the help of the Lord.

The Bishop. Will you be ready with all faithful diligence to banish and drive away all erroneous and strange doctrines, contrary to God's word, and to use both public and private monitions and exhortations, as well to the sick, as to the whole within your cures, as need shall require and occasion be given?

Answer. I will, the Lord being my helper.

The Bishop. Will you be diligent in prayers, and in reading of the holy scriptures, and in such studies as help to the knowledge of the same, laying aside the study of the world and the flesh?

Answer. I will endeavour my self so to do, the Lord being my helper.

The Bishop. Will you be diligent to frame and fashion your own self and your family according to the doctrine of Christ, and to make both your self and them (as much as in you lieth) wholesome examples and spectacles to the flock of Christ?

Answer. I will apply myself, the Lord being my helper.

The Bishop. Will you maintain and set forwards (as much as lieth in you) quietness, peace, and love among all Christian people; and specially among them that are, or shall be, committed to your charge?

Answer. I will so do, the Lord being my helper.

The Bishop. Will you reverently obey your Ordinary, and other chief ministers, unto whom the government and charge is committed over you, following with a glad mind and will their godly admonitions, and submitting your self to their godly judgments?

Answer. I will so do, the Lord being my helper.

⨀ Then shall the Bishop say.

ALMIGHTY God, who hath given you this will to do all these things, grant also unto you strength and power to perform the same, that he may accomplish his work, which he hath begun in you, until the time he shall come at the latter day, to judge the quick and the dead.

¶ After the congregation shall be desired, secret in their prayers, to make humble supplications to God for the foresaid things: for the which prayers there shall be a certain space kept in silence.

¶ That done, the Bishop shall pray in this wise.

¶ Let us pray.

ALMIGHTY God and heavenly Father, which of thine infinite love and goodness towards us hast given to us thy only and most dear beloved Son Jesus Christ, to be our redeemer and author of everlasting life: who, after he had made perfect our redemption by his death, and was ascended into heaven, sent abroad into the world his Apostles, Prophets, Evangelists, Doctors, and Pastors, by whose labour and ministry he gathered together a great flock in all the parts of the world, to set forth the eternal praise of thy holy name: for these so great benefits of thy eternal goodness, and for that thou hast vouchsafed to call these thy servants here present to the same office and ministry of the salvation of mankind, we render unto thee most hearty thanks, we worship and praise thee, and we humbly beseech thee by the same thy Son, to grant unto all us, which either here or else where call upon thy name, that we may shew our selves thankful to thee for these and all other thy benefits, and that we may daily increase and go forwards in the knowledge and faith of thee, and thy Son, by the Holy Spirit; so that as well by these thy ministers, as by them to whom they shall be appointed ministers, thy holy name may be always glorified, and thy blessed kingdom enlarged, through the same thy Son our Lord Jesus Christ: which liveth and reigneth with thee, in the unity of the same Holy Spirit, world without end. Amen.

¶ When this prayer is done, the Bishop with the Priests present shall lay their hands severally upon the head of every one that receiveth orders; the receivers humbly kneeling upon their knees, and the Bishop saying.

RECEIVE the Holy Ghost: whose sins thou dost forgive, they are forgiven; and whose sins thou dost retain, they are retained: and be thou a faithful dispenser of the word of God, and of his holy Sacraments: In the name of the Father, and of the Son, and of the Holy Ghost. Amen.

¶ The Bishop shall deliver to every one of them the Bible in his hand, saying.

TAKE thou authority to preach the word of God, and to minister the holy sacraments in this congregation, where thou shalt be so appointed.

¶ When this is done, the congregation shall sing the Creed, and also they shall go to the Communion, which all they that receive orders shall take together, and remain in the same place where the hands were laid upon them, until such time as they have received the Communion.

¶ The Communion being done, after the last Collect, and immediately before the benediction, shall be said this Collect.

MOST merciful Father, we beseech thee so to send upon these thy servants thy heavenly blessing, that they may be clad about with all justice, and that thy word spoken by their mouths may have such success, that it may never be spoken in vain. Grant also that we may have grace to hear, and receive the same as thy most holy word, and the mean of our salvation, that in all our words and deeds we may seek thy glory, and the increase of thy kingdom, through Jesus Christ our Lord. Amen.

¶ And if the Orders of a Deacon and Priesthood be given both upon one day: then shall all things at the holy Communion be used as they are appointed at the ordering of Priests. Saving that for the Epistle, the whole third Chapter of the first to Timothe shall be read as it is set out before in the order of Priests. And immediately after the Epistle, the Deacons shall be ordered. And it shall suffice the Litany to be said once.

¶ **The form of consecrating of an Archbishop, or Bishop.**

¶ At the Communion.

The Epistle.

THIS is a true saying: if a man desire the office of a Bishop, he desireth an honest work. A Bishop therefore must be blameless, the husband of one wife, diligent, sober, discreet, a keeper of hospitality, apt to teach, not given to over much wine, no fighter, not greedy of filthy lucre: but gentle, abhorring fighting, abhorring covetousness, one that ruleth well his own house, one that hath children in subjection, with all reverence; for if a man cannot rule his own house, how shall he care for the congregation of God? He may not be a young scholar, lest he swell, and fall into the judgment of the evil speaker: he must also have a good report of them which are without, lest he fall into rebuke, and snare of the evil speaker.

The Gospel.

JESUS said to Simon Peter, Simon Johanna, lovest thou me more than these? He said unto him, Yea, Lord, thou knowest that I love thee. He said unto him, Feed my lambs. He said to him again the second time, Simon Johanna, lovest thou me? He said unto him, Yea, Lord, thou knowest that I love thee. He said unto him, Feed my sheep. He said unto him the third time, Simon Johanna, lovest thou me? Peter was sorry because he said unto him the third time, Lovest thou me? And he said unto him, Lord, thou knowest all things, thou knowest that I love thee. Jesus said unto him, Feed my sheep.

¶ Or else out of the tenth chapter of John, as before in the order of Priests.

¶ After the Gospel and Creed ended, first the elected Bishop shall be presented by two Bishops unto the Archbishop of that province, or to some other Bishop appointed by his commission: The Bishops that present him saying.

MOST reverend father in God, we present unto you this godly and well learned man, to be consecrated Bishop.

¶ Then shall the Archbishop demand the Queen's mandate for the consecration, and cause it to be read. And the oath touching the knowledge of the Queen's supremacy shall be ministered to the person elected, as it is set out in the Order of Deacons. And then shall be ministered also the oath of due obedience unto the Archbishop, as followeth.

¶ The Oath of due Obedience to the Archbishop.

IN the name of God, Amen. I *N.* chosen Bishop of the Church and see of .*N.* do profess and promise all due reverence and obedience to the Archbishop, and to the Metropolitical Church of .*N.* and to their successors: so help me GOD through Jesus Christ.

¶ This oath shall not be made at the consecration of an archbishop.

¶ Then the archbishop shall move the congregation present to pray:
saying thus to them.

BRETHREN, it is written in the Gospel of saint Luke, that our Saviour Christ continued the whole night in prayer, or ever that he did choose and send forth his .xii. Apostles. It is written also in the Acts of the Apostles, that the Disciples which were at Antioch did fast and pray, or ever they laid hands upon, or sent forth Paul and Barnabas. Let us therefore, following the example of our Saviour Christ and his Apostles, first fall to prayer, or that we admit and send forth this person presented unto us to the work whereunto we trust the Holy Ghost hath called him.

¶ And then shall be said the Litany, as afore in the order of Deacons.
And after this place: That it may please thee to illuminate all Bishops, &c. he shall say.

THAT it may please thee to bless this our brother elected, and to send thy grace upon him, that he may duly execute the office whereunto he is called; to the edifying of thy Church, and to the honour, praise, and glory of thy name.

Answer. We beseech thee to hear us, good Lord.

¶ Concluding the Litany in the end with this prayer.

ALMIGHTY God, giver of all good things, which by thy Holy Spirit hast appointed diverse orders of ministers in thy Church, mercifully behold this thy servant, now called to the work and ministry of a Bishop, and replenish him so with the truth of thy doctrine and innocency of life, that both by word and deed he may faithfully serve thee in this office, to the glory of thy name, and profit of thy congregation: Through the merits of our Saviour Jesu Christ: who liveth and reigneth with thee and the Holy Ghost, world without end. Amen.

Then the Archbishop sitting in a chair, shall say this to him that is to be consecrated.

BROTHER, forasmuch as holy scripture and the old Canons commandeth, that we should not be hasty in laying on hands, and admitting of any person to the government of the congregation of Christ, which he hath purchased with no less price than the effusion of his own blood: afore that I admit you to this administration whereunto ye are called, I will examine you in certain articles, to the end the congregation present may have a trial and bear witness, how ye be minded to behave your self in the church of God.

Are you persuaded that you be truly called to this ministration, according to the will of our Lord Jesus Christ, and the order of this realm?

Answer. I am so persuaded.

The archbishop. Are you persuaded that the holy scriptures contain sufficiently all doctrine, required of necessity for eternal salvation, through the faith in Jesu Christ? And are you determined, with the same holy scriptures, to instruct the people committed to your charge, and to teach or maintain nothing, as required of necessity to eternal salvation, but that you shall be persuaded may be concluded and proved by the same?

Answer. I am so persuaded and determined by God's grace.

The archbishop. Will you then faithfully exercise your self in the said holy scriptures, and call upon God by prayer for the true understanding of the same, so as ye may be able by them to teach and exhort with wholesome doctrine, and to withstand and convince the gainsayers?

Answer. I will so do, by the help of God.

The archbishop. Be you ready with all faithful diligence to banish and drive away all erroneous and strange doctrine contrary to God's word, and both privately and openly to call upon and encourage other to the same?

Answer. I am ready, the Lord being my helper.

The archbishop. Will you deny all ungodliness and worldly lusts, and live soberly, righteously, and Godly in this world, that you may shew your self in all things an example of good works unto other, that the adversary may be ashamed, having nothing to lay against you?

Answer. I will so do, the Lord being my helper.

The archbishop. Will you maintain and set forward (as much as shall lie in you) quietness, peace and love, among all men; and such as be unquiet, disobedient and criminous within your diocese, correct and punish according to such authority as ye have by God's word, and as to you shall be committed by the ordinance of this realm?

Answer. I will so do, by the help of God.

The archbishop. Will you shew your self gentle, and be merciful for Christ's sake to poor and needy people, and to all strangers destitute of help?

Answer. I will so shew my self by God's help.

The archbishop. Almighty God our heavenly Father, who hath given you a good will to do all these things, grant also unto you strength and power to perform the same: that he accomplishing in you the good work which he hath begun, ye may be found perfect and irreprehensible at the latter day, through Jesu Christ our Lord. Amen.

Then shall be sung or said. Come Holy Ghost. &c. as it is set out in the order of Priests.

That ended, the Archbishop shall say.

Lord hear our prayer.

Answer. And let our cry come unto thee.

Let us pray.

ALMIGHTY God, and most merciful Father, which of thy infinite goodness hast given to us thy only and most dear beloved Son Jesus Christ, to be our redeemer and author of everlasting life: who, after that he had made perfect our redemption by his death, and was ascended into heaven, poured down his gifts abundantly upon men, making some Apostles, some Prophets, some Evangelists, some Pastors, and Doctors, to the edifying and making perfect of his con-

THE[1] ORDERING OF PRIESTS.

gregation: grant, we beseech thee, to this thy servant such grace, that he may evermore be ready to spread abroad thy Gospel and glad tidings of reconcilement to God, and to use the authority given unto him, not to destroy, but to save; not to hurt, but to help: so that he as a wise and faithful servant, giving to thy family meat in due season, may at the last day be received into joy, through Jesu Christ our Lord: who with thee, and the Holy Ghost, liveth and reigneth one God, world without end. Amen.

Then the Archbishop and Bishops present shall lay their hands upon the head of the elected Bishop, the Archbishop saying.

TAKE the Holy Ghost, and remember that thou stir up the grace of God, which is in thee by imposition of hands: for God hath not given us the spirit of fear, but of power, and love, and soberness.

Then the Archbishop shall deliver him the Bible, saying.

GIVE heed unto reading, exhortation and doctrine. Think upon these things contained in this book: be diligent in them, that the increase coming thereby may be manifest unto all men. Take heed unto thy self, and unto teaching, and be diligent in doing them: for by doing this thou shalt save thy self, and them that hear thee. Be to the flock of Christ a shepherd, not a wolf: feed them, devour them not: hold up the weak, heal the sick, bind together the broken, bring again the outcasts, seek the lost. Be so merciful, that you be not too remiss: so minister discipline, that you forget not mercy: that when the chief Shepherd shall come, ye may receive the immarcescible crown of glory, through Jesus Christ our Lord. Amen.

¶ *Then the Archbishop shall proceed to the communion, with whom the new consecrated Bishop with other shall also communicate. And [after] the last Collect, immediately before the benediction, shall be said this prayer.*

MOST merciful Father, we beseech thee to send down upon this thy servant thy heavenly blessing, and so endue him with thy Holy Spirit, that he, preaching thy word, may

[1 A misprint, on this and the next page, for, Consecration of Bishops.]

not only be earnest to reprove, beseech, and rebuke with all patience and doctrine, but also may be to such as believe an wholesome example, in word, in conversation, in love, in faith, in chastity, and purity: that faithfully fulfilling his course, at the latter day he may receive the crown of righteousness, laid up by the Lord the righteous judge: who liveth and reigneth, one God with the Father and the Holy Ghost, world without end. Amen.

¶ **Imprinted at London in powles Churche yarde**
*by Rychard Iugge and Iohn Cawood Printers
to the Quenes Maiestie
Anno. M.D.LIX.*

Cum priuilegio Regiæ Maiestatis.

LIBER

PRECUM PUBLICARUM

SEU

MINISTERII ECCLESIASTICÆ ADMINISTRATIONIS
SACRAMENTORUM, ALIORUMQUE RITUUM

ET

CÆREMONIARUM IN ECCLESIA ANGLICANA.

Cum privilegio Regiæ Majestatis.

Liber Precum
PVBLICARUM, SEV
ministerij Ecclesiasticę administrationis Sacramentorum, aliorumque rituum & cęremoniarum in Ecclesia Anglicana.

Cum prilegio Regiæ
Maiestatis.

[The copy here reprinted is in the possession of the Parker Society.]

ELIZABETH, *Dei gratia Angliæ, Franciæ & Hiberniæ Regina, fidei defensor, &c. Omnibus ad quos præsentes literæ pervenerint, salutem.*

Cum memores officii nostri erga Deum omnipotentem (cujus providentia principes regnant) legibus quibusdam saluberrimis, consensu trium Regni nostri statuum, sancitis, anno regni nostri primo, Regium nostrum assensum libenter præbuerimus: inter quas una lex[1] *lata est, ut Preces publicæ, una, & eadem certa, & præscripta precandi forma, lingua vulgari, & vernacula, passim in ecclesia Anglicana haberentur, quo subditi nostri quid orarent facilius intelligerent, & absurdum illum, diuque in Ecclesia inveteratum errorem, tandem devitarent; fieri enim non potest, ut precationes, supplicationes, aut gratiarum actiones non intellectæ, mentis ardorem aliquando excitent & accendant, cum spiritu & veritate Deus qui spiritus est, non oris tantum strepitu, adorari vult: cui rei etiam addi potest, quod hac cæca ignoratione, superstitiosæ preces, aut res alienæ, non satis idoneæ quæ Deo profunderentur, cordium humanorum scrutatori, sæpenumero ore prophano offerebantur: Notum vobis esse volumus, quod quoniam intelligimus Collegia utriusque Academiæ, Cantabrigiensis & Oxoniensis; Collegium item Novum prope Wintoniam, & Etonense, bonis literis dicata, supplicibus votis petere, ut quo sacrarum literarum monumenta Latina ad uberiorem Theologiæ fructum eis reddantur magis familiaria, eis liceat eadem forma precum Latine uti; omnibus Reipublicæ nostræ membris, quantum in nobis est, consulere, & cum eorum necessitati, qui Latina non intelligunt, tum eorum voluntati qui utranque linguam percipiunt, consulere cupientes, constituimus per præsentes, licitum esse & permissum nostra autoritate & privilegio regali, tam Decano & Sodalitio Ecclesiæ Christi in Academia nostra Oxoniæ, quam Præsidibus, custodibus, rectoribus, magistris & sodalitatibus, omnium & singulorum Collegiorum Cantabrigiæ, Oxoniæ, Wintoniæ, & Etoniæ hoc modo precandi Latine uti publice in Ecclesiis & Sacellis suis, quem nos per nostrum Typographum ædi* [edi] *curavimus in hoc præsenti volumine, convenientem cum Anglicano nostro Publicarum precum libro, jam per universum nostrum Regnum recepto & usitato. Cui item peculiaria quædam in Christianorum funebribus & exequiis decantanda adjungi præcepimus, Statuto illo prædicto de ritu publicarum precum (cujus supra mentionem fecimus), anno primo regni nostri promulgato, in contrarium non obstante.*

Proviso semper, quod in ejusmodi Collegiis, quibus laicorum parochiæ annexæ erunt, ac in reliquis etiam, ad quorum templa laici, eorundem Collegiorum famuli & ministri, sive alii quicunque sive[2] *Latinæ linguæ imperiti, necessario adire debent, his horæ aliquot opportunæ & loca in dictis ecclesiis aut sacellis assignentur, in quibus,*

[1] See p. 27.]
[2] This second 'sive' is a misprint.]

Festis saltem diebus, preces Matutinæ & Vespertinæ legantur & recitentur; & Sacramentorum administrationes suis temporibus Anglice ad laicorum ædificationem celebrari possint. Eadem etiam formula Latina[1] *precandi privatim uti hortamur omnes reliquos Ecclesiæ nostræ Anglicanæ ministros, cujuscunque gradus fuerint, iis diebus, quibus aut non solent, aut non tenentur parochianis suis, ad ædem sacram pro more accedentibus, publice preces vernacula lingua, secundum formam dicti Statuti, recitare.*

In præmissorum autem fidem & testimonium, has literas nostras fieri fecimus patentes.

Dat. apud Palacium nostrum de Westmonasterio, sexto die Aprilis. Anno regni nostri secundo.

[[1] See p. 35.]

Præfatio.

NIHIL *unquam fuit humana sapientia tam bene constitutum, aut constabilitum firmiter, quod processu temporis non labefactaretur & corrumperetur. Et ut de aliis exemplis taceam, hoc manifestum est de forma publicarum precum in Ecclesia, quas vulgus Cultum dei vocare consuevit. De harum origine si quis consultat autenticos scriptores, inveniet non alia ratione institutas esse, quam ut fides, pietasque ac religio Christiana cresceret, & doctrina latius propagaretur. Nam sancti Patres ita rem instituerunt, ut tota Biblia, aut major horum pars semel in anno prælegeretur, hoc consilio, ut clerici & præsertim ministri Ecclesiæ, frequenti lectione & meditatione scripturæ, seipsos excitarent ad pietatem, & instructiores redderentur ad docendam Ecclesiam verbo Dei, & refutandos adversarios veræ doctrinæ; deinde, ut populus ex quotidiana lectione sacrorum librorum in templis, cresceret subinde magis ac magis in vera cognitione Dei & Domini nostri Jesu Christi, & per id accenderetur ad studium & amorem veræ religionis. Sed multis retro ab hinc annis, hæc pia & salutaris Patrum constitutio ita neglecta, mutata & corrupta fuit, additione incertarum historiarum, ut nihil durius dicam, Responsoriorum, Versuum & inutilium repetitionum, commemorationum, & aliarum Synodalium constitutionum, ut semper fere cum inciperetur liber aliquis sacer, priusquam tria aut quatuor capita absolverentur, nihil temporis superesset pro reliqua parte scripti. Ut, exempli gratia, visio Esaiæ prophetæ incipiebatur prima dominica Adventus, ita liber Geneseos dominica Septuagesimæ incipiebatur: sed incipiebatur tantum, quia nunquam finiebatur. Et ad hunc modum fiebat de aliis.*

Præterea, etiamsi Paulus jubeat sacram lectionem fieri lingua populari, ut inde ædificetur Ecclesia, tamen aliquot seculis sacri libri prælegebantur ad Anglos Latine, ut is qui legeret, plerumque daret sine mente sonum, & vox tantum aerem & aures feriret; corda, spiritus & men-

tes, fructu vacarent. Ad hæc, etsi sancti patres diviserunt Psalmos in septem partes, quas Nocturnas preces vocant, ut Psalterium integrum singulis septimanis absolveretur; raro tamen his postremis temporibus huic ordinationi fuit satisfactum, sed omnibus diebus iidem Psalmi repetebantur, aliis interim omnino omissis. Postremo tantus fuit numerus, tanta varietas regularum Picæ[1] *(ut vocabant), tot mutationes in officio ecclesiastico, quod revolutio libri, ad inveniendum quid legeretur, plus negotii & difficultatis haberet, quam lectio hujus quod fuerat inventum. Horum & similium incommodorum consideratione, revocavimus officium Ecclesiasticum ad primam institutionem, juxta consilium sanctorum Patrum. Et ut omnia sint in promptu, præfixum est Calendarium facile intellectu, & in quo, quantum fieri potuit, totius Scripturæ continua lectio proponitur ordine, ita ut nulla sit interruptio aut separatio locorum in sacris Bibliis conjunctorum. Hoc ut commode fieret, necesse fuit omittere Antiphonas*[2], *Responsoria, Invitatoria, & alia quædam similia, quæ disjungebant perpetuum contextum & continuam lectionem scripturæ. Et quia conducit ad hujus ordinis & perpetui contextus sacrorum librorum intellectum, præfigere quosdam Canones, ideo aliquos huic operi præfiximus, qui ut numero pauci, ita intellectione sunt facillimi: sic enim ordo precationum, quantum ad scripturam attinet, dispositus est, ut multo magis conveniat cum consilio institutionis sanctorum Patrum, & multo commodior atque utilior sit, quam fuerit illa qua antea sumus usi. Quod autem majorem habeat utilitatem, vel ex eo facile intelligi potest, quod in eo multa sunt omissa de illis rebus, quæ sunt incertæ, quædam etiam confictæ, nonnullæ superstitiosæ. Et quod in hac*

[1] Note 5 on p. 33, requires some amendment. The body of rules called the 'Pie' was the same as the Ordinale or Directorium Sacerdotum. Monumenta Ritualia, Vol. I. pp. xlii, xlviii. Whatever may be thought, too, of Nicholls's explanation of that term, he clearly erred in confounding Verses with Hymns. Commemorations (of festivals) mean Collects and Antiphons, &c. continued for a day or two after, as the case might be; or an octave of the festival itself.]

[2] The Antiphons, or Anthems, were verses commonly taken from the Psalms, &c. which they preceded or followed, for the purpose of fixing the attention upon them. We find them also introduced in other connexions, as before Collects.]

ordinatione[3] *nihil contineatur præter purum verbum Dei & sacras literas, vel quod in evidente & necessaria consequutione ex istis deducitur, idque hoc ordine, illo idiomate, ut & a lectoribus & auditoribus haud difficile percipi & retineri possit. Est præterea hæc ordinatio commodior propter brevitatem & manifestum ordinem, & paucas regulas apertas; et quia ministris Ecclesiæ nihil opus est aliis libris in publico ministerio, si hunc & sacra biblia teneant, quo fit etiam ut plebecula facilius ferre possit sumptus in coemendis libris in unaquaque Parochia, quam unquam antea. Est & illud in hac ordinatione illustre, & quod omnes ad decorum non solum, sed & utile & necessarium judicant, quod in omnibus hujus regni ecclesiis eædem sunt lectiones & cantiones, cum antea singulæ Diæceses suam habuerint ordinationem, ut alii Sarum, alii Herfordiensem, alii Eboracensem, aut Lincolniensem, &c. sequerentur.*

Si autem quispiam queratur, difficiliorem esse hanc ordinationem, propterea quod oporteat jam omnia ex libro recitare, cum antea ex solo auditu, propter crebram repetitionem, multa addisci possent: is si conferet utilitatem intelligentiæ, quam ex quotidiana lectione sacrorum librorum consequetur, cum labore, facile hanc molestiam devorabit. Quia vero nulla ordinatio tam perspicue proponi potest, de quo non oriantur interdum disputationes in quotidiano usu, constitutum est, ut quoties dubia occurrunt aut incidunt inter ministros, deferatur res ad Episcopum Diæceseos, cujus judicio in hac re acquiescent, modo nihil constituat, quod palam cum hac ordinatione pugnet.

[[3] This word, which often occurs, is probably to be explained by the title of Aless's translation,—Ordinatio Ecclesiæ, &c.]

De Cæremoniis, cur aliæ
QUIDEM ABROGATÆ, ALIÆ
vero retentæ ac receptæ sunt in
Ecclesia nostra Anglicana.

CÆRIMONIAS plærasque omnes, ac sacrorum ritus, quibus in Ecclesia diu jam auctoritas tributa est, ab hominum institutione ac disciplina manavisse, luce clarius est. Harum autem cærimoniarum aliæ pie sancteque ab ortu excogitatæ, diuturnitate post & institutionis ignoratione, versæ fuerunt in eam superstitionem, in qua insunt timores quidam, ac confidentiæ pariter inanes. Aliæ clam in Ecclesiam irrepserunt, effictæ ad quorundam hominum arbitrium, quibus plus desiderii cultus divini, quam cognitionis modi ac rationis recte colendi Deum fuit. Quæ quoniam primo conniventibus cæteris, quibus fuit judicium confirmatius, introductæ fuerunt, in dies singulos in nefarios & flagitiosos abusus adoleverunt. Hæ, non solum quod inutiles sunt, quod iis populus cæcutiit, verum etiam quod gloriæ Dei per has offusæ sunt tenebræ, dignæ existimabantur, quæ exploderentur ac penitus exterminarentur. Aliæ sunt, quas licet ab hominibus ascitas fuisse confitemur; eas tamen retinere optimum visum est, cum propter εὐταξίας & decori ordinis conservationem in Ecclesia (quo erant primum destinatæ), tum potissimum, quia spectant ad ædificationem, ad quam sunt omnia (ut Apostolus tradit) referenda. Et quanquam cæremoniæ alicujus retentio, aut omissio, (quod ad eam ipsam attinet) non magni est momenti: temeraria tamen & fastuosa communis ordinis ac disciplinæ majorum rescissio gravissimam numinis divini reprehensionem incurrit.

Fiant omnia inter vos (inquit Apostolus) decore, & apposito ordine. Ordinis autem hujus constitutio temperatioque neutiquam ad privatos homines spectare potest. Quamobrem conatus rescindendi aut novandi instituta publica, in Ecclesia Christi, non nisi legitime ad eam rem accersito est cuiquam permissus.

Et quoniam his nostris turbulentissimis temporibus, ob vehemens hominum studium, tam ardens in quibusdam cærimoniarum suarum propugnatio sit, ut vel minimam partem earum libenter dimitti non velint; aliis contra aures sint novarum rerum cupiditate adeo prurientes, ut nihil nisi novum ac nuper ascitum possit arridere: non tam illorum libidini, quam rei veritati consulendum esse rati, in Deum primum oculos conjecimus, deinde in utilitatem utrarumque partium. Verum ne quisquam ægre ac iniquo animo ferat cærimoniarum in Ecclesia immutationem, rationes quasdam adduximus, cur a multis ante seculis receptæ quædam antiquentur, aliæ vero observentur. Abolentur nonnullæ ad ingentem & immensam illarum congeriem imminuendam, quæ non multo ante hanc nostram ætatem adeo amplificabantur, ut onus illarum non esset ferendum. Quamobrem divus Augustinus in illa ecclesiæ Christi quasi juventute graviter acerbeque conquestus est, acervum illarum tam infinite excrevisse, ut Christianorum conditio multo esset deterior, ea in re, quam populi Judaici : isque auctor ac consultor fuit, ut tam grave jugum & importunum pondus levaretur, quum primum occasio & temporis opportunitas sedate id fieri posse permitteret. At quid diceret divus Augustinus, si in hæc nostra tempora reservatus, vidisset auctissimum incrementum hodiernarum cærimoniarum, quibuscum illæ nequaquam numero sunt conferendæ? Nostrarum cærimoniarum multitudo adeo erat amplificata, adeo erat abstrusæ & obscuræ significationis, & interdum adeo inutiliter accommodatæ, ut potius tenebras obducerent, involverentque rerum sensa, quam illustrarent beneficia Christi, prolixe & copiose in nos collata. Ad hæc, Christi evangelium non est disciplina egens cærimoniis, æque atque Moysis instituta ; verum est pura & sincera ratio colendi Deum, non in servitute typorum & umbraculorum, sed in spiritus libertate, contenta his solum cærimoniis, quæ poterunt pertinere ad decori ordinis conservationem (quam paulo ante εὐταξίαν appellavimus) & sanctæ morum disciplinæ confirmationem : & sunt præterea aptæ ad excitandos hebetes & somnolentos hominum sensus in recordationem officii sui erga

[1 The diphthong æ is very often indicated by a mark at the bottom of the e (ę), the omission of which has rarely been thought worth noticing in any way, as a misprint.]

Deum, idque clara & patenti notatione, in ædificationem corporis mystici. Postremo, gravissima ratio, quæ ad exterminationem quarundam cærimoniarum nos commovit, fuit, quod hæ partim cæcitas [cæcitate] imperitæ plebis, partim inexplebili eorum avaritia, qui quærebant corradere suum quæstum potius quam gloriam Dei illustrare, in tam horribiles abusus degeneraverunt, ut hi, nisi sublatis ipsis cærimoniis, tolli ulla ratione non possent. Verum jam nunc si qui forte graviter ac moleste ferent, aliquas veterum cærimoniarum non abolitas fuisse: ii si secum ipsi velint reputare, sine certis non posse fieri, ut rerum gerendarum decorum & tranquilla disciplina in ecclesia conserventur, facile deprehendent rationum quædam momenta, quibus poterunt revocari ad saniorem mentem & acrius judicium. Quod si penitus omnes antiquas amovendas esse censebunt, & illarum loco novas substituendas: tum quandoquidem auctores sunt cærimoniarum habendarum, equidem eas, quæ diutino populi assensu & voce receptæ comprobatæque sunt, & apposite possunt servire instituto nostro, respuendo, stultitiam suam manifeste produnt, præsertim cum nostro ævo earum significatio accommodatioque non ignoretur. Hac siquidem clare explorata & percepta, sunt magni æstimandæ ab omnibus, ob admirabilem continuationem, & seriem longinqui temporis, si se ipsi potius concordiæ & consensionis cupidos esse videri volunt, quam introducendi res inusitatas, exoticas & adventitias, id quod (quantum Christianæ religionis diligens quædam procuratio patitur) est sedulo vitandum. Præter hæc, nemo poterit merito & juste de retentis cærimoniis conqueri, nemo succensere. Nam quemadmodum illæ exulant ab ecclesia, quibus populus fœdissime abutebatur, & quibus hominum conscientiæ oppressæ succumbebant; sic hæ retentæ sunt, disciplinæ ac ordinis causa, quæ tamen ita valebunt, ut non solum mutari, sed refigi etiam ac rescindi possint, & ea de re non dabunt se in societatem honoris cum lege divina. Ad hæc, non sunt involutæ aut elingues cerimoniæ nostræ; patent, loquuntur, adeo ut explicata & evoluta sit illarum intelligentia, & propositum non obscurum, quo referuntur. Quo fit, ut credi non possit eas pervertendas fore tempore venturo, æque ac cæteræ, quibus Christiana vita toto cœlo a scopo vitæ, Christo, aberravit. At dicent aliqui fortasse:

Quo sese jactabit hæc audacia? Ecquid præscribetis religionis formas & effigies peregrinis? Neutiquam. Nam neque consuetas illorum cærimonias reprehendimus, neque inducimus novas, utpote quibuscum nihil nobis commercii est; de nostris hominibus duntaxat sumus solliciti. Hoc enim judicio diu jam fuimus, ut convenire opinaremur, ut quælibet respublica utatur his cærimoniis, quas accommodatissimas existimaverit ad illustrandam Dei gloriam, ac ad sevocandum populum a turpitudine ad cœlestem vitam, ab errore & superstitione ad cognitionem & verum cultum; & denique ut excludat alias omnes, quolibet tempore, quas intellexerit abusu indecore deformatas esse, quemadmodum in humanis traditionibus sæpe usu venisse in diversis provinciis intelleximus.

Index & Calendarium, quo
EXPRIMITUR ORDO PSAL-
morum & Lectionum, ad preces Matutinas
& Vespertinas, per totum annum, exceptis quibusdam Festis propriis,
quemadmodum regulæ
subsequentes planius
explicabunt.

Totum Psalterium prælegitur singulis mensibus, & quia non idem est numerus dierum in omnibus, sed aliqui plures, aliqui pauciores dies habent, placuit eos pares facere, quantum ad numerum dierum, hac ratione.

Cuilibet Mensi, quantum ad nostrum institutum attinet, deputantur triginta dies.

Et quia Januarius & Marcius unum & triginta habent dies in Calendariis, & horum medio Februarius viginti octo tantum, ideo is ab unoquoque illorum unum mutuabitur diem. Ita ut Psalterium quod legi debet mense Februario, incipiatur ultimo Januarii & finiatur primo Martii.

Cum autem Maius, Julius, Augustus, October & December, singuli triginta & unum dies habeant, constitutum est, ut psalmi qui penultimo die leguntur, sequenti etiam die, id est ultimo, repetantur, ut Psalterium primo die sequentium mensium possit incipi.

Jam ad intelligendum qui psalmi singulis diebus debeant prælegi, inspice numerum in Calendario, qui adscriptus est psalmis, & tunc quære eundem numerum in hac tabula; quo invento, videbis qui psalmi ad Matutinas & Vesperas debeant recitari.

Quia vero psalmus 118. divisus est in 22 periodos, & prolixior est, quam ut uno tempore legatur, constitutum est, ut una vice quatuor aut quinque periodi tantum legantur, ut in tabula signatum deprehendes.

Hoc autem considerandum est, quod in hac tabula, & in tota ordinatione, ubi mentio fit de numero psalmorum, sequuti simus supputationem veteris[1] translationis, quia Hæbræi, a nono psalmo usque ad 146, aliter numerant quam Latini in vulgata æditione.

[[1] No strict attention has been paid to this, the Psalms being oftener quoted according to the Hebrew notation than that of the Vulgate.]

Sequitur Tabula, monstrans ordinem Psalmorum, ad Matutinas & Vespertinas preces.

	Psalmi.	
dies.	*Matutinæ.*	*Vespertinæ.*
1	1, 2, 3, 4, 5.	6, 7, 8.
2	9, 10.	11, 12, 13.
3	14, 15, 16.	17.
4	18, 19, 20.	21, 22.
5	23, 24, 25.	26, 27, 28.
6	29, 30.	31, 32, 33.
7	34, 35.	36.
8	37, 38, 39.	40, 41, 42.
9	43, 44, 45.	46, 47, 48.
10	49, 50, 51.	52, 53, 54.
11	55, 56, 57.	58, 59, 60.
12	61, 62, 63.	64, 65, 66.
13	67.	68, 69.
14	70, 71.	72, 73.
15	74, 75, 76.	77.
16	78, 79, 80.	81, 82, 83, 84.
17	85, 86, 87.	88.
18	89, 90, 91.	92, 93.
19	94, [95], 96.	97, 98, 99, 100.
20	101, 102.	103.
21	104.	105.
22	106.	107, 108.
23	109, 110, 111, 112.	113, 114.
24	115, 116, 117.	118. *Inde 4 periodi.*
25	*Inde quinque periodi ejusdem.*	*Inde 4 periodi ejusdem.*
26	*Inde quinque periodi ejusdem.*	*Inde 4 ultimi ejusdem.*
27	119, 120, 121, 122, 123, 124.	125, 126, 127, 128, 129, 130.
28	131, 132, 133, 134.	135, 136, 137.
29	138, 139, 140.	141, 142.
30	143, 144, 145.	146, 147, 148, 149, 150.

Ordo Lectionum juxta contextum Bibliorum:

sepositis Psalmis.

VETUS Testamentum prima lectione recitatur in Matutinis & Vesperis: & quolibet anno debet finiri, exceptis quibusdam libris & capitibus, qui omittuntur, propterea quod non sunt tam necessarii quam alii.

Novum Testamentum alteri lectioni inseritur in Matutinis & Vesperis: & singulis annis ter repetitur, una cum Epistolis & Evangeliis, excepta Apocalypsi, ex qua lectiones aliquot festis quibusdam tribuuntur.

Nota. Ut autem scias quæ lectiones quolibet die legi debeant, quære diem mensis in sequenti Calendario. Isthic enim libros & capita invenies lectionum, quæ ad Matutinas & Vesperas recitabuntur.

In festis mobilibus, immobilibus, & Dominicis, quæ proprios habent psalmos & lectiones, relinquuntur psalmi & lectiones nominati in Calendario.

Sciendum est etiam, Collectam, Epistolam, & Evangelium Dominicæ diei repeti per totam septimanam, nisi inciderit festum quod proprium habet officium.

In Bolismo vel bisextili, quo vicesimus quintus dies Februarii in duos dividitur, utriusque diei idem est officium.

Ubicunque principium Lectionis, Epistolæ vel Evangelii non exprimitur, incipiendum est a principio capitis.

Et ubicunque non exprimitur finis Lectionis, legendum est ad finem capitis.

Lectiones Propriæ, quæ pro Primis Lectionibus recitabuntur, per totum annum, diebus Dominicis, ad preces Matutinas & Vespertinas. Aliquot etiam Secundæ lectiones.

Dominicæ Adventus Dom.		
Dominica.	*Matutinæ.*	*Vesperæ.*
1	Esai. 1	Esa. 2
2	5	24
3	25	26
4	30	32
Dominicæ post Natalem Domini.		
1	Esai. 37	Esai. 38
2	41	43
Dominicæ post Epiphaniam.		
1	Esai. 44	Esai. 46
2	51	53
3	55	56
4	57	58
5	59	64
Septuagesima.		
	Gen. 1	Gen. 2
Sexagesima.		
	Gen. 3	Gen. 6
Dominica Quinquagesimæ.		
	Genesis 9	Genesis 12
Dominicæ Quadragesimæ.		
1	Gene. 19	Gene. 22
2	27	34
3	39	42
4	43	45
5	Exod. 3	Exod. 5
6	9	10

Dominica.	Matutinæ.	Vespertinæ.
	Die Paschæ.	
	⎱ Exod. 12 ⎰ Roma. 6	⎱ Exod. 14 ⎰ Acto. 2
	Dominicæ post Pascha.	
1	Num. 16	Num. 22
2	23	25
3	Deut. 4	Deut. 5
4	6	7
5	8	9
	Dominica post Ascensionem Dom.	
	Deut. 12	Deut. 13
	Die Pentecostes.	
	⎱ Deut. 17 ⎰ Act. 10. Aperiens autem Petrus os. &c.	⎱ Deut. 18 ⎰ Act. 19. Factum est autem cum Apollo esset Corinthi. &c.
	Dominica Trinitatis.	
	Gene. 18 Matth. 3	Josue. 1
	Dominicæ post Trinitatem.	
1	Josuæ. 10	Josuæ 23
2	Judi. 4	Judi. 5
3	1. Reg. 2	1. Reg. 3
4	12	13
5	15	16
6	2. Reg. 12	2. Reg. 21
7	22	24
8	3. Reg. 13	3. Reg. 17
9	18	19
10	21	22
11	4. Reg. 5	4. Reg. 9
12	10	18
13	4. Reg. 19	4. Reg. 23
14	Jere. 5	Jere. 22
15	Jerem. 35	Jere. 36
16	Ezech. 2	Ezec. 14
17	16	18
18	20	24
19	Danie. 3	Dan. 6
20	Joel. 2	Mich. 6
21	Abacuc. 2	Prover. 1
22	Prover. 2	3
23	11	12
24	13	14
25	Pro. 15	16
26	17	19

Sequuntur lectiones propriæ Festorum dierum.

Propriæ Lectiones Festorum dierum.

Dies.	Matutinæ.	Vesperæ.
Andreæ apost. Thomæ apost.	Proverb. 20. Proverb. 23	Proverb. 21 Proverb. 24

Die Natalis Domini.

lect.	1 2	Esai. 9. Luc. 2. usque ad hominibus bonæ voluntatis.	Esa. 7. locutus est Dominus ad Ac. Tit. 3. Apparuit bonitas.
Stephani prothomartyris		Proverb. 28 Act. 6. & 7. Stepha. plenus usque, Et post 40.	Eccle. 4 Act. 7. Et completis quadraginta annis.
Joannis Evang.		Ecclesi. 5 Apoca. 1.	Eccle. 6. Apoc. 22.
Innocentium.		Jere. 31. usque ad Audivi Ephraim.	Sapient. 1
Circumcisionis.		Genesis. 17. Roma. 2	Deu.10. & nunc Isra. Coloss. 2.

Die Epiphaniæ.

	1 2	Esa. 60. Luc. 3. Factum est autem cum baptizaretur. &c.	Esa. 69. [49] Joa. 2. Post hæc descendit Capernaum.
Convers. Pauli.		Sapien. 5. Act. 22. usque ad Audiebant autem.	Sapient. 6. Act. 2.

Die Purificationis Mariæ vir.

Mathiæ Aposto.		g[S]apient. 9.	Sapient. 12
Annunci. Mariæ.		Sapient. 19	Ecclesi. 1
Fer. 4. ante pasc.		Ecclesi. 2	Ecclesi. 3
Cœnæ Domini.		Osee. 13	Osee. 14
Parasceves.		Dani. 9	Jere. 31
Vigilia Paschæ.		Gen. 22	Esai. 53
		Zach. 9	Exo. 13
Fer. 2. post pasch.		Exod. 16 Matth. 28	Exod. 17 Act. 3
Feria tertia.	1 2	Exod. 20 Lu. 24. usque ad Et ecce duo ex.	Exod. 32 1 Cor. 15
Marci evang.		Ecclesi. 4	Ecclesi. 5
Philip. & Jacobi.		Ecclesi. 7	Ecclesi. 9

Die Ascensionis Domini.

Fer. 2. post. Pent.	Deut. 10	Deut. 11
Feria tertia.	Deut. 30	Deut. 31
	Deut. 32	Deut. 34
Barnabæ Apost.	Ecclesi. 10 Acto. 14	Ecclesi. 12 Act. 15. usque ad Post aliquot dies.

Dies.	Matutinæ.	Vesperæ.
\multicolumn{3}{c}{Die Joannis Baptistæ.}		
Lect. {1, 2}	{ Malach. 3 { Matth. 3	{ Malach. 4 { Mat. 14. usque ad, Cum audisset.
Petri aposto. {[1], 2}	{ Ecclesi. 15 { Acto. 3	{ Ecclesi. 19 { Acto. 4
Jacobi aposto.	Ecclesi. 21	Ecclesi. 23
Bartholomæi.	Ecclesi. 25	Ecclesi. 29
Matthæi. apost.	Ecclesi. 35	Ecclesi. 38
\multicolumn{3}{c}{Die Michaelis Angeli.}		
Lucæ Evangeli. Simonis & Judæ.	Ecclesi. 39. Eccle. 51 { Eccle[1]. 24, 25	Ecclesi. 44 Job. 1 Job. 42
\multicolumn{3}{c}{Die omnium Sanctorum.}		
Lectio {1, 2}	Sapient. 3. usque ad Quoniam felix est sterilis. &c. Heb. 11. & 12. Sancti per fidem. usque ad, Feratis castigationem.	Sap. 5. usque ad. Et accipiet armaturam zelus illius. Apo. 19. usque ad Et ecce vidi Angelum.

Psalmi proprii festorum.

Die Natalis Domini.

Psalmi.	18. 44. 84	88. 109. 131.

Die Paschæ.

Psalmi.	2. 56. 110.	112. 113. 117.

Die Ascensionis Domini.

Psalmi.	8. 14. 23.[2]	27. 67. 108.

Die Pentecostes.

Psalmi.	47. 68.	103. 144.

Finis.

[1 A misprint for, Job. The figures 1, 2, are inserted in the English Calendar, as pointing out the first and second lessons. See p. 44.]
[2 These Psalms ought to be 20, 23, 67, 107.]

[1560.]   317

Januarius habet xxxi dies.

			Matutinæ.		Vesperæ.	
	ps.		Lect. 1.	2.	Lect. 1.	2.
1	A	Circumcisio[1] Domi.	Gen. 17	Rom. 2.	Deut. 10.	Colo. 2.
2	b		Gen. 1	Mat. 1.	Gen. 2.	Rom. 1
3	c	Genovefæ virg.	3	2	4	2
4	d		5	3	6	3
5	e		7	4	8	4
6	f	Depo. Edwardi Re.	Esai. 60	Luc. 3	Esa.69.[49]	Joan.2.
		Epiphania Domini.				
7	g	Felicis & Jan.	Gen. 9	Mat. 5	Gen. 11	Rom. 5
8	A	Luciani pres. cum so.	12	6	13	6
9	b	Judoci.	14	7	15	7
10	c	Pauli primi heremi.	16	8	17	8
11	d		18	9	19	9
12	e	*Sol in Aquario*.	20	10	21	10
13	f	Hilarii episcopi.	22	11	23	11
14	g	Felicis presbyteri.	24	12	25	12
15	A	Mauri & Isidori.	26	13	27	13
16	b	Marcelli martyris.	28	14	29	14
17	c	Sulpitii episc.	30	15	31	15
18	d	Priscæ virginis.	32	16	33	16
19	e	Ulstani[2] episcopi.	34	17	35	1. Cor. 1.
20	f	Fabiani & Sebast.	36	18	37	2
21	g	Agnetis virginis.	38	19	39	3
22	A	Vincentii martyris.	40	20	41	4
23	b	Emerentianæ virg.	42	21	43	5
24	c	Timothei.	44	22	45	6
25	d	*Conversio Pauli. ap*.	46	Act. 22.	47	Acto. 26
26	e	Polycarpi mart.	48	Mat. 23.	49	1. Cor. 7
27	f	Juliani confess.	50	24	Exod. 1.	8
28	g	Agnetis virginis.	Exod. 2	25	3	9
29	A	Valerii episcopi.	4	26	5	10
30	b	Batildis reginæ.	6	27	7	11
31	c	Saturni[3] & Victoris.	8	28	9	12

[¹ The red letter days are printed in Italics.]
[² A misprint for, Vulstani *or* Wulstani.]
[³ A misprint for, Saturnini. (Nov. 29th.)]

Februarius habet xxviii dies.

			Matutinæ.		Vesperæ.	
	ps.		Lect. 1.	2.	Lect. 1.	2.
1	d	Brigidæ virginis.	Exo. 10	Marci. 1	Exo. 11.	1. Co.13.
2	e	*Purificatio Mariæ*.	12	2	13	14
3	f	Blasii episc. & marty.	14	3	15	15
4	g	Gilberti confessoris.	16	4	17	16
5	A	Agathæ vir. & mar.	18	5	19	2. Co. 1.
6	b	Vedasti & Amandi.	20	6	21	2
7	c	Anguli episcopi.	22	7	23	3
8	d	Pauli episcopi.	24	8	32	4
9	e	Appoloniæ virginis.	33	9	34	5
10	f	Scholastica vir.	35	10	40	6
11	g	*Sol in piscibus*.	Levi. 18	11	Levi. 19	7
12	A	Eulaliæ virginis.	20	12	Nu. 10.	8
13	b	Ulfranni[1] episcopi.	Num. 11	13	12	9
14	c	Valentini episcopi.	13	14	14	10
15	d	Faustini.	15	15	16	11
16	e	Julianæ virginis.	17	16	18	12
17	f	Policronii episcopi.	19	Lu. di. 1	20	13
18	g	Simeonis episc.	21	di. 1.	22	Galat. 1.
19	A	Sabini & Juliani.	23	2	24	2
20	b	Mildredæ virgin.	25	3	26	3
21	c	Sexaginta novem mar.	27	4	28	4
22	d	Cathedra[2] Petri apo.	29	5	30	5
23	e	Policarpi episcopi.	31	6	32	6
24	f	*Mathiæ apostoli*.	33	7	34	Ephe. 1.
25	g		35	8	36	2
26	A	Alexandri episcopi.	Deut. 1	9	Deu. 2.	3
27	b	Augustini episcopi.	3	10	4	4
28	c	Oswaldi epis. & conf.	5	11	6	5

[¹ A misprint for, Vulfranni *or* Wulfranni. (Oct. 15th)]
[² The 'Charyng of S. Petre.']

318   [1560.

Martius habet xxxi dies.

			Matutinæ.		Vespertinæ.	
ps.			Lect. 1.	2.	Lect. 1.	2.
1	d	Davidis episcopi.	30	Deut. 7	Luc. 12	Deut. 8	Ephe. 6
2	e	Cedde epis. & confess.	1	9	13	10	Philip. 1
3	f	Maurini & Asterii.	2	11	14	12	2
4	g	Adriani mary.	3	13	15	14	3
5	A	Foce & Eusebii.	4	15	16	16	4
6	b	Victoris.	5	17	17	18	Colo. 1
7	c	Perpetue.	6	19	18	20	2
8	d		7	21	19	22	3
9	e	Quadraginta mart.	8	23	20	24	4
10	f	*Equinoctium vernum.*	9	25	21	26	1. Tes. 1
11	g	*Sol in Ariete.*	10	27	22	28	2
12	A	Gregorii epi. Roma.	11	29	23	30	3
13	b	Theodori mart.	12	31	24	32	4
14	c	Petri martyris.	13	33	Joan. 1	34	5
15	d	Longini martyris.	14	Josue. 1	2	Josue 2	2. Tes. 1
16	e	Hylarii & Tacoani.	15	3	3	4	2
17	f	Patricii episcopi.	16	5	4	6	3
18	g	Edwardi regis.	17	7	5	8	1. Tim. 1
19	A	Joseph sponsi Mari.	18	9	6	10	2. 3.
20	b	Cuthberti episcopi.	19	11	7	12	4
21	c	Benedicti abbatis.	20	13	8	14	5
22	d	Affrodosii episcopi.	21	15	9	16	6
23	e	Theodori presbyteri	22	17	10	18	2. Tim. 1
24	f	Agapiti martyris.	23	19	11	20	2
25	g	*Annunc. Mariæ virg.*	24	21	12	22	3
26	A	Castorii mary.	25	23	13	24	4
27	b		26	Judic. 1	14	Judic. 2	Tit. 1.
28	c	Dorotheæ virginis.	27	3	15	4	2. 3.
29	d	Victorini.	28	5	16	6	Phile. 1.
30	e	Quirini martyris.	29	7	17	8	Heb. 1.
31	f	Adelmi episcopi.	30	9	18	10	2

Aprilis habet xxx dies.

			Matutinæ.		Vespertinæ.	
ps.			Lect. 1.	2.	Lect. 1.	2.
1	g	Theodore virg.	Judi. 11	Joan. 19	Jud. 12	Heb. 3
2	A	Mariæ Aegyptiacæ.	13	20	14	4
3	b	Richardi confessoris	15	21	16	5
4	c	Ambrosii episcopi	17	Acto. 1.	18	6
5	d	Martiniani ep. mar.	19	2	20	7
6	e	Sixti epis. & mart.	21	3	Ruth. 1	8
7	f	Euphemie.	Ruth. 2	4	3	9
8	g	Egesippi sociorumque	4	5	1. Re. 1.	10
9	A	Perpetui episcopi.	1. Reg. 2	6	3	11
10	b	Passio septem virgi.	4	7	5	12
11	c	Guthliacii[1] confes.	6	8	7	13
12	d	*Sol in Tauro.*	8	9	9	Jaco. 1
13	e	Eufemiæ virginis.	10	10	11	2
14	f	Tiburcii.	12	11	13	3
15	g	Oswaldi archiepisc.	14	12	15	4
16	A	Isidori episcopi.	16	13	17	5
17	b	Aniceti episcopi Ro.	18	14	19	1. Pet. 1
18	c	Eleutherii & Anthi.	20	15	21	2
19	d	Alphegi martyris.	22	16	23	3
20	e	Victoris martyris.	24	17	25	4
21	f	Simonis martyris.	26	18	27	5
22	g	Sotheris.	28	19	29	2. Pet. 1
23	A	*Georgii martyris.*	30	20	31	2
24	b	Ulfridi confes.	2. Reg. 1	21	2. Re. 2	3
25	c	*Marci Evangelist.*	3	22	4	1. Joa. 1
26	d	Cleti episcopi. Ro.	5	23	6	2
27	e	Anastasii episc. Ro.	7	24	8	3
28	f	Vitalis martyris.	9	25	10	4
29	g	Petri Mediolanensis	11	26	12	5
30	A	Deposit. Erken. epis.	13	27	14	2. Joa. 3[2]

[1 A misprint for, Guthlaci.]
[2 A misprint for, 2. 3. Joa.]

[1560.]   319

Maius habet xxxi dies.

ps.			Matutinæ.		Vespertinæ.	
			Lect. 1.	2.	Lect. 1.	2.
1	b		Philippi & Jacobi,		2. Re. 16	Judæ. 1
2	c		Athanasii episcopi.		18	Rom. 1
3	d			2. Re. 15	Acto. 8.	20	2
4	e		Godardi.	17	28	22	3
5	f		Joan. ante port. lat.	19	Math. 1	24	4
6	g		Joan. de Beverlaco.	21	2	3. Re. 2	5
7	A			23	3	4	6
8	b			3. Reg. 1	4	6	7
9	c			3	5	8	8
10	d		Gordiani & Epima,	5	6	10	9
11	e		Anthonii martyris	7	7	12	10
12	f		Sol in Gemini.	9	8	14	11
13	g		Servasii confessoris	11	9	16	12
14	A		Bonifacii martyris.	13	10	18	13
15	b		Isydori martyris	15	11	20	14
16	c		Brandani episcopi.	17	12	22	15
17	d			19	13	4. Re. 2	16
18	e		Dioscori martyris	21	14	4	1. Cor. 1
19	f		Dunstani episcopi	4. Re. 1	15	6	2
20	g		Bernardini.	3	16	8	3
21	A		Helenæ reginæ	5	17	10	4
22	b		Julianæ virginis	7	18	12	5
23	c		Desyderii martyris	9	19	14	6
24	d			11	20	16	7
25	e		Aldemi[1] episcopi	13	21	18	8
26	f		Augustini angl. epi.	15	22	20	9
27	g		Bedæ presbyteri	17	23	22	10
28	A		Germani episc.	19	24	24	11
29	b		Coronis mart.	21	25		12
30	c		Felicis episc. Ro.	23	26	1. Esd. 1	13
30	d		Petronillæ virgin.	25	27	3	14
				1. Esd. 2	28	5	
				4	Mar. 1.		

[1 A misprint for, Aldelmi. (March 31st.)]

Junius habet xxx dies.

ps.			Matutinæ.		Vespertinæ.	
			Lect. 1.	2.	Lect. 1.	2.
1	e		Nichomedis mart.	1. Esd. 6	Mar. 2	1. Esd. 7	1. Cor. [1]5
2	f		Marcellini marty.	8	3	9	[1]6
3	g		Erasmi episc.	10	4	2. Esd. 1.	2. Cor. 1
4	A		Petrocii confess.	2. Esd. 2	5	3	2
5	b		Bonifacii epis. Rom.	4	6	5	3
6	c		Melonis archiepisc.	6	7	7	4
7	d			8	8	9	5
8	e			10	9	11	6
9	f		Gulielmi archiep.	12	10	13	7
10	g		Aestas incipit.	Heste. 1	11	Hest. 2	8
11	A		Barnabæ apostoli.	3	Act. 14	4	Act. 15.
12	b		Sol in Cancro.	5	Mar. 12	6	2. Cor. 9
13	c		Solstitium estivale.	7	13	8	10
14	d			9	14	10	11
15	e		Viti & Modesti.	Job. 2	15	Job. 1.	12
16	f			4	16	3	13
17	g		Botulphi confessoris.	6	Luc. 1.	5	Galat. 1.
18	A		Marci & marcelliani	8	2	7	2
19	b		Gervasii & Prothasii.	10	3	9	3
20	c			12	4	11	4
21	d		walburgæ virg.	14	5	13	5
22	e		Albani mart.	16	6	15	6
23	f		Etheldredæ virg.	19	7	17. 18.	Ephe. 1.
24	g		Nat. Joannis baptista	Mala. 3	Mat. 3.	20	Mat. 14
25	A			23	Luc. 8.	Mala. 4	Ephe. 2
26	b		Joannis & Pau. mar.	26, 27	9	Job. 22	3
27	c		Crescentia.	29	10	24, 25	4
28	d		Leonis episcopi Ro.	31	11	28	5
29	e		Petri apost.		Act. 3.	30	Acto. 4
30	f		Commemora. pauli.	33	Luc. 12	32	Ephe. 6.
						34	

Julius habet xxxi dies.

			Matutinæ.		Vespertinæ.	
ps.			Lect. 1.	2.	Lect. 1.	2.
1	g	Visitatio mariæ virg.	Job. 35.	Luc. 13	Job. 36	Phil. 1.
2	A		37	14	38	2
3	b		39	15	40	3
4	c	Zoæ virg. & marty.	41	16	42	Colo. 1.
5	d	*Dies Caniculares inci-*	Pro. 1.	17	Pro. 2.	2
6	e	*piunt.*	3	18	4	3
7	f		5	19	6	4
8	g		7	20	8	1. Tes. 1.
9	A	Cyrilli episcopi.	9	21	10	2
10	b	Septem fratrum mar.	11	22	12	3
11	c	Benedicti abbatis	13	23	14	4
12	d	Naboris & Felicis.	15	24	16	5
13	e	Privati martyris.	17	Joan. 1.	18	2.Tim.1
14	f	*Sol in Leone.*	19	2	20	2
15	g	Swithini & sociorum.	21	3	22	3
16	A		23	4	24	1. Tim. 1
17	b	Kenelmi regis.	25	5	26	2. 3.
18	c	Armulphi epis.	27	6	28	4
19	d	Rufinæ & Justinæ.	29	7	30	5
20	e	Margaretæ virginis.	31	8	Eccle. 1.	6
21	f	Praxedis virginis.	Eccle. 2	9	3	2 Tim. 1
22	g	Mariæ Magdalenæ.	4	10	5	2
23	A	Appollinaris episco.	6	11	7	3
24	b	Christinæ virgin.	8	12	9	4
25	c	*Jacobi apostoli.*	10	13	11	Tit. 1.
26	d	Annæ matris Mariæ.	12	14	Jerem. 1	2. 3.
27	e	Septem dormientiu m.	Jere. 2.	15	3	Phile. 1.
28	f	Sampsonis episcopi.	4	16	5	Heb. 1.
29	g	Felicis & sociorum.	6	17	7	2
30	A	Abdon & Sennes.	8	18	9	3
31	b	Germani episcopi.	10	19	11	3

[¹ A misprint for, Tes. i.e. Thes.]

Augustus habet xxxi dies.

			Matutinæ.		Vespertinæ.	
ps.			Lect. 1.	2.	Lect. 1.	2.
1	c	Petri ad vincula	Jere. 12	Joan. 20	Jere. 13.	Heb. 4
2	d	Stephani epis. Ro.	14	21	15	5
3	e		16	Acto. 1.	17	6
4	f	Justini presbyteri	18	2	19	7
5	g		20	3	21	8
6	A	Transfigur. Domi.	22	4	23	9
7	b	Festum nominis Jesu.	24	5	25	10
8	c	Ciriaci sociorumque	26	6	27	11
9	d	Romani mart.	28	7	29	12
10	e	Laurentii martyris	30	8	31	13
11	f	Tiburcii martyris	32	9	33	Jacobi.1
12	g	Claræ virginis	34	10	35	2
13	A	Ipoliti & sociorum	36	11	37	3
14	b	*Sol in Virgine.*	38	12	39	4
15	c		40	13	41	5
16	d	Rochi mart.	42	14	43	1. Pet. 1.
17	e		44	15	45. 46	2
18	f	Agapeti² martyris	47	16	48	3
19	g	Magni martyris	49	17	50	4
20	A	Ludovici episcopi	51	18	52	5
21	b	Bernardi confess.	Lame. 1	19	Lame. 2	2. Pet. 1.
22	c		3	20	4	2
23	d	Timothei & Apoli.	5	21	Eze. 2.	3
24	e	*Bartholomæi apost.*	Eze. 3.	22	6	1. Joan.1
25	f	Ludovici Regis.	7	23	13	2
26	g	Severini	14	24	18	3
27	A	Ruffi³ martyris.	33	25	34	4
28	b	Augustini episc.	Dani. 1.	26	Dani. 2.	2. 3. Joa.
29	c	Decollatio Joannis	3	27	4	Judæ. 1
30	d	Felicis & Audacti	5	28	6	Rom. 1
31	e	Paulini episcopi	7	Math. 1	8	

[¹ A misprint for, Tiburcii. (April 14th.)]
[² A misprint for, Agrapiti. (March 24th.)]
[³ A misprint for, Ruffi. (Nov. 28th.)]

[1560.] 321

September habet xxx dies.

ps.			Matutinæ.		Vespertinæ.	
			Lect. 1.	2.	Lect. 1.	2.
1	f	Egidii abbatis.	Dani. 9	Mat. 2	Dani. 10	Rom. 2
2	g	Anthonii martyris.	11	3	12	3
3	A		13	4	14	4
4	b	Bertini abbatis.	Oze. 1	5	Oze. 1. 3	5
5	c		4	6	5, 6.	6
6	d	Eugenii confessoris	7	7	8	7
7	e		9	8	10	8
8	f	Nativitas Mariæ vi.	11	9	12	9
9	g	Æquinoct.autumnale.	13	10	14	10
10	A	Sol in Libra.	Joel. 1	11	Joel 2.	11
11	b	Prothi & Jacincti.	3	12	Amo. 1	12
12	c	Martiniani episcopi.	Amo. 2	13	3	13
13	d		4	14	5	14
14	e		6	15	7	15
15	f		8	16	9	16
16	g	Edithæ virginis.	Abdia. 1	17	Jonas. 1	1 Cor. 1
17	A	Lamberti episcopi.	Jone. 2. 3	18	4	2
18	b	Victoris & Coronæ.	Mich. 1.	19	Mich. 2	3
19	c	Januarii martyris.	3	20	4	4
20	d	Eustachii.	5	21	6	5
21	e	*Mathæi apo. & evan.*	Naum 1	22	Naum 1	6
22	f	Mauricii & sociorum.	3	23	3	7
23	g	Tecle virginis.	Abac. 1.	24	Abac. 2.	8
24	A	Andochini martyris.	3	25	Soph. 1.	9
25	b	Firmini episcopi.	Soph. 2.	26	3	10
26	c	Cypriani & Justinæ.	Agge. 1.	27	Agge. 2	11
27	d	Cosmæ & Damiani.	Zach. 1	28	Zac. 2. 3	12
28	e	Exuperii episcopi.	4, 5.	Mar. 1.	6	13
29	f	*Michaelis archangeli.*	7	2	8	14
30	g	Hieronimi presbyt.	9	3	10	15

[¹ A misprint for, 2.]

October habet xxxi dies.

ps.			Matutinæ.		Vespertinæ.	
			Lect. 1.	2.	Lect. 1.	2.
1	A	Remigii & Bavonis.	Zac. 11.	Mar. 4.	Zac. 12.	1 Co. 16
2	b	Leodegarii episcopi.	13	5	14	2 Cor. 1
3	c	Candidi martyris.	Mala. 1.	6	Mala. 2.	2
4	d	Francisci confessoris.	3	7	4	3
5	e	Apolinaris martyris.	Tob. 1.	8	Tob. 2.	4
6	f	Fidis virginis.	3	9	4	5
7	g	Marci & Marcellini[1].	5	10	6	6
8	A	Pelagiæ virginis.	7	11	8	7
9	b	*Sol in Scorpione.*	9	12	10	8
10	c	Gereonis & sociorum.	11	13	12	9
11	d	Nichasii episc. & mar.	13	14	14	10
12	e	Wilthfridi[2] episcopi.	Judi. 1.	15	Judi. 2	11
13	f		3	16	4	12
14	g	Calixti episc. Ro.	5	Luc. di. 1	6	13
15	A	Ulfranni episcopi.	7	di. 1.	8	Galat. 1.
16	b		9	2	10	2
17	c	Etheldredæ virgi.	11	3	12	3
18	d	*Lucæ evangelistæ.*	13	4	14	4
19	e	Fredeswidæ virg.	15	5	16	5
20	f	Austrobertæ[3] virgi.	Sapi. 1.	6	Sap. 2.	6
21	g	Undecim mil. virgi.	3	7	4	Ephe. 1
22	A	Mariæ Salome.	5	8	6	2
23	b	Romani episcopi.	7	9	8	3
24	c	Maglorii episcopi.	9	10	10	4
25	d	Crispini & crispinia.	11	11	12	5
26	e	Evaristæ episco. Ro.	13	12	14	6
27	f	Florentii martyris.	15	13	16	Philip. 1
28	g	*Symonis & Judæ.*	17	14	Eccle. 1	2
29	A	Narcisci episcopi.	19	15	3	3
30	b	Germani & Capuani.	Eccle. 2	16	5	4
31	c	Quintini episco.	4	17		Colo. 1.

[¹ A misprint for, Marcelliani. (June 18th.)]
[² A misprint for, Wilfridi.]
[³ A misprint for, Austrebertæ.]

[LITURG. QU. ELIZ.]   21

November habet xxx dies.

			Matutinæ.		Vespertinæ.	
ps.			Lect. 1.	2.	Lect. 1.	2.
1	d	Festum omnium sanct.	Sapi. 3.	He.11.12	Sap.4. [5]	Apo. 19.
2	e		Ecclé. 6	Luc. 18	Eccle. 7	Colo. 2.
3	f	Wenefredæ virginis.	8	19	9	3
4	g	Amantii & Vitalis.	10	20	11	4
5	A	Leti presbyteri.	12	21	13	1. Tes.1.
6	b	Leonardi abbatis.	14	22	15	2
7	c	Willibrordi archiep.	16	23	17	3
8	d	Sol in Sagittario.	18	24	19	4
9	e	Theodori.	20	Joan. 1.	21	5
10	f	Martini episcopi.	22	2	23	2. Tes.1.
11	g	Martini episcopi.	24	3	25	2
12	A	Paterni. mart.	26	4	27	3
13	b	Bricii episcopi.	28	5	29	1. Tim.1
14	c	Transl. Erkenwaldi.	30	6	31	2. 3.
15	d	Machuti episcopi.	32	7	33	4
16	e		34	8	35	5
17	f	Hugonis episcopi.	36	9	37	6
18	g		38	10	39	2. Tim.1
19	A	Elizabethæ matro.	40	11	41	2
20	b	Edmundi regis.	42	12	43	3
21	c	Presentatio mariæ.	44	13	45	4
22	d	Ceciliæ virginis.	46	14	47	Titus 1.
23	e	Clementis episc. Ro.	48	15	49	2. 3.
24	f	Grisogoni martyris.	50	16	51	Phil. 1.
25	A	Katherine virginis.	Baruc. 1	17	Baruc. 2	Hebr. 1.
26	b	Lini episcopi Rom.	3	18	4	2
27	c	Agricolæ & Vitalis.	5	19	6	3
28	d	Rufi martyris.	Esai. 1.	20	Esai. 2.	4
29	e	Saturnini.	3	21	4	5
30		Andreæ apostoli.	5	Act. 1.	6	6

December habet xxxi dies.

			Matutinæ.		Vespertinæ.	
ps.			Lect. 1.	2.	Lect. 1.	2.
1	f	Eligii episcopi.	Esai. 7.	Act. 2.	Esa. 8.	Heb. 7.
2	g	Libanii[1].	9	3	10	8
3	A	Barbare virgin.	11	4	12	9
4	b	Osmundi episcopi.	13	5	14	10
5	c	Sabbæ abbatis.	15	6	16	11
6	d	Nicolai episcopi.	17	di. 7	18	12
7	e	Sol in Capricorno.	19	di. 7	20, 21.	13
8	f	Concept. Mariæ vir.	22	8	23	Jacob.1.
9	g	Solstitium hybernum.	24	9	25	2
10	A	Eualiæ[2] virginis.	26	10	27	3
11	b	Damasi episc. Ro.	28	11	29	4
12	c	Pauli episcopi.	30	12	31	5
13	d		32	13	33	1. Petr.1
14	e	Othile[3] virginis.	34	14	35	2
15	f	Valerii episcopi.	36	15	37	3
16	g		38	16	39	4
17	A	Lazari episcopi.	40	17	41	5
18	b	Graciani episcopi.	42	18	43	2. Pet. 1
19	c	Venesiæ virginis.	44	19	45	2
20	d	Julii martyris.	46	20	47	3
21	e	Thomæ apostoli.	48	21	49	1.Joan.1
22	f	Triginta martyrum.	50	22	51	2
23	g	Victoriæ virginis.	52	23	53	3
24	A	Sanctarum virg. 40.	54	24	55	4
25	b	Nativitas Domini.	Esai. 9.	Luc. 22.	Esai. 7.	Tit. 3.
26	c	Stephani prothoma.	56	Act. 6.7.	57	Act. 7.
27	d	Joannis Evangelistæ.	58	Apoc. 1.	59	Apo. 22
28	e	Sanct. Innocentium.	Jere. 31.	Act. 25.	60	1. Joa. 5
29	f		Esai. 61.	26	62	2. Joa. 1
30	g		63	27	64	3. Joa. 1
31	A	Silvestri episc. Rom.	65	28	66	Jude. 1.

[1 A misprint for, Libanii.]
[2 A misprint for, Eulaliæ. (Feb. 12th.)]
[3 A misprint for, Othiliæ.]

De anno & partibus ejus.

ANNUS *proprie est illud spacium temporis, quo sol totum suum Zodiacum sive Signiferum peragrat: quod tempus comprehendit dies 365. & sex horas ferme. Qui dies efficiunt hebdomadas 52 & diem præterea unum.*

Sex illæ horæ quater collectæ integrum diem quarto quoque anno efficiunt intercalandum. Qui dies ita inserendus videbatur, ut temporum ratio Solis itineri perpetuo congrueret; utque Solstitia & Æquinoctia, cæteraque anni tempora, eosdem menses tanquam sedes obtinerent: quodque dies reliqui omnes, adeoque festa Immobilia, quæ vocant, easdem literas retineant, nec suis sedibus pellantur.

Quare in anno quarto legendum est in fine mensis Februarii, videlicet 25[1]*. die, in sede litera* F, *bis Mat. Mat. ut sextus dies Kalendarum (inde anno nomen Bissexto vel Bissextili) bis nominetur, propter diem illum quarto quoque anno ibidem inserendum. Unde prima ex duabus illius anni literis dominicalibus seruit usque ad diem 24 Februarii, secunda vero inde usque ad anni finem.*

Hebdomadæ sive Septimanæ.

Annus Solaris sive Communis habet Hebdomadas 52. & diem unum.

Hebdomada habet dies septem. Horum adpellationes partim a recepto usu ecclesiæ, partim a Judæis & Astrologis ad nos transmissæ sunt, quorum diversitatem hæc tabella ostendit.

Judæi.		Astrologi.		Christiani.	
Prima vel una Sabbatorum.			*Solis.*	*Dominicus dies.*	
Secunda	⎫		*Lunæ.*	*Secunda*	⎫
Tertia	⎪		*Martis.*	*Tertia*	⎪
Quarta	⎬ *Sabbati.*	*Dies*	*Mercurii.*	*Quarta*	⎬ *Feria.*
Quinta	⎪		*Jovis.*	*Quinta*	⎪
Sexta	⎭		*Veneris.*	*Sexta*	⎪
Sabbatum			*Saturni.*	*Septima*	⎭

Cyclus Solaris.

MUTATIO *literæ Dominicalis partim contingit ob reliquum diem super integras hebdomadas, partim ob ἐμβολισμὸν quaternis annis recurrentem,* [et] *non potest ipsa in sua principia revolvi citius, quam viginti*

[1 The intercalary day, or another 24th, on which the letter f was to be repeated, and the feast of S. Matthias a second time kept. This direction is contrary to the one on p. 312, translated from the English Prayer Book.]

octo annorum perpetuo intervallo. Quater enim 7 efficiunt 28. Proinde hic Cyclus literarum Dominicalium complectitur 28 annos, & vocatur Solaris, quia ab ipsius ambitu per signiferum pendet. Cujus initium a Bissextili anno, in quo prior litera Dominicalis G esset, posterior F, non inconcinne factum est, nempe ut anticipatio illa a postrema litera in primam recurreret.

Ipsum Cyclum hic in tabella subjiciemus.

Cycl. sola.	1	2	3	4	5	6	7	8	9	10	11	12	13	14
Lite. dom.	G	E	D	C	B	G	F	E	D	B	A	G	F	D
Bissextilis.	F				A				C				E	

Cycl. sola.	15	16	17	18	19	20	21	22	23	24	25	26	27	28
Lit. Dom.	C	B	A	F	E	D	C	A	G	F	E	C	B	A
Bissextilis.			G				B				D			

Jam ut hujus tabellæ usus sit, tribue anno Domini 1560. unitatem, proximo binarium, tertio inde ternarium, donec ad finem pervenias. Itaque annus hic præsens 1560. currentis cycli solaris est 1, qui pariter cum 1587. anno terminabitur, ita ut anno 88. supra 1500, ordo iterum redeat ad unitatem, atque ita deinceps, quamdiu hic mundus duraverit.

Litera dominicalis ea est, quæ sub ipso Aureo numero posita invenitur. Si duæ occurrerint, est annus Bissextilis. Et litera quæ superiorem locum occupat, est Dominicalis usque ad ferias Matthiæ, quæ inferiorem, usque ad finem anni.

Eadem ratione indagatur Aureus numerus & Epactæ : de quibus vide subjectam tabellam.

Aur. num.	3	4	5	6	7	8	9	10	11	12	13	14	15	16	17	18	19	1	2
Epactæ.	3	14	25	6	17	28	9	20	1	12	23	4	15	26	7	18	29	11	22

De inventione Paschatis,

in perpetuum.

Aure. nume.	A	B	C	D	E	F	G	Lit. Dom.
1	Apr. 9.	10	11	12	6	7	8	
2	Mar. 26.	27	28	29	30	31	Ap. 1	
3	Apr. 16.	17	18	19	20	14	15	
4	Apr. 9.	3	4	5	6	7	8	
5	Mar. 26.	27	28	29	23	24	25	
6	Apr. 16.	17	11	12	13	14	15	
7	Apr. 2.	3	4	5	6	Ma. 31	Apr. 1	
8	Apr. 23.	24	25	19	20	21	22	
9	Apr. 9.	10	11	12	13	14	8	
10	Apr. 2.	3	M. 28	29	30	31	Apr. 1	
11	Apr. 16.	17	18	19	20	21	22	
12	Apr. 9.	10	11	5	6	7	8	
13	Mar. 26.	27	28	29	30	31	25	
14	Apr. 16.	17	18	19	13	14	15	
15	Apr. 2.	3	4	5	6	7	8	
16	Mar. 26.	27	28	22	23	24	25	
17	Apr. 16.	10	11	12	13	14	15	
18	Apr. 2.	3	4	5	M. 30	31	Ap. 1	
19	Ap. 23.	24	28	19	20	21	22	

In loco correspondente numero Aureo & literæ Dominicali, invenies quota die Martii vel Aprilis erit Paschatis dies. Martius notatur hoc modo: Mar. vel M. Aprilis vero hac nota: Apr. vel Ap.

De Festis Mobilibus.

Invento tempore Paschatis, reliquorum Festorum, quæ Mobilia nuncupantur, tempora sine ullo negotio præfiniri possunt, quoniam eodem semper intervallo aut præcedunt πάσχα, aut sequuntur, ut ex hac tabella patet.

$$\left.\begin{array}{l}\text{Septuagesima}\\ \text{Sexagesima}\\ \text{Quinquagesima}\\ \text{Quadragesima}\end{array}\right\} \text{antecedunt Festum Paschatis.} \left\{\begin{array}{l}9\\8\\7\\6\end{array}\right\} \text{hebdomadibus:}$$

$$\left.\begin{array}{l}\text{Rogationes}\\ \text{Pentecoste}\\ \text{Trinitatis}\end{array}\right\} \text{sequuntur Pascha} \left\{\begin{array}{l}5\\7\\8\end{array}\right\} \text{Hebdomadis.}$$

Festum Ascensionis Domini sequitur Dominicam Rogationum proximo die Jovis, seu feria quinta.

Intervallum vocant vulgo spatium inter festum Nativitatis Domini & dominicam Quinquagesimæ comprehensum, quod plærunque præter integras hebdomadas dies aliquot continet, quos appellant Concurrentes.

Dominica prima Adventus semper ea est, quæ Barbaræ festum proxime antecedit.

Immobilia Festa.

Reliqua festa dicuntur Immobilia, quia singula eisdem tum diebus mensium, tum literis septenariis, velut perpetuis sedibus adfixa sunt. De quibus in genere hi versus, quamvis inconditi, non tamen inutiles vulgo circumferuntur:

Sex sunt ad Puri, bis sex sunt usque Philippi.
Ad Jacobum totidem, novem sunt ad Michaelem.
Sex ad Martini, sex ad Natalia Christi.
Adde dies octo, totus complebitur Annus.

Liber precum publicarum, in ecclesia ANGLICANA.

Ordo in Matutinis et Vespertinis precibus servandus.

MATUTINÆ preces & Vespertinæ celebrabuntur in locis Ecclesiarum, Capellarum & Chororum, consuetis, nisi aliter loci Ordinario visum fuerit. Chorus etiam manebit eadem forma, qua superiorum temporum fuit. In principio Matutinarum precum Administrator Sacrorum clara & aperta voce pronunciabit unam aliquam ex sacræ scripturæ sententiis, quæ consequuntur. Post quam subjiciet orationem, quæ Sententiis est apposita. Qui ordo etiam servabitur in exordio precum Vespertinarum.

Sententiæ.

Si impius egerit pœnitentiam pro omnibus peccatis suis quæ operatus est, & custodierit omnia præcepta mea, & fecerit judicium & justiciam, vita vivet, & non morietur. Omnium iniquitatum ejus quas operatus est, non recordabor: dicit Dominus. Ezech. 18.

Iniquitatem meam agnosco, & peccatum meum contra me est semper. Psal. 51.

Averte faciem tuam a peccatis meis: & omnes iniquitates meas dele. Psal. [5]1.

Sacrificium Deo spiritus contribulatus: cor contritum & humiliatum, O deus, ne contemnas. Psal. 51.

Scindite corda vestra, & non vestimenta vestra, & convertimini ad Dominum Deum vestrum, quia benignus & misericors est, patiens & multæ clementiæ, qui se ab inferendo malo contineat. Joel. 2.

Tui Domini Dei nostri est misericordia & propiciatio, quia recessimus a te, & non audivimus vocem Domini Dei nostri, ut ambularemus in lege ejus. Daniel.

Corripe nos, Domine, veruntamen in judicio & non in furore tuo, ne forte ad nihilum redigas nos. Jere. [1]0. Psal.

Pœnitentiam agite; appropinquat enim regnum cœlorum. Math.

Luc. 15.	Surgam, & ibo ad patrem meum, & dicam ei: Pater, peccavi in cœlum & coram te. Jam non sum dignus vocari filius tuus.
Psal. [1] 42.	Non intres in judicium cum servo tuo, Domine, quia non justificabitur in conspectu tuo omnis vivens.
[1.] Joan. 1.	Si nos peccati expertes esse dicimus, fallimus nos ipsos, nec est in nobis veritas.

CHARISSIMI fratres: Sacra scriptura multis in locis nos commonefacit, ut multiplices nostras offensiones & infinita peccata confiteamur & agnoscamus, nec ullam in conspectu Dei dissimulationem adhibeamus, sed errata, quocunque ex genere sint, universa coram Deo denudemus, animo demisso sinceroque contestemur, ut culpæ tam salutaris agnitio veniam ex summa Dei clementia consequatur. Et quanquam peccata nostra semper in oculis Dei collocanda sunt, & nobis lamentabiliter commemoranda; tamen hoc in publico cœtu precipue fieri debet, in quo primum nos summas gracias agere convenit, propter uberrimam Divini numinis munificentiam, quæ nos omni genere beneficiorum cumulavit. Deinde Dei bonitas excellens prædicanda est, attendendæ sunt sacræ scripturæ: postremo precibus ardentissimis emendicandum est a Deo, quicquid animorum status aut corporis requirit. Quapropter omnes vos, qui præsentes hic adestis, per Dei nomen obtestor, ut intimi sensus vestri, cum meo conjuncti pariter, ad cœlestis clementiæ thronum subvolent, & in hunc qui sequitur sermonem succedatur.

Generalis confessio, ab universa congregatione dicenda, genibus flexis.

OMNIPOTENS & clementissime Pater, tanquam oves perditæ peregrinati sumus, & a viis tuis aberravimus. Inventis & concupiscentiis cordis nostri nimium indulsimus: Sacrosanctas leges tuas violavimus. Quæ a nobis facienda fuerant omisimus, & quæ facienda non fuerant admisimus. In nobis nulla est salus. quapropter, O Domine, propitius esto nobis miserrimis peccatoribus. Parce, O Deus, peccata sua confitentibus: misericordiam concede resipiscentibus, juxta promissiones tuas humano generi in Christo Jesu Domino nostro benignissime revelatas. Amplius etiam concede nobis, O clementissime Pater, propter Filium tuum & Servatorem nostrum

Jesum Christum, ut posthac pie, juste, sobrieque vitam nostram instituamus, ad sanctissimi tui nominis gloriam. Amen.

Absolutio per Ministrum solum pronuncianda.

OMNIPOTENS Deus, Pater Domini nostri Jesu Christi, qui non vult mortem peccatoris, sed potius ut recedat a malis suis moribus & vivat; deditque potestatem suis ministris, imo præcipit, ut populo suo pœnitenti absolutionem remissionemque peccatorum suorum plane annunciarent, ipse singulis vere pœnitentibus, & sacrosancto Evangelio haud ficte credentibus, condonat, eosque certissime absolvit. Rogamus ergo, ut ille nobis veram pœnitentiam largiatur, sanctumque suum Spiritum impartiat, ut quod hoc tempore agimus, id illi totum placeat: & reliqua etiam nostra vita adeo pura sit in hoc mundo, & sancta, ut in futuro gaudium consequamur æternum, per Christum Dominum nostrum. *Populus respondebit.* Amen.

Tunc Minister ordietur, alta voce, Orationem Dominicam.

PATER noster qui es in cœlis, Sanctificetur nomen tuum. Adveniat regnum tuum. Fiat voluntas tua, sicut in cœlo, & in terra. Panem nostrum quotidianum da nobis hodie. Et dimitte nobis debita nostra, sicut & nos dimittimus debitoribus nostris. Et ne nos inducas in tentationem. Sed libera nos a malo. Amen. Mat. 6.
Lucæ. 11.

Deinde Minister dicet.

DOMINE, labia nostra aperies.
Responsio. Et os nostrum annunciabit laudem tuam.
Minister. DEUS, in adjutorium nostrum intende.
Responsio. Domine, ad adjuvandum nos festina. Gloria Patri & Filio, & Spiritui sancto: Sicut erat in principio & nunc & semper, & in secula seculorum. Amen. Alleluia.

Tunc canatur Psalmus sequens.

Psalm 95[1].

TUNC sequentur Psalmi, ordine præmonstrato in Tabula, nisi diei assignentur proprii Psalmi. Et ad finem uniuscujusque Psalmi repetatur Gloria Patri & Filio.

[[1] The *Gloria Patri* is appended at length to this, and the second Psalm in the Office for the Visitation of the Sick; after the other Psalms it is abbreviated.]

Post psalmos, duæ Lectiones distincte & clara voce pronuncientur, prior ex Veteri, posterior ex Novo Testamento, ut in Calendario proponuntur, nisi diei assignatæ fuerint propriæ lectiones.

Minister eo modo versa facie stabit, quo commodius audiri possit.

Et initio cujuslibet lectionis, Librum & Caput novi & veteris Testamenti, unde lectio sumitur, indicabit, hoc modo : Primum, Secundum, Tertium vel Quartum. &c. caput Geneseos. Exodi. &c. Matthæi, Marci. &c. ut in Calendario præmonetur.

Et ad finem cujuslibet capitis, sic : Finitur hoc vel illud Caput, talis Libri vel Evangelii, &c.

Et ut facilius intelligatur, in his locis ubi Musica figuralis cani solet, Lectiones, Epistolæ & Evangelia simpliciter & naturali tono, in modum perpetuæ dictionis, distincte legantur.

Post primam lectionem sequetur, per totum Annum.

Canticum. D. Ambrosii et Augustini.

TE Deum laudamus : te Dominum confitemur.

Te æternum Patrem : omnis terra veneratur.

Tibi omnes Angeli, tibi cœli & universæ potestates.

Tibi Cherubin & Seraphin, incessabili voce proclamant,

Sanctus, Sanctus, Sanctus Dominus Deus sabaoth.

Pleni sunt cœli & terra majestatis gloriæ tuæ.

Te gloriosus Apostolorum chorus.

Te Prophetarum laudabilis numerus.

Te Martyrum candidatus laudat exercitus.

Te per orbem terrarum, sancta confitetur Ecclesia.

Patrem immensæ majestatis.

Venerandum tuum, verum, et unicum Filium.

Sanctum quoque paraclitum Spiritum.

Tu rex gloriæ, Christe.

Tu Patris sempiternus es Filius.

Tu ad liberandum suscepturus hominem, non horruisti Virginis uterum.

Tu devicto mortis aculeo, aperuisti credentibus regna cœlorum.

Tu ad dexteram Dei sedes, in gloria Patris.

Judex crederis esse venturus.

Te ergo quæsumus tuis famulis subveni, quos præcioso[1] sanguine redemisti.

Æterna fac cum Sanctis tuis in gloria numerari.

Salvum fac populum tuum Domine : & benedic hæreditati tuæ.

[1 This word is most commonly so spelt throughout.]

Et rege eos, & extolle illos usque in æternum.
Per singulos dies benedicimus te.
Et laudamus nomen tuum in seculum, & in seculum seculi.
Dignare Domine die isto, sine peccato nos custodire.
Miserere nostri Domine : miserere nostri.
Fiat misericordia tua Domine super nos, quemadmodum speravimus in te.
In te Domine speravi, non confundar in æternum.

Aut Hymnus.

BENEDICITE omnia opera Domini Domino, laudate & su- perexaltate eum in secula. *Dani. 3.*

Benedicite angeli Domini Domino, laudate & superexaltate eum in secula.

Benedicite cæli Domino, laudate & superexaltate eum in secula.

Benedicite aquæ omnes quæ super cœlos sunt Domino : laudate & superexaltate eum in secula.

Benedicite omnes virtutes Domini Domino : laudate & superexaltate eum in secula.

Benedicite Sol & luna Domino : laudate & superexaltate eum in secula.

Benedicite stellæ cœli Domino : laudate & superexaltate eum in secula.

Benedicite omnis imber & ros Domino : laudate & superexaltate eum in secula.

Benedicite omnis spiritus Dei Domino : laudate & superexaltate eum in secula.

Benedicite ignis & æstus Domino : laudate & superexaltate eum in secula.

Benedicite frigus & æstas Domino : laudate & superexaltate eum in secula.

Benedicite rores & pruina Domino : laudate & superexaltate eum in secula.

Benedicite gelu & frigus Domino : laudate & superexaltate eum in secula.

Benedicite glacies & nives Domino : laudate & superexaltate eum in secula.

Benedicite noctes & dies Domino : laudate & superexaltate eum in secula.

Benedicite lux & tenebræ Domino : laudate & superexaltate eum in secula.

Benedicite fulgura & nubes Domino : laudate & superexaltate eum in secula.

Benedicat terra Dominum : laudet & superexaltet eum in secula.

Benedicite montes & colles Domino : laudate & superexaltate eum in secula.

Benedicite universa germinantia in terra Domino : laudate & superexaltate eum in secula.

Benedicite fontes Domino : laudate & superexaltate eum in secula.

Benedicite maria & flumina Domino : laudate & superexaltate eum in secula.

Benedicite cete & omnia quæ moventur in aquis Domino : laudate & superexaltate eum in secula.

Benedicite omnes volucres cœli Domino : laudate & superexaltate eum in secula.

Benedicite omnes bestiæ & pecora Domino : laudate & superexaltate eum in secula.

Benedicite filii hominum Domino : laudate & superexaltate eum in secula.

Benedicat Israel Dominum : laudet & superexaltet eum in secula.

Benedicite sacerdotes Domini Domino : laudate & superexaltate eum in secula.

Benedicite servi Domini Domino : laudate & superexaltate eum in secula.

Benedicite spiritus & animæ justorum Domino : laudate & superexaltate eum in secula.

Benedicite sancti & humiles corde Domino : laudate & superexaltate eum in secula.

Benedicite Anania, Azaria, Misael Domino : laudate & superexaltate eum in secula.

Gloria Patri & Filio : et Spiritui sancto.

Sicut erat in principio et nunc & semper : & in secula seculorum. Amen.

Deinde sequatur lectio secunda, qua finita, canatur Hymnus Zachariæ.

Luce. 1. BENEDICTUS Dominus Deus Israel : quia visitavit & fecit redemptionem plebi suæ.

Et erexit cornu salutis nobis : in domo David pueri sui.

Sicut locutus est per os sanctorum : qui a seculo sunt prophetarum ejus.

Salutem ex inimicis nostris : & de manu omnium qui oderunt nos.

Ad faciendam misericordiam cum patribus nostris : & memorari testamenti sui sancti.

Jusjurandum quod juravit ad Abraham patrem nostrum : daturum se nobis.

Ut sine timore de manu inimicorum nostrorum liberati : serviamus illi,

In sanctitate & justitia coram ipso : omnibus diebus nostris.

Et tu puer Propheta Altissimi vocaberis : præibis enim ante faciem Domini, parare vias ejus.

Ad dandam scientiam salutis plebi ejus : in remissionem peccatorum eorum.

Per viscera misericordiæ Dei nostri : in quibus visitavit nos oriens ex alto.

Illuminare his qui in tenebris & in umbra mortis sedent : ad dirigendos pedes nostros in viam pacis.

Gloria Patri & Filio : & Spiritui sancto.

Sicut erat in principio, & nunc & semper : & in secula seculorum. Amen.

Aut Psalmus.

Psalm 100.

Deinde dicatur, Ministro & Populo stantibus

CREDO in Deum Patrem omnipotentem, creatorem cœli & terræ. Et in Jesum Christum Filium ejus unicum Dominum nostrum. Qui conceptus est de Spiritu Sancto, natus ex Maria virgine. Passus sub Pontio Pilato : crucifixus, mortuus, & sepultus, descendit ad inferna. Tertia die resurrexit a mortuis, ascendit ad cœlos, sedet ad dexteram Dei Patris omnipotentis. Inde venturus est judicare vivos & mortuos. Credo in Spiritum sanctum. Sanctam Ecclesiam Catholicam. Sanctorum communionem. Remissionem peccatorum. Carnis resurrectionem. Et vitam æternam. Amen.

Post hæc sequuntur per totum annum, ad Matutinas & Vespertinas, hæ preces, omnium genibus religiose flexis.

Minister. Dominus vobiscum.
Responsio. Et cum spiritu tuo.
Minister. Oremus. Kyrie eleyson, Christe eleyson, Kyrie eleyson.

Deinde a Ministro & tota Ecclesia dicatur alta voce.

Pater noster qui es in Cœlis. &c.

Minister erigens se, dicet.

Ostende nobis Domine misericordiam tuam.
Responsio. Et salutare tuum da nobis.
Minister. Domine salvam fac Reginam.
Responsio. Et exaudi nos cum invocamus te.
Minister. Sacerdotes tui induantur Justitia.
Responsio. Et sancti tui exultent.
Minister. Salvum fac Populum tuum Domine.
Responsio. Et benedic Hæreditati tuæ.
Minister. Da pacem Domine in diebus nostris.
Responsio. Quia non est alius qui pugnet pro nobis, nisi tu Deus noster.
Minister. Cor mundum crea in nobis O Deus.
Responsio. Et Spiritum sanctum tuum ne auferas a nobis.

Has preces sequentur quotidie tres Collectæ. Prima de Die, ea scilicet quæ assignatur dicenda ad Communionem eo die. Altera pro pace. Tertia pro gratia Dei, perseverantia in Fide & vera doctrina. Posteriores autem duæ nunquam mutantur, sed per integrum annum dicuntur ad Matutinas & Vesperas.

Collecta pro Pace.

Minister.

Oremus.

DEUS auctor pacis & amator, quem nosse, vivere; cui servire, regnare est: protege ab omni oppugnatione supplices tuos, ut qui in tua protectione confidimus, nullius hostilitatis arma timeamus. Per Christum Dominum nostrum. Amen.

Collecta pro Gratia.

DOMINE sancte, Pater omnipotens, æterne Deus, qui nos ad principium hujus diei pervenire fecisti, tua nos hodie serva virtute, ut in hac die ad nullum declinemus mortale peccatum, nec ullum incurramus periculum, sed semper ad tuam justitiam faciendam omnis nostra actio tuo moderamine dirigatur. Per Jesum Christum Do. nostrum. Amen.

In festis Natalis Domini, Epiphaniæ, Mathiæ, Paschatis, Ascensionis, Pentecostes, Trinitatis, Joannis Baptistæ, S. Jacobi, S. Bartholomæi, S. Matthæi, Simonis & Judæ, & S. Andreæ, ad Matutinas statim post Benedictus canetur Symbolum Athanasii.

QUICUNQUE vult salvus esse : ante omnia opus est ut teneat Catholicam fidem.

Quam nisi quisque integram inviolatamque servaverit : absque dubio in æternum peribit.

Fides autem Catholica hæc est, ut unum Deum in trininate, & Trinitatem in unitate veneremur.

Neque confundentes personas : neque substantiam separantes.

Alia est enim persona Patris : alia Filii, alia Spiritus sancti.

Sed Patris & Filii & Spiritus sancti una est divinitas : æqualis gloria, coeterna majestas.

Qualis Pater, talis Filius : talis Spiritus sanctus.

Increatus Pater, increatus Filius : increatus Spiritus sanctus.

Immensus Pater, immensus Filius : immensus Spiritus sanctus.

Æternus Pater, æternus Filius : æternus Spiritus sanctus.

Et tamen non tres æterni : sed unus æternus.

Sicut non tres increati, nec tres immensi : sed unus increatus, & unus immensus.

Similiter, omnipotens Pater, omnipotens Filius : omnipotens Spiritus sanctus.

Et tamen non tres omnipotentes : sed unus omnipotens.

Ita Deus Pater, Deus Filius : Deus Spiritus sanctus.

Et tamen non tres dii : sed unus est Deus.

Ita Dominus Pater, Dominus Filius : Dominus Spiritus sanctus.

Et tamen non tres Domini : sed unus est Dominus.

Quia sicut singulatim unamquanque personam Deum ac Dominum confiteri Christiana veritate compellimur : ita tres deos aut dominos dicere catholica religione prohibemur.

Pater a nullo est factus : nec creatus nec genitus.

Filius a Patre solo est : non factus, nec creatus, sed genitus.

Spiritus sanctus a Patre & Filio est : non factus, nec creatus, nec genitus, sed procedens.

Unus ergo Pater, non tres patres; unus Filius, non tres filii : unus Spiritus sanctus, non tres spiritus sancti.

Et in hac trinitate nihil prius aut posterius : nihil majus aut minus, sed totæ tres personæ coæternæ sibi sunt & coæquales.

Ita ut per omnia, sicut jam supra dictum est : & Unitas in trinitate, & Trinitas in unitate veneranda sit.

Qui vult ergo salvus esse : ita de Trinitate sentiat.

Sed necessarium est ad æternam salutem : ut incarnationem quoque Domini nostri Jesu Christi fideliter credat.

Est ergo fides recta, ut credamus & confiteamur : quod Dominus noster Jesus Christus, Dei Filius, Deus & homo est.

Deus est ex substantia Patris ante secula genitus : & homo ex substantia Matris in seculo natus.

Perfectus Deus, perfectus homo : ex anima rationali & humana carne subsistens.

Æqualis Patri secundum divinitatem : minor Patre secundum humanitatem.

Qui licet Deus sit & homo : non duo tamen, sed unus est Christus.

Unus autem non conversione divinitatis in carnem : sed assumptione humanitatis in Deum.

Unus omnino non confusione substantiæ : sed unitate personæ.

Nam sicut anima rationalis & caro unus est homo : ita Deus & homo unus est Christus.

Qui passus est pro salute nostra : descendit ad inferos, tertia die resurrexit a mortuis.

Ascendit ad coelos, sedet ad dexteram Dei Patris omnipotentis : inde venturus est judicare vivos & mortuos.

Ad cujus adventum omnes homines resurgere habent cum corporibus suis : & reddituri sunt de factis propriis rationem.

Et qui bona egerunt, ibunt in vitam æternam : qui vero mala, in ignem æternum.

Hæc est fides Catholica, quam nisi quisque fideliter firmiterque crediderit : salvus esse non poterit.

Gloria Patri & Filio : & Spiritui sancto.

Sicut erat in principio, & nunc & semper : & in secula seculorum. Amen.

Ordo Vesperarum per totum
Annum.

Sacerdos sive Minister dicet.

P_{ATER} noster, qui es in cœlis. &c.

Deinde. Domine, labia nostra aperies.

Responsio. Et os nostrum annunciabit laudem tuam.

Minister. D_{EUS}, in adjutorium nostrum intende.

Responsio. Domine, ad adjuvandum nos festina.

Gloria. &c. Sicut. &c.

Alleluia.

Postea canuntur Psalmi præmonstrati in Tabula, nisi festum fuerit quod proprios habeat Psalmos. Hos sequitur prima Lectio ex veteri Testamento, nisi fuerint propriæ Lectiones Festi.

Deinde canitur.

M_{AGNIFICAT} anima mea Dominum.   Lucæ 1.

Et exultavit spiritus meus : in Deo salutari meo.

Quia respexit humilitatem ancillæ suæ : ecce enim ex hoc beatam me dicent omnes generationes,

Quia fecit mihi magna qui potens est : & sanctum nomen ejus,

Et misericordia ejus a progenie in progenies : timentibus eum.

Fecit potentiam in brachio suo : dispersit superbos mente cordis sui.

Deposuit potentes de sede : & exaltavit humiles.

Esurientes implevit bonis : & divites dimisit inanes.

Suscepit Israel puerum suum : recordatus misericordiæ suæ;

Sicut locutus est ad patres nostros : Abraham & semini ejus in secula.   Gloria. &c.

Vel Psalmus.

Psalm 93.

Lectio Secunda ex novo Testamento : post quam finitam, canatur Canticum Simeonis.   Lucæ 2.

N_{UNC} dimittis servum tuum, Domine : secundum verbum tuum in pace.

[LITURG. QU. ELIZ.]

Quia viderunt oculi mei : salutare tuum.
Quod parasti : ante faciem omnium populorum.
Lumen ad revelationem gentium : & gloriam plebis tuæ Israel.
Gloria patri. &c.   Sicut erat in principio.

Vel Psa. 67.

His finitis, adduntur Symbolum cum aliis suffragiis supra ad Matutinas præscripta, cum tribus Collectis, quarum Prima sit de die : Secunda pro Pace : Tertia pro Dei adjutorio adversus omnia pericula.

Collecta secunda ad Vesperas, pro Pace.

DEUS, a quo sancta desideria, recta consilia, & justa sunt opera, da servis tuis illam quam mundus dare non potest Pacem, ut corda nostra mandatis tuis dedita, & hostium sublata formidine, tempora sint tua protectione tranquilla. Per Jesum Christum Dominum nostrum.

Collecta tertia pro Dei adjutorio adversus omnia pericula.

ILLUMINA, quæsumus, Domine Deus, tenebras nostras, & totius noctis insidias tu a nobis repelle propicius. Per Dominum nostrum Jesum Christum. Amen.

Hæ duæ suprascriptæ Collectæ dicuntur ad Vesperas per totum annum, absque variatione.

Finis Vespertinarum precum.

[1 A misprint for, Vespertinæ.]

Sequitur Letania & Supplicationes, cantandæ diebus Dominicis, feriis quartis, & sextis, atque aliis temporibus, cum per Ordinarios ordinatum fuerit.

PATER[2] de cœlis Deus, miserere nobis miseris peccatoribus.
Pater de cœlis Deus, miserere nobis miseris peccatoribus.

Fili redemptor mundi Deus, miserere nobis miseris peccatoribus.
Fili redemptor mundi Deus, miserere. &c.

Spiritus sancte Deus, a Patre & Filio procedens, miserere nobis miseris peccatoribus.
Spiritus sancte Deus, a Patre. &c.

Sancta, beata, & gloriosa Trinitas, tres personæ, unus Deus, miserere nobis miseris peccatoribus.
Sancta, beata, & gloriosa Trinitas. &c.

Ne memineris Domine iniquitatum nostrarum, vel parentum nostrorum, neque vindictam sumas de peccatis nostris: parce Domine, parce populo tuo, quem redemisti præcioso sanguine tuo, & ne in perpetuum irascaris nobis.
Parce nobis Domine.

Ab omni peccato, malo, & infortunio, ab insidiis diaboli, ab ira tua, & æterna damnatione.
Libera nos Domine.

A cœcitate cordis, Superbia, Ambitione, Hypocrisi, Ira, Odio, Malitia & Discordia.
Libera nos Domine.

A fornicatione & aliis omnibus peccatis mortalibus, & a tentationibus carnis, mundi, & diaboli.
Libera nos Domine.

[[2] The initial P has a curious illumination. A traveller is, seemingly, *giving* a letter to a man chained by the legs, and sitting in front of a hole arched and dark. Is Boner's coal-hole intended? Examinations, &c. of Archdeacon Philpot, pp. 13, 227.]

A fulgure & tempestate, a plaga & pestilentia, fame, bello, latrocinio, & morte subitanea.

Libera nos Domine.

Ab omni seditione & conspiratione, a falsis & hæreticis dogmatibus, a duritia cordis, & contemptu verbi & mandati tui.

Libera nos Domine.

Per mysterium sanctæ incarnationis, nativitatis, circumcisionis, baptismi, jejunii, & tentationis tuæ.

Libera nos Domine.

Per Agonem & sanguineum sudorem, per crucem & passionem, per pretiosam mortem & sepulturam, per gloriosam resurrectionem, & ascensionem tuam in cœlos, & adventum Spiritus sancti.

Libera nos Domine.

In tempore tribulationis & prosperitatis nostræ, in hora mortis & in die judicii.

Libera nos Domine.

Te rogamus, O Deus, nos peccatores exaudias, ut Ecclesiam tuam sanctam Catholicam regere & gubernare digneris.

Te rogamus audi nos.

Ut famulam tuam Elizabetham, Reginam & gubernatricem nostram clementissimam, in vera tui adoratione, in justitia & sanctitate vitæ confirmare & custodire digneris.

Te rogamus audi nos.

Ut ejus mentem in tua fide, tui amore & timore, ut semper in te confidat, & ut in omnibus honorem & gloriam tuam quærat & promoveat, dirigere digneris.

Te rogamus audi nos.

Ut Eam servare & defendere, & ei victoriam contra omnes hostes suos concedere digneris.

Te rogamus audi nos.

Ut Episcopos, pastores & ministros ecclesiæ, vera cognitione & recto intellectu verbi tui illuminare[1], & ut tam doctrina quam vita illud promoveant.

Te rogamus audi nos.

[1 Aless, too, has not, digneris. Did the word drop out in printing? See the next petition but one.]

Ut Consiliarios regios, & totam nobilitatem Regni, gratia, sapientia & intellectu illustrare digneris.
Te rogamus audi nos.

Ut Magistratui nostro benedicere, eique gratiam conferre ut exequatur justitiam, & custodiat veritatem.
Te rogamus audi nos.

Ut populo tuo universo benedicere, eumque servare digneris.
Te rogamus audi nos.

Ut omnibus Gentibus unitatem, pacem, & concordiam donare digneris.
Te rogamus audi nos.

Ut mentes nostras ad verum amorem & timorem tui inflammare, & ad mandatorum tuorum observantiam inclinare velis.
Te rogamus audi nos.

Ut populo incrementum gratiæ, ut verbum tuum humiliter audiat, & puro corde amplectatur, & fructus Spiritus proferat, donare digneris.
Te rogamus audi nos.

Ut errantes & deceptos in viam veritatis revocare digneris.
Te rogamus audi nos.

Ut stantes confirmare, imbecilles sustentare, & cadentes erigere, ac Sathanam sub pedibus nostris conculcare velis.
Te rogamus audi nos.

Ut defendas, juves, consoleris omnes in periculis, necessitatibus, & molestiis constitutos.
Te rogamus audi nos.

Ut peregrinantibus terra marique, parturientibus, ægrotantibus, & infantibus, captivis & incarceratis, succurrere velis.
Te rogamus audi nos.

Ut pupillis & orphanis, viduis, desolatis & oppressis, prospicere digneris.
Te rogamus audi nos.

Ut omnibus hominibus miserearis.
Te rogamus audi nos.

Ut inimicis & persecutoribus nostris ignoscas, & eorum corda ad pœnitentiam convertere velis.
Te rogamus audi nos.

Ut fructus terræ dare & conservare digneris, ut suo tempore pie eis utamur.

Te rogamus audi nos.

Ut veram pœnitentiam & remissionem peccatorum nobis largiri, negligentias & ignorantias nobis condonare, gratiam Sancti Spiritus, & emendationem vitæ nobis donare digneris.

Te rogamus audi nos.

Fili Dei, te rogamus audi nos.

Fili Dei, te rogamus audi nos.

Agnus Dei, qui tollis peccata mundi:

Dona nobis Pacem.

Agnus Dei, qui tollis peccata mundi:

Miserere nobis.

Christe audi nos.

Christe audi nos.

Kyrie eleyson.		Kyrie eleyson.
Christe eleyson.	Resp.	Christe eleyson.
Kyrie eleyson.		Kyrie eleyson.

Pater[1] noster, qui es in cœlis, sanctifi. &c.
Et ne nos inducas in temptationem.

Sed libera nos a malo.

Domine, non secundum peccata nostra facias nobis.

Neque secundum iniquitates nostras retribue nobis.

Oremus.

DEUS misericors Pater, qui contritorum non despicis gemitum, & mœrentium non spernis affectum, adesto precibus nostris, quas tibi in angoribus nostris effundimus, easque clementer suscipere dignare; ut quicquid contra nos diabolicæ atque humanæ moliuntur adversationes, ad nihilum redigatur, & consilio tuæ pietatis elidatur, ut nos tui servi, nullis infestationibus læsi, in ecclesia tua sancta tibi gratias referamus: Per Jesum Christum Dominum nostrum.

Exurge, Domine, adjuva nos, & libera nos propter nomen tuum.

Deus auribus nostris audivimus, Patres nostri annunciaverunt nobis opera admiranda, quæ operatus es in diebus eorum, & in diebus antiquis.

Exurge, Deus, adjuva nos, & libera nos propter honorem tuum.

Gloria Patri. &c. Sicut erat. &c. Amen.

[[1] See p. 72, note 1.]

Ab inimicis nostris libera nos Christe.
>Respice clementer afflictiones nostras.

Aspice dolorem cordis nostri.
>Propicius esto peccatis populi tui.

Benigne audi orationes nostras.
>O Fili David, miserere nobis.

Et nunc & semper dignare exaudire nos, O Christe.
>Christe exaudi nos :
>Exaudi nos clementer Domine Jesu Christe.

Ostende nobis, Domine, misericordiam tuam.
>Sicut speramus in te.

Oremus.

INFIRMITATES nostras, quæsumus, Domine, benigne respice, & propter gloriam nominis tui mala omnia, quæ juste pro peccatis nostris meremur, a nobis clementer averte : & præsta, ut in cunctis adversitatibus omnem nostram fiduciam collocemus in misericordia tua, & tibi semper in puritate vitæ serviamus, ad gloriam tui nominis : Per unicum mediatorem nostrum & advocatum Jesum Christum Dominum nostrum. Amen.

Pro Regina.

O DOMINE Pater noster cœlestis, qui maximus potentissimusque es Rex regum & Dominus dominantium, omnium principum solus & unicus moderator & gubernator, qui ab excelso & summo throno tuo omnes mundi incolas intueris, suppliciter te rogamus, ut Reginam nostram Elizabetham clementer & benigno vultu respicere digneris, & eam tui sancti Spiritus gratia ita adimplere, ut semper ad tuam voluntatem perficiendam dedita, in viis tuis ambulet. Accumula in eam cœlestia tua dona : vitam illi fœlicem & diuturnam largire, ut diu fœliciterque regnet, hostes omnes superet suos, & post hanc vitam gloria perfruatur æterna. Per Christum Dominum nostrum. Amen.

OMNIPOTENS sempiterne Deus, qui facis mirabilia magna solus, prætende super famulos tuos Pontifices & Ministros, & super cunctas congregationes illis commissas, Spiritum gratiæ salutaris, & ut in veritate tibi complaceant, perpetuum eis rorem tuæ benedictionis infunde, per Advocatum & Mediatorem nostrum Jesum Christum. Amen.

Precatio Divi Chrysostomi.

OMNIPOTENS sempiterne Deus, qui nobis gratiam dedisti ut hoc tempore unanimiter congregati, preces nostras ad te offerremus, quique polliceris, ut ubi duo vel tres congregati fuerint in tuo nomine, te eorum supplicationes clementer exauditurum, petimus, ut vota & preces tuorum famulorum, prout tibi videbitur eorum saluti maxime expedire, perficias, & præsta nobis in hac vita tuæ veritatis cognitionem, & in futura, vitam æternam. Amen.

ii. Corinth. xiii.

GRATIA Domini nostri Jesu Christi, charitas Dei, & communicatio sancti Spiritus, sit semper cum omnibus nobis. Amen.

Pro Pluvia petenda, tempore necessitatis.

DEUS pater cœlestis, qui per Filium tuum unigenitum promisisti universis tuum regnum & ejus justitiam quærentibus omnia huic vitæ necessaria, da nobis quæsumus in hac nostra necessitate pluviam & imbres tempestivos, ut terræ fructus, ad corporis nostri consolationem, tui nominis honorem, recipere possimus. Per Jesum Christum Dominum no. Amen.

Pro Aeris serenitate.

DOMINE Deus, qui propter peccata hominis semel submersisti mundum universum, octo hominibus solum exceptis, & postea singulari ductus misericordia, promisisti illum nunquam penitus submergendum; supplices te rogamus, etsi ob iniquitates nostras has pluviæ & aquarum inundationes sumus commeriti, digneris tamen nos ad veram pœnitentiam convertere, & talem nobis tribuere cœli serenitatem, ut terræ fructus tempore opportuno recipiamus, tuoque hoc supplicio admoniti, vitam nostram emendare discamus, atque ob tuam in nos clementiam tuas laudes & honores perpetuo celebrare valeamus. Per Jesum Christum Dominum nostrum. Amen.

Tempore Caritatis & Famis.

DEUS pater cœlestis, cujus beneficio pluvia decidit, terra fit frugifera, animantia crescunt, & pisces multiplicantur:

intuere quæsumus afflictiones populi tui, & largire ut hæc penuria caritasque annonæ, quam nunc justissime propter peccata nostra patimur, bonitate misericordiæ tuæ vertatur in copiam & abundantiam. Hæc nobis, clementissime Pater, concede, propter amorem Jesu Christi Domini nostri, cui tecum & sancto Spiritui laus, honor & gloria in omnem æternitatem. Amen.

Tempore belli.

OMNIPOTENS Deus, Rex regum, & omnium gubernator, cujus potentiæ nulla creatura resistere potest, cui proprium est peccatores punire, & eorum misereri qui vere agunt pœnitentiam, serva & libera nos, suppliciter te petimus, a manu inimicorum, reprime eorum superbiam, minue malitiam, dissipa illorum machinationes & astutias, ut nos tuis armis muniti semper servemur ab omnibus periculis, ad glorificandum te, qui es unicus victoriæ largitor : propter merita unigeniti Filii tui Domini nostri Jesu Christi. Amen.

Tempore pestis, mortalitatis, sive morbi.

OMNIPOTENS Deus, qui tempore Regis David, in ira tua, septuaginta millia hominum interfecisti, & tamen, tuæ misericordiæ memor, conservasti reliquos, miserere nostri miserorum, qui nunc variis morbis & gravi mortalitate affligimur, ut quemadmodum angelis tuis a supplicio inferendo cessare jussisti, ita quoque nunc et hanc pestem a nobis amovere digneris. Per Jesum Christum Dominum nostrum. Amen.

DEUS, cui proprium est misereri semper & parcere, suscipe
  has precationes nostras, ut quos delictorum catena
    misere constringit, clementia tuæ miseri-
      cordiæ libere absolvat, propter me-
        rita Jesu Christi, nostri
          mediatoris unici.
            Amen.

Finis Letaniæ.

Collectæ, Epistolæ,

ac Evangelia, ad sacram Communionem, sive in Cœna Domini dicenda, per totum annum.

Dominica prima Adventus.

Collecta.

DA nobis, quæsumus, omnipotens Deus, ut abjectis operibus tenebrarum, induamur arma lucis in hac mortali vita, in qua Jesus Christus Filius tuus cum magna humilitate ad nos visitandos advenit, ut in extremo die, quo rediturus est cum gloria Majestatis suæ ad judicandos vivos & mortuos, resurgamus ad vitam immortalem. Per Christum Dominum nostrum, qui tecum vivit & regnat in unitate sancti Spiritus, per. &c.

[1] Epistola. ad Roma. Cap. xiii.

NEMINI quicquam debeatis, nisi hoc, ut invicem diligatis......& carnis curam ne agatis ad concupiscentias.

Evangelium. Matthæi. xxi.

ET quum appropinquassent Hierosolymis, & venissent Bethphage ad montem olivarum,......& dixit eis: Scriptum est, Domus mea domus deprecationis vocabitur.

Dominica ii. Adventus.

Collecta.

BENEDICTE Deus, qui effecisti ut quæcunque scripta sunt, ad nostram doctrinam scriberentur, concede nobis, ut ita scripturam attente audiamus, legamus, discamus, & intelligamus, syncereque observemus, ut per patientiam & consolationem scripturarum retineamus spem vitæ æternæ, quam dedisti nobis in servatore nostro Jesu Christo, cui tecum & sancto Spiritui sit honor & gloria, per omnia secula seculorum. Amen.

[[1] Every Epistle and Gospel has marginal references, but it was deemed unnecessary to reprint them.]

Epistola ad Romanos. xv. capite.

QUÆCUNQUE præscripta sunt, in nostram doctrinam præscripta sunt :......in eo gentes sperabunt.

Evangelium Lucæ xxi.

ERUNT signa in Sole & Luna & stellis, & in terris anxietas Gentium per desperationem,...... Cœlum & terra transibunt, verba autem mea non transibunt.

Dominica tertia Adventus.
Collecta.

AUREM tuam, quæsumus, Domine, precibus nostris accommoda, & mentis nostræ tenebras gratia tuæ visitationis illustra, Per Dominum nostrum Jesum Christum. &c.

Epistola. i. Cor. iiii.

SIC nos æstimet homo, ut Ministros Christi, & dispensatores mysteriorum Dei:......& patefaciet consilia cordium, ac tunc laus erit unicuique a Deo.

Evangelium. Matthæi cap. xi.

JOANNES autem cum audisset in carcere facta Christi, missis duobus discipulis suis,......qui præparaturus est viam tuam ante te.

Dominica quarta Adventus.
Collecta.

EXCITA, quæsumus, Domine, potentiam tuam & veni, & magna nobis virtute succurre, ut per auxilium gratiæ tuæ, quod nostra peccata præpediunt, indulgentia tuæ miserationis acceleret. Per Christum Do. &c.

Epistola. Philip. iiii.

GAUDETE in Domino semper, & iterum dico gaudete...... custodiat corda vestra & sensus vestros, per Christum Jesum.

Evangelium. Joannis. i.

ET hoc est testimonium Joannis, quando miserant Judæi ab Hierosolymis sacerdotes & Levitas,......Hæc in Bethabara facta sunt, trans Jordanem, ubi Joannes baptizabat.

In die Natalis Domini.
Collecta.

OMNIPOTENS Deus, qui unigenitum Filium tuum nobis dedisti, ut nostram naturam assumeret, hodiernaque die de pura virgine nasceretur, præsta quæsumus, ut nos regenerati, filiique tui per adoptionem & gratiam facti, tuo sancto Spiritu quotidie renovemur, per eundem Dominum nostrum. &c.

Epistola. ad Hebræos. cap. i.

DEUS olim multifariam, multisque modis loquutus patribus per prophetas,......tu autem idem es, & anni tui non deficient.

Evangelium. Joannis i.

IN principio erat sermo, & sermo erat apud Deum, & Deus erat ille sermo.......& conspeximus gloriam ejus, gloriam velut unigeniti a Patre: plenus gratia & veritate.

Die Sancti Stephani.
Collecta.

DA nobis Domine, quæsumus, ut exemplo sancti Stephani discamus inimicos diligere, qui pro persecutoribus suis precatus est Dominum nostrum Filium tuum, qui tecum vivit & regnat. &c. Amen.

Tunc sequetur collecta de Nativitate Domini, quæ quotidie dicetur usque ad Circumcisionem.

Epistola. Act. vii.

STEPHANUS plenus Spiritu sancto, intentis in cœlum oculis, vidit gloriam Dei,......Et cum hæc dixisset, obdormivit.

Evangelium. Matth. xxiii.

ECCE ego mitto ad vos Prophetas, & Sapientes, & Scribas :......Dico enim vobis, haudquaquam me videbitis posthac, donec dicatis : Benedictus qui venit in nomine Domini.

Die Joannis Evangelistæ.
Collecta.

ECCLESIAM tuam, quæsumus, Domine, benignus illustra, ut beati Joannis Apostoli tui & Evangelistæ illuminata doctrinis, ad dona perveniat sempiterna. Per Dominum nostrum Jesum Christum. &c. Amen.

Epistola. i. Joan. i.

QUOD erat ab initio, quod audivimus, quod vidimus oculis nostris,......quod Deus lux est, & tenebræ in eo non sunt ullæ.

Evangelium. Joan. xxi.

Dixit autem Jesus Petro: Sequere me. Conversus Petrus......quæ si scribantur per singula, nec ipse, opinor, mundus caperet eos qui scriberentur libros.

Die Innocentium.
Collecta.

Deus, cujus hodierna die præconium Innocentes Martyres non loquendo, sed moriendo confessi sunt, omnia in nobis vitiorum mala morti dede, ut fidem tuam, quam lingua nostra loquitur, etiam vita moribus fateatur. Per Dominum nostrum Jesum Christum. &c. Amen.

Epistola. Apocal. xiiii.

Et vidi, & ecce Agnus stans super montem Sion, & cum eo centum quadraginta quatuor millia,......Sine macula enim sunt ante thronum Dei.

Evangelium. Matth. ii.

Angelus Domini apparet in somnis Joseph,......& noluit consolationem admittere, propterea quod non sint.

Dominica post festum Nati[1].
Collecta.

Omnipotens Deus, qui unigenitum. &c.
ut supra in festo Nativitatis.

Epistola. Galatas. iiii.

Dico autem, quamdiu hæres puer est, nihil differt a servo, ...Itaque jam non es servus, sed filius, quod si filius, & hæres Dei per Christum.

Evangelium. Matthæi. i.

Liber generationis Jesu Christi filii David, filii Abraham. ......donec peperisset filium suum primogenitum, & appellavit nomen ejus Jesum.

Die Circumcisionis[2].
Collecta.

Omnipotens Deus, qui unigenitum Filium tuum carnis circumcisionem pati, & Legi subditum esse voluisti, propter hominem, da corda nostra vera & spirituali circumcisione ita

---
[1] The heading on two of the pages is, Die Natalis Domini.
[2] On both sides of the leaf the heading is, Die Sancti Stephani.

discindi, ut mactatis mundanis & carnalibus concupiscentiis, obediamus per omnia divinæ voluntati tuæ. Per eumdem Dominum nostrum.

Epistola. Rom. iiii.

BEATUS vir, cui non imputavit Dominus peccatum........ inanis facta est fides, et irrita facta est promissio.

Evangelium. Lucæ. ii.

ET factum est ut discesserunt ab eis Angeli in cœlum......: vocatum est nomen ejus Jesus, quod vocatum erat ab Angelo, priusquam in utero conciperetur.

Si fuerit Dominica inter festum Epiphaniæ & Circumcisionis, tum recitabitur ipsa Collecta, Epistola & Evangelium, quæ dicebantur in die Circumcisionis.

Die Circumcisionis[1] [Epiphaniæ].

Collecta.

DEUS, qui unigenitum tuum gentibus stella duce revelasti, concede propitius, ut qui te jam ex fide cognovimus, tua gloriosa Deitate post hanc vitam perfruamur, Per Christum Do.

Epistola. Ephe. iii.

HUJUS rei gratia ego Paulus vinctus sum Christi Jesu pro vobis gentibus.......per quem habemus audaciam & aditum cum fiducia, quæ est per fidem illius.

Evangelium. Matthæi. ii.

CUM autem natus esset Jesus in Bethlcem civitate Judææ, temporibus Herodis regis, ecce Magi ab oriente......per aliam viam reversi sunt in regionem suam.

Dominica. i. post Epiphaniam.

Collecta.

VOTA, quæsumus, Domine, supplicantis populi cœlesti pietate prosequere, ut ea quæ agenda sunt, videant, & ad implenda quæ viderint, tua gratia ac virtute commoveantur.

Epistola. Rom. xii.

OBSECRO igitur vos, fratres, per miserationes Dei,....... sic multi unum corpus sumus in Christo, singulatim autem alii aliorum membra.

[1 We have also on one page, as the heading, Die Joannis Baptistæ.]

Evangelium Lucæ. ii.

Et ibant parentes ejus quotannis Hierosolymam, in die festo Paschæ.......Et Jesus proficiebat sapientia & ætate, & gratia apud Deum atque homines.

Dominica secunda.
Collecta.

Omnipotens sempiterne Deus, qui cœlestia simul & terrestria moderaris, supplicationes nostras clementer exaudi, & pacem tuam nostris concede temporibus. Per Christum. &c.

Epistola. ad Rom. xii.

Habentes dona juxta gratiam datam nobis varia :....... non arroganter de vobis ipsis sentientes, sed humilibus vos accommodantes.

Evangelium. Joannis. ii.

Et die tertia nuptiæ fiebant in Cana Galilææ, & erat mater Jesu ibi.......& manifestavit gloriam suam, & crediderunt in eum discipuli ejus.

Dominica tertia.
Collecta.

Omnipotens æterne Deus, infirmitatem nostram propitius respice, atque ad protegendum nos dexteram tuæ majestatis extende. Per Do. &c.

Epistola. Rom. xii.

Ne sitis arrogantes apud vosmetipsos, neque cuipiam malum pro malo reddatis....... Ne vincaris a malo, imo vince bono malum.

Evangelium. Matth. viii.

Cum descendisset autem de monte, sequutæ sunt eum turbæ multæ :.......Et sanatus est famulus ejus in hora illa.

Dominica quarta post Epiphaniam.
Collecta.

Deus, qui nos in tantis periculis constitutos propter humanam fragilitatem scis non posse subsistere : da nobis salutem mentis & corporis, ut ea quæ pro peccatis nostris patimur, te adjuvante vincamus. Per Dominum. &c.

Epistola. Rom. xiii.

OMNIS anima potestatibus supereminentibus subdita sit. ......cui tributum, tributum : cui vectigal, vectigal : cui timorem, timorem : cui honorem, honorem.

Evangelium. Matth. viii.

ET quum esset ingressus navim, sequuti sunt eum discipuli sui :......Et cum vidissent illum, rogabant, ut decederet e finibus ipsorum.

Dominica quinta.

Collecta.

FAMILIAM tuam, quæsumus, Domine, continua pietate custodi, ut quæ sola fiducia gratiæ cœlestis innititur, tua semper protectione muniatur. Per Christum Dominum nostrum.

Epistola. Coloss. iii.

SITIS igitur induti tanquam electi Dei, sancti ac dilecti, viscera miserationum,......omnia in nomine Domini Jesu facite, gratias agentes Deo & Patri per illum.

Evangelium. Matth. xiii.

ASSIMILATUM est regnum cœlorum homini seminanti bonum semen in agro suo :...... triticum vero congregate in horreum meum.

Dominica Septuagesimæ.

Collecta.

PRECES[1] populi tui, quæsumus Domine, clementer exaudi, ut qui juste pro peccatis nostris affligimur, pro tui nominis gloria per misericordiam tuam liberemur. Per Dominum nostrum. &c.

Epistola. i. Cor. ix.

AN nescitis, quod qui in stadio currunt, omnes quidem currunt,......ne quo modo fiat, ut cum aliis prædicarim, ipse reprobus efficiar.

Evangelium. Matth. xx.

SIMILE est regnum cœlorum homini patrifamilias, qui exiit primo statim diluculo,......Multi enim sunt vocati, pauci vero electi.

[1] The illumination of the initial P, represents a traveller in the act of receiving a letter from a venerable looking man, through the bars of a cell in which he is confined.]

Dominica Sexagesimæ.

Collecta.

DEUS, qui conspicis quod ex nulla nostra actione confidimus, concede propitius, ut contra adversa omnia protectionis tuæ benignitate muniamur. Per Jesum Christum Dominum nostrum.

Epistola. ii. Cor. xi.

LIBENTER enim suffertis insipientes, cum sitis sapientes. ......Deus & Pater Domini nostri Jesu Christi, qui est laudandus in secula, novit quod non mentiar.

Evangelium. Lucæ. viii.

CUM autem turba plurima conveniret, & e singulis civitatibus properarent ad eum,......audientes sermonem, retinent, & fructum afferunt per patientiam.

Dominica quinquagesimæ[2].

Collecta.

DEUS, qui nos per Apostolum tuum docuisti, quod omnia opera nostra sine caritate nihil sint, da nobis Spiritum tuum sanctum, qui diffundat in cordibus nostris excellens donum caritatis, verum vinculum pacis & omnium virtutum, & sine qua omnis vivens coram te est mortuus, hoc largire: per Dominum no. &c.

Epistola. i. Cor. xiii.

SI linguis hominum loquar & angelorum, caritatem autem non habeam,......Nunc autem manet fides, spes, caritas, tria hæc, sed maxima in his caritas.

Evangelium. Lucæ. xviii.

ASSUMPSIT autem Jesus duodecim, & ait illis: Ecce ascendimus Hierosolymam,......Et omnis plebs ut vidit, dedit laudem Deo.

Feria. iiii. post quinquages[3].

Collecta.

OMNIPOTENS æterne Deus, qui nihil odisti eorum quæ fecisti, & remittis peccata omnibus pœnitentibus: crea in nobis

[2] One of the pages has, Dominica Quinta, as the heading.]

[3] The heading of one page is, Septuagesimæ; of the other, Die Cinerum.]

cor contritum, ut digne peccata nostra defleamus, & agnoscamus iniquitates nostras, & a te Deo omnis misericordiæ perfectam peccatorum remissionem consequamur. Per Dominum nostrum Jesum Christum. &c.

Lectio Prophetiæ. Joelis. ii.

CONVERTIMINI ad me in toto corde vestro in jejunio, & in fletu, & in planctu.......& dominentur eis nationes. Quare dicunt in populis : Ubi est Deus eorum?

Evangelium. Matthei. vi.

CUM jejunaveritis, ne sitis veluti hypocritæ tetrici....... Nam ubi fuerit thesaurus vester, illic erit & cor vestrum.

Dominica. i[1]. quadragesimæ.

Collecta.

DOMINE Jesu Christe, qui nostra causa quadraginta diebus et quadraginta noctibus jejunasti, da nobis hujusmodi uti abstinentia, ut caro nostra spiritui sit subjecta, & mandatis tuis semper obsequamur in vera justicia & sanctitate, ad gloriam & honorem nominis tui : Qui vivis & regnas. &c.

Epistola. ii. Cor. vi.

QUIN & adjuvantes obsecramus, ne in vacuum graciam Dei receperitis.......ut nihil habentes, & tamen omnia possidentes.

Evangelium. Matth. iiii.

TUNC Jesus subductus fuit in desertum a spiritu, ut tentaretur a diabolo.......Tunc omittit illum diabolus. Et ecce angeli accedebant, ac ministrabant ei.

Dominica Secunda quadr.[2]

Collecta.

DEUS qui conspicis omni nos virtute destitui, interius exteriusque custodi, ut ab omnibus adversitatibus muniamur in corpore, & a pravis cogitationibus mundemur in mente. Per. &c.

Epistola. i. Thessa. iiii.

QUOD superest igitur, fratres, rogamus vos, & adhortamur

[1 The heading on neither side of the leaf mentions what Sunday in Lent it is.]

[2 At the top of one page is, Sexagesima.]

per Dominum Jesum,......Proinde qui rejicit, non rejicit hominem, sed Deum, qui dedit Spiritum suum sanctum in vos.

Evangelium. Matth. xv.

Et digressus illinc Jesus, secessit in partes Tyri & Sidonis.......O mulier, magna est fides tua : fiat tibi sicut vis. Et sanata fuit filia ejus ex eo tempore.

Dominica tertia quadra.

Collecta.

QUÆSUMUS omnipotens Deus, vota humilium respice, atque ad defensionem nostram dexteram tuæ Majestatis extende. Per Jesum Christum Dominum nostrum.

Epistola. Ephesios. v.

SITIS igitur imitatores Dei, tanquam filii dilecti, & ambuletis in dilectione,......Expergiscere qui dormis, & surge a mortuis, & illucescet tibi Christus.

Evangelium. Lucæ. xi.

Et erat Jesus ejiciens dæmonium, & illud erat mutum : ......At ille dixit : Quinimo beati qui audiunt sermonem Dei, & custodiunt illum.

Dominica quarta quadr.

Collecta.

CONCEDE, quæsumus, omnipotens Deus, ut qui ex merito nostræ pravitatis affligimur, tuæ gratiæ consolatione respiremus. Per Jesum Christum Dominum nostrum.

Epistola. Galat. iiii.

DICITE mihi, qui sub lege vultis esse, legem ipsam non auditis ?......Itaque, fratres, non sumus ancillæ filii, sed liberæ.

Evangelium. Joannis. vi.

Post hæc abiit Jesus trans mare Galilææ, quod est Tiberiadis,......Hic est vere Propheta ille, qui venturus est in mundum.

Dominica quinta.

Collecta.

POPULUM tuum, quæsumus, Domine, benigne respice, ut tua magna bonitate dirigatur, & corpore ac animo conservetur. Per Dominum. &c.

Epistola. Heb. ix.

CHRISTUS accedens Pontifex futurorum bonorum,....... ii qui vocati sunt, promissionem accipiant æternæ hæreditatis.

Evangelium. Joannis. viii.

QUIS ex vobis arguit me de peccato?......Jesus autem abscondit se, & exivit e templo.

Dominica proxima[1] Paschæ.

Collecta.

OMNIPOTENS sempiterne Deus, qui humano generi ad imitandum humilitatis exemplum, Salvatorem nostrum carnem assumere, & crucem subire fecisti, concede propitius, ut & pacientiæ ipsius habere documenta, et resurrectionis consortia mereamur. Per eundem Christum dominum nostrum.

Epistola. Philip. ii.

Is enim affectus sit in vobis, qui fuit & in Christo Jesu: ......omnisque lingua confiteatur, quod Dominus sit Jesus Christus, ad gloriam Dei Patris.

Evangelium. Matt. xxvi.

ET factum est cum consummasset Jesus sermones hos omnes, dixit discipulis suis......inter quas erat Maria Magdalene, & Maria Jacobi & Jose mater, & mater filiorum Zebedæi.

Feria Secunda ante Pascha.

Lectio Esaiæ prophetæ. cap. lxiii.

QUIS est iste qui venit de Edom, tinctis vestibus de Bosra :......Facti sumus quasi in principio, cum non dominareris nostri, neque invocaretur nomen tuum super nos.

Evangelium. Mar. xiiii.

ERAT autem pascha, & azymorum dies futuri post biduum. ......Priusquam gallus cecinerit bis, abnegabis me ter. cœpitque flere.

Feria tertia ante Pascha.

Lectio Esaiæ Prophetæ. cap. l.

DOMINUS Deus aperuit mihi aurem, ego autem non contradico, retrorsum non abii.......de manu mea factum est hoc vobis, in doloribus dormietis.

[[1] The heading gives the last four letters of this word twice.]

Evangelium. Mar. xv.

ET confestim diluculo concilio inito, summi sacerdotes cum Senioribus & Scribis ac toto consessu,......At Maria Magdalene, & Maria Jose, spectabant ubi poneretur.

Feria quarta ante pascha.
Epistola. Heb. ix.

SIQUIDEM ubi testamentum est, mors intercedat necesse est testatoris.......rursus absque peccato conspicietur iis, qui illum exspectant in salutem.

Evangelium. Lucæ. xxii.

INSTABAT autem dies festus azymorum, qui dicitur pascha. ......At illi dixerunt: Quid adhuc desideramus testimonium? ipsi enim audivimus ex ore ipsius.

Feria quinta ante pascha.
Epistol. i. Cor. xi.

ILLUD tamen præcipiens, non laudo, quod non in melius, sed in deterius convenitis.......Cetera vero, cum venero, disponam.

Evangelium. Lucæ. xxiii.

ET surgens universa multitudo eorum, duxit illum ad Pilatum.......ac sabbato quidem quieverunt secundum præceptum.

Die Parasceves.
Collectæ.

OMNIPOTENS Deus, familiam tuam quæsumus benigne respice, pro qua Dominus noster Jesus Christus non dubitavit tradi manibus nocentium, & crucis subire tormentum: Qui tecum vivit & regnat cum sancto Spiritu, in secula se. &c.

Alia Collecta.

OMNIPOTENS æterne Deus, cujus Spiritu universum corpus ecclesiæ sanctificatur & regitur, exaudi nos pro universis ordinibus supplicantes, & præsta, ut ab omnibus tibi digne & laudabiliter serviatur. Per d. n. Jesum.

MISERICORS Deus, creator omnium hominum, qui nihil odisti eorum quæ condidisti, neque vis mortem peccatoris, sed ut magis convertatur & vivat, miserere Judæorum, Turcarum,

Infidelium & hæreticorum: aufer ab eis ignorantiam & duriciem cordis, & contemptum verbi tui, & reduc eos, misericors Domine, ad gregem tuum, ut serventur inter reliquias veri Israelis, ut fiat unum ovile & unus pastor Jesus Christus Dominus noster, qui vivit & regnat. &c.

Epistola. Heb. x.

NAM lex umbram obtinens futurorum bonorum, non ipsam imaginem rerum, his hostiis,......sed adhortantes invicem, idque hoc magis, quod videtis appropinquantem diem.

Evangelium. Joan. xviii.

HÆC cum dixisset Jesus, egressus est cum discipulis suis trans torrentem Cedron,......ibi ergo propter parasceven Judæorum, quod in propinquo esset monumentum, posuerunt Jesum.

Vigilia Paschæ.

Epistola. i. Pet. iii.

PRÆSTAT enim, ut bene agentes (si ita velit Dei voluntas) ......qui est ad dextram Dei, profectus in cœlum, subjectis sibi angelis & potestatibus ac virtutibus.

Evangelium. Math. xxvii.

CUM autem vespera facta esset, venit homo dives ab Arimathæa,......Illi autem abientes, munierunt sepulchrum obsignato lapide, adhibitis custodibus.

Die Paschæ.

Ad matutinas, loco Psal. Venite exultemus Domino, Antiphonæ sequentes cantabuntur aut dicentur.

CHRISTUS resurgens a morte, jam non amplius moritur, mors illi ultra non dominabitur. Quod enim mortuus est, semel mortuus propter abolitionem peccati. Quod autem vivit, vivit Deo. Ita existimate vosipsos mortuos quidem esse peccato, viventes autem Deo, Per Jesum Christum Dominum nostrum.

NUNC autem Christus resurrexit a mortuis primitiæ eorum qui dormierunt. Postquam enim per hominem mors, etiam per hominem resurrectio mortuorum. Quemadmodum enim omnes per Adam moriuntur, ita per Christum omnes vivificabuntur.

Collecta.

Deus, qui per unigenitum tuum æternitatis nobis aditum, devicta morte, reserasti, vota nostra quæ præveniendo aspiras, etiam adjuvando prosequere. Per eundem Jesum Christum Dominum nostrum, qui. &c.

Epistola. Coloss. iii.

Itaque si resurrexistis una cum Christo, superna quærite, ...inter quos ambulabatis quondam, cum viveretis in his.

Evangelium. Joan. xx.

Uno vero die Sabbatorum Maria Magdalene venit mane, ...Abierunt ergo rursus discipuli ad semetipsos.

Feria secunda post Pascha.

Collecta.

Deus qui per unigenitum. &c.

ut supra in die Paschæ.

Epistola. Acto. x.

Aperiens autem Petrus os, dixit: Reipsa comperio, quod non sit personarum respectus apud Deum,......quod remissionem peccatorum accepturus sit per nomen ejus, quisquis crediderit in eum.

Evangelium. Lucæ. xxiiii.

Et ecce duo ex illis ibant eodem die in castellum,........ Et illi narrabant quæ gesta erant in via, & quomodo fuisset agnitus ipsis ex fractione panis.

Feria tertia post Pascha.

Collecta.

Omnipotens Pater, qui dedisti Filium tuum, ut pro peccatis nostris moreretur, & pro justitia nostra resurgeret, præsta, ut abjecto fermento malitiæ & nequitiæ, in puritate fidei & vitæ tibi perpetuo serviamus. Per. &c.

Epistola. Acto. xiii.

Viri fratres, filii generis Abrahæ, & qui inter vos timent Deum,........quia opus operor ego in diebus vestris, quod non credetis, si quis enarraverit vobis.

Evangelium. Lucæ xxiiii.

Stetit Jesus ipse in medio discipulorum, & dicit eis: Pax vobis.......Vos autem estis testes horum.

Dominica prima post Pascha.

Collecta.

DEUS qui per unigenitum tuum. &c.

ut supra in die Paschæ.

Epistola. i. Joan. v.

OMNE quod natum est ex Deo, vincit mundum :......Qui habet Filium, habet vitam: qui non habet Filium Dei, vitam non habet.

Evangelium. Joan. xx.

CUM ergo vespera esset die illo, qui erat unus Sabbatorum,......Quorumcunque remiseritis peccata, remittuntur eis: quorumcunque retinueritis, retenta sunt.

Dominica. ii. post Pascha.

Collecta.

OMNIPOTENS Deus, qui dedisti nobis Filium tuum, ut esset & sacrificium pro peccato, & exemplum novæ & æternæ vitæ, da ut gratis mentibus hoc inestimabile beneficium agnoscamus, & exempla vitæ ipsius sanctissimæ perpetuo imitari studeamus. Per eundem Christum. &c.

Epistola. i. Pet. ii.

NAM hæc est gratia, si quis propter conscientiam Dei suffert molestias,......sed conversi estis nunc ad pastorem & curatorem animarum vestrarum.

Evangelium. Joan. x.

DIXIT Jesus discipulis suis: Ego sum Pastor ille bonus. ......illas quoque oportet me adducere, & vocem meam audient: & fiet unum ovile, unus pastor.

Dominica tertia post Pascha.

Collecta.

DEUS, qui errantibus ut in viam possint redire justitiæ, veritatis tuæ lumen ostendis, da cunctis qui christiana professione censentur, & illa respuere quæ huic inimica sunt nomini, & ea quæ sunt apta sectari, Per Jesum Christum Dominum nostrum.

Epistola. i. Pet. ii.

DILECTI, obsecro tanquam advenas ac peregrinos, abstinete

a carnalibus concupiscentiis,......Omnes honorate, fraternitatem diligite, Deum timete, Regem honorate.

Evangelium. Joannis. xvi.

DIXIT Jesus discipulis suis : Pusillum & non videtis me : .....sed iterum videbo vos, & gaudebit cor vestrum, & gaudium vestrum nemo tollit a vobis.

Dominica quarta post Pascha.

Collecta.

DEUS, qui fidelium mentes unius efficis voluntatis, da populo tuo id amare quod præcipis, id desiderare quod promittis, ut inter mundanas varietates ibi nostra fixa sint corda, ubi vera sunt gaudia. Per Christum Do. &c.

Epistola. Jacobi. i.

OMNIS donatio bona, & omne donum perfectum, e supernis est,......cum mansuetudine recipite insitum sermonem, qui potest salvas reddere animas vestras.

Evangelium. Joannis. xvi.

NUNC autem vado ad eum qui misit me, & nemo ex vobis interrogat me, quo vadam......Propterea dixi vobis, quod de meo accipiet, & annunciabit vobis.

Dominica quinta post pascha.

Collecta.

DEUS, a quo bona cuncta procedunt, largire supplicibus tuis, ut cogitemus te inspirante, quæ vera sunt, & te gubernante, eadem faciamus. Per Jesum Christum Dominum nostrum. Amen.

Epistola. Jacobi. i.

SITIS autem effectores sermonis, & non auditores tantum, fallentes vosmetipsos......Invisere orphanos & viduas in afflictione sua, immaculatum seipsum servare a mundo.

Evangelium. Joan. xvi.

AMEN amen dico vobis, quæcunque petieritis Patrem in nomine meo, dabit vobis......In mundo afflictionem habetis: sed bono animo sitis, ego vici mundum.

Die Ascentionis Domini.

Collecta.

CONCEDE, quæsumus, omnipotens Deus, ut qui unigenitum tuum, redemptorem nostrum, ad cœlos ascendisse credimus, ipsi quoque mente in cœlestibus habitemus. Per eundem Dominum nostrum. &c.

Epistola. Acto. i.

SUPERIORE quidem volumine diximus, Theophile, de omnibus quæ cœpit Jesus tum facere,.....quemadmodum vidistis eum euntem in cœlum.

Evangelium. Mar. xvi.

APPARUIT Jesus undecim, & exprobravit illis incredulitatem suam, & cordis duritiem,.....& sermonem confirmante per signa subsequentia.

Dominica[1] post Ascentionem.

Collecta.

DEUS rex gloriæ, qui exaltasti Filium tuum unigenitum Jesum Christum ad dexteram tuam in glorioso regno tuo æternæ vitæ, petimus, ne relinquas nos orphanos, sed mitte nobis Spiritum sanctum Paracletum, qui nos consoletur, & ut nos evehat ad illam gloriam, ad quam Dominus & servator noster Jesus Christus prior ascendit, Qui tecum vivit. &c.

Epistola. i. Petri. iiii.

RERUM omnium finis imminet. Sitis igitur sobrii, & vigilantes ad orandum......cui est gloria & imperium, in secula seculorum. Amen.

Evangelium. Joannis. xv. xvi.

CUM autem venerit Paracletus, quem ego mittam vobis a Patre, Spiritus veritatis,.....reminiscamini eorum, quod ego dixerim vobis.

Die Pentecostes.

Collecta.

DEUS, qui corda fidelium sancti Spiritus illustratione docuisti, da nobis eodem Spiritu recta sapere, & de ejus semper

[1 The heading of the page, (which begins with the Collect,) is, Die Ascentionis; on the previous page, too, we have, as the catch word, the first word of the Collect for Ascension-day.]

sancta consolatione gaudere: Per merita Servatoris nostri Jesu Christi, qui tecum vivit & regnat in unitate ejusdem Spiritus sancti Deus, per omnia secula seculorum. Amen.

Epistola. Acto. ii.

ET quum compleretur dies Pentecostes, erant omnes unanimiter in eodem loco:.....audimus eos loquentes nostris linguis magnifica Dei.

Evangelium. Joannis. xiiii.

SI diligitis me, præcepta mea servate. Et ego rogabo Patrem, & alium consolatorem dabit vobis,.....& sicut mandatum dedit mihi Pater, sic facio.

Feria. ii. Pentecostes.

Collecta.

DEUS, qui corda fidelium. &c.

ut supra in die Pentecostes.

Epistola. Acto. x.

APERIENS autem Petrus os, dixit: Reipsa comperio, quod non sit personarum respectus apud Deum,......Tunc rogaverunt eum, ut remaneret aliquot dies.

Evangelium. Joannis. iii.

SIC Deus dilexit mundum, ut Filium suum unigenitum daret,.....ut conspicua fiant facta ipsius, quod per Deum sint facta.

Feria tertia Pentecostes.

Collecta.

DEUS, qui corda fidelium sancti Spiritus. &c.

ut supra in die Pentecostes.

Epistola. Acto. viii.

CUM autem audissent apostoli qui erant Hierosolymis, quod recepisset Samaria sermonem Dei,.....Tunc imponebant manus super illos, accipiebantque Spiritum sanctum.

Evangelium. Joan. x.

AMEN amen dico vobis, qui non intrat per ostium in stabulum ovium, sed ascendit aliunde,.....Ego veni ut vitam habeant, & abundantius habeant.

Dominica S. Trinitatis.

Collecta.

OMNIPOTENS sempiterne Deus, qui dedisti nobis famulis tuis in confessione veræ fidei æternæ Trinitatis gloriam agnoscere, & in potentia Majestatis adorare unitatem, quæsumus, ut ejusdem fidei firmitate ab omnibus semper muniamur adversis. Qui vivis & regnas Deus, per omnia secula seculorum. Amen.

Epistola. Apocalypsis. iiii.

POST hæc vidi, & ecce ostium apertum in cœlo, & vox prima quam audivi tanquam tubæ loquentis mecum,......& propter voluntatem tuam sunt, & creata sunt.

Evangelium. Joan. iii.

ERAT autem homo ex Pharisæis, Nicodemus nomine, princeps Judæorum......ut omnis qui credit in eum, non pereat, sed habeat vitam æternam.

Dominica prima post Trinit.

Collecta.

DEUS, in te sperantium fortitudo, adesto propicius invocationibus nostris, & quia nihil sine te potest mortalis infirmitas, præsta auxilium gratiæ tuæ, ut in exequendis mandatis tuis & voluntate tibi & actione placeamus. Per Jesum Christum Dominum nostrum.

Epistola i. Joan. iiii.

CARISSIMI, diligamus nos invicem, quia caritas ex Deo est......Et hoc præceptum habemus ab eo, ut qui diligit Deum, diligat & fratrem suum.

Evangelium. Lucæ. xvi.

HOMO quidam erat dives, qui induebatur purpura & bysso, & epulabatur quotidie splendide...... neque si quis ex mortuis resurrexerit, credent.

Dominica. ii. post Trinitat.

Collecta.

SANCTI nominis tui, Domine, timorem pariter & amorem fac nos habere perpetuum, quia nunquam tua gubernatione destituis, quos semel in soliditate tuæ dilectionis instituis. Per Jesum Christum Dominum nostrum. Amen.

Epistola. i. Joannis iii.

NE miremini, fratres mei, si odit vos mundus. Nos scimus, quod translati sumus de morte ad vitam,......Et per hoc scimus, quod manet in nobis e spiritu quem nobis dedit.

Evangelium. Lucæ. xiiii.

HOMO quidam apparaverat cœnam magnam, & vocavit multos :......Dico enim vobis, quod nemo virorum illorum qui vocati sunt, gustabit cœnam meam.

Dominica tertia.

Collecta.

QUÆSUMUS nos, Domine, clementer exaudi, & quibus supplicandi præstas affectum, tribue defensionis auxilium. Per Christum Do. &c.

Epistola. i. Petri. v.

OMNES alius alii vicissim subjiciamini. Humilitatem animi vobis infixam habete :......Ipsi gloria, imperium in secula seculorum. Amen.

Evangelium. Lucæ. xv.

ACCEDEBANT autem ad eum omnes publicani & peccatores, ut audirent illum......Ita dico vobis, gaudium erit coram angelis Dei super uno peccatore resipiscente.

Dominica quarta post Trinit.

Collecta.

PROTECTOR omnium in te sperantium Deus, sine quo nihil est sanctum, nihil validum, multiplica super nos misericordiam tuam, ut te rectore, te duce, sic transeamus per bona temporalia, ut non amittamus æterna. Per Jesum Christum Dominum nostrum. Amen.

Epistola. Roma. viii.

REPUTO, non esse pares afflictiones præsentis temporis ad gloriam quæ revelabitur erga nos......adoptionem exspectantes, redemptionem corporis nostri.

Evangelium. Lucæ. vi.

ESTOTE misericordes, sicut & Pater vester misericors est. Nolite judicare, & non judicabimini......& tunc perspicies ut ejicias festucam, quæ est in oculo fratris tui.

Dominica quinta.

Collecta.

DA nobis quæsumus, ut & mundi cursus pacifice nobis tuo ordine dirigatur, & ecclesia tua tranquilla devotione lætetur. Per Jesum Christum Dominum nostrum.

Epistola. i. Petri. iii.

OMNES sitis unanimes, similiter affecti, fraterna præditi caritate, misericordes, affabiles,......sed Dominum Deum sanctificate in cordibus vestris.

Evangelium. Lucæ. v.

FACTUM est autem, cum turba immineret ei ut audiret verbum Dei,......Et subductus in terram navibus, relictis omnibus, sequuti sunt eum.

Dominica sexta post Trinit.

Collecta.

DEUS, qui diligentibus te bona invisibilia præparasti, infunde cordibus nostris tui amoris affectum, ut te in omnibus & super omnia diligentes, promissiones tuas, quæ omnium desiderium superant, consequamur. Per Jesum Christum Dominum nostrum.

Epistola. Rom. vi.

AN ignoratis, quod quicunque baptizati sumus in Christum Jesum, in mortem ejus baptizati sumus?.....viventes autem Deo, per Christum Jesum Dominum nostrum.

Evangelium. Matt. v.

DIXIT Jesus discipulis suis: Nisi abundaverit vestra justitia plus quam Scribarum & Pharisæorum,......donec persolveris extremum quadrantem.

Dominica vii. post Trinit.

Collecta.

DEUS virtutum, cujus est omne quod est optimum, insere pectoribus nostris amorem tui nominis, & præsta nobis religionis incrementum, ut quæ bona sunt nutrias, & quæ sunt nutrita custodias, Per Jesum Christum Dominum nostrum. &c.

Epistola. Rom. vi.

HUMANUM quiddam dico, propter infirmitatem carnis vestræ......donum autem Dei vita æterna, per Christum Jesum Dominum nostrum.

Evangelium. Mar. viii.

IN diebus illis, cum turba admodum multa esset, nec haberent quod manducarent,.....Erant autem qui comederant, ferme quater mille, & dimisit illos.

Dominica octava post Trinit.

Collecta.

DEUS, cujus providentia in sua[1] dispositione non fallitur, te supplices exoramus, ut noxia cuncta submoveas, & omnia nobis profutura concedas. Per Jesum Christum Dominum nostrum. Amen.

Epistola. Rom. viii.

PROINDE fratres, debitores sumus non carni, ut secundum carnem vivamus:.....Siquidem simul cum eo patimur, ut & una cum illo glorificemur.

Evangelium. Matth. vii.

CAVETE vero vobis a pseudoprophetis, qui veniunt ad vos in vestitu ovium,.....introibit in regnum cœlorum, sed qui fecerit voluntatem Patris mei qui in cœlis est.

Dominica nona post Trinit.

Collecta.

LARGIRE nobis, quæsumus Domine, semper spiritum cogitandi quæ recta sunt, pariter & agendi, ut qui sine te esse non possumus, secundum te vivere valeamus. Per Jesum Christum Dominum nostrum.

Epistola. i. Corint. x.

NOLIM autem vos ignorare, fratres, quod patres nostri omnes sub nube erant,.....imo, faciet una cum tentatione eventum, quo possitis sufferre.

[[1] Aless also has, sua: the Salisbury Missal (1502), sui.]

Evangelium. Lucæ. xvi.

DIXIT Jesus discipulis suis: Homo quidam erat dives, qui habebat dispensatorem,.....ut cum defeceritis, recipiant vos in æterna tabernacula.

Dominica decima post Trin.

Collecta.

PATEANT aures misericordiæ tuæ, Domine, precibus supplicantium, & ut petentibus desiderata concedas, fac eos quæ tibi placita sunt postulare, Per Christum Dominum nostrum.

Epistola. i. Cor. xii.

PORRO de spiritualibus, fratres, nolo vos ignorare. Scitis quod gentes fuistis,.....Sed omnia hæc efficit unus ille & idem Spiritus, dividens peculiariter unicuique sicuti vult.

Evangelium. Lucæ. xix.

ET ut appropinquavit Jesus Hierosolymam, videns civitatem flevit super illam, dicens :.....vos autem fecistis illam speluncam latronum. Et docebat quotidie in templo.

Dominica. xi. post Trinit.

Collecta.

DEUS, qui omnipotentiam tuam parcendo maxime & miserendo[1] manifestas, multiplica super nos misericordiam tuam, ut ad tua promissa currentes cœlestium bonorum facias esse participes. Per Jesum Christum Dominum nostrum.

Epistola. i. Cor. xv.

NOTUM autem vobis facio, fratres, Evangelium quod evangelizavi vobis, quod & accepistis,.....Sive igitur ego, sive illi, sic prædicamus, & sic credidistis.

Evangelium. Luc. xviii.

DIXIT autem Jesus ad quosdam, qui in se confidebant quod essent justi,.....Quia omnis qui se extollit, humiliabitur: & qui se humiliat, extolletur.

Dominica. xii. post Trinit.

Collecta.

OMNIPOTENS sempiterne Deus, qui abundantia pietatis tuæ & merita supplicum excedis & vota, effunde super nos

[1 The Salisbury Missal has, miserando : Aless, as here, miserendo.]

misericordiam tuam, ut dimittas quæ conscientia metuit, & adjicias quæ oratio postulare non audet. Per Jesum Christum Dominum nostrum.

Epistola. ii. Corin. iii.

FIDUCIAM autem hujusmodi habemus per Christum erga Deum, non quod idonei simus ex nobisipsis,.....multo magis excellit administratio justitiæ in gloria.

Evangelium. Mar. vii.

ET Jesus inde surgens abiit in confinia Tyri ac Sidonis, & ingressus domum,.....Bene omnia fecit, & surdos facit audire, & mutos loqui.

Dominica. xiii. Post Trinit.

Collecta.

OMNIPOTENS & misericors Deus, a cujus beneficentia proficiscitur ut tibi a fidelibus tuis digne & laudabiliter serviatur, tribue quæsumus nobis, ut ad promissiones tuas sine offensione curramus. Per Jesum Christum Do. &c.

Epistola. Galat. iii.

ABRAHÆ dictæ sunt promissiones, & semini ejus. Non dicit, Et seminibus :......ut promissio ex fide Jesu Christi daretur credentibus.

Evangelium. Lucæ. x.

BEATI oculi qui vident, quæ vos videtis. Dico enim vobis,.....At ille dixit: Qui exercuit misericordiam in illum. Ait igitur illi Jesus: Vade, & tu fac similiter.

Dominica. xiiii. post Trinit.

Collecta.

OMNIPOTENS sempiterne Deus, da nobis fidei, spei & caritatis incrementum: & ut mereamur assequi quod promittis, fac nos amare quod præcipis. Per Jesum Christum Do. &c.

Epistola. Galat. v.

DICO autem, spiritu ambulate, & concupiscentiam carnis non perficietis......Qui vero sunt Christi, carnem crucifixerunt cum affectibus & concupiscentiis.

[LITURG. QU. ELIZ.]

Evangelium. Lucæ. xvii.

ET factum est, dum Jesus iret Hierosolyman, & ipse transibat per mediam Samariam & Galilæam......Surge, vade, fides tua te servavit.

Dominica xv. post Trinit.

Collecta.

CUSTODI, quæsumus, Domine, ecclesiam tuam miseratione perpetua: & quia sine te labitur humana fragilitas, præsta auxilium gratiæ tuæ, ut ab omnibus abstrahatur noxiis, & ad salutaria cuncta dirigatur. Per Jesum Christum Dominum nostrum. Amen.

Epistola. Galat. vi.

VIDETIS quanta vobis epistola scripserim mea manu..... Gratia Domini nostri Jesu Christi cum Spiritu vestro, fratres, Amen.

Evangelium. Matt. vi.

NEMO potest duobus dominis servire. Aut enim hunc habebit odio,......nam crastinus dies curam habebit sui ipsius. Sufficit sua diei afflictio.

Dominica xvi. post Trinit.

Collecta.

ECCLESIAM tuam, Domine, miseratio continuata mundet & muniat; & quia sine te non potest salva consistere, tuo semper munere gubernetur. Per Jesum Christum Do. &c.

Epistola. Ephe. iii.

QUAPROPTER peto, ne deficiatis ob afflictiones meas, quas pro vobis tolero,.....sit gloria in ecclesia per Christum Jesum, in omnes ætates seculi seculorum. Amen.

Evangelium. Lucæ. vii.

ET factum est deinceps, ibat Jesus in civitatem, quæ vocatur Nain,......Et exiit hic rumor in universam Judæam de eo, & omnem finitimam regionem.

Dominica xvii. post Trin.

Collecta.

TUA nos, Domine, quæsumus, gratia semper præveniat & sequatur, ac bonis operibus præstet esse intentos. Per Jesum Christum. &c.

Epistola. Ephe. iiii.

HORTOR itaque vos ego vinctus in Domino, ut ambuletis ita ut dignum est vocatione qua vocati estis,......& per omnia, & in omnibus vobis.

Evangelium. Lucæ. xiiii.

ET accidit ut introiret Jesus in domum cujusdam principis Pharisæorum Sabbato,......Quia omnis qui se extollit, dejicietur, & qui se dejicit, extolletur.

Dominica xviii. post Trinit.

Collecta.

DA, quæsumus, Domine, populo tuo diabolica vitare contagia, & te solum verum Deum pura mente sectari, Per Jesum Christum Dominum nostrum.

Epistola. i. Cor. i.

GRATIAS ago Deo meo semper pro vobis de gratia Dei, quæ data est vobis per Christum Jesum,......inculpatos in die Domini nostri Jesu Christi.

Evangelium. Matt. xxii.

PHARISÆI autem quum audissent, quod Jesus obturasset os Sadducæis, convenerunt in unum,......neque ausus fuit quisquam ex eo die cum amplius interrogare.

Dominica xix. post Trinit.

Collecta.

DIRIGAT corda nostra, quæsumus, Domine, tuæ miserationis operatio: quia tibi sine te placere non possumus. Per Jesum Christum Dominum nostrum.

Epistola. Ephe. iiii.

HOC itaque dico & testor per Dominum, ne posthac ambuletis,......quemadmodum & Deus per Christum largitus est vobis.

Evangelium. Matt. ix.

ET ingressus Jesus navem, trajecit, ac venit in suam civitatem. Et ecce,......& glorificaverunt Deum, qui dedisset potestatem talem hominibus.

Dominica. xx. Post Trinit.
Collecta.

OMNIPOTENS & misericors Deus, universa nobis adversantia misericors exclude, ut mente & corpore pariter expediti, quæ tua sunt liberis mentibus exequamur, Per Christum Dominum nostrum.

Epistola. Ephe. v.

VIDETE igitur quomodo circumspecte ambuletis, non ut insipientes, sed ut sapientes,.....Subditi vicissim alius alii, cum timore Dei.

Evangelium. Matt. xxii.

DIXIT Jesus discipulis suis : Simile factum est regnum cœlorum homini regi, qui fecit nuptias filio suo.......Multi enim sunt vocati, pauci vero electi.

Dominica xxi. post Trinit.
Collecta.

LARGIRE, quæsumus, Domine, fidelibus tuis veniam placatus & pacem, ut pariter ab omnibus mundentur offensis, & secura tibi mente deserviant, Per Jesum Christum Dominum nostrum.

Epistola. Ephesios. vi.

QUOD superest, fratres mei, sitis fortes per Dominum perque potentiam roboris illius......ut in eo libere loquar, sicut oportet me loqui.

Evangelium. Joan. iiii.

ERAT autem quidam Regulus, cujus filius infirmabatur Capernaum :.....Hoc iterum secundum signum edidit Jesus, cum venisset a Judæa in Galilæam.

Dominica xxii. post Trinit.
Collecta.

FAMILIAM tuam, quæsumus, Domine, continua pietate custodi, ut a cunctis adversitatibus te protegente sit libera, & in omnibus actionibus tuo nomini sit devota. Per Dominum nostrum Jesum Christum. &c.

Epistola. Philip. i.

GRATIAS ago Deo meo in omni memoria vestri, semper in omni precatione mea pro omnibus vobis,.....qui contingit per Jesum Christum, ad gloriam & laudem Dei.

Evangelium. Matt. xviii.

ACCEDENS Petrus ad Jesum, dixit : Domine, quoties peccabit in me frater meus, & remittam ei?.....si non remiseritis suo quisque fratri ex cordibus vestris delicta illorum.

Dominica xxiii post Trinit.

Collecta.

DEUS, nostrum refugium & virtus, adesto piis ecclesiæ tuæ precibus, auctor ipse pietatis, & præsta, ut quod fideliter petimus, efficaciter consequamur. Per Jesum Christum Dominum nostrum.

Epistola. Phil. iii.

ESTOTE pariter imitatores mei, fratres, & considerate eos qui sic ambulant,.....secundum efficatiam, qua potest etiam subjicere sibi omnia.

Evangelium. Matthæi. xxii.

TUNC abeuntes Pharisæi consilium ceperunt, ut illaquearent Jesum in sermone......Et his auditis, mirati sunt: & omisso eo, abierunt.

Dominica. xxiiii. post Trinit.

Collecta.

ABSOLVE, quæsumus, Domine, tuorum delicta populorum, ut a peccatorum nostrorum nexibus, quæ pro nostra fragilitate contraximus, tua benignitate liberemur. Per Jesum Christum Dominum nostrum. &c.

Epistola. Coloss. i.

GRATIAS agimus Deo & Patri Domini nostri Jesu Christi, semper de vobis, cum oramus,.....qui idoneos nos fecit ad participationem sortis sanctorum in lumine.

Evangelium. Matt. ix.

CUM hæc loqueretur illis Jesus, ecce primas quidam venit & adoravit eum, dicens :.....Et emanavit rumor hic in totam terram illam.

Dominica. xxv. Post Trinit.

Collecta.

EXCITA, quæsumus, Domine, tuorum fidelium voluntas [voluntates], ut divini operis fructum propensius exequentes, pietatis tuæ præmia majora percipiant, Per Jesum Christum Dominum nostrum.

Lectio. Jeremiæ. xxiii.

ECCE dies veniunt, dicit Dominus: & suscitabo David germen justum:.....& de cunctis terris, ad quas ejeceram eos illuc: & habitabunt in terra sua.

Evangelium. Joan. vi.

CUM sustulisset ergo oculos Jesus, & vidisset quod multa turba veniret ad se,.....Hic est vere Propheta ille, qui venturus est in mundum.

Si ante Dominicam Adventus Domini plures istis .xxv. acciderint Dominicæ, Collecta, Epistola & Evangelium dicantur, quæ Dominicis inter Epiphaniam & Septuagesimam assignata sunt, & erant omissa.

Die Sancti Andreæ[1] apostoli.

Collecta.

OMNIPOTENS Deus, qui dedisti beato Andreæ Apostolo tuo, ut acerbam & ignominiosam crucis mortem duceret sibi pro magna gloria, tribue ut omnia nobis adversa pro nomine tuo ducamus profutura[2] ad æternam vitam conducibilia. Per Christum Dominum nostrum.

Epistola. Romanos. x.

SI confessus fueris ore tuo Dominum Jesum, & credideris in corde tuo,.....Toto die expandi manus meas ad populum non credentem & contradicentem.

Evangelium. Matt. iiii.

AMBULANS autem Jesus juxta mare Galilææ, vidit duos fratres, Simonem qui vocabatur Petrus,.....At illi protinus relicta navi, & patre suo, sequuti sunt eum.

Die Sancti Thomæ apostoli.

Collecta.

OMNIPOTENS æterne Deus, qui pro confirmatione fidei nostræ beatum Thomam Apostolum de resurrectione Filii tui dubitantem confirmasti, concede nobis, ut vere & sine ulla

[1] On the second page the heading is, Mathias.]
[2] Aless:—profutura, & ad æternam.]

dubitatione credamus in Filium tuum Dominum nostrum Jesum Christum, & ut fides nostra coram te nunquam mereatur reprehensionem. Per eundem Dominum nostrum Jesum Christum Filium tuum, qui tecum vivit & regnat in unitate Spiritus sancti Deus, per omnia secula seculorum.

Epistola. Ephe. ii.

JAM non estis hospites & incolæ, sed concives Sanctorum, ac domestici Dei,......in quo & vos coædificamini in habitaculum Dei per Spiritum.

Evangelium. Joan. xx.

THOMAS autem unus ex duodecim, qui dicitur Didymus, non erat cum eis,......quod Jesus est Christus ille Filius Dei, & ut credentes vitam habeatis per nomen ejus.

Die Conversionis S. Pauli[3].

Collecta.

DEUS, qui universum mundum beati Pauli Apostoli prædicatione docuisti, da nobis quæsumus, ut cujus Conversionem recolimus, per ejus ad te exempla gradiamur. Per Jesum Christum Dominum nostrum.

Epistola. Acto. ix.

SAULUS autem adhuc spirans minas ac cædem adversus discipulos Domini,......& confundebat Judæos, qui habitabant Damasci, affirmans, quod is esset Christus.

Evangelium. Matthæi. xix.

RESPONDENS Petrus, dixit Jesu: Ecce nos reliquimus omnia, & sequuti sumus te:......Multi autem primi erunt novissimi, & novissimi primi.

Die purificationis Mariæ vir.

Collecta.

OMNIPOTENS Deus, majestatem tuam supplices exoramus, ut sicut unigenitus Filius tuus cum carnis nostræ substantia hodie tibi in templo est præsentatus, ita nos facias purgatis mentibus tibi præsentari, & vitam obtinere æternam: Per eundem Jesum Christum Dominum nostrum.

[[3] At the top of one page he is styled, Apostoli.]

Epistola.

Eadem cum illa quæ assignatur diei Dominico.

Evangelium. Luc. ii.

POSTEAQUAM completi fuissent dies purgationis eorum secundum legem Mosi,.....nisi prius videret Christum Domini. Et venit per spiritum in templum.

Die Mathiæ Apostoli.

Collecta.

OMNIPOTENS Deus, qui in locum Judæ traditoris elegisti fidelem servum tuum Mathiam, ut esset unus ex numero duodecim Apostolorum, defende ecclesiam tuam a doctrina pseudoapostolorum, & tribue ut a veris pastoribus gubernetur. Per Jesum Christum Dominum nostrum.

Epistola. Actor. i.

IN diebus his, exurgens Petrus in medio discipulorum, dixit :.....& cecidit sors super Mathiam, & cooptatus est ad numerum undecim Apostolorum.

Evangelium. Matth. xi.

IN illo tempore respondens Jesus dixit : Gratias ago tibi, Pater, Domine cœli & terræ,.....Jugum enim meum commodum est, & onus meum leve est.

Annunciatio beatæ Mariæ.

Epistola. [Collecta.]

MENTIBUS nostris, quæsumus Domine, gratiam tuam benignus infunde, ut qui Filii[1] tui incarnationem cognovimus, per passionem ejus & crucem ad resurrectionis gloriam perducamur : Per eundem Christum Dominum nostrum.

Lectio. Esa. vii.

ET adjecit Dominus loqui ad Achaz, dicens: Pete tibi signum a Domino Deo tuo in profundum inferni,.....ut sciat reprobare malum, & eligere bonum.

Evangelium. Lucæ. i.

IN mense autem sexto, missus est angelus Gabriel a Deo in civitatem Galilææ,.....fiat mihi secundum verbum tuum. Ac discessit ab illa Angelus.

[1] This mutilated sentence is faithfully copied from Aless. The Salisbury Missal:—ut qui *angelo nunciante Christi* filii tui.]

Die S. Marci Evangelistæ.

Collecta.

DEUS, qui beatum Marcum Evangelistam tuum ad Evangelicæ prædicationis gratiam evexisti, tribue quæsumus, nos semper sancto[2] tuo Evangelio proficere, & fidei constantia stabiliri, ut non simus semper pueri, fluctuantes omni vento doctrinæ. Per Jesum Christum Dominum nostrum.

Epistola. Ephe. iiii.

VERUM unicuique nostrum data est gratia juxta mensuram donationis Christi.....incrementum corporis facit, in ædificationem sui ipsius per caritatem.

Evangelium. Joan. xv.

DIXIT Jesus discipulis suis: Ego sum vitis vera, & Pater meus agricola est......ut gaudium meum in vobis maneat, & gaudium vestrum impleatur.

Die Philippi & Jacobi apost.

Collecta.

OMNIPOTENS Deus, cujus vera cognitio vita æterna est, fac nos credere Filium tuum Dominum nostrum Jesum Christum esse viam, & veritatem, & vitam, id quod sancti Apostoli tui Philippus & Jacobus crediderunt & docuerunt. Per eundem Dominum nostrum Jesum. &c.

Epistola. Jacobi. i.

JACOBUS Dei ac Domini Jesu Christi servus, duodecim tribubus quæ sunt in dispertione, salutem......quam promisit Dominus iis, a quibus fuerit dilectus.

Evangelium. Joan. xiiii.

DIXIT Jesus discipulis suis: Ne turbetur cor vestrum. Creditis in Deum,.....ut glorificetur Pater per Filium. Si quid petieritis per nomen meum, ego faciam.

Die Barnabæ Apostoli.

Collecta.

OMNIPOTENS Domine, qui sanctum Apostolum tuum Barnabam singularibus donis sancti Spiritus ornasti, quæsumus,

[2 Aless has, contrary to the English, eius eruditione proficere.]

ne sinas nos destitui multiplicibus donis tuis, aut gratia tua ut illis recte utamur ad laudem & gloriam sanctissimi nominis tui. Per Jesum Christum Dominum nostrum.

Epistola. Acto. xi.

PERVENIT autem rumor ad aures ecclesiæ, quæ erat Hierosolymis, super his:.....quod & fecerunt, mittentes ad seniores per manum Barnabæ ac Sauli.

Evangelium. Joan. xv.

DIXIT Jesus discipulis suis: Hoc est præceptum meum, ut diligatis vos invicem, sicut dilexi vos......ut quicquid petieritis Patrem nomine meo, det vobis.

Die Joannis Baptistæ.

Collecta.

OMNIPOTENS Deus, cujus providentia præcursor Joannes Baptista miraculose natus est, & missus ut præpararet viam Filio tuo prædicatione pœnitentiæ: fac nos ejus doctrinam & sanctam vitam ita imitari, ut agamus veram pœnitentiam juxta ipsius doctrinam, & exemplo ejus constanter fateamur veritatem, & libere crimina reprehendamus, ac patienter pro confessione veritatis mortem perferamus acerbam. Per eundem Jesum Christum Dominum nostrum. &c.

Lectio. Esaiæ. xl.

CONSOLAMINI consolamini popule meus, dicit Deus vester. Loquimini ad cor Hierusalem,.....& in sinu suo levabit: fœtas ipse portabit.

Evangelium. Lucæ. i.

ELIZABETÆ vero impletum est tempus pariendi, & peperit filium......& erat in desertis donec veniret dies, quo ostendendus erat apud Israelitas.

Die Sancti Petri apost.

Collecta.

OMNIPOTENS Deus, qui per Filium tuum Dominum nostrum Jesum Christum beato Petro Apostolo excellentia dona contulisti, & ut gregem tuum diligenter pasceret tertio præcepisti, præsta quæsumus, ut omnes Episcopi & Pastores diligenter doceant Evangelium, & ut populus doctrinæ sit obsequens, quatenus vitam consequatur æternam. Per Jesum Christum Dominum nostrum.

Epistola. Act. xii.

EODEM autem tempore injecit Herodes Rex manus, ut affligeret quosdam de ecclesia......& ex omni expectatione plebis Judæorum.

Evangelium. Mat. xvi.

CUM venisset autem JESUS in partes Cæsareæ ejus, quæ cognominatur Philippi,.....& quicquid solveris in terra, erit solutum in cœlis.

Die Sancti Jacobi apostoli.

Collecta.

MISERICORS Deus, concede, ut sicut sanctus Jacobus Apostolus tuus, relicto patre & omnibus quæ habebat, continuo obediens fuit vocationi Filii tui, & eum est sequutus; ita nos, relictis omnibus mundanis & carnalibus affectibus, semper pareamus mandatis tuis. Per Dominum nostrum Jesum Christum.

Epistola. Act. xi. & xii.

IN his autem diebus supervenerunt ab urbe Hierosolymorum prophetæ Antiochiam,.....videns autem quod gratum esset Judæis, perrexit comprehendere & Petrum.

Evangelium. Matth. xx.

TUNC accessit ad Jesum mater filiorum Zebedæi cum filiis suis adorans,.....sed ut ipse ministraret, utque daret animam suam redemptionem pro multis.

Die S. Bartholomæi apostoli.

Collecta.

OMNIPOTENS sempiterne Deus, qui dedisti apostolo tuo Bartholomæo, ut crederet Evangelio, illudque doceret, da quæsumus ecclesiæ tuæ & amare quod credidit, & prædicare quod docuit. Per Jesum Christum Dominum nostrum.

Epistola. Acto. v.

PER manus autem apostolorum ædebantur signa ac prodigia multa in populo......afferens ægros ac vexatos a spiritibus immundis, qui sanabantur omnes.

Evangelium. Luc. xxii.

FACTA est autem & contentio inter discipulos, quis eorum videretur esse major......& sedeatis super thronos, judicantes duodecim tribus Israel.

Die S. Matthæi Apostoli[1].

Collecta.

OMNIPOTENS Deus, qui per Filium tuum vocasti beatum Matthæum, ut ex publicano Apostolus fieret & Evangelista, da nobis gratiam, ut studium pecuniæ & opum amorem inordinatum relinquamus, & sequamur Filium tuum Dominum nostrum Jesum Christum, qui tecum vivit & regnat in unitate Spiritus sancti Deus, per omnia secula seculorum.

Epistola. ii. Cor. iiii.

PROPTEREA cum ministerium hoc habeamus, ut nostri misertus est Deus, haud degeneramus :......ad illuminationem cognitionis gloriæ Dei, in facie Jesu Christi.

Evangelium. Matt. ix.

ET præteriens Jesus illinc, vidit hominem desidentem ad telonium, Matthæum nomine,......Non enim veni ad vocandum justos, sed peccatores ad pœnitentiam.

Die Michaelis & omnium Angelorum[2].

Collecta.

DEUS, qui miro ordine Angelorum ministeria hominumque dispensas, concede propitius, ut a quibus tibi ministrantibus in cœlo semper assistitur, ab his in terra vita nostra muniatur. Per Christum Dominum nostrum.

Epistola. Apo. xii.

ET factum est prælium magnum in cœlo, Michael & angeli ejus præliabantur cum dracone :......habens iram magnam, sciens quod modicum tempus habet.

Evangelium. Matt. xviii.

IN illo tempore accesserunt discipuli ad Jesum, dicentes : Quis maximus est in regno cœlorum?......semper vident faciem Patris mei, qui in cœlis est.

[1 At the top of the page is, Apost. et Evang.]
[2 The heading of both pages is, Michael Archangelus.]

Die Sancti Lucæ Evang.

Collecta.

OMNIPOTENS Deus, qui Lucam medicum, cujus laus est in Evangelio, ut animarum quoque curam susciperet, ad te vocasti, præsta quæsumus, ut salubribus ejus doctrinæ medicinis omnes animarum nostrarum morbi sanentur. Per Jesum Christum Dominum nostrum.

Epistola. ii. Tim. iiii.

AT tu vigila in omnibus, obdura in afflictionibus: opus perage Evangelistæ,.....quem & tu cave. Vehementer enim restitit sermonibus nostris.

Evangelium. Luc. x.

POST hæc autem designavit Dominus & alios septuaginta, ...edentes & bibentes quæ dantur ab illis. Dignus est enim operarius mercede sua.

Die Simonis & Judæ apost.

Collecta.

OMNIPOTENS Deus, qui ecclesiam super fundamento prophetarum & Apostolorum in ipso summo angulari lapide Christo Jesu ædificasti, da nobis ut per eorum doctrinam in unitate spiritus conjungamur, ut simus tibi semper templum acceptabile: Per eundem Jesum Christum Dominum nostrum.

Epistola. Judæ. i.

JUDAS Jesu Christi servus, frater Jacobi, iis qui in Deo Patre sanctificati sunt,.....dominos vero spernunt, in potestate præditos maledicta congerunt.

Evangelium. Joannis. xv.

HOC est præceptum meum, ut diligatis vos invicem, sicut dilexi vos......Quin & vos testes estis, quia ab initio mecum estis.

Die omnium Sanctorum.

Collecta.

OMNIPOTENS Deus, qui conjunxisti electos tuos in una communione & societate mystici corporis Filii tui Domini nostri Jesu Christi, da ut sanctos tuos in omnibus virtutibus & bonis operibus imitemur, ut ad ineffabile gaudium, quod præparasti iis qui vere te diligunt, perveniamus. Per Jesum Christum Dominum nostrum.

Epistola. Apo. vii.

ECCE ego Joannes vidi alterum angelum ascendentem ab ortu solis..... honor & virtus & fortitudo Deo nostro, in secula seculorum. Amen.

Evangelium. Matth. v.

CUM autem vidisset Jesus turbas, ascendit in montem: & quum consedisset,.....Sic enim persequuti fuerunt prophetas, qui fuerunt ante vos.

Finis Collectarum, Epistolarum, & Evangeliorum totius Anni.

Ordo administrandi Cœnam

Domini, sive Sacram Communionem.

Quotquot cupiunt participes fieri sacræ Communionis, indicabunt nomina sua Pastori, pridie aut mane, priusquam inchoentur Matutinæ, vel immediate post principium matutinarum precum.

Si quis autem eorum fuerit manifeste criminosus, ita ut Ecclesia per eum sit offensa, vel affecit proximum notoria injuria, verbis aut facto, Pastor vocabit eum, & commonefaciet, ne ullo modo audeat accedere ad mensam Domini, donec præbuerit clara indicia suæ resipiscentiæ, & satisfecerit Ecclesiæ, ac illis quos affecit injuria; vel ad minimum, promittat se illis satisfacturum, quam primum commode fieri potest.

Eodem ordine, admonebit pastor eos, inter quos intelligit esse simultates ac odia, nec permittet eos communicare mensæ Domini, donec certior redditus fuerit de eorum reconciliatione. Quod si altera pars dixerit se velle ex animo alteri ignoscere, & ei etiam satisfacere, & altera noluerit accipere satisfactionem, aut deponere iram & odium, Pastor admittet pœnitentem, ablegato pertinace.

Mensa Dominicæ Cœnæ operietur mundo panno lineo: ad cujus mensæ septentrionalem partem minister stans, orabit Precationem Dominicam, in hunc modum:

PATER noster qui es. &c.

cum Collecta sequente.

OMNIPOTENS Deus, cui omne cor patet, & cui omnes affectus animorum cogniti sunt, & quem nihil latet, purifica cogitationes cordium nostrorum, ut per inspirationem sancti Spiritus te ex animo amemus, & debita veneratione celebremus nomen tuum sanctum, Per Jesum Christum Dominum nostrum.

Tunc recitabit sacerdos clare Decem præcepta: & universus populus post singula mandata, genibus flexis, misericordiam Dei implorabit pro violatione illorum, in hunc qui sequitur modum.

Exo. 20.
Deu. 5.

Minister. Deus hæc verba ad hunc modum effatus est. Ego sum Dominus Deus tuus. Deos nullos alios habebis præter me.

Populus. Domine miserere nostri, & dirige corda nostra ad servandam hanc legem.

Minister. Non facies tibi sculptile, neque ullam similitudinem ullius rei quæ est supra in cœlo, aut infra in terra, aut in aquis sub terra: non adorabis ea nec coles. Ego enim Deus tuus fortis zelotes sum, visitans iniquitates patrum in filios, in tertiam & quartam generationem eorum qui oderunt me, & faciens misericordiam in millia, his qui diligunt & custodiunt præcepta mea.

Populus. Domine miserere nostri, &c.

Minister. Non assumes nomen Domini Dei tui in vanum: non enim habebit insontem Dominus eum, qui assumpserit nomen Domini Dei sui frustra.

Populus. Domine miserere nostri. &c.

Minister. Memento ut diem Sabbati sanctifices. Sex diebus operaberis, & facies omnia opera tua, septimo autem die Sabbatum Domini Dei tui est: nullum in eo facies opus, tu & filius tuus & filia tua, servus tuus & ancilla tua, jumentum tuum, & advena qui est intra portas tuas. Sex enim diebus fecit Dominus cœlum & terram & mare, & omnia quæ in eis sunt, & requievit die septimo. Idcirco benedixit Dominus diei Sabbati, & sanctificavit eum.

Populus. Domine miserere nostri. &c.

Minister. Honora patrem tuum & matrem tuam, ut sis longævus super terram, quam Dominus Deus tuus dabit tibi.

Populus. Domine miserere nostri. &c.
Minister. Non occides.
Populus. Domine miserere nostri. &c.
Minister. Non committes adulterium.
Populus. Domine miserere nostri. &c.
Minister. Non furtum facies.
Populus. Domine miserere nostri. &c.
Minister. Non loqueris contra proximum tuum falsum testimonium.

Populus. Domine miserere no. &c.

Minister. Non concupisces domum proximi tui, nec desiderabis uxorem ejus, non servum, non ancillam, non bovem, non asinum, nihil denique quod sit alterius.

Populus. Domine miserere nostri, & quæsumus has omnes leges in cordibus nostris inscribas.

Tunc per ministrum, stantem ad sacram Mensam, legetur Collecta sive oratio diei assignata, una cum altera duarum Collectarum sequentium pro fœlici statu Reginæ.

OMNIPOTENS Deus, cujus regnum est æternum, & potentia infinita, miserere universæ Ecclesiæ, & sic dirige cor electæ famulæ Elizabethæ Reginæ nostræ, ut cognoscat se esse famulam tuam, & ante omnia quærat gloriam & honorem tuum: & ut nos ei subjecti agnoscentes, ut decet, eam a te habere imperium, fideliter ei serviamus, eam honoremus, & obsequamur ipsi cum omni submissione, in te, & propter te, juxta præceptum & ordinationem tuam. Per Jesum Christum Filium tuum, Dominum nostrum, qui tecum. &c.

Alia Collecta.

OMNIPOTENS sempiterne Deus, in cujus manu docemur ex verbo tuo corda regum esse, qui es humilium consolator, & fidelium fortitudo, ac protector in te sperantium, da Reginæ nostræ Elizabethæ, ut super omnia & in omnibus te honoret & amet, & studeat servare populo sibi commisso pacem, cum omni pietate. Per Jesum Christum Dominum nostrum. Amen.

Post has Collectas, sacerdos, seu quis alius minister ad id deputatus, legat Epistolam, in loco ad id assignato, & sic incipiat.

Epistola Sancti N. Apostoli, scripta ad N. capite. &c.

Epistola finita, legatur Evangelium.

Evangelium Sancti N. scriptum cap. N. &c.

Post Evangelium, sequetur Symbolum.

CREDO in unum Deum Patrem omnipotentem, factorem cœli & terræ, visibilium omnium & invisibilium. Et in unum Dominum Jesum Christum Filium Dei unigenitum, & ex Patre natum ante omnia secula. Deum de Deo, Lumen de Lumine:

[LITURG. QU. ELIZ.]

Deum verum de Deo vero, genitum non factum, consubstantialem Patri, per quem omnia facta sunt. Qui propter nos homines & propter nostram salutem descendit de cœlis. Et incarnatus est de Spiritu sancto ex Maria virgine, & homo factus est. Crucifixus etiam pro nobis sub Pontio Pilato, passus & sepultus est. Et resurrexit tertia die secundum scripturas, & ascendit in cœlum, sedet ad dexteram Patris. Et iterum venturus est cum gloria, judicare vivos & mortuos, cujus regni non erit finis. Et in Spiritum sanctum Dominum & vivificantem, qui ex Patre Filioque procedit. Qui cum Patre & Filio simul adoratur & conglorificatur, qui loquutus est per Prophetas. Et unam, Sanctam, Catholicam, & Apostolicam Ecclesiam. Confiteor unum baptisma, in remissionem peccatorum. Et expecto resurrectionem mortuorum, & vitam venturi seculi. Amen.

Post Symbolum sequatur Concio, sive legatur una Homiliarum, vulgari lingua.

Finita Homilia aut Sermone ad populum, Pastor indicabit festos ac jejunos dies, si qui fuerint, sequenti septimana.

Inprimisque hortabitur, ut pauperum meminerint, & eorum inopiam sublevent. Deinde cantentur vel recitentur una vel plures ex sententiis sequentibus.

Mat. 5. Sic luceat lux vestra coram hominibus, ut videant vestra opera bona, & glorificent Patrem vestrum, qui in cœlis est.

Mat. 6. Ne reponatis vobis thesauros in terra, ubi erugo & tinea corrumpit, & ubi fures perfodiunt & furantur; sed recondite vobis thesauros in cœlo, ubi neque erugo neque tinea corrumpit, & ubi fures non perfodiunt neque furantur.

Mat. 7. Quæcunque volueritis ut faciant vobis homines, sic & vos facite illis. Hæc enim est lex & Prophetæ.

Mat. 7. Non omnis qui dicit mihi Domine, Domine, intrabit in regnum cœlorum, sed qui fecerit voluntatem Patris mei, qui in cœlis est.

Luc. 19. Zachæus stans dicebat ad Dominum: Ecce dimidium bonorum meorum, Domine, do pauperibus, & si quid aliquem defraudavi, reddo quadruplum.

1 Cor. 9. Quis militat suis stipendiis unquam? Quis plantat vineam, & de fructu ejus non edit? Aut quis pascit gregem, & de lacte gregis non edit?

1 Cor. 9. Si nos vobis spiritualia seminavimus, magnum est si nos vestra carnalia messuerimus?

An nescitis quod ii qui in sacris operantur, ex sacrificiis 1 Cor. 9.
vivant? Qui sacrario assistunt, una cum sacrario partem
accipiunt? Sic & Dominus ordinavit, ut qui Evangelium
annunciant, ex Evangelio vivant.

Qui sementem facit parce, is parce messurus est. Et 2 Cor. 9.
qui sementem facit libenter ac benigne largiendo, copiose
messurus est, unusquisque secundum propositum cordis, non
ex molestia aut necessitate: nam hilarem datorem diligit
Deus.

Communicet qui catechizatur sermone, ei qui se catechizat, Gal. 6.
omnibus bonis. Ne erretis, Deus non irridetur. Quicquid
enim seminaverit homo, hoc & metet.

Cum tempus habemus, operemur bonum erga omnes, max- 1 Tim. 6.
ime autem ad domesticos fidei.

Est autem quæstus magnus pietas cum animo sua sorte 1 Tim. 6.
contento. Nihil enim intulimus in mundum, videlicet nec
efferre quicquam possumus.

Præcipe his qui divites sunt, ut prompti sint ad largien- 1 Tim. 6.
dum & distribuendum, thesaurizantes sibi ipsis thesaurum,
fundamentum bonum in posterum, ut apprehendant æternam
vitam.

Non est Deus injustus, ut obliviscatur operis vestri, & la- Heb. 6.
boris ex caritate suscepti, quam exhibuistis erga nomen illius,
qui ministrastis sanctis, & ministratis.

Beneficentiæ autem & communionis nolite oblivisci: tali- Heb. 13.
bus enim victimis placetur Deo.

Qui habuerit substantiam hujus mundi, & viderit fratrem 1 Joa. 3.
suum egere, & clauserit viscera sua ab eo, quomodo caritas
Dei manet in eo?

Fac eleemosynam ex substantia tua, & noli avertere fa- Tob. 4.
ciem tuam ab ullo paupere: ita enim fiet, ut nec a te avertatur
facies Domini.

Quo modo potueris, ita esto misericors. Si multum tibi Tob. 4.
fuerit, abundanter tribue: si exiguum tibi fuerit, etiam exiguum libenter impartiri stude. Præmium enim bonum tibi
thesaurizas in die necessitatis.

Fœneratur Domino, qui miseretur pauperis, & vicissitudi- Pro. 13.
nem suam reddet ei.

Beatus vir qui intelligit super egenum & pauperem, in die Psa. 41.
mala liberabit eum Dominus.

Interea ædiles seu alii, quibus illud munus assignabitur, colligent oblatam a populo eleemosynam, & in cistam ad pauperum usum reponent. Singuli item consuetas oblationes & decimas[1] suo tempore Pastori persolvent.

Post hæc minister dicet,

Oremus pro statu universalis Ecclesiæ, hic in terra militantis.

1 Ti. 2.

OMNIPOTENS æterne Deus, qui[2] per Apostolum tuum jubes facere orationes, obsecrationes, deprecationes, & gratiarum actiones pro omnibus hominibus, humiliter te petimus, ut clementer accipias [hæc munera, atque] has preces nostras, quas offerimus divinæ majestati tuæ, supplicantes, ut perpetuo inspires & conserves universæ Ecclesiæ spiritum veritatis & concordiæ. Præsta etiam, ut omnes qui confitentur nomen tuum sanctum, consentiant in fide, & vera doctrina Evangelii, & vivant inter se concordes in caritate. In primis autem te oramus, ut serves & defendas famulam tuam Elizabetham Reginam nostram, ut sub ipsa quietam vitam degamus cum omni pietate & honestate. Da suis consiliariis & universis qui magistratum gerunt, ut sine personarum acceptione administrent justitiam, qua vitia & nequitiæ puniantur & corrigantur; pietas, religio, & virtus crescant, & afficiantur dignis præmiis. Da gratiam, cœlestis Pater, omnibus Episcopis, pastoribus, & his qui curam gerunt animarum, ut tam vita quam doctrina ornent ministerium Evangelii, & administrent sacramenta, juxta institutionem Filii tui. Tribue universo populo gratiam tuam, ut humili animo, & qua decet reverentia, audiant & accipiant sanctum verbum tuum, & tibi serviant in sanctitate & justitia, omnibus diebus vitæ. Submisse etiam te petimus, propter bonitatem tuam, Domine, ut consoleris & succurras omnibus qui sunt in angustiis, doloribus, infirmitatibus, vel aliis adversitatibus constituti. Hæc nobis largire, O Pater, propter Jesum Christum Mediatorem nostrum unicum & Advocatum. Amen.

Si nulla largiatur eleemosyna omittitur (hæc munera atque).

Tunc sequetur hæc exhortatio, certis temporibus, quando presbyter videbit populum negligenter accedere ad sacram Communionem.

[1 The English only has 'the due and accustomed offerings'. See p. 185. and also the last rubric on p. 399.]

[2 Aless, qui nos per.]

CONVENIMUS hodie, dilectissimi fratres, ad alendum nos pastu coenæ dominicæ, ad quam jubeo vos omnes, qui saltem hic adestis, & item obsecro in Domino Jesu Christo, ut non velitis recusare accedere, præsertim tam amanter a Domino ipso vocati ac invitati. Scitis quam graviter & iniquo animo ferri solet, cum quis apparavit opiparum convivium, & mensam conquisitissimis epulis instruxit, adeo ut nihil desit, nisi ut convivæ accumbant, si ii qui vocantur temere & ingrate recusent accedere. Quis e vobis, si secum eo pacto ageretur, non succenseret? Quis non opinaretur immensam fieri sibi injuriam? Quamobrem, dilectissimi in Christo Jesu, cavete, ne subterducentes vos ab hac sacratissima coena, iram Dei in vos devocetis. Facile dici potest abs quovis homine, Nolo communicare, quoniam secus sum impeditus mundanis negotiis: verum hujusmodi excusationes non tam facile recipiuntur & probantur coram Domino. Si quisquam dixerit, Sum gravis peccator, & ideo non ausim accedere: cur quæso non corrigit seipse? cur non resipiscit? Cum Dominus vocat, an non turpe esse ducitis respondere: Nolumus accedere? Quando converteremini ad Dominum, excusabitis vos & dicetis, Non sumus parati? Reputate diligenter apud vos, quam non valebunt ejusmodi fictæ & simulatæ causationes coram Domino. Qui respuerant convivium in Evangelio, quia emerant Luc. 14. villam, vel quia vellent experiri boves quos comparaverant, vel quia contraxerant matrimonium, non excusabantur, sed habebantur coelesti illo epulo indigni. Ego hic adsum, ac pro meo officio invito vos in Domino, exhortor in Christo Jesu, si vestram ipsorum redemptionem amplecti libeat, ut sitis participes hujus religiosissimæ communionis. Et quemadmodum Filius Dei non dedignabatur morte animam profundere in ara crucis pro salute vestra, sic vestrum est una participes esse Communionis, in recordationem mortis illius, prout ipse præcepit. Jam si recusare hanc coenam certum est vobis, saltem perpendite & reputate quam immensam injuriam facitis Deo omnipotenti, & quam grave supplicium imminet cervicibus vestris, ob coenæ contemptionem. Et quoniam tam graviter Dominum offenditis vel ipsa sacrati epuli recusatione, admoneo, hortor ac obsecro vos, ut ad hanc ingratitudinem aliud scelus non adjungatis: quod quidem fiet, si astiteritis tanquam spectatores & admiratores illorum qui communicant, cum sitis interim ipsi exortes. Quid etenim aliud duci poterit hoc, præterquam accumulata quædam & amplificata contemptio & ingratitudo adversus Deum? Equidem magnæ ingratitudinis est denegare cum accerseris, multo vero majoris est cum astas, interim nec edendo nec bibendo degustare ex hac sacrosancta communione cum ceteris. Quæso an non merito duci poterit hæc acerba mysteriorum Christi Domini illusio? Sermo est late patens, & ad omnes pertinens, Accipite & manducate, Accipite & bibite ex hoc omnes, Hoc facite in mei recordationem. Quo ore, imo quo vultu audietis hæc verba? An non est hæc neglectio, contemptio, & irrisio testamenti Dominici? Quamobrem, potius quam hoc admittatis, discedite hinc, & date locum iis, qui pie sunt affecti. Verum inter discedendum, precor a vobis, ut iterum atque iterum cogitetis, abs quo disceditis. Disceditis a mensa Domini, & ab epulo cœlestis pabuli. Has res si diligenter perpenderitis, ad meliorem & saniorem vitam (Deo bene juvante) convertemini. Quam rem ut consequamini, supplices preces immortali Deo, in hac participatione sacræ mensæ, fundemus.

Aliquando etiam dicetur hoc, pro arbitratu presbyteri.

DILECTISSIMI, quandoquidem nostrum est ex animo reddere omnipotenti Deo, cœlesti Patri nostro, gratias, quia dedit Filium suum Servatorem nostrum Jesum Christum, non solum ut moreretur pro nobis, verum etiam ut esset nostrum spirituale pabulum & alimentum, quemadmodum proditum est nobis, cum verbo divino, tum sacramentis corporis & sanguinis sui, tam salutaribus iis qui digne recipiunt, & tam tremendis e contra iis qui recipiunt indigne : meum est exhortari vos, ut diligenter trutinetis amplitudinem & dignitatem hujus sancti mysterii, & ingens periculum indignæ receptionis ejus, & non secus descendere in vos, & explorare conscientias vestras, quam si deberetis sancti ac impolluti adire divinissimum & cœleste epulum, sic ut nullo modo adire liceat vobis, destitutis veste illa nuptiali, quam Dominus poscit in sacra scriptura, dummodo recipi velitis ut digni convivæ hujusmodi cœlestis mensæ. Ratio autem & via ad hanc rem hæc est quam subdo.

Primum oportet explorare vitam & mores vestros ad normam mandatorum Dei, & cuicunque intelligetis vos neutiquam satisfecisse, voluntate, dicto, vel opere, in eo gemere & deplorare impiam vestram vitam, confitentes vos omnipotenti

Mat. 22.

Deo cum firmo & constanti proposito resipiscendi, & non relabendi æque turpiter. Quod si deprehenderitis vestra inique facta ejus farinæ esse, ut non solum in Deum, sed in proximos etiam commissa sint, tum illis quidem conciliabitis vosipsi, parati ad satisfaciendum pro virili in omnes injurias & injustitias illis per vos illatas; nec minus parati ad condonandum omnibus in vos inique patratis, similiter ac veniam erratorum consequi velletis ipsi a Domino. Nam absque hoc sit, receptio hujus sacræ Communionis non solum non conducit, sed adauget potius vestram condemnationem. Et propterea quod non est fas quenquam accedere ad hæc mysteria, nisi solida spe & fiducia misericordiæ divinæ, & sedata ac tranquilla conscientia eo incitatum : idcirco, si quisquam e vobis sit, qui superioribus rationibus non possit pacare suam conscientiam, verum eget ampliore consolatione, tum me petat, aut aliquem alium consultum & eruditum ministrum verbi divini, & nudet vulnus, ut possit recipere spirituale consilium, admonitionem, & solatium, ut conscientiæ levetur onus, & ut ministerio verbi divini consequatur fomentum & beneficium absolutionis, ad pacificationem conscientiæ, & amotionem omnis scrupuli ac hæsitationis.

Tunc Minister recitabit hanc exhortationem.

DILECTI in Domino, qui constituistis communicare corpori & sanguini Domini nostri Jesu Christi, necesse est ut ad memoriam revocetis, quid scripserit sanctus Paulus Corinthiis, & 1 Cor. 11. quomodo exhortetur eos, ut quilibet seipsum probet, & sic de pane illo edat, & de calice bibat. Nam sicut magnum beneficium est spiritualiter manducare corpus, & bibere sanguinem Christi, manere in Christo, & habere Christum in se habitantem, ac unum effici cum ipso; quod contigit illis, qui digne accedunt, id est corde contrito & humiliato, cum vera fide ac fiducia certa misericordiæ promissæ per Christum : ita præsens periculum est, si indigne accedamus, quia efficimur rei corporis & sanguinis Domini, & ad judicium & condemnationem manducamus, propterea quod non discernimus corpus Domini, nec ei debitum habemus honorem. Sed ipsius iram & indignationem nobis accersimus, ac provocamus eum, ut nos puniat diversis plagis, morbis, & morte. Quare si quis blasphemus verbi Dei hostis, adulter, flagrans ira, odio, aut reus alterius criminis sit, is non audeat accedere ad mensam Domini, nisi se ex animo pœniteat, ac omnino constituat emendare vitam, & persuasus sit se esse reconciliatum Deo fiducia misericordiæ propter Christum, & redeat in gratiam cum omnibus hominibus. Sed ante defleat peccata sua quam accedat, ne cum sacrosancto pane simul intret in eum Satanas, sicut in Juda proditore, ut eum repleat omni iniquitate, & perducat ad exitium corporis & animæ. Quare, fratres, vosipsos judicate, ne a Domino judicemini: ejicite ex animis studium peccandi, pœniteat vos serio præteritorum peccatorum, toto pectore confidite Servatori nostro Christo. Diligatis omnes homines ex animo: ita enim efficiemini vere participes horum mysteriorum. Sed ante omnia necesse est, ut maxima cum humilitate & ex corde agamus gratias Deo Patri, & Filio, & Spiritui sancto, quod redemit mundum per passionem & mortem Servatoris nostri Jesu Christi, veri Dei & veri hominis, qui se humiliavit usque ad mortem, mortem autem crucis, pro nobis miseris peccatoribus, habitantibus in tenebris & umbra mortis, ut nos efficeret filios Dei & hæredes vitæ æternæ. Ad hunc enim finem institutum est sacramentum, ut semper memores essemus infiniti amoris magistri & unici mediatoris nostri Jesu Christi, & innumerabilium beneficiorum, quæ per effusionem præciosi sui sanguinis nobis obtinuit, & reliquit in his sacris mysteriis, quasi pignus amoris & perpetuum monumentum suum, scilicet proprium corpus & præciosum sanguinem, ut ex his spiritualiter pascamur, & haberemus æternam consolationem. Ei autem una cum Patre & Spiritu sancto agamus gratias, ut merito debemus, & humiliemus nosmetipsos, ac subjiciamus ejus sanctissimæ voluntati, et studeamus ei obsequi, in vera sanctitate & justitia, omnibus diebus vitæ nostræ.

Deinde minister alloquetur communicaturos his verbis.

Vos quos serio pœnitet de peccatis vestris coram Deo, & reconciliati estis proximis, ac diligitis omnes homines ex animo, & constituistis posthac ducere vitam vestram juxta præcepta Dei, Accedite huc propius, ut percipiatis Sacramentum ad vestram consolationem, confitemini humiliter peccata vestra Deo & Ecclesiæ hic congregatæ in nomine ipsius.

Tunc fiat hæc generalis confessio nomine eorum qui communicaturi sunt, vel per eorum aliquem, vel per unum ex Ministris, aut per ipsum Sacerdotem, omnibus interim genua flectentibus.

OMNIPOTENS Deus, Pater Domini nostri Jesu Christi, conditor omnium rerum, & judex universorum mortalium, nos confitemur & deploramus nostra multiplicia peccata, & innumeras iniquitates, quas subinde per omnem vitam contumaciter designavimus, cogitatione, verbis, facto, contra divinam Majestatem tuam, provocantes justissimam iram & indignationem tuam adversus nos: vere enim ex animo dolemus, & serio nos pœnitet de peccatis nostris: eorum commemoratio est nobis acerbissima, illorum gravitatem ferre non possumus. Miserere nostri, misericordissime Pater, propter Filium tuum Dominum nostrum Jesum Christum. Condona nobis peccata præterita, & benigne concede, ut semper posthac serviamus & placeamus tibi in novitate vitæ, ad laudem & gloriam nominis tui. Per Jesum Christum Dominum nostrum.

Deinde eriget se Sacerdos, & conversus ad populum sic loquetur.

DOMINUS noster Jesus Christus, qui suam potestatem dedit Ecclesiæ, ut absolvat pœnitentes a peccatis ipsorum, & reconciliet cœlesti Patri eos, qui suam fiduciam collocant in Christum, misereatur vestri, remittat & condonet vobis omnia peccata vestra, confirmet & corroboret vos in omni opere bono, & perducat vos ad vitam æternam. Per Jesum Christum Dominum nostrum. Amen.

Sic stans, & ad populum conversus, dicet.

AUDITE, quomodo Christus ad se invitat peccatores, & eos consoletur verbis omni consolatione plenissimis.

Venite (inquit) ad me omnes qui laboratis, & onerati estis, & ego vos requiescere faciam.

Sic Deus dilexit mundum, ut Filium suum unigenitum daret, ut omnis qui credit in eum, non pereat, sed habeat vitam æternam.

Audite etiam quid Sanctus Paulus dicat.

Fidelis sermo, & omni observatione dignissimus, Christus Jesus venit in hunc mundum, ut salvos faceret peccatores.

Et beatus Joannes inquit,

Si quis peccaverit, advocatum habemus apud Patrem, Jesum Christum, & ipse est propitiatio pro peccatis nostris.

Quo finito, Minister cantabit.

SURSUM corda.
Responsio. Habemus ad Dominum.
Minister. Gratias agamus Domino Deo nostro.
Responsio. Dignum & justum est.
Minister. Vere dignum & justum est, æquum & salutare, nos tibi semper & ubique gratias agere, Domine sancte, Pater omnipotens, æterne Deus.

Sequetur propria præfatio diei, si quæ sit assignata, alioqui statim subjungetur.

Ideo cum angelis. &c.

Propriæ Præfationes.

Die nativitatis & septem diebus sequentibus.

QUIA dedisti nobis unicum Filium tuum Dominum nostrum Jesum Christum, quem hodierna die pro nobis nasci voluisti, et per operationem sancti Spiritus fieri verum hominem ex virgine Maria matre sua, sine labe peccati, ut nos ab omni peccato mundaret. Ideo cum Angelis & Archangelis, cum thronis, &c.

Die Paschæ, & septem diebus sequentibus.

ET te quidem omni tempore, sed in hoc potissimum die gloriosius prædicare, cum Pascha nostrum immolatus est Christus. Ipse enim est vere Agnus, qui abstulit peccata mundi: qui mortem nostram moriendo destruxit, & vitam resurgendo reparavit. Ideoque cum Angelis. &c.

Die Ascensionis, & septem diebus sequentibus.

QUI post gloriosam resurrectionem suam omnibus discipulis suis manifestus apparuit, & ipsis cernentibus elevatus est in cœlum, ut nobis præparet[1] locum; & ubi ipse esset, istic nos ascendamus, & cum eo regnemus in gloria. Ideo cum Angelis. &c.

Die Pentecostes, & sex diebus sequentibus.

QUI ascendens super omnes cœlos, sedensque ad dexteram tuam, promissum Spiritum hodierna die in filios adoptionis effudit: qui cum subito & vehementi sonitu de cœlo descendit, & super Apostolos in figura linguarum ardentium resedit, ut induceret in omnem veritatem: contulitque donum linguarum,

[1 The reading of Aless is, præpararet.]

& fortitudinem confitendi, ac prædicandi Evangelium omni nationi, ut ex tenebris erroris ad veram lucem & cognitionem tuam, per Jesum Christum, perveniremus. Quapropter profusis gaudiis totus in orbe terrarum mundus exultat, sed & supernæ virtutes atque Angelicæ potestates hymnum gloriæ tuæ concinunt, sine fine dicentes, Sanctus. &c.

In festo Trinitatis.

QUI cum unigenito Filio tuo, & Spiritu sancto, unus es Deus, unus es Dominus: non in unius singularitate personæ, sed cum trinitate personarum, in unitate substantiæ. Quod enim de gloria tua revelante te credimus, hoc de Filio tuo, hoc de Spiritu sancto, sine differentia discretionis sentimus: quem laudant Angeli atque Archangeli: Cherubin quoque & Seraphin, qui non cessant clamare jugiter una voce, dicentes: Sanctus. &c.

Finis omnium Præfationum.

IDEO cum angelis & archangelis, cum thronis & dominationibus, cumque omni militia cœlestis exercitus, hymnum gloriæ tuæ canimus, sine fine dicentes: Sanctus, sanctus, sanctus Dominus Deus sabaoth. Pleni sunt cœli & terra gloria tua. Osanna in excelsis. Benedictus qui venit in nomine Domini. Osanna in excelsis.

Tunc sacerdos nomine eorum qui communicare volunt sic orabit genibus flexis.

NON accedimus ad hanc mensam tuam, O misericors Domine, fiducia justitiæ nostræ, sed in multitudine miserationum tuarum. Neque enim sumus digni, ut colligamus micas de mensa tua. Sed tu es idem Dominus, cujus semper proprium fuit misereri. Concede igitur, misericors Domine, ut sic edamus carnem Filii tui, & bibamus ejus sanguinem in his sacris mysteriis, ut nostra corpora peccatis inquinata munda fiant perceptione sacratissimi corporis sui, & nostræ animæ laventur in prætioso sanguine suo: ut perpetuo habitemus in eo, & ipse in nobis. Amen.

Postea Sacerdos erigens se dicet.

O DEUS omnipotens, Pater noster cœlestis, qui ex immensa tua misericordia dedisti nobis unicum Filium tuum

Jesum Christum, pro nostra redemptione mortem in cruce pati, ibique unica illa oblatione qua sese semel obtulit, perfectum, plenum, & sufficiens sacrificium, hostiam & satisfactionem integram faceret pro peccatis totius mundi: quique instituit, ac in suo sacrosancto Evangelio præcepit perpetuam memoriam præciosæ suæ mortis celebrare, usque dum rediret. Exaudi nos quæsumus, misericors Pater, & concede, ut nos sumentes has creaturas panis & vini, juxta sacrosanctam institutionem Filii tui, Servatoris nostri Jesu Christi, in memoriam ejus diræ mortis & passionis, participes simus sanctissimi corporis & sanguinis ejus. Qui eadem nocte qua tradebatur, accepit panem, & gratias agens fregit, ac dedit discipulis suis, dicens: Accipite, comedite, hoc est corpus meum, quod pro vobis datur: hoc facite in meam commemorationem. Simili modo, postquam cœnatum est, accepit calicem, & gratias agens dedit illis, dicens: Bibite ex eo omnes: hic est enim sanguis meus novi Testamenti, qui pro vobis & pro multis effunditur, in remissionem peccatorum: hoc facite, quotiescunque biberitis, in meam commemorationem.

> Tunc minister ipse primo recipiet Eucharistiam sub utraque specie: proximo loco tradet reliquis Ministris, si qui adsint, ut eum post adjuvent in communicando populo.
>
> Deinde Minister tradet Eucharistiam populo in manus, genibus flexis, & cum exhibet panem, dicet.

Corpus Domini nostri Jesu Christi, quod pro te traditum est, conservet corpus tuum & animam tuam in vitam æternam.

Accipe & ede hoc, in memoriam quod Christus mortuus sit pro te: fide illum ede, in corde tuo, cum gratiarum actione.

> Minister cum exhibet poculum, dicet.

Sanguis Domini nostri Jesu Christi, qui pro te effusus est, conservet corpus tuum & animam tuam in vitam æternam.

Bibe hoc, in memoriam Christi sanguinem pro te effusum esse, & gratias age.

> Tunc Minister dicet orationem Dominicam, Pater noster. &c.
> Et populus recitabit post illum singulas petitiones.
>
> Deinde dicetur oratio sequens.

O DOMINE cœlestis Pater, nos humiles servi tui supplices rogamus paternam tuam bonitatem, ut hoc nostrum sacrificium laudis, & gratiarum actionis, benigne accipias : humiliter supplicantes, ut propter merita & mortem Filii tui Jesu Christi, & per fidem in illius sanguinem, concedas, ut nos cum universa Ecclesia remissionem peccatorum ceteraque beneficia passionis illius consequamur. Atque hic etiam offerimus, & præsentamus tibi, Domine, nosipsos, animas nostras, & corpora nostra, hostiam rationalem, sanctam, & vivam : humiliter obsecrantes, ut quotquot participes sumus hujus sacrosanctæ Communionis, tua gratia & cœlesti benedictione repleamur. Et quanquam indigni sumus, propter multitudinem peccatorum nostrorum, qui tibi ullum sacrificium offeramus, tamen supplicamus, ut acceptam habeas hanc nostram servitutem, non intuendo nostra merita, sed condonando nostra peccata, per Jesum Christum Dominum nostrum, per quem, & cum quo, in unitate sancti Spiritus, sit tibi, omnipotens Pater, omnis honor & gloria, in omnem æternitatem. Amen.

Vel ista oratio.

OMNIPOTENS æterne Deus, immortales tibi ex animo gratias agimus, quod nos, qui hæc sacrosancta mysteria rite percepimus, pascere digneris spirituali cibo præciosissimi corporis & sanguinis Filii tui Servatoris nostri Jesu Christi, nosque certos reddis horum participatione de tuo favore ac gratia erga nos, & quod sumus vera membra in corpore tuo mystico incorporata, quod est sancta communio omnium fidelium, quodque hæredes sumus secundum spem vitæ æternæ, per merita præciosissimæ mortis & passionis dilectissimi Filii tui. Nos ergo supplices rogamus, O pater cœlestis, ita nos [nobis] tua gratia semper adsis, ut in hac sanctissima communione perseveremus, & omnia hujusmodi opera bona faciamus, quæ tu præparasti ut in eis ambulemus, per Jesum Christum Dominum nostrum, cui cum Spiritu sancto, [et] tibi sit omnis honor & gloria in omnem æternitatem.

Deinde dicatur aut canatur.

GLORIA in excelsis Deo. Et in terra pax, hominibus bonæ voluntatis. Laudamus te, Benedicimus te, Adoramus te, glorificamus te. Gratias agimus tibi, propter magnam gloriam tuam. Domine Deus rex cœlestis, Deus pater omnipotens. Domine Fili unigenite, Jesu Christe. Domine Deus Agnus dei, Filius Patris, Qui tollis peccata mundi, miserere nobis. Qui tollis peccata mundi, suscipe deprecationem nostram. Qui sedes ad dexteram Patris, miserere nobis. Quoniam tu solus sanctus, tu solus Dominus, tu solus altissimus, Jesu Christe. Cum sancto Spiritu, in gloria Dei Patris, Amen.

> Postremo Sacerdos vel Episcopus, si adsit, dimittet eos, hac benedictione.

PAX Dei, quæ superat omnem intellectum, conservet corda vestra & mentes vestras, in cognitione, & amore Dei, & Filii ejus Jesu Christi Domini nostri : & favor omnipotentis Dei, Patris, Filii, & Spiritus sancti, vobis adsit, semperque vobiscum maneat.

> Sequuntur Collectæ dicendæ post offertorium, quando non adsunt communicantes.

ADESTO supplicationibus nostris, misericors Deus, & viam famulorum tuorum in salutis tuæ prosperitate dispone, ut inter omnes hujus vitæ varietates & casus tuo semper protegamur auxilio. Per Dominum nostrum Jesum Christum. &c.

DIRIGERE et sanctificare dignare, Domine sancte Pater omnipotens æterne Deus, hodie corda & corpora nostra in lege tua, & operibus mandatorum tuorum, ut hic & in æternum, te auxiliante, semper sani corpore, salvi animo, esse mereamur. Per Jesum Christum Dominum nostrum.

LARGIRE quæsumus, omnipotens Deus, ut tua sacrosancta verba, quæ externis auribus hodie percepimus, ita cordibus nostris per tuam gratiam intus inserantur, ut fructum bonæ vitæ semper in nobis proferant, ad laudem & gloriam tui nominis. Per Christum Dominum nostrum. Amen.

ACTIONES nostras, quæsumus, Domine, aspirando præveni, & adjuvando prosequere, ut cuncta nostra operatio a te semper incipiat, & per te cœpta finiatur. Per Jesum Christum Dominum nostrum.

Omnipotens Deus, fons omnis sapientiæ, qui non solum quibus rebus opus nobis sit, antequam quicquam petimus, noveris, sed etiam nostram in petendo ignorantiam vides: rogamus tuam clementiam, miserescat te nostrarum infirmitatum; & quæ vel propter indignitatem nostram non audemus, vel propter cœcitatem nostram non possumus, tu ea nobis largiri digneris, per merita Filii tui Domini nostri Jesu Christi, qui tecum vivit & regnat Deus, in omnem æternitatem. Amen.

OMNIPOTENS Deus, qui promisisti te auditurum preces eorum, qui in nomine Filii tui postulant: aures tuas clementer precibus nostris accommoda, & præsta, ut quæ fideliter a te petimus, efficaciter consequamur. Per Dominum. &c.

Diebus festis, si non adsint communicantes, dicentur tamen omnia quæ præscripta sunt, usque ad finem homiliæ, addendo orationem illam generalem pro universali statu totius militantis Ecclesiæ, atque unam aut alteram e Collectis præcedentibus.

Nunquam celebretur cœna Dominica, sine convenienti numero communicantium.

In Cathedralibus Ecclesiis & Collegiis, ubi multi sunt presbyteri & Diaconi, omnes una cum Ministro, singulis Dominicis, simul communicabunt, nisi forte justa de causa eorum quispiam impediatur.

Quisquis autem, ex tota multitudine, ter minimum in anno ad sacram Communionem se præparabit, nominatim autem festo Paschatis, quo etiam tempore singuli consuetas decimas, oblationes, ceteraque debita, suo pastori aut ejus vicario sine fraude persolvet.

Ordo visitationis infirmorum
ET COMMUNIO
eorundem.

Ingrediens Sacerdos domum infirmi dicat.

Pax huic domui, & omnibus habitantibus in ea.

Tunc accedens ad ægrotum, flexis genibus, dicat,

NE reminiscaris, Domine, peccata nostra vel parentum nostrorum. Parce Domine, parce populo tuo, quem redemisti præcioso sanguine tuo, ne in æternum irascaris nobis.

Kyrie eleyson.
Christe eleyson.
Kyrie eleyson.
Pater noster qui es in cœlis. &c.

Minister. Et ne nos inducas in temptationem.
Responsio. Sed libera nos a malo.
Minister. Domine salvum fac servum tuum.
Responsio. Qui suam fiduciam in te collocat.
Minister. Mitte eum[1] Domine angelum[1] de sanctuario tuo.
Responsio. Et potenter defende eum.
Minister. Nihil prævaleat inimicus in eo :
Responsio. Et filius iniquitatis non noceat ei.
Minister. Esto ei Domine turris fortitudinis :
Responsio. A facie inimici.
Minister. Domine exaudi orationem nostram :
Responsio. Et clamor noster ad te veniat.

Oremus.

RESPICE Domine de cœlo, visita servum tuum, respice eum oculis misericordiæ tuæ, consolare eum ut in te certo confidat : defende eum ab insidiis inimici, & serva eum in pace perpetua & quiete. Per Jesum Christum Dominum nostrum. Amen.

[[1] *Eum, angelum,* mistakes for *ei, auxilium.* See Monumenta Ritualia, Vol. I. p. 71. The English Prayer Book has, Send him help : Aless, on the contrary, Mitte ei Domine *angelum* de sanctuario.]

VISITATIO INFIRMORUM.

EXAUDI nos, omnipotens & misericors Deus, extende consuetam misericordiam tuam ad hunc servum tuum ægrotantem: visita illum Domine, ut invisisti socrum Petri, & servum Centurionis: sic visita & restitue hunc sanitati, si ita tibi visum fuerit: vel fac cum ita perferre hanc afflictionem, ut post hanc vitam tecum vivat in æternum. Amen.

Utatur autem ista ad ægrotum exhortatione, vel consimili.

Hoc scias, carissime frater, Christum[2] esse Dominum mortis et vitæ, juventutis, fortitudinis, sanitatis, senectutis, debilitatis, & infirmitatis. Quare persuasum tibi sit, quod quicunque tuus fuerit morbus, is Deo volente & sciente tibi contingat, & quacunque tandem de causa, sive ut probet tuam pacientiam, sive ad exemplum aliorum, ut fides tua in die Domini inveniatur ad laudem, gloriam & honorem Dei, & augmentum fœlicitatis vitæ æternæ, sive etiam ad correctionem & castigationem de aliquo, quod offendit oculos cœlestis Patris: noveris certo, quod si vere te pœniteat peccati, & æquo animo feras hanc afflictionem, confisus in misericordia Dei, promissa propter Filium suum Dominum nostrum Jesum Christum, gratias agens pro hac paterna visitatione, & te humiliter subjicias divinæ ejus voluntati, tibi proderit ad salutem, & promovebit te in recta via, quæ ducit ad vitam æternam.

Si ægrotus fuerit admodum debilis, poterit Minister hic facere finem exhortationis: alioquin perget in sequentibus.

Quare in optimam partem accipias hanc correctionem. Quem enim diligit Dominus, hunc castigat. Imo, ut D. Paulus inquit: Flagellat[3] omnem filium quem recipit. Item si fertis castigationem, offert semetipsum vobis, ut propriis filiis. Quis enim est filius, quem pater non castigat? Si non estis subjecti correctioni, cujus omnes germani filii sunt participes, nothi estis & spurii, non legitimi filii. Quare cum patres nostri carnales nos castigent, & nihilominus obsequimur illis cum omni reverentia, nunquid multo magis debemus obedire spirituali Patri, ut vivamus? Et illi quidem paucis diebus nos correxerunt pro ipsorum voluntate: Ipse vero nos castigat propter nostram utilitatem, ut participes simus suæ

[2 Such is Aless's translation.]
[3 This word begins a page, but the catch word on the previous page is, Facile.]

sanctitatis. Hæc verba, carissime frater, propter nostram consolationem & instructionem scripta sunt, ut pacienter & cum gratiarum actione feramus cœlestis Patris correctionem quancunque, & per quæcunque adversa placuerit illi nos visitare. Neque enim major consolatio Christiano esse debet, quam ut similis fiat imaginis Filii Dei, in perferundis ærumnis & adversis ac infirmitatibus. Quemadmodum igitur Christus ipse non ante ingressus est in gloriam, quam pateretur, sed ante crucifixus est, quam glorificaretur: ita profecto via ad gloriam est pacientia tribulationum; & transitus ad vitam est cum Christo mori, ut una cum ipso resurgamus a morte, & perfruamur vita æterna. Feras igitur tuam infirmitatem æquo animo, & memineris professionis tuæ in baptismo. Cum autem post hanc vitam reddenda sit ratio justo Judici, a quo omnes sine respectu personarum oportet judicari, exhortor te, ut examines te ipsum, & quomodo cum Deo & cum omnibus hominibus tecum convenit, ut dum te ipsum accusas & judicas, pro peccatis invenias misericordiam apud cœlestem Patrem propter Christum, & ne accuseris aut damneris in tremendo judicio. Recitabo igitur articulos fidei, ut noris utrum vere credas illa, quæ Christianum credere oportet.

Hic sacerdos recitabit articulos Symboli, dicens in hunc modum.

CREDIS in Deum Patrem omnipotentem, creatorem cœli & terræ? &c.

Quemadmodum fit in Baptismate.

Tunc examinabit illum sacerdos, num sit in caritate cum omnibus hominibus, exhortans illum, ut ex toto corde condonet illis, a quibus injuria affectus fuerit. Et si aliquos ipse offenderit, aut injuria affecerit, precetur ut sibi condonent.

Et si ante non condiderit testamentum, tunc condat, &[1] dicat, quæ ei debentur, & vicissim quæ debeat, propter quietem posteritatis & amicorum. Sæpe autem in concionibus divites & potentes moneat, de condendo testamento dum valent.

Hic ne omittatur, quin Minister agat cum infirmo de eleemosyna danda pauperibus.

Si ægrotus sentit suam conscientiam gravatam esse aliqua in re, de illa sacerdoti privatim confiteatur: & finita confessione, Minister utetur hac forma absolutionis.

[[1] The arrangement of what follows is different in the English Prayer Book; but the transposition is due to Aless, from whom this rubric, as almost the whole service, was verbally copied.]

1560.] VISITATIO INFIRMORUM. 403

Dominus noster Jesus Christus, qui dedit potestatem Ecclesiæ absolvendi a peccatis pœnitentes, & credentes Evangelio, ipse ex infinita misericordia indulgeat tibi peccata tua: ego vero autoritate ipsius mihi commissa absolvo te ab omnibus peccatis, in nomine Patris & Filii, & Spiritus sancti. Amen.

<small>Deinde Minister recitabit subsequentem Collectam, dicens.</small>

Oremus.

O Misericordissime Domine, qui juxta multitudinem misericordiæ tuæ deles peccata pœnitentium, ita ut eorum amplius non memineris, aperi oculos misericordiæ tuæ super hunc famulum tuum, qui petit misericordiam & remissionem peccatorum ex toto pectore. Renova, amantissime Pater, quicquid in eo subversum est fraude & malitia satanæ, vel carnali concupiscentia, & fragilitate humana: conserva & custodi hoc ægrotum membrum in unitate Ecclesiæ: vide contritionem ejus, respice lachrymas, pœnasque mitiga aut amove, ut placet divinæ voluntati tuæ. Et quia in tua misericordia tantum confidit, noli imputare ei priora peccata, sed cum eo in gratiam redi, propter merita dilectissimi Filii tui Domini nostri Jesu Christi.

<small>Tunc oret Minister hunc Psalmum. [l]xxi.</small>
Antiphona.

Salvator mundi, salva nos. Qui per crucem & præciosum sanguinem redemisti nos, adjuva nos, te rogamus, O Deus.

Collecta.

Omnipotens Deus, qui est fortitudo omnium in se sperantium, cui omnia in cœlo & in terra & subtus terram obediunt, nunc & semper sit tibi protector, & faciat cognoscere & sentire, quod non sit aliud nomen datum sub cœlo hominibus, in quo & per quod tu recipias salutem & sanitatem, præter nomen Domini nostri Jesu Christi.

<small>Si videtur commodum, dicatur etiam hic Psalmus, pro usitata[2], ante hæc tempora, visitatione.</small>

Psalmus. xiiii.[3]

[[2] The reference is to the Prayer Book of 1549. See Liturgies of K. Edward VI. p. 140.]

[[3] Aless has, xiiii instead of, xii.]

Communio Infirmorum.

Cum omnes mortales subjecti sint infinitis periculis, infirmitatibus, & ærumnis, & semper incerti sint, quando ex hac vita erit emigrandum: Ideo ut semper sint parati, & in expectatione mortis, quandocunque Deus voluerit, Pastor subinde, sed præsertim pestis tempore, admoneat parochianos, ut frequenter communicent sacramento corporis & sanguinis Domini. Sic enim cavebitur, ne cum subito fuerint correpti morbo, soliciti sint pro sacra Communione.

Verum si infirmus non poterit venire in Ecclesiam, & petit sibi dari Sacramentum in domo sua, significabit tum demum postridie[1] aut primo mane parocho, quot cum ipso una velint communicare.

Quod si contingat eodem die Cœnam Domini in Ecclesia celebrari, tunc sacerdos in cœna tantum sacramenti servabit, quantum sufficit ægroto: & mox finita cœna, una cum aliquot ex his qui intersunt, ibit ad ægrotum, & primo communicabit cum illis, qui assistunt ægroto, & interfuerunt cœnæ, & postremo cum infirmo.

Sed primo fiat generalis confessio, & absolutio, cum Collecta[2], ut supra est præscriptum.

Sed si infirmus illo die petat communionem, quo non celebratur cœna, tunc sacerdos in loco decenti, in domo ægroti, celebrabit Cœnam, hoc modo.

Oremus.

OMNIPOTENS æterne Deus, conditor humani generis, qui quos diligis corrigis, & castigas omnem filium quem recipis, quæsumus, ut miserearis huic servo tuo infirmo, & præsta, ut pacienter hanc infirmitatem ferat, & recuperet sanitatem, si ita tibi videbitur, & quandocunque hinc emigraverit, immaculatus perveniat ad vitam sempiternam.

[1 This misprint for *pridie* occurs first in Aless. The English Prayer Book has, over night.]

[2 The Collect meant appears to be that on p. 403. But see Liturgies of K. Edward VI. p. 141.]

Epistola. Heb. xii.

FILI mi, ne neglexeris correptionem Domini, neque deficias, cum ab eo argueris. Quem enim diligit Dominus, corripit: flagellat autem omnem filium quem recipit.

Evangelium. Joan. v.

AMEN amen dico vobis, qui sermonem meum audit, & credit ei qui misit me, habet vitam æternam, & in condemnationem non veniet, sed transivit a morte in vitam.

Minister. Dominus vobiscum.
Responsio. Et cum spiritu tuo.
Minister. Sursum corda. &c.

usque ad finem, ut supra dictum est.

CUM venitur ad distributionem Sacramenti corporis & sanguinis Christi, Sacerdos primo communicet, deinde alii cum ægroto, qui sese ad hoc præpararunt.

Si eodem tempore visitatur, & recepturus sit Sacram communionem ægrotus, licebit sacerdoti (quo citius officium utrumque absolvat) Visitationis finem facere, cum ventum fuerit ad Psalmum, *In te Domine speravi*, atque mox inchoare officium Sacræ communionis.

Sepultura.

SACERDOS procedet obviam feretro, ad ingressum Cœmeterii, & dicat, aut ministri & clerici qui cum eo sunt, canant, euntes ad sepulchrum, has Antiphonas.

Joannis xi.

EGO sum resurrectio, & vita. Qui credit in me, etiamsi mortuus fuerit, vivet: & omnis qui vivit & credit in me, non morietur in æternum.

Job xix.

SCIO quod Redemptor meus vivit, & in novissimo die de terra surrecturus sum. Et rursum circundabor pelle mea, & in carne mea videbo Deum. Quem visurus sum ego ipse: & oculi mei conspecturi sunt, & non alius.

i. Timo. vi.

NIHIL intulimus in mundum, videlicet nec efferre quicquam possumus: sed habentes alimenta, & quibus tegamur, his contenti erimus.

Job i.

Dominus dedit, Dominus abstulit: sicut Domino placuit, ita factum est: sit nomen Domini benedictum.

Cum ventum est ad sepulchrum, dum cadaver paratur imponendum, dicatur aut canatur.

Job xiiii.

Homo natus de muliere, brevi vivens tempore, repletur multis miseriis. Qui quasi flos egreditur & conteritur, & fugit velut umbra, & nunquam in eodem statu permanet.

Antiphona.

Media vita in morte sumus: quem quærimus adjutorem, nisi te Domine? qui pro peccatis nostris juste irasceris. Sancte Deus, Sancte fortis, Sancte & misericors Salvator, amaræ morti ne tradas nos. Tu Domine, qui cognoscis occulta cordium nostrorum, noli claudere aures tuæ misericordiæ ad preces nostras, sed parce nobis, sanctissime Deus, fortis, misericors salvator, & judex æquissime, ne derelinquas nos in hora mortis nostræ.

Dum cadaver terra injecta operitur, sacerdos dicat.

Cum Deo visum sit ex immensa sua misericordia animam carissimi fratris nostri nunc defuncti ad se suscipere, corpus suum sepulchro committendum curamus, terram terræ, cinerem cineribus, pulverem pulveribus, cum certa & constanti spe resurrectionis ad vitam æternam: Per Dominum nostrum Jesum Christum, qui transformabit corpus humilitatis nostræ, configuratum corpori claritatis suæ, juxta potentiam operationis suæ, qua potest sibi subjicere omnia.

Tum recitatur Antiphona.

Apo. [1]4. Audivi vocem de cœlo, dicentem mihi: Scribe: Beati mortui, qui in Domino moriuntur a modo. Etiam dicit Spiritus, ut requiescant a laboribus suis.

Deinde legatur Lectio. i. Cor. xv.

Col. 1.
2 Thes. 4. Christus surrexit ex mortuis: primitiæ eorum qui dor-

mierant, fuit.......cum sciatis quod labor vester non est inanis in Domino.

Finita epistola, Minister dicet.

Kyrie eleyson.
Christe eleyson.
Kyrie eleyson.
Pater noster qui es in cœlis. &c.

Minister. Et ne nos inducas in temptationem.
Responsio. Sed libera nos a malo.

Minister.
Oremus.

OMNIPOTENS Deus, apud quem vivunt spiritus illorum, qui hinc decesserunt, & quocum animæ electorum, postquam exuerunt onus hujus carnis, lætitia & fœlicitate fruuntur: gratias agimus tibi immensas, propterea quod expedire voluisti N. nostrum fratrem, ex ærumnis hujus mundi impii, precantes ut placeat infinitæ tuæ bonitati brevi explere numerum electorum tuorum, & maturare gloriam regni tui, ut nos una cum fratre nostro, & omnibus aliis vita defunctis in vera fide & confessione nominis tui, consequamur perfectam absolutionem, & beatitudinem, tum corporis tum animæ, in tua perpetua & sempiterna gloria. Amen.

Collecta.

MISERICORS Deus, Pater Domini nostri Jesu Christi, qui est resurrectio vitæ, in quem quicunque crediderit, vivet, etiamsi moriatur; & quicunque vivit & credit in ipsum, in omnem æternitatem non morietur: qui nos docuit etiam, per sanctum apostolum suum Paulum, ut non tristaremur, tanquam ii qui spem non habent, illorum causa qui dormiunt in ipso: supplices te petimus, O Pater, ut nos suscites a morte peccati ad vitam justitiæ, ut quum decedimus ab hac vita, quiescamus in ipso, prout spes est nostrum fratrem quiescere, & ut in communi illa resurrectione extremi diei reperiamur accepti coram te, & recipiamus illam benedictionem, quam dilectus tuus Filius enunciabit omnibus iis, qui diligunt ac verentur te, dicens: Venite benedicti filii Patris mei, recipite regnum illud, quod vobis paratum fuit ab origine mundi. Largire hoc, quæsumus te, misericors Pater, per Jesum Christum mediatorem ac servatorem nostrum. Amen.

Ordo Baptismi te-

nendus in Ecclesia.

Veteres prodiderunt scriptores, Baptismi sacramentum olim non solitum fuisse publice exhiberi, nisi bis quotannis, hoc est, ad solenne Paschatis, & Pentecostes. His autem temporibus publice administrabatur coram publico populi concilio, qui mos hac nostra tempestate obsoletus & antiquatus, & si multas ob causas in pristinum locum restitui non potest, consultissimum tamen esse duximus, tam affine ejus vestigium & imaginem retinere, quam temporis ratio pateretur. Quamobrem admonendus est populus, Baptismum publicum non permitti certis de causis, nisi Dominicis, ac Festis diebus, quando populi conventus est frequentissimus, partim, ut concio illa possit testari eorum qui loti sunt in Ecclesiam Christi novitiam insitionem, partim, ut in Baptismo infantium, cuilibet eorum qui astant, veniat in mentem voti ac professionis suæ adversus Deum, quam ille in se receperat in propria lotione. Qua de re convenit etiam ut Baptismus vernaculo sermone administretur. Verum ne qua, de re non magni momenti, velitatio suboriatur, meminerint hæc dicta esse de publico Baptismo. Possunt enim pueri (si necessitas id efflagitet) domi baptizari, sine ulla temporis observatione, dummodo caute id fiat, conservatis præcipuis ac necessariis Baptismi circumstantiis.

Publicus Baptismus.

Cum infantes baptizandi sunt vel Dominico, vel alio aliquo festo, tum parentes ea de re pastorem præmonebunt, vel nocte pridiana, vel mane, ante exordium matutinarum precum, & tum Susceptores ac Susceptrices cum populo apud fontem adesse convenit, statim a posteriore lectione matutinarum aut vespertinarum precum, prout Minister decreverit. Tum Minister cum his astans, interrogabit eos, ecquid infans baptizatus sit an non? Si negaverint, tunc Minister sic dicet.

DILECTISSIMI, quandoquidem omnis homo tum concipitur, tum paritur in peccato, & Servator noster Christus dicit, neminem posse introire in regnum Dei, nisi sit regeneratus, & renatus ex aqua & Spiritu sancto: obtestor vos, ut invocetis Deum Patrem, in Domino nostro Jesu Christo, ut per immensam suam misericordiam dignetur concedere his infantibus id quod sua vi & natura consequi non possunt, ut baptizentur aqua & Spiritu sancto, & recipiantur in sanctam Christi Ecclesiam, & fiant membra viva ejusdem.

Tunc Minister dicet. Oremus.

OMNIPOTENS & æterne Deus, qui ineffabili tua misericordia Noah ac ejus familiam e diluvio servavisti, qui sine periculo deduxisti populum tuum Israelem per Mare rubrum, eo figurans sacrosanctum tuum Baptismum, qui sacra lotione dilecti Filii tui Jesu Christi sanctificavisti fluvium Jordanis, & omnes alias aquas, in mysticam peccati ablutionem: nos te precamur per infinitam clementiam tuam, ut pie intuearis in hos infantes, sanctifices, & laves eos tuo Spiritu sancto, ut liberi ab ira tua recipiantur in arcam ecclesiæ Christi, ut solidi fide, spe læti, & dilectione firmi, sic superent undas hujus turbulentissimi mundi, ut ad extremum in regionem æternæ vitæ perveniant, quo tecum regnent in omnem æternitatem: per Christum Jesum Dominum nostrum. Amen.

OMNIPOTENS & immortalis Deus, præsidium omnium in angustia constitutorum, scutum omnium tuam opem implorantium, vita credentium & mortuorum resurrectio: te invocamus, horum infantium causa, ut illi accedentes ad tuum baptismum, remissionem peccatorum per spiritualem regenerationem consequantur. Recipe eos, O Deus, & sicuti pollicitus es per dilectum Filium tuum, dicens: Petite, & accipietis, quærite, & invenietis, pulsate, & aperietur vobis: ita nobis præbe nunc qui te poscimus, inveniamus qui quærimus, aperi januam nobis pulsantibus, ut hi infantes sempiternam benedictionem tuæ cœlestis lotionis assequantur, & ad illud tuum æternum regnum perveniant, Per Christum Dominum nostrum. Amen.

Tunc dicet Minister.
Audite verba evangelii scripti per divum Marcum, capite Decimo.

ATTULERUNT ad Jesum pueros, ut tangeret illos: discipuli vero increpabant eos qui adducebant. Cum vidisset autem Jesus, indignatus est, & dixit illis: Sinite pueros venire ad me, ne prohibete illos, talium enim est regnum Dei. Amen dico vobis, Quicunque non acceperit regnum Dei tanquam puer, haudquaquam ingredietur in illud. Et cum cepisset illos in ulnas, impositis manibus super illos, benedixit eis.

Post lectum evangelium, presbyter hanc brevem admonitionem pronunciabit super verbis evangelii.

AMICI, auditis hoc in evangelio verba Servatoris nostri Christi, invitantis ad se puerulos, & reprehendentis illos, qui eos a se arcebant, ac postremo suadentis hominibus, ut imitentur illorum innocentiam. Intelligitis per gestus, & acta externa, ejus immensam benevolentiam in illos. Brachiis siquidem arcte complexus est illos, manus imposuit, & benedixit. Ne dubitetis igitur, verum firmiter credite, eum benigne recepturum hos qui hic adsunt infantes, amplexaturum eos misericordiæ suæ brachiis, donaturum eis æternæ vitæ benedictionem, effecturumque eos cœlestis regni sui consortes. Quamobrem nos minime nescii favoris, quem cœlestis Pater noster gerit in hos infantes, illustrati ac patefacti per Filium ejus Jesum Christum, ac nihil omnino hæsitantes, quin magni pendat hunc nostrum conatum in adducendo hos infantes ad suum sacrum baptismum, per fidem & affectum reddamus illi immortales gratias, dicentes.

OMNIPOTENS & æterne Deus, cœlestis Pater, gratias tibi supplices agimus, quod vocare nos dignatus es ad agnitionem gratiæ ac favoris tui, & fidei[1] in te. Precamur autem, ut hanc cognitionem in nobis adaugeas, ac stabilias hanc fidem in omnem æternitatem: infundas in hos infantes Spiritum sanctum tuum, ut possint renasci, & fieri hæredes æternæ redemptionis, per Dominum nostrum Jesum Christum, qui vivit & regnat tecum, ac cum sancto Spiritu, & in præsens & in posteritatem. Amen.

Tunc Minister alloquetur Susceptores, & susceptrices, in hanc formam.

DILECTISSIMI amici, attulistis huc hos infantes, ut baptisarentur; vota fecistis, ut Dominus noster Jesus Christus dignaretur recipere eos, manus imponere in eos, eis benedicere, remittere eis peccata sua, tribuere eis regnum cœleste, ac sempiternam vitam. Audivistis præterea Dominum nostrum Jesum Christum pollicitum esse in evangelio, se præstaturum hæc omnia, ad quæ vota fecistis: quæ quidem pollicitatio

[[1] We might have expected *fidem*, the reading of all the later Latin Prayer Books; *fidei*, however, is also in Aless, and, particularly, in Hermann's Simplex ac pia Deliberatio, &c., fol. LXXIIII.]

rata ac firma futura est. Qua de re, pro hoc promisso, hos infantes oportet spondere per vos, suos fidejussores, se deserturos diabolum, & omnia ejus opera, & constanter credituros verbo evangelico, & obsequenter servaturos ejus præcepta.

Tunc Minister interrogabit Susceptores ac Susceptrices hæc, quæ sequuntur.

DETESTARIS diabolum & omnia ejus opera, inanem pompam & gloriam mundi, una cum omnibus desideriis ejusdem, [et] impias carnis libidines, sic ut eas vel sequi, vel ab his duci, te non sis permissurus?

Responsio. Detestor ea omnia.

Minister. CREDIS in Deum Patrem omnipotentem, creatorem cœli & terræ: & in Jesum Christum Filium ejus unicum, Dominum nostrum, conceptum ex Spiritu sancto, natum ex Maria virgine? Credis eundem passum fuisse sub Pontio Pilato, crucifixum, mortuum, sepultum, ac descendisse ad inferos, & tertia die resurrexisse a mortuis? Credis eum ascendisse in cœlum, & sedere ad dexteram Dei Patris omnipotentis, & illinc iterum venturum esse, in fine sæculi, ad judicandum vivos & mortuos? Credis item in Spiritum sanctum? Credis sanctam catholicam Ecclesiam, sanctorum communionem, remissionem peccatorum, carnis resurrectionem, & æternam vitam post mortem?

Responsio. Omnia hæc firmiter credo.

Minister. Vis baptisari in hanc fidem?

Responsio. Cupio.

Tunc Minister dicet.

CONCEDE, misericors Deus, sic veterem Adamum in his infantibus posse sepeliri, ut novus Adam possit in his suscitari. Amen.

Concede, ut omnes carnis concupiscentiæ in his extinguantur, & ea quæ sunt Spiritus, in eis vegetentur, ac augeantur. Amen.

Concede, ut potentiam & vim consequantur vincendi, ac triumphandi, adversus Satanam, mundum, & carnem. Amen.

Largire, ut quisquis tibi dicatus sit, officii nostri ministerio, imbuatur cœlesti virtutum dono, ac in omnem æternitatem remuneretur. O benedicende Domine, qui vivis, & regis omnia, in secula. Amen.

OMNIPOTENS, & sempiterne Deus, cujus carissimus Filius, Jesus Christus, in ablutionem peccatorum nostrorum, e latere profudit aquam & sanguinem, imposuitque discipulis suis, ut irent doctum omnes nationes, & baptizatum eos in nomen Patris, & Filii, & Spiritus sancti, intuere quæsumus vota hujus tuæ concionis, & largire, ut omnes tui famuli, qui baptizabuntur in hac unda, recipiant plenitudinem omnis gratiæ, ac connumerentur in censu fidelium ac electorum liberorum tuorum, per Jesum Christum, Dominum nostrum. Amen.

Hic Minister infantem in manus suscipiet, & nomen quæret: deinde nomine appellans, tinget illum in aquam, sed consulte & caute, dicens.

N. Ego baptizo te, in nomine Patris, & Filii, & Spiritus sancti. Amen.

Verum, si puer sit imbecillus, ac languidus, tum sat erit, aliquid aquæ in illum effudisse, ad modum superiorem, dicens.

N. Ego baptizo te, in nomine Patris, & Filii, & Spiritus sancti. Amen.

Tunc Minister cruce signabit infantes fronte, dicens.

Nos recipimus hunc (vel hanc) infantem in societatem gregis Christi, & insignimus illum (vel illam) crucis monumento, in signum, ut eum nunquam pudeat confessionis fidei Christi crucifixi, sed robuste pugnaturum sub ejus insigni, adversus peccatum, mundum, & diabolum, & permansurum Christi fidelem militem et famulum, usque ad vitæ exitum.

Tunc Minister dicet.

QUANDOQUIDEM nunc, carissimi fratres, hi infantes sunt regenerati, & insiti in corporis Christi ecclesiam & societatem: agamus gratias Deo pro his beneficiis, & uno animorum consensu precemur omnipotenti Deo, ut illi ducant reliquum vitæ suæ secundum hunc ingressum.

Tunc dicetur.

Pater noster qui. &c.

Tunc Minister dicet.

HABEMUS tibi ex animo immortales gratias, misericors Pater, eo quod placuit tibi regenerare hunc (vel hanc) infantem tuo sancto Spiritu, recipere eum in proprium filium per adoptionem, & inserere in tuam sanctam concionem. Suppliciter etiam te petimus, ut concedas, ut is (vel ea) mortuus (vel mortua) peccato, & vivens justitiæ, & sepultus (vel sepulta) cum Christo in ejus mortem, cruci affigat veterem hominem, & penitus exterminet corpus peccati, ut quemadmodum factus (vel facta) est particeps mortis Filii tui, sic fiat item particeps resurrectionis suæ, quo tandem cum reliqua sancta societate fiat hæres tui regni sempiterni, per Christum Dominum nostrum. Amen.

Ad extremum, Minister convocans Susceptores ac Susceptrices, hanc sequentem cohortationem efferat.

QUANDOQUIDEM infantes hi polliciti sunt per vos, se deserturos Satanam, & omnia ejus opera, contra vero credituros in Deum, & servituros ei: recordandum est vobis vestrum esse procurare, ut hi infantes agnoscant, quam primum possunt, quam celebre votum, promissum, & professionem susceperint. Et ut has res exactius cognoscant, exhortabimini, ut sæpe adeant conciones. Potissimum autem efficietis, ut sedulo ediscant Symbolum Apostolorum, Dominicam orationem, cum præceptis Decalogi, lingua vernacula, & cætera etiam quæ Christiano homini sunt percipienda & credenda in salutem animarum, & ut probe educentur ad degendum piam & Christianam vitam, memores perpetuo, quod baptismus effigiat nobis nostram professionem, ad insistendum in vestigiis Christi Servatoris nostri, & ad induendum ejus imaginem, ut quemadmodum is mortuus fuit & resurrexit pro nobis, ita nos qui baptizamur, moreremur a peccato, & resurgeremus justitiæ, continuo trucidantes omnes nostros malos & depravatos affectus, & in dies singulos progredientes in omni probitate & vitæ sanctimonia.

Minister imperabit, ut infantes perducantur ad Episcopum, ut confirmentur ab ipso, quam primum poterunt lingua vernacula dicere Articulos fidei, Orationem Dominicam, & Decem præcepta, & penitius perceptum & comprehensum tenuerint Catechismum, prout hic paulo infra habetur.

Baptismus privatus.

De his qui baptizantur domi, necessitate nos eo impellente.

Pastores ac ministri Ecclesiæ sæpe admonebunt populum, ne differant baptismum infantium ultra Dominicam, aut alia Festa, quæ proxime sequuntur natalem puerulorum, sine gravi causa, eaque relata ad ministros, & ab his probata.

Admonebunt etiam, ut absque ratione gravi, & necessitate, non baptizent infantes privatim intra domesticos parietes, & ut (cum necessitas eos ad hoc protruserit) hanc sequantur formam.

Primum, qui præsentes fuerint, invocent Deum, dicentes orationem Dominicam, si occasio permiserit. Tunc aliquis vel tinget infantem in aquam, vel effundet aquam super illum, adjungens hæc verba.

N. EGO baptizo te, in nomine Patris, & Filii, & Spiritus sancti. Amen.

Hoc peracto, ne ambigant quicquam de pueruli Baptismo. Est siquidem legitime & satis absolute baptizatus, neque eget Baptismi repetitione in templo. Verum si infans, qui hoc pacto baptizabatur, revaluerit, expedit, ut in templum adducatur hujus rei gratia, ut Minister vestiget & exploret, ecquid infans sit legitime baptizatus. Quod si hi, qui adducunt infantem ad templum, confiteantur eum baptizatum esse, tum Minister eam rem trutinabit per hæc interrogata.

PER quem baptizatus est is infans?

Quinam aderant, interim dum baptizaretur?

Utrum implorarent opem, & auxilium divinum, in illis angustiis?

Qua re ac materia baptizabant?

Quibus verbis baptizabatur infans?

Utrum opinentur puerum legitime & perfecte baptizatum fuisse?

Quod si Minister deprehenderit per eorum responsa, qui puerum afferebant, omnia pro natura rei fuisse peracta, tum non repetet pueruli Baptismum, verum recipiet eum, ut unum ex ovili Christiano, dicens.

CERTO recte præstititis officium vestrum hac in re, justumque ordinem retinuistis in baptismo hujus infantis, qui natus in originali peccato, & sub ira divina, nunc est per Lavacrum regenerationis in Baptismo in censum liberorum Dei relatus, & hæres factus æternæ vitæ. Nam Dominus noster Jesus Christus non detinet gratiam & misericordiam suam ab hujusmodi [infantibus], verum amantissime accersit & invitat ad se, quemadmodum sanctum evangelium in nostrum solatium testatur, hoc pacto.

Evangelium. Mar. x.

ATTULERUNT ad Jesum. &c. Ut supra in publico Baptismate.

Post lectum evangelium, pronunciabit Minister admonitionem, ut in publico Baptismate.

AMICI. &c. Ut supra, donec perventum est ad postremam sententiam, quæ sese sic habebit. Quamobrem nos minime nescii favoris, quem cœlestis noster Pater gerit in hos infantes, illustrati ac patefacti per Filium ejus Jesum Christum, agamus illi gratias per fidem & pium affectum, & dicamus orationem, quam Dominus ipse docuit, & ad testationem fidei nostræ recitemus articulos comprehensos in symbolo.

Hic Minister cum Susceptoribus & Susceptricibus, dicet.

PATER noster qui es. &c.

Tunc Minister interrogabit nomen infantis, quo quidem per Susceptores & Susceptrices indicato, is dicet.

DETESTARIS tu, vice & loco hujus infantis, diabolum. &c Ut supra.

Responsio. Detestor ea omnia.

Minister. ECQUID profiteris nomine hujus infantis, hanc fidem? nempe te credere in Deum Patrem. &c.

Quæst. Ecquid credis ejus nomine in Spiritum sanctum? &c.

Responsio. Omnia hæc firmissime credo.

Tunc Minister dicet.

Oremus.

OMNIPOTENS & æterne Deus, Pater cœlestis, agimus tibi gratias, quod dignatus es vocare nos in agnitionem gratiæ tuæ, ac fidei[1] in te. Adauge quæsumus hanc notitiam, & confirma hanc in nobis fidem: dona huic infanti Spiritum tuum, ut renatus, & effectus hæres sempiternæ redemptionis per Dominum nostrum Jesum Christum, perseveret famulus tuus, & consequatur promissa tua, Per eundem Dominum nostrum Jesum Christum Filium tuum, qui tecum vivit & regnat in unitate ejusdem Spiritus sancti in secula. Amen.

Tunc Minister hac exhortatione utetur ad Susceptores & Susceptrices.

QUANDOQUIDEM hic infans. &c.

ut supra, servato numero singulari.

Verum, si hi, qui afferunt infantes ad templum, ambigue respondeant ad interrogata, & dicant se nescire quid cogitaverint, fecerint, aut dixerint in eo metu & mentis anxietate (ita uti sæpe fit) tum baptizet

[[1] See p. 410, note 1.]

eum minister juxta formam Baptismi publici, excepto quod inter tingendum infantem in fontem utetur hac verborum ratione.

Si tu non sis adhuc baptizatus .N. ego baptizo te, in nomine Patris, & Filii, & Spiritus sancti. Amen.

Confirmatio Puerorum,

cui insertus est Catechismus.

Ut Confirmatio administretur cum fructu, & ad ædificationem eorum, qui eam recipiunt, juxta doctrinam sancti Pauli, qui præcipit, ut omnia fiant in ecclesia ad ædificationem, commodum videtur, ut nemo posthac confirmetur, nisi qui lingua materna possit recitare articulos fidei, precationem Dominicam, & Decalogum, & respondere ad quæstiones in hac brevi Catechesi propositas, cum de aliqua interrogati fuerint ab Episcopo, vel alio designato ab ipso. Hoc ut statueremus, monemur his rationibus.

Primo, ut pueri propriam fidem confiteantur, & se ratam habere testentur confessionem, quam Patrini eorum nomine fecerunt in Baptismo, & ut ipsimet proprio ore atque consensu coram ecclesia confirmare & rata habere ea possint; & promittant se per gratiam Dei omnia illa velle fideliter præstare, quæ proprio ore profitentur.

Deinde, quia Confirmatio adhibetur baptisatis per impositionem manuum, & precem publicam, ut recipiant donum fortitudinis ad resistendum omnibus tentationibus, & assultibus carnis, mundi & Diaboli, placuit illo tempore exhiberi, quo per ætatem experiri possunt, quænam sint illæ tentationes, per quas sollicitantur ad peccatum.

Tertio, quia hoc convenit cum institutione primitivæ Ecclesiæ, quæ decrevit, eos tantum esse confirmandos, qui erant adulta ætate, ut illi sufficienter edocti in Christiana religione aperte profiterentur suam propriam fidem, & promitterent obedientiam Deo.

Et ne quis putet, noxiam esse pueris dilationem Confirmationis usque dum adoleverint, is certo sciat ex manifesto verbo Dei pueros post Baptismum habere omnia necessaria ad salutem, & absque dubio servandos esse.

Catechesis, qua puer instituitur

priusquam ad Confirmationem producitur.

Quod est tibi nomen? Responsio .N. vel N.

Quæst. Quis indidit tibi hoc nomen? Responsio. Patrini, in Baptismo, quo factus sum membrum Christi, filius Dei, & hæres vitæ æternæ.

Quæstio. Quid promiserunt pro te Compatres & Commatres?

Responsio. Tria meo nomine polliciti sunt.

Primum, quod renunciarem Diabolo, mundo, & carnalibus concupiscentiis.

Deinde, ut crederem omnes Articulos fidei Christianæ

Tertio, quod vellem obsequi præceptis Dei, & ei servire in sanctitate & justitia, omnibus diebus vitæ meæ.

Quæstio. Nonne putas te esse astrictum ut credas atque facias illa, quæ ipsi tuo nomine promiserunt?

Responsio. Ita certe: atque id Dei auxilio sum facturus; & gratiam ago ex animo cœlesti Patri, qui me ad hanc gratiam per Dominum nostrum Jesum Christum vocavit, eumque toto pectore precor, ut porro largiatur mihi gratiam, ut in ea perseverem usque ad finem vitæ.

Quæstio. Recita articulos Fidei.

Resp. Credo in Deum Patrem omnipotentem. &c.

Qu. Quid præcipue didicisti ex his articulis fidei?

Resp. Primum, didici credere in Deum Patrem, qui creavit cœlum & terram.

Deinde in Deum Filium, qui me redemit, & totum genus humanum.

Tertio, in Spiritum sanctum, qui me sanctificat, & universum electum populum Dei.

Qu. Cum responderis, Patrinos nomine tuo promisisse te servaturum esse præcepta Dei, dic quot sunt?

Resp. Decem.

Quæstio. Quæ sunt?

Resp. Ea quæ Dominus recensuit Exodi vicesimo, dicens: Ego sum Dominus Deus vester, qui eduxi te de terra Ægypti, ex domo servitutis. &c. ut supra, ante Communionem.

Quæstio. Quid potissimum ex his præceptis discis?

Resp. Duo: Primum, quid Deo: Alterum, quid proximo debeam.

Quæstio. Quid Deo debes?

Re. Fidem, timorem, amorem ex toto corde, tota mente, anima, & omnibus viribus: cultum, gratiarum actionem, ut omnem fiduciam meam in eum collocem, eum invocem, glorificem, nomen & verbum suum sanctum honore afficiam, ac serviam ei omnibus diebus vitæ meæ.

Quæstio. Quid vero debes proximo?

Resp. Ut amem eum perinde ac me ipsum: & ut faciam omnibus hominibus, prout velim mihi fieri ab illis: ut honore afficiam Patrem & Matrem, eis succurram & subveniam, ut obediam Regi[1] & ipsius Ministris, ut me subjiciam meo Magistratui, Doctoribus, Pastori spirituali, et Magistro, ut me modeste geram & reverenter erga majores & meliores, ut nullum lædam verbo aut facto, ut sim fidelis & justus in omnibus negotiis, ut nulli invideam, nullum odiam, ut manus contineam a furto, linguam a maledicentia & obtrectatione, ut me ipsum castum & sobrium servem; ne concupiscam aliorum bona, sed discam meo labore mihi victum parare, & ut Deo obediam in quacunque vocatione, ad quam me dignabitur vocare.

Quæstio. Cum scire debeas, te ista ex tuis viribus & sine speciali Dei gratia præstare non posse, ac propterea continuo orandum esse pro gratia, dic mihi, bone puer, Orationem Dominicam.

[[1] Haddon ought to have substituted *Reginæ* for Aless's *Regi.*]

Resp. Pater noster qui es in cœlis. &c.
Quæstio. Quid petis a Deo hac precatione?
Res. Peto ut cœlestis Pater, dator omnis boni, det mihi & omnibus hominibus, ut eum colamus, ei serviamus, & obediamus, ut donet nobis omnia quæ necessaria sunt ad hanc vitam, remittat nobis peccata, ac ut defendat nos in omnibus periculis corporis & animæ. Postremo, ut nos liberet ab omni peccato, ab insidiis Diaboli, & morte æterna. Credo etiam Deum Patrem pro sua bonitate & misericordia hoc facturum per Dominum nostrum Jesum Christum, ideoque dico Amen: id est, ita fiet.

Finis Catechismi.

Quum pueri possint vulgari & materna lingua recitare Articulos fidei, Precationem Dominicam, & Decalogum, et respondere ad quæstiones in hac brevi Catechesi propositas, cum interrogati fuerint ab Episcopo, vel alio designato ab ipso, tunc adducentur ad Episcopum per aliquem qui futurus sit ejus Patrinus; quod fieri debet, ut unusquisque puerorum possit habere testem suæ confirmationis.

Episcopus confirmabit puerum hoc modo.

Confirmatio.

Episcopus. Adjutorium nostrum in nomine Domini.
Responsio. Qui fecit cœlum & terram.
Episcopus. Sit nomen Domini benedictum.
Responsio. Et nunc, & in perpetuum.
Episcopus. Domine, exaudi orationem nostram.
Responsio. Et clamor noster ad te perveniat.

Episcopus.
Oremus.

OMNIPOTENS & immortalis Deus, qui dignatus es regenerare hos tuos famulos per aquam & Spiritum paracletum, & tribuisti eis veniam omnium delictorum suorum, robora eos, te quæsumus, Domine, spiritu consolationis, & indies adauge & exaggera in iis donum gratiæ tuæ varium & multiplex, largire spiritum sapientiæ & intellectionis, spiritum consilii et internæ fortitudinis, spiritum scienciæ & veræ pietatis, & comple eos, O Deus, spiritu sancti timoris tui. Amen.

Hic Minister imponet manum suam in quemlibet puerum separatim, dicens.

PROTEGE, Domine, puerum hunc tua cœlesti gratia, ut

1560.] CONFIRMATIO PUE. 419

perseveret tuus in omnem ætatem, & in dies singulos multiplica in eo Spiritum sanctum tuum magis magisque, donec pervenerit ad tuum regnum sempiternum. Amen.

Tunc Episcopus dicet.

Oremus.

OMNIPOTENS & immortalis Deus, qui facis nos & velle & efficere quæ sunt bona & accepta tuæ majestati: nos te supplices petimus horum puerorum gratia, in quos (sanctorum apostolorum tuorum exemplo) manus imposuimus, ut reddas eos certos hoc signo tui favoris & dilectionis in eos. Sit, oramus, tua paterna manus semper super eos, sit Spiritus tuus semper cum eis, & sic præluceat, & manu ducat eos in cognitionem & obsequium verbi tui, ut ad postremum æternam vitam consequantur, per Dominum nostrum Jesum Christum, qui tecum & cum sancto Spiritu vivit & regnat unus Deus, immutabili æternitate. Amen.

Tunc Episcopus benedicet pueris his verbis.

BENEDICTIO omnipotentis Dei Patris, & Filii, & Spiritus sancti, sit super vos, & maneat semper vobiscum. Amen.

Pastor cujuslibet Parrochiæ, aut aliquis alius deputatus, die Dominico aut Festo, dimidia hora ante Vesperas, examinabit & instituet pueros in templo de aliqua parte Catechismi, facta ante intimatione: & omnes patresfamiliæ & matresfamiliæ curabunt liberos, servos & ancillas eo venire, & respondere Parrocho ad interrogata, donec Catechesin didicerint.

Quoties etiam Episcopus significaverit se velle confirmare pueros, Parrochus intimabit Episcopo nomina eorum, quos judicarit sufficienter institutos in Catechismo.

Nemo autem admittatur ad Communionem, nisi ante fuerit confirmatus.

De solenni Matrimonio.

Primo, nomina contrahentium tribus Dominicis[1] intimentur, populo præsente, ut hactenus in more fuit. Si autem in diversis habitaverint personæ Parrochiis, non admittantur ad matrimonii solenni-

[[1] Aless left 'or holy dayes' untranslated, and this omission was not supplied by Haddon.]

zationem, nisi in utraque Parrochia facta fuerit legitima intimatio, & alter Parrochus alterum de hoc certiorem reddiderit. Die constituto ad nuptias conveniant Sponsus & Sponsa cum amicis in medio Ecclesiæ, ante Chorum, ubi Minister sic verba faciet.

CARISSIMI, hic coram Deo in ecclesia ipsius convenimus, ad conjungendum hunc Virum & hanc mulierem matrimonio, quod honorifice ab ipso Deo institutum est in Paradiso, cum adhuc integra esset natura, ad significandum mysterium conjunctionis Christi cum Ecclesia. Hunc ordinem Christus ornavit & honoravit sua præsentia, & primo suo miraculo, quod ædidit in Cana Galilææ. Paulus etiam ita celebrat, quod sit honorabile inter omnes homines conjugium, & thorus immaculatus. Non est igitur contemnendum a nobis, aut leviter, temere, petulanter, & tantum propter explendam libidinem, brutorum (quæ ratione carent) & pecudum more, arripiendum a quolibet ebrio, sed debita qua decet reverentia, cum gravi deliberatione, a sobriis cum timore Dei: diligenter considerando causas, propter quas Deus conjugium instituit. Harum una est procreatio prolis, & educatio ad timorem & disciplinam Domini. Altera est, ut sit remedium contra peccatum carnalis concupiscentiæ, & scortationem, ut conjuges in matrimonio caste vivant, & seipsos incontaminatos servent, ut membra corporis Christi. Tertia est societas, mutuum auxilium, consolatio, consilium, ut alter alteri adsit, tam in prosperis quam in adversis. In hoc sacrosancto ordine hæ personæ adveniunt conjungendæ. Quare si quis adest, qui justam causam habet, propter quam non debent copulari, is nunc dicat, aut posthac in perpetuum taceat.

Tunc conversus ad sponsum et sponsam dicat.

Vos admoneo extremi judicii, in quo stabitis ad tribunal Christi, quem nihil latet, ut si alter de altero aut seipso scit impedimentum, quominus valeat hoc matrimonium inter vos, fateamini, & hoc certo vobis persuadeatis, quod quoruncunque matrimonium non probatur verbo Dei, Deum hos non conjungere, nec eorum conjugium esse legitimum.

Si adest aliquis qui allegat impedimentum, quominus conjungi possint matrimonio lege Dei & hujus Regni, & offert se cum sponsoribus ad solvendas impensas matrimonii, si non probaverit quod objicit, differatur solemnizatio matrimonii: Si nihil in contrarium adferatur, tunc dicat Minister Sponso.

N. Vis habere hanc personam N. ut sit tua legitima uxor, ut cum ea vivas juxta Dei ordinationem in sacro matrimonio? Vis eam amare, consolari, honorare, & conservare sanam & aegrotam, & repudiare omnem aliam, & te illi soli servare quamdiu vivas?

Respondeat. Volo.

Tunc conversus ad mulierem dicet.

N. Vis habere hunc N. ut sit tibi legitimus maritus, & cum eo vivere juxta Dei ordinationem in sancto matrimonio, ei obedire, servire, amare & honorare ipsum, servare eum sanum & aegrotum, &, posthabitis omnibus aliis, te illi soli custodire toto tempore vitae vestrae?

Respondeat. Volo.

Tunc Minister dicet.

Quos[1] Deus conjunxit, homo non separet.

Post, Minister, accepta sponsa a Parentibus, tradet ejus dextram Sponso, & jubebit ut dent mutuam fidem, dicente viro:

Ego N. accipio te N. ut sis mea uxor, ut habeam & retineam ab hoc die, inter prospera & adversa, sive ditior sive pauperior, aegra aut sana fueris, ut amem & foveam, donec mors nos separaverit, juxta ordinationem divinam: & in signum trado tibi meam fidem.

Tunc mulier, accipiens dextram viri, dicat.

Ego N. accipio te N. ut sis meus maritus, ut habeam & retineam ab hoc die, & deinceps, inter prospera & adversa, sive ditior sive pauperior, sanus aut aeger fueris, ut te amem & foveam, tibi obediam, donec mors nos separaverit, juxta ordinationem Dei, & in signum trado tibi meam fidem.

Tunc vir det mulieri annulum, & alia munera, aurum & argentum, & ponet super librum, cum consueto ministris debito salario, quem Minister manu tenet, ac Presbyter, accepto annulo, tradet viro, ut imponat quarto digito mulieris, dicens:

Hoc annulo te mihi despondeo, hoc aurum & argentum tibi dono, cum meo corpore te honoro, & omnibus fortunae bonis te amplifico, in nomine Patris, & Filii & Spiritus sancti. Amen.

[[1] The insertion of this sentence, instead of a translation of, "Who giveth this Woman to be married to this Man?" is also an error copied from Aless.]

Vir[1] relinquens annulum in quarto digito sinistræ manus sponsæ, Minister dicet.

Oremus.

O æterne Deus, creator & conservator humani generis, dator omnis gratiæ spiritualis, & auctor æternæ vitæ, da benedictionem servis tuis, huic viro & huic mulieri, quibus nos in tuo nomine benedicimus, ut quemadmodum Isaac & Rebecca fideliter inter se vixerunt, ita hæ personæ certo præstent & servent votum, & conventionem inter sese mutuo factam, cujus hic annulus datus & receptus est signum & testimonium, & ut in perpetuo amore ac pace permaneant, & vitam ducant juxta legem tuam, per Dominum nostrum Jesum Christum. Amen.

Tunc sacerdos, jungens eorum dextras, dicat.

Quos Deus conjunxit, homo non separet.

His peractis, Minister dicet populo.

Cum N. & N. consenserint in sacrum matrimonium, & hoc coram Deo, & Ecclesia hic congregata, sint testati, & mutuam fidem tradiderint, hancque donatione & acceptione annuli, auri & argenti, ac dextrarum conjunctione confirmarint, declaro & pronuncio eos esse conjuges, in nomine Patris, & Filii, & Spiritus sancti. Amen.

Tunc Minister addet hanc benedictionem.

Deus Pater, Deus Filius, Deus Spiritus sanctus, vos benedicat, defendat & custodiat. Misericors Dominus vos suo favore respiciat, & repleat omni benedictione spirituali & gratia, ut sic una in hac præsenti vita vivere possitis, et postea vitam habeatis æternam.

Tunc ingrediantur Chorum, Ministris aut clericis recitantibus Psalmum cxxvii.

Beati omnes qui timent Dominum. &c.

Aut hunc Psalmum lxvi.

Deus misereatur nostri, & benedicat nobis.

Sponsus & Sponsa interea genu flectant juxta mensam Domini, & Minister stans conversus ad eos oret.

Kyrie eleyson.
Resp. Christe eleyson.

[1 Aless omits the rubric, and thus is not answerable for its Latinity.]

Mini. Kyrie eleyson.
Pater noster qui es in cœlis. &c.
Et ne nos inducas in tentationem.
Responsio. Sed libera nos a malo.
Minister. Domine, salvum fac servum & ancillam tuam.
Responsio. Qui suam fiduciam in te collocant.
Minister. Mitte eis, Domine, auxilium de sancto.
Responsio. Et defende eos in æternum.
Minister. Esto illis turris fortitudinis.
Responsio. A facie inimici.
Minister. Domine, exaudi orationem nostram.
Responsio. Et clamor noster ad te perveniat.

Oremus.

DEUS Abraham, Deus Isaac, Deus Jacob, benedic servis tuis, & insere mentibus eorum semen vitæ æternæ, ut quæcunque ex verbo tuo utiliter didicerint, opere perficiant. Respice, Domine, de sanctuario tuo, & de excelso cœlorum habitaculo, super eos, & benedicito illis. Et sicut misisti benedictionem tuam super Abraham & Saram, ad ingentem eorum consolationem, ita dignare benedicere his servis tuis, ut obsequentes mandatis tuis, & sub tua protectione securi, perseverent in amore tuo ad finem usque vitæ, per Dominum nostrum Jesum Christum.

Oratio hæc sequens omitti debet, si mulier fuerit annosa aut sterilis, alioquin dicatur.

CŒLESTIS et misericors Pater, cujus dono humanum genus multiplicatur, & conservatur, adsis quæsumus his servis tuis cum benedictione, ut sint fœcundi in propagatione prolis, & ut ducant vitam cum pietate & honestate, ut videant filios filiorum, usque ad tertiam & quartam generationem, in laudem & gloriam sanctissimi nominis tui, per Dominum nostrum Jesum Christum Filium tuum. Amen.

DEUS, qui ex omnipotentia tua cuncta de nihilo creasti, quique post aliarum rerum ordinationem voluisti, ut ex Viro condito ad imaginem tuam Mulier formaretur, & in eorum conjunctione docuisti eos[2] non licere ulli hos separare, quos tu conjunxeras: O Deus, qui statum conjugum consecrasti ad

[2 This is Aless's reading.]

significandum excelsum mysterium conjunctionis Christi cum Ecclesia, respice clementer super hos servos tuos, & præsta, ut Sponsus iste juxta tuam ordinationem amet suam Sponsam, ut Christus dilexit Ecclesiam, & pro qua seipsum tradidit: & ut vicissim hæc sponsa suum complectatur amore sponsum, & redamet: ut Rachael sit sapiens, ut Rebecca fidelis, & ut Sara obediens: cum omni quiete, sobrietate, & concordia imitetur sanctas matronas. Benedic Domine utrique, & tribue frui vita æterna, per Dominum nostrum Jesum Christum Filium tuum, qui tecum vivit & regnat in unitate Spiritus sancti Deus, per omnia secula. &c. Amen.

Tunc Minister dicet.

OMNIPOTENS[1] Deus, qui initio condidisti primos parentes nostros Adam & Evam, & benedixisti illis, atque in matrimonio conjunxisti, effundat super vos divitias gratiæ tuæ, sanctificet & benedicat vos, ut illi corpore & animo placeatis, & vitam ducatis suavem & sanctam. Amen.

Deinde sequetur Communio, & cum lectum fuerit Evangelium, sequatur sermo de officiis conjugum, aut loco Concionis hæc dici possint.

Vos qui estis conjuges, aut qui matrimonium contrahere posthac constituistis, audite quid Scriptura dicat de officiis conjugum, quid vir mulieri debeat, & contra, mulier suo viro.

Paulus ad Ephesios v. præcipit conjugibus.

Viri, diligite uxores vestras, sicut Christus Ecclesiam dilexit, & obtulit semetipsum pro illa, ut illam sanctificaret, & purificaret lavacro aquæ per verbum, ut exhiberet sibi gloriosam Ecclesiam, non habentem maculam, neque rugam, aut aliquid simile, sed ut esset sancta & irreprehensibilis. Sic viri diligere debent uxores, ut propria sua corpora.

Qui diligit uxorem, seipsum diligit. Nemo enim carnem propriam unquam odio habuit, sed diligit & fovet, sicut Christus Ecclesiam. Nam sumus membra corporis ipsius, os

[[1] The translation of Aless is worth giving entire, as exhibiting both his strange treatment of the original, and the source of Haddon's errors:—Omnipotens Deus, qui initio condidisti primos parentes nostros Adam et Evam, et benedixisti illis, atque in matrimonio conjunxisti, effunde super nos divitias gratiæ tuæ, sanctifica et ✠ benedicito illis, ut tibi corpore et animo placeant, et vitam ducant suavem et sanctam, Amen.]

de ossibus, & caro de carne ejus : propterea relinquet vir patrem & matrem, & adhærebit uxori suæ, et erunt duo in carne una. Mysterium hoc magnum est, in Christo scilicet, & in Ecclesia, & tamen unusquisque vestrum diligat suam uxorem, sicut seipsum. Ad eundem modum Paulus præcipit ad Colossenses. Viri, diligite uxores vestras, & ne sitis amarulenti erga eas. Et beatus Petrus, Apostolus Christi, qui & ipse fuit maritus, præcipit maritis. Viri, cohabitate uxoribus vestris juxta scientiam, habentes honorem uxori, tanquam infirmiori vasculo, ut cohæredes gratiæ, vitæ, ne impediantur precationes vestræ.

> Hactenus audivistis, quid Vir debeat uxori suæ, jam uxores audiant suum officium, et quid debeant maritis.

Sanctus Paulus Apostolus, in prænominata epistola ad Ephesios, ita vobis præcipit. Uxores propriis viris subditæ sint, veluti Domino, quoniam vir est caput uxoris, quemadmodum & Christus est caput Ecclesiæ, & idem est, qui salutem dat corpori. Itaque quemadmodum ecclesia subdita est Christo, sic uxores suis viris subditæ sint in omnibus. Et rursus ad Colossenses ait. Uxores, subditæ estote propriis viris, sicut decet in Domino.

Beatus etiam Petrus sic vos instituit. Uxores, subditæ sitis viris vestris, ut etiam illi viri, qui non auscultant Evangelio, per uxorum conversationem sive prædicationem lucrifiant, dum considerant castam conversationem vestram, cum timore conjunctam : quarum ornatus sit non forensis, qui situs sit in intricatis capillis, & auri ornamentis, aut decore vestium, sed interius in corde bono, sine pravitate, ut spiritus sit placidus ac quietus, qui coram Deo preciosissimum est ornamentum. Nam ad hunc modum etiam illæ sanctæ mulieres, sperantes in Deo, sese ornabant, & subditæ erant viris suis. Quemadmodum Sara obedivit Abrahæ, vocans eum dominum, cujus factæ estis filiæ, dum benefacitis, & non metuitis vobis pro ulla turpitudine.

Observandum, quod desponsati debeant participes fieri mensæ Domini.

Gratiarum actio pro
mulieribus post partum.

Mulier cum in templo venerit, genu flectat quodam in loco commodo, prope mensam Domini, cui astans minister hæc aut his similia dicat:

CUM placuerit Deo ex infinita sua bonitate te in partu servare, debes ei ex animo gratiam agere, & orare.

Tunc recitabit Minister Psalmum cxx. dicens:

LEVAVI oculos meos in montes. &c.

usque ad finem Psalmi.

Kyrie eleyson.
Resp. Christe eleyson.
Kyrie eleyson.
Pater noster qui es in cœlis. &c.
Et ne nos inducas in tentationem.
Responsio. Sed libera nos a malo.
Minister. Domine, salvam fac famulam tuam.
Responsio. Deus meus, sperantem in te.
Minister. Esto ei turris fortitudinis.
Responsio. A facie inimici.
Minister. Domine, exaudi orationem nostram.
Responsio. Et clamor noster ad te perveniat.

Oremus.

OMNIPOTENS Deus, qui liberasti hanc famulam tuam periculis parturientium, præsta, quæsumus, misericors Pater, ut per gratiam tuam fideliter inserviat suæ vocationi in hac præsenti vita, ut particeps fiat vitæ æternæ, per Dominum nostrum. &c. Amen.

Mulier offeret oblationes solitas, juxta morem hactenus observatum, & præterea communicet, si adsint communicantes.

[Die Cinerum Cærimoniæ.

POST Matutinas signo dato per campanam, ut populus conveniat, et decantata Letania, Parrochus populum alloquatur:

Fratres, in primitiva Ecclesia fuit utilis disciplina, ut initio Quadragesimæ rei manifestorum criminum ejicerentur ex Ecclesia, ut agerent publicam pœnitentiam, et ut alii eorum exemplo admoniti sibi caverent. Hujus publicæ pœnitentiæ vice, interim dum hæc restitui possit, quod optare debemus, visum est hoc tempore conducibile ad pietatem, ut præsentibus vobis legantur comminationes et execrationes contra impœnitentes ex 27. capite Deuter. & aliis locis scripturæ, ut ad quamlibet sententiam respondeatis, Amen.

Hoc fine, et propter hanc causam, ut vos admoniti de gravissima ira Dei contra peccatum, excitemini ad veram pœnitentiam, et ut in hoc corruptissimo seculo circumspectius vivatis, ac vitetis peccata, propter quæ vos, ut ipsi fatemini, divinitus estis excommunicati.

Maledictus vir, qui fecerit sculptile, aut conflatile, quæ sunt Domino abominanda, et posuerit in loco aliquo, quo colantur opera manuum suarum.

Et respondebit omnis populus: Amen.

Maledictus[1] pater et mater ejus.
Maledictus vir, qui abstulerit, aut loco moverit, signum finis, & termini terræ, aut agri proximi sui.
Maledictus qui errare fecerit cœcum de via.
Maledictus qui in judicio oppresserit advenam vel viduam.
Maledictus qui clam percusserit proximum suum.
Maledictus qui condormierit uxori proximi sui.
Maledictus qui accipit munera ad effundendum sanguinem innocentem.
Maledictus qui ponit fiduciam suam in homine, et ponit carnem brachium suum, et cor ejus discedit a Domino.
Maledicti immisericordes, scortatores, adulteri, avari, simulachrorum cultores, maledici, ebriosi, et violenti.

Et respondebit omnis populus: Amen.

Adhortatio.

Cum igitur, ut Propheta inquit, maledicti sint omnes, qui declinant Psalm. 118. a mandatis Dei, meminerimus tremendi judicii Dei, impendentis capitibus nostris, et quod præsto est præ foribus, et convertamur ad Dominum corde contrito et humiliato, in jejuniis, lachrymis, et orationibus, facientes dignos fructus pœnitentiæ. Nam securis ad radicem arboris jam posita Matth. 3. est, et omnis arbor, quæ non fert fructum bonum, excidetur, et in ignem mittetur. Horrendum enim est incidere in manus Dei viventis; pluet Hebr. 10. enim super peccatores laqueos, ignem et sulphur: spiritus procellarum Psalm. 10. pars calicis eorum. Egredietur enim Dominus de loco sancto suo, ut Malach. 3. visitet iniquitatem habitantium in terra. Quis feret diem adventus ejus? Cujus ventilabrum in manu sua est, ut purget aream suam, et Matth. 3. congregabit triticum in horreum suum; paleas vero exuret igne inextinguibili. Dies enim Domini, sicut fur in nocte, veniet, & cum 1 Thess. 5. dixerint pax et securitas, repentinus eis superveniet interitus, sicut dolores partus invadunt parturientem, nec effugient. Tunc revelabitur ira Dei in die iræ et revelationis justi judicii Dei, quam impii et

[1 A serious error exists in this sentence.]

obstinati sibi ipsis thesaurisant, juxta duritiem suam, et impœnitens cor suum, quo bonitatem, et patientiam, ac longanimitatem Dei, eos ad pœnitentiam invitantis, contemnunt. Tunc clamabunt ad me, et non exaudiam, quærent me, et non invenient, quia oderunt scientiam, nec receperunt disciplinam Domini; sed abhorruerunt a consilio meo, et correctionem meam despexerunt: tunc nimis sero pulsabunt post clausum ostium, et petent misericordiam in die judicii. O terribilis vox justi judicis, quæ contra eos pronunciabitur. Nam dicetur ad illos: Ite maledicti in ignem æternum, qui paratus est Diabolo et angelis suis. Ideo, fratres, operemur dum dies est, quia veniet nox, in qua nemo poterit operari. Dum lucem habemus, credamus in lucem, ne abjiciamur in tenebras exteriores, ubi erit fletus et stridor dentium. Non abutamur bonitate Dei, nos ad pœnitentiam invitantis, et promittentis veniam, modo ad eum convertamur in corde contrito et spiritu humiliato, quia, etsi peccata nostra rubicunda sint ut purpura, tamen ut nix dealbantur. Convertimini a peccatis vestris, dicit Dominus, et iniquitates vestræ non erunt vobis exitio. Abjicite a vobis omnem impietatem, quam fecistis, Facite vobis corda nova. Quare moriemini in peccatis vestris? Nolo enim mortem peccatoris, dicit Dominus, sed magis ut convertatur, et vivat. Etsi enim peccavimus, tamen habemus advocatum Jesum Christum justum, et ipse est propiciatio pro peccatis nostris. Vulneratus est enim propter iniquitates nostras, et afflictus propter scelera nostra. Convertamur igitur ad eum, quia misericors est, persuadentes nobis ipsis, quod nos expectet, et paratus sit recipere revertentes, et ignoscere nobis, si vera pœnitentia redeamus, si nos ei subjicimus, et volumus ambulare in viis ejus, si suave jugum et onus suum leve velimus ferre, ut eum sequamur in humilitate, patientia, caritate, quæramus semper gloriam ejus, et quilibet diligenter in sua vocatione Deo inserviat. Hæc si fecerimus, liberabit nos Christus a maledictione legis, et ab æterna ira, quæ eveniet illis, qui ad sinistram stabunt, et nos ad dextram collocabit, et benedicet illa dulcissima benedictione: Venite benedicti a Patre meo, possidete regnum, quod vobis paratum est ante conditum mundum: ad quod nos ex infinita sua misericordia perducere dignetur. Amen.

Proverb. 1.

Tunc genu flexo, orabunt Psalmum [50].

Miserere mei Deus, secundam magnam misericordiam tuam.

Kyrie eleison.
Christe eleison.
Kyrie eleison.

Pater noster, qui es in cœlis. &c.	Responsio.
Et ne nos inducas in tentationem.	Sed libera nos a malo.
Domine, salvos fac servos tuos.	Deus meus, sperantes in te.
Mitte eis auxilium de sancto.	Et defende illos in æternum.
Adjuva nos, Deus Salvator noster.	Et propter gloriam nominis tui libera nos, et propicius esto propter nomen sanctum tuum.
Domine, exaudi orationem meam.	Et clamor meus ad te perveniat.

Preces nostras, quæsumus Domine, clementer exaudi, et confitentium tibi parce peccatis, ut quos conscientia delictorum accusat, indulgentia propiciationis tuæ absolvat, per Dominum nostrum.

Omnipotens et misericors Deus, qui contritorum non despicis gemitus, et nihil odisti eorum quæ feceras, qui non vis mortem peccatoris, sed magis ut convertatur, et vivat; ignosce clementer peccatis nostris, recipe et consolare nos, qui laboramus et onerati sumus pondere peccatorum. Tibi proprium est misereri, ad te solum pertinet remittere peccata Parce Domine, parce populo tuo, quem redemisti. Non intres in judicium cum servis tuis, qui sumus terra et pulvis. Sed averte a nobis iram tuam, quia nostram miseriam agnoscimus, et ex animo de peccatis dolemus. Accelera ut auxilieris nobis in hoc seculo, ut tecum in æternum vivamus in futuro, per Dominum. &c.

Antiphona.

Converte nos, Domine, et convertemur: propicius esto, Domine, populo tuo, qui ad te convertitur in jejuniis, lachrymis et precibus, quia es misericors, et plenus miserationum, longanimis, et paratus ad ignoscendum. Tu parcis peccatoribus, et in ira misericordiæ recordaris. Parce Domine, parce populo tuo, et ne des hæreditatem tuam ad opprobrium. Exaudi nos Domine, quia benigna est misericordia tua, et juxta multitudinem miserationum tuarum respice nos.]

Finis.

Excufum Londini apud Reginaldum
Wolfium, Regiæ Maieſt.
in Latinis typo-
graphum.
Cum priuilegio Regiæ Maieſtatis.

pite regnum illud, quod vobis paratum fuit ab origine mundi. Largire hoc, quæsumus te, misericors Pater, per Jesum Christum mediatorem ac servatorem nostrum. Amen.

Finis libri publicarum Precum Ecclesiæ Anglicanæ.

[1 A misprint for, Sepultura. See p. 408.]

D. Augustinus

De civitate Dei, libro primo,

capite. 12.

CURATIO funeris, conditio sepulturæ, pompa exequiarum, magis sunt vivorum solatia, quam subsidia mortuorum.

In commendationibus

Benefactorum.

Ad cujusque termini finem, commendatio fiat fundatoris, aliorumque clarorum virorum, quorum beneficentia Collegium locupletatur. Ejus hæc sit forma.

Primum recitetur clara voce Oratio dominica.

PATER noster qui es in cœlis. &c.

Deinde recitentur tres Psalmi.
- Exaltabo te Deus meus rex. Psalmus. 144.
- Lauda anima mea Do. 145.
- Laudate Dominum, quoniam bonus. Psalmus. 146.

Posthæc legatur caput 44. Ecclesiastici.

His finitis, sequatur concio, in qua concionator Fundatoris amplissimam munificentiam prædicet: quantus sit literarum usus ostendat: quantis laudibus afficiendi sunt, qui literarum studia beneficentia sua excitent: quantum sit ornamentum Regno doctos viros habere, qui de rebus controversis vere judicare possunt: quanta sit scripturarum laus, & quantum illæ omni humanæ auctoritati antecedant, quanta sit ejus doctrinæ in vulgus utilitas, & quam late pateat: quam egregium & regium sit (cui Deus universæ plebis suæ curam commisit) de multitudine ministrorum verbi laborare, atque hi ut honesti atque eruditi sint, curare: atque alia ejus generis, quæ pii & docti viri cum laude illustrare possint.

Hac Concione perorata, decantetur.

BENEDICTUS Dominus Deus Israel.

Ad extremum hæc adhibeantur.

Minister. IN memoria æterna erit justus.
Responsio. Ab auditu malo non timebit.
Minister. Justorum animæ in manu Dei sunt.
Responsio. Nec attinget illos cruciatus.

Oremus.

DOMINE Deus, resurrectio & vita credentium, qui semper es laudandus, tam in viventibus, quam in defunctis, agimus tibi gratias pro fundatore nostro .N. ceterisque benefactoribus nostris, quorum beneficiis hic ad pietatem & studia literarum alimur: rogantes, ut nos his donis ad tuam gloriam recte utentes, una cum illis ad resurrectionis gloriam immortalem perducamur. Per Christum Dominum nostrum. Amen.

Celebratio cœnæ

Domini, in funebribus, si amici & vicini defuncti communicare velint.

Collecta.

MISERICORS Deus, Pater Domini nostri Jesu Christi, qui es resurrectio & vita, in quo qui credidit, etiamsi mortuus fuerit, vivet; & in quo qui crediderit & vivit, non morietur in æternum: quique nos docuisti per sanctum Apostolum tuum Paulum, non debere mœrere pro dormientibus in Christo, sicut ii qui spem non habent resurrectionis: humiliter petimus, ut nos a morte peccati resuscites ad vitam justitiæ, ut cum ex hac vita emigramus, dormiamus cum Christo, quemadmodum speramus hunc fratrem nostrum, & in generali resurrectione, extremo die, nos una cum hoc fratre nostro resuscitati, & receptis corporibus, regnemus una tecum in vita æterna. Per Dominum nostrum Jesum Christum.

Epistola.   i. Thess. iiii.

NOLO vos ignorare, fratres, de his qui obdormierunt,...... Proinde consolemini vos mutuo sermonibus his.

Evangelium.   Joan. vi.

DIXIT Jesus discipulis suis, & turbis Judæorum: Omne quod dat mihi Pater......habeat vitam æternam, & ego suscitabo eum in novissimo die.

[LITURG. QU. ELIZ.]

Vel hoc Evangelium. Joan. v.

DIXIT Jesus discipulis suis, & turbis Judæorum : Amen, Amen, dico vobis, qui sermonem meum audit......qui vero mala egerunt, in resurrectionem condemnationis.

*Excuſum Londini apud Reginaldum
Volfium, Regiæ Maiest.
in Latinis typo-
graphum.*

Cum priuilegio Regiæ Maieſtatis.

THE[1] NEW CALENDAR.

1561.

[1 The original has, of course, no title.
The copy here followed is bound up with the second edition of Elizabeth's English Prayer Book in the University Library, Cambridge. It must have been printed by Jugge and Cawode.]

¶ The Order how

the rest of holy scripture (beside
the Psalter) is appointed
to be read.

THE Old Testament is appointed for the first Lessons at Morning and Evening Prayer, and shall be read through every year once, except certain Books and Chapters, which be least edifying, and might best be spared, and therefore are left unread.

The New Testament is appointed for the Second Lessons at Morning and Evening Prayer, and shall be read over orderly every year thrice, beside the Epistles and Gospels: except the Apocalypse, out of the which there be only certain Lessons appointed upon divers Proper Feasts.

And to know what Lessons shall be read every day: Find the day of the Month in the Calendar following, and there ye shall perceive the Books and Chapters that shall be read for the Lessons both at Morning and Evening Prayer.

And here is to be noted, that whensoever there be any proper Psalms, or Lessons, appointed for the Sundays, or for any Feast, moveable or unmoveable: Then the Psalms and Lessons appointed in the Calendar, shall be omitted for that time.

Ye must note also, that the Collect, Epistle, and Gospel, appointed for the Sunday, shall serve all the week after, except there fall some Feast that hath his proper.

When the years of our Lord may be divided into four even parts, which is every fourth year: then the Sunday letter leapeth, and that year the Psalms and Lessons which serve for the .xxiii. day of February shall be read again the day following, except it be Sunday, which hath proper Lessons of the Old Testament, appointed in the Table serving to that purpose.

Also, wheresoever the beginning of any Lesson, Epistle, or Gospel, is not expressed, there ye must begin at the beginning of the Chapter.

And wheresoever is not expressed how far shall be read, there shall you read to the end of the Chapter.

Item, so oft as the first Chapter of Saint Mathie[1] is read either for Lesson or Gospel: ye shall begin the same at. The birth of Jesus Christ was on this wise. &c. And the third Chapter of Saint Luke's Gospel shall be read unto. So that he was supposed to be the Son of Joseph.

[1 1596, Matthewe.]

1561.]   437

¶ Proper Lessons to be read for the first Lessons, both at Morning prayer[1] and Evening prayer, on the Sundays throughout the Year, and for some also the second Lessons.

Sundays of Advent.	Mattins.[2]	Evensong.[3]
The First	Esai. 1	Esai. 2
ii	5	24
iii	25	26
iv	30	32
Sundays after Christmas.	Mattins.	Evensong.
The First	37	38
ii	41	43
Sundays after the Epiphany.	Mattins.	Evensong.
The First	44	46
ii	51	53
iii	55	56
iv	57	58
v	59	64
Septuages.	Genesis 1	Genesis 2
Sexagesim.	3	6
Quinquage.	9	12
Lent.		
i Sunday	19	22
ii	27	34
iii	39	42
iv	43	45
v	Exod. 3	Exod. 5
vi	9	10
Easter day.	Mattins.	Evensong.
i Lesson	Exod. 12	Exod. 14
ii Lesson	Roma. 6	Acte. 2
¶ Sundays after Easter.		
The First	Nume. 16	Nume. 22
ii	23	25
iii	Deuter. 4	Deut. 5
iv	6	7
v	8	9

	Mattins.	Evensong.
Sunday after Ascension day.	Deut. 12	Deut. 13
Whitsunday.		
i Lesson	Deuter. 16	Wisdome. 1
ii Lesson	Acts 10	Acts 19
	Then Peter opened his. &c.	It fortuned when[4] Apollo went to Corinth. &c. unto. After these things.
Trinity Sunday.	Mattins.	Evensong.
i Lesson	Gene. 18	Josue. 1
ii Lesson	Math. 3	
Sundays after the[5] Trinity.		
The First	Josue. 10	Josue 23
ii	Judic. 4	Judic. 5
iii	1 King. 2	1 King. 3
iv	12	13
v	15	16[6]
vi	2 King. 12	2 King. 21
vii	22	24
viii	3 King. 13	3 King. 17
ix	18	19
x	21	22
xi	4 King. 5	4 King. 9
xii	10	18
xiii	19	23
xiv	Jerem. 5	Jerem. 22
xv	35	36
xvi	Ezech. 2	Ezech. 14
xvii	16	18
xviii	20	24
xix	Daniel 3	Daniel 6
xx	Joel 2	Miche. 6
xxi	Abacuk. 2	Proverb. 1
xxii	Proverb. 2	3
xxiii	11	12
xxiv	13	14
xxv	15	16
xxvi	17	19

[1] 1578 and 1596 omit, prayer.]
[3] 1578, *For Euening.* And so elsewhere.]
[4] 1596, that while Apollo was at Corin. &c.]
[5] 1596, after Trinitie.]

[2] 1578, *For Morning.* And so elsewhere.]

[6] 1596, xvii.]

Lessons proper for holy days.

	Mattins.	Evensong.		Mattins.	Evensong.
S. Andrew. S. Thomas the Apostle.	Prover. 20 23	Prover. 21 24	Purification of the Virgin Mary.	Wisdom 9	Wisdom 12
			Saint Mathie.	Wisdom 19	Eccle. 1
Nativity of Christ.			Annunciation of our Lady.	Eccle. 2	Eccle. 3
i Lesson	Esai. 9	Esai. 7. God spake once again to Achas. &c.	Wednesday afore Easter.	Osee 13	Osee 14
ii Lesson	Luke 2. unto. And unto men of good will.	Titu. 3. The kindness and love, &c.	Thursday afore Easter.	Daniel 9	Jere. 31
S. Steven.			Good Friday.	Gene 22	Esai. 53
i Lesson	Pro. 28	Eccle. 4	Easter Even.	Zachari. 9	Exod. 13
ii Lesson	Act 6 & 7. Stephen full of faith and power, &c. unto. And when xl. years, &c.	Acte 7. And when forty years were expired, there appeared unto Moses, &c. unto Stephen full of the holy, &c.	Monday in Easter week.		
			i Lesson	Exodi. 16	Exod. 17
			ii Lesson	Mat. 28	Act 3
			Tuesday in Easter week.		
			i Lesson	Exod. 20	Exod. 32
			ii Lesson	Luke 24 unto And behold two of them.	1 Corin. 15
Saint John.					
i Lesson	Eccle. 5	Eccle. 6			
ii Lesson	Apoca. 1	Apoca. 22			
Innocents.[1]	Jere 31, unto Moreover I heard Ephraim.	Wisdom 1	S. Mark.	Eccle. 4	Eccle. 5
			Philip[4] & Jacob.	Eccle. 7	Eccle. 9
Circumcision day.[2]			Ascension Day.	Deute. 10	4 King. 2
i Lesson	Gene 17	Deu. 10. And now Israel, &c.	Monday in Whitsun week.		
ii Lesson	Roma. 2	Colloss. 2	i Lesson	Gene. 11 unto These are the generation[5] of Sem.	Num. 11 Gather unto me lxx. men, &c. unto Moses and the elders returned.
Epiphany day.[3]					
i Lesson	Esai. 60	Esai. 49			
ii Lesson	Luke 3 unto So that he was supposed to be the son of Joseph.	John. 2 unto After this he went to Capernaum.	ii Lesson	1 Cor. 12	
Conversion of S. Paul.			Tuesday in Whitsun week.		
i Lesson	Wisdom 5	Wisdom 6		1 King. 19 David came to Saul[6] in Ramatha, &c.	Deute. 30
ii Lesson	Acte 22 unto They heard him.	Act 26			

[1 1596, Innocents day.]
[3 1596, Epiphanie.]
[5 1596, generations.]
[6 A misprint for, Samuel. 1596, to Samuel, to Rama, &c.]

[2 1596, Circumcision.]
[4 See p. 448, note 3.]

[1561.] 439

	Mattins.	Evensong.		Mattins.	Evensong.
S. Barnabe. i Lesson ii Lesson	Eccle. 10 Acte 14	Eccle. 12 Act. 15 unto After certain days.	Saint Matthew. Saint Michael. S. Luke.	Eccle. 35 39 51	Eccle. 38 44 Job 1
Saint John Baptist. i Lesson ii Lesson	Mala. 3 Math. 3[1]	Mala. 4 Math. 14 unto When Jesus heard.	S.[3] Simon & Jude. i Lesson All Saints. i Lesson	24. 25 Wisdom. 3 unto Blessed is rather the barren.	Job 42 Wisdome. 5 unto His jealousy also.
Saint Peter. i Lesson ii Lesson S. James. Saint Bartholomew.	Eccle. 15 Acts 3 Eccle. 21 25	Eccle. 19 Acts 4 Eccle. 23[2] 29	ii Lesson	Hebr. 11. 12 Saints by faith, unto If you endure chastening.	Apoca. 19 unto And I saw an Angel stand.

Proper Psalms on certain days.

	Mattins.	Evensong.		Mattins.	Evensong.
Christmas day.	Psal. 19 45 85	Psal. 89 110 132	Ascension day.	Psal. 8 15 21	Psal. 24 68 108
Easter day.	2 57 111	113 114 118	Whit Sunday.	45[4] 67[5]	104 145[6]

[1 1596, xiii. A misprint.]   [2 1596, xxii.; but 23 in the Calendar against July the 25th.]
[3 1596 omits, S.]   [4 See p. 44, note 2.]   [5 1578, lxviii. 1596, xlvii.]
[6 There follows in 1596—The Table for the order of the Psalmes, to be saide at Morning and Evening Prayer. After this comes immediately the Calendar.]

The[1] Almanack.

The Years of our Lord.	The Golden Number.	Dominical Letter.	Septuagesima.	[2] First day of Lent.	Easter day.	Rogation Week.	Ascension.[3]	Whit Sunday.	Advent Sunday.
1561	4	E.	2 Februa.	19 Febru.	6 April	12 Maii	15 Maii	25 Maii	30 Novem.
1562	5	D.	25 Janua.	11	29 March	4	7	17	29
1563	6	C.	7 Febru.	24	11 April	17	20	30	28
1564	7	B. A.	30 Janu.	16	2	8	11	21	3 Decem.
1565	8	G.	18 Febru.	7 March	22	28	31	10 June	2
1566	9	F.	10	27 Febru.	14	20	25	2	1
1567	10	E.	26 Janu.	12	30 March	5	8	18 Maii	30 Novem.
1568	11	D. C.	15 Febru.	3 March	18 April	24	27	6 June	28
1569	12	B.	6	23 Febru.	10	16	19	29 Maii	27
1570	13	A.	22 Janu.	8	26 March	1	4	14	3 Decem.
1571	14	G.	11 Febru.	28	15 April	21	24	3 June	2
1572	15	F. E.	3	20	6	12	15	25 Maii	30 Novem.
1573	16	D.	18 Janua.	4	22 March	27 April	30 April	10 Maii	29
1574	17	C.	7 Febru.	24	11 April	17 Maii	20 Maii	30	28
1575	18	B.	30 Janua.	16	3	9	12	22	27
1576	19	A. G.	19 Febr.	7 March	22	28	31	10	2 Decem.
1577	1	F.	3	20 Febru.	7	13	16	26	1
1578	2	E.	26 Janu.	12	30 March	5	8	18	30 Novem.
1579	3	D.	15 Febru.	4 March	19 April	25	28	7 Junii	29
1580	4	C. B.	31 Janua.	17 Febru.	3	9	12	22	27
1581	5	A.	22	8	26 March	1	4	14	3 Decem.
1582	6	G.	11 Febru.	28	15 April	21	24	3 Junii	2
1583	7	F.	27 Janu.	13	31 March	6	9	19 Maii	1
1584	8	E. D.	16 Febru.	3 March	19 April	25	28	7 Junii	29 Novem.
1585	9	C.	7	24 Febru.	11	17	20	30 Maii	28
1586	10	B.	30 Janu.	16	3	9	12	22	27
1587	11	A.	12 Febru.	1 March	16	22	25	4 Junii	3 Decem.
1588	12	G. F.	4 Febru.	21 Febru.	7	13	16	26 Maii	1
1589	13	E.	26 Janu.	12 Febru.	30 March	5	8	18	30 Novem.
1590	14	D.	15 Febru.	4 March	19 April	25	28	7 June	29

[[1] 1596, An.]   [[2] 1596, The first.]   [[3] 1596, Ascension day.]

Note, that the supputation of the year of our Lord, in the Church of England, beginneth the .xxv. day of March, the same day supposed to be the first day upon which the world was created, and the day when Christ was conceived in the womb of the Virgin Mary.

1578. ¶ *Of the Golden number.* The Golden number is so called, because it was written in the Kalender with letters of golde, right at that daye whereon the Moone changed: and it is the space of 19. yeeres, in the which the Moone returneth to the selfe same daye of the yeere of the Sunne: and therefore it is also called the Cycle of the Moone, in the which the Solstices and Equinoctials doe returne to all one point in the Zodiaque.

To finde it euerie yeere, you must adde one yeere to the yeere of Christ (for Christ was borne one yeere of the 19. already past) then diuide the whole by 19, and that which resteth is the Golden number for that yeere; if there be no surplusage, it is then 19.

¶ *The Epact.* *Epactæ hemeræ* in Greeke, doeth signifie in Englishe, dayes set betwene, and therefore the 11. dayes and 3 houres, that are added to the yeere of the Moone, are called *Epactæ,* and are added to make the yeere of the Moone, which is but 354. dayes, iust with the yeere of the Sunne, which hath 365. dayes and a quarter.

To finde out the Epact of eche yeere, doe thus. To the Epact[1] of the yeere that last went before that yeere for which you would finde the Epact, adde 11. and the summe of these two make the Epact. If it surmount 30. then take 30. out, and that which resteth aboue 30, is the Epact you desire.

¶ *The vse of the Epact.* To knowe howe olde the Moone is at any time for euer by the Epact, doe thus: Adde unto the dayes of your moneth, wherein you woulde knowe this, the Epact, and as many dayes moe as are monethes from March to that moneth, including both monethes, out of the which Substract 30. as often as you may, the age remaineth: if nothing remaine, the Moone changeth that day.

¶ For the more ease of the Reader, we have placed hereouer an Almanacke, inclusively comprehending, not onely howe to finde the Epact for the space of xxxii. yeeres to come, but also the Golden number afore specified, together with the Dominicall letter, Leape yeere, and vii. other moueable feastes, or dayes in the yeere, during the same time, as may appeare.

Note, that the Golden number and Dominicall letter doeth change euery yeere the first day of Januarie, and the Epact the first day of March for euer. Note also, that the yeere of our Lorde beginneth the xxv. day of March, the same day supposed to be the first day vpon which the worlde was created, and the day when Christ was conceived in the wombe of the virgin Marie.

[1] The Epact for 1578 was xxii.]

To find Easter for ever.

Golden Number.	A	B	C	D	E	F	G
I	April 9	10	11	12	6	7	8
II	March 26	27	28	29	30	31	April 1
III	April 16	17	18	19	20	14	15
IV	April 9	3	4	5	6	7	8
V	March 26	27	28	29	23	24	25
VI	April 16	17	11	12	13	14	15
VII	April 2	3	4	5	6	Mar. 31	April 1
VIII	April 23	24	25	19	20	21	22
IX	April 9	10	11	12	13	14	8
X	April 2	3	March 28	29	30	31	April 1
XI	April 16	17	18	19	20	21	22
XII	April 9	10	11	5	6	7	8
XIII	March 26	27	28	29	30	31	25
XIV	April 16	17	18	19	13	14	15
XV	April 2	3	4	5	6	7	8
XVI	March 26	27	28	22	23	24	25
XVII	April 16	10	11	12	13	14	15
XVIII	April 2	3	4	5	Mar. 30	31	April 1
XIX	April 23	24	18	19	20	21	22

When ye have found the Sunday Letter in the uppermost line, guide your eye downward from the same, till ye come right over against the prime, and there is shewed both what month, and what day of the month, Easter falleth that year.

Septuagesima		9
Sexagesima	before Easter	8
Quinquagesima		7
Quadragesima		6
Rogations		5
Whitsunday	after Easter	7
Trinity Sunday		8

before Easter — weeks.
after Easter — weeks.

¶ These to be observed for Holy days, and none other.'

That is to say: All Sundays in the year. The days of the Feasts of the Circumcision of our Lord Jesus Christ. Of the Epiphany. Of the Purification of the blessed Virgin. Of Saint Mathie[1] the Apostle. Of the Annunciation of the blessed Virgin. Of Saint Mark the Evangelist. Of Saint Philip & Jacob the Apostles. Of the ascension of our Lord Jesus Christ. Of the Nativity of Saint John Baptist. Of Saint Peter the Apostle. Of Saint James the Apostle. Of Saint Bartholomew Apostle. Of Saint Mathew the Apostle. Of Saint Michael the Archangel. Of Saint Luke the Evangelist. Of Saint Simon and Jude the Apostles. Of All Saints. Of Saint Andrew the Apostle. Of Saint Thomas the Apostle. Of the Nativity of our Lord. Of Saint Stephen the Martyr. Of Saint John the Evangelist. Of the holy Innocents. Monday and Tuesday in Easter week, and[2] Monday and Tuesday in Whitsun week.

¶ A brief declaration when every Term beginneth and endeth.

Be it known that Easter Term beginneth always the .xviii. day after Easter, reckoning Easter day for one : and endeth the Monday next after the Ascension day.

Trinity Term beginneth .xii. days after Whitsunday, and continueth xix. days.

Michaelmas Term beginneth the .ix. or .x. day of October, and endeth the .xxviii. or .xxix. day of November.

Hilary Term beginneth the .xxiii. or .xxiv. day of January, and endeth the .xii. or .xiii. day of February.

In Easter Term, on the Ascension day. in Trinity Term, on the Nativity of Saint John Baptist. in Michaelmas Term, on the feast of All Saints. in Hilary Term, on the Feast of the Purification of our Lady: the Queen's Judges of Westminster do not use to sit in Judgment, nor upon any Sundays.

[1 1596, Matthias.]   [2 1596 omits, and.]

January hath xxxi. days[1].

Sun	riseth / falleth	hour	8² mi. 3. / 3 mi. 57.	Psalms.	Morning Prayer.		Evening Prayer.	
					1 Lesson.	2 Lesson.	1 Lesson.	2 Lesson.
³3 A	Kalend.	Circumcision[4]......		1	Gen. 17	Roma. 2	Deut. 10	Coloss. 2
b	4 No.	....		2	Gene. 1	Math. 1	Gene. 2	Roma. 1
11 c	3 No.	....		3	3	2	4	{2
d	Prid. No.	....		4	5	3	6	3
19 e	Nonas.	....		5	7	4	8	4
8 f	8 Id.	Epiphany............		6	Esay 60	Luke 3	Esai 49	1⁷ Joh. 2
g	7 Id.	....		7	Gene. 9	Math. 5	Gene. 12	Roma. 5
16 A	6 Id.	Lucian................		8	13	6	14	6
5 b	5 Id.	....		9	15	7	16	7
c	4 Id.	Sol⁵ in Aquario.....		10	17	8	18	8
13 d	3 Id.	....		11	19	9	20	9
2 e	Prid. Id.	....		12	21	10	22	10
f	Idus.	Hillary...............		13	23	11	24	11
10 g	19 Kl.	Februarii.............		14	25	12	26	12
A	18 Kl.	....		15	27	13	28	13
18 b	17 Kl.	....		16	29	14	30	14
7 c	16 Kl.	....		17	31	15	32	15
d	15 Kl.	Prisca................		18	33	16	34	16
15 e	14 Kl.	....		19	35	17	37	1 Cor. 1
4 f	13 Kl.	Fabian...............		20	38	18	39	2
g	12 Kl.	Agnes...............		21	40	19	41	3
12 A	11 Kl.	Vincent..............		22	42	20	43	4
1 b	10 Kl.	....		23	44	21	45	5
c	9 Kl.	....		24	46	22	47	6
9 d	8 Kl.	Conver. Paul........		25	Wisd. 5	Act. 22	Wisd. 6	Act. 26
e	7 Kl.	....		26	Gene. 48	Mat. 13⁶	Gen. 49	1 Cor. 7
17 f	6 Kl.	....		27	50	24	Exod. 1	8
6 g	5 Kl.	....		28	Exod. 2	25	3	9
A	4 Kl.	....		29	4	26	5	10
14 b	3 Kl.	....		30	7	27	8	11
3 c	Prid. Kl.	....		1	9	28	10	12

[¹ 1596, The Moone xxx.]
[² In 1596 the time of the Sun's rising and falling varies throughout.]
[³ 1596 has quite a different set of Golden Numbers. It has also a column, which comes second, for the days of the month.]
[⁴ Red letter days are marked in Italics.]
[⁵ In 1596 this is placed against the twelfth day of the month.]
[⁶ A misprint for, xxiii.]   [⁷ A misprint for, Joh. ii.]

1578. JANUARIE.

1. The first day of this moneth, Noah, after he had bene in the Arke 150 dayes, began to see the toppes of the high mountaines. *Gene.* 7. 24. and 8. 3, 5.

Also as vpon this day, Christ was circumcised according to the Lawe. *Luke* 2. 21.

6. The Magians as vpon this day (hauing ben guided vnto Beth-lehem by the direction of a starre) worshipped Christ, and offered vnto him golde, mirrhe, and frankensence. *Matth.* 2. 1. *usque* 13.

Also as vpon this day, Christ was baptized by John in Jordan, being about xxx. yeeres of age. *Matth.* 3. 13. *Luke* 3. 21, 23.

Also Christ as vpon this day, wrought his first miracle, in turning water into wine, at a marriage in Cana of Galile. *John* 2. 2, 11.

10. Nebuchad-nezzar the king of Babel as vpon this day, besieged the Citie of Jerusalem. 2 *Kings* 25. 1. *Jere.* 52. 4.

17. The good Prince Scanderbeg king of Epyrus, a scourge to the Turke, as vpon this day, died. 1466.

22. The Duke of Somerset as vpon this day, was beheaded. 1552.

25. Caius Caligula, his wife and daughter, as vpon this day, were slaine. *Anno Do.* 42.

27. Saint Paul, as vpon this day, of a persecuter was conuerted, as he iourneyed vnto Damascus. *Actes* 9. 3.

1561.]   445

¶ February hath xxviii. days[1].

Sun { riseth / falleth } hour { 7 mi. 14. / 4 mi. 46. }				Psalms.	Morning Prayer.		Evening Prayer.	
					1 Lesson.	2 Lesson.	1 Lesson.	2 Lesson.
	d	Kalend.	Fast	2	Exod. 11	Marke 1	Exod. 12	1 Cor. 13
11	e	4 No.	*Puri. Mary*.........	3	Wi sd. 9	2	Wisd. 12	14
19	f	3 No.	Blasii..................	4	E xo. 13	3	Exo. 14	15
8	g	Prid. No.	....	5	15	4	16	16
	A	Nonas.	Agathe.	6	17	5	18	2 Cor. 1
15	b	8 Id.	....	7	19	6	20	2
5	c	7 Id.	....	8	21	7	22	3
	d	6 Id.	Sol[2] in Piscibus.....	9	23	8	24	4
13	e	5 Id.	....	10	32	9	33	5
2	f	4 Id.	....	11	34	10	Levit. 18	6
	g	3 Id.	....	12	Levi. 19	11	20	7
10	A	Prid. Id.	....	13	26	12	Nume. 11	8
	b	Idus.	....	14	Num. 12	13	13	9
17	c	16 Kl.	Valentine...............	15	14	14	16	10
7	d	15 Kl.	Martii..................	16	17	15	20	11
	e	14 Kl.	....	17	21	16	22	12
15	f	13 Kl.	....	18	23	Luke [3]1	24	13
4	g	12 Kl.	....	19	25	di. 1.	27	Galath. 1
	A	11 Kl.	....	20	30	2	31	2
12	b	10 Kl.	....	21	32	3	35	3
1	c	9 Kl.	....	22	36	4	Deut. 1	4
	d	8 Kl.	....	23	Deut. 2	5	3	5
9	e	7 Kl.	Fast	24	4	6	5	6
	f	6 Kl.	*S. Mathias*............	25	Wisd. 19	7	Eccle. 1	Ephes. 1
17	g	5 Kl.	....	26	Deut. 6	8	Deut. 7	2
6	A	4 Kl.	....	27	8	9	9	3
	b	3 Kl.	....	28	10	10	11	4
14	c	Prid. Kl.	....	29	12	11	15	5

[1 1596, The Moone xxix.]
[2 1596 has this against the eleventh day of the month.]
[3 1596, Lu. di. i.]

1578. FEBRUARIE.

2. As vpon this day, Christ our Saviour was offered vnto the Lord in the Temple at Jerusalem, and his mother, the Virgin Marie, was purified according to the law. *Luke* 2. 22.

8. As vpon this day, the Romanes began their spring, after Plinie.

9. As vpon this day, Noah (fourtie daies after he had seene the toppes of the mountaines) sent out of the Arke the Rauen, and after the Doue, of the which only the Doue returned. *Gene*. 8. 7, 8.

14. The Jewes, as vpon this day, slewe three hundreth of their enemies, in Shushan, but yet on the spoyle they layd not their hand. *Ester* 9. 15.

15. The Jewes kept this day for a feast, because nowe the sappe riseth in the trees.

16. The learned Clerke, Philip Melanthon, as vpon this day, was borne. *Anno* 1497.

17. Noah, as vpon this day, sent out of the Arke againe the Doue, which returning vnto him, brought an Oliue branche in her bill, whereby he knewe, that the waters were abated vpon the earth. *Gene*. 8. 10, 11.

18. Martin Luther, the seruant of God, died as vpon this day. *Anno* 1546.

22. Martin Luther his body, as vpon this day, was translated to Witemberg, and buried in the chappell of the Castell there.

25. Noah, as vpon this day, sent the Doue out of the Arke the third time, and she returned no more. *Gene*. 8. 12.

¶ March hath xxxi. days[1].

Sun			hour		Psalms.	Morning Prayer.		Evening Prayer.	
		riseth falleth		6 mi. 18. 5 mi. 42.		1 Lesson.	2 Lesson.	1 Lesson.	2 Lesson.
3	d	Kalend.	Davyd............		30	Deu. 16	Luke 12	Deute. 17	Ephe. 6
	e	6 No.	Cedde		1	18	13	19	Philip. 1
11	f	5 No.			2	20	14	21	2
	g	4 No.			3	22	15	24	3
19	A	3 No.			4	25	16	26	4
8	b	Prid. No.			5	27	17	28	Coloss. 1
	c	Nonas.	Perpetue.		6	29	18	30	2
16	d	8 Id.			7	31	19	32	3
5	e	7 Id.			8	33	20	34	4
	f	6 Id.			9	Josue. 1	21	Josue 2	1 Thes. 1
13	g	5 Id.			10	3	22	4	2
2	A	4 Id.	Gregory..........		11	5	23	6	3
	b	3 Id.	Sol in Ariete....		12	7	24	8	4
10	c	Prid. Id.			13	9	John 1	10	5
	d	Idus.			14	23	2	24	2 Thes. 1
18	e	17 Kl.			15	Judg. 1	3	Judg. 2	2
7	f	16 Kl.	Aprilis[2]........		16	3	4	4	3
	g	15 Kl.	Edward		17	5	5	6	1 Tim. 1
15	A	14 Kl.			18	7	6	8	2. 3.
4	b	13 Kl.			19	9	7	10	4
	c	12 Kl.	Benedict........		20	11	8	12	5
12	d	11 Kl.			21	13	9	14	6
1	e	10 Kl.			22	15	10	16	2 Tim. 1
	f	9 Kl.	Fast		23	17	11	18	2
9	g	8 Kl.	Annun. of Ma...		24	Eccle. 2	12	Eccle. 3	3
	A	7 Kl.			25	Judg. 19	13	Judg. 20	4
17	b	6 Kl.			26	Judi. 21	14	Ruth 1	Titus. 1
6	c	5 Kl.			27	Ruth 2	15	3	2. 3.
	d	4 Kl.			28	4	16	1 King. 1	Phile. 1
14	e	3 Kl.			29	1 King. 2	17	3	Hebre. 1
3	f	Prid. Kl.			30	4	18	5	2

[1 1596, The Moone xxx.]
[2 1596 has this more correctly against the previous day.]

1578. MARCH.

3. As vpon this day, the Temple of Jerusalem was finished and holied, 597. yeeres before Christ his birth. *Ezra* 6. 15. and I *Esdr.* 7. 5.

10. As vpon this day, Christ being on the other side of Jordan, was aduertised of the sicknesse of Lazarus. *John* 11. 3.

13. As on this day, was the fast of Ester. *Ester* 3. 12. and 4. 16.

16. As vpon this day, Lazarus was raised from death. *John* 11. 44.

20. As vpon this day, Christ entred into Jerusalem. *John* 12. 14, 15.

22. Marie Magdalen, as on this day, annointed Christ with precious oyntment. *John* 12. 3. *Matth.* 26. 7, 12.

24. Christ held his last supper, as vpon this day, and was taken. *Matth.* 26. 20.

25. Christ was crucified, dead and buried, as vpon this day. *Luke* 23. 33. *Mark* 15. 25. *Mat.* 27. 35.

This day also, was the day of preparation. *John* 19. 31, 42.

26. Christ as on this day, lay in the Sepulchre. *Matth.* 27. 62.

27. As vpon this day, was the resurrection of Christ. *Matth.* 28. 1, 2. *Luke* 24. 1.

Also as vpon this day, Jehoachin, king of Judah, was deliuered out of prison, by Euil Merodach King of Babylon, who after had his allowance at the Kinges table, all the dayes of his life. ii *King* 25. 27, 29, 30.

1561.]   447

❡ April hath xxx. days[1].

Sun					Psalms.	Morning Prayer.		Evening Prayer.	
		riseth falleth	hour	6 mi. 17. 6 mi. 43.		1 Lesson.	2 Lesson.	1 Lesson.	2 Lesson.
	g	Kalend.	....		1	1 King. 6	Joh. 19	1 King. 7	Hebre. 3
11	A	4 No.	....		2	8	20	9	4
	b	3 No.	Richard........		3	10	21	11	5
19	c	Prid. No.	Ambrose........		4	12	Acte 1	13	6
8	d	Nonas.	....		5	14	2	15	7
16	e	8 Id.	....		6	16	3	17	8
5	f	7 Id.	....		7	18	4	19	9
	g	6 Id.	....		8	20	5	21	10
13	A	5 Id.	....		9	22	6	23	11
2	b	4 Id.	Sol in Tauro[3]		10	24	7	25	12
	c	3 Id.	....		11	26	8	27	13
[2]	d	Prid. Id.	....		12	28	9	29	Jacobi. 1
	e	Idus.	....		13	30	10	31	2
18	f	18 Kl.	Maii...........		14	2 King. 1	11	2 King. 2	3
7	g	17 Kl.	....		15	3	12	4	4
	A	16 Kl.	....		16	5	13	6	5
15	b	15 Kl.	....		17	7	14	8	1 Petr. 1
4	c	14 Kl.	....		18	9	15	10	2
	d	13 Kl.	Alphege.......		19	11	16	12	3
12	e	12 Kl.	....		20	13	17	14	4
1	f	11 Kl.	....		21	15	18	16	5
	g	10 Kl.	....		22	17	19	18	2 Pet. 1
9	A	9 Kl.	S. George.....		23	19	20	20	2
	b	8 Kl.	....		24	21	21	22	3
17	c	7 Kl.	Mark Evan.....		25	Eccl. 4	22	Eccle. 5	1 John 1
6	d	6 Kl.	....		26	2 Kin. 23	23	2 Kin. 24	2
	e	5 Kl.	....		27	3 Kin. 1	24	3 King. 2	3
14	f	4 Kl.	....		28	3	25	4	4
3	g	3 Kl.	....		29	5	26	6	5
	A	Prid. Kl.	....		30	7	27	8	2. 3 Jo.

[1 1596, The Moone xxix.]   [2 10, omitted.]
[3 1596 has this one day later.]

1578. APRIL.

1. In this first day, Noah opened the couer of the Arke. *Gene.* 8. 13. Also as vpon this day, Moses reared the Tabernacle. *Exod.* 40. 2, 17.
4. Christ, as vpon this day, which was eyght dayes after his resurrection, appeared to his disciples, Thomas also being present. *John* 20. 26.
6. Joshua and the Jewes camped before Jordan, the space of three dayes. *Joshua* 3. 1.
10. The Israelites as vpon this day, passe Jordan with a great multitude, the yeere before the Natiuitie of our Lord Jesus Christ 1457. *Joshu.* 3. 17. and 4. 1, 11.
11. Joshua circumcised the people nigh Jericho. *Joshua* 5. 3.
13. King Ahashuerosh as vpon this day, commanded all ye Jewes to be slaine. *Ester* 3. 11, 13.
14. The Israelites vpon this day kept passouer, and Man ceased. *Joshua* 5. 10, 12.
15. Moses, as on this day, brought the Israelites out of Egypt. *Exod.* 12. 37, 41.
16. As on this day, they departed from Succoth into the desert of Etham. *Exo.* 13. 20. *Nom.* 33. 6.
17. As on this day, they passed into the mountaines and daungerous places. *Exodus* 14. 2. *Nomb.* 33. 7.
18. As on this day they went through the red Sea. *Exod.* 14. 29. *Nomb.* 33. 8.
19. As on this day, they wander in the desert of Shur, and came to Marah. *Ex.* 15. 22. *Nom.* 33. 8.

❧ May hath xxxi. days[1].

Sun { riseth / falleth } hour { 5 mi. 48. / 7 mi. 13.			Psalms	Morning Prayer.		Evening Prayer.	
				1 Lesson.	2 Lesson.	2 Lesson.	2 Lesson.
11	b	Kalend.	Philip & Ja..........	1	Eccle. 7	Acte. 8[3].	Eccle. 9	Judas 1
19	c	6 No.	....	2	3 King. 9	28	3 King. 10	Roma. 1
8	d	5 No.	Inven. of the Cro...	3	11	Math. 1	12	2
	e	4 No.	....	4	13	2	14	3
16	f	3 No.	....	5	15	3	16	4
5	g	Prid. No.	John Evang..........	6	17	4	18	5
	A	Nonas.	....	7	19	5	20	6
13	b	8 Id.	....	8	21	6	22	7
2	c	7 Id.	....	9	4 King. 1	7	4 King. 2	8
	d	6 Id.	....	10	3	8	4	9
10	e	5 Id.	Sol in Gemini[2]......	11	5	9	6	10
	f	4 Id.	....	12	7	10	8	11
18	g	3 Id.	....	13	9	11	10	12
7	A	Prid. Id.	....	14	11	12	12	13
	b	Idus.	....	15	13	13	14	14
15	c	17 Kl.	Junii............	16	15	14	16	15
4	d	16 Kl.	....	17	17	15	18	16
	e	15 Kl.	....	18	19	16	20	1 Cor. 1
12	f	14 Kl.	Dunstane.	19	21	17	22	2
1	g	13 Kl.	....	20	23	18	24	3
	A	12 Kl.	..........,..........	21	25	19	1 Esd.1[4]	4
9	b	11 Kl.	....	22	1 Esd. 3	20	4	5
	c	10 Kl.	....	23	5	21	6	6
17	d	9 Kl.	....	24	7	22	9	7
6	e	8 Kl.	....	25	2 Esd. 1	23	2 Esd. 2	8
	f	7 Kl.	Augustine	26	4	24	5	9
14	g	6 Kl.	....	27	6	25	8	10
3	A	5 Kl.	....	28	9	26	10	11
	b	4 Kl.	....	29	13	27	Hester 1	12
11	c	3 Kl.	....	30	Hester 2	28	3	13
	d	Prid. Kl.	....	30	4	Mark 1.	5	14

[1 1596, The Moone xxx.]   [2 In 1596 this is placed later by one day.]
[3 This lesson was appointed by the Prayer Book of 1549, and appeared invariably in the Calendar from that year until the last review.]   [4 1596, i. Esdr. ii.]

1578. MAY.

1. As vpon this day, Moses and Aaron numbred the people of Israel, the second yeere after their comming out of Egypt. *Nom.* 3 and 4 *Chapters.*
5. As vpon this day, Christ ascended into heauen, in the sight of his Apostles, and many others. *Mark* 16. 19. *Actes* 1. 9.
10. God commaunded Noah, as vpon this day, to carrie foode into the Arke for himselfe his houshold, and for such as were preserued with him. *Gene.* 6. 21.
14. Those that had not kept the feast of Passeouer the first day of the first moneth, kept it as vpon this day of the second moneth. *Nomb.* 9. 11. and so did Hezekiah. 2 *Chron.* 30. 15.
15. As vpon this day, ye Jewes kept their Whitsontide. And also as vpon the same day, God sent the Jewes Quailes for their foode. *Exod.* 16. 13. *Nomb.* 11. 31.
16. God, as vpon this day, rained ye foode Man from heauen. *Exod.* 16. 13, 14, 15.
17. Noah, as vpon this day, at God's commaundment entred the Arke. *Gen.* 7. 7, 11.
20. As vpon this day, ye Israelites departed from Sinai. *Nomb.* 10. 11, 12.
22. As vpon this day, part of the Israelites, for their murmuring, were consumed with fire. *Nomb.* 11. 1.
27. Noah, as vpon this day, was commaunded by God, to go forth of the Arke. *Gene.* 8. 14, 16.

[1561.] 449

☾ June hath xxx. days[1].

Sun { riseth / falleth }	hour { 4 mi. 48. / 8 mi. 13. }	Psalms.	Morning Prayer.		Evening Prayer.	
			1 Lesson.	2 Lesson.	1 Lesson.	2 Lesson.
e	Kalend.	Nichomede[2].........	1	Hester 6	Mark 2	Hester 7	1 Cor. 15
19 f	4 No.	....	2	8	3	9	16
8 g	3 No.	....	3	Job 1	4	Job 2	2 Cor. 1
16 A	Prid. No.	....	4	3	5	4	2
5 b	Nonas.	Boniface...............	5	5	6	6	3
c	8 Id.	....	6	7	7	8	4
13 d	7 Id.	....	7	9	8	10	5
2 e	6 Id.	....	8	11	9	12	6
f	5 Id.	....	9	13	10	14	7
10 g	4 Id.	....	10	15	11	16	8
A	3 Id.	Barnabe apo.........	11	Eccle. 10	Act. 14	Eccle. 12	Actes 15
18 b	Prid. Id.	Sol in Cancro.........	12	Job 17.18	Mar. 12	Job 19	1[5] Cor. 9
7 c	Idus.	Solsticium æstivum	13	20	13	21	10
d	18 Kl.	[3]	14	22	14	23	11
15 e	17 Kl.	....	15	24. 25	15	26. 27	12
4 f	16 Kl.	....	16	28	16	29	13
g	15 Kl.	....	17	30	Luke. 1	31	Galath. 1
12 A	14 Kl.	....	18	32	2	33	2
1 b	13 Kl.	....	19	34	3	35	3
c	12 Kl.	Edwarde...............	20	36	4	37	4
9 d	11 Kl.	....	21	38	5	29[4]	5
e	10 Kl.	....	22	40	6	41	6
17 f	9 Kl.	Fast	23	42	7	Prov. 1	Ephes. 1
6 g	8 Kl.	John Baptist.	24	Mala. 3	Mat. 3	Mal. 4	Math. 14
A	7 Kl.	....	25	Prov. 2	Luk. 8	Prov. 3	Ephes. 2
14 b	6 Kl.	....	26	4	9	5	3
3 c	5 Kl.	....	27	6	10	7	4
d	4 Kl.	Fast	28	8	11	9	5
11 e	3 Kl.	S. Peter apo.........	29	Eccle. 15	Act. 3	Eccle. 19	Act. 4
f	Prid. Kl.	....	30	Prov. 10	Luke 12	Prov. 11	Ephe. 6

[[1] 1596, The Moone xxix.]
[[3] Julii, omitted.]
[[5] A misprint for, ii.]
[[2] 1596 has, Nicomede, against the third day.]
[[4] A misprint for, xxxix.]

1578. JUNE.

1. The people of Israel, as vpon this day, came vnto yᵉ mount Sinai, which afterward was called the hill of Casius, and there taried almost a yeere, as apeareth, *Exod.* 19. 1. *Nomb.* 10. 11. *Deut.* 1. 19.
6. The Temple of Diana in Ephesus, which amongst all Panims Temples was the most magnificent and renoumed, as vpon this day, was consumed with fire liiii yeeres before the Natiuitie of Jesus Christ.
20. Godfrey and Baldwine with their Christian armie, as vpon this day, ouercame the Persians at Antiochia, in a memorable conflict. *Benedic. de Aculf.*
23. The King Ahashuerosh, as on this day, sent forth a proclamation throughout all his countrey and prouinces, in yᵉ favour of the Jewes, and against Haman and his conspiration, as apeareth, *Ester.* 8. 9. &c.
25. As on this day, was the conflict at Mersbrough, betweene the Emperour Henrie the fourth and Rodolfe duke of Sueuia, stickled forth by the Pope. *Anno* 1080.
27. After the flood had been fourtie dayes vpon the earth, the waters were so increased, that Noah's arke was lifted vp as vpon this day, aboue the earth. *Gene.* 7. 17.

[LITURG. QU. ELIZ.]

450   [1561.

ℭ July hath xxxi. days[1].

Sun				Psalms.	Morning Prayer.		Evening Prayer.	
{ riseth falleth }		hour { 4 mi. 53. 8 mi. 7. }			1 Lesson.	2 Lesson.	1 Lesson.	2 Lesson.
19	g	Kalend.	....	1	Prov. 12	Luke 13	Pro. 13	Philip. 1
8	A	6 No.	Visitaci. Ma.[3]	2	14	14	15	2
	b	5 No.	....	3	16	15	17	3
16	c	4 No.	Martin	4	18	16	19	4
5	d	3 No.	....	5	20	17	21	Coloss. 1
	e	Prid. No.	....	6	22	18	23	2
13	f	[2]	Dog days	7	24	19	25	3
2	g	8 Id.	....	8	26	20	27	4
	A	7 Id.	....	9	28	21	29	1 Tessa. 1
10	b	6 Id.	....	10	31	22	Eccle. 1	2
	c	5 Id.	....	11	Eccle. 2	23	3	3
18	d	4 Id.	....	12	4	24	5	4
7	e	3 Id.	Sol in Leone........	13	6	John 1	7	5
	f	Prid. Id.	....	14	8	2	9	2 Tess. 1
15	g	Idus.	Swithune	15	10	3	11	2
4	A	17 Kl.	Augusti	16	12	4	Jere. 1	3
	b	16 Kl.	....	17	Jere. 2	5	3	1 Tim. 1
12	c	15 Kl.	....	18	4	6	5	2. 3.
1	d	14 Kl.	....	19	6	7	7	4
	e	13 Kl.	Margaret............	20	8	8	9	5
9	f	12 Kl.	....	21	10	9	11	6
	g	11 Kl.	Magdalen	22	12	10	13	2 Tim. 1
17	A	10 Kl.	....	23	14	11	15	2
6	b	9 Kl.	Fast	24	16	12	17	3
	c	8 Kl.	James apo.	25	Eccle. 21	13	Eccle. 23	4
14	d	7 Kl.	Anne	26	Jer. 18	14	Jere. 19	Titus 1
3	e	6 Kl.	....	27	20	15	21	2. 3
	f	5 Kl.	....	28	22	16	23	Phile. 1
11	g	4 Kl.	....	29	24	17	25	Hebre. 1
	A	3 Kl.	....	30	26	18	27	2
19	b	Prid. Kl.	....	30	28	19	29	3

[1 1596, The Moone xxx.]
[2 Nonas, omitted.]
[3 In 1596 this comes one day earlier: so also the next three.]

1578. JULY.

6. The vi. day of this moneth, the Josias of our age, Edward the sixt, King of England, dyed. *Anno.* 1553.

8. John Hus was burnt as on this day, at the councell holden at Constance, for professing the Gospel of our Lord Jesus. *Anno* 1415.

9. As on this day, Jerusalem was besieged by the king of Babel, the space of eighteene moneths, and at length was taken. 2 *Kings* 25. 3. and Zedekiah's son slayne before his face, and after had his owne eyes put out. *Jeremi.* 39. 2, 7.

12. As on this day was the birth of C. Julius Cæsar, the first Emperour of Rome, of whome this moneth is so called.

15. About this time the great Sweat began in England. *Anno* 1551.

17. As on this day, Moses in his anger, being thereunto prouoked by the Idolatrie of the people, brake the two Tables of stone, which hee had receyued of the Lorde in the mount. *Exod.* 32. 19.

19. As on this day, the great hurt by fire began at Rome in Neroe's reigne.

23. As on this day, Pope Alexander the third treadeth upon Frederick Barbarossa the Emperour.

27. As vpon this day, the Athenians receyved a great ouerthrowe in Sicilia, of the Syracusians.

1561.]   451

☞ August hath xxx. days[1].

Sun { riseth falleth } hour { 4 mi. 37. 7 mi. 23. }	Psalms	Morning Prayer.		Evening Prayer.	
		1 Lesson.	2 Lesson.	1 Lesson.	2 Lesson.

8	c	Kalend.	Lammas...............	1	Jere. 30	John 20	Jere. 31	Hebr. 4
16	d	4 No.		2	32	21	33	5
5	e	3 No.		3	34	Actes 1	35	6
	f	Prid. No.		4	36	2	37	7
13	g	Nonas.		5	38	3	39	8
2	A	8 Id.	Transfigu.............	6	40	4	41	9
	b	7 Id.	The Name of Je....	7	42	5	43	10
10	c	6 Id.		8	44	6	45. 46	11
	d	5 Id.		9	47	7	48	12
18	e	4 Id.	Laurence.............	10	49	8	50	13
7	f	3 Id.		11	51	9	52	Jacob. 1
	g	Prid. Id.		12	Lament.1	10	Lament.2	2
15	A	Idus.		13	3	11	4	3
4	b	19 Kl.		14	5	12	Ezech. 2	4
	c	18 Kl.	Sol in Virgine[2]....	15	Ezech. 3	13	6	5
12	d	17 Kl.		16	7	14	13	1 Peter 1
1	e	16 Kl.	Septembris...........	17	14	15	18	2
	f	15 Kl.		18	33	16	34	3
9	g	14 Kl.		19	Daniel 1	17	Dani. 2	4
	A	13 Kl.		20	3	18	4	5
17	b	12 Kl.		21	5	19	6	2 Peter 1
6	c	11 Kl.		22	7	20	8	2
	d	10 Kl.	Fast	23	9	21	10	3
14	e	9 Kl.	Bartho. apo.	24	Eccle. 25	22	Eccle. 29	1 John 1
3	f	8 Kl.		25	Dani. 11	23	Dani. 12	2
	g	7 Kl.		26	13	24	14	3
11	A	6 Kl.		27	Ose. 1	25	Ose. 2. 3	4
	b	5 Kl.	Augustine	28	4	26	5. 6	5
19	c	4 Kl.	Behead. of Joh......	29	7	27	8	2.3. Joh.
8	d	3 kl.		30	9	28	10	Jude 1
	e	Prid. Kl.		30	11	Math. 1	12	Roma. 1

[1 1596, The Moone xxix.]
[2 This and the following are out of their places: 1596 puts them three days higher.]

1578. AUGUST.

1. Aaron as vpon this day, being 123 yeeres olde, dyed vpon the mountaine Hor, 40 yeeres after the children of Israel's coming out of Egypt. *Nomb.* 20. 25, 28. and 33. 38, 39.

7. Nebuzar-adan, as on this day, setteth ye citie and Temple of Jerusalem on fire. 2 *King* 25. 8, 9.

8. Henrie the 4. Emperour, as on this day dyed with sorowe, constrained thereunto by the Pope's iniuries.

10. Titus soldiours, as on this day, set the Citie and Temple of Jerusalem on fire, sithens which time neither of them haue euer bin reedified. *Joseph. lib.* 6. *Chap.* 26.

As on this day also, Ezra the Scribe entreth into Jerusalem with a great multitude of the Jewes, and is honorably receaued of those that about 50 yeeres before, came thither with Zerubbabel before the incarnation of Christ, 596 yeeres. *Ezra.* 7. 9.

26. Darius being slaine Alexander, as vpon this day, obtaineth the Empire of Asia, and the same day, ye monarchie was translated from the Persians vnto the Greekes. 1. *Macca.* 1. 1.

27. Religion, as on this day, was reformed, according to God's expresse truth, in the most renoumed citie of Geneva. 1535.

29. The citie Buda in Hungarie, as on this day, yeelded vnto ye Turke in the yeere of our Lord God, 1526.

452   [1561.

☾ September hath xxx. days.[1]

Sun	riseth falleth	hour	5 mi. 36. 6 mi. 24.	Psalms.	Morning Prayer 1 Lesson.	Morning Prayer 2 Lesson.	Evening Prayer 1 Lesson.	Evening Prayer 2 Lesson.
16 f	Kalend.		Gyles	1	Ose 13	Math. 2	Ose 14	Roma 2
5 g	4 No.		....	2	Joel 1	3	Joel 2	3
A	3 No.		....	3	3	4	Amos[5]	4
13 b	Prid. No.		....	4	Amos 2	5	3	5
2 c	Nonas.		Dog days en.........	5	4	6	5	6
d	8 Id.		....	6	6	7	7	7
10 e	7 Id.		[2]	7	8	8	9	8
f	6 Id.		Nati. Mar...........	8	Abdias 1	9	Jonas 1	9
18 g	5 Id.		....	9	Jo. 2. 3	10	4	10
7 A	4 Id.		....	10	Miche 1	11	Miche 2	11
b	3 Id.		....	11	3	12	4	12
15 c	Prid. Id.		....	12	5	13	6	13
4 d	Idus.		Sol in Libra[3].......	13	7	14	Naum 1	14
e	18 Kl.		Holy cross...........	14	Naum 2	15	3	15
12 f	17 Kl.		Æquinoctium.......	15	Abacu 1	16	Abacu 2	16
1 g	16 Kl.		Autumnale.	16	3	17	Sopho. 1	1 Cor. 1
A	15 Kl.		Lambert..............	17	Soph. 2	18	3	2
9 b	14 Kl.		....	18	Agge 1	9[4]	Agge 2	3
c	13 Kl.		....	19	Zacha. 1	20	Za. 2. 3	4
17 d	12 Kl.		.... Fast.	20	4. 5	21	6	5
6 e	11 Kl.		S. Mathew.	21	Eccle. 35	22	Eccle. 38	6
f	10 Kl.		....	22	Zach. 7	23	Zach. 8	7
14 g	9 Kl.		....	23	9	24	10	8
3 A	8 Kl.		....	24	11	25	12	9
b	7 Kl.		....	25	13	26	14	10
11 c	6 Kl.		Cyprian...............	26	Mala. 1	27	Mala. 2	11
d	5 Kl.		....	27	3	28	4	12
19 e	4 Kl.		....	28	Toby 1	Mark 1	Toby 2	13
8 f	3 Kl.		S. Michael..........	29	Eccle. 39	2	Eccle. 44	14
g	Prid. Kl.		Hierom.	30	Toby 3	3	Tob. 4	15

[1 1596, The Moone xxix.]   [2 1578, *Nati. of Eliza.*]
[3 1596 places it higher by one day.]   [4 A misprint for, 19.]   [5 1, omitted.]

1578. SEPTEMBER.

2. Augustus Cæsar this day, ouerthrew Antonius and Cleopatra, in a battel by sea at Actium, 28 yeeres before Christ was borne. *Dion.*

7. Our Soueraigne Lady QUEENE ELIZABETH, was borne as vpon this day, at Greenewich. *Anno.* 1532 [1533].

8. Jerusalem was as vpon this day, sacked with fire and sworde, and vtterly rased, 73. yeeres after the birth of Christ: who prophesied the same 40. yeeres before. *Matth.* 24. 2, 34. *Joseph. lib.* 7. *chap.* 26.

13. Titus the Emperour, sonne to Vespasian, as vpon this day died, after Christes birth 83. yeeres.

14. Chrysostome being chased out of his Church of Constantinople, as vpon this day, died.

18. Domitian the Emperour as vpon this day, was slaine, by ye treason of his wife and seruaunts.

20. The noble Oratour L. Crassus, as vpon this day, died of a pleurisie. *Cicero. lib.* 3. *de Orat.*

23. Octauius Cesar, as vpon this day, was borne 60. yeeres before the Natiuitie of Christ. *Gel. lib.* 15. *chap.* 7.

24. Angelus Politian, as vpon this day, died, *Anno.* 1509.

25. As vpon this day, Nehemiah finished the walles of Jerusalem, 444. yeeres before Christ. *Nehe.* 6. 15.

30. As vpon this day, Pompeius surnamed the great, was borne, before Christ, 103. yeeres.

[1561.]   453

❡ October hath xxxi. days[1].

Sun riseth/falleth	hour	6 mi. 35. / 5 mi. 25.	Psalms:	Morning Prayer 1 Lesson.	Morning Prayer 2 Lesson.	Evening Prayer 1 Lesson.	Evening Prayer 2 Lesson.
16 A	Kalend.	Remige...............	1	Tobi. 5	Mark 4	Tobi. 6	1 Cor. 16
5 b	6 No.	....	2	7	5	8	2 Cor. 1
13 c	5 No.	....	3	9	6	10	2
2 d	4 No.	....	4	11	7	12	3
e	3 No.	....	5	13	8	14	4
10 f	Prid. No.	Fayth	6	Judith [3]	9	Judi. 2	5
g	Nonas.	....	7	3	10	4	6
18 A	8 Id.	....	8	5	11	6	7
7 b	7 Id.	Dennis...............	9	7	12	8	8
c	6 Id.	....	10	9	13	10	9
15 d	5 Id.	....	11	11	14	12	10
4 e	4 Id.	....	12	13	15	14	11
f	3 Id.	Edwarde............	13	15	16	16	12
12 g	Prid. Id.	Sol in Scorpio[2]......	14	Wisd. 1	Luk. di. 1	Wisd. 2	13
1 A	Idus.	....	15	3	di. 1.	4	Galat. 1
b	17 Kl.	Novemb.............	16	5	2	6	2
9 c	16 Kl.	Etheldrede	17	7	3	8	3
d	15 Kl.	*Luke Evan.*	18	Eccle. 51	4	Job 1	4
17 e	14 Kl.	....	19	Wisd. 9	5	Wisd. 10	5
6 f	13 Kl.	....	20	11	6	12	6
g	12 Kl.	....	21	13	7	14	Ephe. 1
14 A	11 Kl.	....	22	15	8	16	2
3 b	10 Kl.	....	23	17	9	18	3
c	9 Kl.	....	24	19	10	Eccle. 1	4
11 d	8 Kl.	Crispine	25	Eccle. 2	11	3	5
e	7 Kl.	....	26	4	12	5	6
19 f	6 Kl.	Fast.	27	6	13	7	Philip. 1
8 g	5 Kl.	*Simon & Jude*	28	Job 24. 25	14	Job 42	2
A	4 Kl.	....	29	Ecc. 8	15	Eccle. 9	3
16 b	3 Kl.	....	30	10	16	11	4
5 c	Prid. Kl.	Fast.	30	12	17	13	Coloss. 1

[1 1596, The Moone xxx.]
[2 In 1596 it is against the twelfth day of the month.]   [3 1, omitted.]

1578. OCTOBER.

1. The feast of Trumpets was kept this day. *Leuit.* 23. 24.
Also Pompeius and his armie, as vpon this day, was discomfited by Cesar.
4. The Jewes fast and mourne, as on this day, for the death of Gedaliah. *Jere.* 41. 1, 2.
10. As on this day the fast of reconciliation, the onely fast commaunded by God, was kept. *Leuit.* 23. 27.
11. As on this day was the first conflict of the Tigurines with ye fiue Townes of Heluetia, wherein Zwinglius was slaine. *Anno.* 1532.
15. As on this day, the Jewish feast of Tabernacles was kept, lasting 7. dayes. *Leuit.* 23. 34.
17. As on this day, Noah's Arke, after 160. daies, rested on the mountaines Ararat, in Armenia. *Gene.* 8. 4.
21. As on this day, the Jewish great feaste of palmes was kept.
22. This day, ye feast of holy conuocation was kept.
23. As on this day, the Jewes which returned from the captiuitie of Babylon, made a newe couenant with God. *Nehe.* 9. 1.
Also Titus, sonne to Vaspasian, after the destruction of Jerusalem, slaieth 3000. Jewes on the birth day of his brother Domitian. *An.* 73.
31. This day, in the yeere of our Lord God 1517. & CI. yeeres after ye death of John Hus, Martin Luther gaue his propositions in ye Uniuersitie of Witemberg, against ye Pope's pardons.

❡ November hath xxx. days [1].

Sun	riseth falleth	hour	7 mi. 34. 4 mi. 26.	Psalms.			Morning Prayer.		Evening Prayer.	
							1 Lesson.	2 Lesson.	1 Lesson.	2 Lesson.
	d	Kalend.	All Saints		1		Wisd. 3	He. 11. 12	Wisd. 5	Apo [5]. 19
13	e	4 No.			2		Eccle. 14	Lu. 18	Eccle. 15	Coloss. 2
2	f	3 No.			3		16	19	17	3
	g	Prid. No.			4		18	20	19	4
10	A	Nonas.			5		20	21	21	1 The. 1
	b	8 Id.	Leonard		6		22	22	23	2
18	c	7 Id.			7		24	23	25 [4]	3
7	d	6 Id.			8		27	24	28	4
	e	5 Id.			9		29	Joh. 1	30	5
15	f	4 Id.			10		31	2	32	2 The. 1
4	g	3 Id.	S. Martin		11		33	3	34	2
	A	Prid. Id.	Sol in Sagittario		12		35	4	36	3
12	b	Idus.	Bryce		13		37	5	38	1 Tim. 1
1	c	18 Kl.	Decembris		14		29 [3]	6	40	2. 3
	d	17 Kl.	Machute		15		41	7	42	4
9	e	16 Kl			16		43	8	44	5
	f	15 Kl.	Hugh		17		45	9	46	6
17	g	14 Kl.	Init. reg. Elizabet.[2]		18		47	10	48	2 Tim. 1
6	A	13 Kl.			19		49	11	50	2
	b	12 Kl.	Edmund King		20		51	12	Baruc. 1	3
14	c	11 Kl.			21		Baruc. 2	13	3	4
3	d	10 Kl.	Cycelia		22		4	14	5	Titus 1
	e	9 Kl.	Clement		23		6	15	Esai. 1	2. 3
11	f	8 Kl.			24		Esai. 2	16	3	Phil. 1
	g	7 Kl.	Katherine		25		4	17	5	Hebre. 1
19	A	6 Kl.			26		6	18	7	2
8	b	5 Kl.			27		8	19	9	3
	c	4 Kl.			28		10	20	11	4
16	d	3 Kl.	Fast.		29		12	21	13	5
5	e	Prid. Kl.	Andrew Apo.		30		Prov. 20	Acte. 1	Pro. 1	6

[1 1596, The Moone xxix.]
[2 This event ought to have been assigned to the seventeenth day, as in 1578 and 1596.]
[3 A misprint for, 39.]
[4 Note, that the beginning of the xxvi. chapter of Ecclesi. (unto) But when one is, &c. must be read with the xxv. chapter.]
[5 1596, Reu.]

1578. NOUEMBER.

10. This day happened the woful slaughter of Varna, where Ladislaus king of Hungarie was slaine by the Turke *Anno.* 1444. Also as vpon this day Martin Luther was borne. *Anno.* 1483.

15. Jeroboam, after that he had turned the people from ye obedience of Rehoboam their king vnto him self, deuised and ordained this day to be kept holy of the people, and because they should not goe vnto Jerusalem to worship, he caused two golden calues to be set vp, the one at Dan, and the other at Bethel, and so he & the people committed Idolatrie. 1 *Kings.* 12. 32, 33.

16. As vpon this daye Tiberius Cesar was borne, before the birth of Christ 39 yeeres.

17. As vpon this day, began most prosperously our most Soueraigne Ladye QUEENE ELIZABETH, to reigne ouer vs, *anno.* 1558. whom we beseech God long to continue in that gouernment.

18. Titus as vpon this day, vsed no lesse crueltie against the Jewes his prisoners, in the citie of Beryte in Syria, keeping the birth day of his father Vespasian, then he did on the birth day of his brother Domitian. *Joseph. Lib.* 7. *Chap.* 20.

1561.]   455

☞ December hath xxxi. days[1].

Sun	riseth / falleth	hour	8 mi. 12. / 3 mi. 48.	Psalms.	Morning Prayer.		Evening Prayer.	
					1 Lesson.	2 Lesson.	1 Lesson.	2 Lesson.
f	Kalend.	....		1	Esai. 14	Actes 2.	Esai. 15	Hebr. 7
13 g	4 No.			2	16	3	17	8
2 A	3 No.			3	18	4	19	9
10 b	Prid. No.			4	20. 21	5	22	10
c	Nonas.			5	23	6	24	11
18 d	8 Id.	Nicholas.........		6	25	di. 7	26	12
7 e	7 Id.			7	27	di. 7	28	13
f	6 Id.	Concep. Ma.		8	29	8	30	James 1
15 g	5 Id.			9	31	9	32	2
4 A	4 Id.			10	33	10	34	3
b	3 Id.			11	35	11	36	4
12 c	Prid. Id.	Sol in Capricor......		12	37	12	38	5
1 d	Idus.	Lucie		13	39	13	40	1 Pet. 1
e	19 Kl.	Januarii		14	41	14	42	2
9 f	18 Kl.			15	43	15	44	3
g	17 Kl.	O Sapient		16	45	16	46	4
17 A	16 Kl.			17	47	17	48	5
6 b	15 Kl.			18	49	18	50	2 Pet. 1
c	14 Kl.			19	51	19	52	2
14 d	13 Kl.	Fast.		20	53	20	54	3
3 e	12 Kl.	Thomas Apo.........		21	Prov. 23	21	Prov. 24	1 Joh. 1
f	11 Kl.			22	Esai. 55	22	Esai. 56	2
11 g	10 Kl.			23	57	23	58	3
A	9 Kl.	Fast.		24	59	24	60	4
19 b	8 Kl.	Christmas		25	Esai. 9	Luk. 22[2]	Esai. 7	Titu. 3
8 c	7 Kl.	S. Stephen...........		26	Prov. 28	Ac. 6. 7	Eccl. 4	Act. 7
d	6 Kl.	S. John		27	Eccle. 5	Apoca[3]. 1	Eccl. 6	Apo[4]. 22
16 e	5 Kl.	Innocents		28	Jer. 31.	Act. 25	Wisd. 1	1 Joh. 5
5 f	4 Kl.			29	Esai. 61	26	Esai. 62	2 Joh. 1
g	3 Kl.			30	63	27	64	3 Joh. 1
13 A	Prid. Kl.	Silvestre..........		30	65	28	66	Judi.[5] 1

[1 1596, The Moone xxx.]
[3 1596, Reuel.]
[5 A misprint for, Jude.]

[2 A misprint for, 2.]
[4 1596, Reu.]

1578. DECEMBER.

9. In the yeere of our Lord God, 1437. Sigismund King of Hungarie, and Emperour of Rome, as on this day dyed.

15. Antiochus Epiphanes, as on this day, placed the Idole of Jupiter vpon ye Altar of God in Jerusalem. 1. *Macca*. 1. 57.

16. Ezra as on this day, commaundeth ye Israelites to leaue their strange wiues. *Ezra*. 10. 11. and 1. *Esdr*. 9. 8, 9.

25. Christ borne as on this day, of the Virgin Marie, in the yeere from the worldes creation 4018.

Antiochus Epiphanes entred also as vpon this day into Jerusalem, with a great armie, and spoyled it. *Joseph. lib*. 12. *chap*. 6.

Also he caused sacrifice on this day to be made vpon the Altar, which was in the steade of the Altar of sacrifices, looke 1. *Macca*. 1. 62.

26. Steuen was stoned to death by the Jewes, for professing Christ, in the yeere after Christ his ascension. *Acts*. 7. 58, 59.

27. As vpon this day Saynt John the Euangelist, being of the age of lxxxix. yeeres, died at Ephesus, in the reigne of Traiane the Emperour, xxx. yeeres after the destruction of Jerusalem.

28. This day Herod slewe the Innocents, two yeeres after the birth of Christ, among whom he had thought to haue murthered Christ. *Mat*. 2. 16, 17, 18.

A LIST OF OCCASIONAL FORMS OF PRAYER AND SERVICES,

FOR THE MOST PART, PUBLICLY AND AUTHORITATIVELY USED DURING THE

REIGN OF QUEEN ELIZABETH.

I. 1560. A FORM OF PRAYER commanded to be used for her majesty's safety, and the good estate of the nation, and of the religion professed therein.

There is extant (Bibl. Lans. 6. art. 62) a letter from Parker to Cecil, dated the 23rd of July, 1563, wherein he tells him of his having prescribed for the inhabitants of his own cathedral city in their distresses, 'that comon prayer, that was apointed in the Gwises tyme, alteringe a fewe wordes in the same.' Wright's Elizabeth and her Times, Vol. i. p. 134. The Form to which the archbishop alludes, Strype, without ever having seen it, supposes (Parker, p. 131) to have been put forth 'about the Year 1559 or 1560,' when Elizabeth was in great fear lest, by having introduced French troops into Scotland, the duke of Guise and his brother should be meditating 'the conquest of our crowne for their Neece the Queene of *Scottes*.' Camden (p. 657.) (Kennet's Collection). Zurich Letters, second edition, pp. 103, 106. The English attacked Scotland by sea and land in January 1560, and peace was proclaimed on Sunday, July the 7th. Stow's Annals, pp. 1085, 1093.

II. 1560. A SHORTE FOURME AND ORDER to be vsed in Common prayer thrise a weke, for seasonable wether, and good successe of the Common affaires of the Realme : meate to be vsed at this presente and also heareafter when like occasyon shall arryse, by the discrecyon of the Ordinaries within the prouince of Canturburye. [Grindal's Register, St Paul's Cathedral, fol. 4, b.]

This Form was sent by the archbishop to Grindal, bishop of London, (ibid., fol. 7, a), 'on Sondaye beinge the vii. daye of Julye.' During the summer of 1560 'the foule wether' was sorely felt in Germany and France, as well as in England. Wright's Elizabeth, Vol. i. p. 40. Grindal, in a letter to Cecil respecting the plague of 1563 (Remains, p. 259), most probably refers to this same 'time of unseasonable weather,' and to the religious observances then enjoined. No complete copy of any kind has been discovered. Herbert, however, (see his Ames, p. 726,) had met with one ; for he gives 'Richard Jugge,' as the name of the printer, and 'octavo,' as the size. Strype (Parker, p. 90) has likewise no more than the commencement of the preface.

III. 1562. A PRAYER to be vsed for the presente estate in [the] churches, at the ende of the latanie, on Sondaies, Wednesdaies, and Frydaies, throughe the whole Realme. [Grindal's Register, St Paul's Cathedral, fol. 26, a.]

We may read this Prayer in Strype's Annals, Vol. i. p. 248. Elizabeth, having made a compact with the French protestants to aid them against the Guisian faction, in September and October sent over into Normandy a large body of men under the command of Dudley, earl of Warwick. Camden, p. 390. Davila, (Aylesbury's translation,) p. 139. See also Strype, ibid. p. 327, where we are told, that on Nov. the 14th prayers were commanded to be offered up on three successive days for the English army then about to engage in battle with the duke of Guise.

IV. 1563. A FOURME to be vsed in Common prayer twyse aweke, and also an order of publique fast, to be vsed euery Wednesday in the weeke, duryng this tyme of mortalitie, and other afflictions, wherwith the Realme at this present is visited. Set forth by the Quenes Maiesties speciall commaundement, expressed in her letters hereafter folowyng in the next page. xxx Julii. 1563. Jugge and Cawood. Quarto. Collates F in fours. [Archbishop Harsnet's Library, Colchester.]

This, the commonest of all the Forms, which served as the basis of those issued for a somewhat similar reason in 1593, 1603, and 1625, has with the Homily been already reprinted by the Parker Society in the 'Remains of Archbishop Grindal,' its author, who had meant it simply for his 'own cure.' See pp. 75—110, 258—261. The plague was brought into England by our soldiers, on their return from Newhaven, or Havre de grace, of which town the French protestants, according to agreement, had the year before put Elizabeth in possession. There is an account of several circumstances connected with the composition of the Form, and likewise a minute description of it, as well in Strype's Parker, p. 131—134, as in his Grindal, pp. 70—73. Holinshed, p. 1206. Stow, p. 1112. Herbert's Ames, p. 721.

V. 1563. A FORME OF MEDITATION, very meete to be daylye vsed of house holders in their houses, in this daungerous and contagious time. Set forth accordyng to the order in the Quenes maiesties Iniunction. Alexander Lacy. n. d. Octavo. Collates A in eight. [Archbishop Harsnet's Library, Colchester.]

The plague of 1563 occasioned this publication, of which we have a reprint in Grindal's Remains, pp. 477—484. Is it not the 'short Meditation to be used in private houses,' of which the bishop writes to Cecil (ibid. p. 264) in a letter dated August the 21st? It would seem, too, to have been put out by authority, notwithstanding its not coming from the office of the queen's printers. Herbert's Ames, p. 1005. In 1580, after the earthquake, the householders were similarly provided with suitable devotions. See p. 464.

VI. 1563. THANKSGEUING TO GOD for w^{h}drawing & ceasing the plage. [Strype's Grindal, Appendix, p. 7. The British Museum, Bibl. Lans. 116. art. 27.]

The manuscript 'prayer or collect,' 'wth ye Secretaries corrections,' belonging to this Form, (which seems to have been set forth in the middle of December,) is thus indorsed, though the first sentence shews it to relate simply to the 'Abatement of the plague,' under which title the whole Form was reprinted in Grindal's Remains, pp. 111—114. Strype, misled by the indorsement, considered it to be the last Service on account of the plague, and mentions its having been 'sent to the Secretary about the seventh of *March*,' [1564]. Grindal, p. 84. Here, however, we need not doubt of his being wrong, both from the fact above mentioned, and from the contents of one of Grindal's letters. See his Remains, p. 265.

VII. 1564. A SHORT FOURME OF THANKESGEUYNG TO GOD for ceassing the contagious sicknes of the plague, to be vsed in Common prayer, on Sundayes, Wednesdayes, and Frydayes, in steade of the Common prayers, vsed in the time of mortalitie. Set forth by the Byshop of London, to be vsed in the Citie of London, and the rest of his diocesse, and in other places also at the discretion of the ordinary Ministers of the Churches. Jugge and Cawood. n. d. Quarto. Collates A in four. [Archbishop Sancroft's Collection in the Library of Emmanuel College, Cambridge.]

We have this Form in the same work as the two others about the plague, pp. 115—120. The mortality 'was not fullie ceassed' in London: having in August been above a thousand a week, by the end of January, 1564, the date of the Form, it had only just sunk under a hundred. Holinshed, p. 1206. Zurich Letters, p. 188. Herbert's Ames, p. 721. When Strype printed his Grindal, he had either quite overlooked, or was ignorant of, the present Office. In his Parker, on the contrary, he describes it (p. 135); but still it could scarcely have been seen by him in its original state: for, immediately after, he quotes its title, (transferring the Form itself to the Appendix,) as if it were the composition of bishop Cox, and solely for his own diocese of Ely. That it came at first from Grindal, how widely soever adopted, and that it was designed to terminate the religious exercises of the period, may be made manifest by two letters, no. xxv and xxvii, published in his Remains. A second copy, with a date, is in the State Paper Office.

VIII. 1565. A FORME *to be evsed in Common praier* euery Wednesdaie and Fridaie, within the citie and Dioces of Sarum: to excite al godly people to praie vnto God for the deliuerie of those Christians, that are now inuaded by the Turke. London. *Jhon Waley.* n. d. Quarto. Collates A in four. [The Cathedral Library, Salisbury.]

Malta, 'the key of that part of Christendom,' and since 1525 the residence of the knights of St John of Jerusalem, was attacked in 1565 by the Turks with a formidable fleet and army. They came in sight of the island on the 18th of May, resolved to destroy 'the Lord Great Master' and his knights. Strype's Grindal, p. 103.—A copy of this same Form, and by the same printer, for the diocese of Norwich, exists at Lambeth. Dr Williams's manuscript also furnishes us with the title of another for the London diocese, adding 'Printed by authority.' It was from this last, that Strype made his quotation. See his Annals, Vol. i. p. 465. They had all a common original: moreover, the public nature of the present Form is shewn by its being incorporated entire into the next but one; from the commencement of the preface to which we also learn, that prayers for the Maltese were, in 1565, commonly put up throughout the kingdom.

1565. A SHORT FORME OF THANKESGEUING TO GOD IX. for the delyuerie of the Isle of *Malta* from the inuasion and long siege therof by the great armie of the Turkes both by sea and lande, and for sundry other victories lately obteined by the christians against the saide Turkes, to be vsed in the common prayer within the prouince of Canturburie, on Sondayes, Wednesdaies, and Fridaies, for the space of syx weekes next ensuinge the receipt hereof. *Set forthe by the most Reuerend father in God, Matthew, by Goddes prouidence Archebyshop of Canturburie, Primate of all Englande and Metropolitane.* · London. Wyllyam Seres. 1565. Quarto. Collates A in four, last page blank. [The Cathedral Library, Salisbury.]

Dr Williams's manuscript mentions this Form. The collect has been quoted by Strype (Annals, Vol. i. p. 466), and Collier (Vol. ii. p. 505). It was published about the middle of October, after news had arrived of the Turks having been compelled to abandon their enterprise against Malta, with the loss of about thirty thousand men. Grindal (Remains, p. 287) clearly compiled the Form, and to him Strype (Grindal, p. 103) assigns its authorship, though in his Annals he gives it to Parker. Herbert's Ames, p. 726.

1566. A FOURME to be vsed in Common prayer, euery X. Sunday, Wednesday, and Fryday, through the whole Realme: To excite and stirre all godly people to pray vnto God for the preseruation of those Christians and their Countreys, that are nowe inuaded by the Turke in Hungary or elswhere. *Set foorth by the most Reuerende father in God, Mathewe Archbyshop of Canterbury, by the aucthoritie of the Queenes Maiestie.* Jugge and Cawood. n. d. Quarto. Collates A, A ii., and B, in fours, last page blank. [Lambeth.]

Hungary had 'of long tyme ben as a moste stronge wall and defence to all Christendome.' Strype (Parker, pp. 232, 233) has printed a portion of the preface, and the prayer commencing 'O Lorde God of hostes,' &c. Herbert (Ames, p. 721) assigns to this Form the date 1565, and adds, 'Again next year;' but he may have been misled by the copy in archbishop Sancroft's collection, which was certainly seen by him, and has 1565 written on the title-page. The very first sentence of the preface will prove the earlier date to be wrong. There are copies of the Form at Colchester, in the Bodleian, and at Salisbury.

XI. 1569. THE PRAYER. [The King's Library, British Museum.]

The rising of the earls of Northumberland and Westmoreland in the north, November the 14th, 1569, caused 'An Homilie against disobedience and wylfull rebellion' to be put forth, at the end of the first part of which we find this Prayer. Afterwards we have it, as at present, subjoined to all the six parts of the Homily. Camden, pp. 421—423. See Zurich Letters, second edit. pp. 329, 331, 341.

XII. 1570. A THANKES GEUYING for the suppression of the last rebellion. [The King's Library, British Museum.]

As the rebellion terminated with the flight of the two earls, and "sundrie of their principall gentlemen," into Scotland on the 20th of December, 1569, there could have been no time to publish this Thanksgiving before the early part of the next year. Stow, p. 1125. Strype fancies Parker to have written it. Annals, Vol. i. p. 552. It, doubtless, came out originally by itself on a broadside, though now to be found, like the Prayer, only in a copy by Jugge and Cawood of the Homily above mentioned. Herbert's Ames, p. 726.

XIII. 1572. ¶ A FOURME OF COMMON PRAYER to be vsed, and so commaunded by aucthoritie of the Queenes Maiestie, and necessarie for the present tyme and state. 1572. 27. Octob. Richarde Jugge. Quarto. Collates C ii. in fours, last leaf blank. [Archbishop Harsnet's Library, Colchester.]

The horrible massacre of the French hugonots on St Bartholomew's day by order of Charles the ninth, and the terrors consequent thereupon, which oppressed all true protestants, occasioned this Form, whence Strype (Parker, pp. 358, 359) has given us two prayers. Wright's Elizabeth, Vol. i. p. 438. In Wilkins' Concilia (Vol. iv. p. 272) is Parker's letter to Sandys, bishop of London, on transmitting it to him for publication through the province of Canterbury. Herbert's Ames, p. 723. Many copies of the Form still exist.

XIV. 1576. A FOURME OF PRAYER WITH THANKES GEUYING to be vsed euery yeere, the 17. of Nouember, beyng the day of the Queenes Maiesties entrie to her raigne. Richard Jugge. n.d. Quarto. Collates B i. in eights, last page blank. [The Library at Westminster Abbey.]

1578. A FOURME OF PRAYER WITH THANKES GIUING, to be vsed of all the Queenes Maiesties louing subiects euery yeere, the 17. of Nouember, being the day of her Highnesse entry to her kingdome. *Set forth by authoritie.* Christopher Barker. 1578. Quarto. Collates C in eights, last page blank.

The second of the Canons of 1640 (Cardwell's Synodalia, p. 392) informs us, that 'our own most religious princes since the Reformation have caused the days of their inaugurations to be publicly celebrated by all their subjects with prayers and thanksgivings to Almighty God.' And the same language was afterwards held by James II., when sanctioning, in 1685, the Form of prayer and thanksgiving for his own accession, which he had caused the bishops to compose. Cardwell's History of Conferences, p. 384. On the contrary, Dr Thomas Holland, Regius Professor of Divinity at Oxford, when preaching at Paul's Cross on November the 17th, 1599, declared 'the first public celebrity' of the day, with respect to Elizabeth, (and, as it would seem by implication, the first public celebrity of the day, with respect to any of our sovereigns,) to have been 'instituted in Oxford about the twelfth year of her reign by Dr Cooper, being then there Vice-Chancellor, after Bishop of Lincoln, and by remove from thence Bishop of Winchester; from whence this institution flowed by a voluntary current over all this realme.' Ellis's Letters, Second Series, Vol. iii. p. 160. A quotation from Edmund Bunny, which evidently supports this view, will appear hereafter, as a note to the very commencement of the Form for 1576. Bohun, too, in his character of Elizabeth (p. 310) makes a similar assertion about its popular origin. However, though the observance of the festival, according to Dr Holland, had been thus commenced as early as 1570, the regular religious part of it dates only from 1576, when Elizabeth had reigned 'now by the space of these eighteen yeeres;' and not until 1578 have the copies '*Set forth by authoritie*' on the title-page. The latter circumstance may be of little moment, especially as they all came equally from the royal printer: still, archbishop Sancroft, in his endeavours to prove the contemporary writer, Bohun, to be wrong, undesignedly draws from its occurrence at all an inference favourable to the correctness of the Canon, and, therefore, of James's Order, which latter, indeed, he may have drawn up himself. 'Without all Doubt,' he says, 'there was a Letter from ye Q to ye ABp to compose, & to her printer to publish this Office.' See a manuscript note in the volume marked 1, 4, 35, belonging to his collection.

A second copy for 1576 is in bishop Cosin's library, Durham; whilst another, printed by Christopher Barker for the following year, is at

Lambeth: copies of the Service, as definitely arranged in 1578, are not of extreme rarity. Strype has twice given us the prayer 'O Lord God, most merciful Father,' &c. (Annals, Vol. ii. p. 452, and Vol. iii. p. 355); and the second time, (in the Appendix, p. 135,) we have also a large portion of the metrical Anthems first appended in 1578, though all of them do not belong to every copy of that date. Herbert's Ames, p. 1079.

xv. 1580. THE ORDER OF PRAYER upon Wednesdayes and Frydayes, to auert and turne Gods wrath from vs, threatned by the late terrible earthquake, to be vsed in all parish churches. Whereof the last prayer is to be vsed of all housholders with their whole families. *Set foorth by authoritie.* Christopher Barker. 1580. Quarto. Collates F in fours, last three pages blank. [The University Library, Cambridge.]

1580. THE ORDER OF PRAYER, and other exercises, vpon Wednesdayes and Frydayes, to auert and turne Gods wrath from vs, threatned by the late terrible earthquake: to be vsed in all Parish Churches and housholdes throughout the Realme, by order giuen from the Queenes Maiesties most honorable priuie Counsell. Christopher Barker. 1580. Quarto. Collates F in fours, last leaf blank.

The history of these Forms requires a few words of explanation. From the Minutes of the privy council we learn, that on the 22nd of April a letter was directed to be sent 'to yᵉ B. off London touchinge the fast & prayers apointed for the earthquake.' The answer to this letter seems to be one dated also on the 22nd, which will be given at the beginning of the Form now reprinted. In his reply Aylmer presses the general adoption of that 'alredie presented' by him to lord Burleigh, as 'the compyling of a new forme of prayer would aske a long tyme.' On the following day the privy council wrote to the archbishop Grindal, (see his Remains, p. 416,) requiring the existing 'good and convenient order of prayer' to be 'used in all other dioceses of this realm.' Accordingly, on the 30th of April (ibid. p. 415), he gave directions for carrying the wishes of the privy council into effect 'throughout the whole diocese of Canterbury.'

Thus Strype erred, both in affirming the present Order to have proceeded at all from Grindal (see his Life, p. 248), and in supposing the diocese of London to have had a Form of its own. Annals, Vol. ii. p. 669. Aylmer's life (Oxford edition), p. 51. Herbert, also, erred, who (Ames, p. 1089), quoting the first words of the title, expressly declares the latter Form to have been intended for the province of York, whereas it was only a more authoritative publication of the other, of that which Aylmer had originally printed for the use of his own diocese. That Grindal was not necessarily the compiler of the Form alluded to by the privy council, notwithstanding the tenor of their language, may even be inferred from

Elizabeth using similar language in 1563 to the archbishop of York, as well as of Canterbury, in relation to the first Service for the plague, (see her letters prefixed,) which Grindal himself, then bishop of London, had composed. Strype (Grindal, p. 248.) reprints Camden's description of the earthquake, of which, as was to be expected, there is also a minute account in the Form subsequently issued for general use. Of this latter copies exist in archbishop Sancroft's collection, and in bishop Cosin's library. Strype (Annals, Vol. ii. p. 668.) notices the '*godlie Admonition*,' which is annexed, but which was likewise put out separately. Herbert's Ames, pp. 613, 1080.

1580. A PRAYER for the estate of Christes Church: to be vsed on Sundayes. Quarto. [Bishop Cosin's Library, Durham.] XVI.

The writer of Dr Williams's manuscript affirms, that this Prayer was put out in 1580 for the earthquake. It was, however, an independent publication, beginning on A iii, the fly-leaf and title-page being gone; or, if we suppose the first signature to be wrong, collating A in four, last page blank. None of the copies compared has a colophon, and they are uniformly imperfect. Strype's Annals, Vol. ii. p. 668.

1585. ¶ A PRAYER for all Kings, Princes, Countreyes, and people, which doe professe the Gospel: And especially for our soueraigne Lady Queene Elizabeth, vsed in her Maiesties Chappell, and meete to bee vsed of all persons within her Maiesties Dominions. XVII.

¶ A PRAYER AND THANKESGIUING for the Queene, vsed of all the Knights and Burgesses in the High Court of Parliament, and very requisite to bee vsed and continued of all her Maiesties louing subiectes.

♰ A PRAYER vsed in the Parliament onely. C[hristopher] B[arker.] n. d. Quarto. Contains pp. 7. [Archbishop Sancroft's Collection, Cambridge.]

These three Prayers were occasioned by the treason of a Welchman, Dr Parry, who had engaged to shoot Elizabeth whilst out riding, 'animated thereunto by the Pope and his Cardinals.' He was betrayed by his accomplice, Nevil, and, being a member of parliament, hanged, drawn, and quartered, in the presence of the two houses, in Palace-yard, the 2nd of March, 1585. Foulis's History of Romish Treasons and Usurpations, pp. 437—444. Strype (Annals, Vol. iii. p. 260.) notices all the Forms, which in the Appendix (pp. 99, 100.) he has quoted entire. Herbert's Ames, p. 1090. They always begin upon H i, without any title-page, as if part of a larger publication. The copy of them in the Bodleian, indeed, actually occurs at the end of 'A true and plaine declaration of the horrible Treasons, practised by William Parry,' &c.,

[LITURG. QU. ELIZ.]

printed at London by C. B., referred to by Strype (ibid. p. 282), and given in the continuation of Holinshed, p. 1382, *et seq*. Herbert's Ames, p. 1082.

XVIII. 1585. AN ORDER OF PRAIER AND THANKES-GIUING, for the preseruation of the Queenes Maiesties *life and salfetie: to be vsed of the* Preachers and Ministers of the Dioces of Winchester. *With a short extract of* William Parries voluntarie confession, written with his owne hand. *London. Ralfe* Newberie. n. d. Quarto. Collates A in four. [The British Museum.]

Cooper, bishop of Winchester, drew up this Form. The '*Praier for the Queene*' is printed by Strype (Annals, Vol. iii. p. 261), because it has 'several historical Remarks, as well as a devout Spirit in it.'

XIX. 1585. A PRAYER OF THANKSGEUINGE for the deliuerance of hir ma^{tie} from ye murderous intention of D. Parry. [The British Museum, Bibl. Lans. 116. art. 29.]

In Strype (Annals, Vol. iii. Appendix, p. 101) we have this Prayer, which was 'to be used, as it seems, in the Churches.' The manuscript was sent to the lord treasurer Burghley, who corrected it in a few places. No original *printed* copy of the Prayer has been found.

XX. 1585. SUPPLEX AD DIVINAM MAIESTATEM ORATIO, *pro defensione nostri aduersus Satanæ carnificumque* suorum diritatem & malitiam, adeo truciter in *populum* DEI *desæuientium*. n. d. Broadside. [Archbishop Sancroft's Collection, Cambridge.]

This Prayer bears neither printer's name, nor date: a date, however, has been written upon it by Sancroft. It possibly did not possess any public authority; but, being too curious to be entirely omitted, will occur as a note to the Form, which Babington's conspiracy occasioned.

XXI. 1585. A NECESSARY AND GODLY PRAYER, appointed by the right Reverend father in God, John [Aylmer], lord bishop of London, to be used throughout that dioces on Wednesdayes and Fridayes, for the turning away of God's wrath, as well concerning this untemperate weather by rain lately fallen upon the earth, and scarcity of victualls, as also all other plagues and punishments: most needfull to be used in every houshold throughout the Realme, 1585.

Besides other evils, 'fears arising from foreign enemies, the Queen of Scots, and the plots laid for Queen Elizabeth's life,' were then causing the nation much disquietude. Strype (Aylmer, p. 81.) has the first sentence of the Prayer; and it occupies, he says, seven pages. Did he see it in Aylmer's Register, which he enumerates in his list of books consulted (Bibl. Lans. 1195), but which is no longer forthcoming; or rather in Dr Williams's library, from whose manuscript the title has been here copied? See likewise Strype's Annals, Vol. iii. p. 293.

1585. CERTAINE PRAYERS AND OTHER GODLY EXERCISES, XXII. for the *seuenteenth of Nouember: Wherein we solemnize the blessed reigne of our gracious Soueraigne Lady* Elizabeth, by the prouidence and grace of God, of England, Fraunce & Ireland Queene. &c. Christopher Barker. 1585. Quarto. Collates E in fours.

The present Order of prayer, compiled by Edmund Bunny, subdeacon of York, is somewhat similar to that mentioned under the year 1576, but must by no means be confounded with it. It was designed to promote the religious observance of the accession day, 'especially,' as he remarks, 'in these partes where I am resident.' Though dedicated to archbishop Whitgift, it was entirely a private publication. Strype's Annals, Vol. iii. p. 355. Herbert's Ames, p. 1083. Copies are not uncommon. One peculiarity distinguishes this Form: its Psalms are set down much more according to the express words of Scripture, than in the other Forms of the period.

1586. A MOST NECESSARY AND GODLY PRAYER, for the XXIII. preseruation of the right honourable the Earle of Leicester, Lieuetenant Generall of her Maiesties Armie in the Lowe Countries, and all his faythfull well-wyllers and followers in these affayres, that God of hys mercy may prosper them in these hys good begunne exployts. Very necessarye to be vsed in thys perrilous tyme, of all her maiesties louing subiects and well-willers. Walter Mantell. 1585. Quarto. Collates A in four. [Archbishop Sancroft's Collection, Cambridge.]

The earl of Leicester embarked at Harwich on the 8th of December, 1585; wherefore we seem obliged to assign the publication of the Prayer to the first part of the next year. Camden, p. 510. The warlike expedition now undertaken was thought to require some justification: accordingly, 'a Declaration of the causes moouing the Queene of Enggland to giue aide to the Defence of the People afflicted and oppressed in the lowe Countries,' dated '*the first of October*,' had been previously published by Christopher Barker. Ibid. pp. 654—659. Strype's Whitgift, pp. 228—231. This Prayer, set forth, probably, by the Puritans, whose party Leicester greatly favoured, will be printed with the Form for 1587.

1586. AN ORDER FOR PUBLIKE PRAYERS to be vsed on XXIV. *Wednesdayes and Frydayes in euery* Parish Church within the Prouince of Canterburie, conuenient for this present time: *Set forth by authoritie.* Christopher Barker. n. d. Quarto. Collates F in fours. [Archbishop Sancroft's Collection, Cambridge.]

 A very common Form. Strype quotes a portion of the preface, and refers the Service itself to the year 1590. Whitgift, p. 359. But, since the business was transferred to Barker's Deputies about 1588 (Herbert's Ames, p. 1076), and thus the Form could not have come in 1590 from Barker's own office, the historian has manifestly erred; as he did by putting *Charles*, instead of Christopher, for the christian name of the printer. The true date is, doubtless, four years earlier; and the Lambeth copy really has 1586 written, in what seems a contemporary hand, on the title-page. As additional arguments, the preface to the next Form contains at the end a reference to 'prayers alreadie of late set foorth,' which can be none other than the present; whilst the Prayer issued in 1587 mentions 'the Homilies of repentance, fasting, and almes deedes, lately published.' From Strype's Annals, too (Vol. iii. p. 391), we actually find the nation to have been at the same time apprehensive of a Spanish invasion, and afflicted with a dearth, in the summer of 1586. See also Stow, p. 1241, and Herbert's Ames, pp. 1083, 1087.

XXV. 1586. AN ORDER OF PRAYER AND THANKSGIUING, for the preseruation of her Maiestie and the Realme, from the traiterous and bloodie practises of the Pope, and his adherents: to be vsed at times appointed in the Preface. *Published by authoritie.* Christopher Barker. 1586. Quarto. Collates B in fours. [Archbishop Sancroft's Collection, Cambridge.]

 Wilkins (Concilia, Vol. iv. p. 319.) gives us Whitgift's letter to Aylmer, bishop of London, dated the 24th of August, concerning the publication of this Form among the bishops of his province. It was caused by the apprehension, in the beginning of the month, of Ballard and Babington, with the other conspirators in that plot, which cost the queen of Scots her life, 'she being tryed as one of them that had an hand in it, as without doubt she had.' Bohun, p. 155. Sandys's twenty-first sermon (Parker Society edition, p. 403) was preached on the same occasion. Strype's Annals, Vol. iii. p. 417. Fourteen of the traitors, including the two above named, were hanged in St Giles's fields, their accustomed place of meeting, on the 20th and 21st of September. Camden, pp. 515—518. Stow, pp. 1217—1220. Herbert's Ames, p. 1083. There is another copy of the Form in the library of Westminster Abbey, and a third at Salisbury.

XXVI. 1587. A PRAYER AND THANKSGIUING fit for this present: and *to be vsed in the time of* Common prayer. Christopher Barker. 1587. Quarto. Collates A in four, last leaf blank. [Archbishop Harsnet's Library, Colchester.]

Drake's brilliant successes at Cadiz and elsewhere in April and May 1587, and the fortunate check which those successes gave to the Spanish preparations against England, are related by Camden, p. 540, and by Stow, p. 1242. The Armada was in consequence delayed for a year.

Herbert (Ames, p. 1186.) refers to 'A praier dayly vsed in Stepney parishe,' as printed by John Wolf this year.

1588. A PRAYER meete to be sayd of all true Subiectes XXVII for our Queene Elizabeth, and for the present state. London. Richard Iones. n. d. Broadside.

No public authority, we presume, can be assigned to this Prayer, which is printed both in French and English: still, the petitions and suffrages, whereby it is preceded, shew clearly, that its composer intended it for common use. Sancroft, in whose collection it exists, has arranged it between the Services for 1587 and 1588: most probably, it belongs to the latter year.

1588. A FOURME OF PRAYER, NECESSARY for the present XXVIII. time and state. The Deputies of Christopher Barker. 1588. Quarto. Collates C in fours, last page blank. [The British Museum.]

A republication, with some additions, of the Form for 1572. The archbishop's circular letter to his suffragans, announcing the printing of it by reason of 'the daungerousnes of the tyme,' is dated July the 10th. Whitgift's Register, Lambeth, part 1. fol. 148, b. The 19th of July the Spanish fleet was first 'discouered neare vnto ye Lizard' (Stow, p. 1249); and on the 23rd a letter was sent by the privy council (see their Minutes) to Whitgift, praying him to direct every bishop and pastor within his province 'to move their auditories and parishioners to join in Publyke Prayer to Almightie God the giver of victoryes to assist us against the malice of our enemies.' Strype (Annals, Vol. iii. p. 518.) quotes one of the prayers. Herbert's Ames, p. 1084. This was also in Scotland 'a time of publick Humiliation,' and of religious observances. Spotiswoode's History of Scotland, part i. p. 370.

1588. A PSALME AND COLLECT OF THANKESGIUING, not XXIX. vnmeet for this present time: to be said or sung in Churches. The Deputies of Christopher Barker. 1588. Quarto. Collates A in four. [Archbishop Sancroft's Collection, Cambridge.]

The first public expression of joy on account of the dispersion and flight of the Armada took place at Paul's Cross on the 20th of August; and on September the 8th several banners were displayed there during the sermon. The 30th of September the privy council (see their Minutes) by her majesty's command summoned the bishops of Sarum and Lincoln (Piers and Wickham) to court, to preach thanksgiving sermons. Moreover, on November the 3rd, they sent a letter to the archbishop of

Canterbury, and to the 'Deane and Chapter of the Byshoprick of Yorke,' requiring them 'to appoint some speciall daye for giuinge publike and general thankes unto God for his gratyous fauor extended towarde vs.' Not, therefore, before tuesday, November the 19th, was 'kept holy day throughout the Realme,' to celebrate the complete overthrow of the Armada; and only on the following sunday Elizabeth herself went in state to St Paul's for the same purpose. Stow, pp. 1259, 1260. We have a large portion of the collect in Strype (Annals, Vol. iii. p. 526). The Rev. W. Maskell has another copy of this Form. 'The [Scottish] King caused solemn Thanksgiving for this deliverance to be given to God in all Churches of the Kingdom, beginning in his own Court for an ensample to others.' Spotiswoode, part i. p. 272.

XXX. 1588. A GODLY PRAYER for the preseruation of the Queenes Maiestie, and for her *Armies both by sea and land, against the enimies of the Church and this Realme of England*. London. John Wolfe for Thomas Woodcocke. 1588. Broadside. [Archbishop Harsnet's Library, Colchester.]

Anthony Marten, one of the Sewers of her majesty's most honourable Chamber, wrote this Prayer, which Strype (Annals, Vol. iii. Appendix, p. 229.) has printed. It was read, he says (ibid. p. 528), 'at the Queen's Chapel, and elsewhere,' being published soon after the defeat of the Armada, whilst the kingdom apprehended a similar danger for the ensuing year. Mr Lathbury (Spanish Armada, p. 66), on the contrary, assigns this Prayer to 'the time when the invasion was [first] expected.'

XXXI. 1589. A FORME OF PRAYER, thought fitte to be dayly vsed in the English Armie in France. The Deputies of Christopher Barker. 1589. Quarto. Collates B in fours, last page blank. [Archbishop Sancroft's Collection, Cambridge.]

In September 1589, Elizabeth both assisted Henry the fourth against the popish League with 'a greater sum than, as he declared, he had ever seen before,' and sent him a reinforcement of four thousand men commanded by Peregrine lord Willoughby. Camden, p. 556. Herbert's Ames, p. 1085.

XXXII. 1590. A FOURME OF PRAYER, necessarie for the *present time and* state. The Deputies of Christopher Barker. 1590. Quarto. Collates D in fours. [Lambeth.]

As another Spanish invasion was expected this year, on the 6th of March, 1589 [1590], Whitgift wrote to the bishops of his province (Strype's Life, p. 317), requiring them, not only to have in readiness the arms, which in 1588, in consequence of a circular letter from himself, dated May the 29th, themselves and their clergy had prepared, but to cause public prayers to be used throughout their dioceses thrice a week at least, 'according to such order as was taken at the last intended invasion: untill you shall receave further direction from me.' See his Register, Lambeth, part 1. fol. 163, b. Camden, p. 558. The present Form, therefore, may have been issued shortly afterwards by the archbishop, though the last prayer shews, that it was also connected with the assistance then being rendered to the cause of protestantism, and, most likely, in France.

XXXIII. 1590. CERTAINE PRAIERS to be vsed at this present time for the good *successe of the French King* against the enemies of Gods true religion and his State. The Deputies of Christopher Barker. 1590. Quarto. Collates A in four. [Archbishop Sancroft's Collection, Cambridge.]

Elizabeth in 1590 again furnished money to Henry the fourth in those domestic wars, which he was obliged still to wage with his refractory subjects and their Spanish allies. Camden, p. 558.

XXXIV. 1590. A PRAYER vsed in the Queenes Maiesties house and Chappell, for *the prosperitie of the French King, and his nobilitie, assayled by a multitude of notorious* rebels that are supported and waged by great forces of forraines. 21 Aug. An. 1590. The Deputies of Christopher Barker. Broadside. [Archbishop Harsnet's Library, Colchester.]

We have this Prayer in Strype (Annals, Vol. iv. p. 41). Henry the fourth, with whom were 'the chief nobility of France,' defeated the League and their allies at Yvry, March the 14th, and re-invested Paris in the beginning of May. Having almost forced the city through famine to capitulate, on the 30th of August he was compelled to raise the blockade by the duke of Parma, who hastily brought an army against him from the Netherlands, whereof he was governor. Davila, p. 944. Herbert's Ames, p. 1710.

XXXV. 1593. CERTAINE PRAIERS collected out of a fourme of godly Meditations, set foorth by her Maiesties authoritie in the great Mortalitie, in the fift yeere of her Highnesse raigne, and most necessarie to be vsed at this time in the like present visitation of Gods heauie hand for our manifold sinnes, and commended vnto the Ministers and people of London, by the Reuerend Father in God, *John* [Aylmer], Bishop of London, &c. *July*. 1593. The Deputies of *Christopher Barker*. Quarto. Collates B in fours.

There died of the plague, and other diseases, this year in London and its suburbs, nearly twenty thousand persons; whence Bartholomew fair was not kept, and the Judges were obliged to hold Michaelmas Term at St Alban's. Camden, p. 574. Stow, p. 1274. Herbert's Ames, p. 1086. Copies of the Form are at Durham and Colchester.

XXXVI. 1594. An Order for Prayer and Thankes-giuing (necessary to be vsed in *these dangerous times*) *for* the safetie and preseruation of her Maiesty and this realme. *Set forth by Authoritie.* The Deputies of *Christopher Barker.* 1594. Quarto. Collates C in fours. [Archbishop Sancroft's Collection, Cambridge.]

Spanish machinations against Elizabeth's life, and the unnatural treasons of her fugitive Roman Catholic subjects in the Netherlands, originated this Form, as the second prayer will teach us. That there was ample reason for issuing it, may be learnt from the '*admonition*,' which, in one of the three editions, is lengthened by the insertion of a very remarkable passage. Bohun, pp. 129—165. Bacon's works (edit. 1753), Vol. i. pp. 537—543. Herbert's Ames, p. 1088.

XXXVIII. 1596. A prayer set forth by authoritie to be vsed for the prosperous successe of hir Maiesties Forces and Nauie. The Deputies of Christopher Barker. 1596. Broadside. [The Bodleian.]

A powerful armament, under the joint command of Robert, earl of Essex, and Charles Howard, lord admiral of England, sailed from Plymouth, on the first of June 1596, for Cadiz, to counteract the great preparations there making by Philip the second for an invasion of England and Ireland. Stow, pp. 1282—1293. There is another copy of this Prayer at Colchester.

XXXVIII. 1596. A Prayer made by the queene at the departure of the fleet. [Lambeth MSS. no. 250.]

According to Stow (p. 1284), Elizabeth wrote a prayer in 1596 'for the good successe of the fleete, and sent it to the Generals, commanding that it should be daily saide throughout all the fleete.' No trace, however, of the Prayer seems now to exist, unless it was the same which will be found under this date, notwithstanding its having been originally designed solely for her private devotions.

XXXIX. 1596. A Prayer of thanksgiuing, and for continuance of good successe to her Maiesties Forces. *Set foorth by authoritie.* The Deputies of Christopher Barker. 1596. Broadside. [The British Museum, Bibl. Lans. 116. art. 30.]

The original draft of this Prayer may be seen in the same place as the Prayer itself. It is dated '3rd July 1596,' indorsed 'Forme of a Prayer for ye Queen thanking God for ye succes of ye fleet,' and corrected by two persons, one of whom was the lord treasurer Burghley. Cadiz had been taken by the English fleet on the 21st of June. Camden, p. 592. Strype has printed the Prayer in his Annals (Vol. iv. p. 262). Two copies of it exist in archbishop Harsnet's library. Herbert's Ames, p. 1088.

1597. CERTAINE PRAYERS set foorth by Authoritie, to XL. be vsed for the prosperous successe of her Maiesties Forces and Nauy. *The Deputies of Christopher* Barker. 1597. Quarto. Collates C in fours. [Archbishop Harsnet's Library, Colchester.]

These arose out of the design of Philip the second to make a descent upon Ireland. For Elizabeth immediately prepared a fleet and army, which sailed from Plymouth on the 9th of July, 1597, under the chief command of Robert, earl of Essex, to destroy the new Armada assembled at Corunna and Ferrol, and to take the Azores. Camden, p. 597. Bacon, Vol. i. pp. 547, 548. Herbert's Ames, p. 1088.

1598. AN ORDER FOR PRAYER AND THANKESGIUING XLI. (necessary to bee vsed in these dangerous times) for the safetie and preseruation of her Maiestie and this Realme. *Set foorth by Authoritie* Anno 1594. And renewed with some alterations upon the present occasion. The Deputies of Christopher Barker. 1598. Quarto. Collates D in fours, last page blank. [The Rev. W. Maskell.]

The '*admonition to the Reader*' minutely explains all the circumstances of Squire's extraordinary treason, the particular cause why this adaptation of a previous Form was arranged and published. Only a single copy has been met with; but the Form is mentioned in Dr Williams's manuscript, and was once in his library.

1599. A PRAYER for the good successe of her Maiesties XLII. Forces in Ireland. The Deputies of Christopher Barker. 1599. Broadside.

The earl of Essex, the newly appointed lord deputy of Ireland, arrived at Dublin on the 17th of April, 1599. Camden, pp. 614—616. Wilkins (Concilia, Vol. iv. pp. 360, 361, 367.) has three documents relating to this war against Tyrone, the first two for contributions from ecclesiastical persons towards the carrying of it on, the last, dated January the 25th, 1601 [1602], for thanksgivings on account of its satisfactory termination. Zurich Letters, (second edition,) p. 555. Herbert's Ames, p. 1089.

1599. A PRAYER for the Prosperous Proceedings, and XLIII. good successe of the Earle of Essex and his company in their present expedition in Ireland against Tyrone, and his adherent rebels there, fit to be used by all loyall subjectes, as well of that countrey, as in England. John Norden. London. 1599.

The present Form, like the one put forth in the beginning of 1586 for the earl of Leicester, could only have been a private publication. Dr Williams's manuscript has furnished the title, as Herbert furnished the title of that which precedes it.

XLIV.   1601. CERTAINE PRAYERS fit for the time. *Set foorth by authoritie.* Robert Barker. 1600. Quarto. Contains pp. 11. [Archbishop Sancroft's Collection, Cambridge.]

Strype (Annals, Vol. iv. pp. 354—356.) has printed two of these Prayers, which were intended to commemorate a great deliverance of the queen and kingdom from the dangerous rebellion of the earl of Essex, 'of late greatly feared to have entered England by force of armes.' Stow, p. 1310. Essex's outbreak took place on sunday the 8th of February, 1601; and he was beheaded in the Tower on the 25th, which was Ashwednesday. Bacon, Vol. i. p. 568. In quoting the title Strype adds 'to be used thrice a week on the prayer days in the churches;' and also, 'Composed upon her Entrance upon a new Century, viz. 1600,' to which circumstance the last two Prayers certainly do allude. In his Whitgift, however (p. 544), he seems to assert two distinct Forms to have been put forth, one for each of the events above mentioned. At Lambeth there is another copy of the Prayers.

A SHORT FORM AND ORDER to be used in Common prayer II. thrice a week for seasonable weather, and good success of the Common affairs of the Realm : meet to be used at this present, and also hereafter, when like occasion shall arise, by the discretion of the Ordinaries within the province of Canterbury.

The[1] preface.

WE be taught by many and sundry examples of holy Scriptures, that, upon occasion of particular punishments, afflictions, and perils, which God of his most just judgments hath sometimes sent among his people, to shew his wrath against sin, and to call his people to repentance and to the redress of their lives, the Godly have been provoked, and stirred up, to more fervency and diligency in prayer, fasting, and alms-deeds, to a more deep consideration of their consciences, to ponder their unthankfulness. &c. *As in print commonly to be seen. &c.*

[1 This preface would appear to have been verbally reprinted in the Form for 1563. See p. 479.]

III. A PRAYER to be used for the present estate in [the] churches, at the end of the litany, on Sundays, Wednesdays, and Fridays, through the whole Realm.

O MOST mighty Lord God, the Lord of hosts, the governor of all creatures, the only giver of all victories, who alone art able to strengthen the weak against the mighty, and to vanquish infinite multitudes of thine enemies with the countenance of a few of thy servants, calling upon thy name, and trusting in thee: defend, O Lord, thy servant, and our governor under thee, our queen Elizabeth, and all thy people committed to her charge: and especially at this [time], O Lord, have regard to those her subjects, which be sent over the Seas to the aid of such, as be persecuted for the profession of thy holy name, and to withstand the cruelty of those, which be common enemies, as well to the truth of thy eternal word, as to their own natural prince, and countrymen, and manifestly to this Crown and Realm of England, which thou hast of thy divine providence assigned, in these our days, to the government of thy servant our Sovereign, and gracious queen. O most merciful Father, if it be thy holy will, make soft and tender the stony hearts of all those, that exalt them selves against thy truth, and seek to oppress this crown and Realm of England, and convert them to the knowledge of thy Son, the only saviour of the world, Jesus Christ, that we and they may jointly glorify thy mercies: lighten, we beseech thee, their ignorant hearts, to embrace the truth of thy word; else so abate their cruelty, O most mighty Lord, that this our christian Region, with others that confess thy holy gospel, may obtain by thy aid and strength, surety from our enemies, without shedding of christian and innocent blood, whereby all they, which be oppressed with their tyranny, may be relieved, and all which be in fear of their cruelty, may be comforted: and finally, that all christian Realms, and specially this Realm of England, may by thy defence and protection enjoy perfect peace, quietness, and security, and that we for these thy mercies jointly all together, with one consonant heart and voice, may thankfully render to thee all laud and praise, and in one godly concord and unity amongst our selves may continually magnify thy glorious name, who with thy Son our saviour Jesus Christ, and the Holy Ghost, art one eternal, almighty, and most merciful God: To whom be all laud and praise, world without end. Amen.

IV. A FORM to be used in Common prayer twice a week, and also an order of public fast, to be used every Wednesday in the week, during this time of mortality, and other afflictions, wherewith the Realm at this present is visited.

Set forth by the Queen's Majesty's special commandment, expressed in her letters hereafter following in the next page. xxx[1]. July. 1563.

By the Queen.

MOST Reverend father in God, right trusty and right well-beloved, we greet you well. Like as Almighty God hath of his mere grace committed to us, next under him, the chief government of this Realm and the people therein: So hath he, of his like goodness, ordered under us sundry principal ministers, to serve and assist us in this burden. And therefore considering the state of this present time, wherein it hath pleased the most highest, for the amendment of us and our people, to visit certain places of our Realm with more contagious sickness than lately hath been : For remedy and mitigation thereof, we think it both necessary and our bounden duty, that universal prayer and fasting be more effectually used in this our Realm. And understanding that you have thought and considered upon some good order to be prescribed therein, for the which ye require the application of our authority, for the better observation thereof amongst our people, we do not only commend and allow your good zeal therein ; but do also command all manner our Ministers, Ecclesiastical or Civil, and all other our Subjects, to execute, follow, and obey such Godly and wholesome orders, as you, being Primate of all[2] England, and Metropolitan of this[2] province of Canterbury, upon Godly advice and consideration, shall uniformly devise, prescribe, and publish, for the universal usage of Prayer, Fasting, and other good deeds, during the time of this visitation by sickness and other[3] troubles.

Given under our Signet, at our Manor of Richmond, the first day of August, the fifth year of our reign.

To the most Reverend father in God, our right trusty and right well-beloved, the Archbishop of Canterbury and Primate of all England.

[[1] The Form was first 'exercised' in London and Fulham on Wednesday the 18th of August. Grindal's Remains, pp. 261, 265.]

[[2] This same Form, printed by the same parties, was likewise issued for the province of York (Strype's Parker, p. 135. Grindal's Remains, p. 264), the queen's letters being altered by the omission of 'all,' and by the substitution of 'that prouince of York.']

[[3] Parker, writing to Cecil on the 23rd of July (Bibl. Lans. 6.

¶ The Preface.

WE be taught by many and sundry examples of holy Scriptures, that upon occasion of particular punishments, afflictions, and perils, which God of his most just judgment hath sometimes sent among his people, to shew his wrath against sin, and to call his people to repentance and to the redress of their lives, the Godly have been provoked and stirred up to more fervency and diligence in prayer, fasting, and alms-deeds, to a more deep consideration of their consciences, to ponder their unthankfulness and forgetfulness of God's merciful benefits towards them, with craving of pardon for the time past, and to ask his assistance for the time to come, to live more Godly, and so to be defended and delivered from all further perils and dangers. So king David in the time of plague and pestilence, which ensued upon his vain numbering of the people, prayed unto God with wonderful fervency, confessing his fault, desiring God to spare the people, and rather to turn his ire to himward, who had chiefly offended in that transgression. The like was done by the virtuous kings, Josaphat and Ezechias, in their distress of wars and foreign invasions. So did Judith and Hester fall to humble prayers in like perils of their people. So did Daniel in his captivity, and many other moe in their troubles. Now therefore calling to mind, that God hath been provoked by us to visit us at this present with the plague and other grievous diseases, and partly also with trouble of wars: It hath been thought meet to set forth by public order some occasion to excite and stir up all godly people within this Realm, to pray earnestly and heartily to God, to turn away his deserved wrath from us, and to restore us as well to the health of our bodies by the wholesomeness of the air, as also to Godly and profitable peace and quietness. And although it is every Christian man's duty, of his own devotion to pray at all times: yet for that the corrupt nature of man is so slothful and negligent in this his duty, he hath need by often and sundry means to be stirred up and put in remembrance of his duty. For the effectual accomplishment whereof, it is ordered and appointed as followeth.

First, that all Curates and Pastors shall exhort their Parishioners to endeavour themselves to come unto the Church, with so many of their families as may be spared from their necessary business, (having yet a prudent respect in such assemblies to keep the sick from the whole, in places where the plague reigneth,) and they to resort, not only on Sundays and holidays, but also on Wednesdays and Fridays, during the time of these present afflictions, exhorting them, there reverently and Godly to behave themselves, and with penitent hearts to pray unto God to turn these plagues from us, which we through our unthankfulness and sinful life have deserved.

art. 62), describes 'the Realm' as 'molested vniuersallie by warre, and perticularlie at London by pestilence, and partlie here at Canterburie by famyn.']

Secondly, that the said Curates shall then distinctly and plainly read the general confession appointed in the book of Service, with the residue of the Morning prayer, using for both the Lessons the Chapters hereafter following. That is to say:

For the first Lesson, one of these Chapters, out of the old Testament.

The 2. Kings. Cap. 24. Leviticus. 26. Deuteronom. 28. Hieremy. 18. Unto these words: Let us. &c., and .22. 2. Para. Cap. 34. Esay. 1. Ezechiel. 18. and .19. Joel. 2. 2. Esdras. 9. Jonas the .2. and .3. Chapter together. Which Chapters would be read orderly on Sundays, Wednesdays, and Fridays.

And for the second Lesson, one of these Chapters, out of the new Testament.

Mathewe. 3. 6. 7. 24. 25. Luke. 13. Actes. 2. beginning at these words: Ye men of Israel, hear these words. To the end of the Chapter. &c. Rom. 2. 6. 12. 13. Galath. 5. Ephesians. 4. 5. 1. Tim. 2. Apoca. 2.

The order for the Wednesdays.

¶ On Wednesdays (which be the days appointed for general fast, in such form as shall hereafter be declared) after the Morning prayer ended, as is aforesaid, the said Curates and Ministers shall exhort the people assembled, to give them selves to their private prayers and meditations. For which purpose a pause shall be made of one quarter of an hour and more, by the discretion of the said Curate. During which time, as good silence shall be kept as may be.

That done, the Litany is to be read, in the midst of the people, with the additions of prayer hereafter mentioned.

Then shall follow the ministration of the Communion, so oft as a just number of Communicants shall be thereto disposed, with a Sermon[1], if

[1 'The conformable, as well as the non-conformable divines, *kept these dayes* of fasting, but with this disadvantage. Many of the conformists only read prayers and preached not, whenas the non-conformists also preached, and had therefore generally great auditories, so that they preaching, and the people (many of whom were of condition) coming to hear them, under the protection of authority, at their publick fasts and thanksgivings, got such assurance and boldnesse, that they continued to hear, and the ministers continued to preach at the same, or some other, place, after the fasts and thanksgiving dayes were ended. And some of those dayes they turned into stated lectures, and in many of those places this liberty of preaching and hearing was not totally infringed of many yeares after, if ever.' 'So that the preaching of the gospell, and the open visible profession of religion, gained much advantage upon these occasions, as it did in London in the great plague in 1665, and was not easily nor speedily controlled, or utterly checked.' The above remarks

it can be, to be made by such as be authorised by the Metropolitan or Bishop of the Diocese, and they to entreat of such matters especially as be meet for this cause of public prayer: or else, for want of such Preacher, to read one of the Homilies hereafter appointed, after the reading of the Gospel, as hath been accustomed. And so the Minister commending the people to God with the accustomed benediction, shall dimiss them.

If there be no Communion, then on every of the said Wednesdays after the Litany, the .x. Commandments, the Epistle, Gospel, the Sermon or Homily done: the general usual prayer for the state of the whole Church shall be read, as is set forth in the book of Common prayer. After which shall follow these two prayers:

Almighty God, the fountain of all wisdom. &c.   And,
Almighty God, which hast promised. &c. With the accustomed benediction.

¶ The Order for Fridays.

¶ On Fridays shall be only the Morning prayer, and the Litany, with the prayers now appointed to be annexed to the same.

¶ Homilies to be read in order on Wednesdays.

1. First, an Homily entitled, an Homily concerning the Justice of God in punishing of impenitent sinners. &c. Newly now set forth for that purpose.
2. The .viii. Homily of the first Tome of Homilies, entitled, Of the declining from God.
3. The .ix. Homily of the same Tome, entitled: An exhortation against the fear of death.
4. The Homily of Fasting, in the second Tome of Homilies.
5. The Homily of Prayer, in the same Tome.
6. The Homily of Alms deeds, in the same Tome.
7. The Homily of Repentance, in the same Tome also.

When these Homilies are once read over, then to begin again, and so to continue them in order.

After the end of the Collect in the Litany, which beginneth with these words: We humbly beseech thee, O Father. &c. shall follow this Psalm, to be said of the Minister, with the answer of the people.

¶ The[2] Psalm to be said in the Litany, before one of the

out of Dr Williams's MS. do not seem intended to be confined to the Form for 1593, which gave occasion to them, and which was taken from this (see p. 471), but to be applied generally.]

[[2] This Psalm may be seen in Bull's Christian Prayers (p. 162), but copied from the York Form.]

prayers newly appointed. Whereof one verse to be said of the Minister, and another by the people, clerk, or clerks.

Psal. 95.

1. O COME, let us humble our selves, and fall down before the Lord, with reverence and fear.

2. For he is the Lord our God: and we are the people of his pasture, and the sheep of his hands.

Osee 6.

3. Come therefore, let us turn again unto our Lord; for he hath smitten us, and he shall heal us.

Acts 3.

4. Let us repent, and turn from our wickedness: And our sins shall be forgiven us.

Jona. 3.

5. Let us turn, and the Lord will turn from his heavy wrath, and will pardon us, and we shall not perish.

Psal. 51.

6. For we knowledge our faults: and our sins be ever before us.

Lament. 3.

7. We have sore provoked thine anger, O Lord: thy wrath is waxed hot, and thy heavy displeasure is sore kindled against us.

8. Thou[1] hast made us hear of the noise of wars, and hast troubled us by the vexation of enemies.

Esay 64.

9. Thou hast in thine indignation stricken us with grievous sickness, and by and by we have fallen as leaves beaten down with a vehement wind.

Judith 8.
Job 11.
Sap. 11.

10. In deed we acknowledge that all punishments are less than our deservings: But yet of thy mercy, Lord, correct us to amendment, and plague us not to our destruction.

11. For thy hand is not shortened, that thou canst not help: neither is thy goodness abated, that thou wilt not hear.

Esay 65.

12. Thou hast promised, O Lord, that afore we cry thou wilt hear us: whilst we yet speak, thou wilt have mercy upon us.

13. For none that trust in thee shall be confounded: neither any that call upon thee shall be despised.

Toby 3.
Job 5.
Osee 6.

14. For thou art the only Lord, who woundest and dost heal again, who killest, and revivest, bringest even to hell, and bringest back again.

Psal. 22.

15. Our fathers hoped in thee, they trusted in thee, and thou didst deliver them.

16. They called upon thee, and were helped: they put their trust in thee, and were not confounded.

[1 The York Form, omitting this, makes the next verse the response, and carries on the change to the end of the Psalm. This was done by the express direction of Grindal. See his Remains, p. 265.]

O Lord, rebuke not us in thine indignation: neither 17.
chasten us in thy heavy displeasure. _{Psal. 6.}

O remember not the sins and offences of our youth: but according to 18.
thy mercy think thou upon us, O Lord, for thy goodness. _{Psal. 25.}

Have mercy upon us, O Lord, for we are weak: O Lord, 19.
heal us, for our bones are vexed.

And now in the vexation of our spirits, and the anguish of our souls, 20.
we remember thee, and we cry unto thee: hear, Lord, and have mercy. _{Baruc. 3. Jona. 2.}

For thine own sake, and for thy holy name sake, incline 21.
thine ear, and hear, O merciful Lord. _{Dani. 9.}

For we do not pour out our prayers before thy face, trusting in our 22.
own righteousness: but in thy great and manifold mercies.

Wash us throughly from our wickedness: and cleanse us 23.
from our sins.

Turn thy face from our sins, and put out all our misdeeds. 24.

Make us clean hearts, O God: and renew a right spirit 25.
within us.

Help us, O God of our salvation, for the glory of thy name: O deliver 26.
us, and be merciful unto our sins for thy name's sake. _{Psal. 79.}

So we that be thy people, and sheep of thy pasture, shall 27.
give thee thanks for ever, and will always be shewing forth
thy praise, from generation to generation.

Glory be to the Father. &c.

¶ After this Psalm, shall be said by the Curate or Minister openly and
with an high voice, one of these three prayers following. And after
that, orderly the rest of the Collects appointed in the Litany. At
which time the people shall devoutly give ear, and shall both with
mind and speech to themselves assent to the same prayers.

¶ A [2] Prayer, containing also a Confession of sins. Which is to be said
after the Litany, as well upon Sundays, as Wednesdays and Fridays.

O ALMIGHTY, most just and merciful God, we here acknowledge our selves most unworthy to lift up our eyes unto heaven; for our conscience doth accuse us, and our sins do reprove us. We know also that thou, Lord, being a just judge, must needs punish the sins of them which transgress thy law. And when we consider and examine all our whole life, we find nothing in our selves, that deserveth any other thing but eternal damnation. But because thou, O Lord, of

[[2] Knox's Book of Common Order furnished this Prayer, and almost in the same words. See p. 263, note 4.]

thy unspeakable mercy, hast commanded us in all our necessities to call only upon thee, and hast also promised, that thou wilt hear our prayers, not for any our desert (which is none) but for the merits of thy Son our only Saviour Jesus Christ, whom thou hast ordained to be our only mediator and intercessor: we lay away all confidence in man, and do flee to the throne of thy only mercy, by the intercession of thy only Son our Saviour Jesu Christ. And first of all, we do most lament and bewail, from the bottom of our hearts, our unkindness and unthankfulness towards thee, our Lord, considering, that besides those thy benefits which we enjoy as thy creatures, common with all mankind, thou hast bestowed many and singular special benefits upon us, which we are not able in heart to conceive, much less in words worthily to express. Thou hast called us to the knowledge of thy Gospel. Thou hast released us from the hard servitude of Sathan. Thou hast delivered us from all horrible and execrable Idolatry, wherein we were utterly drowned, and hast brought us into the most clear and comfortable light of thy blessed word, by the which we are taught how to serve and honour thee, and how to live orderly with our neighbours in truth and verity. But we, most unmindful in times of prosperity of these thy great benefits, have neglected thy commandments, have abused the knowledge of thy Gospel, and have followed our carnal liberty, and served our own lusts; and through our sinful life have not worshipped and honoured thee, as we ought to have done. And now, O Lord, being even compelled with thy correction, we do most humbly confess that we have sinned, and have most grievously offended thee by many and sundry ways. And if thou, O Lord, wouldst now, being provoked with our disobedience, so deal with us as thou might, and as we have deserved, there remaineth nothing else to be looked for, but universal and continual plagues in this world, and hereafter eternal death and dampnation, both of our bodies and of our souls. For if we should excuse ourselves, our own consciences would accuse us before thee, and our own disobedience and wickedness would bear witness against us. Yea, even thy plagues and punishments, which thou dost now lay upon us in sundry places, do teach us to acknowledge our sins. For seeing, O Lord, that thou art just, yea, even justice itself, thou punishest no people without desert. Yea, even at this present, O Lord, we see thy hand terribly stretched out to plague us and punish us. But although thou shouldest punish us more grievously than thou hast done, and for one plague send an hundreth; if thou shouldst pour upon us all those the testimonies of thy most just wrath, which in times passed thou pouredst on thy own chosen people of Israel: yet shouldst thou do us no wrong, neither could we deny but we had justly deserved the same. But yet, O merciful Lord, thou art our God, and we nothing but dust and ashes: Thou art our Creator, and we the work of thy hands: Thou art our Pastor, we are thy flock: Thou art our Redeemer, and we thy people redeemed: Thou art our heavenly Father, we are thy children. Wherefore punish us not, O Lord, in thine anger, but chasten us in thy mercy. Regard not the horror of our sins, but the repentance thereof. Perfit that work which thou hast begun in us, that the whole world may know, that thou art our God and merciful deliverer. Thy people of Israel often times offended thee, and thou most justly afflicted them: but as oft as they returned to thee, thou didst receive them to mercy. And though their sins were never so great, yet thou always turned away thy wrath from them, and the punishment prepared for them, and that for thy covenant sake, which thou made with thy servants, Abraham, Isaac, and Jacob. Thou hast made the same covenant with us (O heavenly Father), or rather a covenant of more excellency and efficacy, and that, namely, through the mediation of thy dear Son Jesus Christ our Saviour, with whose most precious blood it pleased thee that this covenant should be, as it were, written, sealed, and confirmed. Wherefore, O heavenly Father, we, now casting away all confidence in our selves, or any other creature, do flee to this most holy covenant and Testament, wherein our Lord and Saviour Jesus Christ, once offering himself a sacrifice for us on the cross, hath reconciled us to thee for ever. Look therefore, O merciful God, not upon the sins which we continually commit; but upon our Mediator and peace-maker, Jesus Christ, that by his intercession thy wrath may be pacified, and we again by thy fatherly countenance relieved and comforted. Receive us also into thy heavenly defence, and govern us by thy holy Spirit, to frame in us a newness of life, therein to laud and magnify thy blessed name for ever, and to live every of us according to the several state of life whereunto thou, Lord, hast ordained us. And although we are unworthy, O heavenly Father, by means of our former foul life, to crave any thing of thee: yet because thou hast commanded us to pray for all men, we most humbly here upon our knees beseech thee, save and defend thy holy Church, be merciful, O Lord, to all common weals, Countries, Princes, and Magistrates, and especially to this our Realm, and to our most gracious Queen and Governour, Queen Elizabeth. Increase the number of Godly Ministers, endue them with thy grace to be found faithful and prudent in their office. Defend the Queen's Majesty's Council, and all that be in authority under her, or that serve in any place by her commandment for this Realm. We commend also to thy fatherly mercy all those that be in poverty, exile, imprisonment, sickness, or any other kind of adversity, and namely those whom thy hand now hath touched with any contagious and dangerous sickness, which we beseech thee, O Lord, of thy mercy (when thy blessed will is) to remove from us, and in the mean time grant us grace and true repentance, stedfast faith, and constant patience, that whether we live or die, we may always continue thine, and ever praise thy holy name, and be brought to the fruition of thy Godhead. Grant us these, and all other our humble petitions (O merciful Father) for thy dear Son's sake, Jesus Christ our Lord. Amen.

Or else in the stead of the other, this Prayer may be used, and so to use the one one day, and the other another.

O ETERNAL and everliving GOD, most merciful Father, which of thy great longsuffering and patience hast hitherto suffered and borne with us most miserable offenders, who have so long strayed out of thy way, and broken all thy laws and commandments, and have, neither by thy manifold benefits bestowed upon us unworthy and unthankful sinners, nor by the voice of thy servants and Preachers, by continual threatenings out of thy holy word, hitherto been moved, either as thy children, of love to return unto thee our most gracious Father, either for fear of thy judgments, as humble and lowly servants to turn from our wickedness. And therefore, most righteous Judge, thy patience being (as it were) overcome at the last with our obstinate unrepentance, thou hast most justly executed those thy terrible threats now partly upon us, by plaguing us so (with most dreadful and deadly sickness) (with troubles of wars) (with penury and scarceness of food and victual), whereby great multitudes of us are daily afflicted and consumed. We beseech thee, O most merciful Father, that in thy wrath thou wilt remember thy old great mercies, and to correct us in thy judgments, and not in thy just anger, lest we be all consumed and brought to nought. Look not so much upon us and upon our deservings, O most righteous Judge, to take just vengeance on our sins: but rather remember thy infinite mercies, O most merciful Father, promised to us by thy dearly beloved Son our Saviour Jesus Christ, for whose same[1], and in whose name, we do earnestly and humbly crave mercy and forgiveness of our sins, and deliverance from this horrible sickness, being thy just punishment and plague for the same. And as thy holy word doth testify, that thy people of all ages, being justly plagued for their sins, and yet in their distress unfeignedly turning unto thee, and suing for thy mercy, obtained the same: So likewise we, most worthily now afflicted with grievous and dreadful plagues for our iniquities, pray thee, O most merciful Father, to grant us thy heavenly grace, that we may likewise both truly and unfeignedly repent, and obtain thy mercy, and deliverance from the same, which we beseech thee, O Father of all mercies, and God of all consolation, to grant us, for the same Jesus Christ's sake, our only Saviour, Mediator and Advocate. Amen.

¶ Note to pray against any of these plages as they shall touch us.

This Prayer may be said every third day.

It had been the best for us, O most righteous Judge, and our most merciful Father, that in our wealths and quietness, and in the midst of thy manifold benefits continually bestowed upon us most unworthy sinners, we had of love hearkened to thy voice, and turned unto thee, our most loving and gracious Father: For in so doing, we had done the parts of good and obedient loving children. It had also been well, if at thy dreadful threats out of thy holy word continually pronounced unto us by thy servants our preachers, we had of fear, as corrigible servants, turned from our wickedness. But, alas! we have shewed hitherto our selves towards thee, neither as loving children (O most merciful Father) neither

[[1] A misprint. The York Form has, sake.]

as tolerable servants, O Lord most mighty. Wherefore now we feel thy heavy wrath, O most righteous Judge, justly punishing us with grievous and deadly sickness and plagues[1]; we do now confess and acknowledge, and to our most just punishment do find in deed, that to be most true, which we have so often heard threatened to us out of thy holy scriptures, the word of thy eternal verity: that thou art the same unchangeable God, of the same justice that thou wilt, and of the same power that thou canst, punish the like wickedness and obstinacy of us impenitent sinners in these days, as thou hast done in all ages heretofore. But the same thy holy Scriptures, the word of thy truth, do also testify, that thy strength is not shortened but that thou canst, neither thy goodness abated but that thou wilt, help those that in their distress do flee unto thy mercies, and that thou art the same God of all, rich in mercy towards all that call upon thy name, and that thou dost not intend to destroy us utterly, but fatherly to correct us; who hast pity upon us, even when thou dost scourge us, as by thy said holy word, thy gracious promises, and the examples of thy saints in thy holy Scriptures expressed for our comfort, thou hast assured us. Grant us, O most merciful Father, that we fall not into the uttermost of all mischiefs, to become worse under thy scourge; but that this thy rod may by thy heavenly grace speedily work in us the fruit and effect of true repentance, unfeigned turning and converting unto thee, and perfect amendment of our whole lives; that, as we through our impenitency do now most worthily feel thy justice punishing us, so by this thy correction we may also feel the sweet comfort of thy mercies, graciously pardoning our sins, and pitifully releasing these grievous punishments and dreadful plagues. This we crave at thy hand, O most merciful Father, for thy dear Son our Saviour Jesus Christ's sake. Amen.

¶ A short meditation to be said of such as be touched in affliction.

Jerem. 14.

O FATHER, doubtless our own wickedness do reward us: but do thou, O Lord, according to thy name. Our oft transgressions and sins be many. Against thee have we sin-

[1] The composition of the prayer in Knox's Book of Common Order, entitled 'A Prayer in time of Public Affliction,' is evidently to be referred to this same 'noisome and destroying plague.']

ned, yet art thou the comforter and helper of thy humble subjects in the time of their trouble. For thou, O Lord, art in the mids of us, and thy name is called upon us. Forsake us not, O God, forsake us not for the merits of thy only Son our Saviour Jesus Christ, to whom, with thee and the Holy Ghost, be all honour and glory. Amen.

¶ Psalms which may be sung or said before the beginning, or after the ending of Public Prayer.

1	2	3	4	5	6
13	15	25	26	30	32
46	51	67	79	84	91
102	103	107	123	130	143
147					

The Order for the general Fast.

¶ It is most evident to them that read the Scriptures, that both in the old Church under the law, and in the Primitive Church under the Gospel, the people of God hath always used general Fasting, both in times of common calamities, as War, Famine, Pestilence. &c. and also when any weighty matter, touching the estate of the Church or the common wealth, was begun or intended. And it can not be denied, but that in this our time, wherein many things have been reformed according to the doctrine and examples of God's word, and the Primitive Church, this part for fasting and abstinence, being always in the Scripture, as a necessary companion, joined to fervent prayer, hath been too much neglected.

Wherefore, for[2] some beginning of redress herein, it hath been thought meet to the Queen's Majesty, that in this contagious time of sickness, and other troubles, and unquietness, according to the examples of the Godly king Josaphat, and the king of Ninive, with others, a general Fast should be joined with general Prayer, throughout her whole Realm, and to be observed of all her godly Subjects, in manner and form following. 2 Par. 20. Jonas. 3.

1. First, it is ordained, that the Wednesday of every week shall be the day appointed for this general Fast.

2. Secondly, all persons between the age of .xvi. years and .lx. (sick folks, and labourers in harvest or other great labours, only excepted) shall eat but one only competent and moderate meal upon every Wednesday. In which said meal shall be used very sober and spare diet, without variety of kinds of meat, dishes, spices, confections, or wines, but only such as may serve for necessity, comeliness, and health.

[2 Grindal, in a letter to Cecil dated August the 21st, assigns the reason for his insertion of these words: "Surely my opinion hath been long, that in no one thing the adversary hath more advantage against us, than in the matter of fast, which we utterly neglect: they have a shadow." See his Remains, p. 265.]

3.   Item, in that meal it shall be indifferent to eat flesh or fish, so that the quantity be small, and no variety or delicacy be sought. Wherein every man hath to answer to God, if he in such Godly exercises either contemn Public order, or dissemble with God, pretending abstinence, and doing nothing less.
4.   Item, those that be of wealth and ability, ought that day to abate and diminish the costliness and variety of their fare, and increase therewith their liberality and alms towards the poor, that the same poor, which either in deed lack food, or else that which they have is unseasonable and cause of sickness, may thereby be relieved and charitably succoured, to be maintained in health.
5.   Last of all, this day, being in this manner appointed for a day of general Prayer and Fasting, ought to be bestowed by them, which may forbear from bodily labour, in prayer, study, reading or hearing of the Scriptures, or good exhortations. &c. And when any dulness or weariness shall arise, then to be occupied in other godly exercises: But no part thereof to be spent in plays, pastimes, or idleness, much less in lewd, wicked, or wanton behaviour.

When[1] there is a Sermon, or other just occasion, one of the Lessons may be omitted, and the shortest of the three prayers appointed in the Litany by this order may be said, and the longest left off.

Forasmuch as divers Homilies, appointed before to be read in this form of Common prayer, are contained in the second Tome of Homilies now lately set forth by the Queen's Majesty's authority: Therefore it is ordered, that the Churchwardens of every parish shall provide the same second Tome or book of Homilies with all speed, at the charges of the parish.

[[1] In the Form for 1593 we have the following direction:—6. Admonition is heere lastly to be giuen, that on the fasting day they haue but one Sermon at Morning Prayer, and the same not aboue an houre long, to auoyde the inconuenience that may growe by abuse of fasting: as some make it a faction more then religion, and other, with ouermuch wearines and tediousnesse, keepe the people a whole day together, which in this time of contagion is more dangerous in so thicke and close assemblies of the multitudes.—To the above passage Dr Williams's MS. gives us this note: The Puritans: many of them began the fast about ten in the forenoon, and continued it without intermission till 3 or 4 in the afternoone, which they thought the most edifying course, and most agreeable to the nature of the Ordinance; but this course, it seemes, was offensive, and in this sort prohibited.]

¶ An[2] Homily concerning the Justice of God, in punishing of impenitent sinners, and of his mercies towards all such as in their afflictions unfeignedly turn unto him. Appointed to be read in the time of sickness.

The most righteous God, and the same our most merciful Father, abhorring all wickedness and impiety, and delighting in all righteousness and innocency, and willing that we his people and children should herein be conformed, and become like to our God and heavenly Father, that we might be also partakers of his inheritance and everlasting kingdom; in his holy Scriptures, containing the perfect rule of righteousness, and written for our learning and direction towards his said kingdom, both by great threatenings doth continually fear[3] us from all impiety and wickedness so displeasant to him, and also by most large and gentle promises, like a loving father, doth provoke and entice us to righteousness and holiness so acceptable unto him; and so leaveth nothing unassayed, no way unproved, whereby he might save us from perpetual destruction, and bring us to life everlasting. To this end, all those threatenings of temporal punishments and plagues, whereof the Scriptures be so full, are to be referred, that we, for fear of temporal punishments refraining from all unrighteousness, might also escape eternal pain and dampnation, whereunto it would finally bring us, if we should not by repentance turn from the same, and return unto our God and most merciful Father, who would not the destruction and death of sinners, but rather that they should convert and be saved. Gen. 12. d⁴. Job 36. a. Psal. 7. 12. 119. Esay 26. c. Jer. 30. b. Job 5. c. Tob. 3. d. 2 Pet. 3. b.

But when he perceiveth that neither gentleness can win us, as his loving children, neither fear and threatenings can amend us, as being most stubborn and rebellious servants; at the last he performeth in deed that, which he hath so oft threatened, and of fatherly sufferance and mercy so long, upon hope of amendment, deferred, his longanimity and patience being now overcome with our stony hardness and obstinate impenitency. After this sort, we shall find by the holy Scriptures and histories Ecclesiastical, that he hath dealt with his people of all ages, namely, the Israelites, whom in sundry other places, but especially in the .26. of Leviticus, and .28. of Deuteronomium, as well by fair promises, as by menaces, he laboureth to bring to due obedience of his law, which is perfect righteousness. If (saith he) thou hear the voice of the Lord thy Levit. 26. Deut. 28.

---

[2] This Homily, composed for the occasion by Alexander Nowell, dean of St Paul's (Grindal's Remains, p. 253), was printed as part of the preceding Form. In the Form for the province of York it is divided into two parts, and somewhat varies in other respects: the differences of reading are noted in their proper places.]

[3] Fear: affright, terrify.]

[4] The chapters were anciently subdivided by letters.]

God, and keep his commandments, all these blessings shall come upon thee: Thou shalt be blessed in the city, and in the field. The seed of thy body, the fruit of thy earth, the increase of thy cattle, shall be blessed. &c. Thou shalt have seasonable weather, fruitful ground, victory of thy enemies, and after, quiet peace in thy coasts, and I will be thy loving Lord and God, thy aid and defender, and thou shalt be my beloved people. But if thou wilt not hear the voice of the Lord thy God, nor keep his commandments, but despise his laws. &c. all these curses shall come upon thee: Thou shalt be cursed in the city and in the field, thy barn, all thy storehouses shall be cursed, the fruit of thy body, of thy cattle, and of thy ground, shall be cursed, thou shalt be cursed going out and coming in. The Lord shall send thee famine and necessity, he shall strike thee with agues, heats, and colds, with pestilences, and all other evil diseases, yea, and with all the botches and plagues of Egypt. He shall make heaven over thee, as it were, of brass, and the earth which thou treadest on, as it were iron. He shall send thee unseasonable weather. &c. wars, and overthrow thee at thine enemies' hands, and thy carrion shall be a prey to the birds of the air, and the beasts of the earth, and there shall be no man to drive them away: and so forth, many mo most horrible evils and mischiefs, written at large in those two Chapters, where ye may see how lovingly on the one part he promiseth to the obedient, and how terribly on the other part he threateneth the disobedient, and how largely and at length he prosecuteth the matter, specially in the threatenings and menaces, most meet for the Jews, a people ever stiff-necked and rebellious. And in deed the whole writings of the prophets, and universally of all the Scriptures, be nothing else but like callings to true obedience, and to repentance from our transgressions, by like promises and threatenings, yea, and greater also, as by promise of life everlasting to the faithful obedient, and penitent, and contrarily, of everlasting damnation and death to the stubborn, rebellious, and impenitent sinners. And to prosecute this matter, when the Jews were monished, remonished, prayed, threatened, so oft by so many prophets, and all in vain: did not the Lord at the last bring upon them all those evils which he had threatened, namely, famine, war, and pestilence, as ye may read at large in the books of Judges, Kings, and Chronicles, in the Lamentations of Jeremie, namely, the .2. .4. and .5. Chapters, and in other places of the Prophets and the old Testament, containing the descriptions of extreme famines, horrible wars and captivities, and dreadful plagues, whereby God punished and afflicted his people for their sins and rebellion against him most sharply? Yea, and when all this could not amend them, but that they waxed worse under the rod and correction: did he not at the last, which is most horrible, utterly destroy them with famine, war, and pestilence, and carried the rest into captivity, and destroyed utterly their cities and countries, according to the prophecy of Esay, and as our Saviour Christ likewise in the Gospel foresheweth of the miserable destruction and ruin of their cities and temple, so horrible, that one stone should not be left upon another? In like manner, the same immutable God proceeded aforetime with the Christians of Asia, Affricke, and Grece; he sent them like Prophets, learned doctors, and holy saints, saint Clement, Ignatius, Tertullian, Cyprian, Origine, Gregorius, Basil, Chrysostome, Augustine, and many mo, who out of holy Scriptures likewise warned and warned them again, to turn from their sins, and to return to God; unto whom after, when they would not be warned with words, he sent them the swords of the Goths, Hunnes, Vandales, Saracens, and Turks, he sent them likewise famines, and pestilences, and finally, when neither threats nor punishments could amend them by those nations, and especially the Saracens and Turks, he hath either utterly destroyed them, or else made them most miserable captives of the miscreants[1] Turks, under them to be in all unspeakable slavery and misery: and that which is most horrible of all, where their forefathers worshipped Christ the Saviour of the world, to serve in his stead filthy and dampned Machomet, the deceiver of the world.

Goths.

Now to come to our times (most dearly beloved in our Saviour Christ) hath not God likewise begun this order of proceeding with us Christians of this age? Hath he not sent amongst us his Prophets and preachers, who out of God's holy word have continually called us to repentance, continually denounced unto us, that he is the same immutable God, of the same justice that he will, and of the same power that he can, persecute the same wickedness and impenitency with like punishments and plagues? In the which also he hath used his wonted clemency, in denouncing evils before he bring them upon us, that by speedy repentance we might avoid and escape them. And hath he not, I pray you, prosecuted the same his proceedings with us also continuing in impenitency, by sending us sundry plagues at sundry times, wars, famines, exiles, horrible fires? And hath he not now at the last, after almost .xx. years' patience and forbearing of us, sent us the pestilence, which of all sicknesses we most fear and abhor, as indeed it is to be feared? Seeing we have so long despised his justice, requiring our innocency, he can not but visit with his justice, punishing our iniquity, and that he doth more justly execute upon us, than he did upon his people of any time before us: for that we, besides the warning of his Scriptures, and preachers of his word, by so many examples of the punishments of all former ages for like vices, have not been amended or moved to any repentance. Wherefore now at the last he hath sent to us, that could never in health by any means be brought to the obedience of him, horrible sickness, and the dreadful fear of death, present at our doors and before our eyes. We, that could never skill of compassion towards the misery of others, are now ourselves by his just judgments fallen into extreme misery. We, that have not visited and comforted the sick, according to God's will, are now fallen into such sickness, that the nearest of our friends refuse to visit us. We, that could never be brought from the love of this world, are now most justly brought in fear suddenly to leave and depart out of this world. We, that loved our

[1] Miscreants: infidels, unbelievers.

wicked mammon so much, that we could not find in our hearts to bestow any part thereof upon the relief of our poor brethren and sisters, are now brought in fear suddenly to lose it altogether, and ourselves also with it, by sudden and dreadful death of our bodies, and, for the abusing of it, in danger and dread to lose our souls also everlastingly. We, that set all our delight in gathering together and heaping of worldly muck, in building of fair houses, and purchasing of lands, as though we should live for ever, are now justly put in fear of loss of life, and all with it, at the short warning of .2. or .3. days, and often not many mo hours. All those doctrines of the vanity of this transitory life and world, set out in the Scriptures in so many places, preached unto us in so many sermons, which we yet could never hitherto by hearing believe, are now put in practice in deed, and set before our eyes, and all our senses, to see and perceive most certainly. Wherefore, unless we now at the last repent, I see not what time is left for repentance. It had been the best in deed, as we have been oft forewarned, to have turned to our heavenly Father in time of quietness, for love of our Father, rather than fear of the rod; for that had been in deed the part of loving and good children: but not to be mended with stripes is now the part not of servants that be corrigible, but of indurate and desperate slaves. Let us not (O dearly beloved) fall into the uttermost of all mischiefs, that we should be incorrigible with punishment also, and worse under the scourge, as were those stiff-necked Jews; who when, first after threatenings, and then after plagues of war, famine, and pestilence, they remained indurate and incorrigible; lastly, as he by his holy Prophets had threatened them, he overthrew them as a high wall down to the ground, and dashed them all to pieces as an earthen vessel, that their ruin might be without help, and their destruction remediless. Which most horrible mischief that we may avoid, let us avoid the cause thereof: contempt, obstinacy, and hardness of heart, in God's most just wrath and scourge now used for our correction. There is yet no cause, for all this, why we should despair or distrust: but rather that we should turn from our sins, and return to our merciful Father, craving pardon and deliverance at his hand.

For the declaration whereof, it shall be shewed out of the Scriptures: First, that God doth not punish us in this world, and send us these miseries and sickness, of hatred, to destroy us, but of love, mercifully to correct us. And out of infinite places, it shall suffice to rehearse a few notable, serving for this purpose. And here the testimony of Job, a man both sore punished and most favoured of God, hath a worthy place, who, well understanding God's goodness and mercy, even in his grievous punishments, Blessed or happy (saith he) is the man whom God punisheth. Therefore refuse not thou the chastening of the Almighty. For though he make a wound, he giveth a plaster; though he smite, his hand maketh whole again. He shall deliver thee in six troubles, and in the seventh there shall no evil come unto thee. In hunger, he shall feed thee from death, and

[¹ The reference is wrong. The York Form has 30, which is equally wrong.]

in the wars, he shall deliver thee from the power of the sword; and so forth, how God in dearth and destruction will help and save, and how that such correction keepeth us from sinning. And again, in the .36. Chapter, God by punishing and nourtering[2] of men, roundeth[3] them (as Job 36. a. it were) in the ears, warneth them to leave off their wickedness, and to amend. If they now take heed and serve him, they shall wear out their days in prosperity, and their years in prosperity and joy. And Toby, a man likewise exercised in afflictions, saith: Blessed is thy name, Tob. [1]3. c. O God of our fathers, who, when thou art angry, shewest mercy, and in time of trouble forgivest the sins of them that call upon thee. And by and by after: This may every one that worshippeth thee look for of a certainty, that if his life be put to trial, he shall be crowned; if he be in trouble, he shall be delivered; if he be under correction, he shall come to thy mercy. For thou delightest not in our destruction; for after tempest thou sendest calm, and after mourning and weeping thou bringest joy and rejoicing: thy name, O God of Israel, be blessed for ever. And in the .6. Chapter of Osee, God saith: In their adversity Osee. 6. a. they shall seek me and say: Come, let us turn again unto the Lord, Esay 26. for he hath smitten, and he shall heal us, he hath wounded us, and he shall bind us up again. After two days shall he quicken us, and the third day shall he raise us up, so that we shall live in his sight. Then shall we have understanding, and endeavour ourselves to know God. And in the third Chapter of the Proverbs: My son (saith Salomon) Pro. 3. b. despise not the chastening of the Lord, neither faint when thou art rebuked of him; for whom the Lord loveth, him he chasteneth, yea, and delighteth in him, even as a father in his own son. The apostle to the Hebrues hath the like most comfortable doctrine, which he yet amplifieth more, saying: Ye have forgotten the exhortation, which Hebr. 12. b. speaketh unto you as unto children: My son, despise not thou the chastening of the Lord, neither faint when thou art rebuked of him; for whom the Lord loveth, him he chasteneth, yea, and scourgeth every son that he receiveth. If ye endure chastening, God offereth himself unto you as unto sons. What son is he whom the Father chasteneth not? If ye be not under correction, whereof all are partakers, then are ye bastards and not sons. Therefore, seeing we have had fathers[4] of our flesh, which corrected us, and we gave them reverence: shall we not much rather be in subjection unto the Father of spirits, and live? And they verily for a few days nourtered us after their own pleasure: but he nourtereth us for our profit, to the intent that he may minister of his holiness unto us. No manner chastening for the present time seemeth to be joyous, but grievous: Nevertheless[5] afterward, it bringeth the quiet fruit of righteousness unto them which are exercised

---

[2 Nourtering *or* nurturing: chastening. Psalm xciv. 10. Prayer Book version.]

[3 Round *or* rown: whisper.]

[4 our corporall fathers correcting vs, and we gaue.]

[5 Yet afterward.]

Apoca. 3. d. thereby. And[1] in the .3. of the Revelation Christ saith : As many as I love, I rebuke and chasten; be zealous therefore, and repent. And
Rom. 8. g. S. Paul declareth, that neither trouble nor peril, neither life nor death, nor any other thing, can separate us from the love of God, if we through
1 Cor. 11. g. Christ trust in his mercy. And the first to the Corinthians, he teacheth, that God doth punish and correct us in this wretched world, that we should not be condempned with the wicked world.

Secondly, it is most comfortable to call to remembrance such places of the Scriptures, as contain God's merciful promises made to all such as in their trouble unfeignedly call unto him for help; whereof certain be
Deut. 4. c. hereunder noted, for the more readiness to have them before our eyes. In the .4. of Deuter. as God threateneth to bring the Jews into all miseries, if they do disobey him: So, saith he, if thou then in thy greatest distress do turn unto the Lord thy God, and hear his voice, and seek him, thou shalt find him, if thou seek him with all thy heart and soul. For the Lord thy God is a merciful God; he will not forsake thee,
Deut. 30. a. nor destroy thee. And in the .30. Chapter of the same book: If (saith the Lord) for thy sins the curses written in this book do light upon thee, and thou, moved with repentance of thy heart, turn unto the Lord, and obey his commandments, with all thy heart and with all thy soul, the Lord thy God shall bring thee again out of captivity, and will

[[1] And Christe sayth, As many as I loue, I rebuke and chasten: be zelous therefore and repent. And Saint Paul declareth, that neither trouble nor perill, neither lyfe nor death, nor any other thing, can separate vs from the loue of God. And he teacheth, that God doth punishe and correct vs in this wretched worlde, that we should not be condempned with the wicked in the worlde to come, but rather by our repentaunce and obedience be the children of God, and so made partakers of the kyngdome of heauen, through our Lorde and sauiour Jesus Christe, to whom with the father and the holy ghost be all honour and glory for euer. Amen.

⁌ *The seconde part of the Homelie.*

We haue (good people) in the former part of this exhortation (concernyng our turnyng to God) opened to you of the seueritie and iustice of God, and also declared howe God by his great goodnesse yet so tempereth his rod and punishment of iustice, that though the wicked by their obstinacie begin their hell here in such punishment, yet the godly by taking the rod of his iustice in repentaunce haue much commoditie thereof, that it beginneth not onlye chyldelie and reuerent feare to his maiestie, but also strongly moueth vs to an earnest and stable purpose of lyuing more agreeablie to his honour and our duetie. Nowe the more to recount this our duetie to our Lorde God, I wyll secondly in a fewe wordes set before you some part of gods mercifull promises towarde such (as with all their heart turne to him.) In the .4. of Deuteronomium where God threatneth (for our example) to bring the Jewes into all miseries, yf they do disobey him: so sayth he agayne, If thou in thy great distresse.]

THE JUSTICE OF GOD.

have compassion[2] upon thee, and will turn and fet[3] thee again from all the nations, among which the Lord thy God shall have scattered thee. Though thou were cast unto the extreme parts of heaven, even from thence will the Lord thy God gather thee, and from thence will he fet thee. And the Lord thy God will bring thee into the land, which thy fathers possessed, and thou shalt enjoy it. And he will shew thee kindness, and multiply thee above thy fathers. And the Lord thy God will circumcise thine heart, and the heart of thy seed, that thou mayst love the Lord thy God with all thy heart, and with all thy soul, that thou mayst live. And the Lord thy God will put all these curses upon thine enemies, and on them that hate thee, and that persecute thee. But thou shalt turn and hearken unto the voice of the Lord, and do all his commandments, which I command thee this day. And the Lord thy God will make thee plenteous in all the works of thy hands, in the fruit of thy body, and in the fruit of thy cattle, and in the fruit of thy land, for thy wealth. For the Lord will turn again and rejoice over thee, to do thee all good, as he rejoiced over thy fathers. The book of Psalms is very plentiful of such comfortable promises. Psalm .50. Call Psal. 50. a. upon me in the time of thy trouble, and I will deliver thee (saith the Lord) and thou shalt honour me. Psalm .86. Thou, Lord, art good Psal. 86. a. and gracious, and of great mercy unto all them that call upon thee. And by and by: In the time of my trouble I will call upon thee, for thou hearest me. In the .91. Psalm be large promises of God's help Psal. 91. a. and deliverance, yea, and that expressly from the plague and pestilence, and all other evils. Psalm .145. The Lord is nigh to all them that call Psal. 145. d. upon him, yea, all such as call upon him faithfully[4]. And Salomon, in 3 Reg. 8. d. dedicating of his Temple, testifieth, that if either in war, or famine, or pestilence, or any other plague for our sins, we do convert unto God, and ask mercy, that we shall obtain it. And God, appearing to him, 2 Para. 6 [7]. doth promise and assure the same. Which promise of God the good ^{c.} king Jehosaphat doth repeat in the .2. of Paralipomenon and the .20. 2 Par. 20. b. Chapter, and, according to the same, in his distress obtaineth God's mercy and help. And the Lord by his prophet Jeremy saith: If that people, Jere. 18. a. against whom I have thus devised, convert from their wickedness, I will repent of the plague that I devised to bring upon them. Again, When I take in hand to build or to plant a people or a kingdom, if the same people do evil before me, and hear not my voice, I will repent of the good that I devised to do for them. And in another place: Ye shall Jere. 29. c. cry[5] unto me, ye shall go and call upon me, and I shall hear you; ye shall seek me and find me, yea, if so be that you seek me with your whole heart, I will be found of you (saith the Lord) and will deliver you. And again, in another place: I heard Ephraim that was led away Jere. 31. d. captive complain on this manner: O Lord, thou hast corrected me, and

[2] compassion vpon thee: and the Lorde thy God wyll bring thee.]
[3] Fet: fetch. See Nares's Glossary.]
[4] faythfully. And the Lorde by his prophete Jeremie.]
[5] crye vnto me, and I shall heare.]

[LITURG. QU. ELIZ.]

thy chastening have I received[1] as an untamed calf. Convert thou me, and I shall be converted, for thou art my Lord God. Yea, as soon as thou turnest me, I shall reform myself, and[2] when I understand, I shall smite upon my thigh. And by his Prophet Ezechiel he saith: If the ungodly will turn away from all his sins that he hath done, and keep all my commandments, and do the thing that is equal and right; doubtless he shall live and not die. As for all his sins that he did before, they shall not be thought upon, but in his righteousness that he hath done he shall live. For have I any pleasure in the death of a sinner, (saith the Lord God,) but rather that he convert and live? And shortly after again: When the wicked man turneth away from his wickedness that he hath done, and doth the thing which is equal and right, he shall save his soul alive. For insomuch as he remembereth himself, and turneth him from all the ungodliness that he hath used, he shall live and not die. And again: Wherefore be converted, and turn you clean from all your wickedness; so shall there no sin do thee harm. Cast away from you all your ungodliness that ye have done, make you new hearts, and a new spirit. Wherefore will ye die, O ye house of Israel? seeing I have no pleasure in the death of him that dieth, (saith the Lord God:) turn you then, and ye shall live. And likewise by his Prophet Joel: Although an horrible destruction be threatened to be at hand; yet (saith the Lord) turn unto me with all your hearts, with fasting, weeping, and mourning, rent your hearts and not your clothes, turn you unto the Lord your God; for he is gracious and merciful, and of great compassion, and ready to pardon wickedness. And anon: Every one that calleth upon the name of the Lord shall be saved. And the Lord himself testifieth, that he hath performed these his promises accordingly, saying: Thou calledst upon me in troubles, and I delivered thee, and heard thee, what time as the storm fell upon thee. Yea, and it is so accustomed unto God to help those that in their troubles flee unto him for succour, that he is, as it were, by a special name called in the Scriptures the helper and refuge in the day of trouble, the Father of mercies, the God of all comfort; that thereby we might in our distress be the more encouraged to sue to the throne of his heavenly grace, whereunto our Saviour most lovingly calleth all such as feel the burthen of adversity, and their sins withal.

Now it remaineth, for the third part, rehearsal be made of certain examples of such as being in trouble, and trusting to God's merciful promises, called upon him, and were delivered. And first, of David, a man wonderfully exercised in worldly troubles, to his eternal health and salvation; who confesseth, that God was ever his helper and deliverer, when he called upon him, in trouble, sickness, or any other adversity, and that in very many places of the Psalter, a number whereof are noted in the margents. Yea, when he was in desperate state concerning all worldly help, crying out, that the snares and sorrows of death had com-

[1 receaued. Conuert.]
[2 This part of the quotation is not in the York form.]

passed him round about, and that the pains of hell had come upon him, and taken hold of him; that he would yet call upon the name of the Lord, beseeching him to deliver his soul, and that God out of his holy temple would not fail to hear, and speedily to help and save him. And notably and directly to this purpose, the same king David, as is testified in the .2. book of Kings, and .24. chapter, when .70. thousand were in three days slain with the plague for his and their sins, making most humble confession of his offence, and earnest prayer for mercy and pardon, obtained the same, and the plague at God's commandment suddenly ceased. Ezechias, and the people with him, in their great distress, whereunto they were brought for their sins, called upon the merciful Lord, and he heard, and holp them, not remembering their sins. Jonas, when by disobedience he had offended God, and was swallowed up of the Whale, yet by prayer he was delivered even out of the belly of hell, as he himself speaketh, that none, even in most desperate state, should distrust in God's mercy and help. The Jews also, ever most stubborn and rebellious against God, yet when they, being afflicted most worthily, did in their distress call upon the Lord for mercy and help, he heard and relieved them, as appeareth by all the scriptures of the old Testament; but especially and notably the .107. Psalm, which rehearseth the manifold rebellions of that nation against their Lord and God, and the sundry afflictions that he therefore sent upon them. But ever this verse, as it were the burden of the Psalm or song, is oftentimes among[3] rehearsed: But they cried to the Lord in their trouble, and he delivered them from their distress. And in the end of the Psalm is added, that they that be wise will consider these examples, and thereby understand the mercies of the Lord, in like distress to flee thereunto. The like rehearsal of God's mercies, shewed unto them when they in their troubles called upon him, is in the book of Nehemias, or .2. of Esdras, and the .9. chapter. How mercifully relieved God Ismael and his mother in their great distress! What mercy was shewed to wicked Manasses, truly repenting! Likewise to Nabuchodonosor, turning unto the Lord in his trouble! How graciously is the prodigal son received of his father in his extreme misery, procured by his own wickedness! How mercifully is the thief pardoned, even in the miserable end of his most wicked life! Yea, all those diseases which the Gospel recordeth to be so miraculously cured by our Saviour Christ, in such as sued to him for health, and by faith trusted to obtain the same; what be they else but testimonies to us of our like relief in our grievous sickness, if with like faith we call to him for help? For it is the same Lord of all, rich in mercy towards all that call upon him: Neither is his hand shortened or weakened, that he can not, nor his goodness abated or diminished, that he will not, now help his servants that in their distress do flee to his mercy and goodness. For it is now also true, as it was then, when it was written of the sheep and penny lost and found again, and that there is more joy in heaven upon one sinner repenting, than upon .99. righteous.

[[3] Among (it), that is, in the course of it.]

I have more largely prosecuted this part, for that I thought it necessary that we should be instructed by the doctrine of God's word, his merciful promises, and the comfortable examples of his saints in their troubles; that God doth punish us in this wretched world, that we be not dampned with the wicked world, and that he will not refuse nor reject such as, being punished for their sins, do unfeignedly in their distress return unto him. For where[1] our negligence in coming to him heretofore in the time of our quietness might now in the day of our trouble come into our minds, to the great disquieting of our fearful consciences: I thought it expedient to stir up and erect our good hope in his mercies in the time of our troubles by the manifold, most sweet, and assured comforts of the holy Scriptures, written for our doctrine and consolation, both at all times, and specially in the time of affliction; for then is that heavenly medicine most necessary, when our disease doth most grieve and fear us, which we should undoubtedly receive at God's merciful hand to our eternal health, if we, according to the above written doctrines, promises, and examples, do unfeignedly turn to the Lord our God in these days of our affliction: unfeignedly, I say, not for the time of affliction only, as mariners in the tempest, neither as dogs returning again to their vomit; but to remain such in health and security, as in sickness and danger we promised to be, and all the days of our life hereafter, being delivered from fear of all plagues, to serve the Lord our God sincerely and continually in all holiness and righteousness acceptable to him. Wherefore I thought good to admonish us, that we do not by dissembling with God, who can not be deceived, deceive ourselves: but that, as the Lord would have this plague not to be an utter destruction unto us, but to be our fruitful correction, as by the doctrine and examples above rehearsed appeareth; so we of this cross might win that gain, and gather that fruit, which may be healthful unto us, as it was to those godly saints, which were before under like correction and chastisement of the Lord. Therefore let us learn by this affliction to mourn for our sins, to hate and forsake sin, for the which God doth thus shew his anger and displeasure against us. For when shall we mourn for our sins, if not now in the time of mourning? When shall we hate them, if not now when they so grievously wound us, and bring us to present danger of double death, both of body and soul, if we flee not from them? When shall we forsake sin in our life, if we cleave to it now when life forsaketh, or is most like to forsake us? And if we shall enter into particularities: when will we forsake our pride, if not now when all glory is falling into the dust? When will we leave our envy, malice, hatred, and wrath, if not now when we are going to the grave, where all these things take an end? When will we give over our gluttony, if not now when we must forego the belly and whole body also? When will we leave our fleshly lusts, if not now when our flesh shall turn to dust? When will we give over the cares of this life, if not now when we shall cease to live? When will we cease from our usury, if not now when we must lose both the

[¹ Where: whereas.]

increase and the stock wholly? When shall we willingly give over the love of wicked mammon, if not now when we can not hold nor use it, but, will we nill we, we must part from it? Wherefore, either now let us make us friends of it, who may receive us into the heavenly tabernacles, or else there is no hope that we ever will. When shall we relieve the poor in their need, if not now, thereby to provoke the Lord to succour us in this our great distress? When will we awake, that we sleep not in death, if not now at the point of death? When shall we ever truly remember the last times, thereby to avoid sin, if not now in the last times[2] themselves? And as we ought now in affliction to flee all wickedness; so ought we to learn the love of righteousness, whereunto of long by gentleness God hath drawn us, and now by his just punishment meaneth to drive us. Let us learn the fear of God, now punishing us, which by his long sufferance and patience heretofore was almost clean gone out of our hearts. For there be special promises that he will hear them that fear him. And when will we fear him, if not now when he punisheth us? Let us learn patience, knowing that affliction in the children of salvation worketh patience, patience bringeth trial, trial hope, and hope shall not suffer us to be confounded. For the short evil of our troubles in this world, patiently taken, worketh in us an exceeding high and everlasting weight of glory in the world to come. Let us learn the contempt of this wretched life and wicked world, with all her trifling and uncertain joys, and manifold and horrible evils. For when shall we understand that this life is as a vapour, as a shadow passing and fleeing away, as a fading flower, as a bull[3] rising on the water, if not now in the decaying, passing, and vanishing away of it? When shall we forsake this wicked world, if not now when it forsaketh us? Let us learn the desire of heaven, and the life to come, where be both many and most great and certain joys, mingled with no evils, no plagues of famine, war, pestilence, or other sickness, and miseries, whereof this wretched life is full, as we now by experience prove.

To conclude, let us, giving over all wickedness, now at the last, when we are in most greatest danger to give over ourselves, and helping the needy and poor, that the Lord in our necessities may relieve us; let us, I say, now at the last, turn unto the Lord our God, and call for help and mercy, and we shall be heard and relieved, according to the doctrine of God's word, and his merciful promises made unto us, and after the examples foreshewed to us out of the holy scriptures afore declared, and in infinite other places, to our great comfort. For if, as God by affliction goeth about, as our heavenly schoolmaster, to teach us thus to flee from sin, and to follow righteousness, to contemn this world, and to desire the life to come, with such other Godly lessons; so we, like his good disciples,

Psal. 145. d.
Rom. 5. a.
2 Cor. 1. b.
Jacob. 1. a.
2 Cor. 4. d.
Jacob. 4.
Job [7.]
Esay 58. b.
Dani. 4. e.

[2] That the end of the world drew near, was a very common notion in the middle of the sixteenth century. See p. 504. Becon's Works, Prayers, &c., Parker Society edition, p. 624. Preface to Bale's Declaration. Latimer's Works, Vol. i. pp. 172, 364.]

[3] Bull (*bulla*): bubble.]

do well learn the same, we shall not need much to fear this plague as dreadful and horrible, but with the blessed man of God, Job, to trust in him, yea, though he should kill us bodily, and patiently to take our sickness as God's good visitation and fatherly correction, and in it quietly and constantly to commit ourselves wholly to the holy will of our most merciful Father, by our Saviour Christ, whether it be to life or death, knowing that he is the Lord of life and death, and that whether we live or die, we be the Lord's, for it can not perish which is committed unto him. In whom they that believe, though they die, shall live, and in whom all that live and trust faithfully in his mercy, shall not die eternally; and by whom, through our Saviour Christ, all that die in him have life everlasting, which I beseech the same our most merciful heavenly Father, for the death of our Saviour Jesus Christ, to grant unto us all: Unto whom with the Father and the Holy Ghost, one eternal majesty of the most glorious God, be all honour, glory, and dominion, world without end. Amen.

Job 13. c.
Deute. 32. f.
Sapien. 16.
Rom. 14.
John 18. b.

¶ Imprinted at London in Powles Church yarde by Rycharde Jugge and John Cawood, Printers to the Quenes Maiestie.

Cum priuilegio Regiæ Maieſtatis.

A FORM OF MEDITATION, very meet to be daily used of v. house holders in their houses, in this dangerous and contagious time.

Set forth according to the order in the Queen's[1] majesty's Injunction.

¶ Imprinted at London without Aldersgate, in little Britain street, by Alexander Lacy.

The master kneeling with his family in some convenient place of his house, perfumed before with Frankincence, or some other wholesome thing, as Juniper, Rosemary, Rose water and Vinegar, shall with fervent heart say, or cause to be said, this that followeth. The servants and family to every petition shall say: Amen.

Meditation.

WE read in thy holy word (O Lord) what blessings thou hast of thy mercy promised to them that live obediently according to thy blessed will and commandments: we read also the curses that thy justice hath pronounced against such as despise thy word, or negligently pass not to live thereafter. Deut. 28. Levi. 26.

And, among the rest of thy heavy curses, thou threatenest by name the plague, and the Pestilence, with other noisome and most painful diseases, to such as forsaking thee worship strange gods, and follow their own vain fantasies, in stead of thy sacred ordinances.

We find also, how extremely thine own people the Jews, have oftentimes felt the performance of these thy bitter threatenings, and that for sundry and divers offences.

Because they loathed Manna, and were not contented with thy miraculous provision, but would have Quails, and other dainty victuals to content their luxurious appetites, thou slewest so many with a sudden and mighty plague that the place of their burial was named thereof, and called the Graves of lust. Num. 11.

Also for murmuring against the ministers of thy word Moses and Aaron, thou destroyedst with a sudden plague xiiii. thousand and more, besides those traitors, whom the earth swallowed for their rebellion: And had not Aaron entreated for them, and gone between the quick and the Num. 16.

[1] Grindal (Remains, p. 258) writing to Cecil respecting the previous Form, says:—It is to be considered by you in what form the fast is to be authorised, whether by proclamation, or by way of injunction or otherwise; for it must needs pass from the queen's majesty.]

dead, thou wouldest have consumed them all, as thou wast minded to have done before, when they despised the plentiful land which thou hadst promised them (had not Moyses stayed thy wrath), when thou saidst: I will strike them with the pestilence, and utterly destroy them.

<small>Num. 14.</small>

<small>1 Reg. 4. 5. 6. 7.</small>
Furder, when they had lost thine Ark through their own sins, and the sins of their Priests the keepers thereof, after that the Philistines were forced through thy plaguing hand religiously to send it home again, thou stroockest with the plague fifty thousand of the Bethsamites thy people, for rashly presuming to look into the same, not having thy warrant so to do.

<small>2 Reg. 24.</small>
In the time of king David, thou destroyedst three score and ten thousand of thy people in three days, with thy wasting plague of Pestilence: moved thereto by the transgression of David, whom for the sins of his people thou sufferedst to be tempted and subdued with a vain curiosity to number the people.

<small>1 Cor. 11.</small>
Also shortly after the death of that immaculate lamb our Saviour, thou sufferedst the plague to reign among the members of his body (the church of the Corinthians) for not worthily preparing themselves, and for misusing the Sacrament of the body and blood of our Saviour Jesus Christ, and many died therefore: as thy holy Apostle saint Paul hath taught us.

Since which time, O Lord, as the monuments of thy church and other chronicles do declare, thou hast from time to time so plagued with pestilence not only cities, but also whole countries for these and other like causes, that we may justly look for the coming of our Saviour: so many and so horrible Pestilences have been among us already.

All which causes, O Lord, for the which thou hast so afflicted thy people, are through the malice of Satan and our wilful consenting unto him grown so ripe in us, that were it not for the exceeding greatness of thy mercy and compassion, we should all presently perish, and that worthily, so horrible and outrageous are our iniquities.

For we loathe not only the plentiful provision of wholesome victuals and apparel, which thou hast given us for our bodies more abundantly than to many nations, travailing by all means to get wherewith to pamper our flesh, with wines, spices, silks, and other vain costly delighting things; but the precious Manna of our souls, thy holy word and sacraments, we can not away with: we are so full that we are glutted therewith.

We so little esteem the heavenly kingdom, which our Saviour hath so dearly prepared and kindly promised to us, that we abhor it, and are ready to stone those few that commend it, and exhort us for our own good to travel thitherward: better liking and crediting those false prophets, the Epicures and papists, that with their lies discourage us therefrom.

What murmuring and grudging make we against the ministers of thy sword and word, which thou of thy especial goodness hast in mercy given us! How despise we our Bishops and Preachers, and other ministers of thy holy sacraments, whom thou hast commanded us to reverence and honour!

Did not we, through our wicked lives, wretchedly lose the Ark of thy holy word and the true ministration of thy sacraments not many years agone, which the popish Philistines took from us? And now, when thou through thy plagues laid upon them hast miraculously sent it us again; see how bold we be with the Bethsamites unreverently to receive it.

For many make of it a gazing-stock[1] to serve their eyes and tongues, rather than a law to obey and follow in their lives.

Yea, the knowledge of thy truth, goodness, and mercy, breedeth in many of us a careless security, and a contempt of thy holy ordinances. For we presume upon thy mercy and promises, not regarding the conditions, nor any of thy commandments, which in our baptism we vowed to observe. Yea, we make thy Gospel a cloke of our covetousness: under colour whereof we seek our own lucre, and hide all our wicked and filthy practices.

If the Corinthians deserved to be plagued for abusing thy holy Sacrament, how much more are we worthy of fierce wrath, that not only abuse it, but also abhor and contemn it, because it is ministered as it ought! For thou knowest, O Lord, what a sort[2] there are, which, bewitched with the Devil and the Pope's doctrine, do utterly abhor Christ's holy communion, and, saving for fear of the law[3], would never come at it: In what sort these receive, and how they be prepared, is not unknown unto thee. How rashly also, and unadvisedly, and unprepared, the common multitude do frequent it, partly appeareth in that many of them never forgive old offences, nor reconcile themselves, nor in any thing do amend their old sins and vices.

Seeing then that we, Lord, the common sort and multitude, do thus abound in all kind of wickedness, how can it be, but that thou of thy justice must suffer our Magistrates to offend also in somewhat, to the end thou mayest justly take vengeance on our sins?

For these manifold heaps of sins and wickednesses, O Lord, thou hast justly at this present sent this dangerous Pestilence among us, as thou hast often and long time threatened by the mouths of thy faithful preachers, who continually have called upon us to stay thy wrath by earnest repentance and amendment of life: But we have alway been deafer and deafer; the delight in our sins not only stopped our ears, but also hardened our hearts, against their hearty and friendly admonitions: And in that we now, O Lord, do begin to feel and acknowledge our sins, it cometh more of thy rigor in plaguing us, than of any good inclination of our selves. Mollify therefore, O Lord, our flinty hearts with the suppling moisture of thy holy Spirit: Make us to reverence thee as

[1 Apparently, a reference to the permission allowed the congregation from 1552 to 1662 of standing 'by as gasers and lokers on them that do communicate.' See p. 187. Grindal's Remains, p. 267. Clay's Prayer Book Illustrated, p. 112.]

[2 Sort: multitude.]

[3 See p. 30; and also the last rubric on p. 198.]

children for love of thy mercies, and not to dread thee like slaves, for fear of punishment. Amen.

O dear Father, reclaim us thy lost children; O merciful Saviour, pity us thy putrified members; O Holy Ghost, repair us, thy decayed Temples; O holy, blessed and glorious Trinity, have mercy upon us miserable sinners. Amen.

Grant us, O Lord, such true repentance, as may through the blood of our Saviour blot out the stains of our heinous iniquities. Forgive us our sins, O Lord, forgive us our sins, for thine infinite mercy's sake. Amen.

Forgive us our blasphemies, Idolatries, and perjuries, forget our vain and outrageous oaths. As thou hast by thy rigor and plagues forced us to acknowledge thee to be our just and righteous Lord, so let us through thy mercy and forgiveness feel thee to be our mild and loving Father: and give us grace for ever hereafter to reverence this thy glorious name. Amen.

Take from us, O God, the care of worldly vanities, make us contented with necessaries: Pluck away our hearts from delighting in honours, treasures, and pleasures of this life; and engender in us a desire to be with thee in thy eternal kingdom. Give us, O Lord, such taste and feeling of thy unspeakable joys in heaven, that we may alway long therefore, saying with thine elect: Hasten thy kingdom, O Lord, take us to thee. Amen.

Make us, O Lord, obedient to thy will revealed in thy holy word; make us diligent to walk in thy commandments; forgive us our contempt and murmuring against the Magistrates and Ministers which thou hast in thy mercies appointed; make us obedient unto their godly laws and doctrine. Save and preserve, O Lord, thine anointed, our Queen Elizabeth, that she in thy grace and fear may long reign among us.

Give peace to all Christian nations: Move us by thy Spirit to love one another, as the members of one body, that we may all do thy will here in earth, as it is in heaven. Amen.

Dig out of us, O Lord, the venomous roots of covetousness and concupiscence: or else so repress them with thy grace, that we may be contented with thy provision of necessaries, and not to labour as we do with all toil, sleight, guile, wrong, and oppression, to pamper ourselves with vain superfluities. Feed our souls, O Lord, daily with the true Manna of thy heavenly word, and with the grace of thy holy sacraments. Give us grace continually to read, hear, and meditate thy purposes, judgments, promises, and precepts, not to the end we may curiously argue thereof, or arrogantly presume thereupon, but to frame our lives according to thy will: that by keeping the covenants we may be sure of the promises; and so make our election and vocation certain through our constant faith, and virtuous and godly living. Amen.

Conform us, O Lord, to the image of our Saviour; so burn our hearts with the flames of love, that no envy, rancour, hatred, or malice, do remain in us, but that we may gladly forgive whatsoever wrong is or shall be either maliciously or ignorantly done or said against us. And here,

Lord, in thy presence (thy Majesty is every where) we forgive whatsoever hath been by any man practised against us, beseeching thee of thy goodness likewise to forgive it. And further, for thy mercies' sake, and for our Saviour Jesus Christ's sake, we beseech thee, O dear Father, to forgive us those horrible and damnable sins, which we have committed against thy Majesty; for which thou hast now justly brought this Pestilence and plague upon us: let the ceasing thereof, we beseech thee, certify us of thy mercy and remission. Amen.

We know, O Lord, the weakness of ourselves, and how ready we are to fall from thee: suffer not therefore Satan to shew his power and malice upon us, for we are not able to withstand his assaults. Arm us, O Lord, alway with thy grace, and assist us with thy holy Spirit, in all kinds of temptation. Amen.

Deliver us, O dear Father, from all evils both bodily and ghostly: Deliver, O Lord, from trouble of conscience all that are snarled[1] in their sins: Deliver, O Lord, from all fear of persecution and tyranny our brethren that are under the Cross for profession of thy word: Deliver, O merciful Father, those that for our sins and offences are already tormented with the rage of Pestilence: Recover those, O Lord, that are already stricken, and save the rest (of this my household) from this grievous infection. Amen. Grant this, O dear Father, for our Saviour Jesus Christ's sake, to whom with thee and the Holy Ghost be all honour and glory, world without end. Amen.

¶ End with the Lord's prayer.

¶ A prayer to God to cease the Plague.

O Lord God, which for our innumerable sins dost here fatherly correct us, to the end we should not feel the rigour of thy severe judgment in eternal condemnation: We humbly submit ourselves unto thy grace and pity, beseeching thee for our Lord Jesus Christ's sake, that although we have justly deserved this plague now laid upon us, yet it may please thee in the multitude of thy mercies to withdraw thy rod from us. Grant us, O Lord, true repentance of our sins, which (as it did in that good king Ezechias) may deliver us from the plague laid upon us, and cause those that be sick to recover. Or if thou have determined to take a number of us out of the miseries of this present world, give us the comfort of thy holy Spirit, that may make us glad and willing to come unto thee. Give us grace, O Lord, so to prepare ourselves, that we may be ready, with the wise Virgins, to enter into life with our Saviour Christ, whensoever it shall please thee to call us. Grant us this, O dear Father, for Jesus Christ's sake, our only mediator and advocate. To whom with thee and the Holy Ghost be all honour and glory, world without end. Amen.

[1 Snarle: entangle, as a skein of silk or thread.]

FINIS.

VI. THANKSGIVING TO GOD for withdrawing[1] and ceasing the plague.

The Psalm.

Psal. 147.
1. O praise the Lord, for it is a good thing to sing praises unto our God: yea, a joyful and pleasant thing it is to be thankful.

Psal. 105.
2. O give thanks unto the Lord, and call upon his name, and tell the people what he hath done.

Psal. 92.
3. For it is a good thing to give thanks unto the Lord, and to sing praises unto thy name, O most Highest:

4. To tell of thy loving kindness early in the morning, and of thy truth in the night season.

Psal. 13.
5. We will sing of the Lord, because he hath dealt so lovingly with us: yea, we will praise the name of the Lord most Highest.

Psal. 30.
6. We will magnify thee, O Lord: for thou hast set us up, and not made our foes to triumph over us.

Psal. 92.
7. For thou, Lord, hast made us glad through thy works: and we will rejoice in giving praise for the operation of thy hands.

Psal. 30.
8. For, O Lord our God, we cried unto thee, and thou hast healed us.

9. Thou hast brought our souls out of hell: thou hast kept our life from them, that go down to the pit.

Psal. 86.
10. For great is thy mercy towards us, and thou hast delivered our souls from the nethermost hell.

Psal. 68.
11[2]. Praised be the Lord daily, even the God which helpeth us, and poureth his benefits upon us.

Psal. ciii.
12. The Lord is full of compassion and mercy, longsuffering, and of great goodness.

[[1] The present title is similarly circumstanced with that prefixed to the first of Sir John Mason's prayers, composed in 1568. See p. 516. The terms employed are not to be taken absolutely, but must be limited and explained in each by the obvious purport of the composition, to which they refer.]

[[2] In Strype this is numbered 12, which makes the last verse the 28th. Perhaps it is a mere typographical error.]

13. Gracious is the Lord, and righteous: yea, our God is merciful. Psal. 116.

14. For his wrath endureth but the twinkling of an eye, and in his pleasure is life: heaviness may endure for a night, but joy cometh in the morning. Psal. 30.

15. He will not alway be chiding, neither keepeth he his anger for ever. Psal. ciii.

16. He hath not dealt with us after our sins, nor rewarded us according to our wickedness.

17. For look, how wide the east is from the west, so far hath he set our sins from us.

18. For like as a father pitieth his children, even so is the Lord merciful to them that fear him.

19. For he knoweth whereof we be made: he remembereth that we are but dust.

20. For thou, Lord, art good and gracious, and of great mercy unto all them that call upon thee. Psal. 86.

21. Thou hast forgotten the offence of thy people, and covered all their sins. Psal. 85.

22. Thou hast taken away all thy displeasure, and turned thyself from thy wrathful indignation.

23. Thou hast turned our heaviness to joy: thou hast put off our sackcloth, and girded us with gladness. Psal. 30.

24. Turn thee, again, O Lord, at the last, and be gracious unto thy servants. Psal. 90.

25. O satisfy us with thy mercy, and that soon: so shall we rejoice and be glad all the days of our life.

26. Comfort us again, after the time that thou hast plagued us: and for the year wherein we have suffered adversity.

27. Shew thy servants thy work, and their children thy glory: and the glorious majesty of the Lord our God be upon us. Prosper thou the work of our hands upon us, O prosper thou our handy work.

Glory be to the Father, and to the Son, and to the Holy Ghost:

As it was in the beginning. &c.

[A Psalm[1] compiled out of the Book of Psalms, and appointed by the Bishop to be used in public, upon the abatement of the Plague.

Psal. 123.
1. UNTO thee, O Lord, lift we up our eyes, O thou that dwellest in the heavens.
2. Even as the eyes of servants look unto the hands of their masters, and as the eyes of a maiden unto the hands of her mistress: even so our eyes wait upon the Lord our God until he have mercy upon us.

Psal. 18.
3. In our trouble we have called upon the Lord: with our voice we complained unto our God, and our prayers entered into his ears, and he heard us out of his holy temple.

Psal. 3.
4. Many there were that did say of our souls, There is no help for them in their God.

5. But salvation belongeth unto thee, O Lord, and thy blessing is upon thy people.

Psal. 27.
6. We will tarry the Lord's leisure with patience, and put our trust in him, and he will comfort our hearts.

Psal. 9.
7. They that know thy name, O Lord, will put their trust in thee, for thou hast never failed them that seek thee.

Psal. 147.
8. Thou healest those that are broken in heart, and givest medicine to heal their sickness.

Psal. 79.
9. Finish, therefore, O Lord, the work of thy mercy, that thou hast begun in us: save the residue that are appointed to death.

Psal. 17.
10. Shew thy marvellous loving kindness to us, thou that art the saviour of them that put their trust in thee.

Psal. 143.
11. Quicken us, O Lord, for thy name's sake: for thy mercy's sake bring our souls out of trouble.

Psal. 90.
12. The glorious majesty of our God be upon us: prosper thou the work of thy hands upon us, O prosper thou the work of thy hands.

Psal. 7.
13. God is a righteous Judge, strong and patient, and God is provoked every day.
14. If a man will not turn, he will whet his sword; he hath bent his bow, and made it ready, and ordaineth his arrows against the wicked and ungodly.

[[1] This Psalm, if Strype is correct, does not belong to the Service here given: still, he clearly refers it to Grindal, and to the present period. See his Life, p. 82; and the Appendix, p. 6. Can it have constituted part of some similar Form, put forth on the same occasion by another bishop for his own diocese?]

15. Let us therefore always set God before our eyes: Let us stand in awe and sin not: Let us offer up the sacrifice of righteousness, and put our trust in the Lord. ^{Psal. 4.}

16. Let us have an eye unto the laws of the Lord, and keep his ways, and not forsake our God, as the wicked doth. ^{Psal. 18.}

17. Let us live uncorrupt before him, and eschew our own wickedness.

18. Let us come near unto his house, even in the multitude of his mercies, and in his fear let us worship toward his holy temple. ^{Psal. 5.}

19. Then he will lift up the light of his countenance upon us, and bless us. ^{Psal. 4.}

20. Then may we lay ourselves down in peace and take our rest: for it is the Lord only that maketh us dwell in safety.

21. For thou, O Lord, wilt give thy blessing unto the righteous, and with thy favourable kindness wilt thou defend him, as with a shield. ^{Psal. 5.}

22. O how plentiful is thy goodness, which thou hast laid up for them that fear thee, and that thou hast prepared for them that put their trust in thee, even before the sons of men. ^{Psal. 3[1].}

23. Thanks be to the Lord: for he hath shewed us marvellous great kindness in a mighty city.

24. We will thank the Lord, because he hath given us warning: we will sing of the Lord, because he hath dealt lovingly with us: Yea, we will praise the name of the Lord most High. ^{Psal. 16.}

25. Let all them that put their trust in the Lord rejoice: they shall ever be giving of thanks, because thou defendest them: they that love thy name shall be joyful in thy salvation. ^{Psal. 5.}

26. The Lord liveth, and blessed be our gracious helper: and praised be the God of our salvation, which hath delivered us from the snares of death. ^{Psal. 18.}

Glory be to the Father, and to the Son, and to the Holy Ghost:

As it was in the beginning, is now, and ever. &c.]

The Prayer or Collect.

WE yield thee hearty thanks, O most merciful Father, that it hath pleased thee in thy wrath to remember thy mercy, and partly to mitigate thy severe rod of this terrible plague, wherewith thou hast hitherto most justly scourged us for our wickedness, and most mercifully revoked us from the same:

calling us (who in health and prosperity had clean forgotten both thee and ourselves) by sickness and adversity to the remembrance both of thy justice[1] and judgment, and of our miserable frailness and mortality; and now, lest we by the heaviness of thine indignation should have utterly despaired, comforting us again by the manifest declaration of thy fatherly inclination to all compassion and clemency. We beseech thee to perfect the work of thy mercy graciously begun in us: And forasmuch as true health is, to be sound and[2] whole in that part, which in us is most excellent and like to thy Godhead, we pray thee thoroughly to cure and heal the wounds and diseases of our souls[3], grievously wounded and poisoned, by the[4] daily assaults and infections of the old serpent Satan, with the deadly plagues of sin and wickedness: by[5] the which inward infection of our minds[6] these outward diseases of our bodies have by the order of thy justice, O Lord, issued and followed[7], that we, by thy fatherly goodness and benefit, obtaining perfect health both of our minds and bodies, may render unto thee therefore continual and most hearty thanks, and that, by flying from[8] sin, we may avoid thine anger[9] and plagues, and ever hereafter, in innocency and godliness of life studying to serve and please thee, may both by our words and works always glorify thy holy name. Which we beseech thee to grant us, O Father of mercies and God of all consolation, for thy dear Son, our only Saviour and Mediator, Jesus Christ's sake. Amen.

[1 terrible justice. These notes shew the original readings of the manuscript copy.]
[2 and well at ease.]   [3 sickly souls.]
[4 the great murtherer and old serpent.]   [5 from.]
[6 minds, as it were out of a most corrupt sink, these.]
[7 flowed.]   [8 of sin from henceforth.]
[9 anger, and ever.]

1564.] 513

A SHORT FORM OF THANKSGIVING TO GOD for ceasing the VII. contagious sickness of the plague, to be used in Common prayer, on Sundays, Wednesdays, and Fridays, in stead of the Common prayers, used in the time of mortality. Set forth by the Bishop of London, to be used in the City of London, and the rest of his diocese, and in other places also at the discretion of the ordinary Ministers of the Churches.

After the end of the Collect in the Litany, which beginneth with these words: We humbly beseech thee, O Father. &c. shall follow this Psalm, to be said of the Minister, with the answer of the people.

LORD[10], thou art become gracious unto thy Land, thou 1. hast turned away the afflictions of thy servants. Psal. 85.

Thou hast taken away all thy displeasure, and turned thyself from 2. thy wrathful indignation.

For if thou, Lord, hadst not helped us, it had not failed, 3. but our souls had been put to silence. Psal. 94.

But when we said, our feet have slipped, thy mercy, O Lord, helped 4. us up.

In the multitude of the sorrows that we had in our hearts, 5. thy comforts have refreshed our souls.

Our souls waited still upon the Lord, our souls hanged upon his help, 6. our hope was always in him. Psal. 62. 63.

In the Lord's word did we rejoice, in God's word did we 7. comfort ourselves.

For the Lord said: Call upon me in the time of trouble, and I will 8. hear thee, and thou shalt praise me. Psal. 50.

So when we were poor, needy, sickly, and in heaviness, 9. the Lord cared for us : he was our help and our Saviour ac- Psal. 40. 69. cording to his word.

In our adversity and distress he hath lift up our heads, and saved us 10. from utter destruction. Psal. 27.

He hath delivered our souls from death, he hath fed us in 11. the time of dearth, he hath saved us from the noisome pesti- Psal. 33. 91. lence.

[[10] The psalm has been reprinted once before in Bull's Christian Prayers, p. 164. It occurs, too, in a Form for 1625, put forth on a similar occasion.]

[LITURG. QU. ELIZ.]

<small>Psal. 27.</small> 12. Therefore will we offer in his holy Temple the oblation of thanksgiving with great gladness: we will sing and speak praises unto the Lord our Saviour.

<small>Psal. 106.</small> 13. We will give thanks unto the Lord, for he is gracious, and his mercy endureth for ever.

<small>Psal. 86. 103.</small> 14. The Lord is full of compassion and mercy, long-suffering, plenteous in goodness and pity.

<small>Psal. 57. 108.</small> 15. His mercy is greater than the heavens, and his gracious goodness reacheth unto the clouds.

<small>Psal. 103.</small> 16. Like as a father pitieth his own children: even so is the Lord merciful unto them that fear him.

<small>Psal. 71.</small> 17. Therefore will we praise thee and thy mercies, O God; unto thee will we sing, O thou holy one of Israel.

<small>Psal. 98.</small> 18. We will sing a new song unto thee, O God, we will praise the Lord with psalms of thanksgiving.

<small>Psal. 47.</small> 19. O sing praises, sing praises unto our God: O sing praises, sing praises unto our king.

20. For God is the King of the Earth, sing praises with understanding.

21. We will magnify thee, O God our King, we will praise thy name for ever and ever.

22. Every day will we give thanks unto thee, and praise thy name for ever and ever.

23. Our mouth shall speak the praises of the Lord, and let all flesh give thanks to his holy name for ever and ever.

<small>Psal. 21. 72.</small> 24. Blessed be the Lord God of Israel for ever: and blessed be the name of his Majesty, world without end. Amen. Amen.

After this Psalm, shall be said by the Minister openly, and with an high voice, the Collect following.

The Collect.

O HEAVENLY and most merciful Father, what mind or what tongue can conceive or give thee worthy thanks for thy most great and infinite benefits, which thou hast bestowed, and dost daily bestow upon us, most unworthy of this thy so great and continual goodness and favour, though we should bestow all our life, power, travail, and understanding thereabouts only and wholly? When we were yet as clay is in the potter's hands, to be framed at his pleasure, vessels of honour or dishonour: of thy only goodness without our deserving (for how could we deserve any thing, before we were any thing?) thou hast created and made us of nothing, not dumb beasts void of reason, not vile vermins creeping upon the earth; but the noblest and most honourable of all thy worldly creatures, little inferior to thy heavenly Angels, endued with understanding, adorned with all excellent gifts, both of body and of mind, exalted to the dominion over all other thy earthly creatures, yea, the sun and the moon with other heavenly lights appointed to our service, enriched with the possession of all things, either necessary for our use, or delectable for our comfort. And as thou hast made us so excellent of nothing, so hast thou restored us, being lost, by thy Son our Saviour Jesus Christ, dying for us upon the cross, both more marvellously and mercifully than thou didst first create us of nothing; besides that thou dost continually forgive and pardon our sins, into the which we do daily and hourly fall most dangerously, yea, deadly also, dampnably, and desperately, were not this thy present and most ready help of thy mercy. And what have we, that we have not by thee? or what be we, but by thee? All which unspeakable benefits thou hast, like a most loving father, bestowed upon us, that we thereby provoked might, like loving children, humbly honour and obediently serve thee, our good and most gracious Father. But forsomuch as we have dishonoured thee by and with the abusing of thy good gifts, thou dost even in this also, like a father correcting his children whom he loveth, when they offend, no less mercifully punish us for the said abuse of thy gifts, than thou didst bounteously before give them unto us; scourging us sometime with wars and troubles, sometimes with famine and scarcity, sometime with sickness and diseases, and sundry other kinds of plagues, for the abusing of peace, quietness, plenty, health, and such other thy good gifts, against thy holy word and will, and against thy honour and our own health, to thy great displeasure and high indignation: As thou now of late terribly, but most justly and deservedly, plagued us with contagious, dreadful and deadly sickness; from the which yet thou hast most mercifully, and without all deservings on our part, even of thine own goodness, now again delivered us and saved us. By the which thy most merciful deliverance, and especially[1] in

[1] This passage respecting the queen was inserted by the positive direction of Cecil. Grindal's Remains, p. 268.

The following two prayers, as not being devoid of interest, are

that, amongst other thy great and manifold benefits, it hath
pleased thee of thine eternal goodness, most mercifully and

added here from the Bibl. Lans. 116. articles 25, 28. The first is expressly stated to be in 'Mr Threasorer [of Elizabeth's household], Sr Joh. Mason's hand.' The second, written probably by the same individual, ends with a notice, which clearly shews, that Cecil (whose corrections they both exhibit) had ordered them to be composed: 'I haue sent yor honour this prayer againe, because nowe I haue made it, as you woulde me to doo.' Strype has given them in the Appendix to the first volume of his Annals, and says (p. 517), they were 'used, I suppose, with the rest at the accustomed Times of Prayer before her.'

An English prayer for Quene Eliz. being recouered of dangerous
sicknes. 1563.

O MOST mercifull Sauiour Jesu Christe, who being here vppon the earthe, by curing of all kinde of bodilie diseases, and perdoning the synnes of all suche as beleaued in the, didest declare vnto the worlde that thou art the onlie Phisician both of the bodie and the soule : and whan thou waste rebuked by the Pharisies for accompaninge of synfull persons, thou didest planelie by expresse words testifie the same, saynge that sooche as were hoole had noo nede of a Phisician, but those that were sycklie : behold here, O most gracious Jesu, a cure mete for thie diuine power and mercie, a person vppon whom euen from her infancie thou hast bestowed great and innumerable benefites, and haste sett her in high honour and estate in thys worlde, and that of thie speciall grace and goodnes onlie, wth out anie her deseruinge at all : but now, O Lorde, ether to the ende that moche worldlie prosperitie shulde not make her to forgett her feeffe and her duitie towards the, or els for that, that she beinge by thie goodnes maide a prince ouer thie people, hath not in dede soo well as she ought to haue done remembred and acknowleged that she was thie subiecte and handmayden ; nether hath, accordinge to her bonden duitie, bene thankfull to the as her most louinge and beneficiall Sauiour, nor obedient to the as her most gracious and soueraigne lorde : or for other causes to thie diuine wisdome best knowen, thou hast now of late, o lorde, for her admonition and correction striken thie said seruante wth dangerous syknes and bodilie infirmitie euen to the vere poynt of deathe, and hast withall abashed her soule allsoo wth dyvers trobles and terrors of mynde, and by her danger hast terrified the holle realme and people of England, whose quietnes and securitie dependeth, nexte after the, vppon the healthe of thie saide seruant. And yet in thie iudgement thou hast, O Lorde, according to thie accustomed goodnes, remembred thie mercie, delyueringe thie said seruant, aboue all humane reason and liklihoode, from the present danger of deathe : declaring as well by her soodan and great syckness, as by thie steadie healpe and succoure in danger allmost desperat, thie diuine power ioyned wth thie vnspekable goodnes and mercie. Finishe, O most mercifull Sauiour, the worke of thie seruant's healthe wch thou hast graciouslie begonne : accom-

miraculously, not only heretofore to deliver our most gracious Queen and governour from all perils and dangers, yea, even from the gates of death; but now also to preserve her from this late most dangerous contagion and infection. Like as thou hast exceedingly comforted our sorrowful hearts: so we for the same do yield unto thee, as our bounden duty is, our most humble and hearty thanks, O most merciful Father, by thy dear Son our Saviour Jesus Christ, in whose name we pray thee to continue this thy gracious favour towards us, and stay us in thy grace, defending us against the assaults of Sathan, that we continually enjoying thy favour, with the

plishe the cure wch thou hast mercifullie taken in hande; heale her soule by perdoninge her vnthankfulnes towards the, her forgettfullnes of the, and all other her synnes committed ageinst the: cure her mynde by framinge it to the obedience of thie wyll, with pacient takinge and quiett acceptation of this sycknes, sent from the, to her iust ponishment for disobeyinge the, and to her holsome and necessarie admonition, for her forgettfulnes of the and vnthankfullnes towards the: and wth all make her bodie also throughlie hoole and sounde from all this sycknes and infirmitie: that thie seruant obteininge perfect healthe as well of mynde, as bodie, she, and wth her all thie people of England, may bothe be instructed by this danger to acknolege and feare thie iuste iudgements, and for her delyuerie from the said danger, and the obteininge of perfecte healthe, may continuallie magnifie thie mercie, rendering all laude, prayse and thanksgyvinge to the, and thin heauenlie Father, wth the hoolie gohste, one immortall maiestie of the most glorious God, to whom belongeth all dominion, honour and glorie worlde wth out ende. Amen.

A prayer for ye Quene being sicke. 21 July, 1568.

O MOST iust God and mercyfull Father which of thy iustice doest punnishe vs with sicknes for our synnes, and yet of thy mercy wilst not vs to dye for the same, and therfore of thy mere goodnes hast delyuered thy seruant our most gracious Quene from hir extreme danger of deathe, which she and we have deserued for our synnes, and wherunto of thy iustice and power she hath bene browght in token, if thow so woldest, thow couldest, iustly haue suffred hir to dye in the same: we most hartely thanke thee that thow woldest not doo against hir as thow mightest of thy iustice, but what thow wilst of thy mercye in releeuing hir of hir sicknes. And most earnestly we besech thee, O Lord, make hir to growe into perfect health, and hir and vs alwaye to be most thankfull for it, she and we in praysing thee contynually for thy infynit mercye shewed herein, and in folowing thy holy commaundmentes, we with hir taking this hir sicknes to be thy louing chasticement to calle vs all from synne wholy to obey thee and thy worde through Jesus Christ thy Sonne and our Lord. Amen.

health of our souls, which is the quietness of our consciences, as a taste here in earth of thy heavenly joys, and as a pledge of thy eternal mercy, may always in this life render therefore all laud and honour to thee, and after this transitory and miserable life may ever live and joy with thee, through the same our only Saviour and Mediator, Jesus Christ, thy only Son, who with thee and the Holy Ghost, one immortal majesty of the most glorious God, is to be praised and magnified, world without end. Amen.

Psalms[1] *which may be sung or said* before the beginning, or after the ending of public prayer.

Psal. 34. 95. 96. 100. 103. 107.
Psal. 116. 118. 145. 146. 147. 148.

Imprinted at London in Powles Churchyarde, by
𝕽𝖎𝖈𝖍𝖆𝖗𝖉 𝕵𝖚𝖌𝖌𝖊 𝖆𝖓𝖉 𝕵𝖔𝖍𝖓 𝕮𝖆𝖜𝖔𝖔𝖉,
𝕻𝖗𝖎𝖓𝖙𝖊𝖗𝖘 𝖙𝖔 𝖙𝖍𝖊 𝕼𝖚𝖊𝖓𝖊𝖘
𝕸𝖆𝖎𝖊𝖘𝖙𝖎𝖊[2].

Cum priuilegio Regiæ Maieſtatis.

[1 This rubric, as reprinted in Grindal's Remains, p. 120, from the State Paper Office Copy, is as follows:—*Psalmes whereof may be vsed, in stede of the ordinary* Psalmes in the Morning Prayer, one, two, or three, in order, according to the length thereof: And also one of the same may be said or songe in the beginning or endyng of publique prayer.]

[2 The copy just quoted has here the date 22. *Januarii.* 1563. The same date is also on the title-page of the Emmanuel copy, but in writing. Still, the publication of the Form did not take place before Wednesday the 26th. Ibid. p. 267.]

A Form *to be used in common prayer* every VIII. Wednesday and Friday, within the city and Diocese of Sarum: to excite all godly people to pray unto God for the delivery of those Christians that are now invaded by the Turk.

¶ *Imprinted at London
by Jhon Waley.*

The Preface.

FORASMUCH as the Isle of *Malta* (in old time called *Melite*, where S. Paul arrived when he was sent to Rome) Acts xxviii. lying near unto Sicily and Italy, and being as it were the key of that part of Christendom, is presently invaded with a great Army and navy of Turks, infidels and sworn enemies of christian religion, not only to the extreme danger and peril of those Christians that are besieged, and daily assaulted in the holds and forts of the said Island, but also of all the rest of the countries of Christendom adjoining; it is our parts, which for distance of place cannot succour them with temporal relief, to assist them with spiritual aid: that is to say, with earnest, hearty, and fervent prayer, to Almighty God for them, desiring him after the examples of Moses, Josaphat, Exod. xvii. Ezechias, and other godly men, in his great mercy to defend iiii. Reg. xix. and deliver Christians professing his holy name, and in his Justice to repress the rage and violence of Infidels, who by all tyranny and cruelty labour utterly to root out not only true Religion, but also the very name and memory of Christ our only Saviour, and all christianity; and if they should prevail against the Isle of *Malta*, it is uncertain what further peril might follow to the rest of Christendom. And although it is every christian man's duty, of his own devotion to pray at all times, yet for that the corrupt nature of man is so slothful and negligent in this his duty, he hath need by often and sundry means to be stirred up, and put in remembrance of his duty. For the effectual accomplishment whereof it is ordered and appointed as followeth.

First, that all Pastors and Curates shall exhort their Parishioners to endeavour themselves to come unto the Church, with as many of their family as may be spared from their necessary business, and they to resort thither, not only upon Sundays and holy days, but also upon Wednesdays and Fridays, during this dangerous and perilous time: exhorting them there reverently and godly to behave themselves, and with penitent minds, kneeling on their knees, to lift up their hearts, and pray to the merciful God to turn from us, and all Christendom, those plagues and punishments, which we and they through our unthankfulness and sinful lives have deserved.

Secondly, that the said Pastors and Curates shall then distinctly and plainly read the general confession appointed in the book of service, with the residue of the morning prayer unto the first lesson.

Then for the first lesson shall be read one of the chapters hereafter following, or so much thereof as is appointed.

Exod. xiiii. Exod. xv. unto these words: And Miriam a Prophetess. &c. Exod. xvii. beginning at these words: Then came Amelech and fought with Israel. &c. Judges. vii. The first of the Kings. xxiii. beginning at these words: Then came the Ziphites to Saul. &c. unto the end of the chapter. iiii. of the Kings. vii. iiii. of the Kings. xix. The second of the Chronicles, or Paralipomenon. xx.

After that, instead of *Te Deum, laudamus,* that is to say, We praise thee, O God, shall be said the .li. Psalm: Have mercy upon me, O God. &c.

Then immediately after shall be said the Creed: I believe in God the Father. &c. and after that, the accustomed prayers following, unto the end of the Morning prayer.

That done, the Litany shall be said in the mids of the people, unto the end of the Collect in the same Litany, which beginneth with these words: We humbly beseech thee, O Father. &c. And then shall follow this Psalm to be said of the Minister with the answer of the people.

¶ *The Psalm.*

Psal. lxxix. and lxxiv.

O God, the Heathen are come into thine inheritance: thine adversaries roar in the mids of thy congregations, and set up their banners for tokens.

They have set fire upon thy holy places, and have defiled the dwelling Psal. lxxiv.
place of thy name, and destroyed them even unto the ground.

The dead bodies of thy servants have they given to be Psal. lxxix.
meat unto the fowls of the air, and the flesh of thy Saints
unto the beasts of the land.

Their blood have they shed like water on every side of Hierusalem, Psal. lxxix.
and there was no man to bury them.

And so we are become an open shame to our enemies, a Psal. lxxix.
very scorn and derision unto them that are round about us.

Lord, how long wilt thou be angry? Shall thy jealousy burn like Psal. lxxix.
fire for ever?

O God, wherefore art thou absent from us so long, why Psal. lxxiv.
is thy wrath such against the Sheep of thy pasture?

O remember not our old sins, but have mercy upon us, and that soon, Psal. lxxix.
for we are come to great misery.

But think upon the congregation, whom thou hast pur- Psal. lxxiv.
chased, and redeemed of old.

Help us, O God of our salvation, for the glory of thy name: Oh Psal. lxxix.
deliver us, and be merciful unto our sins for thy name's sake.

Wherefore do the Heathen say: Where is now their God? Psal. lxxix.

Lift up thy feet, that thou mayest utterly destroy every enemy, which Psal. lxxiv.
hath done evil in thy Sanctuary.

Pour out thine indignation upon the Heathen, that have Psal. lxxix.
not known thee: and upon the Kingdoms, that have not called
upon thy name.

Let the vengeance of thy servants' blood, that is shed, be openly Psal. lxxix.
shewed upon the Heathen in our sight.

Let the sorrowful sighing of the prisoners come before Psal. lxxix.
thee, according to the greatness of thy power, preserve thou
those that are appointed to die.

And as for the blasphemy (wherewith our enemies have blasphemed Psal. lxxix.
thee) reward thou them (O Lord) seven fold into their bosom.

So we that be thy people, and sheep of thy pasture, shall Psal. lxxix.
give thee thanks for ever: and will alway be shewing forth
thy praise from generation to generation.

Glory be to the Father. &c. As it was in the. &c.

¶ After the Psalm the prayer following shall be said by the minister
alone, with a high voice, at saying whereof the people shall devoutly
give ear, and shall both with mind and speech to themselves assent
to the same prayer.

¶ *The prayer.*

O ALMIGHTY and everlasting God, our heavenly Father, we thy disobedient and rebellious children, now by thy just judgment sore afflicted, and in great danger to be oppressed, by thine and our sworn and most deadly enemies the Turks, Infidels, and Miscreants, do make humble suit to the throne of thy grace, for thy mercy, and aid against the same our mortal enemies: for though we do profess the name of thy only Son Christ our Saviour, yet through our manifold sins and wickedness we have most justly deserved so much of thy wrath and indignation, that we can not but say, O Lord correct us in thy mercy and not in thy fury. Better it is for us to fall into thy hands, than into the hands of men, and especially into the hands of Turks and Infidels thy professed enemies, who now invade thine inheritance. Against thee, O Lord, have we sinned, and transgressed thy commandments: against Turks, Infidels, and other enemies of the Gospel of thy dear Son Jesus Christ, have we not offended, but only in this, that we acknowledge thee, the eternal Father, and thy only Son our Redeemer, with the Holy Ghost, the comforter, to be the only true Almighty and everliving God. For if we would deny and blaspheme thy most holy name, forsake the Gospel of thy dear Son, embrace false religion, commit horrible Idolatries, and give ourselves to all impure, wicked, and abominable life, as they do; the devil, the world, the Turk, and all other thine enemies would be at peace with us, according to the saying of thy Son Christ: If you were of the world, the world would love his own. But therefore hate they us, because we love thee: therefore persecute they us, because we acknowledge thee, God the Father, and Jesus Christ thy Son, whom thou hast sent. The Turk goeth about to set up, to extol, and to magnify that wicked monster and damned soul Mahumet above thy dearly beloved Son Jesus Christ, whom we in heart believe, and with mouth confess, to be our only Saviour and Redeemer. Wherefore awake, O Lord our God and heavenly Father, look upon us thy children, and all such Christians as now be besieged and afflicted, with thy fatherly and merciful countenance: and overthrow and destroy thine and our enemies, sanctify thy blessed name emonges us, which they blaspheme, establish

John xv.

thy kingdom, which they labour to overthrow: suffer not thine enemies to prevail against those, that now call upon thy name, and put their trust in thee, lest the Heathen and Infidels say: Where is now their God? But in thy great mercy save, defend, and deliver all thy afflicted Christians in this and all other invasions of these Infidels, that we and they that delight to be named Christians may continually laud, praise, and magnify thy holy name, with thy only Son Jesus Christ, and the Holy Ghost, to whom be all laud, praise, glory, and empire for ever and ever. AMEN.

¶ Psalms which may be sung or said before the beginning, or after the ending of public prayer.

ii. iii. vii. x. xi. xiv. xxii. xxvii. xlvi. lii. lvi. lxx. lxxiiii. lxxxiii. lxxxx. lxxxxiiii. cxxi. cxxiii. cxxx. cxl.

IX. A SHORT FORM OF THANKSGIVING TO GOD for the delivery of the Isle of *Malta* from the invasion and long siege thereof by the great army of the Turks both by sea and land, and for sundry other victories lately obtained[1] by the christians against the said Turks, to be used in the common prayer within the province of Canterbury, on Sundays, Wednesdays, and Fridays, for the space of six weeks next ensuing the receipt hereof.

Set forth by the most Reverend father in God, Matthew by God's providence Archbishop of Canterbury, Primate of all England and Metropolitan.

Psalm 50.

Call upon me in the day of trouble; so will I deliver thee, and thou shalt glorify me.

¶ After the end of the Collect in the Litany which beginneth with these words: We humbly beseech thee, O Father. &c. shall follow this Psalm to be said of the minister, with the answer of the people.

We praise thee, O Lord, with our whole hearts, and we will speak of thy marvellous works.

We will be glad and rejoice in thee, we will sing praises unto thy name, O most high.

For that our enemies are turned back, are fallen and perished at thy presence.

For that thou hast rebuked the heathen, and destroyed the wicked, and brought their destruction to an end.

Thou hast been a refuge for the poor, a refuge in due time, even in affliction.

Thou hast delivered us from our strong enemy, and from them that hated us, for they were too strong for us.

We have sinned with our fathers, we have committed iniquity, and done wickedly.

Nevertheless the Lord hath saved us for his name's sake, that he might make his power to be known.

O our deliverer from our enemies, even thou hast set us

[1 No doubt, in Hungary (see p. 527), which Solyman the magnificent had himself invaded with another army.]

up from them that rose against us : thou hast delivered us from the cruel man.

Great deliverance hast thou given us, and shewed us great mercy in the day of our calamity.

Though we said in our haste, we were cast out of thy sight, yet thou heardest the voice of our prayer, when we cried unto thee.

Thou rememberedst us in our base estate, and rescuedst us from our oppressors.

O God, the proud were risen against us, and the assemblies of violent men sought our souls, and did not set thee before their eyes.

They said in their hearts, Let us destroy them altogether, there is no help for them in God.

If the Lord had not been on our side, may we now say : if the Lord had not been on our side, when Infidels rose up against us;

They had swallowed us up quick, when their wrath was kindled against us.

But praised be the Lord, which hath not given us as a prey unto their teeth, nor suffered our enemies to triumph over us.

Let us therefore confess before the Lord his loving kindness, and his wonderful works before the sons of men.

Let us exalt him in the congregation of the people, and praise him in the assembly of the Elders. Psal. 72.[2]

Blessed be the Lord God of Israel, which only doth wondrous things, and blessed be the name of his majesty for ever. Amen. Amen.

¶ After this Psalm shall be said by the minister openly, and with an high voice, the Collect following.

The Collect.

O HEAVENLY and most merciful Father, the defender of those that put their trust in thee, the sure fortress of all them that flee to thee for succour : who of thy most just judgments for our disobedience against thy holy word, and for our sinful and wicked living, nothing answering to our holy profession, which hath been an occasion that thy holy name hath been

[[2] The margin is somewhat damaged, so that the other references have disappeared.]

blasphemed emonges the heathen, hast of late most sharply corrected and scourged our christian brethren thy servants with terrible wars and dreadful invasions of most deadly and cruel enemies, Turks and Infidels: But now of thy fatherly pity and merciful goodness, without any desert of ours, even for thine own name's sake, hast, by thy assistance given to divers Christian princes and potentates, at length, when all our hope was almost past, dispersed and put to confusion those Infidels, being thine and our mortal enemies, and graciously delivered thy afflicted and distressed Christians in the Isle of *Malta* and sundry other places in Christendom, to the glory and praise of thy name, and to the exceeding comfort of all sorrowful Christian hearts: We render unto thee most humble and hearty thanks for these thy great mercies shewed to them that were thus afflicted and in danger; we laud and praise thee, most humbly beseeching thee to grant unto all those that profess thy holy name, that we may shew ourselves in our living thankful to thee for these and all other thy benefits: Endue us (O Lord) and all other Christian people with thy heavenly grace, that we may truly know thee, and obediently walk in thy holy commandments, lest we again provoke thy just wrath against us: Continue thy great mercies towards us, and as in this, so in all other invasions of Turks and Infidels, save and defend thy holy Church, that all posterities ensuing may continually confess thy holy name, praising and magnifying thee with thy only Son Jesus Christ, and the Holy Ghost, to whom be all laud, praise, glory and empire, for ever and ever.   Amen.

¶ Imprynted at London by Wylyam Seres, dwellinge at the west
end of Paules, at the sygne of
the Hedgehogge.

¶ Cum priuilegio ad imprimendum solum.

Anno. 1565.

A FORM to be used in common prayer, every Sunday, Wed- x.
nesday, and Friday, through the whole Realm: To
excite and stir all godly people to pray unto God
for the preservation of those Christians and their Countries, that are now invaded by the Turk in Hungary,
or elsewhere.

Set forth by the most Reverend father in God, Matthew, Archbishop of
Canterbury, by the authority of the Queen's Majesty.

The Preface.

WHERE as the Turks the last year most fiercely assailing the Isle of *Malta*, with a great army and navy, by the grace and assistance of Almighty God (for the which we with other Christians at that time by our hearty prayers made most humble suit) were from thence repelled and driven, with their great loss, shame and confusion; they, being inflamed with malice and desire of vengeance, do now by land invade the kingdom of Hungary (which hath of long time been as a most strong wall and defence to all Christendom) far more terribly and dreadfully, and with greater force and violence, than they did either the last year, or at any time within the remembrance of man: It is our parts, which for distance of place cannot succour them with temporal aid of men, to assist them at the least with spiritual aid, that is to say, with earnest, hearty, and fervent prayer to Almighty God for them, desiring him, after the examples of Moses, Josaphat, Ezechias, and other *Exod.* xvii. godly men, in his great mercy to defend, preserve, and deliver Christians, iiii. *Reg.* xix. professing his holy name, and to give sufficient might and power to the Emperor's excellent Majesty, as God's principal minister, to repress the rage and violence of these Infidels, who by all tyranny and cruelty labour utterly to root out not only true religion, but also the very name and memory of Christ our only Saviour, and all Christianity. And forsomuch as if the Infidels, who have already a great part of that most goodly and strong kingdom in their possession, should prevail wholly against the same (which God forbid) all the rest of Christendom should lie as it were naked and open to the incursions and invasions of the said savage and most cruel enemies the Turks, to the most dreadful danger of whole Christendom; all diligence, heartiness, and fervency is so much the more now to be used in our prayers for God's aid, how far greater the danger and peril is now, than before it was. And although it is every Christian man's duty, of his own devotion to pray at all times: yet for that the corrupt nature of man is so slothful and negligent in this his duty, he hath need by often and sundry means to be stirred up, and put in remembrance of his duty.

For the effectual accomplishment whereof, it is ordered and appointed as followeth.

First, that all Parsons and Curates shall exhort their parishioners to endeavour themselves to come unto the Church, with as many of their family, as may be spared from their necessary business: And they to resort thither, not only upon Sundays and holidays, but also upon Wednesdays and Fridays, during this dangerous and perilous time: exhorting them there reverently and godly to behave themselves, and with penitent minds, kneeling on their knees, to lift up their hearts, and pray to the merciful God to turn from us, and all Christendom, those plagues and punishments, which we and they through our unthankfulness and sinful lives have deserved.

Secondly, that the said Parsons and Curates shall then distinctly and plainly read the general confession appointed in the book of Service, with the residue of the Morning prayer, unto the first lesson.

Then for the first Lesson shall be read one of the Chapters hereafter following, or so much thereof as is appointed.

Exod. xiiii. *Exod.* xvii. beginning at these words: *Then came Amelech and fought with Israel.* &c. *Josue* x. Unto these words: *And laid great stones on the Cave's mouth, which remain until this day. Judges* vii. i *kyng* xvii. iiii *kyng* vii. iiii *kyng* xix. *The second of the Chronicles, or Paralipomenon* xx. Unto these words: *And his God gave him rest on every side. Act.* xii.

After that, instead of *Te Deum laudamus,* that is to say: We praise thee, O God: shall be said the li. Psalm: Have mercy upon me, O God. &c.

Then immediately after, upon Wednesdays and Fridays, shall be said the Creed. I believe in God. &c. And after that the accustomed prayers following, unto the end of the Morning prayer. And upon Sundays, the second Lessons shall be read, as they are ordinarily appointed with the rest of the Morning prayer.

That done, the Litany shall be said in the mids of the people, unto the end of the Collect in the same Litany, which beginneth with these words: *We humbly beseech thee, O Father.* &c. And then shall follow one of these Psalms in their order, to be said of the Minister according to the order of the days, with the answer of the people.

¶ *The Psalm.*

HEAR our prayer, O Lord, consider our desire: hearken unto us for thy truth and righteousness sake. *Psal.* cxliii.

Oh hearken then to the voice of our calling, our King and our God: for unto thee will we make our prayer. *Psal.* v.

O God, the Heathen are come into thine inheritance: thine adversaries roar in the mids of thy congregations, and set up their banners for tokens. *Psal.* lxxix. & lxxiv.

They have set fire upon thy holy places, and have defiled the dwelling place of thy name: and destroyed them even unto the ground. *Psal.* lxxiv.

The dead bodies of thy servants have they given to be meat unto the fowls of the air: and the flesh of thy saints unto the beasts of the land. *Psal.* lxxix.

Their blood have they shed like water on every side of Hierusalem: and there was no man to bury them. *Psal.* lxxix.

And so we are become an open shame to our enemies: a very scorn and derision unto them that are round about us. *Psal.* lxxix.

Lord, how long wilt thou be angry? Shall thy jealousy burn like fire for ever? *Psal.* lxxix.

O God, wherefore art thou absent from us so long? why is thy wrath so kindled against the sheep of thy pasture? *Psal.* lxxiv.

Oh remember not our old sins, but have mercy upon us, and that soon: for we are come to great misery. *Psal.* lxxix.

But think upon the congregation: whom thou hast purchased and redeemed of old. *Psal.* lxxiv.

Help us, O God of our salvation, for the glory of thy name: Oh deliver us, and be merciful unto our sins, for thy name's sake. *Psal.* lxxix.

Wherefore do the Heathen say, Where is now their God? *Psal.* lxxix.

Make haste that thou mayst utterly destroy every enemy: which hath done evil in thy sanctuary. *Psal.* lxxiv.

Arise, O GOD: maintain thine own cause: remember how the wicked man blasphemeth thee daily. *Psal.* lxxiv.

Pour out thine indignation upon the Heathen that have not known thee: and upon the kingdoms that have not called upon thy name. *Psal.* lxxix.

O let the vengeance of thy servants' blood that is shed: be openly shewed upon the Heathen in our sight. *Psal.* lxxix.

Deliver us from our enemies, O God: defend us from them that rise up against us. *Psal.* lix.

[LITURG. QU. ELIZ.]

Psal. xxxv.   Let them be confounded and put to shame: let them be turned back and brought to confusion, that imagine mischief against us.

Psal. lxxix.   So we that be thy people, and sheep of thy pasture, shall give thee thanks for ever: and will alway be shewing forth thy praise from generation to generation.

Glory be to the Father, and to the Son, and to the Holy Ghost.

As it was in the beginning, is now, and ever shall be, world without end, Amen.

Or this Psalm.

Psal. ii.   THE Heathen do furiously rage together, and the Kings of the earth stand up, and rulers take counsel together: against the Lord, and against his anointed.

Psal. xi.   The ungodly bend their bows, and make ready their arrows within the quiver: that they may shoot at those that call upon the name of the Lord.

Psal. xciv.   They smite down thy people, O Lord: and trouble thine heritage.

Psal. iii.   Lord, how are they increased that trouble us! many are they that rise against us.

Psal. iii.   Many one there be, that say of our souls: There is no help for them in their God.

Psal. x.   The ungodly are so proud, that they care not for God: neither is God in all their thoughts, nor his judgments in their sight.

Psal. x.   They have said in their hearts, Tush, God hath forgotten: he hideth away his face, and he will never see it.

Psal. xxv.   For thy name's sake, O Lord, be merciful unto our sins: for they are great.

Psal. xxv.   Turn thee unto us and have mercy upon us: for we are desolate and in great misery.

Psal. x.   Stand not so far off, O Lord: neither hide thy face in the needful time of trouble.

Psal. xxvii.   Hearken unto our voice, O Lord, now when we cry unto thee: arise, O Lord God, and lift up thine hand, and forget not thy people.

Psal. x.   Wherefore should the wicked blaspheme God? while he doth say in his heart, Tush, thou God carest not for it.

Psal. x.   O take the matter into thy hand: thy people commit themselves unto thee, for thou art their helper in their distress.

Break thou the power of the wicked and malicious: smite all our enemies upon the cheek bone, and break the teeth of the ungodly. *Psal.* x. *Psal.* iii.

Rain snares, fire and brimstone, storm and tempest upon them: and let this be their portion to drink. *Psal.* xi.

Recompense thou their wickedness, and destroy them in their own malice: yea, the Lord our God shall destroy them, and deliver us. *Psal.* xciv.

And we shall give thanks unto the Lord according to his great mercies: and will praise the name of the Lord the most high. *Psal.* vii.

We will declare thy name unto our brethren: in the mids of the congregation will we praise thee, and magnify thy salvation world without end. *Psal.* xxii.

Glory be to the Father. &c.
As it was in the beginning. &c.

¶ *Or this.*

O Lord, many dogs are come about us: and the councell of the wicked layeth siege against us. *Psal.* xxii.

Many Oxen do compass us: fat bulls of Basan close us in on every side. *Psal.* xxii.

They gape upon us with their mouths: as it were ramping and roaring Lions. *Psal.* xxii.

Our enemies are daily in hand to swallow us up: for they be exceeding many that fight against us, O thou most high. *Psal.* lvi.

O remember not the sins and offences of our youth and times past: but according to thy mercy think upon us, O Lord, for thy goodness. *Psal.* xxv.

For thou, O Lord, art our defender: thou art our health, and our salvation. *Psal.* iii.

O Lord our God, in thee have we put our trust: save us from all them that persecute us, and deliver us. *Psal.* vii.

Lest they devour our souls like Lions, and tear them in pieces: whiles there is none to help. *Psal.* vii.

Save us from these Lions' mouths: and from among the horns of the Unicorns. *Psal.* xxii.

Oh deliver not the soul of thy turtle dove unto the multitude of the enemies: and forget not thy poor congregation for ever. *Psal.* lxxiv.

And our praises shall be of thee in the great congrega- *Psal.* xxii.

tion: our vows will we perform in the sight of them that fear thee.

Psal. xxii. And all the ends of the world shall remember themselves, and be turned unto the Lord: and all the kindreds of the nations shall worship before him.

Glory be to the Father. &c.

As it was in the beginning. &c.

After the Psalm, the prayer following shall be said by the Minister alone, with a high voice. At saying whereof, the people shall devoutly give ear, and shall both with mind and speech to themselves assent to the same prayer.

The prayer.

ALMIGHTY and everliving God, our heavenly Father, we thy disobedient and rebellious children, now by thy just judgment sore afflicted, and in great danger to be oppressed, by thine and our sworn and most deadly enemies, the Turks, Infidels, and miscreants, do make humble suit to the throne of thy grace, for thy mercy and aid against the same our mortal enemies. For though we do profess the name of thy only Son Christ our Saviour, yet through our manifold sins and wickedness we have most justly deserved so much of thy wrath and indignation, that we can not but say: O Lord, correct us in thy mercy, and not in thy fury. And better it is for us to fall into thy hands, than into the hands of men, and especially into the hands of Turks and Infidels, thy professed enemies, who now invade thine inheritance. Against thee (O Lord) have we sinned, and transgressed thy commandments: Against Turks, Infidels, and other enemies of the Gospel of thy dear Son Jesus Christ have we not offended, but only in this, that we acknowledge thee, the eternal Father, and thy only Son our redeemer, with the Holy Ghost, the comforter, to be one only true, almighty, and everliving God. For if we would deny and blaspheme thy most holy name, forsake the Gospel of thy dear Son, embrace false religion, commit horrible Idolatries, and give ourselves to all impure, wicked, and abominable life, as they do; the devil, the world, the Turk, and all other thine enemies would be at

John xv. peace with us, according to the saying of thy Son Christ: If you were of the world, the world would love his own. But therefore hate they us, because we love thee; therefore persecute they us, because we acknowledge thee God the Father, and Jesus Christ thy Son, whom thou hast sent. The Turk goeth about to set up, to extol, and to magnify that wicked monster and damned soul Mahumet, above thy dearly beloved Son Jesus Christ, whom we in heart believe, and with mouth confess to be our only saviour and redeemer. Wherefore awake, O Lord our God and heavenly Father, and with thy fatherly and merciful countenance look upon us thy children, and all such Christians, as are now by those most cruel enemies invaded and assaulted: overthrow and destroy thine and our enemies, sanctify thy blessed name among us, which they blaspheme, establish thy kingdom, which they labour to overthrow: suffer not thine enemies to prevail against those that now call upon thy name and put their trust in thee, lest the Heathen and Infidels say: Where is now their GOD? But in thy great mercy save, defend, and deliver all thy afflicted Christians, in this and all other invasions of these infidels, and give to the Emperor[1] thy servant, and all the Christian army now assembled with him, thy comfortable might and courage, that we and they that delight to be named Christians, may enjoy both outward peace, and inwardly laud, praise, and magnify thy holy name for ever, with thy only Son Jesus Christ, and the Holy Ghost, to whom be all laud, praise, glory and empire for ever and ever. Amen.

¶ *This prayer to be said at Evening prayer, immediately after the Collect of the day.*

O LORD God of hosts, most righteous Judge, and most merciful Father: These dreadful dangers and distresses wherein other Christian men our brethren and neighbours do now stand, by reason of the terrible invasions of most cruel and deadly enemies the Turks, Infidels, and miscreants, do set before our eyes a terrible example of our own worthy deserts, by our continual sinning and offending against thy great majesty and most severe justice; and do also put us in remembrance, here in this our Realm of England, of our most deserved thanks for our great tranquillity, peace, and

[1] Maximilian II. lay then encamped in the vicinity of Raab, with the main body of his army, to watch the motions of the Turks, who, under Solyman, again entered Hungary in the spring of 1566. Coxe's House of Austria, Vol. II. p. 322.]

quietness, which we by thy high benefit, and preservation of
our peaceable Prince, whom thou hast given us, do enjoy:
Whiles others in the like or less offences, than ours are against
thy majesty, are by thy righteous judgments so terribly
scourged, these thy fatherly mercies do set forth thy unspeakable patience which thou usest towards us thy ingrate
children, as well in the same thy gracious benefits of such
our peace and tranquillity, as in thy wholesome warnings of
us by thy just punishments of others, less offenders than we
be. For the which thy great benefits bestowed upon us
without all our deserving, as we praise thy Fatherly goodness
towards us: so being stricken in our minds with great dread
of thy just vengeance, for that we do so little regard the
great riches of thy Fatherly goodness and patience towards
us, we most humbly beseech thee to grant us thy heavenly
grace, that we continue no longer in the taking of thy
manifold graces and goodness in vain. And upon deep compassion of the dreadful distresses of our brethren and neighbours the Christians, by the cruel and most terrible invasions
of these most deadly enemies the Turks; we do make and
offer up our most humble and hearty prayers before the
throne of thy grace, for the mitigation of thy wrath, and
purchase of thy pity and fatherly favour towards them: and
not only towards them, but to us also by them; forsomuch
as our danger or safety doth follow upon success of them:
Grant them and us thy grace, O most merciful Father, that
we may rightly understand, and unfeignedly confess our sins
against thy majesty, to be the very causes of this thy just
scourge, and our misery: grant us true and hearty repentance
of all our sins against thee, that, the causes of thy just offence
being removed, the effects of these our deserved miseries may
withal be taken away. Give to thy poor Christians, O Lord
God of hosts, strength from heaven, that they, neither respecting their own weakness and paucity, nor fearing the
multitude and fierceness of their enemies, or their dreadful
cruelty, but setting their eyes and only hope and trust upon
thee, and calling upon thy name, who art the giver of all victory,
may by thy power obtain victory against the infinite multitudes and fierceness of thine enemies, that all men understanding the same to be the act of thy grace, and not the deed of
man's might and power, may give unto thee all the praise

and glory : and specially thy poor Christians (by thy strong hand) being delivered out of the hands of their enemies, we for their and our own safety with them may yield and render unto thee all lauds, praises, and thanks, through thy Son, our Saviour Jesus Christ, to whom with thee and the Holy Ghost, one eternal God of most sacred majesty, be all praise, honour and glory, world without end. Amen.

¶ *Or this Collect of the Litany following.*

O ALMIGHTY God, king of all kings, and governour of all things, whose power no creature is able to resist, to whom it belongeth justly to punish sinners, and to be merciful to them that truly repent : save and deliver us (we humbly beseech thee) from the hands of our enemies : abate their pride, asswage their malice, and confound their devices, that we, being armed with thy defence, may be preserved evermore from all perils, to glorify thee, which art the only giver of all victory, through the merits of thy only Son Jesus Christ our Lord. Amen.

¶ *Psalms which may be sung or said before the beginning or after the ending of public prayer, or before and after Sermons.*

ii. iii. vii. x. xi. xxii. *unto the end of these words :*

In the mids of the congregation will I praise thee.

xxvii. xlvi. lii. lvi. lxx. lxxiiii. lxxxiii. xci. xciiii. cxxi. cxxiii. cxl.

IMPRINTED AT LON-
don in Powles Churchyarde by Ri-
charde Iugge, and Iohn Cawood, Printers to the Queenes
Maieſtie.

¶ Cum priuilegio Regiæ Maieſtatis.

XI. ¶ *THE PRAYER*[1].

O MOST mighty God, the Lord of hosts, the governour of all creatures, the only giver of all victories, who alone art able to strengthen the weak against the mighty, and to vanquish infinite multitudes of thine enemies with the countenance of a few of thy servants calling upon thy name, and trusting in thee: Defend, O Lord, thy servant, and our governour under thee, our Queen Elizabeth, and all thy people committed to her charge. O Lord, withstand the cruelty of all those which be common enemies as well to the truth of thy eternal word, as to their own natural prince and country, and manifestly to this crown and Realm of England, which thou hast of thy divine providence assigned in these our days to the government of thy servant, our sovereign, and gracious Queen. O most merciful Father, if it be thy holy will, make soft and tender the stony hearts of all those that exalt themselves against thy truth, and seek either to trouble the quiet of this Realm of England, or to oppress the crown of the same; and convert them to the knowledge of thy Son the only saviour of the world, Jesus Christ, that we and they may jointly glorify thy mercies. Lighten, we beseech thee, their ignorant hearts, to embrace the truth of thy word; or else so abate their cruelty (O most mighty Lord), that this our Christian region, with others that confess thy holy gospel, may obtain by thine aid and strength surety from all enemies, without shedding of christian blood, whereby all they which be oppressed with their tyranny may be relieved, and they which be in fear of their cruelty may be comforted: and finally, that all christian Realms, and specially this Realm of England, may by thy defence and protection continue in the truth of the Gospel, and enjoy perfect peace, quietness, and security; and that we for these thy mercies

[1 See p. 476. This prayer, and the fourth part of the 'Homilie against disobedience and wylfull rebellion,' were appended to a Form of prayer, which Charles the first caused to be printed at Oxford in 1643 by the university printer, Leonard Lichfield, for a 'solemne Fast the second *Friday* in every moneth, beginning on the tenth day of November.']

jointly all together with one consonant heart and voice may thankfully render to thee all laud and praise, that we, knit in one godly concord and unity amongst our selves, may continually magnify thy glorious name, who with thy Son our Saviour Jesus Christ, and the Holy Ghost, art one eternal, almighty, and most merciful God: To whom be all laud and praise, world without end. Amen.

XII. ¶ *A THANKSGIVING for the suppression of the last rebellion.*

O[1] HEAVENLY, and most merciful Father, the defender of those that put their trust in thee, the sure fortress of all them that flee to thee for succour: who of thy most just judgments for our disobedience and rebellion against thy holy word, and for our sinful and wicked living, nothing answering to our holy profession, whereby we have given an occasion that thy holy name hath been blasphemed amongst the ignorant, hast of late both sore abashed the whole Realm and people of England with the terror and danger of rebellion, thereby to awake us out of our dead sleep of careless security; and hast yet by the miseries following the same rebellion more sharply punished part of our countrymen, and Christian brethren, who have more nearly felt the same; and most dreadfully hast scourged some of the seditious persons with terrible executions[2], justly inflicted for their disobedience to thee, and to thy servant their sovereign, to the example of us all, and to the warning, correction, and amendment of thy servants, of thine accustomed goodness turning always the wickedness of evil men to the profit of them that fear thee: who, in thy judgments remembering thy mercy, hast by thy assistance given the victory to thy servant our Queen, her true nobility, and faithful subjects, with so little, or rather no effusion of Christian blood, as also might justly have ensued, to the exceeding comfort of all sorrowful christian hearts; and that of thy fatherly pity, and merciful goodness only, and even for thine own name's sake, without any our desert at all. Wherefore we render unto thee most humble and hearty thanks for these thy great mercies shewed unto us, who had deserved sharper punishment; most humbly beseeching thee to

[¹ See p. 525.]
[² Stow (p. 1125) says, on 'the fourth and fift of Januarie [1570], did suffer at Durham to the number of threescore and sixe Constables and other: then sir *George Bowes*, Marshall, finding many to be faultors [guilty] in the foresaid rebellion, did see them executed in euery market towne and other places, betwixt Newcastle and Wetherby, about 60. miles in length, and 40. miles in breadth, as himselfe reported unto me.']

grant unto all us that confess thy holy name, and profess the true and perfect religion of thy holy Gospel, thy heavenly grace to shew our selves in our living, according to our profession: that we, truly knowing thee in thy blessed word, may obediently walk in thy holy commandments, and that we, being warned by this thy fatherly correction, do provoke thy just wrath against us no more; but may enjoy the continuance of thy great mercies toward us, thy right hand, as in this, so in all other invasions, rebellions, and dangers, continually saving and defending our Church, our Realm, our Queen and people of England; that all our posterities ensuing, confessing thy holy name, professing thy holy Gospel, and leading an holy life, may perpetually praise, and magnify thee, with thy only Son Jesus Christ our Saviour, and the Holy Ghost: to whom be all laud, praise, glory, and empire for ever and ever. Amen.

XIII. ¶ A FORM OF COMMON PRAYER to be used, and so commanded by authority of the Queen's Majesty, and necessary for the present time and state. 1572. 27. *Octob.*

The Preface.

FIRST, that all Parsons and Curates shall every Sunday, at convenient times, exhort their parishioners to endeavour themselves to come to the Church, with as many of their family, as may be spared from their necessary business : and they to resort thither, not only upon Sundays and Holydays, but also upon Wednesdays, and Fridays, specially in Cities and great Towns, during these dangerous and perilous times of the troubles in Christendom ; exhorting them there reverently and godly to behave themselves, and with penitent minds, kneeling on their knees, to lift up their hearts, and pray to the merciful God, to turn from us of this Realm, and all the rest of Christendom, those plagues and punishments, which we and others through our unthankfulness and sinful lives have deserved.

Secondly, that the said Parsons and Curates, shall then distinctly and plainly read the general confession appointed in the book of service, with the residue of the morning prayer, unto the first Lesson.

Then for the first Lesson shall be read one of the Chapters hereafter following, or so much thereof as is appointed.

Any of these Chapters may be read for the first Lesson, at the disposition of the Minister, in the week days : and upon the Sunday or holy days for the second Lessons.

Matthew the third, the whole Chapter.

Matthew the fifth, (to this place,) Ye are the salt of the earth.

Matthew the sixt, whole.

Matthew the seventh, whole.

Matthew the tenth, (beginning,) Behold, I send you forth as sheep. &c. *to the end.*

Matthew the sixteenth, whole.

Matthew the four and twentieth, whole.

Matthew the five and twentieth, whole.

Luke the fifteenth, whole.

Luke the seventeenth, (beginning,) When he was demanded of the Pharisees. &c. *to the end.*

Luke the eighteenth, (unto) They brought unto him also infants. &c.

Luke the one and twentieth, whole.

Acts the ninth, (unto) And it came to pass, as Peter walked through all quarters.

Romans the second Chapter, whole.
Romans the twelfth Chapter, whole.
Romans the thirteenth Chapter, whole.

Ephesians the fifth, (unto) Wives submit yourselves unto your own husbands.

Thessalonians. i. Epistle. ii. Chapter, (beginning) For ye brethren became followers of the church of God. *to the end.*

Thessalonians. i. Epistle. iiii. Chapter, (beginning) But I would not have you to be ignorant brethren. *to the end.*

Thessalonians. i. Epistle. v. Chapter, whole.
Timothy. i. Epistle. ii. Chapter, whole.

After that, in stead of *Te Deum laudamus,* that is to say, *We praise thee, O God,* shall be said the li. Psalm, *Have mercy upon me, O God. &c.*

Then immediately after, upon Wednesdays and Fridays, shall be said the Creed, *I believe in God. &c.* and after that the accustomed prayers following, unto the end of the morning prayer. And upon Sundays the second lessons shall be read as they are ordinarily appointed, with the rest of the morning prayer.

That done, the Litany shall be said in the midst of the people, unto the end of the Collect in the same Litany, which beginneth with these words, *We humbly beseech thee, O Father. &c.* and then shall follow one of these Psalms in their order, to be said of the Minister, according to the order of the days, with the answer of the people.

A prayer for the forgiveness of sins[1].

O COME, let us humble ourselves : and fall down before the Lord our maker, with reverence and fear. *Psal.* 95.

[1 This prayer may be compared with the psalm in the Service for 1563. See p. 482.]

A PRAYER.

Osee 6.
Acts 3.
Let us repent and turn from our wickedness, and turn again unto our Lord : and our sins shall be forgiven us.

Jonas 3.
Osee 6.
Let us turn, and the Lord will turn from his heavy wrath: he hath smitten us, and he will heal us, he will pardon us, and we shall not perish.

Psal. 5[1].
We acknowledge our faults, O Lord : and our sins are ever before our sight.

Lam. 51[5].
We have sore provoked thine anger, O Lord : thy wrath is waxed hot, and thy heavy displeasure is sore kindled against us.

Psal. 6.
But rebuke us not, O Lord, in thine indignation : neither chasten us in thy heavy displeasure.

Judith 8.
Job 11.
Sapi. 11.
In deed we acknowledge that all punishments are less than our deserving : but yet of thy mercy, Lord, correct us to amendment, and plague us not to our destruction.

Psal. 25.
O remember not the sins and offences of our youth, and times past, but according to thy mercy think upon us, O Lord, for thy goodness.

Psal. 10.
Stand not so far off, O Lord : neither hide thy face in the needful time of trouble.

Psal. 25.
Turn thee unto us, and have mercy upon us : for we are desolate and in great misery.

Baruc. 3.
Jonas 2.
And now in the vexation of our spirits, and the anguish of our souls : we remember thee, and we cry unto thee, hear, Lord, and have mercy.

Dan. 9.
For we do not pour out our prayers before thy face, trusting in our own righteousness : but in thy great and manifold mercies.

Psal. 25.
For thine own sake, and for thy holy name's sake, incline thine ear, and hear : and be merciful to our sins, for they are great.

Psal. 79.
Help us, O God of our salvation, for the glory of thy Name : O deliver us, and save us for thy name's sake.

Psal. 79.
So we that be thy people, and sheep of thy pasture, shall give thee thanks for ever : and will be always shewing forth thy praise from generation to generation.

Glory be to the Father. &c. As it was in the. &c.

Prayers for true repentance and mercy.

MOST merciful Father, who hast in thy holy word, the word of truth, promised mercy unto sinners that do repent and turn unto thee, and hast by thy terrible examples of thy just anger, being executed upon people and countries round about us, called us, and most mercifully moved us to repentance, and by thy patience and long suffering of us hitherto, hast graciously granted us time and space to repent: grant also, we beseech thee, both to them and us grace truly to repent, and unfeignedly to turn unto thee with amendment of life, and to trust in thy mercies, and safely to rest under thy continual protection from all enemies and evils, both bodily and ghostly, through our Saviour Jesus Christ, who with thee and the Holy Ghost liveth and reigneth one God, world without end. Amen.

Another for the same.

WE have sinned, Lord, we have sinned grievously, we have done unjustly, we have lived wickedly: we are sorry therefore, O Lord, yea, we are most sorry, that we are no more sorry for our sins: but thou, Lord GOD, Father of all mercies, we humbly beseech thee, be not angry with us for ever for our great and manifold sins, neither deal with us according to our deserts, neither reward us according to our wickedness; but even for thy self, O Lord God, and for thy holy name's sake, for thy most gracious assured promises made unto penitent sinners in thy holy word, the word of truth, for thy infinite mercies which are in thy dearly beloved Son Jesu Christ our Saviour, for his sake, for his death and precious blood, be merciful unto us sinners; and so we, who have most grievously offended thy divine majesty, shall continually magnify thy great and infinite mercy, through our Saviour Jesus Christ, to whom with thee and the Holy Ghost be all honour and glory, world without end. AMEN.

A prayer to be delivered from our enemies.

O HEARKEN to the voice of our prayer, our King and our God: for unto thee do we make our complaint. *Psal.* 5.

O Lord, the counsel of the wicked conspireth against us: and our enemies are daily in hand to swallow us up. *Psal.* 22.

They gape upon us with their mouths: as it were ramping and roaring lions. *Psal.* 22.

But thou, O Lord, art our defender: thou art our health and our salvation. *Psal.* 3.

Psal. 7.	We do put our trust in thee, O God: save us from all them that persecute us, and deliver us.
Psal. 10.	O take the matter into thy hand, thy people commit themselves unto thee: for thou art their helper in their distress.
Psal. 7. & 22.	Save us from the Lions' mouths, and from the horns of the Unicorns: lest they devour us, and tear us in pieces, while there is none to help.
Psal. 74.	O deliver not the soul of thy Turtle dove unto the multitude of the enemies: and forget not thy poor congregation for ever.
Psal. 59.	Deliver us from our enemies, O God: defend and save us from them that imagine mischief, and rise up against us.
Psal. 7.	And we shall give thanks unto thee, O Lord, according to thy great mercies: and will praise the name of the Lord most high.
Psal. 22.	We will declare thy name unto our brethren: in the mids of the congregation will we praise thee, and magnify thy salvation world without end.

Glory be to the Father, and to the Son: and to the Holy Ghost.

As it was in the beginning, is now, and ever shall be: world without end. Amen.

The Collect of the Litany in the time of war.

The prayer following for the Queen must be said every day for the second Collect after the Psalm.

A thanksgiving and prayer for the preservation of the Queen, and the Realm.

O GOD, most merciful Father, who in thy great mercies hast both given unto us a peaceable princess, and a gracious Queen, and also hast very often and miraculously saved her from sundry great perils and dangers, and by her government hast preserved us and the whole Realm from manifold mischiefs and dreadful plagues, wherewith nations round about us have been and be most grievously afflicted: have mercy upon them, O Lord, and grant us grace, we beseech thee, for these thy great benefits, that we may be thankful and obedient unto thee, to fly from all things that may offend thee, and provoke thy wrath and indignation against us, and to order our lives in all things that may please thee; that thy servant our sovereign Lady, and we thy people committed to her charge, may by thy protection be continually preserved from all deceits and violences of enemies, and from all other dangers and evils both bodily and ghostly, and by thy goodness may be maintained in all peace and godliness: grant this, O merciful Father, for thy dear Son's sake our Saviour Jesus Christ; to whom with thee, and the Holy Ghost, one God immortal, invisible, and only wise, be all honour and glory for ever and ever. Amen.

A prayer for deliverance from enemies.

Hear our prayer, O Lord, consider our desire: hearken unto us for thy truth and mercy's sake. *Psal.* 14.

Lord, how are they increased that trouble us: many are they that rise against us. *Psal.* 3.

The ungodly bend their bows, and make ready their arrows within the quiver: that they may shoot at those that call upon the name of the Lord. *Psal.* 11.

They smite down thy people, O Lord: and trouble thine heritage. *Psal.* 104.

The dead bodies of thy servants have they given to be meat unto the fowls of the air: and the flesh of thy saints unto the beasts of the land. *Psal.* 79.

Their blood have they shed like water on every side of Hierusalem: and there was no man to bury them. *Psal.* 79.

And we that live are become an open shame to our enemies: a very scorn and derision unto them that are round about us. *Psal.* 79.

O Lord, why is thy wrath such against the sheep of thy pasture? how long wilt thou be angry? shall thy jealousy burn like fire for ever? *Psal.* 74. & 79.

Wherefore should the ungodly say, Where is now their God: there is now no more help for them in their God? *Psal.* 79.

Oh remember not our old sins, but have mercy upon us, and that soon: for we are come to great misery. *Psal.* 79.

O let the sorrowful sighing of the prisoners come before thee, according to the greatness of thy power: preserve thou those sely[1] souls, that are appointed to die. *Psal.* 79.

O Lord, think upon the congregation of thy people, whom thou hast purchased and redeemed of old: O deliver us, and save us, for the glory of thy name. *sal.* 74.

And our praises shall be of thee in the great congregation: our vows will we perform in the sight of them that fear thee. *Psal.* 22.

[[1] Sely: simple, inoffensive.]

[LITURG. QU. ELIZ.]

Psal. 22. And all the ends of the world shall remember themselves, and be turned unto the Lord: and all the kindreds of the nations shall worship before him.

Glory be to the Father. &c.
As it was in the beginning. &c.

A prayer.

O MOST righteous God, and most merciful Father, who as well by the dreadful plagues and afflictions of nations round about us, as by long suffering and saving of us, and by manifold benefits bestowed upon us, hast shewed thy severity in punishing or trying of them, and thy mercy in sparing and blessing of us: we most humbly and heartily beseech thee, in thy justice to remember thy mercy towards them, and to save them, and to grant unto us grace not to despise the riches of thy patience and goodness towards us, neither by hardness of heart and impenitency to heap upon ourselves vengeance in the day of vengeance; but that we, being taught by the example of their punishment to fear thy justice, and moved by thy long suffering and blessing of us to love thy goodness, may by true repentance for our sins, and with all our souls, hearts, and minds, unfeignedly turning unto thee in newness of life, both escape thy wrath and indignation, and enjoy the continuance and increase of thy favour, grace, and goodness, through our Saviour Jesus Christ, thy only Son, to whom with thee and the Holy Ghost, one God of most glorious majesty, be all honour and glory world without end. AMEN.

Or this.

O LORD our God and heavenly Father, look down, we beseech thee, with thy fatherly and merciful countenance upon us thy people, and poor humble servants, and upon all such Christians as are anywhere persecuted and sore afflicted for the true acknowledging of thee to be our God, and thy Son Jesus Christ, whom thou hast sent, to be the only Saviour of the world: save them, O merciful Lord, who are as sheep appointed to the slaughter, and by hearty prayer do call and cry unto thee for thy help and defence: hear their cry, O Lord, and our prayer for them, and for our selves; deliver those that be oppressed, defend such as are in fear of cruelty, relieve them that be in misery, and comfort all that be in sorrow and heaviness, that by thy aid and strength they and we may obtain surety from our enemies, without shedding of Christian and innocent blood. And for that, O Lord, thou hast commanded us to pray for our enemies, we do beseech thee, not only to abate their pride, and to stay the fury and cruelty of such as either of malice or ignorance do persecute them which put their trust in thee, and hate us, but also to mollify their hard hearts, to open their blinded eyes, and to lighten their ignorant minds, that they may see and understand, and truly turn unto thee, and embrace thy holy word, and unfeignedly be converted unto thy Son Jesus Christ, the only Saviour of the world, and believe and love his Gospel, and so eternally to be saved. Finally, that all Christian Realms, and specially this Realm of England, may by thy defence and protection enjoy perfite peace, quietness, and security, and all that desire to be called and accounted Christians, may answer in deed and life to so good and godly a name; and jointly altogether in one godly concord and unity, and with one consonant heart aud mind, may render unto thee all laud and praise, continually magnifying thy glorious name, who with thy Son our Saviour Jesus Christ, and the Holy Ghost, art one eternal, almighty, and most merciful God, to whom be all laud and praise, world without end. AMEN.

¶ Imprinted at Lon-
don, in Powles Churchyarde by Ri-
charde Iugge printer to
the Queenes Ma-
ieftie.

Cum priuilegio Regiæ Maieftatis.

XIV. A[1] FORM OF PRAYER WITH THANKS GIVING, to be used every year, the 17th of November, being the day of the Queen's Majesty's entry to her reign.

1. Tim. 2. Chap. Verse 1.

¶ I exhort you therefore, that first of all, prayers, supplications, intercessions, and giving of thanks be made for all men: for Princes, and for all that are in authority, that we may live a quiet and peaceable life, in all godliness and honesty; for that is good and acceptable in the sight of God our Saviour.

A[2] form of prayer.

Morning prayer is to be begun as in the book of Common prayer, unto the end of the psalm beginning, O[3] come let us. &c.

[[1] The following extract from the Epistle to Whitgift, prefixed by Edmund Bunny to his Form for the 17th of November (see p. 467), favours the notion, that Elizabeth made no express provision for, at least, the religious celebration of that day.

'Whereas therefore euery yeere, when that day commeth, we resort to the Church to giue thankes vnto God, and otherwise testifie that we haue good cause to reioyce therein: the more that such doings of ours do witnes against vs, that it is but due debt in vs, the more do I thinke it conuenient that order shoulde be taken for the continuance of the exercise begunne in your Graces Predecessors time [Grindal]: for the better accomplishment whereof, especially in these partes where I am resident, I thought it my duetie to make some triall of myself, to see how farre it would please the Lorde (of his wonted mercies) to blesse me therein. In which kinde of want, though my selfe be not able to make any sufficient supplie; yet, when I sawe howe to make a proffer towards it, little though it were, I, thought not good to let it slippe, not knowing whereunto by the goodnes of God (if it would please him to imploy some others thereabouts that are more able) it might be able to grow in the ende.']

[[2] In, and from, 1578 the whole Service was printed according to the tenor of the following rubric. This note shews how it then commenced.

An order for morning prayer, to be vsed the 17. of Nouember.
1 Tim. 2. vers. 1.
I exhort you therefore, &c. *as above.*
¶ You shall vnderstand, that euery thing in this booke is placed in order, as it shall be vsed, without turning to and fro, sauing the three

1576.]   A FORM OF PRAYER.   549

Then shall follow these special psalms.
Psalms xxi. lxxxv. cxxiiii.
¶ The first Lesson, taken out of the xvii. xviii. xix. and xx. Chapters of the second Book of the Chronicles.

JEHOSAPHAT the son of Asa reigned over Juda. And the Lord was with him, because he walked in the former ways of his father David, and sought not Baalim: But sought the Lord God of his father, and walked in his commandments, and not after the doings of Israel. And the Lord stablished the kingdom in his hand, and all Juda brought him presents, so that he had abundance of riches and honour. And he lift up his heart unto the ways of the Lord, and he put down yet more of the high places and groves out of Juda. In the third year of his reign, he sent to his Lords, even to Benhail, Obadia, Zacharia, Nethanel, and to Michaia, that they should teach in the cities of Juda: And with them he sent Levites, even Semeia, Nethania, Zebadia, Asael, Semiramoth, Jehonathan, Adonia, Tobia, and Tobadonia, Levites; and with them Elisama and Joram, Priests. And they taught in Juda, and had the book of the law of God with them, and went about throughout all the cities of Juda, and taught the people. And the fear of the Lord fell upon all the kingdoms of the lands that were round about Juda, and they fought not against Jehosaphat. _{2 Chro. ch. 17. vers. a. 1. 3. &c.⁴}

And when Jehosaphat, taking part with Achab in his wars against the king of Syria, was in great danger to be slain, he cried unto the Lord, and the Lord helped him, and chased his enemies away from him: but wicked Achab, king of Israel, was there slain. _{2 Chron. ch. 18. vers. a. 3. & e. 31. &c.}

lessons taken out of the old Testament, of which you may chuse anie one, as you thinke best, for the first lesson at this morning praier. And in Cathedrall Churches, the minister may vse either of the other two for the first lesson at euening praier.

¶ *First the Minister shall, with a loude voyce, pronounce some one of these three sentences, as in the booke of common prayer.*

At what time soeuer a sinner doeth repent him of his sinne from the bottome of his heart, I will put all his wickednesse out of my remembrance, saith the Lord. Ezech. 18.

Rent your hearts and not your garments, and turne to the Lorde your God, because hee is gentle and mercifull, he is pacient, and of much mercy, and such a one that is sorie for your afflictions. Joel 2.

If we say that we haue no sinne, we deceive ourselues, and there is no trueth in us.

Dearely beloued brethren, &c.]

[³ In 1578, when, as just mentioned, all the parts were given entire, this psalm had the *Gloria Patri*, but not the three others.]

[⁴ These references are to the Bishops' Bible, which, in its earlier editions, had always both letters and figures, whilst the Geneva version never had any thing but figures, to mark the divisions of chapters.]

2 Chron. ch. 19. vers. a. 1. 4. &c.

And Jehosaphat came home again in peace to Hierusalem, and dwelt there. And Jehosaphat went out to the people from Beerseba to Mount Ephraim, and brought them again unto the Lord God of their fathers. And he set Judges in the Land, throughout all the strong cities of Juda, city by city, and said to the Judges, Take heed what ye do: for ye execute not the judgments of man, but of God, which is with you in the judgment. Wherefore now let the fear of the Lord be upon you, and take heed, and be doing *the thing that pleaseth him*: for there is no unrighteousness with the Lord our God, that he should have any respect of persons, or take rewards. Moreover, in Hierusalem did Jehosaphat set of the Levites, and of the Priests, and of the ancient fathers over Israel, in the judgment and cause of the Lord, and they returned again to Hierusalem. And he charged them, saying, Thus shall ye do in the fear of the Lord faithfully, and with a pure heart: What cause so ever come to you of your brethren, that dwell in their cities, between blood and blood, between law and commandment, between statutes and ordinances; ye shall warn them that they trespass not against the Lord, and so wrath come upon you, and your brethren: thus do, and ye shall not offend. And behold, Amaria the high priest is among you in all matters of the Lord, and Zebadia the son of Ismael, a ruler of the house of Juda, for all the king's matters: there be officers of the Levites also before you: take courage to you therefore, and be doing *manfully*, and the Lord shall be with such as be good.

2 Chron. ch. 20. vers. a. 1. 2. 3.

a. 5. c. 18. d. 22. &c.

After this there came an exceeding great army of the Moabites and Ammonites against Jehosaphat. And Jehosaphat feared, and set himself to seek the Lord, and proclaimed fasting throughout all Juda. And he, with all Juda and the inhabitants of Hierusalem, prayed, and fell before the Lord, worshipping the Lord. And the enemies fell out amongst themselves, and slew one another, until they were all destroyed. And Jehosaphat and his people had the spoil of goods, raiment, and jewels, more than they could carry away. And they blessed the Lord, and called the place the valley of blessing unto this day. And they returned to Hierusalem with great joy and gladness. And the fear of GOD fell on the kingdoms of all lands, when they had heard that the Lord fought against the enemies of Israel. And so the Realm of Jehosaphat was in tranquillity, and his God gave him rest on every side.

Or this may be the first Lesson.

The history of King Hezekia, taken out of the fourth book of Kings, the 18. 19. and 20. Chapters.

4 Reg. ch. 18. vers. a. 1. 3.

HEZEKIAH the son of Ahaz, reigned over Juda, and he did that which is right in the sight of the Lord, according to all as did David his father.

4.

He put away the high places, and brake the images, and cut down the groves, and all-to[1] brake the brasen serpent that Moses had made: for unto those days the children of Israel did burn sacrifice to it, and he

5.

called it Nehustan. He trusted in the Lord God of Israel, so that after

[[1] all-to: completely, altogether.]

him was none like him among all the kings of Juda, neither were there any such before him. For he clave to the Lord, and departed not from him, but kept his commandments which the Lord commanded Moses. And the Lord was with him, so that he prospered in all things which he took in hand: and he resisted the king of Assyria, and served him not. Therefore in the fourteenth year of king Hezekia, did Sennacherib king of Assyria, come up against all the strong cities of Juda, and took them. And he sent word to king Hezekia by his captain Rabsakeh, who said, Tell Hezekia, thus saith the great king, even the king of Assyria, What confidence is this thou hast? Or on whom dost thou trust, that thou rebellest against me? If ye say, Ye trust in the Lord our God, is not that he, whose high places and whose altars Hezekia hath put down? And Rabsakeh stood, and cried unto the Jews that stood upon the walls, with a loud voice, saying, Hear the words of the great King, even the King of Assyria, Thus saith the King, Let not Hezekia beguile you, for he shall not be able to deliver you out of my hands: neither let Hezekia make you to trust in the Lord, saying, The Lord shall surely deliver us, and this city shall not be given over into the hands of the king of Assyria. Hearken not unto Hezekia, for he beguileth you, saying, The Lord shall deliver us. Hath any[2] one of the gods of the nations delivered his land out of the hand of the King of Assyria? Where is the God of Hamath, of Arphad, and where is the God of Sepharvaim, Hena, and Iva? Did they deliver Samaria out of mine hands? And what god is among all the gods of the nations, that hath delivered his land out of mine hand? Shall the Lord deliver Hierusalem out of mine hand?

When king Hezekia heard of these words, he rent his clothes, and put on sackcloth, and came into the house of the Lord, and sent Eliakim, which was the Steward of the houshold, and Sobna the Scribe, and the Elders of the Priests clothed in sack, to Isai the Prophet, the son of Amos: And they said unto him, Thus saith Hezekia: This day is a day of tribulation, and of rebuke and blasphemy. Peradventure the Lord thy God will hear all the words of Rabsakeh, whom the King of Assyria, his master, hath sent to rail on the living God, and to rebuke him with words which the Lord thy God hath heard: and lift thou up thy prayer for the remnant that are left. So the servants of King Hezekia came to Isai. And Isai said unto them, So shall you say to your master, Thus saith the Lord, Be not afraid of the words which thou hast heard, with which the young men of the King of Assyria have railed on me. Behold, I will put him in another mind, and he shall hear tidings, and so return to his own land, and I will bring to pass that he shall fall upon the sword, even in his own land. And when Sennacherib had word that Thirhaka, King of Ethiopia, was come out to fight against him, he departed, and sent messengers unto Hezekia, saying, Thus speak to Hezekia, king of Juda, saying, Let not thy God deceive thee, in whom thou trustest, saying, Hierusalem shall not be delivered into the hand of the King of Assyria.

[² All the editions have, euery.]

11.	Behold, thou hast heard what the Kings of Assyria have done to all lands, how they have utterly destroyed them: and shalt thou escape? And
14.	Hezekia received the letter of the hand of the messengers, and read it: and Hezekiah went up into the house of the Lord, and laid it abroad
15.	before the Lord. And Hezekia prayed before the Lord, and said, O Lord God of Israel, which dwellest between the Cherubims, thou art God alone over all the kingdoms of the earth, thou hast made heaven
16.	and earth. Lord, bow down thine ear, and hear: open, Lord, thine eyes (I beseech thee) and see, and hear the words of Sennacherib which
17.	hath sent (this man) to rail on the living God. Of a truth, Lord, the kings of Assyria have destroyed nations, and their lands, and have
18.	set fire on their gods: for they are no gods, but the work of the hands of man, even of wood and stone: and they destroyed them. Now
19.	therefore, O Lord our God, I beseech thee, save thou us out of his hand, that all the kingdoms of the earth may know that thou only art the
20.	Lord God. And Isai, the son of Amos, sent to Hezekia, saying, Thus saith the Lord God of Israel: That which thou hast prayed me con-
E. 32.	cerning Sennacherib king of Assyria, I have heard it. Wherefore thus saith the Lord concerning the king of Assyria, He shall not come to this city, nor shoot an arrow into it, nor come before it with shield, nor
33.	cast a bank against it, but shall go back again the way he came, and shall
34.	not come into this city, saith the Lord. For I will defend this city to
35.	save it, for mine own sake, and for David my servant's sake. And the self same night the Angel of the Lord went out, and smote in the host of the Assyrians an hundred four score and five thousand; and when the remnant were up early in the morning, behold, they were all dead
36.	corses. And so Sennacherib, king of Assyria, avoided and departed,
37.	and went again and dwelt at Ninive. And as he was in a temple worshipping Nisroch his God, Adramelech and Saresar, his own sons, smote him with the sword, and they escaped into the land of Armenia,
4 Reg. 20. ch. vers. a. 1.	and Asarhaddon his son reigned in his stead. About that time was Hezekia sick unto death; and the Prophet Isai, the son of Amos, came to him, and said unto him, Thus saith the Lord, Put thine house into
2.	an order, for thou shalt die, and not live. And Hezekia turned his
3.	face to the wall, and prayed unto the Lord, saying, I beseech thee (O Lord) remember now how I have walked before thee in truth, and with a perfect heart, and have done that which is good in thy sight:
4.	and Hezekia wept sore. And afore Esai was gone out into the middle
5.	of the court, the word of the Lord came to him, saying, Turn again and tell Hezekia, the captain of my people, Thus saith the Lord God of David, thy father, I have heard thy prayer, and seen thy tears, and behold, I will heal thee, so that on the third day thou shalt go up to
6.	the house of the Lord. And I will add unto thy days yet fifteen years, and I will deliver thee and this city out of the hand of the king of Assyria, and will defend this city, for mine own sake, and for David
7.	my servant's sake. And Esai said, Take a lump of dried figs: and they took and laid it on the sore, and he recovered, and had exceeding much honour and riches.

A FORM OF PRAYER.

The sum of the history of king Josia, taken out of the fourth book of the Kings, the 22. and 23. Chapters, and the 2. of the Chronicles, the 34. Chapter. *Or this may be the first Lesson.*

JOSIA reigned in Hierusalem, and he did that which was right in the sight of the Lord, and walked in the ways of David his father, and bowed neither to the right hand nor to the left. In the eight year of his reign, when he was yet a child, he began to seek after the God of David his father: and in the twelfth year he began to purge Juda and Hierusalem from the high places, groves, carved images, and images of metal. And they brake down the altars of Baalim, even in his presence, and other images, that were in greater honour than they, he caused to be destroyed: and the groves, carved images, and images of metal, he brake, and made dust of them, and strawed it upon the graves of them that had offered to them. And he burnt the bones of the Priests upon the altars of them, and cleansed Juda and Hierusalem. And in the eighteenth year of his reign, when he had purged the land and the temple, he sent Saphan the Scribe, to Helkia the high Priest, that he should see the decayed places of the temple repaired with such money as the keepers of the porch of the house of the Lord had gathered of the people.

And Helkia, as he was about the king's commandment, found in the temple the book of the law of the Lord, and delivered it unto Saphan, who brought it unto the king, and read in it before him. When the king had heard the words of the book of the law, he rent his clothes, and commanded Helkia the priest, with certain others, saying, Go ye, and inquire of the Lord for me, and for the people, and for all Juda, concerning the words of the book that is found; for great is the wrath of the Lord that is kindled against us, because our fathers have not hearkened to the words of this book, to do according to all that which is written therein for us.

So Helkia, the high Priest, with others, went unto Hulda, the Prophetess, and they communed with her. And she answered them, Thus saith the Lord God of Israel, Tell the man that sent you to me, Thus saith the Lord, Behold, I will bring evil upon this place, and on the inhabiters thereof, even all the words of the book, which the king of Juda hath read, because they have forsaken me, and have burnt incense to other gods, to anger me with all the works of their hands: my wrath therefore is kindled against this place, and shall not be quenched. But to the king of Juda, which sent you to ask counsel of the Lord, so shall ye say, Thus saith the Lord God of Israel, Because thine heart did melt, and because thou hast humbled thyself before the Lord, when thou heardest what I spake against this place, and against the inhabiters of the same, how that they should be destroyed and accursed, and hast rent thy clothes, and wept before me, that I also have heard, saith the Lord. Behold therefore, I will receive thee unto thy fathers, and thou shalt be put into thy grave in peace, and thine eyes shall not see all the evil which I will bring upon this place: And they brought the king word again.

4 Reg. ch. 23. vers. a. 1.
2.   And then the king sent, and there gathered together unto him all the Elders of Juda, and of Hierusalem. And the king went up into the house of the Lord, with all the men of Juda, and all the inhabiters of Hierusalem, with the Priests and Prophets, and all the people, both small and great: and he read in the ears of them all the words of the book of the
3. covenant, which was found in the house of the Lord. And the king stood by a pillar, and made a covenant before the Lord, that they should walk after the Lord, and keep his commandments, his witnesses, and his statutes, with all their heart, and with all their soul, and make good the words of the said covenant that were written in the foresaid book: and all the people consented to the covenant.
4. And the King commanded Helkia, the high Priest, and the inferior Priests, and the keepers of the ornaments, to bring out of the temple of the Lord all the vessels that were made for Baal, for the groves, and for all the host of heaven: and he burnt them without Hierusalem, in the fields of Cedron, and carried the ashes of them into
5. Bethel. And he put down the Priests of Baal, whom the kings of Juda had founded to burn incense in the high places and cities of Juda, that were round about Hierusalem, and also them that burnt incense unto Baal, to the Sun, to the Moon, to the Planets, and to all the host of heaven. And
24. moreover, all workers with spirits, and soothsayers, images, idols, and all the abominations that were spied in the land of Juda, and in Hierusalem, these did Josia put out of the way, to perform the words of the law, which were written in the book that Helkia the Priest found in the house
25. of the Lord. Like unto him was there no king before him, that turned to the Lord with all his heart, with all his soul, and all his might, according to all the law of Moses, neither after him arose there any such as he.

In[1] Cathedral and Collegiate Churches, one of the former Lessons omitted at Morning prayer may be read for the first Lesson at Evening prayer.

Then, *We praise thee, O God. &c.*

The[2] second Lesson. The xiii. to the Romans.

Then[3] the Psalm, *O be joyful. &c.* with the belief and the Lord's prayer, as is in the book of Common prayer.

Then shall be said.

Minister. O Lord, shew thy mercy upon us.
People. And grant us thy salvation.
Minister. O Lord, save the Queen.
People. Who putteth her trust in thee.

[1 For the wording, and position, of this rubric from 1578, see p. 549. note 2.]

[2 1578, The second Lesson, taken out of the Epistle of S. Paul to the Romanes, the xiii. Chapter.]

[3 1578, Or the c. Psalme. The Form in archbishop Harsnet's library, issued for 1590, contains the same error (Or), derived from copying the Prayer Book too closely.]

Minister. Send her help from thy holy place.
People. And evermore mightily defend her.
Minister. Let the enemies have none advantage on her.
People. Let not the wicked approach to hurt her.
Minister. Indue thy ministers with righteousness.
People. And make thy. &c. *as in the book of Common prayer.*

Then the Collect for the Queen, beginning, *O Lord our heavenly Father, high and mighty.* &c. as it is in the Litany[4].

It is ordered, that the Litany shall not be omitted the seventeenth day of November, though it fall upon Monday, Tuesday, Thursday, or Saturday. And that immediately after the collect beginning, *We humbly beseech thee.* &c. this Psalm and prayer following be said.

O COME hither, and hearken, all ye that fear God : and we will tell you what he hath done for our souls. Psal. 66. c. 14.

When men of power were gathered against us, and lay in wait for our souls : they took counsel together, saying, God hath forsaken them, persecute them, and take them, for there is none to deliver them. Psal. 59. a. 3. & 71. b. 9. 10.

Our enemies closed us in on every side : they gaped upon us with their mouths, as it were ramping and roaring Lions, seeking to devour us, and to swallow us up. Psal. 22. b. 12. & 56. a. 1. 2.

We were counted even as sheep appointed to be slain : many of us were for thy sake killed all the day long. Psal. 44. d. 20.

And many went astray in the wilderness, wandering hungry and thirsty in strange lands : our souls fainted in us, and were brought low, even unto the very dust. Psal. 107. a. 4. & 44. d. 22.

For why? The snares and sorrows of death compassed us : and the overflowings of ungodliness made us afraid. Psal. 18. a. 3. 4.

Then we made our complaint unto our God, and cried unto the Lord in our trouble : and he heard the voice of our prayer out of his holy temple, and delivered us out of our distress. Psal. 18. a. 5. & 107. b. 12.

He gathered us home again out of the lands : from the East, and from the West, from the North, and from the South. Psal. 107. a. 3.

He delivered our souls from death, our eyes from tears, and our feet from falling : he hath set us at liberty, he hath light our candle ; the Lord our God hath made our darkness to be light. Psal. 116. b. 8. & 4. a. 1. & 18. d. 27.

[4 In 1578, the collects for Peace and Grace followed that for the queen.]

Psal. 18. g. 47.
& 59. c. 16.

Wherefore we will give thanks unto thee, O Lord, and sing praises unto thy name : we will sing of thy power, and praise thy mercy betimes in the morning; for thou hast been our defence and refuge in the time of trouble.

Psal. 118.

O give thanks unto the Lord, for he is gracious : and his mercy endureth for ever.

Glory be to the Father, and to the Son, and to the Holy Ghost.

As it was in the beginning, is now, and ever shall be, world without end. Amen.

Let us pray.

O[1] Lord God, most merciful Father, who as upon this day, placing thy servant our Sovereign and gracious Queen

[[1] As an accompaniment to this prayer, may be added from the Bibl. Lans. 116. art. 24, 'The prayer for the Q. on her byrthe daye' (September the 7th), though both its date and author are unknown:

O Lorde, the hope and strengthe of Israell, the onely planter and preseruer of Princes, and the rocke of sure defence for all that trust in thee : wee thine vnworthy seruants accepted in him, in whome thowe arte well pleased, doe offer vp o^r sacrifice of praise and thankesgiuing for all the daungers wee haue escaped hauing soe iustlye deserued them, and for all the good thinges receiued, being so vnworthye of them. Among all other and aboue the reste, wth tearful hartes and humble handes lifted vp wth reuerence toward thy mercy seat, wee blesse and praise thy holy name, for that precious jewell of inestimable price, to witt the blessed spirit and being of thine humble seruant, our moste gratious Soverayn, whose sacred person according to thy word we doe reuerentlye repute and call the Breath of our nostrils, the Annoynted of the Lord, by whose breath we liue, and by whose Life we breathe. And now, Lorde, since it hathe pleased thee, in thy foreseeing prouidence, for the safety and comfort of so many thousands to giue to thine annoynted a princely birth and being, and by the right hand of Loue, by soe many dangers to lead the same along to that place of regall dignity, of wch thowe haste saide, Euen I haue sett my Kinge upon my holy mount of Sion; wee most humbly and earnestly entreat thy heauenly Ma^{ty} that our woorkes may not impare thy woorkes, nor o^r sinnes impeach her safety. But [as] there is a plante wch thine owne right hand hath planted, so lett the eye of thy prouidence continually watch ouer her, and the arme of thy protection mightely defend her, that the Boars out of the forest, nor the Lyon out of the wood, nor any subtle Leopard out of the way of Ashur, may haue anie power to hurt the smallest Leafe of this thy princelye Plant. But so shadow her and compasse her wth the wings of thye Cherubims, that her highthe and State may be as the Cedars of Lebanon,

Elizabeth in the kingdom, didst deliver thy people of England from danger of war and oppression, both of bodies by tyranny, and of conscience by superstition, restoring peace and true religion, with liberty both of bodies and minds, and hast continued the same thy blessings, without all desert on our part, now by the space of these *eighteen years: we who are in memory of these thy great benefits assembled here together, most humbly beseech thy fatherly goodness to grant us grace, that we may in word, deed, and heart, shew ourselves thankful and obedient unto thee for the same: and that our Queen through thy grace may in all honour, goodness, and godliness, long and many years reign over us, and we obey and enjoy her, with the continuance of thy great blessings, which thou hast by her thy minister poured upon us: This we beseech thee to grant unto us, for thy dear Son Jesus Christ's sake, our Lord and Saviour. Amen[2].

*Increase this number, according to the years of, her Majesty's reign.

For[3] the Epistle of the day, read i Pet. ii. beginning at the xi. verse, *Dearly beloved, I beseech you.* &c. to the xviii. verse, ending with these words: *Fear God, Honour the king.*

her strength and long continuance as the Okes of Bashan, her perpetuall flourishing as the Palme tree, and her glorie as the Rose plantes in the Vale of Jericho. And lett those riuers that runne oute of the Sanctuary, euermore flowe and ouerflowe round about her, as doth the Riuer Jordan at the tyme of haruest. And soe, O heauenly Father, to conclude our thankful prayer, we most humbly besech the in thy beloued, to pleade her cause with them that striue wth her, and to fight against those that fight against her, and by the sure and secret motions of thy most holy Spirit to saye vnto her Soule, I am thy Sauiour. Bless them that blesse her. Curse them that curse her. Lett the day of her birth be as the sweet influence of the Pleiades, and the day of their birth, as Arcturus and Orion. Lett the day of her birth be as the Sunn when he riseth in his mighte, and the day of their birth as the Moone in her way. Lett her rise. Lett them fall. Lett her flourish. Lett them perish. That the rude world may see and saye, thy promise is performed, Them that honor me, I will honor; and they that despise me, shall be despised. Theis things, O heauenly Father, we besech thee graunte to vs and to thy whole Church, for Jesus Christ his sake o^r Lord and onely Saueour. Amen.]

[² The Forms from 1578 have, after this prayer, and immediately preceding the Communion service, the prayer, Almighty and everlasting God, which only workest great marvels, &c.: that *In the time of any common plague or sickness:* the prayer of Chrysostom; and the benediction.]

[³ 1578, The collect for the queen is that beginning, Almighty God, whose kingdom is everlasting, &c.: the collect for the day, that for the five and twentieth Sunday after Trinity.]

For the Gospel, read Matth. xxii. beginning at the xvi. verse. *And they sent out unto him their disciples with the Herodians.* &c. to the xxiii. verse, ending with these words, *They marvelled, and left him, and went their way*[1].

The[2] xxi. Psalm in Metre before the sermon, unto the end of the vii. verse. And the c. Psalm after the sermon.

Finis.

¶ Imprinted at Lon-
don by Richarde Iugge, Printer
to the Queenes Maieſtie.

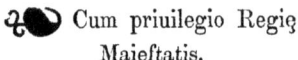 Cum priuilegio Regię
Maieſtatis.

A thanksgiving, to be sung as the 81. Psalm.

1 Be light and glad, in God rejoice,
   which is our strength and stay:
Be joyful and lift up your voice,
   for this most happy day[3].
Sing, sing, O sing unto the Lord,
   with melody most sweet:
Let heart and tongue in one ac-
     cord,
   as it is just and meet.

2 Sing laud unto the Lord above,
   serve him with glad intent:
O clap your hands in sign of love,
   for this which he hath sent.
Sing praise, sing praise with Harp
     and Lute,
   with joy let us be seen:
Before our God let none be mute,
   but laud him for our Queen.

3 Sound out the trump courage-
     ously,
   Blow as on solemn days:
Both high and low, come fill the
     sky
   with sweet resounding praise.
For why? when we were bound in
     thrall,
   and eke in grief did stand,
The Lord did set us free from all
   by this his servant's hand.

4 Ourselves therefore we wholly
     bind,
   A Sacrifice to be,
In token of our thankful mind
   (O God most dear) to thee.
To thee we cry, and also give
   most high thanks, laud and praise,

[1] After the Creed came in 1578, the first sentence from the Offertory: the prayer for the Church Militant: the collect, Almighty God, which hast promised, &c.; and the blessing.]

[2] Instead of this rubric, we have, in 1578, the metrical Thanksgiving which follows.]

[3] Queen's day is still kept as a holiday at the Exchequer, and at Westminster and Merchant Tailors' Schools. Nicholas's Chronology of History, p. 168, note.]

For thy good gifts which we receive,
   both now and all our days.
5 When we in grief did cry and call,
   thou holpst us by and by,
And thou didst set us free from thrall,
   O God, our God most high.
Thy mercy therefore will we sing,
   and praise thy holy Name,
For working of so great a thing:
   O Lord, preserve the same.

6 Blessed art thou, O Lord of hosts,
   Our shield and buckler tried:
Thy Name be prais'd in all the coasts,
   throughout the world so wide.
Vouchsafe this inward sacrifice,
   to thee (O Lord) we call:
Our hearty thanks do not despise,
   we yield our souls and all.

7 For thou through love, when we were lost,
   didst send to seek therefore:
This silly bark of ours, so tost,
   thou broughtst full safe to shore.
When we through blindness went astray,
   with burdens sore opprest,
Thou sentst and set us in the way,
   that leads us to thy rest.

8 We praise thee therefore, Lord, on high,
   with heart and hearty cheer:
To thee we sing, we call, we cry,
   O Lord our God most dear.
Thou art the worker of my wealth,
   Our safeguard and our stay:
O Lord, grant this our country health,
   on thee we wait alway.

---

9 To thee (O God) we yield all praise,
   thou art our help alone:
To thee it is we sing always,
   to thee and else to none.
Then bow to us (good Lord) thine ear,
   and hear us when we cry:
Preserve thy Church now planted here,
   and watch it with thine eye.

10 Lord, keep Elizabeth our Queen,
   defend her in thy right:
Shew forth thyself, as thou hast been,
   her fortress and her might.
Preserve her grace, confound her foes,
   and bring them down full low:
Lord, turn thy hand against all those,
   that would her overthrow.

11 Maintain her Sceptre as thine own,
   for thou hast plac'd her here:

And let this mighty work be known *The second part.*
   to nations far and near.
A noble ancient Nurse, O Lord,
   in England let her reign:
Her grace among us do afford,
   for ever to remain.

12 Indue her (Lord) with virtue's store,
   rule thou her royal Rod:
Into her mind thy Spirit pour,
   and shew thyself her God.
In truth upright, Lord, guide her still,
   thy Gospel to defend;
To say and do what thou dost will,
   and stay where thou dost end.

13 Her counsel (Lord) vouchsafe to guide,
   with wisdom let them shine,
In godliness for to abide,
   as it becometh thine:
To seek the glory of thy name,
   their country's wealth procure,

And that they may perform the
    same,
Lord, grant thy Spirit pure.

14 So will we sing unto thee, Lord,
    betime, ere day be light;

And eke declare thy truth abroad,
    when it doth draw to night.
To thee, O Father, with the Son,
    and Spirit be therefore
All glory now, as hath been done,
    from henceforth evermore. Amen.

FINIS.[1]

An[2] Anthem or prayer for the preservation of the Church, the Queen's Majesty, and the Realm, to be sung after Evening prayer at all times.

Save, Lord, and bless with good increase
Thy Church, our Queen and Realm in peace.

As for thy gifts we render praise,
So, Lord, we crave still blessed days:
Let thy sweet word and Gospel pure
With us, dear God, for aye endure.
With prosperous reign increase it
    still,   [fill.
That sound thereof the world may
    Save, Lord, and bless with good
        increase
        Thy Church, our Queen and
        Realm in peace.

That vine thy right hand planted
    hath,
Preserve, O Lord, from enemies'
    wrath;
And those that practise Sion's spoil,
With mighty arm (Lord) give them
    foil.
Thy Church and Kingdom, Christ,
    we pray,
Increase and build from day to day.
    Save, Lord, and bless with good
        increase
        Thy Church, our Queen and
        Realm in peace.

Like as thy grace our Queen hath
    sent,
So bless her rule and government,
Thy glory chiefly to maintain,
And grant her long and prosperous
    Reign:
All foes confound, and Rebels eke,
That Prince or Church's harm
    would seek.
    Save, Lord, and bless with good
        increase
        Thy Church, our Queen and
        Realm in peace.

This English Isle, and people all,
Preserve, for Christes blood we call.
Grant peace t' enjoy thy blessings
    now,
Because none fights for us but thou.
So shall we live to praise thee then,
Which likewise grant. Amen,
    Amen.
    Save, Lord, and bless with good
        increase
        Thy Church, our Queen and
        Realm in peace.

[[1] In a copy of the Accession service belonging to the British Museum, the colophon, with the date 1578, is placed here, because it has neither the Anthem, nor the Song of rejoicing.]

[[2] Christopher Barker had a licence in 1578 for printing this Anthem. Herbert's Ames, p. 1089.]

1578.]   561

A song of rejoicing for the prosperous Reign of our most gracious Sovereign Lady Queen Elizabeth.

Made to the tune of the 25. Psalm.

G Give laud unto the Lord,
    And praise his holy name :
O O let us all with one accord
    Now magnify the same.
D Due thanks unto him yield,
    Who evermore hath been
S So strong defence, buckler, and shield,
    To our most Royal QUEEN.

A And as for her this day,
    Each where about us round,
V Up to the Sky right solemnly
    The bells do make a sound :
E Even so let us rejoice
    Before the Lord our king ;
T To him let us now frame our voice
    With cheerful hearts to sing.

H Her Majesty's intent,
    By thy good grace and will,
E Ever, O Lord, hath been most bent
    Thy Law for to fulfil.
Q Quite thou that loving mind
    With love to her again :
U Unto her as thou hast been kind,
    O Lord so still remain.

E Extend thy mighty hand
    Against her mortal foes :
E Express and shew that thou wilt stand
    With her against all those.
N Nigh unto her abide,
    Uphold her Sceptre strong :
E Eke grant with us, a joyful guide,
    She may continue long.

                    I. C.

AMEN.

Imprinted at London

by Christopher Barker, Printer to the Queenes Maieſtie.

Cum priuilegio.

xv. The[1] Order of Prayer upon Wednesdays and Fridays, to avert and turn God's wrath from us threatened by the late terrible earthquake, to be used in all Parish Churches.

Whereof the last prayer is to be used of all housholders with their whole families.

Set forth by authority.

Imprinted at London by Christopher Barker, Printer to the Queen's Majesty.

[1 The following letter (Bibl. Lans. 30. art. 49.) is worth reprinting, as well on account of the information which it furnishes respecting the present Order, as because it clearly establishes the fact, that Strype, notwithstanding he consulted it, misunderstood the circumstances of the case. See p. 464.

My verie good L. I receued yor letters at the verie instant when I was redie to departe from Fulham to sitt in the Consistorie [Convocation]; besechinge the same to hold me excused, in that I could not returne my answer thereto soe speedelie as my duetie required. As touchinge the matte^r I cannot but much thank God for yor L. care, to haue all thinges donne as much as might be to the Capacitie and edifynge of the people. But fo^r y^t in my simple judgm^t, vnder yor L. correccion, yt were requisit, the state of the tyme wth the mallic of o^r Enemies considered, wch commonlie vpbraid vs, that we neue^r fast, and seldom pray, wthout further delaye to geue some ordre and direccion to stirre vp the people to devocion, and to turne awaye Godes wrath threatened by the late earthquake. And for that the complying of a new forme of prayer would aske a long tyme, I think if it might so please yor honorable L. yt would doe much good, if the forme alredie presented to yor L. myght be followed, speciallie for that the people is presentlie much moued wth the p^{r}sent warninge, and are of such nature, as commonlie they make it but a ix. daies wondre; for, as he saith, *Cito arescit lacryma:* and we maie saye that *Multo citius indolescit animus.* Therefore it were necessarie that it were done out of hand. But what shall seeme best to yo^u I wilbe readie to followe. I did not send it to yor L. written, because I ment it but onelie to my owne diocesse; and also because I hadd followed yor L. instruccions from hir Matie, wch would not haue anie solempne matte^r made of it. And likewise the forme of praye^r vpon hir Matie daye [November the 17th, see p. 549] hath the psalmes as they stand in the Psalter wthout alteracion of verses.

1580.]   563

The[2] Order of prayer for Wednesdays and Fridays.

First, the Minister shall use the order set down in the book of Common Prayer, to the end of O come, let us sing unto the Lord.
Then shall follow these three Psalms, the 30. 46. and 91.
Also for the first Lesson, some one of these three chapters, the 1. or 2. of Joel, or the 58. of Isaiah, and after that, Te Deum *or* Benedicite, *with a Chapter of the New Testament for the second Lesson, according to the book aforesaid.*
Then after the Litany shall be said this prayer, Oh Eternal, mighty, and most loving Father. &c.
Then shall be read the Homily of repentance, or a part thereof, as in the book of homilies it is divided, if there be no sermon.
Also after the sermon, or homily, shall be sung the 46. Psalm in Metre.
Moreover, that the Preachers and Curates do exhort their flock to refrain those ii. days weekly from one meal, and to bestow the value or some part thereof (as God shall stir up their devotion) upon the poor, teaching them that such alms is more acceptable to God, than that which cometh by constraint of law[3].
Also that they call upon their parishioners to cause their family every night, before their going to bed, all together to say the prayer set out for that purpose, meekly kneeling upon their knees.

Psal. 30.[4]   *Psal. 46.*   *Psal. 91.*

Then shall be read, for the first Lesson, some one of these three Chapters following.

The i. Chapter of Joel.   The ii. Chapter of Joel
The lviii. Chapter of Isaiah.

And soe right humblie I take my leaue of yor honorable L. From my howse in *London*, this xxiith of *Aprill*, 1580.

Y^r L. humbly to command in X^o.

JOHN LONDON.

To the right honorable and my
singule^r good L. the L. high
Treasore^r of England.]

[2 In the Form put forth for both provinces, it is,—The order of prayer, and other exercises vpon Wednesdayes and Frydayes, to be vsed throughout the Realme by order aforesaide.]

[3 See p. 593, note 1.]

[4 The *Gloria Patri* does not come after any of these psalms, which, like the lessons, are printed entire.]

A prayer to be used of all housholders, with their whole family, every Evening before they go to bed, that it would please God to turn his wrath from us, threatened in the last terrible earthquake.

Set forth by authority.

OH eternal, mighty, and most loving Father, which hast no desire of the death of a sinner, but that he convert and live, and unto whom nothing is so pleasant as the repentant, contrite and sorrowful heart of a penitent person: for thou art that kind Father that fallest most lovingly upon the neck of the lost son, kissest, embracest and feastest him, when he returneth from the puddle of pleasures and swill of the swine, and disdainest not the repentant prayer of thy poor and sinful servants, whensoever with true faith they return and call upon thee, as we have most comfortable examples in David, Manasses, Magdalene, Peter, and the thief upon the gibbet: we most heartily and humbly beseech thy fatherly goodness, to look down from the throne of thy mercy-seat upon us most miserable and sinful slaves of Satan, which with fearful and trembling hearts do quake and shake at the strange and terrible token of thy wrath and indignation appearing most evidently unto us, by thy shaking and moving of the earth, which is thy footstool; whereby (if we be not utterly destitute of grace) we be warned that thy coming down amongst us, to visit our sins in most terrible manner, can not be far off, seeing thou treadest so hard upon this thy footstool the earth, which we most shamefully have polluted and defiled with our most wicked, sinful, and rebellious lives, notwithstanding thy continual crying and calling upon us by thy servants, the Prophets and preachers, by whom we have learned to know thy will, but have not followed it; we have heard much and done little, yea, nothing at all; but like most perverse and unthankful children have made a mock of thy word, derided thy ministers, and accounted thy threatenings trifles, and thy warnings of no weight or moment: wherefore we have justly deserved to taste most deeply of the bitter cup of thy anger and vengeance, by wars, famine, pestilence, yea, and eternal death, if thou shouldest not temper the rigour of thy justice with the mildness of thy mercy. But such is thy fatherly affection towards us, that thou shewest thyself slow to anger, long suffering, and of much patience and mercy. Yea, thou art a thousand times more ready to forget and forgive, than we to ask and require forgiveness. Therefore, though we be not worthy of the least mite of thy mercy, yet, gracious Lord, look not upon us and our sins, but upon thy own self and thy Son Jesus Christ, the fountain of grace, the treasure of mercy, the salve of all sickness, the Jewel of joy[1], and the only haven of succour and safety: by him we come to thee, in him and for him we trust to find that we have lost, and gain that he hath got: he is the scale[2] of Jacob, by whom we climb up to thee, and thou by the Angels of thy mercy comest down to us: him we present unto thee, and not ourselves, his death and not our doings, his bloody wounds and not our detestable deservings, whose merits are so great, as thy mercy can not be little, and our ransom so rich, that our beggarly and beastly sins are nothing in thy sight, for the great pleasure and satisfaction that thou takest of his pains and passion. Turn this Earthquake, O Lord, to the benefit of thine elect, as thou didst when thou shookest the prison, loosedst the locks, fetters, and chains of thy servants, Paul and Silas, and broughtest them out of prison, and converted their keeper: so, gracious Lord, strike the hearts of tyrants with the terror of this thy work, that they may know that they are but men, and that thou art that Sampson, that for their mocking and spiting of thee and thy word can shake the pillars of their palaces, and throw them upon the furious Philistines' heads. Turn thy wrath, O Lord, from thy children that call upon thy Name, to the conversion or confusion of thine enemies that defy and abhor thy Name, and deface thy glory. Thou hast knocked long at their doors, but they will not open to let thee in: burst open therefore the brasen gates of their stony hearts, thou that art able of stones to raise up children to Abraham: and, finally, so touch our hearts with the finger of thy grace, that we may deeply muse upon our sinful lives, to amend them, and call for thy mercy to forgive and pardon them, through Christ our Lord, who liveth with thee, and the

[1 The title of one of Becon's treatises. See his works, Catechism, &c., p. 411.]
[2 Scale: ladder.]

Holy Ghost, three persons and one eternal God, to whom be all dominion and glory, with praise and thanksgiving, for ever and ever. Amen.

Psalm xlvi.

1 The Lord is our defence and aid,
The strength whereby we stand.
When we with woe are much dismayed,
He is our help at hand.

2 Though th' earth remove, we will not fear,
Though hills so high and steep
Be thrust and hurled here and there,
Within the sea so deep.

3 No, though the waves do rage so sore,
That all the banks it spills;
And though it overflow the shore,
And beat down mighty hills.

4 For one fair flood doth send abroad
His pleasant streams apace,
To fresh the city of our God,
And wash his holy place.

5 In midst of her the Lord doth dwell,
She can no whit decay:
All things against her that rebel,
The Lord will truly stay.

6 The heathen flock the kingdoms fear,
The people make a noise:
The earth doth melt and not appear,
When God puts forth his voice.

7 The Lord of hosts doth take our part,
To us he hath an eye:
Our hope of health with all our heart
On Jacob's God doth lie.

8 Come here and see with mind and thought
The working of our God:
What wonders he himself hath wrought
Throughout the earth abroad.

9 By him all wars are hush'd and gone,
Which countries did conspire:
Their bows he brake and spears each one,
Their chariots brent with fire.

10 Leave off therefore (saith he) and know,
I am a God most stout,
Among the heathen high and low,
And all the earth throughout.

11 The Lord of hosts doth us defend,
He is our strength and tower:
On Jacob's God do we depend,
And on his mighty power.

To Father, Son, and Holy Ghost,
All glory be therefore;
As in beginning was, is now,
And shall be evermore.

Imprinted at London by Christopher Barker
Printer to the Queenes
Maieftie.
1580.
Cum Priuilegio.

The[1] Report of the Earthquake.

On Easter Wednesday, being the sixt of April, 1580, *somewhat before six of the clock in the afternoon, happened this great Earthquake whereof this discourse treateth: I mean not great in respect of long continuance of time, for (God be thanked) it continued little above a minute of an hour, rather shaking God's rod at us, than smiting us according to our deserts: Nor yet in respect of any great hurt done by it within this Realm: For although it shook all houses, castles, churches, and buildings, every where as it went, and put them in danger of utter ruin; yet within this Realm (praised be our Saviour Christ Jesus for it) it overthrew few or none that I have yet heard of, saving certain stones, chimneys, walls, and pinnacles of high buildings, both in this City and in divers other places: Neither do I hear of any Christian people that received bodily hurt by it, saving two children in London, a boy and a girl: the boy, named* THOMAS GRAY, *was slain out of hand, with the fall of a stone shaken down from the roof of a Church[2]; and the girl (whose name was* MABEL EVERITE), *being sore hurt there at the same present by like casualty, died within few days after: But I term it great in respect of the universalness thereof almost at one instant, not only within this Realm, but also without, where it was much more violent and did far more harm; and in respect of the great terror which it then strake into all men's hearts where it came, and yet still striketh into such as duly consider how justly* GOD *may be offended with all men for sin, and specially with this realm of England, which hath most abundantly tasted of God's mercy, and most unthankfully neglected his goodness, which yet still warneth us by this terrible wonder, what far more terrible punishments are like to light upon us ere long, unless we amend our sinful conversation betimes.*

A[3] godly Admonition for the time present.

MANY and wonderful ways (good christian reader) hath God in all ages most mercifully called all men to the knowledge of themselves,

[1 This Report does not appear to have belonged to the Form intended solely for the diocese of London: it is found, however, in that for the provinces of Canterbury and York, where it occupies its present position, and whence it has been now transcribed.]

[2 Christchurch, near Newgate, where 'they were hearing a Sermon.' Dr Williams's MS.]

[3 When published by itself, the Admonition was thus entitled:— A Discourse containing many wonderful examples of God's Indignation poured upon divers people for their intollerable sins, which Treatise may be read instead of some part of the Homily [p. 563], where there is no Sermon. Dr Williams's MS.]

and to the amendment of their Religion and conversation, before he have laid his heavy hand in wrathful displeasure upon them. And this order of dealing he observeth, not only towards his own dear children, but also even towards the wicked and castaways : to the intent, that the one sort turning from their former sins, and becoming the warer all their life after, should glorify him the more for his goodness in not suffering them to continue in their sins unreformed, to their destruction ; and that the other sort should be made utterly unexcusable for their wilful persisting in the stubbornness of their hard and froward hearts, against all his friendly and fatherly admonitions.

He called *Cayne* to repentance, before he punished him for shedding his brother's blood, and gave him a long time to have bethought himself in.

He warned the old world a hundred year and more, before he brought the flood upon the Earth.

He chastised the Children of *Israel* divers ways, ere he destroyed them in the wilderness.

He sent Hornets and wild Beasts, as foregoers of his host, into the land of Canaan, before he rooted out the old inhabiters thereof.

He punished not *David* for his murder and advoutry[1], until he had first admonished him by his Prophet.

He removed not the *Israelites* into captivity, until all the warnings of his Prophets, and all the former corrections which he had used in vain to reform them, did shew them to be utterly past hope of amendment.

Before the last destruction of *Jerusalem*, there went innumerable signs[2], tokens, and wonders.

Finally, God never poured out his grievous displeasure and wrath upon any Nation, Realm, City, Kingdom, State, or Country, but he gave some notable forewarning thereof by some dreadful wonder.

To let pass the examples of foreign Nations, which are many and terrible : what plagues, pestilences, famines, diseases, tempests, overflowing of waters both salt and fresh, and a number of other most prodigious tokens happened successively long time together, before the displacing of the Britons by the hands of our ancestors, for their neglecting of God's word[3] preached and planted many hundred years among them ! Likewise, what great warnings did GOD give to our forefathers, in divers Princes' reigns, before the alteration of the State, both by the *Danes*, and also by *William* the Conqueror ! Again, even in these our days, how manifestly hath God threatened, and still doth threaten our contempt of his holy Religion, and our security and sound sleeping in

---

[1 Advoutry : adultery.]

[2 See Josephus de Bello Judaico, Lib. iv. cap. 4. § 5 : Lib. vi. cap. 5. § 3. Taciti Histor. Lib. v. cap. 13.]

[3 See the Historia (cap. 19, &c.), as well as Epistola, of Gildas. Bede (Hist. Eccles. Lib. i. cap. 14.) repeats his account, and in nearly the same words. See also Becon's works, Prayers, &c. pp. 10, 11.]

sin, shewing us evident tokens of his just displeasure near at hand, both abroad and at home!

I will not speak of the great civil Wars, nor of the horrible and unnatural massacres of good men, betrayed under the holiest pretences[4], which have been of late years in the Countries bordering upon us: because such dealings, being pleasant to such as seek blood, are taken for no wonders. Neither will I stand upon the rehearsal of the strange things that befel in the Realm of *Naples* in the year 1566: nor of the Earthquake, whereby a great part of the City *Ferrara* in *Italy* was destroyed in the year 1570: or of the miraculous sights that were seen in *France* about *Mountpellier* the year 1573: or of the like terrible sight that appeared little more than a year ago at *Prague*, the chief City of *Bohemia*: nor of divers other things[5] which have happened in foreign Countries within the compass of these few years: because it will perchance be thought, that those tokens concern the Countries where they befel, and not us.

Well, I will not say, *That whatsoever things have been written aforetimes, were written for our learning, that we might learn to beware by other men's harms.*

We have signs and tokens ynow at home, if we can use them to our benefit.

What shall we say to the sore Famine which happened in the time of our late sovereign Lady *queen Mary*[6], which was so great, that men were fain to make bread of Acorns, and food of Fern roots? or to the particular Earthquake, in the time of our most gracious sovereign Lady that now is, which transposed the bounds of men's grounds, and turned a Church to the clean contrary situation[7]? or to the monstrous[8] births both of Children and Cattle? or to the unseasonableness of the seasons of some years, altering (after a sort) Summer into Winter, and Winter into Summer? or to the wonderful new Star so long time[9] fixed in Heaven?

[4 The flattering attentions and false hopes, whereby the choicest of the Hugonots were allured to Paris in 1572, are well known.]

[5 See Strype's Annals, Vol. II. p. 510: Zurich Letters, second edition, p. 396. The *Physica Curiosa* of P. Gaspar Schottus, 1662, records a great variety of natural prodigies.]

[6 The year 1557 was remarkable, both for the great scarcity of corn in England before harvest, and for the extraordinary abundance of it afterwards. Stow, p. 1068. Pilkington, p. 611.]

[7 Camden (Kennet's Collection), p. 433, tells us of 'a hill with a rock of stones at the foot of it,' which rose from the earth at Kinnaston in Herefordshire, on the 17th of February, 1571, and 'walked from Saturday evening till Monday noon.' He gives a particular description of its devastations, among which was the throwing down of a chapel which stood in its way: he only says, however, that a yew-tree, standing in the churchyard, was removed from the west to the east.]

[8 See Zurich Letters, p. 156.]

[9 In November, 1572, a luminous body, brighter than Jupiter, ap-

or to the strange appearings of Comets, the often Eclipses of Sun and Moon, the great and strange fashioned lights seen in the firmament in the night times[1] the sudden falling and unwonted abiding of unmeasurable abundance of Snow[2], the excessive and untimely rains and overflowing of waters[3], the greatness and sharp continuance of sore frosts, and many other such wonderful things, one following in another's neck? Shall we say that none of these also do concern us? or rather more truly, that because they be gone and past (Oh over great security and blindness of heart) we have clean forgotten them, or at leastwise make no great account of them, according [to] our common Proverb, *that a wonder lasteth with us but nine days*?

Therefore, lest we should want either proof of the certainty of God's irrevocable judgments, or argument of his continual merciful dealing towards us, or matter wherewith to convict us of our excessive unthankfulness: behold, he sendeth us now lastly this Earthquake that befel the sixt day of this Month, not so hurtful in present operation, as terrible in signification of things to come. For the tried experience of all ages teacheth us, and the writings of the wise and learned (specially of holy Scripture) do assuredly witness unto us, that such tokens are infallible forewarnings of God's sore displeasure for sin, and of his just plagues for the same, where amendment of life ensueth not.

And although there be peradventure some, which (to keep themselves and others from the due looking back into the time erst misspent, and to foade[4] them still in the vanities of this world, lest they should see their own wretchedness, and seek to shun God's vengeance at hand) will not stick to deface the apparent working of God, by ascribing this miracle to some ordinary causes in Nature: Yet notwithstanding, to the godly and well disposed, which look advisedly into the matter, pondering the manner of this Earthquake throughly, and considering the manner of our dealings from the late restitution of the Gospel unto this day, and conferring the same with the manner of God's favourable dealing with us, and with his ordinary dealing in cases where his truth hath been planted, and groweth to be contemned; it must needs appear to be the very finger of God, and as a messenger of the miseries due to such deserts.

For, first of all, whereas naturally Earthquakes are said to be engendered by wind gotten into the bowels of the earth, or by vapours bred and inclosed within the hollow caves of the earth, where, by their

peared in Cassiopea's chair. It continued there full sixteen months, but at the end of eight months began gradually to grow less. Camden, p. 446. Strype's Annals, Vol. II. p. 173.]

[1 Stow, the great chronicler of prodigies, (p. 1149), seems to describe the lights here meant, as visible on the 14th and 15th of November, 1574. Ibid. p. 1164.]

[2 In February and April, 1579. Holinshed, pp. 1271, 1272.]

[3 See Zurich Letters, pp. 343, 455: Holinshed, pp. 1222—1224.]

[4 Foade *or* Fode: supply with food, feed. See Nares's Glossary.]

striving and struggling of themselves to get out, or being haled outward by the heat and operation of the Sun, they shake the earth for want of sufficient vent to issue out at: If this Earthquake had risen of such causes, it could not have been so universal, because there are many places in this Realm, which by reason of their substantial soundness and massy firmness are not to be pierced by any winds from without, nor have any hollowness wherein to conceive and breed any such abundance of Vapours, specially in places far distant from the Sea, or from Rivers, moors, marishes, fens, or light and open soils.

Neither could it have been in so many places universally at one instant both by sea and land. For the striving thereof within the ground, taking his beginning at some certain place, and proceeding forward to get a vent, would have required some space of time to have attained to so many places so far off, or else have broken out with great fury in some place that had been weakest.

Again, whereas in Earthquakes that proceed of natural causes, certain signs and tokens are reported to go before them, as, a tempestuous working and raging of the sea, the weather being fair, temperate and unwindy, calmness of the air matched with great cold; dimness of the Sun for certain days before; long and thin streaks of Clouds appearing after the setting of the Sun, and the weather being otherwise clear; the troubledness of water even in the deepest wells, yielding moreover an infected and stinking savour; and lastly, great and terrible sounds in the earth, like the noise of groanings or thunderings, as well afore as after the quaking: We find not that any such foretoken happened against the coming of this Earthquake. And therefore we may well conclude (though there were none other reason to move us), that this miracle proceeded not of the course of any natural causes, but of God's only determinate purpose, who maketh even the very foundations and pillars of the earth to shake, the mountains to melt like wax, and the seas to dry up, and to become as a dry field, when he listeth to shew the greatness of his glorious power in uttering his heavy displeasure against sin.

But put the case, that some natural causes or secret influences had their ordinary operations in this Earthquake, whereof notwithstanding there is not any sufficient likelihood: shall we so gaze upon the mean causes, that we shall forget or let slip the chief and principal causes? Know we not (after so long hearing and professing of the Gospel) that a Sparrow lighteth not on the ground without God's providence? That the neglecting of his loving kindness, and the continuing in sin without amendment, provoke his vengeance? And yet that he, of his own fatherly free goodness, doth ever give warning before he striketh? Surely we can not but know it, yea, and see it too, unless the god of this world hath so blinded our eyes, that we will not see it. For it is daily and almost hourly told us by the Ministers of his word, and the Bible lieth always open for us to read it ourselves, that as the only original cause and well-spring of all plagues and punishments is Sin; so the plagues and punishments themselves, and the orderly disposing, directing, and guiding of all causes to their due ends and effects, is the only work of God, who, to make all offenders unexcusable (as I said before) doth often cause even the very Elements and senseless creatures to foreshew in most terrible manner, even by their natural operations, the approaching of his just vengeance. And truly, as it is said in the Psalm, their speaking and talking unto us is not softly and whisperingly, as that the voices of them cannot be heard; but contrariwise, they be so loud in our ears, so manifest to our eyes, and so sensible to our feeling, that (unless we be stony and steely hearted, or given over to a lewd mind,) they cannot but be grievous to our hearts, and terrible to our consciences.

[xix. 3]

Now then, shall we think this rare and unaccustomed miracle, such as no man living nor none of our forefathers have ever seen or heard of, to be a thing of no importance, as happening by chance, or grounded upon some natural cause, and not rather as a messenger and summoner of us to the dreadful Judgment-seat of the almighty and ever living God?

Let us enter into ourselves, and examine our time past. Since the sharp trial which God made of us in the reign of Queen *Mary,* (at which time we vowed all obedience to God, if he would vouchsafe to deliver us again from the bondage of the Romish Antichrist into the liberty of the Gospel of his Son Jesus Christ,) he, hearkening effectually to our request, hath given us a long resting and refreshing time, blessed with innumerable benefits both of body and soul: For peace, health, and plenty of all things necessary for the life of man, we have had a golden world above all the residue of our neighbours bordering round about us.

The word of truth hath been preached unto us early and late without let or disturbance. And because our prosperity hath made us to play the wanton children against God, he hath chastised us in the mean season with many fatherly corrections.

We have been taught, instructed, exhorted, encouraged, allured, entreated, reproved, rebuked, upbraided, warned, threatened, nurtured, and chastised. To be short, there is not that mean whereby we might be won to the obeying and loving of our God, whether it were by favourable mildness or moderate rigour, but he hath ministered the same most mercifully and seasonably unto us. And what are we the better for all this?

Have we so profited in this School, that of covetous we be become liberal? of Proud and Envious, Meek and Lowly? of Lecherous, Chaste? of Gluttons, Measurable feeders? of Drunkards, Sober? of Wrathful and testy, Mild and patient? of Cruel and hard-hearted, Pitiful and gentle? of Oppressors, Relievers? and of Irreligious, Serviceable to God?

Have we so put off the old man, and so clothed ourselves with the new, in living sincerely according to the doctrine we profess, that neither the enemies of Christ's Church nor our own consciences can reprove us? Then need we not to be afraid of any signs from the Heaven above, nor of any tokens from the earth beneath: for we have builded our houses wisely upon the rock, which neither wind, water, nor Earthquake, no, nor Sathan himself, with all his Fiends, can shake down or impair.

But, alas! it is far otherwise with us: we have grown in godliness as the Moon doth in light, when she is past the full. For who seeth not the emulation that remaineth still among us for excess of apparel, fare, and building? Who perceiveth not the disdain of superiors to their inferiors, the grudge and heart-burning of inferiors towards their superiors, and the want of love in all states one towards another?

Who complaineth not of corruption in Officers, yea, even in Officers of Justice[1], and Ministers of the law? Is it not a common byword, (but I hope not true, though common) that *as a man is friended, so the law is ended*?

In Youth there was never like looseness and untimely liberty, nor in Age like unstaidness and want of discretion, nor the like carelessness of duty in either towards other.

The Boy mateth the man of aged gravity, and is commended for that which he deserveth to be beaten for.

Servants are become Master-like, and fellows with Masters: and Masters, unable to master their own affections, are become servants to other folks' servants, yea, and to their own servants too.

Men have taken up the garish attire, and nice behaviour of Women: and Women, transformed from their own kind, have gotten up the apparel and stomachs[2] of men: and as for honest and modest Shamefacedness, the preferrer of all Virtues, it is so highly misliked, that it is thought of some folks scarce tolerable in children.

Hatred, Malice, Disdain, and desire of Revenge for the weight of a feather, are the virtues of our young Gentlemen in commendation of their manhood and valiantness.

Deep Dissimulation and Flattery are counted Courtly behaviour: Might overcometh Right: and Truth is troded under foot.

Idleness and Pride bring daily infinite numbers to that point, that they had rather rob and be shamefully hanged, than labour and live with honesty.

Usury, the consumer of private states, and the confounder of Common weals, is become a common (and in some men's opinions commendable) trade to live by.

Faithfulness is fled into exile, and Falsehood vaunteth himself in his place, till he have gotten great sums of money into his hand, that he may play the Bankeroute, to the undoing of such as trust him.

The Sabboth days and holy days ordained for the hearing of God's word to the reformation of our lives, for the administration and receiving of the Sacraments to our comfort, for the seeking of all things behooveful for body or soul at God's hand by Prayer, for the minding of his benefits, and to yield praise and thanks unto him for the same, and finally, for the special occupying of ourselves in all spiritual exercises, is spent full

[1 See p. 505: also Remains of Latimer, Vol. I. pp. 127, 145, 157.]
[2 Stomachs: minds, dispositions.]

heathenishly, in taverning, tippling, gaming, playing and beholding of Bear-baiting and Stage plays, to the utter dishonour of God, impeachment of all godliness, and unnecessary consuming of men's substances, which ought to be better employed.

The want of orderly Discipline and Catechizing hath either sent great numbers, both old and young, back again into Papistry, or let them run loose into godless Atheism.

And would God that we which call others to obedience, shewing them the way, and rebuking their vices, might not be justly charged to be as Trumpets, which with their sound encourage other men to the battle, but fight not themselves! Nay, would God, that in all degrees some such as ought to be Lanterns of Light, and Ring-leaders to Virtue, were not infectors of others by their evil example!

[i. 6.] I fear me, that if the Prophet Esay were here alive, he would tell us, as he sometime told the Jews, that from the crown of our head to the sole of our foot there is no whole or sound part in our body, but that all is full of sores, blains, and blotches. Think we then that such doing shall scape unpunished, or such buildings stand unshaken? Well may we deceive ourselves in so hoping: but God deceiveth not, neither is deceived.

[Matt. xv. 13 iii. 10.] It is written, that every plant which our heavenly Father hath not planted, shall be plucked up by the roots; and that every tree which beareth not good fruit, shall be cut down, and cast into the fire.

The Axe is laid to the root of the tree: and the longer that God's vengeance is in coming, the sorer it smiteth when it is come.

[Prov. i. 24— 31.] Terrible and most true is this saying of his by the mouth of Salomon: *Forasmuch as I have called, and you have refused; and I have stretched out my hands, and you have not regarded it; but have despised all my counsel, and set my correction at nought: therefore will I also laugh at your destruction, and mock ye when the thing that ye fear cometh upon you; even when the thing that ye be afraid of breaketh in upon you like a storm, and your misery like a tempest. When trouble and heaviness come upon you on all sides: then shall ye call upon me, but I will not answer you, ye shall seek me early, but ye shall not find me: even because ye hated knowledge, and did not choose the fear of the Lord. Ye would none of my counsel, but hated my correction: and therefore shall ye eat the fruit of your own ways, and be filled with your own inventions.*

Soothly it is a dreadful thing to fall into the hands of the Lord. For as he is merciful, so is he also just, and in all his determinations he is utterly unchangeable. And (as the Prophet Jeremy sayeth) *When sentence is once gone forth of his presence, it shall not return without performance.*

Wherefore let us not be as horses and mules which have no understanding: neither let us tarry till Judgment be sent forth unto victory. But let us consider the time of our visitation, and while we have time, let us use it to our benefit.

So long as God calleth unto us, so long as he entreateth us, so long as he teacheth, allureth, exhorteth, or warneth us, yea, so long as he doeth as yet but threaten us; so long the gate is still open for us, so as he will hear us if we call, and be found of us if we seek him. But if he once hold his peace, and begin to smite, then it is too late to call back his hand, our crying will not boot us.

Therefore, while we have respite, and while it is called to-day, let us not harden our hearts as in the provocation, and as in the day of Temptation in the wilderness; but let us hearken to his voice, and, forsaking the lusts and the wicked imaginations and devices of our own hearts, let us turn to the Lord our God with hearty repentance and unfeigned amendment of life, lest (beside other meaner plagues both of body and mind) our Candlestick be removed, our light quenched, Christ's Gospel taken from us, and we for our unthankfulness be cast out with our children into utter darkness, and in the terrible day of Judgment hear this dreadful sentence of the just Judge pronounced against us: Depart from me, ye workers of wickedness, which hardened your hearts against me, and made your faces as hard as brass, at such time as my long sufferance waited for you, provoking you by mildness and patience to amendment.

FINIS.

XVI. A PRAYER for the estate of Christ's Church: to be used on Sundays.

O[1] GRACIOUS GOD and most merciful Father, thou that art the God of all comfort and consolation: we poor and wretched sinners acknowledge against ourselves, that we are unworthy to lift up our eyes to heaven: so horrible and great are the sins that we have committed against thee, both in thought, word, and deed. But thou art that God whose property is always to have mercy, and thou hast extended thy mercy unto us in thy beloved Son our Saviour Christ Jesus, in whom thou hast loved us before the foundation of the world was laid: and to the end thou mightest advance thine own mercy, in a good and happy time hast called us, by the preaching of thy blessed and holy Gospel, to repentance, preferring us before many and great nations to be a people consecrate unto thee, to hold forth thy righteousness, and to walk in obedience before thee all the days of our lives. In this persuasion of faith, and by him, good Father, we present ourselves before thee, renouncing all our sins and corruptions, and trusting only in him and his righteousness, beseeching thee for his sake to hear us, and to have mercy upon us. Thou hast made an holy promise unto us, that shall be performed, that at what time soever a sinner doth repent him of his sin from the bottom of his heart, thou wilt hear him: And that whosoever calleth upon thee in his Name, thou wilt grant all his requests. Our sins therefore do grieve us at the very heart, and we are displeased with ourselves for them; yea, we loathe ourselves for the frailties and transgressions that cleave so fast unto us. Wherefore, good Father, hear us, and accept the sacrifice of thy Son, as a most sufficient satisfaction for them, and behold us in his righteousness. Go forward with that excellent work that thou hast begun in us, and never leave us, till thou have made it perfect, till the day of Jesus Christ. Increase our knowledge, and give us a lively sense to discern sweet from sour, and sour from sweet, good from evil, and evil from

[[1] This prayer may be compared with the one commencing on p. 483.]

good; that sin and superstition deceive us not under the cloke of religion and virtue. O Lord, this must be thy work: for we confess that our reason is blind, our will is froward, our wits crafty to deceive our selves, our understanding and all our natural powers quite alienated and estranged from thee. It must be the seed of thy word, by the quickening of thy Spirit, that must lead us to newness of life, that must work in us the excellent hope of immortality, and make us to live to righteousness: and therefore put to thy helping hand: Let thy gracious goodness never fail us, to the increase of all heavenly virtues, and continual growth and gain to godliness. And because the Ministry of thy word is the ordinary mean for the attaining of this unspeakable blessing: we beseech thee, Let us never lack that excellent help: Let our bodies rather famish than our souls, yea, let us rather lack all worldly things, than that most precious Jewel of thy holy word and comfortable Gospel preached to our salvation. And therefore, thou that art the Lord of the harvest, send forth labourers into thy harvest, and double thy Spirit upon thy servants, making them as brasen walls against thine enemies, giving them courage and boldness to do thy message, yea, and that to Kings and Princes, that they being called and sent of thee, in the assured persuasion of their offices, may not fear the faces of any mortal creatures, nor be dismayed with any transitory majesty[2]. Good Lord, make thy word sharp in their mouths to an effectual operation, that sin may be cut down, and thy righteousness may flourish: Grant to them the fear of thy Name: Let their lips, O Lord, preserve knowledge, and their lives shine in holiness to the stopping of the mouths of their adversaries, and drawing many by their example to thy blessed and holy religion. Bow the hearts of all Kings and Princes of the earth to the obedience of thy dearly beloved Son Christ Jesus: If otherwise they shew by plain effects, that they belong not to thy fold, good Lord, let them feel thy hand, and find against whom they set themselves: let the blood of thy Saints, which they shed

[[2] 'As they did now, when the Terrour of God tooke hold upon them, pray for the Restitution of Discipline [see also p. 574], so in a time of great Judgements in King James the first's Reigne, they tooke certain petitions out of this Prayer for the Church, made and used during this Earthquake.' Dr Williams's MS.]

without mercy, make them drunken to perdition. In mean time assist those that thou callest to this trial, that they may feel thy help and comfort amidst all their sufferings, whilst they shall be assured to be blessed when they suffer for righteousness' sake, and to reign with thy Son, when they fulfil his sufferings in their flesh, and carry in their bodies the scars and marks of his wounds. O Lord, sanctify their blood, that it may water thy Church, and bring a mighty increase and gain to thyself, and a decrease and loss to the kingdom of Antichrist, and to the Princes of the earth, who are become his slaves and butchers. And herein (good Lord) by special name we beseech thee for the Churches of France, Flanders, and of such other places: help them after their long troubles[1], as thou shalt see to be best for them, in the advancing of thine own glory. And now (Lord) particularly we pray unto thee for this Church of England, that thou wilt continue thy gracious favour still towards it, to maintain thy Gospel still amongst us, and to give it a free passage. And to that end save thy servant Elizabeth our Queen; grant her wisdom to rule this mighty people, long life and quietness round about her; detect all the traitorous practices of her enemies, devised against her and thy truth. O Lord, thou seest the pride of thine enemies: and though by our sins we have justly deserved to fall into their hands, yet have mercy upon us, and save thy little flock. Strengthen her hand, to strike the stroke of the ruin of all their superstition, to double into the bosom of that rose-coloured whore that which she hath poured out against thy Saints, that she may give that deadly wound not to one head, but to all the heads of that cruel beast; that the life that quivereth in his dismembered members yet amongst us may utterly decay, and we, through that wholesome discipline, easy yoke, and comfortable sceptre of Jesus Christ, may enjoy his great righteousness, that thy Church may flourish, sin may abate, wicked men may hang their heads, and all thy children be comforted. Strengthen her hand, and give her a swift foot to hunt out

[[1] These troubles were now of more than twenty years' continuance. But, from 1560, the Hugonots had been arrayed, as a great party, in open hostility against the catholic authorities; the inhabitants of the Low Countries, on the contrary, not so long. Davila (Aylesbury's translation), p. 43. Camden, pp. 416, 443. Zurich Letters, pp. 412, 431.]

the bulls of Basan, and the devouring beasts that make havoc of thy flock. And because this work is of great importance, assist her with all necessary helps, both in giving her godly, wise, and faithful counsellors, as also in ministering to her such inferior rulers and officers as may sincerely, uprightly, and faithfully do their duties, seeking first thy honour and glory, then the commonwealth and quiet of this realm: that we may long enjoy thy truth, with her, and all other thy good blessings that in so great mercy thou hast bestowed upon us, with growth in goodness, gain in godliness, and daily bettering in sincere obedience. Good Lord, comfort those that feel the heavy burthen of their sins, and have no assurance in present feeling of that blessed inheritance thou hast purchased for them. Bless all such (if it be thy good will) whom thou hast united and knit unto us in any league of familiarity or affinity, that we may rejoice in the best bond, and only in this, that we are made partakers of one inheritance. Be merciful unto thy people of England which confess thy name, and make us not a byword among the heathen, as our sins have deserved. Turn away thy wrath which thy terrible tokens do threaten toward us, and turn us unto thy self; remove us not out of thy presence, but let thy fatherly warnings move us to repentance. And thus (good Lord) commending our several necessities unto thee, who best knowest both what we want, and what is meet for us, with giving thee humble and hearty thanks for all thy mercies and benefits; we knit up these our prayers with that prayer that Jesus Christ our Lord and master hath taught us. *Our Father, which art in heaven, &c.*

This prayer may be used after the Creed which followeth the Epistle and Gospel.

XVII. ¶ A Prayer for all Kings, Princes, Countries, and people, which do profess the Gospel: And especially for our sovereign Lady Queen Elizabeth, used in her Majesty's Chapel, and meet to be used of all persons within her Majesty's Dominions.

O Lord God of hosts, most loving and merciful Father, whose power no creature is able to resist, who of thy great goodness hast promised to grant the petitions of such as ask in thy Son's name: we most humbly beseech thee to save and defend all Princes, Magistrates, kingdoms, countries, and people, which have received and do profess thy holy word and Gospel, and namely this Realm of England, and thy servant Elizabeth our Queen, whom thou hast hitherto wonderfully preserved from manifold perils and sundry dangers, and of late revealed and frustrated the traitorous practices and conspiracies of divers against her: for the which, and all other thy great goodness towards us, we give thee most humble and hearty thanks, beseeching thee in the name of thy dear Son Jesus Christ, and for his sake, still to preserve and continue her unto us, and to give her long life and many years to rule over this land. O heavenly Father, the practices of our enemies, and the enemies of thy word and truth, against her and us, are manifest and known unto thee. Turn them, O Lord, if it be thy blessed will, or overthrow and confound them for thy name's sake: suffer them not to prevail: take them, O Lord, in their crafty wiliness that they have invented, and let them fall into the pit which they have digged for others. Permit them not ungodly to triumph over us: discomfort them, discomfort them, O Lord, which trust in their own multitude, and please themselves in their subtle devices and wicked conspiracies. O loving Father, we have not deserved the least of these thy mercies which we crave: for we have sinned and grievously offended thee, we are not worthy to be called thy sons: we have not been so thankful unto thee as we should, for thy unspeakable benefits poured upon us: we have abused this long time of peace and prosperity: we have not obeyed thy word: we have had it in mouth, but not in heart; in outward appearance, but not in deed: we have lived carelessly: we have not known the time of our visitation: we have deserved utter destruction. But thou, O Lord, art merciful, and ready to forgive. Therefore we come to thy throne of grace, confessing and acknowledging thee to be our only refuge in all times of peril and danger: and by the means of thy Son we most heartily pray thee to forgive us our unthankfulness, disobedience, hypocrisy, and all other our sins, to turn from us thy heavy wrath and displeasure, which we have justly deserved, and to turn our hearts truly unto thee, that daily we may increase in all goodness, and continually more and more fear thy holy name: so shall we glorify thy name, and sing unto thee in Psalms and Hymns, and spiritual songs: and thy enemies and ours shall know themselves to be but men, and not able by any means to withstand thee, nor to hurt those whom thou hast received into thy protection and defence. Grant these things, O Lord of power, and Father of mercy, for thy Christ's sake, to whom with thee and thy Holy Spirit be all honour and glory for ever and ever. Amen.

¶ A prayer and thanksgiving for the Queen, used of all the Knights and Burgesses in the High Court of Parliament, and very requisite to be used and continued of all her Majesty's loving subjects.

O ALMIGHTY and most merciful God, which dost pitch thy tents round about thy people, to deliver them from the hands of their enemies, we thy humble servants, which have ever of old seen thy salvation, do fall down and prostrate ourselves with praise and thanksgiving to thy glorious name, who hast in thy tender mercies from time to time saved and defended thy servant Elizabeth, our most gracious Queen, not only from the hands of strange children, but also of late revealed, and made frustrate, his bloody and most barbarous treason, who being her natural subject, most unnaturally violating thy divine ordinance, hath secretly sought to shed her blood, to the great disquiet of thy Church, and utter discomfort of our souls: his snare is hewn in pieces, but upon thy servant doth the crown flourish. The wicked and bloodthirsty men think to devour Jacob, and to lay waste his dwelling-place: But thou (O God) which rulest in Jacob, and unto the ends of the world, dost daily teach us still to trust in thee for all thy great mercies, and not to forget thy merciful kindness shewed to her, that feareth thy name. O Lord, we confess to thy glory and praise, that thou only hast saved us from destruction, because thou hast not given her over for a prey to the wicked: her soul is delivered, and we are escaped. Hear us now, we pray thee, O most merciful Father, and continue forth thy lovingkindness towards thy servant, and evermore to thy glory and our comfort keep her in health, with long life, and prosperity, whose rest and only refuge is in thee, O God of her salvation. Preserve her, as thou art wont, preserve her from the snare of the enemy, from the gathering together of the froward, from the insurrection of wicked doers, and from all the traitorous conspiracies of those, which privily lay wait for her life. Grant this, O heavenly Father, for Jesus Christ's sake, our only mediator and advocate. Amen.

Jo. Th.

A prayer used in the Parliament only.

O MERCIFUL God and Father, forasmuch as no counsel can stand, nor any can prosper, but only such as are humbly gathered in thy name, to feel the sweet taste of thy Holy Spirit, we gladly acknowledge, that by thy favour standeth the peaceable protection of our Queen and Realm, and likewise this favourable liberty granted unto us at this time to make our meeting together: Which thy bountiful goodness we most thankfully acknowledging, do withal earnestly pray thy divine Majesty so to incline our hearts, as our counsels may be subject in true obedience to thy holy word and will. And sith it hath pleased thee to govern this Realm by ordinary assembling the three estates of the same: our humble prayer is, that thou wilt graff in us good minds to conceive, free liberty to speak, and on all sides a ready and quiet consent to such wholesome laws and Statutes, as may declare us to be thy people, and this Realm to be prosperously ruled by thy good guiding and defence: so that we and our posterity may with cheerful hearts wait for thy appearance in judgment, that art only able to present us faultless before God our heavenly Father: to whom with thee our Saviour Christ, and the Holy Spirit, be all glory both now and ever. Amen.

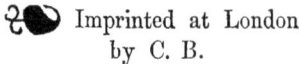

Imprinted at London
by C. B.

Cum priuilegio.

AN ORDER OF PRAYER AND THANKS GIVING for the preservation of the Queen's Majesty's life and safety: to be used of the Preachers and Ministers of the Diocese of Winchester.

With a short extract of William Parry's voluntary confession, written with his own hand.

Imprinted at London by Ralfe Newberie.

The Direction how to use this Order.

FIRST, where any Preacher is, the next Sunday after the receiving of this order, he shall make a Sermon of the authority and Majesty of Princes, according to the word of God, and how straight duty of obedience is required of all good and Christian subjects, and what a grievous and heinous thing it is both before God and man traitorously to seek their destruction, and the shedding of their blood, which are the Anointed of God, set up by him to be the Ministers of his justice and mercy to his people. In the end of which Sermon he shall set forth and declare the brief notes of the confession of the wicked purpose conceived of late by Doctor Parry, to have murdered the Queen's Majesty, animated thereunto by the Pope and his Cardinals, as you may see it set down here following. Last of all, he shall say the prayer here prescribed for that purpose, and desire the people to lift up their hearts to God together with him. After the prayer, there shall be sung or said the xxj. *Psalm, or some other Psalm to the like effect.*

A Short extract of a voluntary confession, made by William Parry, written with his own hand, the [1] *of February.* 1584.

William Parry, Doctor of Law, carrying an offensive mind against the state, by reason of his conviction, in a trial of life and death at Newgate, for the attempting of the murdering of one Hugh Hare, for the which notwithstanding he received her Majesty's most gracious pardon, and thereupon departing the Realm, in the year 1582, for that he conceived no hope of advancement here, because he was in his own opinion a pretended Catholic, and had

---

[1 The date of his letter to the queen, containing this confession, and written from the Tower, is the 14th. Strype's Annals, Vol. III. Appendix, p. 104.]

not in 22. *years received the Communion. At his being in the parts beyond the seas, having first reconciled himself to the Church of Rome at Paris, and then at Milan, conceived with himself a mean (as he pretended) to relieve the Catholics of this Realm, which was by killing of the Queen's Majesty.*

And nothing stayed him in this conceit, but only to be assured in conscience, that it was lawful and meritorious, and before the execution thereof to receive absolution from the Pope. For his assurance, or rather settling of his conscience herein, he received full satisfaction, first from an old Jesuit in Venice; next from the Pope's Ambassador, resident there, then from other good fathers (as he termeth them) in Lyons and Paris, and lastly, was encouraged to proceed therein by the Nuncio to the Pope, resident at Paris, who promised him, after he assented to that wicked enterprise, to recommend him at the altar, and also to procure the like to be done generally through Paris, which was accordingly performed in general terms, by Recommending of one that had taken upon him to do some dangerous enterprise, tending greatly to the advancement of the Catholic religion. *The said Nuncio did also convey the said Parry's letters directed to the Pope, and to the Cardinal*[1]*; by the which he did signify to them his full resolution to proceed in his enterprise, and for his better success in the same prayed his benediction Apostolical, whereunto answer was made by letters written in Rome by the Cardinal, dated the last of January, which he received from him when the Court lay at Greenwich, in March last.*

The tenor of those letters was a commendation of his enterprise, an allowance thereof, an absolution in his holiness' name of all his sins, and a request to go forward in it, in the name of God.

Which letters confirmed his resolution to kill her Majesty, and made it clear in his conscience, that it was lawful and meritorious, as he setteth down in his said confession. Whereupon he insinuated himself into the Court, and by ways and means sought to win credit, &c. to the intent

[[1] The cardinal Como, or, of Como, was prime minister to the Pope. The other personages referred to were named Palmio, Campeggio or Campeius, and Ragazzoni.]

to bring his wicked purpose to pass. Which at sundry times he had done, had not the gracious providence of God, by strange means, interrupted his purpose.

A Prayer for the Queen.

O ETERNAL God and merciful Father, with humble hearts we confess that we are not able, either by tongue to utter, or in mind to conceive, the exceeding measure of thine infinite goodness and mercy towards us wretched sinners, and towards this our noble Realm and natural country. Not many years since, when for our unthankful receiving of the heavenly light and truth of thy Gospel we were justly cast into thraldom and misery, and thrust again under the kingdom of darkness, so that our consciences lay groaning under the heavy burdens of error, superstition, and idolatry; even then, even then, O Lord, thou didst vouchsafe of thy great goodness, not only without our desert, but far beyond our hope and expectation, to preserve for us thy faithful servant our gracious prince and Sovereign Queen Elizabeth, and to save her from the jaws of the cruel Tigers, that then sought to suck her blood, and to work to us perpetual tyranny and bondage of conscience. This thou didst, O gracious Lord, undoubtedly, that she might be to this thy church of England a sweet and tender nurse, and that this realm under her happy government might be a blessed Sanctuary, and place of refuge for thy poor afflicted Saints, in these dangerous days persecuted and troubled in many countries for the profession of thy Gospel: yea, and that this our benefit and their comfort might be the more assured, thy divine providence from time to time hath many ways mightily and miraculously preserved and kept her from the crafty, cruel, and traitorous devices of her bloody adversaries, and the deadly enemies of thy Gospel, which with barbarous cruelty have sought to extinguish the light thereof, by shedding her Majesty's most innocent blood: but this thy gracious goodness and mighty providence never so apparently shewed itself at any one time, as even within these few days, when a traitorous subject, never injured or grieved by her, but sundry times holpen, relieved, and countenanced far above his state and worthiness, had of long time retained a wicked and devilish purpose, and often sought occasion and opportunity to lay violent hands upon her royal person, and to have murdered her. But still the vigilant eye of thy blessed providence did either prevent him by some sudden interruption of his endeavour, or by the majesty of her person and princely behaviour towards him didst strike him so abashed, that he could not perform his conceived bloody purpose. And at the last this wretched villany was by thy means disclosed, and his own tongue opened to confess his detestable and wicked intent. For this thy inestimable goodness towards us (O heavenly Father) with humble hearts and minds we thank thee : and bless thy name for ever and ever. For assuredly if thou hadst not been now on our side (as the prophet David saith), the whole floods and waves of wickedness had overwhelmed us, and we had been sunk into the bottomless pit of infinite and unspeakable miseries. We beseech thee therefore (O Lord), that thou wilt bless us so with thy grace, that we may be rightly and truly thankful to thee : that is, not in word only, but in deed also, daily studying to frame our lives according to the direction of thy holy word, which thou hast sent among us : And that her Majesty, thus feeling the mighty hand of thy providence fighting for her safety, may more boldly and constantly with an heroical spirit stand in the protection and defence of thy blessed Church, which by thy word thou hast planted among us. And lastly, that the cruel spirits of Antichrist, that seek the subversion of the Gospel, may by the hand of thy justice feel what it is to set to sale for money the innocent blood of thine anointed Princes, which thou hast prepared and set up, to be the nurses and protectors of thy truth : Grant this, O heavenly Father, for Jesus Christ's sake, thy only Son our Saviour, to whom, with thee and the Holy Ghost, be given all honour and glory, world without end.

A[1] PRAYER OF THANKSGIVING for the deliverance of her xix. majesty from the murderous intention of D. Parry.

O[2] ETERNAL God and merciful Father, we thy unworthy Creatures most humbly do confess, that we are not able with our tongues to utter, nor in our hearts to conceive, the exceeding measure of thine infinite goodness, graces, and favours in this later age shewed to this Noble Realm, in that thou (O Lord) hast in most dangerous times, a few years past, by thy goodness and providence, beyond expectation of man, directed and preserved the tender and noble person of our now Sovereign lady Elizabeth, by thy grace, according to her right, to come to this kingdom and Royal seat of her noble father, and by her, being therein stablished, as thy dear beloved chosen servant[3], to deliver us thy people, that were as Captives to Babylon, out of bondage and thraldom[4], and to restore us again to the free fruition of the Gospel of thy Son our Saviour Christ; for the enjoyment whereof now these[5] many years, we do confess and acknowledge that beyond all our deserts, yea truly, O Lord, when we by our daily unthankfulness for[6] the benefit of thy Gospel, and by our sinful lives, contrary to our bold profession, have most justly provoked thee to withdraw thy favour from us, thou, O Lord, with thy merciful favour and mighty power did[7] strength thy good blessed servant, our most gracious queen, constantly against the roaring and threatenings of the mighty of the world, to persist in maintenance of us her subjects and thy unworthy servants to draw out our days in all manner of prosperity, peace, and wealth; but most singularly, in a peaceable freedom, to enjoy the

[1 Had not this Prayer been properly authorised for public use, according to Strype's notion (see p. 466), we can scarcely understand why it should have been altered, and incorporated into the Form issued on account of Babington's conspiracy.]

[2 See p. 585.]

[3 minister. These notes shew the readings of the uncorrected manuscript.]

[4 thraldom of the Enemies of thy true Churche.]

[5 now many.]

[6 of.]   [7 hast strengthened.]

blessed benefits of thy holy word, against the mighty roaring of Bulls and Tigers, the Enemies of thy Church, daily conspiring round about us, and partly amongst ourselves, against this Realm, and specially against the royal person of our blessed queen, thy humble servant, and true Handmaid, whose estate being in the expectation of the number of wicked persons many times in great and secret dangers, yet thou, Lord, that art the Lord of lords, and King of kings, of thy heavenly goodness hast always preserved and defended her by many miraculous means: And as we have good cause to think, by many other means, and at many other times, than to us are yet known, but yet of late time we have fully felt thy marvellous goodness by the discovery of some Attempts most apparently taken in hand against her person, by certain wicked unnatural subjects, the stay whereof only hath proceeded, good Lord, by thy most continual tender and fatherly Care over her, thy dear beloved Daughter and servant, and not by the wit, providence, or strength, of any worldly Creature, as was most notably to be seen the last year to have been Sommervile.[1] attempted by one malicious and furious person resolutely prepared, by persuasion of others, wicked Traitors, to have committed a bloody fact upon her person, but marvellously by thy ordinance (O Lord God) discovered, by the troubled desperate conscience of the very Malefactor, and so most happily stayed: for the which thy blessed favour then shewed, if we were not so thankful to thee, O Lord, as we ought to have been, yet, Lord God, we are now most urgently stirred up to acknowledge our most bounden duties of praise and thanksgiving, by a very late manifestation of thy singular favour so largely above that former, as, all wonderful circumstances considered, we may compare it with any Example of thy most wonderful kindness shewed to any Kings or Nations of old time, testified to us in thy Holy Scriptures: For, Lord God, what can be added to this thy secret favour now lastly shewed to her, when neither she being the queen of the whole realm, nor we being in number an exceeding multitude of her subjects, could imagine, or once think of the same, much less have withstanded it[2], in that a miserable wretched unna-

[1] For an account of this man see the notes to the Form put forth in 1594.]

[2] the same.]

tural born subject, a man in truth of no religion (as now appeareth), under colour seeking to be a diligent and most careful servant to our gracious Queen, and pretending to discover to her, by his own privity, how her person was in danger of murdering, and how the same might be withstood, he himself did of long time, even whilst he had gotten credit with her Majesty, and with her Court, determine very often most desperately and resolutely to have with his own cursed hands destroyed her Majesty's sacred person: and if, Lord, thy mighty and unsearchable power had not at many times diverted his desperate heart, and his bloody hand, by reverence of the Majesty of her person, as by his own voluntary confession is declared; we do now perceive, with trembling of our hearts, that she could not at sundry times by the space of one whole year[3] and more have escaped the danger of violence[4], wickedly and resolutely by him intended. Wherefore we now thy humble creatures, acknowledging our unworthiness of these great graces, beseech thee, O Lord, that thou wilt, without regard of our former unthankfulness, shew thy mercy to us, and continue thy blessings over us, that we may for these so unspeakable benefits be more thankful than we have been, not only in words, but in deeds also, according to the direction of thy Holy word, whereof we, under the protection of our gracious Queen, by thy ordinance have by the Ministry of many thy good servants had plentiful instruction: and we do firmly hope in thy great goodness, that our Sovereign Lady the Queen, thy humble servant, having so notable proofs of thy special providence in her whole life, besides thy unknown works of favour towards her far above that which thou shewest to many other Princes, shall by her continual thankfulness, and by constancy in serving of thee and maintaining of thy Holy Word, procure to herself and us the continuance of these thy favourable graces, still to preserve her from all manner of open or secret perils, which the Enemies of thy word are known to intend against her, whereby her years may be prolonged, as far as it may please thee to grant, by the course of nature, to any other prince in this world, for the maintenance of the glory of thy Son Jesus Christ and of his Gospel, and for continuance of us thy people her natural subjects in the due fear and service of

[3 together.]   [4 violent death.]

thee, and in our natural obedience to her, whereby we and our posterity may enjoy such peace, as we have had these many years under her Majesty's government, far above any like example, in any age by past, either in this our natural Country, or any other within the limits of Christendom. Grant this, grant this, O heavenly Father, for Jesus Christ's sake, thy only Son our Saviour, to whom with thee and the Holy Ghost be given all honour and glory, world without end. Amen.

AN ORDER FOR PUBLIC PRAYERS to be used on Wednes- xxiv. days and Fridays in every Parish Church within the Province of Canterbury, convenient for this present time:

Set forth by authority.

Imprinted at London by Christopher Barker, Printer to the Queen's most excellent Majesty.

Cum gratia & Privilegio.
Regiæ Majestatis.

The Preface.

THE Fatherly care and goodness, which Almighty God by his Prophets in many places declared unto his people, never appeared more abundantly toward any nation, than of late years it hath done toward this Realm of England. For when we were in thraldom and captivity under the tyranny of Rome, and carried away with the false worshipping of God, he, by our gracious Sovereign, delivered us: he planted the elect and chosen vine of his gospel among us, by law and authority: he raised up servants to dig and delve about this vineyard, that it might prosper: he hath continually fenced us from our enemies on all sides, by his gracious and mighty providence: beyond the reach of man's policy he hath revealed their conspiracies, defeated their purposes, and made frustrate their counsels and devices: he hath erected a watch-tower of wise and godly government: he hath shed down from heaven, and blessed us with his manifold graces, as well of spiritual gifts, as of all plenty of earthly creatures. And for these his manifold benefits he hath looked for some fruits at our hands according to our duties, that his name by our good doings might be glorified: but, as the world seeth, and our own consciences accuse us, we have yielded little other than sour and unsavoury grapes, unpleasant unto God, and moving him to wrath toward us, that is, contempt of his word, worldly security, infidelity, hypocrisy, using religion only for a shew, and dishonouring the name of God and profession of the Gospel in deed, with the practice of all manner of wickedness. Seeing therefore his mercy and goodness will not allure us, the Arm of his justice will be stretched out against us: For he can abide nothing less than the contempt of his word and merciful calling. Remember the words of God uttered by Jeremy the Prophet in the 7. Chapter, *Because you have done all these works, and I rose up early* [v. 13.]

and spake unto you, but when I spake, you would not hear, neither when I called would ye answer: Therefore will I do unto this house, whereupon my Name is called, wherein also ye trust, even to the place which I gave to you and to your fathers, as I have done to Silo; and I will cast you out of my sight, as I have cast out all your brethren, &c. Let us therefore remember ourselves in time, and call upon God with earnest repentance, before he turn his face clean from us: let us follow the good counsel of the blessed Prophet Esay, *Seek the Lord while he may be found, call upon him while he is nigh us*: let the wicked man forsake his wicked ways, and the evil man his naughty cogitations, and return unto the Lord, and he will have mercy upon us. *Let us return unto God: for he is ready to forgive.* Yea, God himself calleth us by the Prophet Joel: *Turn unto the Lord* (saith he) *with all your heart, with fasting, with weeping, and with mourning; rent your hearts and not your clothes, and turn unto the Lord your God: For he is gracious and merciful, slow to anger, and of great kindness, and repenteth him of the evil that he hath purposed.* Let us therefore embrace the mercy of God while it is offered: he hath not yet stretched out his arm against us: only as a merciful Father he hath shaken the rod of his justice toward us, to wake us out of the deep slumber of our security. The Lord God grant, that in time we may take warning thereby, and not harden our hearts, and make stiff our necks against our gracious God! These are therefore in the fear of God to charge the watchmen of the Lord's city, diligently and carefully to sound the Trumpet in Sion, to gather the people together, to teach them in sackcloth and ashes to repent, to will them inwardly to rent their hearts, and not outwardly their garments only: sanctify the congregation, assemble the elders, call the young ones, and even those that suck the breast. Let the bridegroom and his spouse, let them that live in delicacy and pleasure of this life, in what state or condition soever they be, high or low, cast away their mirth and solace, and come and weep and cry with bitter repentance before the mighty God, saying, Spare thy people (O Lord) and give not thine heritage and beloved vineyard into reproach, that the wicked seed of Antichrist rule over it. Let not the enemies of thy truth say among themselves, Where is now their God, in whom they have put their trust? Then undoubtedly will the Lord be jealous over this land, and spare his people; yea, the Lord will answer, and say unto his people, Behold, I will send you corn, and wine, and oil, and you shall be satisfied therewith, and I will no more make you a reproach among mine enemies, and I will remove far from you the Northern army, that is, the Antichristian power, and I will drive him into a land barren and desolate, with his face toward the East sea, and his end to the uttermost sea, and his stink shall come up, and his corruption shall ascend, because he hath exalted himself against the truth of God. Fear not (O land), but be glad and rejoice, for the Lord will do great things for thee. This godly admonition was given to the prince, priests, and people, with great zeal and earnestness by Joel the prophet, in the days of that good king *Ezechiah*, and is the only way to turn away the wrath of God from us, and to obtain the continuance of his gracious goodness toward us, and his divine protection over us in all our difficulties and distresses.

That therefore this admonition or exhortation may take the better effects in men's hearts, it is ordered and straitly charged, that in every parish where there is a preacher allowed by the Ordinary, that every Sunday in some public Sermon he shall put the people in remembrance of God's exceeding benefits and blessings bestowed upon us these many years, and of our unthankful receiving and using of the same ; and exhort them to sincere and true repentance, and that in such sort, as they declare the inward affection of their hearts with the outward exercises of prayer, fastings, and alms-deeds, that the world may testify and see that they truly return to their Lord God. In other places, where such sufficient and discreet preachers be not, the Ministers upon the same days shall read some part of these Homilies following, distinctly and reverently, that the people may be moved thereby to the effect of that which is before mentioned. Moreover, upon the Wednesdays and Fridays the Ministers in every Parish shall say Divine service morning and evening, in such sort as hereafter followeth: at which Service one of every house in the parish shall be present. And if either the Ministers shall be negligent in doing their duties appointed unto them in this service, or the people disobedient in coming or resorting to this godly exercise, the Churchwardens and other discreet men of the Parish are required to complain thereof unto the Ordinary, that the slackness of each party may be corrected. The people also at each time of assembly would be admonished to make their charitable contributions to the relief of the poor, at the least according to the order of the Statute[1].

The order of this book.

First, the Confession, as it is in the Book of Common prayer, with some one or two of the sentences of Scripture set before the same.

Then two or three of these Psalms following in order.

Psalm vi. x. xxv. xxxviii. xli. li. xxxi. xxxiv. xxxvii. cxii. cxliii. cxlv.

Then some one of these Chapters following: Esai. v. lviii. lix. lxv. Ezechiel xvii. Zachar. vii. Joel i. ii. Jonas iii. Luke xvi. xxi. Matthew xxv. i John iii.

[[1] An act of parliament passed in the fifth year of Elizabeth's reign (cap. 2) ordered, that very soon after Midsummer-day, 'when the people are at the Churche at Dyuine Seruice,' parish officers duly appointed on the previous Sunday should ask 'gentelly' such as were of ability, what they would give weekly towards the maintenance of the poor, and write the sums they mentioned against their names in a book. Doubtless there were many who endeavored to frustrate this merciful enactment.]

[LITURG. QU. ELIZ.]

Then the Litany, with the prayer appointed to be said in the time of dearth and famine: and the next Prayer following for the time of War.

And if there be a convenient number of hearers upon any of the work-days in the Church, then one of these *Homilies* may be read, if there be no Sermon[1].

❧ *An Homily*[2] *of repentance, and of true reconciliation unto God.*

THERE is nothing that the Holy Ghost doth so much labour in, &c.

❧ *An Homily of fasting.*

THE life which we live in this world, &c.

❧ *An Homily of Alms-deeds and mercifulness toward the poor and needy.*

AMONGST the manifold duties that Almighty God requireth, &c.

The second part of the Sermon of Alms-deeds.

YE have heard before (dearly beloved), &c.

The third part of the Homily of Alms-deeds.

YE have already heard two parts, &c.

[1 Whitgift's coat of arms, impaling the arms of the see of Canterbury, occurs here in some copies. But this circumstance does not militate against our assigning to the Form the date 1586 (see p. 468); since armorial bearings, as the documents at Herald's College shew, were really granted to him by Sir *Gilbert* Dethick, the 19th of May, 1577, whilst bishop of Worcester, not, as stated by Strype (Life, p. 3), the 4th of July, 1588, by Sir *William* Dethick.]

[2 These Homilies are all printed entire.]

An ORDER OF PRAYER AND THANKSGIVING, for the preserva-   XXV.
tion of her Majesty and the Realm, from the traitorous
and bloody practises of the Pope, and his adherents:
to be used at times appointed in the Preface.

Ecclesiastes 10.

¶ Wish the king no evil in thy thought, and speak no hurt of the rich in thy privy chamber: for the birds of the air shall carry thy voice, and with their feathers shall they bewray thy words.

Eodem.

¶ He that diggeth a pit shall fall therein himself, and whoso breaketh down the hedge, a serpent shall bite him.

Proverbs 21.

¶ There is no wisdom, there is no understanding, there is no counsel against the Lord.

The horse is prepared for the day of battle: but the Lord giveth victory.

Published by authority.

¶ Imprinted at London, by Christopher Barker, Printer to the Queens most excellent Majesty. 1586.

¶ The Preface.

CONSIDERING the great peace and quietness, wherewith God hath continually blessed this noble Realm of England, since the time that it pleased him by the hand of her Majesty to have the sincere truth of the Gospel of our Saviour planted among us, and his great blessings of all sorts, wherewith he hath enriched us, and given us our hearts' desires to our comfort, and the admiration of our neighbours round about us: It were too great impiety, not to shew ourselves daily thankful for these great mercies, and not to crave the continuance of God's holy hand over us. But weighing further, with what peril of violent death, by means of wicked popish practices, our gracious sovereign hath maintained the truth, which we profess, upon whose life (next under God) the profession of the same in this land, and the continuance of the lives and welfare of us her faithful Subjects, do depend; and knowing that the Almighty most miraculously hath preserved her highness from all treason hitherto intended against her most Royal person, and kept our blood from flowing in every street like water, our Cities and Houses from sacking, and the whole Land from extreme ruin: with what zeal ought every one of us to be inflamed to praise the Lord for the detecting and confusion of our secret foes, whom his right hand hath bruised! and how ought we to detest that doctrine, which bringeth forth so traitorous and bloody fruits!

Moses and *Miriam*, and the whole host of Israel, had never greater cause to sing unto the Lord for the overthrow of *Pharaoh* and his army: nor *Debora* and *Barac* for the victory of *Sisera*: nor *Judith*, and the citizens of *Bethulia* for the end of *Holofernes*[1] and the flight of his host, than we

[[1] This allusion is not unlikely to have been suggested by a little book, which the Roman Catholics printed at Douay in 1578, and reprinted at London in 1580, entitled 'A Treatise of Schisme,' wherein the ladies about the court were thus exhorted: "Judith foloweth, whose godlye and constant wisdome if our Catholike gentlewomen would folowe, they might destroye Holofernes [Elizabeth] the master heretike, and amase all his retinew." The printer of this seditious and traitorous publication, William Carter, also then 'the chief Printer for the *Romanists*,' was hanged, drawn, and quartered for his offence at Tyburn, on the 11th of January, 1584. Camden, p. 497. Lingard, Vol. VIII. p. 429. A similar allusion is contained in the Latin prayer (see p. 466), which will now be given:

XX.   O Summa MAJESTAS, VIRTUS, et POTENTIA, noster solus qui vivas et videas Anglorum DEUS, quanta ferocitate nunc temporum immanis humani generis adversarius ille Satan in asseclis suis (tuis autem conjuratis hostibus apertis), omni fraudum, contumeliarum, atque insidiarum molimine et insultu, CHRISTI Evangelium verosque ejusdem professores (quoad possint) opprimentibus, sanguinem nostrum quam omnia malentibus, passim frendeat ac furiat. Tu autem omnipotens et benignissime PATER adjuva populum tuum sperantem in te: Per te fortescat tua Judith in protectione suæ plebis et Bethuliæ, fratrumque suorum deflende afflictorum ex atroci tyrannide ferocientis illius misereque fascinati Holofernis, atque contra execrandum ejus (quod colit) Idolum, perfidum veritatis desertorem, blasphemum illum Zennacherib: ut tua Famula populusque suus non expavescat unquam ad eorum arma, licet in tuorum perniciem ad amussim exacuta ac intentissime stricta: Quoniam revera, quamvis mundo gigantes videantur robustissimi et tela fortia, in conspectu tamen tuo vecordes et ignavi fiunt nani et spicula junci. Constringe tu DEUS noster gentem infidam, contumacem et religioni tuæ sedulo rebellantem: Per te corruat sacrilegus ille malignantium cœtus, et Ecclesia in impietate fundata, flagitiis constructa, fraudibus suffulta: Aut si fieri possit, ô clementissime PATER, effice, ut hi repudiato suo atheismo tandem aliquando resipiscant, agnoscentes Majestatem et Evangelium CHRISTI tui, in cujus veritate apud ceteros Christiani orbis fratres, cum caritate mutua in gratiam et religionis unitatem redeant, atque coalescant in eadem. Exeras interim, ô FORTITUDO nostra, caput tuum in tuorum tutelam, hostium autem confusionem: Tu propitius DEUS noster, qui adeo in

Psal. 34.   angustiis non deseras tuos, ut castra etiam figat Angelus tuus circum eos qui te timeant, et eripiat eos. Suscipe causam tuam, ô DEUS, quæ nunc agitur, quo videant gentes quod non sit, ut Consilium neque adeo Concilium (ne Tridentinum quidem illud spurium et scelestum) adversus DOMINUM aut adversus CHRISTUM ejus, ita nec Deus ullus præ-

have for the wonderful preservation of the life of our most gracious *Queen,* and thereby for our own safety. Wherefore, let every one that feareth the Lord among us, not only with the *Jews* in the book of *Esther* yearly hold a memorial with great joy of so notable deliverance, but daily in common assemblies have this great goodness in remembrance, and pray that God will not suffer the light of *Israel* to be quenched, but that it will still please him to preserve his anointed from the peril of the sword, and to give her long and happy days, to the glory of his Name, to the comfort of his chosen, and to the stablishing of his truth in this Land, till the coming of his Son in the clouds of Heaven. That this may the better be accomplished, this little book is by authority published, daily to be used in *Common prayer,* where any is, or otherwise at such times as are by law appointed for *Divine Service: viz.* the Prayer, and one or two of the *Psalms* following, according to the discretion of the Minister, and likewise to be adjoined unto those prayers, that are already of late set forth[2], for turning from us the scarcity of victual, and war, at such times as they are appointed to be read in the Church.

¶ *The prayer.*

O ETERNAL God and merciful Father, we thy unworthy creatures most humbly do confess, that we are not able with our tongues to utter, nor in our hearts to conceive, the exceeding measure of thine infinite goodness in this latter age shewed to this Noble Realm, in that thou (O Lord) hast in most dangerous times, by thy providence, beyond expectation of man, preserved the Noble person of our now Sovereign Lady Elizabeth, by thy grace: First, according to her right to come to this kingdom and Royal seat of her Noble father, and next, by her (being therein established) to deliver us thy people, that were as captives to Babylon, out of thraldom of the enemies of thy true Church, and to restore us again to the free fruition of the Gospel of thy Son our Saviour Christ. For the enjoying whereof now many years, we do confess and acknowledge, that when we by our daily unthankfulness, and by our sinful lives, have most justly provoked thee to

terquam TU : In cujus manu sunt omnes fines terræ, et altitudines montium tu quidem conspicis; atque solus qui vivas, regnes, ac sis : Cui uni voluntas, imperium, honor, gloria, laus et gratiarum actio in perpetuum.
2 *Timoth.* 2.
Novit Dominus qui sunt sui.]

[² See p. 591.]

withdraw these thy favours from us, thou (O Lord) with thy mighty power didst strengthen thy servant, our most gracious Queen, constantly against the threatenings of the greatest of the world to persist in maintenance of us in all manner of prosperity, peace and wealth: But most singularly in a peaceable freedom, to enjoy the blessed benefits of thy holy word against the mighty enemies of thy Church daily conspiring against this Realm, and especially against the Royal person of our gracious Queen, thy humble servant and true handmaiden, whose estate being in the opinion of a number of wicked persons many times in great and secret dangers, yet thou (O Lord) of thy heavenly goodness hast always preserved and defended her by many miraculous means, and (as we have good cause to think) by many other means, and at many other times, than to us are yet known. But yet, besides thy preservation of her person from the attempt of two[1] wicked persons, that suffered for the same of late years, even now in this present time, when we had no thought, that any would have minded[2] such a wicked fact, we have fully felt the power of thy miraculous goodness, by the discovery of sundry wicked Conspirators, very secretly bent and combined to make desperate attempts against her life, and against the peaceable estate of thy Church and this Realm. The stay whereof only hath proceeded (good Lord) by thy most continual, tender and fatherly care over her, in the strange discovering, and the manner of apprehending of the malefactors, being many, and not by the wit or strength of any worldly creature. For otherwise than by thy special goodness, we do now perceive, and that with trembling of our hearts, that she could not at sundry times have escaped the danger of violent death, wickedly and resolutely against her intended; so that we may truly say with *David* in his Psalm, *That all men that see it, shall say, This hath God done: for they shall perceive, that it is his work.* Wherefore we now, thy humble creatures, acknowledging our unworthiness of these great graces, beseech thee (O Lord) that

[1 Somerville and Parry are the persons intended, as may be seen by referring to p. 588, where this prayer is printed in its original state. The former, however, died in prison by his own hand after condemnation.]

[2 Minded: turned their minds to, thought about.]

thou wilt, without regard of our former unthankfulness and contempt of thy word, shew thy mercy to us, and continue thy blessings over us, that we may, for these so unspeakable benefits, be more thankful than we have been, not only in words, or as hearers, but in deeds also, as doers of thy will, according to the direction of thy holy word. And that it would please thee still to hold this thy blessed hand over our *Queen Elizabeth*, and preserve her *Royal* person from all manner of open or secret perils, whereby her years may be prolonged, as far as it may please thee to grant, by the course of *Nature*, for the maintenance of thy glory, and of thy Son *Jesus Christ*, and of his *Gospel*, and for continuance of us thy people her natural subjects in the due fear and service of thee, and in our natural obedience to her; whereby we and our posterity may still enjoy such peace, as we have had these many years, under her Majesty's government, far above any like example in any age by-past. Grant this (O heavenly Father) for *Jesus Christ's* sake, thy only Son our Saviour, to whom with thee and the Holy Ghost be all honour and glory, world without end. Amen.

The first Psalm.

WE rejoice in thy strength, (O Lord :) exceeding glad are we of thy salvation. [Psal. 21.]

Thou hast given us our hearts' desire : and hast not denied the request of our lips.

Thou hast prevented us with the blessings of goodness : and hast made us glad with the joy of thy countenance.

For the ungodly had drawn out the sword, and had bended their bow : to cast down the poor and needy, and to slay such as be of a right conversation. [Psal. 37.]

Their sword shall go through their own heart : and their bow shall be broken.

All thine enemies shall feel thine hand : thy right hand shall find out them that hate thee. [Psal. 22 [21].]

Thou shalt make them like a fiery oven in the time of thy wrath : the Lord shall destroy them in his displeasure, and the fire shall consume them.

Their fruit shalt thou root out of the earth : and their seed from among the children of men.

For they intended mischief against thee: and imagined such a device, as they are not able to perform.

Therefore hast thou put them to flight: and the strings of thy bow hast thou made ready against the face of them.

Psal. 36.   Thy mercy (O Lord) reacheth unto the heavens: and thy faithfulness unto the clouds.

Thy righteousness standeth like the strong mountains: and thy judgments are like the great deep.

Thou, Lord, dost save both man and beast: how excellent is thy mercy, O Lord! and the children of men shall put their trust under the shadow of thy wings.

O continue forth thy loving kindness unto them that know thee: and thy righteousness unto them that are true of heart.

O let not the foot of pride come against us: and let not the hand of the ungodly cast us down.

Withdraw not thou thy mercy from us, O Lord: let thy lovingkindness and thy truth alway preserve us.

But let the ungodly perish, let thine enemies consume as the fat of lambs: yea, even as the smoke let them consume away.

Psal. 79.   So we that be thy people, and sheep of thy pasture shall give thee thanks for ever: and will alway be shewing forth thy praise from generation to generation.

The second Psalm.

Psal. 140.   DELIVER us, O Lord, from the evil men: and preserve us from the wicked men.

Which imagine mischief in their hearts: and stir up strife all the day long.

The proud have laid a snare for us, and spread a net abroad with cords: yea, and set traps in our ways.

Psal. 64.   They courage themselves in mischief: and common among themselves, how they may lay snares, and they say no man shall see them.

They imagine wickedness and practise it: that they keep secret among themselves, every man in the deep of his heart.

Psal. 140.   But let not the ungodly have their desire, O Lord: let not their mischievous imaginations prosper, lest they be too proud.

Thou, O Lord, shalt suddenly shoot at them with a swift arrow: that they shall be wounded.

And all men that see it, shall say, *This hath God done:* for they shall perceive, that it is his work.

Praised be the Lord daily, even the God that helpeth us: Psal. 68. and poureth his benefits upon us.

He is our God, even the God of whom cometh *Salvation:* God is the Lord by whom we escape death.

He hath given victory unto us: and hath delivered Psal. 144. *David* his servant from the peril of the sword.

O that men would therefore praise the Lord for his Psal. 107. goodness: and declare the wonders that he doth for the children of men.

That they would exalt him in the congregation of the people: and praise him in the seat of the Elders.

That they would offer unto him the sacrifice of thanksgiving: and tell out his works with gladness.

Then shall our sons grow up as the young plants: and [Psal. 144.] our daughters be as the polished corners of the Temple.

Our garners shall be full and plenteous with all manner of store: our sheep shall bring forth thousands, and ten thousands in our streets.

Our oxen shall be strong to labour, there shall be no decay: no leading into captivity, and no complaining in our streets.

Happy are the people that be in such a case: yea, blessed are the people, that have the Lord for their God.

The third Psalm.

WE will magnify thee, O God our King: and will praise Psal. 145. thy Name for ever and ever.

Every day will we give thanks unto thee: and praise thy name for ever and ever.

Great is the Lord, and marvellous worthy to be praised: there is no end of his greatness.

One generation shall praise thy works unto another: and declare thy power.

The memorial of thine abundant kindness shall be shewed: and men shall sing of thy righteousness.

The Lord is righteous in all his ways: and holy in all his works.

The Lord is nigh unto all that call upon him: yea, all such as call upon him faithfully.

He will fulfil the desire of them that fear him: he also will hear their cry, and will help them.

The Lord preserveth all them that love him: but scattereth abroad all the ungodly.

Psal. 138. Though we walk in the midst of trouble, yet shall he refresh us: he shall stretch forth his hand upon the furiousness of our enemies, and his right hand shall save us.

Psal. 116. The snares of death compassed us round about: and the pains of hell gat hold upon us.

But thou, Lord, hast delivered our souls from death: our eyes from tears, and our feet from falling.

Psal. 30. Thou hast turned our heaviness into joy: thou hast put off our sackcloth, and girded us with gladness.

Therefore shall every good man sing of thy praise without ceasing: O God, we will give thanks unto thee for ever.

The fourth Psalm.

Psal. 106. O GIVE thanks unto the Lord, for he is gracious: and his mercy endureth for ever.

Who can express the noble acts of the Lord: or shew forth all his praise?

For we have sinned with our Fathers: we have done amiss and dealt wickedly.

We have not regarded thy wonders, nor kept thy great goodness in remembrance: but have been disobedient to thy holy will.

Nevertheless he hath holpen us for his name's sake: that he might make his power to be known.

Psal. 11. For lo, the ungodly hath bent their bow, and made ready their arrows within the quiver: that they might privily shoot at us.

Psal 22. Many Oxen purposed to have come about us: fat *Bulls* of *Basan* intended to close us in on every side.

They gaped upon us with their mouths: as it were ramping and roaring lions.

The counsel of the wicked laid siege against us: they set traps in our ways.

Psal. 35. They had privily laid their net to destroy us without a cause: yea, even without a cause had they made a pit for our soul.

But thou (O Lord) hast delivered our soul from the sword: thy darling from the power of the dog. *Psal. 22.*

Thou hast saved us from the Lion's mouth: thou hast heard us from amongst the horns of the *Unicorns*.

A sudden destruction is come upon them unawares, and the net that they had laid privily, hath catched themselves: they are fallen into their own mischief. *Psal. 35.*

They are confounded and put to shame, that did seek after our soul: they are turned back and put to confusion, that imagined mischief for us.

Wherefore praise the Lord, ye that fear him: magnify him all ye of the seed of *Jacob*, and fear him all ye of the seed of *Israel*. *Psal. 22.*

For he hath not despised, nor abhorred the low estate of the poor: he hath not hid his face from him, but when we called unto him, he heard us.

Therefore our praise is of thee in the great *Congregation:* our vows will we perform in the sight of them that fear him.

Glory be to the Father, to the Son. &c.

Hereunto also may be added, at the discretion of the Minister, the lxxxiii. *the* ciii. *and the* cxxiiii. *Psalms. And for the first Lesson, when he shall see occasion, he may read one of these Chapters: viz. Exod.* xv. *Judg.* v. *Esther* vi. vii. viii. *and* ix.

XXVI. A PRAYER AND THANKSGIVING fit for this present: and to be used in the time of Common prayer.

Imprinted at London by Christopher Barker, Printer to the Queen's most excellent Majesty. 1587.

Cum privilegio.

A prayer and thanksgiving fit for this present: and to be used in the time of Common prayer.

O LORD God of hosts, most loving and merciful Father, we thy humble servants prostrate ourselves before thy divine Majesty, instantly beseeching thee of thy gracious goodness to be merciful to thy Church militant here upon earth, many ways vexed and tormented by the malice of Satan and his members, and at this time, as it were, environed on every side with strong and subtle adversaries. We confess and acknowledge, O Lord, (with all humble and hearty thanks) the wonderful and great benefits which thou hast bestowed upon this thy Church and people of England, in giving unto us not only peace and quietness, but also in preserving our most gracious Queen thy handmaid so miraculously from so many perils and dangers, and in granting her good success against the attempts of her adversaries: for the which so wonderful and great benefits, we humbly beseech thee to stir up our dull minds to such thankfulness and acknowledging of thy mercies as becometh us, and as may be acceptable unto thee. O Lord, let thine enemies know, and make them confess, that thou hast received England into thine own protection. Set (O Lord, we pray thee) a hedge about it, and evermore mightily defend it. Let it be a comfort to the afflicted: a help to the oppressed: a defence to thy Church and people persecuted abroad. And, forasmuch as thy cause is now in hand, we beseech thee to direct and go before such as have taken the same upon them. Pitch thy tents about them, and grant unto them (O Lord) so good and honourable victories, as thou didst to Abraham and his company, against the four mighty kings[1]: to Josua against the five kings, and against Amalech: and as thou usest to do to thy children when they please thee. We acknowledge all power,

[1 The following prayer for the earl of Leicester (see p. 467) contains a similar reference:

Lord Jesus Christ, Son of the living God, who was crucified for our sins, and rose again for our justification, and, ascending up into heaven, sittest now at the right hand of the Father, with full power and authority, ruling and disposing all things according to thy glorious and gracious purpose. We, most miserable and sinful creatures, prostrate ourselves and our prayers before thy divine Majesty, beseeching thy gracious goodness, according to thy accustomed mercy, to be merciful to thy poor Church militant, miserably vexed in this world, by the malice of Sathan and his brood, enemies to all Christian peace and concord, so that thy little flock is distressed on every side. Notwithstanding (O merciful Father) so many strifes and debates of men, among so many brands of discord, tossed to and fro by the devils, enemies of truth, having neither rest without, nor peace within: we humbly confess, yielding all thanks unto thy divine Majesty, that this Island of ours, by thy direction from above, hath been so peaceably and quietly governed by her Majesty, that it hath been like a golden Cup in thy gracious hand; for which mercy of thine, as it is more sweet unto us than to other our neighbours, so we beseech thee to stir up our dull minds to such thankfulness and acknowledging of thy mercies, that all the enemies of thy truth may still (though with weeping hearts) confess, because of the continuance of thy goodness towards us, that thou hast made *England* a chosen shaft, and put him in thy quiver. And forasmuch (O Lord) as this discord abroad reacheth almost to the throat of our Church and commonweal, and that the enemies, O Lord, especially those that have the mark of Antichrist, seek to build like the Moth in another man's possession and garment, and seek to swallow up thy people as a grave; make, O Lord (we pray thee), a hedge about us and thy house, and let thy Church be like *Salomon's* bed, about the which there was always a watch, and let the fruit of the English Church be meat unto others, and the leaf thereof medicinable unto thy afflicted and scattered people. Break, O Lord, the *Hydra* his heads, or strangle him within his cave, that he do no more hurt: and that our prayers may be more welcome to thy gracious presence, grant unto us thy Holy Spirit, that every one of us may unfeignedly sorrow for our sins, and confess the majesty of thy word, and our great contempt of thy workmen, before thou do seal this great and known sum with some sharp and notable plague. And forsomuch as thy cause is now taken in hand by our gracious Sovereign, we beseech thee that thou wilt direct and go before her, and her noble wise Counseller, the honourable Earl of Leicester, her highness' Lieutenant in those Countries, and grant unto him so good and honourable victories, as *Josua* had against the five Kings, which sought to destroy the *Gabaonites:* fight for him, strength and victory to come from thee. Some put their trust in chariots, and some in horses; but we will remember thy name, O Lord our God. Thou bringest the counsel of the heathen to nought, and makest the devices of the people to be of none effect. There is no king that can be saved by the multitude of an host, neither is any mighty man delivered by much strength: A horse is but a vain thing to save a man. Therefore we pray unto thee, O Lord: thou art our help and our shield. And, that our prayers may be the more effectual and acceptable unto thee, grant unto us, we beseech thee, true repentance for our sins past, namely for our unthankfulness, contempt of thy word, lack of compassion towards the afflicted, envy, malice, strife and contention among our selves, and for all other our iniquities. Lord, deal not with us as we have deserved: but of thy great

sweet Saviour, as thou didst for *Abraham*, when he overcame the four mighty Kings, which conquered the Kings of the five Cities, and destroyed the men of *Sodom* and *Gomora*: and grant that as *Josua* overcame *Amalech*, that sought to hinder the children of *Israel*, by the prayer of *Moses*, that our noble Counseller, valiant Soldier, and faithful servant to her Majesty, may prevail and vanquish thy enemies, which disturb thy peace, and afflict our poor neighbours of the Low Countries, and that through our earnest prayers and hearty tears, which we most humbly and with unfeigned hearts pour forth before thy divine Majesty, who, seeking not to climb by pride, lest he should fall, but as a faithful member of thy Church, laboureth to defend thy truth and thy glorious Gospel. We confess, O heavenly Father, all power to come from thy seat: neither the Trumpets of Rams' horns wherewith *Jerico* fell, nor *Samson's* jaw bone, nor *David's* stone, nor the Pitchers of *Gedion* have power or strength to prevail without thee. The voice of the Lord breaketh the Cedars, yea, thou, O Lord, breakest the Cedars of *Lebana*. Therefore, O Lord, take the wicked by the heel, disclose the juggling of that popish unholy league. Bruise them, O Lord, with a Sceptre of iron, and break them in pieces like a Potter's vessel; that all thy faithful Children may confess and say, The roaring of the Lion, the voice of the Lioness, and the teeth of the Lion's whelps are broken. Grant also (O Lord) that the soldiers and faithful followers of thy religious Captain may so behave themselves in thy fight, that thou mayest have a pleasure in them, because they fear thy name, and fight thy battle: send thy holy Angel to pitch his Tent amongst them, and ever mightily defend them. Let them, O Lord, love together like Brethren, fight together like Lions, and not fear to die together like men. We beseech thee unite and sanctify them to thee, that they may war like faithful soldiers on earth, and enjoy the peace thou hast provided for them in this world, and in the world to come, for ever and ever. *Amen.*]

goodness and mercy do away our offences. O Lord, give good and prosperous success to all those that fight thy battle against the enemies of thy Gospel: shew some token continually for our good, that they which hate us may see it and be confounded; and that we, thy little and despised flock, may say with good King David, *Blessed are the people whose God is the Lord Jehovah, and blessed are the folk that he hath chosen to be his inheritance.* These and all other graces necessary for us, grant (O heavenly Father) for Jesus Christ's sake, our only Mediator and Redeemer. Amen.

Hereunto may be added the Collect of the Litany appointed to be used in the time of war. And other prayers heretofore published upon the like occasions, according to the discretion of the Minister. And when there are no Sermons, then to read one of the Homilies of repentance, fasting, and alms-deeds, lately published [1].

Some of these Psalms may be said or sung at the days and times before mentioned, after the prayer.

	Psal.	
2	46	83
20	56	94
21	70	140
33		

One of these Chapters may be read on Wednesdays and Fridays, at the discretion of the Curate.

Lessons.

Exod. 14.	Judg. 7.	2 Kin. 19.
Exod. 17. begin at the 8. ver.	1 Sam. 17.	2 Chron. 20. unto the verse 30.
Josua 10. until the 28. verse.	2 King 7.	Act. 12.

It were very convenient, and to be wished, that every one should forbear one meal at the least every week, over and above the ordinary appointed fasting days: to the end they might be more able to relieve the poor, and be more apt to prayer, hearing of the word, and other godly exercises.

[1 See p. 594.]

XXVIII.   A FORM OF PRAYER, necessary for the present time and state.

Imprinted at London by the Deputies of Christopher Barker, Printer to the Queen's most excellent Majesty. 1588.

The[1] Preface.

WE be taught by many and sundry examples of holy Scriptures, that upon occasion of particular punishments, afflictions and perils, which God of his most just judgment hath sometimes sent among his people, to shew his wrath against sin, and to call his people to repentance, and to the redress of their lives, the godly have been provoked and stirred up to more fervency and diligence in prayer, fasting and alms-deeds, to a more deep consideration of their consciences, to ponder their unthankfulness and forgetfulness of God's merciful benefits towards them, with craving of pardon for the time past, and to ask his assistance for the time to come, to live more godly, and so to be defended and delivered from all further perils and dangers. So king David in the time of plague and pestilence, which ensued upon his vain numbering of the people, prayed unto God with wonderful fervency, confessing his fault, desiring God to spare the people, and rather to turn his ire to him-ward, who had chiefly offended in that transgression. The like was done by the virtuous kings Josaphat and Ezechias in their distress of wars and foreign invasions. So did Judith and Hester fall to humble prayers in like perils of their people. So did Daniel in his captivity, and many other mo in their troubles. Now therefore, calling to mind, that God hath been provoked by us many and sundry ways, and doth after a sort threaten us with wars and invasion: it behoveth us to pray earnestly and heartily to God, to turn away his deserved wrath from us, and as well to defend us from the fierceness and fury of our enemies, (which combine and conspire together against us,) as also from all other plagues and punishments, which our unthankfulness and contempt of his word hath justly deserved. And although it is every christian man's duty, of his own devotion to pray at all times: yet for that the corrupt nature of man is so slothful and negligent therein, he hath need by often and sundry means to be stirred up, and put in remembrance of the same.

It is therefore meet and requisite: First, that all Curates and Pastors should exhort their Parishioners to endeavour themselves to come unto the Church, with so many of their families as may be spared from their necessary business, and they to resort not only on Sundays and Holidays,

[[1] This is copied almost entirely from the Form issued in 1563. See p. 479.]

but also on Wednesdays and Fridays, and at other times likewise during the time of these imminent dangers, exhorting them there reverently and godly to behave themselves, and with penitent hearts to pray unto God to turn these plagues from us, which we through our unthankfulness and sinful life have deserved.

Secondly, that the said Curates then distinctly and plainly read the general confession appointed in the book of Service, with the Litany and residue of the Morning prayer, using according to their discretions some of the Psalms and prayers hereafter following, and for the first lesson some of these Chapters: Exodus 14. Exodus 17. begin at the 8. verse. Josua 10. until the 28. verse. Judges 7. 1 Samuel 17. 2 Kings 7. 2 Kings 19. 2 Chron. 20. unto the verse 30.

Finally, it is very requisite, that in their Sermons and exhortations they should move the people to abstinence and moderation in their diet, to the end they might be the more able to relieve the poor, to pray unto God, to hear his holy word, and to do other good and godly works.

A [2]prayer for the forgiveness of sins. [1572.]

O COME, let us humble ourselves : and fall down before the Lord our maker, with reverence and fear. *Psal. 95.*

Let us repent and turn from our wickedness, and turn again unto our Lord: and our sins shall be forgiven us. *Osee 6. Acts 3.*

[[2] In the summer of 1588, Christopher Stile 'Collected and gathered togither,' whilst John Wolfe printed, four 'Psalmes of Inuocation vpon God, To preserue her Maieftie and the people of this lande, from the power of our enemies.' They were followed by 'A Godly Prayer, Wherein is desired aide of God against his enimies, forgiuenesse of sinnes, and to turne his plagues, as well of the sword, as penurie, which be due for sinne, farre from this land.' The subjoined passage from a copy in archbishop Harsnet's library, will shew the spirit of the publication : "We the people of England are thy people, O Lord, and thou art our God : we are thy flocke, and thou art our shepeheard : we are thy children, and thou art our Father. Be merciful vnto vs thy children: tender vs thy flocke, and defend vs thy English nation. Turne thy wrath vpon the nations that haue not knowne thee, and that doe not call vpon thy name : and turne it we pray thee vpon the Antechristians host, send forth thine angel stil to scatter them, as sometime thou didst in the host of *Senacherib* for *Iudah* and *Hezechiah* in his time. Let the blast of the trumpets blowne by our Gedeon stil strike a terror in the harts of the Antechristian Madianites, with their combined powers, and let be hard the sounding of thy host in the aire to the amasing of the Spanish Assyrians, that they and theirs may be a pray for our *Elizabeth*, and our English host : or sinke them in the sea, as thou didst *Pharao* and his host in pursuing thy Israel, to bring them into their seruitude, that so our *Elizabeth* and all her faithfull subiects may sing the songes of triumph to thy diuine maiestie, that giuest victorie to Kinges."]

[LITURG. QU. ELIZ.]

Jonas 3. *Osee* 6.	Let us turn, and the Lord will turn from his heavy wrath: he hath smitten us, and he will heal us, he will pardon us, and we shall not perish.
Psal. 5[1].	We acknowledge our faults, O Lord: and our sins are ever before our sight.
*Lamen.*51[5].	We have sore provoked thine anger, O Lord: thy wrath is waxed hot, and thy heavy displeasure is sore kindled against us.
Psal. 6.	But rebuke us not, O Lord, in thine indignation: neither chasten us in thy heavy displeasure.
Judith 8. *Job* 11. *Sapi.* 11.	Indeed we acknowledge that all punishments are less than our deserving: but yet of thy mercy, Lord, correct us to amendment, and plague us not to our destruction.
Psal. 25.	O remember not the sins and offences of our youth, and times past, but according to thy mercy think upon us, O Lord, for thy goodness.
Psal. 10.	Stand not so far off, O Lord: neither hide thy face in the needful time of trouble.
Psal. 25.	Turn thee unto us, and have mercy upon us: for we are desolate and in great misery.
Baruc. 3. *Jonas* 2.	And now in the vexation of our spirits, and the anguish of our souls: we remember thee, and we cry unto thee; hear, Lord, and have mercy.
Dan. 9.	For we do not pour out our prayers before thy face, trusting in our own righteousness: but in thy great and manifold mercies.
Psal. 25.	For thine own sake, and for thy holy name's sake, incline thine ear and hear: and be merciful to our sins, for they are great.
Psal. 79.	Help us, O God of our salvation, for the glory of thy name: O deliver us, and save us for thy name's sake.
Psal. 79.	So we that be thy people, and sheep of thy pasture, shall give thee thanks for ever: and will be always shewing forth thy praise from generation to generation.

Glory be to the Father, &c. As it was in the, &c.

A prayer to be delivered from our enemies. [1572.]

Psal. 5.	O HEARKEN to the voice of our prayer, our King and our God: for unto thee do we make our complaint.
Psal. 22.	O Lord, the counsel of the wicked conspireth against us: and our enemies are daily in hand to swallow us up.

They gape upon us with their mouths : as it were ramp- *Psal. 22.*
ing and roaring lions.

But thou, O Lord, art our defender: thou art our health and our *Psal. 3.*
salvation.

We do put our trust in thee, O God : save us from all *Psal. 7.*
them that persecute us, and deliver us.

O take the matter into thy hand, thy people commit themselves unto *Psal. 10.*
thee : for thou art their helper in their distress.

Save us from the Lions' mouths, and from the horns of *Psal. 7. & 22.*
the Unicorns : lest they devour us, and tear us in pieces,
while there is none to help.

O deliver not the soul of thy Turtle dove unto the multitude of the *Psal. 74.*
enemies: and forget not thy poor congregation for ever.

Deliver us from our enemies, O God : defend and save *Psal. 59.*
us from them that imagine mischief, and rise up against us.

And we shall give thanks unto thee, O Lord, according to thy great *Psal. 7.*
mercies : and will praise the name of the Lord most high.

We will declare thy name unto our brethren : in the *Psal. 22.*
mids of the congregation will we praise thee, and magnify
thy salvation world without end.

Glory be to the Father, and to the Son, and to the Holy Ghost.

As it was in the beginning, is now, and ever shall be,
world without end. Amen.

A prayer for deliverance from enemies. [1572.]

HEAR our prayer, O Lord, consider our desire : hearken *Psal. 143.*
unto us for thy truth and mercy's sake.

Lord, how are they increased that trouble us : many are they that *Psal. 3.*
rise against us.

The ungodly bend their bows, and make ready their *Psal. 11.*
arrows within the quiver : that they may shoot at those that
call upon the name of the Lord.

They smite down thy people, O Lord : and trouble thine heritage. *Psal. 104.*

The dead bodies of thy servants have they given to be *Psal. 79.*
meat unto the fowls of the air : and the flesh of thy saints
unto the beasts of the land.

Their blood have they shed like water on every side of Hierusalem : *Psal. 79.*
and there was no man to bury them.

And we that live are become an open shame to our *Psal. 79.*

enemies: a very scorn and derision unto them that are round about us.

Psal. 74. & 79. O Lord, why is thy wrath such against the sheep of thy pasture? how long wilt thou be angry? shall thy jealousy burn like fire for ever?

Psal. 79. Wherefore should the ungodly say, Where is now their God? there is now no more help for them in their God.

Psal. 79. Oh remember not our old sins, but have mercy upon us, and that soon: for we are come to great misery.

Psal. 79. O let the sorrowful sighing of the prisoners come before thee, according to the greatness of thy power: preserve thou those that are appointed to die.

Psal. 74. O Lord, think upon the congregation of thy people, whom thou hast purchased and redeemed of old: O deliver us and save us, for the glory of thy name.

Psal. 22. And our praises shall be of thee in the great congregation: our vows will we perform in the sight of them that fear thee.

Psal. 22. And all the ends of the world shall remember themselves, and be turned unto the Lord: and all the kindreds of the nations shall worship before him.

Glory be to the Father, and to the, &c.

As it was in the beginning, is now, &c.

Prayers for true repentance and mercy. [1572.]

MOST merciful Father, who hast in thy holy word, the word of truth, promised mercy unto sinners that do repent and turn unto thee, and hast by thy terrible examples of thy just anger, being executed upon people and countries round about us, called us, and most mercifully moved us to repentance, and by thy patience and long suffering of us hitherto hast graciously granted us time and space to repent: grant also, we beseech thee, both to them and us, grace truly to repent, and unfeignedly to turn unto thee with amendment of life, and to trust in thy mercies, and safely to rest under thy continual protection from all enemies and evils, both bodily and ghostly, through our Saviour Jesus Christ, who with thee and the Holy Ghost liveth and reigneth one God, world without end. *Amen.*

Another for the same. [1572.]

WE have sinned, Lord, we have sinned grievously, we have done unjustly, we have lived wickedly; we are sorry therefore, O Lord, yea, we are most sorry, that we are no more sorry for our sins: but thou, Lord God, Father of all mercies, we humbly beseech thee, be not angry with us for ever for our great and manifold sins, neither deal with us according to our deserts, neither reward us according to our wickedness; but even for thyself, O Lord God, and for thy holy name's sake, for thy most gracious assured promises made unto penitent sinners in thy holy word, the word of truth, for thy infinite mercies which are in thy dearly beloved Son Jesu Christ our Saviour, for his sake, for his death and precious blood, be merciful unto us sinners; and so we, who have most grievously offended thy divine Majesty, shall continually magnify thy great and infinite mercy, through our Saviour Jesus Christ, to whom with thee and the Holy Ghost be all honour and glory, world without end. *Amen.*

Another prayer, to be delivered from our enemies.

O[1] LORD God of hosts, most loving and merciful Father, we thy humble servants prostrate ourselves before thy divine Majesty: most heartily beseeching thee, to grant unto us true repentance for our sins past, namely for our unthankfulness, contempt of thy word, lack of compassion towards the afflicted, envy, malice, strife and contention among ourselves, and for all other our iniquities. Lord, deal not with us as we have deserved, but of thy great goodness and mercy do away our offences, and give us grace to confess and acknowledge, O Lord, with all humble and hearty thanks, the wonderful and great benefits which thou hast bestowed upon this thy Church and people of England, in giving unto us without all desert of our part, not only peace and quietness, but also in preserving our most gracious Queen thine handmaid so miraculously from so many conspiracies, perils, and dangers, and in granting her good success against the attempts of her adversaries: for the which so wonderful and great benefits we humbly beseech thee to stir up our dull

[[1] This Prayer varies very little from that on p. 604.]

minds to such thankfulness and acknowledging of thy mercies as becometh us, and as may be acceptable unto thee. We do instantly beseech thee of thy gracious goodness to be merciful to thy Church militant here upon earth, many ways vexed and tormented by the malice of Satan and his members, and at this time, as it were, compassed about with strong and subtle adversaries. And especially, O Lord, let thine enemies know, and make them confess that thou hast received England (which they most of all for thy gospel sake do malign) into thine own protection. Set, we pray thee (O Lord), a wall about it, and evermore mightily defend it. Let it be a comfort to the afflicted, a help to the oppressed, a defence to thy Church and people persecuted abroad. And forasmuch as thy cause is now in hand, we beseech thee to direct and go before our Armies both by sea and land, bless and prosper them, and grant unto them, O Lord, so good and honourable success and victories, as thou didst to Abraham and his company against the four mighty kings, to Josua against the five kings and against Amalech, to David against the strong and mighty armed giant Goliah, and as thou usest to do to thy children, when they please thee. We acknowledge all power, strength, and victory to come from thee : some put their trust in chariots, and some in horses, but we will remember thy name, O Lord our God. Thou bringest the counsel of the heathen to nought, and makest the devices of the people to be of none effect. There is no king that can be saved by the multitude of an host, neither is any mighty man delivered by much strength. A horse is but a vain thing to save a man: therefore we pray unto thee, O Lord, thou art our help and our shield. O Lord, give good and prosperous success to all those that fight thy battle against the enemies of thy ‘ Gospel, shew some token continually for our good, that they which hate us may see it and be confounded; and that we thy little and despised flock may say with good King David, Blessed are the people whose God is the Lord Jehovah, and blessed are the folk that he hath chosen to be his inheritance. These and all other graces necessary for us grant, O heavenly Father, for Jesus Christ's sake, our only Mediator and Redeemer.

In the time of war.

O ALMIGHTY God, King of all kings, and governor of all things, whose power no creature is able to resist, to whom it belongeth justly to punish sinners, and to be merciful to them that truly repent: save and deliver us (we humbly beseech thee) from the hands of our enemies: abate their pride, assuage their malice, and confound their devices, that we, being armed with thy defence, may be preserved evermore from all perils, to glorify thee, which art the only giver of all victory, through the merits of thy only Son Jesus Christ our Lord.

A prayer for the same. [1572.]

O MOST righteous GOD, and most merciful Father, who as well by the dreadful plagues and afflictions of nations round about us, as by long suffering and saving of us, and by manifold benefits bestowed upon us, hast shewed thy severity in punishing, or trying of them, and thy mercy in sparing and blessing of us: we most humbly and heartily beseech thee, in thy justice to remember thy mercy towards them, and to save them, and to grant unto us grace not to despise the riches of thy patience and goodness towards us, neither by hardness of heart and impenitency to heap upon ourselves vengeance in the day of vengeance; but that we, being taught by the example of their punishment to fear thy justice, and moved by thy long suffering and blessing of us to love thy goodness, may by true repentance for our sins, and with all our souls, hearts, and minds, unfeignedly turning unto thee in newness of life, both escape thy wrath and indignation, and enjoy the continuance and increase of thy favour, grace, and goodness, through our Saviour, Jesus Christ, thy only Son, to whom with thee and the Holy Ghost, one God of most glorious majesty, be all honour and glory, world without end. *Amen.*

Another prayer for the same. [1572.]

O LORD our God and heavenly Father, look down, we beseech thee, with thy fatherly and merciful countenance upon us thy people, and poor humble servants, and upon all such Christians as are any where persecuted, and sore afflicted for the true acknowledging of thee to be our God, and thy Son Jesus Christ, whom thou hast sent, to be the only Saviour of the world: save them, O merciful Lord, who are as sheep appointed to the slaughter, and by hearty prayer do call and cry unto thee for thy help and defence: hear their cry, O Lord, and our prayer for them, and for ourselves; deliver those that be oppressed, defend such as are in fear of cruelty, relieve them that be in misery, and comfort all that be in sorrow and heaviness, that by thy aid and strength they and we may obtain surety from our enemies, without shedding of Christian and innocent blood. And for that, O Lord, thou hast commanded us to pray for our enemies, we do beseech thee, not only to abate their pride, and to stay the fury and cruelty of such as either of malice or ignorance do persecute them which put their trust in thee, and hate us, but also to mollify their hard hearts, to open their blinded eyes, and to lighten their ignorant minds, that they may see and understand, and truly turn unto thee, and embrace thy holy word, and unfeignedly be converted unto thy Son Jesus Christ, the only Saviour of the world, and believe and love his Gospel, and so eternally to be saved. Finally, that all Christian Realms, and specially this Realm of England, may by thy defence and protection enjoy perfect peace, quietness, and security, and all that desire to be called and accounted Christians may answer in deed and life to so good and godly a name; and jointly all together in one godly concord and unity, and with one consonant heart and mind, may render unto thee all laud and praise, continually magnifying thy glorious name, who with thy Son our Saviour Jesus Christ, and the Holy Ghost, art one eternal, Almighty, and most merciful God, to whom be all laud and praise, world without end. *Amen.*

A prayer.

BE[1] merciful (O Father of all mercies) to thy Church

[1] There is considerable similarity, as to its tenor, between this prayer, and one of which Sancroft has preserved an early manuscript copy in his volume marked 3. 4. 30. What the archbishop deemed worth preserving, it has been thought right to reprint. The prayer, which is undated, commences somewhat abruptly. See p. 580.

Increase owr fayth, O Lord, and strengthen yt: graunt that we never distrust in thy mercies, nor decline from thy truth, nor fear the power of

universal, dispersed throughout the whole world: and grant
that all they that confess thy holy name, may agree in the
truth of thy holy word, and live in godly concord and unity.
And specially be merciful to such as are under persecution for
the testimony of their conscience, and profession of the gospel
of thy Son our Saviour Jesus Christ. Repress (O Lord) the
rage and tyranny of such as are bent to bloodshed, and mind
nothing but murther: and save and deliver those silly souls,
which (as sheep) are appointed to the shambles and slaughter.
And namely be merciful to thy Church and Realm of England: to thy servant our Sovereign and gracious Queen
ELIZABETH, whose life (O Lord) long and long preserve
from all the conspiracies and evils, which the craft and malice
of the devil, Antichrist, or other wicked men hath or can devise against her (as hitherto most graciously thou hast done).

anie adversarie, nether anie vaine feare: but that we put our whole trust
and confidens in the, and depend vppon the wholie and onelie, not vppon
man, nether anie kynde of creature. Mollifie owr hard hartes, work in
vs true repentans: forgyve vs all owre synnes: clensse owr hartes and
thowghtes frome all filthinesse, vanities, worldlinesse, and incline the same
to thi lawes and testimonies. Continew, O Lord, thy most holie word and
gospell in this realme of England, graunt that we may trulie and thank-
fullie embrace yt: Convert the ennemies of yt (yf yt be thy wyll)
dissipate there cownsailles, confound there devices. Preaserve Eliz. owr
Quene, gyve her long life, and manie yeares to rule over vs. Govern her,
O Lorde, and her whole counsail w^t thy holie Spirite, that thorow^t they
may be directyd to thy glorie, and profyte and peace of this church and
commonwealth. Gyve peace to thy church frome externall trobles and
persecutions (yf yt be thy blessed wyll) and from domesticall discord and
dissention: kepe yt from the spoyler, frome oppression and wrong, and
vs that be the ministers of yt, deal not w^t vs as we have deservyd: but
graunte that we may more faythfullie and more diligentlie walk in owr
vocations, and do our duties then heatherto we have done. Discomforte,
O Lord, confownd, or ells convert, all such as maling [malign] owr state
wch are the ministers of thy word, desyer owr spoyle and seke our dis-
creadite: all Simonites, wch bye and sell, or vnfytlie bestow livinges and
offices ordeynyd for the ministers and preachers of thy word: all spoylers
and oppressors of thy people, by what color and preatens soever they do
yt: all vniust Judges and wickyd magistrates, wch take bribes and re-
wardes, and have respect of persons: and all such as hinder Justice and
discorage those wch trulie and faythfulli execute the same: all papists
and haters of thy word and gospell. Finallie, O Lord, we vmblie beseech
the to graunt that those wch professe thy word and gospell may have the
same, as well in hart as in mouthe, in dede as in owtward apparens: for
thy name sake and for thy Christes sake. Amen.]

Be merciful (O Lord) to the Queen's most honourable Council, giving them grace to counsel and to execute that which may be to thy honour and glory, to the edifying of the Church of thy Son our Saviour Jesus Christ, and to the benefit and safety of the realm. Be merciful also (O Lord) to the clergy, nobility, Judges, magistrates, people, and commonalty of this realm, granting to every one thy heavenly grace, that they may in their vocation do their duties, to the honour and glory of thy name, the benefit of this church and realm, and to the salvation of their own souls. Grant this (O Lord) to us most unworthy sinners for the worthiness of thy dear Son our Saviour Jesus Christ, to whom with thee and the Holy Ghost be all honour and glory, world without end. *Amen.*

A thanksgiving and prayer for the preservation of the Queen and the Realm. [1572.]

O GOD, most merciful Father, who in thy great mercies hast both given unto us a peaceable princess, and a gracious Queen, and also hast very often and miraculously saved her from sundry great perils and dangers, and by her government hast preserved us and the whole Realm from manifold mischiefs, and dreadful plagues, wherewith nations round about us have been and be most grievously afflicted: have mercy upon them, O Lord, and grant us grace, we beseech thee, for these thy great benefits, that we may be thankful and obedient unto thee, to fly from all things that may offend thee, and provoke thy wrath and indignation against us, and to order our lives in all things that may please thee; that thy servant our sovereign Lady, and we thy people committed to her charge, may by thy protection be continually preserved from all deceits and violences of enemies, and from all other dangers and evils both bodily and ghostly, and by thy goodness may be maintained in all peace and godliness: grant this, O merciful Father, for thy dear Son's sake our Saviour Jesus Christ, to whom, with thee and the Holy Ghost, one God immortal, invisible, and only wise, be all honour and glory for ever and ever. Amen.

A PSALM AND COLLECT OF THANKSGIVING, not unmeet XXIX. for this present time: to be said or sung in Churches.

At London. Printed by the Deputies of Christopher Barker, Printer to the Queen's most excellent Majesty. 1588.

A Psalm of thanksgiving.

O COME hither, and hearken, all ye that fear God, and we will tell you what he hath done for our souls. *Psal.*66.c.14[1].

For we may not hide his benefits from our children, and to the generation to come, and to all people we will shew the praises of the Lord, his power also, and his wonderful works, that he hath done for us. *Psal.* 78. a. 4.

When the Kings and Rulers of the earth, and Nations round about us, furiously raged, and took counsel together against God, and against his anointed. *Psal.* 2. a. 1.

When[2] men of another devotion than we be, (*men bewitched by the Romish Antichrist,*) men drowned in idolatries and superstitions, hated us deadly, and were maliciously set against us, for our profession of the word of God, and the blessed Gospel of our Saviour Christ. *Psal.* 144. b.7. *Matt.*10. d.29. & 24. b 9. 10. *Psal.* 115. a.4. *Psal.* 55. a. 3.

They cast their heads together with one consent, they took their common counsel, and were confederate, and imagined mischief, against thy people, O Lord God. *Psal.* 83. a. 3. 5. *The council of Trent, and the holy league.*

They secretly laid wait, they privily set snares and nets, they digged pits for our souls, thinking that no man should see them. *Psal.* 35. b. 7. & 56. b. 6. & 64. a. 5. 6. & 83. b. 3.

They communed of peace, and prepared for most cruel war; for they think that no faith nor truth is to be kept with us, but that they may feign, dissemble, break promise, swear, and forswear, so they may deceive us and take us unwares, and oppress us suddenly. *Psal.* 12. a. 1. 2. 3. & 14. b. 5. 6. *Psal.* 59. b. 7. c. 12. & 120. a. 2. & 140. a. 2, 3, b. 9.

[1 See p. 549, note 4.]

[2 Dr Williams's MS. quotes the present passage to illustrate a remark on Christopher Stile's publication (p. 609, note 2) : " In this, and most of these Forms they terme the Pope Antichrist, and acknowledge their desert to be plagued, persecuted, and troubled, ' by the sword of forren power stirred vp against vs by the Romish antechrist, the Pope.' "]

Psal. 3. a. 1. 2.
Psal. 22. c. 12.
16. & 59. a. 3.
& 69. a. 4.
 And indeed innumerable multitudes of these most subtle and cruel enemies, and too mighty for us, came suddenly upon us, by sea and by land, when we looked not for them.

Psal. 17. b. 12.
Psal. 22. c. 13.
& 56. a. 1. 2.
Psal. 27. a. 2.
 They came furiously upon us, as it were roaring and ramping Lions, purposing to devour us, and to swallow us up: they approached near unto us, even to eat up our flesh.

Psal. 74. b. 8.
& 83. a. 4.

Israel.
 They said in their hearts, Let us make havoc of them altogether, let us root them out that they be no more a people, and that the name of *England* may be no more had in remembrance.

Psal. 27. c. 15.
Psal. 55. a. 3.
Psal. 124. a.
1. 2. &c.
Psal. 94. c. 17.
 And surely their coming was so sudden, their multitude, power, and cruelty so great, that had we not believed verily to see the goodness of God, and put our trust in his defence and protection, they might have utterly destroyed us.

Psal. 56. a. 3.
& 107. b. 6.
& 108. c. 12.
 But though we had great cause to be afraid, yet we put our whole trust in God: we cried unto the Lord in our trouble and distress; we said, Help us, O Lord our God, for vain is the help of man.

Psal. 60. c. 11.
12. & 108. c.
12. 13.
 We said, We commit ourselves wholly unto thee; according to the greatness of thy power, preserve us, O Lord, who are appointed to die.

Psal. 81. b. 7.
& 18. d. 34. 35.
37.
Psal. 48. a. 5. 6.
 And the Lord inclined his ear and heard us, and gave courage to the hearts, and strength to the hands, of our captains and soldiers, and put the enemies in fear.

Psal. 10. c.
12. 14.
Psal. 35. a. 1.
 The Lord arose, and took the cause (*which indeed was his own*) into his own hands, and fought against them, that fought against us.

Psal. 11. b. 6.
Psal. 18. c. 11.
12. 13.
 The Lord scattered them with his winds, he confounded and disappointed their devices and purposes of joining their powers together against us.

Psal. 48. a. 6.
& 83. c. 15.
Psal. 35. a. 5. 6.
Exod. 15. a.
4. 5.
 The Angel of the Lord persecuted them, brought them into dangerous, dark, and slippery places, where they wandering long to and fro, were consumed with hunger, thirst, cold, and sickness: the sea swallowed the greatest part of them.

Psal. 7. c. 15. 16.
Psal. 35. b. 8.
Psal. 9. c. 15.
16. 17. 18.
Psal. 9. b. 9.
Psal. 18. d. 17.
Psal. 44. b. 12.
d. 22.
 And so the Lord repressed the rage and fury of our cruel enemies, intending nothing but bloodshed and murther, and turned the mischief which they purposed against us upon their own heads; and delivered and saved us, who were as sheep appointed to the shambles and slaughter.

Psal. 64. b. 9.
Psal. 107. f. 42.
4. 5.
 This was the Lord's doing, and it is marvellous in our

and in our enemies' sight, and in the eyes of all people; *Psal.118.d.23.*
and all that see it shall say, This is the Lord's work.

God is our king of old: the help that is done by sea and *Psal. 74. c.13.*
by land, is his. *Psal. 107. d 22. 23. &c.*

It is God that giveth deliverance unto Princes, and that *Psal. 144. b. 10.*
rescueth our *QUEEN* from the hurtful sword, and saveth *David.*
her from all dangers and perils.

We will therefore give thanks, whom the Lord hath re- *Psal. 107. a. 2.*
deemed, and delivered from the hand of the enemy.

We will confess before the Lord, and praise him for his *Psal.107.d.21.*
goodness: and declare the wonders that he doth for the
children of men.

We will offer unto him the sacrifice of thanksgiving: and d. 22.
tell out his works with gladness.

We will exalt him also in the Congregation of the peo- *Psal.107.c.32.*
ple, and praise him in the presence of the Elders.

O sing unto the Lord a new song: for he hath done *Psal. 98. a. 1.*
marvellous things.

With his own right hand, and with his holy arm: hath a. 2.
he gotten himself the victory.

O give thanks unto the Lord, and call upon his name: *Psal. 105. a. 1.*
tell the people what things he hath done.

O let your songs be of him, and praise him: and let a. 2.
your talking be of all his wondrous works.

Rejoice in his holy name: let the hearts of them rejoice a. 3.
that seek the Lord.

And thou, my soul, be joyful in the Lord: let it rejoice *Psal. 35. b. 9.*
in his salvation.

All my bones shall say, Lord, who is like unto thee, b 10.
which deliverest the oppressed from them that be too strong
for them: yea, and them that are in distress from them
that seek to spoil them?

Blessed be the Lord God, even the God of Israel: which *Psal. 72. c. 18.*
only doth wondrous things.

And blessed be the name of his majesty for ever and c. 19.
ever: and all the earth shall be filled with the glory of his
majesty. Amen. Amen.

Glory be to the Father, and to the Son: and to the
Holy Ghost.

As it was in the beginning, is now, and ever shall be:
world without end. Amen.

A¹ *Collect of thanksgiving.*

WE cannot but confess, O Lord God, that the late terrible intended invasion of most cruel enemies was sent from thee to the punishment of our sins, of our pride, our covetousness, our excess in meats and drinks, our security, our ingratitude, and our unthankfulness towards thee, for so long peace, and other thy infinite blessings continually poured upon us, and to the punishment of other our innumerable and most grievous offences continually committed against thy divine majesty. And indeed our guilty consciences looked for (even at that time) the execution of thy terrible justice upon us, so by us deserved. But thou, O Lord God, who knowest all things, knowing that our enemies came not of justice to

[¹ In 1610 Thomas Sorocold, rector of St Mildred's in the Poultry, gave to the world a 'handfull of flowers, picked, sorted, and tyed up into a bundle,' entitled 'Supplications of Saints.' The book contained also three prayers by Queen Elizabeth, 'carying in matter pithe, in stile maiestie, and in words true deuotion,' one of which will not be inappropriately placed here.

Queen Elizabeth's Prayer of Thanksgiving, for the overthrow of the *Spanish Navy*, sent to invade ENGLAND, *Anno* 1588.

MOST omnipotent Creator, Redeemer, and Conserver. When it seemed most fit time to thy worthy Providence to bestow the workmanship of this world's Globe: with thy rare judgment, thou didst divide into four singular parts the form of all this Mould, which aftertime hath termed Elements: all they serving to continue in orderly Government of all the mass. Which all, when of thy most singular bounty, and never yerst seen care, thou hast this year made serve for instruments to daunt our foes, and to confound their malice; I most humbly, with bowed heart, and bended knees, do render my humblest acknowledgments, and lowliest thanks: And not the least, for that the weakest Sex hath been so fortified by thy strongest help, that neither my people need find lack by my weakness, nor Foreigners triumph at my ruin: Such hath been thy unwonted grace in my DAYS, as, though Sathan hath never made Holy-day in practising for my life and state, yet thy mighty hand hath overspread both with the shade of thy wings, so that neither hath been overthrown, nor received shame, but abide with blessing, to thy most glory, and their greatest ignominy. For which, Lord, of thy meer goodness, grant us grace to be hourly thankful, and ever mindful. And if it may please thee to pardon my request, give us thy continuance in my days of like goodness; that my years never see change of such grace to me, but especially to this my kingdom: which, LORD, grant (for thy Son's sake) may flourish many ages after my end. Amen.]

punish us for our sins committed against thy divine majesty (whom they by their excessive wickedness have offended, and continually do offend, as much or more than we), but that they came with most cruel intent and purpose to destroy us, our cities, towns, country and people, and utterly to root out the memory of our nation from off the earth for ever; and withal, wholly to suppress thy holy word and blessed gospel of thy dear Son our Saviour Jesus Christ, which they (being drowned in idolatries and superstitions) do hate most deadly, and us likewise, only for the profession of the same, and not for any offences against thy divine majesty, or injuries done to themselves: wherefore it hath pleased thee, O heavenly Father, in thy justice to remember thy mercies towards us, turning our enemies from us and that dreadful execution which they intended towards us into a fatherly and most merciful admonition of us, to the amendment of our lives; and to execute justice upon our cruel enemies, turning the destruction which they intended against us upon their own heads. For the which the same thy most gracious protection of us, and all other thy graces, without all our desert, continually and most plenteously poured upon our Church, our QUEEN, our Realm and people of England, we beseech thee add, and pour also the grace of gratitude and thankfulness into our hearts: that we never forgetting, but bearing in perpetual memory, this thy merciful protection and deliverance of us from the malice, force, fraud, and cruelty of our enemies, and all other thy benefits most plenteously poured upon us, may enjoy the continuance of thy fatherly goodness towards our Church, our QUEEN, our Realm and people of England, and continually magnify thy holy and most glorious name: which we do beseech thee, O heavenly Father, to grant to us most unworthy sinners, for the worthiness of thy dear Son our Saviour Jesus Christ; to whom with thee, and the Holy Ghost, one God of most glorious majesty, be all honour and glory world without end. Amen.

FINIS.

xxx. A [1] GODLY PRAYER for the preservation of the Queen's majesty, and for her *Armies both by sea and land, against the enemies of the Church and this Realm of England.*

O LORD God, heavenly Father, thou Lord of hosts, without whose providence nothing proceedeth: and without whose mercy nothing is saved: in whose hand is the heart of Princes: and all their actions ordered by thy special providence: have mercy on thine afflicted church, and especially regard thy servant *Elizabeth*, our most excellent Queen, to whom thy dispersed flock do fly, in the anguish of their souls, and in the zeal of thy truth. Behold how princes do band themselves against her, because she endeavoureth to purge thy sanctuary, and that thy holy church may live in security. Consider, O Lord, how long thy servant hath laboured to them for peace, but how proudly they prepare themselves to battle. Arise therefore, maintain thine own cause, and judge thou between her and her enemies. She seeketh not her honour but thine, nor the dominion of others, but in defence of herself; nor the shedding of Christian blood, but the saving of poor afflicted souls. Come down therefore, come down and deliver thy people by her. To vanquish is all one with thee by few or by many, by want or by wealth, by weakness or by strength. O possess the hearts of our enemies with a fear of thy servant. The cause is thine, the enemies thine, the honour, victory, and triumph shall be thine. O consider the end of our enterprises, be present with us in our Armies, and make a joyful peace for thy Christians: and [2] now since, in this extreme necessity, thou hast put into the heart of *Debora* to send forth men of war to restrain the pride of *Cisera*, bless thou all their attempts by sea and by land; grant them one heart, one mind, and one strength to defend our queen, her kingdom, and thy true religion: give them wisdom, wariness, and courage, that they

[[1] Strype's reprint differs in a few trifling particulars from the present one. His, however, was taken from Marten's own work, this from the broadside.]

[[2] This passage goes far to confirm Mr Lathbury's opinion as to the exact time when the Prayer was published. See p. 470.]

may speedily prevent the devices, and valiantly withstand the forces, of all our enemies, that the fame of thy Gospel may be spread to the end of the world: We crave this in thy mercy, O Father, for the precious death of thy dear Son, Jesus Christ our Lord. Amen[3].

Imprinted at London, by John Wolfe, for Thomas Woodcocke. 1588.

[3 The prayer numbered xxvii., which, in deference, as was supposed, to the authority of archbishop Sancroft, has been connected with 1588 (see p. 469), would scarcely seem, even from the passages quoted below, to refer at all to the occurrences of that year. The writer had evidently in his mind the prayer printed on p. 522.

They... determining to deliuer vs ouer to the tyranny of that shamelesse sinfull man of Rome, and the bloudy sword ... conspire against thee, O God, like hipocrites, against our Queene like Traitors, against our common countrey like spoylers, against vs euen as Cain did against Abel. But thy great goodness hath deuised better for vs, then they do: Thou hast spared vs, whom they would haue spoyled. Thy wisdom hath vnfolded their wickednes....... worke out the good worke which thou hast begon among vs. Confound and bring to naught the attemptes of these and the like enemies, as thou didest at Babel. Infold them in the folly of their owne counsels, as thou didest Achitophel. By thine Angell smite their force, as thou didest to Senacheribe. In their desperate attemptes let them be drowned, as was Pharao. In their treasons ouertake them, as thou didest Absalon. If any of them are to be conuerted, turne them as thou didest Manasses. Otherwise, let them feele their due punishment, as did Dathan with his conspirators; that of these also may be left an example of thy iustice to the posteritie.]

XXXI. A FORM OF PRAYER, thought fit to be daily used in the English Army in France.

Imprinted at London by the Deputies of Christopher Barker, Printer to [the] Queen's most excellent Majesty. 1589.

After the Confession, Absolution, and the Lord's prayer; say these psalms following, or one of them. And then the prayers following, or one of them, together with the prayers in the Litany made for the time of war, and with the prayer for her Majesty there also: or some other to that effect.

¶ *A confession of sins.*

ALMIGHTY and most merciful Father, we have erred and strayed from thy ways like lost sheep, we have followed too much the devices and desires of our own hearts, we have offended against thy holy Laws, we have left undone those things which we ought to have done, and we have done those things which we ought not to have done, and there is no health in us. But thou, O Lord, have mercy upon us miserable offenders, spare thou them, O God, which confess their faults, restore thou them that be penitent, according to thy promises declared unto mankind in Christ Jesu our Lord; and grant, O most merciful Father, for his sake, that we may hereafter live a godly, righteous, and sober life, to the glory of thy holy name. Amen.

ALMIGHTY God, the Father of our Lord Jesus Christ, which desireth not the death of a sinner, but rather that he may turn from his wickedness, and live, and hath given power and commandment to his ministers, to declare and pronounce to his people, being penitent, the absolution and remission of their sins: he pardoneth and absolveth all them which truly repent, and unfeignedly believe his holy Gospel. Wherefore we beseech him to grant us true repentance and his holy Spirit, that those things may please him which we do at this present, and that the rest of our life hereafter may be pure and holy, so that at the last we may come to his eternal joy, through Jesus Christ our Lord.

Our Father, which art in heaven, hallowed be thy Name. Thy kingdom come. Thy will be done in earth, as it is in heaven. Give us this day our daily bread. And forgive us our trespasses, as we forgive them that trespass against us. And lead us not into temptation. But deliver us from evil. Amen.

¶ *The Psalm.*

We have heard with our ears, O God, our fathers have told us: what thou hast done in their time of old. *Psalm 44.*

How thou hast driven out the heathen with thy hand, and planted them in: how thou hast destroyed the Nations, and cast them out. *Psalm 44.*

For they gat not the land in possession through their own sword: neither was it their own arm that helped them. *Psalm 44.*

But thy right hand, and thine arm, and the light of thy countenance: because thou hadst a favour unto them. *Psalm 44.*

Thou art my king, O God: send help unto Jacob. *Psalm 44.*

Through thee will we overthrow our enemies: and in thy name will we tread them under that rise up against us. *Psalm 44.*

For I will not trust in my bow: it is not my sword that shall help me. *Psalm 44.*

But it is thou, that savest us from our enemies, and puttest them to confusion that hate us. *Psalm 44.*

We make our boast of God all the day long: and will praise thy Name for ever. *Psalm 44.*

Be not thou far off, O Lord: put us not to confusion, go forth with our Armies.

Make our enemies to turn their backs upon us.

Suffer us not to be rebuked of our Neighbours: to be laughed to scorn, and had in derision of them, that are round about us.

Make us not a byword among the heathen: up, Lord, and sleep not, awake and be not absent from us.

Hide not thy face from us: forget not our trouble.

Arise and help us, and deliver us for thy mercy's sake. *Psalm 44.*

¶ *Another Psalm.*

Hearken to the voice of our prayer, our King and our God: for unto thee do we make our complaint. *Psalm 5.*

Psalm 22.	O Lord, the counsel of the wicked conspireth against us: and our enemies are daily in hand to swallow us up.
Psalm 22.	They gape upon us with their mouths, as it were ramping and roaring Lions.
Psalm 3.	But thou (O Lord) art our defender: thou art our health, and our salvation.
Psalm 7.	We do put our trust in thee, O God: save us from all them that persecute us, and deliver us.
Psalm 10.	O take the matter into thy hand, thy people commit themselves unto thee: for thou art their helper in their distress.
Psalm 7. & 22.	Save us from the Lions' mouths, and from the horns of the Unicorns: lest they devour us, and tear us in pieces, while there is none to help.
Psalm 74.	O deliver not the soul of thy Turtle-dove unto the multitude of the enemies: and forget not thy poor congregation for ever.
Psalm 59.	Deliver us from our enemies, O God: defend and save us from them that imagine mischief, and rise up against us.
Psalm 7.	And we shall give thanks unto thee (O Lord) according to thy great mercies; and will praise the name of the Lord most high.
Psalm 22.	We will declare thy Name unto our brethren: in the mids of the congregation will we praise thee, and magnify thy salvation, world without end.

Glory be to the Father, and to the Son: and to the Holy Ghost.

As it was in the beginning, is now, and ever shall be: world without end. Amen.

Psalm 115.[1]

A prayer.

O LORD God of Hosts, most mighty and merciful Father, who in thy unspeakable wisdom and mercy hast gathered unto thyself a Church truly professing thine holy Name and Gospel: We do here most humbly acknowledge, that through our manifold sins and offences against thy heavenly Majesty, committed by unthankful receiving of thy holy word, and by wicked led lives, we have made ourselves unworthy of the least of these and other thy singular blessings hitherto very abundantly poured upon us. Nevertheless (O heavenly Father) with an assured confidence relying upon thy promises, we make bold to draw near unto the throne of thy grace,

[[1] This Psalm has not the *Gloria Patri.*]

humbly craving forgiveness of our sins, and the continuance of thy blessings upon us, and upon all Princes, Countries, and Commonwealths, that have received and do embrace thine holy Gospel. Therefore, being cast down in soul, we do bewail our iniquities, setting the bitter death and precious bloodshed of thy dear Son Christ Jesus betwixt us and thy just wrath conceived against us. Turn (O Lord) thy wrathful indignation from us: And forasmuch as it is not for these our sins, that our enemies in their purpose have thus banded themselves against us, but for the sincere profession of thy word and Gospel; with thy mighty arm confound, and bring to nought, the devices, power, and strength, of all such, as set themselves against the same. Thou knowest (O Lord) how the heathen, and such as hold of superstitious vanities, do everywhere rush into thine inheritance, to make thy chosen Jerusalem, even thy Church, a desolate heap of stones, to lay waste thy holy Sanctuary; yea, even to give up the flesh of thy dear children to the birds of the air, and the slain carcases of thy saints to the beasts of the field. Wherefore (most mighty God of Hosts) which art the Lord of glory and power, that canst arm the most base and meanest of thy creatures to the overthrow of all the mighty of the world, that be enemies to us for thy truth's sake: Avance thyself like a mighty Giant with a swift and terrible judgment against them: frustrate the counsels of all their *Achitophels:* break them down with an iron rod like an earthen vessel: send an host of Angels to scatter their armies both by sea and land: confound them as thou didst the host of the *Assyrians:* Let thine own sword fight for us and devour up them: be thou as fire unto them, and let them be as stubble before thee. Finally, let them be as *Oreb* and *Zeb:* yea, like unto *Zebah* and *Salmanah,* and be made as dung on the face of the earth. Send (good Lord) upon them the spirit of fear and trembling, that they may fly before the host of thine Israel as chaff before the wind, to the end they may be discomfited, and overthrown by thy mighty hand. Neither give thou us up (O Lord) to be a prey to their teeth, or a byword and reproach to such as hate the true profession of the Gospel: For we do only rest assured under the shadow of thy wings. Protect us in mercy as the apple of thine eye, and mercifully pour upon us the spirit of wisdom, foresight, counsel, strength and courage: that, in full assurance of thine heavenly help fighting for us, ten of us may chase an hundred, and an hundred of us put to flight a thousand of them. Be thou (O Lord) our continual refuge and strong rock of defence: Let thine holy Angels pitch their tents round about us, that we may know thine holy hand both stretched out for our help, and strongly set against them: teach our hands to war, and our fingers to fight: prosper that we shall take in hand, O prosper thou our handy work, and make us always to rejoice in thy salvation and deliverance: that so all such as love not the truth of thy Gospel, hearing thereof, may be discomforted; and that thy fear may fall upon them, to the perpetual glory of thy holy name: That we, escaping the rage and fury of those which seek after our lives, may in thine holy Church here militant, and after in the Church triumphant in heaven, eternally sing praises to thee our heavenly Father, the only giver of all victory. Grant these things for thy Son Christ Jesus' sake: to whom with thee and the Holy Ghost, three persons and one eternal, immortal, invisible, and only wise God, be all honour, praise, glory and dominion now and for ever. Amen.

¶ *Another prayer.*

MOST mighty God, and merciful Father: Forasmuch as thou hast promised to maintain and defend the cause of thy Church, so dearly purchased and redeemed, even with the precious blood of thy dearly beloved Son: we, thy humble servants, confessing our own unworthiness through the infinite number of our wilful transgressions, do at this time prostrate ourselves here before thy divine Majesty, and, wholly relying upon thy promises, most heartily beseech thee through the merits of Jesus Christ our Saviour, to protect us this day and ever hereafter from the fury of our enemies, to pardon our sins past, and to have mercy upon us. Thou knowest, O Lord, how they that fight against us have entered into a league, and combined themselves, never to desist, until they have destroyed all such as profess thy Gospel, and laid the glory of *Sion* in the dust. And though our offences do most justly deserve, that we should be delivered to the edges of their swords: Yet seeing that they do hate us only for thy cause, and that we are noted in the world for such as outwardly profess thy name, and the true doctrine of the Gospel of thy Son our Saviour Christ, save us in thy mercy (O heavenly Father) from the cruelty of these conspirators: cast a fear and trembling into their hearts, take our cause into thine own hands, go before our host, fight our battles, and subdue them: So shall they have no cause to insult over thy true Church, and over us thy servants, nor to say with the old enemies, *Where is now their God?* And we thy penitent and most humble suppliants will from henceforth declare thy Name with cheerful heart unto our brethren: in the midst of the Congregation we will ever praise thee, and magnify thy salvation, world without end.

Grant this, O merciful Father, not for our own sakes, but for thy dear Son's sake, our Lord and Saviour Jesus Christ: to whom with thee and the Holy Ghost, three persons and one God, be all honour, glory, power, and dominion now and for ever. Amen.

A prayer for the Queen's Majesty.

O LORD our heavenly Father, high and mighty, King of Kings, Lord of Lords, the only ruler of Princes, which dost from thy throne behold all the dwellers upon earth, most heartily we beseech thee with thy favour to behold our most gracious Sovereign Lady, Queen Elizabeth, and so replenish her with the grace of thy Holy Spirit, that she may alway incline to thy will, and walk in thy way: endue her plenteously with heavenly gifts, grant her in health and wealth long to live, strengthen her, that she may vanquish and overcome all her enemies, and finally after this life she may attain everlasting joy and felicity, through Jesus Christ our Lord. Amen.

O ALMIGHTY God, King of all Kings, and governour of all things, whose power no creature is able to resist, to whom it belongeth justly to punish sinners, and to be merciful to them that truly repent: save and deliver us (we humbly beseech thee) from the hands of our enemies; abate their pride, assuage their malice, and confound their devices: that we, being armed with thy defence, may be preserved evermore from all perils, to glorify thee which art the only giver of all victory, through the merits of thy only Son Jesus Christ our Lord.

XXXII. A[1] FORM OF PRAYER, necessary for the present time and state.

Imprinted at London by the Deputies of Christopher Barker, Printer to the Queen's most excellent Majesty. 1590.

¶ *A confession of sins.*

ALMIGHTY and most merciful Father, we have erred and strayed from thy ways like lost sheep, we have followed too much the devices and desires of our own hearts, we have offended against thy holy Laws, we have left undone those things which we ought to have done, and we have done those things which we ought not to have done, and there is no health in us: but thou, O Lord, have mercy upon us miserable offenders, spare thou them, O God, which confess their faults, restore thou them that be penitent, according to thy promises declared unto mankind in Christ Jesu our Lord, and grant, O most merciful Father, for his sake, that we may hereafter live a godly, righteous, and sober life, to the glory of thy holy name. Amen.

ALMIGHTY God, the Father of our Lord Jesus Christ, which desireth not the death of a sinner, but rather that he may turn from his wickedness and live, and hath given power and commandment to his ministers to declare and pronounce to his people, being penitent, the absolution and remission of their sins: he pardoneth and absolveth all them which truly repent, and unfeignedly believe his holy Gospel. Wherefore we beseech him to grant us true repentance and his Holy Spirit, that those things may please him which we do at this present, and that the rest of our life hereafter may be pure and holy, so that at the last we may come to his eternal joy, through Jesus Christ our Lord.

OUR Father which art in heaven, hallowed be thy Name. Thy kingdom come. Thy will be done in earth, as it is in

[1] This is almost entirely made up from the Forms for 1588 and 1589.]

heaven. Give us this day our daily bread. And forgive us our trespasses, as we forgive them that trespass against us. And lead us not into temptation. But deliver us from evil. Amen.

A prayer for the forgiveness of sins.

O COME, let us humble ourselves: and fall down before the Lord our maker, with reverence and fear. Psal. 95.

Let us repent and turn from our wickedness, and turn again unto our Lord: and our sins shall be forgiven us. Osee 6. Acts 3.

Let us turn, and the Lord will turn from his heavy wrath: he hath smitten us, and he will heal us, he will pardon us, and we shall not perish. Jonas 3. Osee 6.

We acknowledge our faults, O Lord: and our sins are ever before our sight. Psal. 51.

We have sore provoked thine anger, O Lord: thy wrath is waxed hot, and thy heavy displeasure is sore kindled against us. Lamen. 5.

But rebuke us not, O Lord, in thine indignation: neither chasten us in thy heavy displeasure. Psal. 6.

In deed we acknowledge that all punishments are less than our deserving: but yet of thy mercy, Lord, correct us to amendment, and plague us not to our destruction. Judith 8. Job 11. Sapi. 11.

O remember not the sins and offences of our youth, and times past, but according to thy mercy think upon us, O Lord, for thy goodness. Psal. 25.

Stand not so far off, O Lord: neither hide thy face in the needful time of trouble. Psal. 10.

Turn thee unto us, and have mercy upon us: for we are desolate and in great misery. Psal. 25.

And now in the vexation of our spirits, and the anguish of our souls: we remember thee, and we cry unto thee; hear, Lord, and have mercy. Baruc. 3. Jonas 2.

For we do not pour out our prayers before thy face, trusting in our own righteousness: but in thy great and manifold mercies. Dan. 9.

For thine own sake, and for thy holy name's sake, incline thine ear and hear: and be merciful to our sins, for they are great. Psal. 25.

Help us, O God of our salvation, for the glory of thy name: O deliver us, and save us for thy name's sake. Psal. 9.

Psal. 79.	So we that be thy people, and sheep of thy pasture, shall give thee thanks for ever: and will be always shewing forth thy praise from generation to generation.

Glory be to the Father, &c. As it was in the, &c.

A prayer for deliverance from our enemies.

Psal. 143.	HEAR our prayer, O Lord, consider our desire: hearken unto us for thy truth and mercy's sake.
Psal. 3.	Lord, how are they increased that trouble us: many are they that rise against us.
Psal. 11.	The ungodly bend their bows, and make ready their arrows within the quiver: that they may shoot at those that call upon the name of the Lord.
Psal. 104.	They smite down thy people, O Lord: and trouble thine heritage.
Psal. 79.	The dead bodies of thy servants have they given to be meat unto the fowls of the air: and the flesh of thy saints unto the beasts of the land.
Psal. 79.	Their blood have they shed like water on every side of Jerusalem: and there was no man to bury them.
Psal. 79.	And we that live are become an open shame to our enemies: a very scorn and derision unto them that are round about us.
Psal. 74. & 79.	O Lord, why is thy wrath such against the sheep of thy pasture? how long wilt thou be angry? shall thy jealousy burn like fire for ever?
Psal. 79.	Wherefore should the ungodly say, Where is now their God: there is now no more help for them in their God?
Psal. 79.	O remember not our old sins, but have mercy upon us, and that soon: for we are come to great misery.
Psal. 79.	O let the sorrowful sighing of the prisoners come before thee, according to the greatness of thy power: preserve thou those that are appointed to die.
Psal. 74.	O Lord, think upon the congregation of thy people, whom thou hast purchased and redeemed of old: O deliver us, and save us, for the glory of thy name.
Psal. 22.	And our praises shall be of thee in the great congregation: our vows will we perform in the sight of them that fear thee.

And all the ends of the world shall remember themselves, and be turned unto the Lord: and all the kindreds of the nations shall worship before him. *Psal. 22.*

Glory be to the Father, and to the, &c.
As it was in the beginning, is now, &c.

Psalms.

WE have heard with our ears, O God, our fathers have told us: what thou hast done in their time of old. *Psalm 44.*

How thou hast driven out the Heathen with thy hand, and planted them in: how thou hast destroyed the Nations, and cast them out. *Psalm 44.*

For they gat not the land in possession through their own sword: neither was it their own arm that helped them. *Psalm 44.*

But thy right hand, and thine arm, and the light of thy countenance: because thou hadst a favour unto them. *Psalm 44.*

Thou art my king, O God: send help unto Jacob. *Psalm 44.*

Through thee will we overthrow our enemies: and in thy name will we tread them under that rise up against us. *Psalm 44.*

For I will not trust [in] my bow: it is not my sword that shall help me. *Psalm 44.*

But it is thou, that savest us from our enemies: and puttest them to confusion that hate us. *Psalm 44.*

We make our boast of God all the day long: and will praise thy name for ever. *Psalm 44.*

Be not thou far off, O Lord: put us not to confusion, go forth with our Armies.

Make our enemies to turn their backs upon us.

Suffer us not to be rebuked of our Neighbours: to be laughed to scorn, and had in derision of them, that are round about us.

Make us not a byword among the heathen: up, Lord, and sleep not, awake and be not absent from us.

Hide not thy face from us: forget not our trouble.

Arise and help us: and deliver us for thy mercy's sake. *Psalm 44.*

Another Psalm.

O HEARKEN to the voice of our prayer, our King, and our God: for unto thee do we make our complaint. *Psalm 5.*

O Lord, the Counsel of the wicked conspireth against us: and our enemies are daily in hand to swallow us up. *Psalm 22.*

Psalm 22.	They gape upon us with their mouths, as it were ramping and roaring Lions.
Psalm 3.	But thou (O Lord) art our defender: thou art our health, and our salvation.
Psalm 7.	We do put our trust in thee, O GOD: save us from all them that persecute us, and deliver us.
Psalm 10.	O take the matter into thy hand, thy people commit themselves unto thee: for thou art their helper in their distress.
Psalm 7. & 22.	Save us from the Lions' mouths, and from the horns of the Unicorns: lest they devour us, and tear us in pieces while there is none to help.
Psalm 74.	O deliver not the soul of thy Turtle-dove unto the multitude of the enemies: and forget not thy poor congregation for ever.
Psalm 59.	Deliver us from our enemies, O God: defend and save us from them that imagine mischief, and rise up against us.
Psalm 7.	And we shall give thanks unto thee (O Lord) according to thy great mercies: and will praise the name of the Lord most high.
Psalm 22.	We will declare thy Name unto our brethren: in the mids of the congregation will we praise thee, and magnify thy salvation world without end.

Glory be to the Father, and to the Son: and to the Holy Ghost.

As it was in the beginning, is now, and ever shall be: world without end. Amen.

Psalm 115.[1]

A prayer.

O LORD God of Hosts, most mighty and merciful Father, who in thy unspeakable wisdom and mercy hast gathered unto thyself a Church, truly professing thine holy Name and Gospel: We do here most humbly acknowledge, that through our manifold sins and offences against thy heavenly Majesty, committed by unthankful receiving of thy holy word, and by wicked led lives, we have made ourselves unworthy of the least of these and other thy singular blessings, hitherto very abundantly poured upon us. Nevertheless (O heavenly Father) with an assured confidence relying upon thy promises, we make bold to draw near unto the throne of thy grace, humbly craving forgiveness of our sins, and the

[[1] The *Gloria Patri* does not follow this Psalm.]

continuance of thy blessings upon us, and upon all Princes, Countries, and Commonwealths, that have received and do embrace thine holy Gospel. Therefore, being cast down in soul, we do bewail our iniquities, setting the bitter death and precious bloodshed of thy dear Son Christ Jesus betwixt us and thy just wrath conceived against us. Turn (O Lord) thy wrathful indignation from us : And forasmuch as it is not for these our sins, that our enemies in their purpose have thus banded themselves against us, but for the sincere profession of thy word and Gospel; with thy mighty arm confound and bring to nought the devices, power, and strength of all such, as set themselves against the same. Thou knowest (O Lord) how the heathen, and such as hold of superstitious vanities, do everywhere rush into thine inheritance, to make thy chosen Jerusalem, even thy Church, a desolate heap of stones, to lay waste thy holy Sanctuary ; yea, even to give up the flesh of thy dear children to the birds of the air, and the slain carcases of thy saints to the beasts of the field. Wherefore (most mighty God of Hosts) which art the Lord of glory and power, that canst arm the most base and meanest of thy creatures to the overthrow of all the mighty of the world, that be enemies to us for thy truth's sake : Avance thyself like a mighty Giant with a swift and terrible judgment against them : frustrate the counsels of all their *Achitophels:* break them down with an iron rod like an earthen vessel : send an host of Angels to scatter their armies both by sea and land : confound them as thou didst the host of the *Assyrians:* Let thine own sword fight for us and devour up them : be thou as fire unto them, and let them be as stubble before thee. Finally, let them be as *Oreb* and *Zeb*, yea, like unto *Zebah* and *Salmanah*, and be made as dung on the face of the earth. Send (good Lord) upon them the spirit of fear and trembling, that they may flee before the host of thine Israel, as chaff before the wind, to the end they may be discomfited and overthrown by thy mighty hand. Neither give thou us up (O Lord) to be a prey to their teeth, or a byword and reproach to such as hate the true profession of the Gospel : For we do only rest assured under the shadow of thy wings. Protect us in mercy as the apple of thine eye, and mercifully pour upon us the spirit of wisdom, foresight, counsel, strength and courage : that, in full assurance of thine heavenly help fighting for us, ten of us may chase an hundred, and an hundred of us put to flight a thousand of them. Be thou (O Lord) our continual refuge and strong rock of defence: Let thine holy Angels pitch their tents round about us, that we may know thine holy hand both stretched out for our help, and strongly set against them: teach our hands to war, and our fingers to fight: prosper that we shall take in hand, O prosper thou our handy work, and make us always to rejoice in thy salvation and deliverance: that so all such as love not the truth of thy Gospel, hearing thereof, may be discomforted; and that thy fear may fall upon them, to the perpetual glory of thy holy name: That we, escaping the rage and fury of those, which seek after our lives, may in thine holy Church here militant, and after in the Church triumphant in heaven, eternally sing praises to thee our heavenly Father, the only giver of all victory. Grant these things for thy Son Christ Jesus' sake: to whom with thee and the Holy Ghost, three persons and one eternal, immortal, invisible, and only wise God be all honour, praise, glory, and dominion now and for ever. Amen.

Another prayer.

MOST mighty God and merciful Father, Forasmuch as thou hast promised to maintain and defend the cause of thy Church, so dearly purchased and redeemed, even with the precious blood of thy dearly beloved Son: we thy humble servants, confessing our own unworthiness through the infinite number of our wilful transgressions, do at this time prostrate ourselves here before thy divine Majesty, and, wholly relying upon thy promises, most heartily beseech thee through the merits of Jesus Christ our Saviour, to protect us this day and ever hereafter, from the fury of our enemies, to pardon our sins past, and to have mercy upon us. Thou knowest, O Lord, how they that fight against us have entered into a league, and combined themselves, never to desist, until they have destroyed all such as profess thy Gospel, and laid the glory of *Sion* in the dust. And though our offences do most justly deserve, that we should be delivered to the edges of their swords; yet seeing that they do hate us only for thy cause, and that we are noted in the world for such as outwardly profess thy name, and the true doctrine of the Gospel of thy

Son our Saviour Christ, save us in thy mercy (O heavenly Father) from the cruelty of these conspirators: cast a fear and trembling into their hearts, take our cause into thine own hands, go before our host, fight our battles, and subdue them: So shall they have no cause to insult over thy true Church, and over us thy servants, nor to say with the old enemies, *Where is now their God?* And we thy penitent and most humble suppliants will from henceforth declare thy Name with cheerful heart unto our brethren: in the midst of the Congregation we will ever praise thee, and magnify thy salvation, world without end.

Grant this (O merciful Father) not for our own sakes, but for thy dear Son's sake, our Lord and Saviour Jesus Christ: to whom with thee and the Holy Ghost, three persons and one God, be all honour, glory, power, and dominion now and for ever. Amen.

A prayer for the Queen's Majesty.

O LORD our heavenly Father, high and mighty, King of Kings, Lord of Lords, the only ruler of Princes, which dost from thy throne behold all the dwellers upon earth, most heartily we beseech thee with thy favour to behold our most gracious sovereign Lady, Queen Elizabeth, and so replenish her with the grace of thy Holy Spirit, that she may alway incline to thy will, and walk in thy way: endue her plenteously with heavenly gifts, grant her in health and wealth long to live, strengthen her, that she may vanquish and overcome all her enemies, and finally after this life she may attain everlasting joy and felicity, through Jesus Christ our Lord. Amen.

O ALMIGHTY God, King of all Kings, and governour of all things, whose power no creature is able to resist, to whom it belongeth justly to punish sinners, and to be merciful to them that truly repent: save and deliver us (we humbly beseech thee) from the hands of our enemies, abate their pride, assuage their malice, and confound their devices: that we, being armed with thy defence, may be preserved evermore from all perils, to glorify thee which art the only giver of all victory, through the merits of thy only Son Jesus Christ our Lord.

Prayers for true repentance and mercy.

MOST merciful Father, who hast in thy holy word, the word of truth, promised mercy unto sinners that do repent and turn unto thee, and hast by thy terrible examples of thy just anger, being executed upon people and countries round about us, called us, and most mercifully moved us to repentance, and by thy patience and long suffering of us hitherto hast graciously granted us time and space to repent: grant also, we beseech thee, both to them and us grace truly to repent, and unfeignedly to turn unto thee with amendment of life, and to trust in thy mercies, and safely to rest under thy continual protection from all enemies and evils both bodily and ghostly, through our Saviour Jesus Christ, who with thee and the Holy Ghost liveth and reigneth one God world without end. *Amen.*

Another for the same.

WE have sinned, Lord, we have sinned grievously, we have done unjustly, we have lived wickedly; we are sorry therefore, O Lord, yea, we are most sorry, that we are no more sorry for our sins: but thou, Lord God, Father of all mercies, we humbly beseech thee, be not angry with us for ever for our great and manifold sins, neither deal with us according to our deserts, neither reward us according to our wickedness; but even for thyself, O Lord God, and for thy holy name's sake, for thy most gracious assured promises made unto penitent sinners in thy holy word, the word of truth, for thy infinite mercies which are in thy dearly beloved Son Jesu Christ our Saviour, for his sake, for his death and precious blood, be merciful unto us sinners, and so we, who have most grievously offended thy divine Majesty, shall continually magnify thy great and infinite mercy, through our Saviour Jesus Christ, to whom with thee and the Holy Ghost be all honour and glory world without end. *Amen.*

Another prayer to be delivered from our enemies.

O LORD God of hosts, most loving and merciful Father, we thy humble servants prostrate ourselves before thy divine Majesty: most heartily beseeching thee to grant unto us true repentance for our sins past, namely for our unthankfulness, contempt of thy word, lack of compassion towards the afflicted, envy, malice, strife and contention among ourselves, and for all other our iniquities. Lord, deal not with us as we have deserved, but of thy great goodness and mercy do away our offences, and give us grace to confess and acknowledge, O Lord, with all humble and hearty thanks, the wonderful and great benefits which thou hast bestowed upon this thy Church and people of England, in giving unto us, without all desert of our part, not only peace and quietness, but also in preserving our most gracious Queen thine handmaid so miraculously from so many conspiracies, perils and dangers, and in granting her good success against the attempts of her adversaries: for the which so wonderful and great benefits we humbly beseech thee to stir up our dull minds to such thankfulness and acknowledging of thy mercies as becometh us, and as may be acceptable unto thee. We do instantly beseech thee of thy gracious goodness to be merciful to thy Church militant here upon earth, many ways vexed and tormented by the malice of Satan and his members, and at this time, as it were, compassed about with strong and subtil adversaries. And especially, O Lord, let thine enemies know, and make them confess, that thou hast received England (which they most of all for thy Gospel sake do malign) into thine own protection. Set, we pray thee (O Lord), a wall about it, and evermore mightily defend it. Let it be a comfort to the afflicted, a help to the oppressed, a defence to thy Church and people persecuted abroad. And forasmuch as thy cause is now in hand, we beseech thee to direct and go before our Armies both by sea and land; bless and prosper them, and grant unto them, O Lord, so good and honourable success and victories, as thou didst to Abraham and his company against the four mighty kings, to Josua against the five kings, and against Amalech, to David against the strong and mighty armed giant Goliah, and as thou usest to do to thy children when they please thee. We acknowledge all power, strength and victory to come from thee: some put their trust in chariots, and some in horses, but we will remember thy name, O Lord our God. Thou bringest the counsel of the heathen to nought, and makest the devices of the people to be of none effect. There is no king that can be saved by the multitude of an host, neither is any mighty man delivered by

[LITURG. QU. ELIZ.]

much strength. A horse is but a vain thing to save a man: therefore we pray unto thee, O Lord; thou art our help and our shield. O Lord, give good and prosperous success to all those that fight thy battle against the enemies of thy Gospel, shew some token continually for our good, that they which hate us may see it and be confounded; and that we thy little and despised flock may say with good King David, Blessed are the people whose God is the Lord Jehovah, and blessed are the folk that he hath chosen to be his inheritance. These and all other graces necessary for us, grant, O heavenly Father, for Jesus Christ's sake, our only Mediator and Redeemer.

An other prayer for the same.

O LORD our God and heavenly Father, look down, we beseech thee, with thy fatherly and merciful countenance upon us thy people and poor humble servants, and upon all such Christians as are any where persecuted and sore afflicted for the true acknowledging of thee to be our God, and thy Son Jesus Christ, whom thou hast sent, to be the only Saviour of the world: save them, O merciful Lord, who are as sheep appointed to the slaughter, and by hearty prayer do call and cry unto thee for thy help and defence: hear their cry, O Lord, and our prayer for them, and for our selves: deliver those that be oppressed: defend such as are in fear of cruelty: relieve them that be in misery, and comfort all that be in sorrow and heaviness: that by thy aid and strength they and we may obtain surety from our enemies, without shedding of Christian and innocent blood. And for that, O Lord, thou hast commanded us to pray for our enemies, we do beseech thee, not only to abate their pride, and to stay the fury and cruelty of such as either of malice or ignorance do persecute them which put their trust in thee, and hate us, but also to mollify their hard hearts, to open their blinded eyes, and to lighten their ignorant minds, that they may see and understand, and truly turn unto thee, and embrace the holy word, and unfeignedly be converted unto thy Son Jesus Christ, the only Saviour of the world, and believe and love his Gospel, and so eternally to be saved. Finally, that all Christian Realms, and especially this Realm of England, may by thy defence and protection enjoy perfect peace, quietness, and security, and all that desire to be called and accounted Christians, may answer in deed and life to so good and godly a name; and jointly altogether in one godly concord and unity, and with one consonant heart and mind, may render unto thee all laud and praise, continually magnifying thy glorious name, who with thy Son our Saviour Jesus Christ, and the Holy Ghost, art one eternal, almighty, and most merciful God, to whom be all laud and praise, world without end. Amen.

A prayer.

BE merciful (O Father of all mercies) to thy Church universal, dispersed throughout the whole world: and grant that all they that confess thy holy name, may agree in the truth of thy holy word, and live in godly concord and unity. And specially be merciful to such as are under persecution for the testimony of their conscience, and profession of the gospel of thy Son our Saviour Jesus Christ. Repress (O Lord) the rage and tyranny of such as are bent to bloodshed, and mind nothing but murther: and save and deliver those silly souls, which (as sheep) are appointed to the shambles and slaughter. And, namely, be merciful to thy Church and realm of England: to thy servant our Sovereign and gracious Queen ELIZABETH, whose life (O Lord) long and long preserve from all the conspiracies and evils, which the craft and malice of the devil, Antichrist, or other wicked men hath or can devise against her (as hitherto most graciously thou hast done.) Be merciful (O Lord) to the Queen's most honourable council, giving them grace to counsel and to execute that which may be to thy honour and glory, to the edifying of the Church of thy Son our Saviour Jesus Christ, and to the benefit and safety of the realm. Be merciful also (O Lord) to the clergy, nobility, Judges, magistrates, people, and commonalty of this realm, granting to every one thy heavenly grace, that they may in their vocation do their duties, to the honour and glory of thy name, the benefit of this Church and realm, and to the salvation of their own souls. Grant this (O Lord) to us most unworthy sinners for the worthiness of thy dear Son our Saviour Jesus Christ, to whom with thee and the Holy Ghost be all honour and glory world without end. Amen.

A thanksgiving and prayer for the preservation of the Queen and the Realm.

O GOD, most merciful Father, who in thy great mercies hast both given unto us a peaceable princess and a gracious Queen, and also hast very often and miraculously saved her from sundry great perils and dangers, and by her government hast preserved us and the whole Realm from manifold mischiefs and dreadful plagues, wherewith nations round about us have been and be most grievously afflicted: have mercy upon them, O Lord, and grant us grace, we beseech thee, for these thy great benefits, that we may be thankful and obedient unto thee, to fly from all things that may offend thee, and provoke thy wrath and indignation against us, and to order our lives in all things that may please thee; that thy servant our sovereign Lady, and we thy people committed to her charge, may by thy protection be continually preserved from all deceits and violences of enemies, and from all other dangers and evils both bodily and ghostly, and by thy goodness may be maintained in all peace and godliness: grant this, O merciful Father, for thy dear Son's sake, our Saviour Jesus Christ, to whom with thee, and the Holy Ghost, one God immortal, invisible, and only wise, be all honour and glory for ever and ever. Amen.

A prayer.

O ALMIGHTY God and heavenly Father, who for the great iniquity which aboundeth in these latter days art justly provoked to send forth the heavy executioners of thy fierce wrath, the very fore-runners of the coming of thy Son, these cruel, unchristian, and unnatural wars, which have set the whole world out of course; nation rising against nation, people against people, and the same people against itself: We give thee (as we are bound) most hearty thanks, for that thou hast spared us thine unworthy servants so long, and not suffered us as yet to feel the grievousness of this universal plague in that measure, that our neighbours have done; but hast hitherto delivered us and blessed us, under the government of our true, natural, and gracious Queen, with a long and a wonderful peace. Our sins (we confess) are no less, if not greater than our neighbours': our unthankfulness much more: so that we must needs acknowledge thine undeserved mercy to be the greater in affording us this unspeakable benefit. Nevertheless, because their enemies and ours are all one, and the chief cause of their malice the same: We together with them (as true members of the same Communion) most entirely beseech thy divine Majesty to forgive our former transgressions and unthankfulness, and to be merciful unto us and them in assuaging the malice of our common enemies, confounding their blind and cruel devices, and in delivering of us from their cruel and bloody designments. And that the rather, because they are confederate with Antichrist, and sworn against the truth: and in the pride of their heart and confidence of their own strength they seek the suppression of thy Gospel, and the overthrow of all such as do profess it. Convert them (O Lord) if it be thy will: make them to see the madness and wickedness of their enterprise, and that they do but kick against the prick: to the end they may give over the pursuit of their bad cause, abstain from shedding Christian blood, and in time kiss thy Son in humility, whom in pride they have hitherto so unadvisedly impugned. Otherwise, if they go on in their malicious wickedness, and continue in their bloody purposes: We beseech thee to weaken their hands, to astonish their hearts, to infatuate their counsels, and to confound them; that they never be able to devise or execute any thing prejudicial to the cause of thy Gospel, or the weal of thy children. Establish (O Lord) in their hearts and kingdoms all such Princes and Governours, as profess and favour thy Gospel: and especially preserve in long life and prosperity thy servant our gracious Queen Elizabeth: that by her and them, as thy ministers, thy truth may have the upper hand, thy Gospel flourish, and all we with one voice say: *Happy are the people, that be in such a case: yea, blessed are the people, which have the Lord for their God.* Grant this (O heavenly Father) for thy Son our Saviour Jesus Christ his sake. Amen.

Another[1] prayer.

O MOST mighty Lord God, the Lord of Hosts, the governour of all creatures, the only giver of all victories, who

[[1] See p. 650, note 1.]

alone art able to strengthen the weak against the mighty, and to vanquish infinite multitudes of thine enemies with the countenance of a few of thy servants, calling upon thy Name, and trusting in thee: Defend, O Lord, thy Servant and our Governour under thee, our Queen Elizabeth, and all thy people committed to her charge. And especially at this time, O Lord, have regard to those her Subjects, which be sent to withstand the cruelty of those, which be common enemies as well to the truth of thy eternal word, as to this Crown and Realm of England, which thou hast of thy divine providence assigned in these our days to the government of thy servant, our sovereign and gracious Queen. O most merciful Father, if it be thy holy will, make soft and tender the stony hearts of all those, that exalt themselves against thy truth, and seek to oppress this Crown and Realm of England, and convert them to the knowledge of thy Son, the only Saviour of the world, Jesus Christ, that we and they may jointly glorify thy mercies. Lighten, we beseech thee, their ignorant hearts to embrace the truth of thy word: Or else so abate their cruelty, (O most mighty Lord,) that this our Christian region, with others that confess thy holy Gospel, may obtain by thy aid and strength surety from our enemies, without shedding of Christian and innocent blood: Whereby all they, which be oppressed with their tyranny, may be relieved, and all which be in fear of their cruelty, may be comforted. And finally, that all christian Realms, and especially this Realm of England, may by thy defence and protection enjoy perfect peace, quietness, and security: And that we, for these thy mercies, jointly altogether, with one consonant heart and voice, may thankfully render to thee all laud and praise, and in one godly concord and unity amongst our selves may continually magnify thy glorious name, who with thy Son our Saviour Jesus Christ, and the Holy Ghost, art one eternal, Almighty and most merciful God. To whom be all laud and praise, world without end. Amen.

CERTAIN PRAYERS to be used at this present time, for the xxxiii. good success of the French King, against the enemies of God's true religion and his State.

Imprinted at London, by the Deputies of Christopher Barker, Printer to the Queen's most excellent Majesty. Anno Domini 1590.

A[1] prayer.

O LORD God of hosts, most mighty and merciful Father, who in thy unspeakable wisdom and mercy hast gathered unto thyself a Church truly professing thy holy name and Gospel: We do here most humbly acknowledge, that through our manifold sins and offences against thy heavenly majesty, committed by unthankful receiving of thy holy word, and by wicked led lives, we have made ourselves unworthy of the least of these and other thy singular blessings hitherto very abundantly poured upon us. Nevertheless (O heavenly Father) with an assured confidence, relying upon thy promises, we make bold to draw near unto the throne of thy grace, humbly craving forgiveness of our sins, and the continuance of thy blessings upon us, and upon all princes, countries and common wealths that have received and do embrace thine holy Gospel, and that at this time fight thy battles against the adversaries of thy Gospel, and those that uphold the kingdom of Antichrist. Therefore, being cast down in soul, we do bewail our iniquities, setting the bitter death and precious bloodshed of thy dear Son Christ Jesus betwixt us and thy just wrath conceived against us and them. Turn (O Lord) thy wrathful indignation from us and them: And forasmuch as it is not for our sins that our enemies in their purpose have thus banded themselves against us, but for the sincere profession of thy word and Gospel; with thy mighty arm confound and bring to nought the devices, power, and strength of all such as set themselves against the same. Thou knowest

[[1] This and the next prayer are included, though not in exactly the same words, in the Forms for 1589 and 1590.]

(O Lord) how the heathen and such as hold of superstitious vanities, even at this present, in *France* and elsewhere, do rush into thine inheritance to make thy chosen Jerusalem, even thy Church, a desolate heap of stones, to lay waste thy holy sanctuary, yea, even to give up the flesh of thy dear children to the birds of the air, and the slain carcases of thy Saints to the beasts of the field. Wherefore, most mighty God of hosts, which art the Lord of glory and power, that canst arm the most base and meanest of thy creatures to the overthrow of all the mighty of the world that be enemies for thy truth's sake: advance thyself, like a mighty Giant, with a swift and terrible judgment against them; frustrate the counsels of all their Achitophels, break them down with an iron rod like an earthen vessel, send an host of Angels to scatter their armies, confound them as thou didst the host of the Assyrians, let thine own sword fight for thy servants, and devour up their enemies: be thou as fire unto them, and let them be as a stubble before thee. Finally, let them be as *Oreb* and *Zeb*, yea, like unto *Zebah* and *Salmanah*, and be made as dung on the face of the earth. Send (good Lord) upon them the spirit of fear and trembling, that they may flee before the host of thine *Israel*, as chaff before the wind, to the end they may be discomfited and overthrown by thy mighty hand; neither give thy servants (O Lord) to be a prey unto their teeth, or a by-word and reproach to such as hate the true profession of thy Gospel: for we do only rest assured under the shadow of thy wings. Protect in mercy as the apple of thine eye, and mercifully pour upon those armies that fight against the enemies of the Gospel the spirit of wisdom, foresight, counsel, strength, and courage, that, in full assurance of thine heavenly help fighting for them, ten of them may chase an hundred, and an hundred of them put to flight a thousand of their adversaries. Be thou (O Lord) their continual refuge and strong rock of defence; let thy holy Angels pitch their tents round about them, that they may know thy holy hand both stretched out for their help, and strongly set against their and our enemies. Teach their hands to war, and their fingers to fight: prosper that which they take in hand, O prosper thou their handy work, and make them always to rejoice in thy salvation and deliverance; that so all such as love not the truth of thy Gospel, hearing thereof, may be discomfited, and that thy fear may fall upon thine enemies to the perpetual glory of thy holy name, and that we, escaping the rage and fury of those which seek after our lives and the overthrow of thy truth, may in thy holy Church here militant, and after in the Church triumphant in heaven, eternally sing praises to thee our heavenly Father, the only giver of all victory. Grant these things for thy Son Christ Jesus' sake, to whom with thee and the Holy Ghost, three persons, and one eternal, immortal, invincible, and only wise God, be all honour, praise, glory, and dominion, now and for ever. *Amen.*

A[1] *prayer.*

MOST mighty God and merciful Father, forsomuch as thou hast promised to maintain and defend the cause of thy Church so dearly purchased and redeemed, even with the precious blood of thy dearly beloved Son: We thy humble servants, confessing our own unworthiness, through the infinite number of our wilful transgressions, do at this time prostrate our selves here before thy divine majesty, and, wholly relying upon thy promises, most heartily beseech thee through the merits of Jesus Christ our Saviour, to protect and strengthen thy Servants our brethren in *France,* that are now ready to fight for the glory of thy name. Thou knowest (O Lord) how the adversaries, that come to fight against them, have entered into a league, and combined themselves together, never to desist until they have destroyed all such as profess thy Gospel, and laid the glory of thy *Sion* and *Temple* in the dust. And although both our and their offences do most justly deserve, that both they and we should be delivered to the edge of the sword: yet seeing that these conspirators and rebellers do hate thy servants only for the cause of thy truth, and that they are noted in the world for such as outwardly profess thy name, and the true doctrine of the Gospel of thy Son our Saviour Christ; save them in thy mercy (O heavenly Father) from the cruelty of their enemies, cast a fear and trembling into the hearts of their adversaries, take the cause of thy Gospel into thine own hands: go before them, fight the battles of thy children, and subdue their enemies: so shall that proud generation have no cause to insult over thy

[[1] When this prayer comes last, its title is *Another.* See p. 650, n. 1.]

true Church, and over thy servants, nor to say with thy old enemies, *Where is now their God?* And we thy penitent and most humble suppliants, that do here at this time make intercession both for our brethren and for ourselves, will from henceforth declare thy name with cheerful hearts in the midst of the congregation; we will ever praise thee and magnify thy salvation, world without end. Grant this (O merciful Father) for thy dear Son's sake, our Lord and Saviour Jesus Christ, to whom with thee and the Holy Ghost, three persons and one God, be all honour, glory, power and dominion, now and for ever. Amen.

Another[1].

O MOST mighty Lord God, the Lord of hosts, the governour of all creatures, the only giver of all victories, who alone art able to strengthen the weak against the mighty, and to vanquish infinite multitudes of thine enemies with the countenance of a few of thy servants calling upon thy name, and trusting in thee: Defend, O Lord, thy servant the[2] *French King;* and especially at this time give him power, to withstand the cruelty of those which be common enemies as

[1 In archbishop Harsnet's copy this prayer is placed first, but, as the next note will shew, not without material variations. Its title there is, 'A prayer to be vsed in euery parish *Church at Morning and Euening prayer,* during the time of these present troubles in France.' It was likewise published alone by the Deputies of Christopher Barker, in its altered state, with the same title, and, most probably, for the same occasion, on a broadside, one of which is also at Colchester. Thus we have four modifications of the prayer originally put forth in 1562. See pp. 476, 536, 645.]

[2 the most Christian king, the *French King,* and specially at this time giue him power to withstand the crueltie of all his enemies, as well forreners, as notorious rebels to his crowne and Realme, which thou hast of thy diuine prouidence assigned vnto him in these our dayes. O most mercifull Father, (if it be thy holy will) plucke downe those ambitious and rebellious heartes that exalt themselues against their natural Lord and King. Conuert them to the knowledge of their offences, that in so iust a cause for so noble a King, a friend to our soueraigne Lady & Queene, both these realmes may liue in amitie, and bee ioyned in strength to withstand the rage and crueltie of such as, not content with their own, aspire to depriue others of their kingdomes. Abate therefore their crueltie, (O most mightie Lorde,) that such Christian Regions as desire the peace of thy Church, may obtaine by thy aide and strength.]

well to the truth of thine eternal word, as to his Crown and Realm, which thou hast of thy divine providence assigned unto him in these our days. Most merciful Father, if it be thy holy will, make soft and tender the stony hearts of all those, that exalt themselves against thy truth, and seek to oppress the professors thereof. Convert them to the knowledge of thy Son, the only Saviour of the world, Jesus Christ, that we and they may jointly glorify thy mercies: lighten (we beseech thee) their ignorant hearts to embrace the truth of thy word, or else so abate their cruelty, (O most mighty Lord,) that such Christian regions as confess the holy Gospel, may obtain by thy aid and strength surety from their enemies without shedding of Christian and innocent blood, whereby all they that be oppressed with their tyranny may be relieved, and all which be in fear of their cruelty may be comforted. And finally, that all Christian Realms, and specially this Realm of England, may by thy defence and protection enjoy perfect peace, quietness, and security. And that we for these thy mercies jointly altogether, with one consonant heart and voice, may thankfully render to thee all laud and praise, and in one godly concord and unity amongst ourselves may continually magnify thy glorious name, who with thy Son, our Saviour Jesus Christ, and the Holy Ghost, art one eternal, Almighty, and most merciful God, to whom be all laud and praise, world without end. Amen.

XXXIV. A PRAYER used in the Queen's Majesty's house and Chapel, for the *prosperity of the French King and his nobility, assailed by a multitude of notorious* rebels that are supported and waged[1] by great forces of foreigns[2]. 21 Aug. An. 1590.

O MOST mighty God, the only protector of all Kings and Kingdoms, we thy humble servants do here with one heart, and one voice, call upon thy heavenly grace, for the prosperous estate of all faithful Christian Princes, and namely at this time, that it would please thee of thy merciful goodness to protect by thy favour, and arm with thine own strength, the most Christian King, the French King, against the rebellious conspirations of his rebellious subjects, and against the mighty violence of such foreign forces, as do join themselves with these rebels, with intention not only to deprive him most unjustly of his kingdom, but finally to exercise their tyranny against our Sovereign Lady, and this her Kingdom and people, and against all other, that do profess the Gospel of thy only Son our Saviour Jesus Christ.

Now (O Lord) is the time, when thou mayest shew forth thy goodness, and make known thy power; for now are these rebels risen up against him, and have fortified themselves with strange forces, that are known to be mortal enemies both to him and us. Now do they all conspire and combine themselves against thee, O Lord, and against thy anointed. Wherefore, now, O Lord, aid and maintain this just cause; save and deliver him, and his army of faithful subjects, from the malicious cruel bloody men: send him help from thy holy Sanctuary, and strengthen him out of Zion. O Lord, convert the hearts of his disloyal subjects, bring them to the true and due obedience of Jesus Christ. Command thy enemies not to touch him, being thy Anointed, professing thy holy gospel, and putting his trust only in thee: break asunder their bands, that conspire thus wickedly against him; for his hope is in thee: let his help be by thee: be unto him as thou wast to king David, whom thy right hand had exalted, the God of his

[1 Waged: hired, kept in pay.]
[2 Spaniards.]

salvation, a strong castle, a sure bulwark, a shield of defence, and place of refuge. Be unto him counsel and courage, policy and power, strength and victory : defend his head in the day of battle, comfort his armies, his true faithful Noble men, the princes of his blood, and all other his faithful subjects: Strengthen them to join their hearts and hands with him; associate unto him such as may aid him to maintain his right, and be zealous of thy glory. Let thy holy Angel stand in circuit about his Realm, and about his loyal people, that the enemies thereof, though they be multiplied in number, though they exalt themselves with horses and horsemen, though they trust to their numbers, to their shield, and glory in their strength; yet they may see with Elizeus the unresistable army of angels, which thou canst send for the defence of thy inheritance, and that thy enemies may know and confess, that thy power standeth not in multitude, nor thy might in strong men : but thou (O Lord) art the help of the humble, the defender of the weak, the protector of them that are forsaken, and the saviour of all those who put their trust in thee. [2 Kings vi. 17.]

O merciful Father, we acknowledge thy gracious goodness in our own former deliverance[3] from the like kind of enemies and rebels, against thy anointed our Sovereign Lady and Queen, professing thy Gospel : so will we do in this, and be as joyful of it, and no less thankful for it, and make the same to be for ever an occasion unto us of our more faithful subjection to our own dread Sovereign : Whom (Lord) we beseech thee now and evermore most mercifully to bless with health of body, peace of Country, purity of religion, prosperity of Estate, and all inward, and outward, earthly happiness, and heavenly felicity. This grant (merciful Father) for the glory of thine own name, and for Christ Jesus' sake, our mediator and only Saviour. Amen.

Imprinted at London by the Deputies of Christopher Barker,
Printer to the Queenes most excellent Maiestie.

[[3] In 1569. See p. 462.]

XXXVI. AN ORDER FOR PRAYER AND THANKSGIVING (necessary to be used in these dangerous times) for the safety and preservation of her Majesty and this realm.

Set forth by Authority.

LONDON.

Printed by the Deputies of Christopher Barker, Printer to the Queen's most excellent Majesty. 1594.

An admonition to the Reader.

There have been sundry, but *heathen men* (as *Plato* and others), being no better instructed than the lame reach of reason could guide them, nor any clearer enlightened, than by the dimmed glimpse of nature, who nevertheless arrived thus far, as to know and acknowledge that God, who is above all, extendeth his careful providence over all, and especially in preservation of Kingdoms, and of other politic societies, and of their Governours and Rulers. *For that which may be known of God, is manifest* Rom. 1. ver. (saith Saint Paul) *among them: for God hath opened it unto them. For* 19, 20. *his invisible things being understood by his works through the creation of the world, are seen: that is, both his eternal power and Godhead, so that they are without excuse.* Then how much more must all *Christians*, to whom the *Day-star* hath in greater brightness and measure appeared, and the treasures of *God* the *Father* in his Son *Christ Jesu* been opened, acknowledge this his providence, and reverently adore and magnify that good *God*, which to the heap of all other his mercies towards them addeth this blessing and protection of *Magistracy* and government, whereby men live peaceably with all honesty in this life!

But if ever any nation, yea, if all the nations in the world besides, have cause with thankfulness to acknowledge this kind of benefit, surely we the people of *England* have most just and abundant occasion, of all others, to perform this duty unto God. First, for placing over us our most gracious dread Sovereign Lady *Queen Elizabeth,* by whose happy government we have so long breathed from the burden of intolerable miseries of *scarcity, bloodshed,* and spiritual *bondage,* under which afore we lay grovelling, and pitifully groaned. Then, for preserving these her Realms and dominions so long in the true profession of the Gospel, and in peace and tranquillity, notwithstanding the sundry privy conspiracies and open hostilities practised, both inward and outward, for the interruption of our quiet repose and holy profession. Thirdly, for protecting so long and so often her sacred royal person from the cruel and bloody hands of such and so many several detestable and treacherous Conspirators. And likewise for the Lord's provident and watchful eye over her and us, and for the wonderful happy discoveries of so manifold cruel designments so closely plotted against her innocent life, and so dangerously against her *Highness'* Realms and dominions. Which mischievous devices as they have all flowed from none other fountain, than from that city of seven hills, the *See* of *Rome*, and seat of the *Beast*, not in regard of any desert of ours, but because we have abandoned the cup of spiritual abominations, wherewith these have long intoxicated the kings of the earth: So have they been continually projected, carried forward, and managed by idolatrous *Priests* and *Jesuits* his creatures, the very loathsome *Locusts* that crawl out of the bottomless pit. Howbeit they have been and are mightily seconded by certain *Potentates* of the earth[1], who do nothing else but serve themselves of that idolatrous *Romish religion*, as of a Mask and stalking-horse, therewith to cover the unsatiable ambition, wherewith they are possessed, of usurping[2] other men's *kingdoms*. For if we will first particularly cast our eyes upon the variable conspiracies that have been entered into but against her Highness' realms: shall we not find the treason of the two *Pooles*[3], of *Felton*[4], and of the late Duke of *Northfolk*[5];

Apocal. 13. & 17.

[[1] The two other editions mentioned in the next note have not these four words, "*Potentates* of the earth."]

[[2] There exist three editions of this Order, but only one has the following long enumeration of conspirators. The other two (which are in the University library, Cambridge, and at Lambeth) differ from each other merely in the arrangement of the type, and in the number of pages, one containing C in fours, the other D iii. In both the Admonition goes on thus, " of vsurping the *kingdoms* of other Princes.

Which their most dangerous and desperate plots and enterprises, God of his great mercie hath hitherto most happily discouered to his infinite glorie, and our vnspeakeable comfort. So that it may aptly, &c."]

[[3] In October, 1562, Arthur Pole, and his brother Edmund, (great grandsons of George, duke of Clarence, Edward the fourth's brother,) with others, were apprehended on a charge of conspiring, by means of a French army landing in Wales, to depose Elizabeth, and set on the throne Mary, queen of Scots, who was to marry Edmund, and create Arthur duke of Clarence. They were tried on the 26th of February, 1563, but, though found guilty, were all pardoned. Carte, Vol. III. p. 408. Zurich Letters, second edition, p. 172.]

[[4] Pope Pius V., he who even desired to 'shed his blood in an expedition against England,' issued, February the 25th, 1570, a bull, excommunicating the heretic Elizabeth, and absolving her subjects from their oaths of allegiance. This bull one John Felton affixed to the gates of the bishop of London's palace in St Paul's church-yard, May the 25th, and on the 8th of August was hanged for his offence before the same gates. Camden, p. 428. Foulis, p. 433. Zurich Letters, pp. 341, 349.]

[[5] Thomas Howard, duke of Norfolk, a protestant since he 'knew what religion meant,' the pupil of John Foxe, the martyrologist, to whom he left 'Twenty pound a yeare,' was beheaded on Tower hill, the 2nd of June, 1572, five months after condemnation, for a second time intending to marry Mary, queen of Scots, and thereby further her designs

of *Throgmorton*[1], of *Englefield*[2], of *Paget*, of *Shelley*, and *Stanley*[3], and *Yorke*[4], and of all the seminary *Priests*[5], and *Jesuits*, to have been tickled up by Romish busses and practices, and to have been carried forward by their own gross dotage upon that absurd religion?

on the English throne. Camden, pp. 437-440. Wright's Elizabeth, Vol. I. pp. 402, 406. Zurich Letters, p. 320. Two warrants for his execution had first been signed and revoked. Lingard, Vol. VIII. pp. 89, 90.]

[1 John Throckmorton of Norwich was hanged the 30th of August, 1570, for having endeavoured, about a month before, to raise a rebellion in the county, in order, amongst other things, to set the duke of Norfolk at liberty on his first imprisonment. Camden, pp. 428, 429. Zurich Letters, p. 342. Perhaps, however, the Throckmorton alluded to was rather Francis, a gentleman of Cheshire, apprehended November the 7th, 1583, and put to death at Tyburn in the usual manner the 10th of July, 1584, nearly two months after conviction, because he had striven to bring about an invasion of England by the Catholic powers, so that Mary might be delivered from prison, and Elizabeth deposed. Thomas lord Paget, engaged in the same plot, fled into France. Camden, pp. 497, 498. The ship, wherein this nobleman escaped, William Shelley provided, who, being thus connected with the conspiracy, was cast into prison, and in 1586 condemned for treason. Ibid. pp. 504, 553. Lingard, Vol. VIII. p. 188.]

[2 Sir Francis Englefield had been one of queen Mary's privy council, and her master of the horse; but, retiring on the accession of Elizabeth to Flanders, was taken into the pay of Spain, of which court he became a great favourite. Strype's Annals, Vol. I. pp. 370—374: Vol. II. p.27. In 1594 he was still engaged in plotting against Elizabeth. Camden, p. 576.]

[3 Though a Roman catholic, Sir William Stanley was by the earl of Leicester left in charge of Deventer in Holland, which city having betrayed to the Spaniards in the beginning of 1587, 'upon a principle of conscience,' he thenceforth became a pensioner of Philip the second. Carte, Vol. III. p. 599. Lingard, Vol. VIII. p. 264, note.]

[4 Rowland Yorke, 'a Man of a loose and dissolute Behaviour,' whom the earl of Leicester had appointed governor of a fort near Zutphen, not only turned traitor himself, but was the cause why his neighbouring commander, Sir William Stanley, did the same. Soames's Elizabethan Religious History, pp. 350-353.]

[5 The English clergy, who had withdrawn from their own country on account of religion, were formed into a society after the manner of a college, first at Douay, in 1568, then, on being banished from the Netherlands in 1575, at Rheims, and in 1579 at Rome. Camden, p. 476. These establishments, whose members are not to be confounded with the Jesuits, were called Seminaries, being designed 'to nourish and bring up persons to become seedmen in the tillage of sedition.' Stow, p. 1266. Fuller, Book ix. p. 84. Ranke's History of the Popes, Book v. chap. 7.]

As for those other attempts against her dominions, which have not stayed themselves in the bare terms of conspiracy only, but have also broken further into open rebellion and hostility; they likewise have no less been blown up by that brood of *Massing Priests*, being unnatural subjects (for the most part) of these *kingdoms*. For was not *Moreton*[6] a Priest sent from the *Pope's* own side to stir up the two Earls and others unto the Northern rebellion? Did not *Saunders*[7] second his bookish treasons even with banner displayed, and by commotion in *Ireland*? And doth not that *carnal arch-traitor Allen*[8] proclaim to the world unto his own everlasting reproach, that he and others excited the *King* of *Spain's* invincible *Navy* (vainly so surnamed) by invasion to have conquered his own native country, and to have swallowed us all up? Yea, and in all those their latter hidden, hellish and damnable designs against her Ma-

[[6] In 1569 Pius V. sent Dr Nicholas Morton, a Yorkshireman, from Rome into the northern parts of England, to stir up a rebellion there, by declaring on his authority (in anticipation of his famous bull) to the two principal catholic nobles, the earls of Northumberland and Westmoreland, that Elizabeth was a heretic, and thus had no right to the kingdom. Soames, pp. 107, 108.]

[[7] Nicholas Saunders, (more truly *Slanders*—Fuller, Book IX. p. 169,) 'that indefatigable writer, as well as warrior,' besides other treatises, put out one, *De visibili Monarchia Ecclesiæ;* and also another, *De Origine et Progressu schismatis Anglicani;* whose errors and falsehoods have been amply exposed by Burnet, at the end of the first two volumes of his History of the Reformation. Strype's Whitgift, p. 47. Zurich Letters, p. 418. 'D. Sanders, a lewde scholler and subiect of *England*, a fugitiue and a principall companion and conspirator with the traitors and rebels at *Rome*, was by the *Pope's* speciall commission a commaunder, as in forme of a Legate, and sometime a treasorer or paymaster for those warres: which D. Sanders, in his booke of his Church Monarchie, did afore his passing into *Ireland* openly by writing gloriously allowe the foresaid Bull of *Pius Quintus* against her Maiestie, to be lawfull.' See a Tract published in 1583 to prove that the executions of Priests by Elizabeth were 'for Treason and not for Religion.' Saunders, being sent by Gregory XIII. to Ireland with a consecrated banner, landed, about the 1st of July, 1579, at Smerwick, in Kerry, in company with a small body of soldiers under James Fitzmaurice, whose brother, the earl of Desmond, 'the Pope's great champion,' he soon persuaded to rebel. Camden, pp. 472, 495. Foulis, p. 390. Ellis's Letters, Second Series, Vol. III. pp. 92-97.]

[[8] William Allen, generally called the cardinal of England, died at Rome, October the 16th, 1594. It was, doubtless, in allusion to his ecclesiastical dignity, that the Admonition styles him '*carnall*,' a species of wit not uncommon in the sixteenth century. He retired from the kingdom very soon after Elizabeth's accession. 'His learning and piety were very great, and he laboured very usefully for the defence of the Catholic religion against the Heretics.' Du Pin's Eccles. Hist. of the 16th century, Vol. II. p. 152. Ranke, Book v. chap. 12.]

[LITURG. QU. ELIZ.]

jesty's own person and life, such *Priests* have also been the principal stirrers and agents under their unholy father. *Somerfield*[1] and *Arden*, were not they drawn into that action by *Hall* the Priest? *Parry*[2] by Cardinal *Como*, and by certain English fugitive Priests at *Millaine* and *Paris*, and also by *Allen's* traitorous writings? *Babington*[3] and all the other bloody conspirators, his complices, by *Ballard* the Priest? So *Lopez*[4] his late purposed empoisoning is said to have been first plotted and set forward in *Spain* by *Parsons*[5] the Jesuit Friar. And *Patrick o'Cullen*[6], *Laton, Kale, Poule Wheele*[7], and, sundry others very lately were animated by *Holt, Hart, Sherwood*[8], and other priests, the detestable instruments of the Bish. of *Rome*, and of the king of *Spain's* most dishonourable intended executions.

[[1] Somerfield is clearly an error for Somer*ville*. This 'furious yong man of Warwickshire' (see p. 588), with Arden, his father-in-law, their two wives, and Hall, a priest, were arraigned on December the 16th, 1583, and condemned for conspiring against the queen's life. Somerville strangled himself in prison, Arden was hanged and quartered in Smithfield on the 20th of December, and the rest were spared. Stow, p. 1176.]

[[2] For Dr William Parry, and his abetter cardinal Como, see pp. 465, 584.]

[[3] Babington and Ballard have been mentioned on p. 468.]

[[4] Dr Roderigo Lopez, a Portuguese, suspected to be a Jew, but outwardly a Christian, and the queen's domestic physician, was tried on the last day of February, 1594, at Guildhall, for contriving her majesty's destruction by poison, and on June the 7th hanged at Tyburn. Stow, pp. 1274, 1278.]

[[5] Parsons, 'a turbulent, insidious, and intriguing Jesuit,' resided sometimes at Rome, sometimes in Spain. He came to England in disguise with Campion, in 1580, charged ' by speciall authoritie to execute the sentence of the bul' of 1570. Foulis, pp. 679-688.]

[[6] Patrick o'Cullen, an Irish fencing-master, bribed, like many others, by the traitorous fugitives in the Netherlands, to destroy the queen, was tried at Westminster for that offence on March the 1st, 1594, and hanged at Tyburn on the following day. Camden, p. 577.]

[[7] Nothing has been found respecting *Laton, Kale,* and *Poule Wheele*. Were they among those enumerated by Bacon, Vol. I. p. 538?]

[[8] In 1585 Elizabeth commanded all Jesuits, and priests belonging to seminaries, of whom some were condemned, and others in danger of the law, 'to quit England within forty days, under pain of being dealt with as traitors; in the same manner as the protestant preachers had been driven out of the dominions of so many catholic princes.' Ranke, Book v. chap. 12. Among these was 'John Heart, the most learned of them all.' Camden, p. 497. Holinshed (p. 1380.) prints a document, signed on the 3rd of February by this man and others, acknowledging that their deportation to Normandy had been managed with great kindness and courtesy.]

These and some other complots we see how desperately they have been attempted, yet (thanked be God) are not achieved: how perilously plotted, but are not perfected: how secretly devised, yet most happily hitherto discovered to God's infinite glory, and our unspeakable comfort. So that it may aptly be verified, that her Majesty's life hath all this while been sustained *in manu Altissimi*, and that under the shadow of his wings she hath not miscarried. All which whosoever he be that will attentively weigh and consider, and cannot see the very finger of God mightily working herein by his providence and mercy, no doubt, he is insensible blockish: who seeth, and will not acknowledge it, is wilfully malicious: but who acknowledgeth, and also tasteth of the sweet blessings that are enjoyed thereby, and is not most heartily thankful to God therefore, is extremely impious, and doth but add this ungratefulness unto the mass of all his other wickedness, even unto his own greater damnation. Let every of us therefore who have good will to *Sion*[9], turn from our wicked ways, and from the evil that is betwixt our hands, and incessantly with heart and voice yield most humble and hearty thanks to God our deliverer. But let it not be for a day or two only, whiles the intended wound doth (as it were) present itself fresh and green before the eyes of our minds; but continually, even so long as we may justly imagine the same devil, in his imps, still to rage and to be prest[10] to devour us; so long as *our habitation is amongst the Tents of Mesech*, and our *souls amongst Lions, who hunt after our lives*, and do greedily seek to *give our Dearling to the dog, and to lay our honour in the dust*: to the intent, that (if it be so God's good will) our joy may long and long be redoubled and trebled unto us under the happy government of so gracious a *Sovereign*. Which our bounden duty that it may the more frequently and fruitfully be performed of us; it hath been thought meet to publish this form of prayer for the continuance of God's mercies towards us, and of thanksgiving for his unspeakable goodness in detecting so many conspiracies, and averting so great mischiefs intended against us. Which duty of praying and thanksgiving there is no doubt but every true hearted *English* man and faithful *Subject* will both privately and publicly from the bottom of his heart perform.

Psalm 20[11].	*Psalm* 27.	*Psalm* 33.
Psalm 21.	*Psalm* 31.	*Psalm* 91.

Prayers for the preservation of the Queen's Majesty.

ALMIGHTY and everlasting God, Creator and Governor of all the world, by whom *Kings* do bear rule, and under whose

[[9] Instead of, *Sion*, each of the other editions has, "the truth of the Gospel."]

[[10] Prest (*prêt*): ready.]

[[11] None of these Psalms, though given at length, has the *Gloria Patri*.]

providence they are wonderfully and mightily oftentimes protected from many fearful dangers, by which the malice of *Satan* and his wicked imps do seek to intrap them : We give unto thy heavenly majesty most humble and hearty thanks, for that it hath pleased thee, of thine infinite mercy and goodness in *Christ Jesu*, so wonderfully to uphold, deliver and preserve thine *Hand-maid,* our most dread and Sovereign Queen *Elizabeth*, so many and sundry times, from the cruel and bloody treacheries of desperate men, who address themselves to all wickedness; and at this time especially, wherein her innocent life was shot at by divers wicked designments of blood-thirsty wretches and traitors. And we do most humbly, and from the bottom of our hearts, pray and beseech thee in *Christ Jesu*, to continue this thine unspeakable goodness towards her and this realm, and evermore to defend and protect them. O Lord, dissipate and confound all practices, conspiracies, and treasons, against her, against this realm of *England,* and against the truth of thine *holy word* here taught and professed. Smite our enemies (good Lord) upon the cheek-bone, break the teeth of the ungodly, frustrate their counsels, and bring to nought all their devices. Let them fall into the pit, that they have prepared for us: Let a sudden destruction come upon them unawares; and the net that they have laid for others privily, let it catch themselves, that they may fall into their own mischief. Let them be ashamed and confounded together, that seek after her life to destroy it. Let them be driven backward and put to rebuke, that wish us evil: so that the whole world and all posterity may see and know, how mightily with thy fatherly care and providence thou watchest over and defendest those, which put their trust in thee, and are in the hand of the most highest, and dwell under the shadow of the Almighty: And that those which seek thee may be joyful and glad in thee, and all such as love thy *Salvation* may say alway, *The Lord be praised*. Grant this (O most loving and merciful Father) for thy dear Son's sake, *Jesus Christ* our Lord and only *Saviour*. Amen.

Psal. 2. [3].

Psal. 7.
Psal. 35.

Psal. 40.

Psal. 91.

Psal. 40.

Another.

O ALMIGHTY and eternal God, creator and governor of the whole world, unto whom all power belongeth over all creatures both in heaven and earth, who spake the word, and they were made, commanded, and all things were created, and by whom alone it is, that not only all *Kings* and *Princes* do rule and govern the people committed to their charge, but are likewise by thy divine providence and mighty protection (so long as it seemeth best to thy godly wisdom) defended and delivered, even in the midst of all their perils and dangers, out of the hands of all their enemies: We yield unto thee most humble and hearty thanks, for that it hath pleased thy gracious goodness, according to thine accustomed favour towards her, still to preserve and defend thy well beloved *Hand-maid* and our most gracious *Queen Elizabeth*, from all the wicked conspiracies, traitorous attempts, and devilish devices, which either the foreign and professed enemies abroad, or else her most unloyal, desperate, and rebellious *Subjects* at home, were able at any time to devise and practise against her. But especially (O Lord) at this time, as just occasion is offered unto us all, we all even from the bottom of our hearts praise thy holy name, and give thee most hearty and unfeigned thanks for this thy late and most happy delivery of her *Majesty's* most royal person from all those manifold treasons, which were most wickedly invented and cruelly attempted against her: most humbly beseeching thee, of thine infinite goodness and mercy, still to continue thy fatherly protection over her, daily to increase and multiply thy heavenly blessings and graces upon her. Be thou ever unto her (*O Lord God* of hosts) even a strong rock and tower of defence against the face of all her enemies, which either openly abroad, or secretly at home, go about to bring her life unto the grave, and lay her honour in the dust. Disclose their wicked counsels, and make frustrate all their devilish practices in such sort, as that all the world may learn and know, that there is no counsel, no wisdom, no policy against the Lord. And if it be thy will (*O Lord*), either give them grace in time to see how in vain they still kick against the pricks, and do seek to depose her whom thou dost exalt, and so acknowledge and repent them of these their sins, and thus convert them in thy mercy: or else in thy just judgments (if with the wilful, obstinate, and reprobate sinners, they still harden their hearts and will not repent) let all the enemies (*O Lord*), let all the malicious and deadly enemies of thine anointed servant, and our most gracious Queen *Elizabeth,* perish together. Let them fall into the ditch which they have digged for others, and be taken in their own nets: but let her Majesty (*O Lord*) ever escape them, that all the world may see how dear and precious in thy sight the life of this thine anointed is, who doth not so much as imagine this evil against them, that thus continually thirst after her blood. Wherefore (*O Lord* our God, King of kings and Lord of all lords, unto whose eyes all things are open, and from whom no secrets are hid, who only knowest all the devices and thoughts of men, and searchest out the depth of their hearts) thou knowest (*O Lord*) that nothing at any time hath been more dear unto thine anointed *Hand-maid Elizabeth,* our Queen, than the public good and benefit of thy Church, and the godly peace and unity of all good *Christians* among themselves. We beseech thee therefore of thy great goodness (*O Lord*) still to look down from heaven, and behold her with thine eye of pity and compassion, daily with thy mighty power and stretched out arm to save and deliver her from all her enemies, preserve and keep her as the apple of thine own eye, and grant unto her (O most merciful Father) a long, prosperous, and happy reign over us, and prolong her days as the days of heaven here upon earth, that she may be an old mother in *Israel,* and see her desire upon all thine and her enemies, though in number never so many, or in power never so mighty. And finally, after this life, give unto her everlasting life, through *Jesus Christ* thine only Son, and our only *Saviour.*

Another.

O MOST gracious God and our most loving and merciful Father, which hast not only created us, and all things by thy power, but hast also continued our preservation by thy holy providence, therein working wonderfully, revealing things hidden and secret, as thou dost discover the bottoms and foundations of the deep: how can we worthily praise thy goodness, or sufficiently declare thy loving kindness, which thou hast at all times shewed unto us thy servants in the land of the living? We magnify thy glorious name: thou hast a mighty arm; strong is thy hand, and high is thy right hand, yea, thy wisdom is infinite. The proud have risen against thee, O Lord, and against thine anointed, our Sovereign under thee, and against thy people that call upon thy name: but thou hast cast them down from time to time, and scattered them abroad, for thy mercy endureth for ever. They have taken wicked counsels together, saying, None shall be able to espy it: but thou hast opened them, and brought them out of darkness into light; for thou art God alone which destroyest the wisdom of the wise, and castest away the understanding of the prudent: therefore do we worship thee and praise thy holy Name, rejoicing continually in thy strength and thy salvation; for thou art the glory of our power, and by thy favour and loving kindness are we preserved. Our shield and defence belongeth to thee (O Lord of hosts), and our gracious Prince to thee, O thou Holy one of Israel. And because thou hast loved her for thy name's sake, and the glory of thy kingdom upon the earth, and us also thy people to whom thou hast given her and many excellent blessings together with her righteous government, thou hast many times also preserved and kept her, as the apple of thine eye, from the mischievous imaginations and cruel hands of thine and her enemies, and from the secret practices of those that have endeavoured to rise up against her. Thou (O Lord) hast preserved her Honour from the ignominy, her life from the cruelty, and her Crown from the tyranny of the wicked, her estate from ruin, her peace from disturbance, her kingdom and her people from being a prey to the malignant. The foot of pride hath come against us, but the hand of iniquity hath not cast us down. Therefore do we rejoice before thee, and be glad in thee, yea, our songs do we make of thy name, O thou most Highest, and will be ever setting forth thy praise and thy glory, thy might and thy mercy, from one generation to another. Only, O Lord, forsake us not in this time of our age, until we have shewed thy strength to this generation, and thy power to all that are yet for to come. And albeit, if thou, Lord, in thy displeasure do mark among us all what is done amiss, there is none that can abide it, yet forsake us not, nor leave us, O God of our salvation. Give courage and constancy to our Sovereign to persevere in perils: prudence and wisdom to her Council, wisely to foresee and discover the subtil sleights and dangers of all enemies: faithfulness and fortitude to the Nobles of the land, duty and obedience to us all that are under her. Forgive also, we most humbly pray thee thorow thy fatherly kindness in Jesus Christ, the multitude of our sins and transgressions against thy divine majesty, and thy commandments, and according to the multitude of thy mercies do away all our offences, that the light and candle of thy servant *Elizabeth*, our gracious Queen and Governor, which is our life in the light of thy countenance, and the breath of our nostrils, be not put out, but may still shine and burn bright, illumined by the beams of thy heavenly grace. Protect her (O Lord), we still beseech thee, in safety, save her in majesty, keep her in peace, guide her in counsel, and defend her in danger: bless her, Lord, in all temporal and celestial blessings in Christ, that she may still bless thee: for in death no man remembereth thee, and who shall give thee thanks in the pit? Detect and reveal still the foundations and buildings of all treasons and conspiracies, both at home and abroad; and herein (O Lord) either convert the wicked hearts and secret conceits from their wicked imaginations, or confound their devices, and make them as the untimely fruit that they never see the sun. Say (O Lord) to her soul, as sometime thou didst to *Abraham* the father of the Faithful, I am thy buckler and thy exceeding great reward; and, as thou didst sometime to the soul of thy servant *David*, I am thy salvation, with my holy oil have I anointed thee. Therefore my hand shall hold thee fast, and mine arm shall stablish thee. The enemy shall not be able to do thee violence, the son of wickedness shall not hurt thee. I will beat down thy foes before thy face, and plague them that hate thee. Hear, Lord, and save us, O King of heaven, when we call upon thee: and so shall we all, both Prince and people, dwell still under the shadow of thy wings, protected by thy power, and preserved by thy providence, and ordered by thy governance, to thy everlasting praise, and our unspeakable comfort in Jesus Christ, to whom with thee, O Father and God of all consolation, and the holy Spirit of sanctification, be all honour and glory both now and for ever. Amen.

1596.]

A Prayer set forth by authority to be used for the xxxvii. prosperous success of her Majesty's Forces and Navy.

Not unto us (O Lord) not unto us, but unto thy name give the glory, by beholding of us thy servants graciously at this time, against whom the proud are risen up, and the enemies have conspired and banded themselves. It is thy might and Majesty alone (O Lord) that putteth down all the ungodly of the earth like dross, that stilleth the raging of the Sea, and the noise of his waves, and the madness of the people, that breaketh the bow and knappeth the spear in sunder, and burneth the Chariots in the fire. Arise then (O Lord) to our defence, and break the power and counsels of thine and our enemies, and make them like those people that became as the chaff before the wind, when they conspired and went out against those whose shield and buckler, whose castle of defence, whose God and Saviour thou wast from everlasting. And bless, good Lord, (we most humbly beseech thee) the people of our land provided to withstand their tyranny, and to stand for the just defence of thy servants and people of this kingdom. Encourage all our hearts (O heavenly King and Prince of power) with joy and gladness in thy saving health, and the hands of our armies with strength and constancy. And as thou art the God of hosts, so bless our hosts and companies by sea and by land, by giving them victory in battle and strength in conflict to overcome. So shall we confess to the praise of thy Name, that it is not our bow nor our sword that hath saved us, but thy holy hand and outstretched arm. And all the world shall know, that it is thy favour that prospereth, and thy power that overcometh, and thy blessing that preserveth thy Church from hostility and tyranny, and us thy people from destruction. Hear us (O Lord our defender) for the glory of thy holy Name, through Jesus Christ our blessed Saviour and Redeemer. Amen.

Imprinted at London by the Deputies of Christopher Barker, Printer to the Queenes most excellent Maieſtie.

Anno Domini. 1596.

xxxviii. A[1] Prayer made by the queen at the departure of the fleet.

MOST omnipotent: Maker and guider of all our worlds' mass, that only searchest and fadomest the bottom of all our hearts' conceits, and in them seest the true original of all our actions intended: thou that by thy foresight dost truly discern, how no malice of revenge, nor quittance of injury, nor desire of bloodshed, nor greediness of lucre, hath bred the resolution of our now set out Army, but a heedful care and wary watch, that no neglect of foes, nor over surety of harm, might breed either danger to us, or glory to them: These being grounds, thou that didst inspire the mind, we humbly beseech with bended knees, prosper the work, and with best forewinds guide the journey, speed the victory, and make the return the advancement of thy glory, the triumph of their fame, and surety to the realm, with the least loss of English blood. To these devout petitions, Lord, give thou thy blessed grant[2].

[[1] 'The queen composed two prayers, one for her own use, the other to be daily used in the fleet during the expedition. The former may be seen in Birch, ii. 18, with a letter to Essex from sir Robert Cecil.' Lingard, Vol. VIII. p. 324. It has been printed also, (under different titles, and not without variations,) in Sorocold and Strype, the latter (Annals, Vol. IV. p. 216.) supposing it to belong to 1595, if not to 1594, whilst Sorocold, who lived so much nearer the time, with more correctness refers it expressly to 1596. See p. 472.]

[[2] The two prayers, which follow, are unconnected with the object of this volume: still, as being attributed to Elizabeth, their insertion, appears allowable. The first is her prayer just before proceeding to her coronation, the 14th day of January, 1559. Holinshed (p. 1180), and Heylin (Elizabeth, p. 106), have printed it. The second, which exists in the Bibl. Lans. 116. art. 26, indorsed 'the Q. prayer after a progress, Aug. 15, [1574], being then a Bristow' [Bristol], is likewise in the State Paper Office, (Domestic Elizabeth,) whence the present copy was procured. Zurich Letters, p. 480.

HER highness, being placed in her chariot within the Tower of London, lifted up her eyes to heaven, and said:

O Lord almighty, and everlasting God, I give thee most hearty thanks, that thou hast been so merciful unto me, as to spare me to behold this joyful day. And I knowledge, that thou hast dealt as wonderfully with me, as thou didst with thy true and faithful servant Daniel the prophet, whom thou deliveredst out of the den, from the cruelty of the greedy raging Lions: even so was I overwhelmed, and only by thee delivered. To thee therefore be only thanks, honour and praise for ever. Amen.

The Queenes Prayer.

I RENDER unto Thee (O mercifull and heavenly Father) most humble and hearty thanks for thy manifold mercies so abundantly bestowed upon me, as well for my creation, preservation, regeneration, and all other thy benefites and great mercies exhibited in Christ Jesus, but especially for thy mightie protection and defence over me, in preserving me in this long and dangerous journey, as also from the beginning of my life unto this present hower, from all such perills as I should most justly have fallen into for mine offences, haddest Thou not, O Lord God, of thy great goodness and mercy preserved and kept me. Continue this thy favorable goodness toward me, I beseech Thee, that I may still likewise be defended from all adversity both bodily and ghostly: but specially, O Lord, keep me in the soundness of thy faith, fear, and love, that I never fall away from Thee, but continue in thy service all the daies of my life. Stretch forth, O Lord most mightie, thy right hand over me, and defend me from mine enemys, that they never prevayle against me. Give me, O Lord, the assistance of thy Spiritt, and comfort of thy Grace, truly to know Thee, intirely to love Thee, and assuredly to trust in Thee. And that as I do acknowledge to have received the Government of this Church and Kingdome at thy hand, and to hold the same of Thee, so graunt me grace, O Lord, that in the end I may render up and present the same unto Thee, a peaceable, quiett, and well ordered State and kingdome, as also a perfect reformed Church, to the furtherance of thy Glory. And to my subjects, O Lord God, graunt, I beseech thee, faithfull and obedient hearts, willingly to submit themselves to the obedience of thy Word and Commandments, that we altogether being thankfull unto Thee for thy benefitts received, may laud and magnifie thy Holy Name world without end. Graunt this, O mercifull Father, for Jesus Christes sake our only Mediatour and Advocate. Amen.]

XXXIX. A Prayer of Thanksgiving, and for continuance of good success to her Majesty's Forces.

O[1] Lord God of Hosts, everlasting and most merciful Father, we thine unworthy creatures do yield unto thy divine Majesty all possible praise and humble[2] thanks for thine infinite benefits[3], which thou hast of long time plentifully poured upon thine Handmaiden and humble servant, our Sovereign Lady the Queen, and upon her[4] whole Realm, and us her Subjects the people of this Kingdom: and namely, O Lord, for that graciously respecting us in the merits of thy dear Son our Saviour, and by his intercession passing over and forgiving our manifold sins[5], thou hast this present Summer so favourably conducted the Royal Navy and Army sent to the Seas[6] by our Gracious Queen (not for any other worldly respects, but only for defence of this Realm, and us thy people, against the mighty preparations of our Enemies threatening our ruin,) by safely directing them unto places appointed, and by strengthening[7] the Governors and Leaders of the same with counsel and resolution, and blessing them with notable victories both by Sea and Land, whereby the insolencies[8] and pride of our Enemies, which sought our conquest and subversion, is by these late victories notably daunted[9], repulsed, and abased. Grant unto us (most merciful Father) the grace[10]

[1 The following notes will point out the original readings of the author's manuscript; such corrections thereof, as first suggested themselves, being placed within crotchets.]

[2 hartie.]

[3 spirituall and temporall, wch by the mediation of thy sonne o^r lord Jesus Christ o^r Redemer thou hast.]

[4 her subiects.]

[5 and transgressions.]

[6 seas, for defence of this Realme and vs thy people, by savelie directinge.]

[7 enduinge the Gouuerno^{rs} and Leaders wth Counsell and Courage.]

[8 pride, and mightenes of that nation of Spaine, wch hateth vs mortallie and secketh most greedelie o^r Conquest.]

[9 and abassed to o^r [great] comfort.]

[10 of hartie and unfeined repentance to the amendment of o^r liues past, and wth due.]

A PRAYER OF THANKSGIVING.

with due thankfulness to acknowledge thy [11] fatherly goodness extended upon us by the singular favour shewed to thy Servant [12] and Minister our Sovereign Lady and Queen. And for thy holy Name [13] continue these thy wonderful blessings [14] still upon us, to defend us against our Enemies, and [15] bless us with thy graceful hand to the endless praise of thy holy Name, and to our lasting [16] joy. And direct our Armies by thy providence and favourable support, to finish these late victories to the honour of our Sovereign [17] and safety of her Realm, that hath most carefully made the same able to overmatch her Enemies: So as the Noble men [18], and all others serving in the same Navy and Army under their charge, [19] may with much honour, triumph, and safety return home to their Countries, and give thee due thanks for thy special favours marvellously shewed unto them in preserving of them [20] all this Summer time from all contagion and mortality by sword or sickness, notwithstanding their force and violence most manfully exercised against their Enemies, to the vanquishing of [21] great numbers both by Sea and Land, and to the destruction of their most mighty Ships [22], that heretofore have attempted to invade this Realm, and of their Forts and Castles, and waste of their notable substances of their riches [23], without hurting any person

[11 all thy.]
[12 oʳ Soueraine Ladie the [and noble] Queene.]
[13 sake, for thy Gospell, and thine eternall sonnes sake continue.]
[14 vppon vs, to defend vs [still] against.]
[15 and to blesse vs wᵗʰ continuance of peace to the endlesse.]
[16 perpetual comfort. And for this purpose wee beseeche thee gratious Lord for vs and oʳ Armies [whersoevʳ by sea or land] to continewe still thy fauoʳ, as in great mercie thou diddest in old time promise to be to thy people of Israele, that is, be thou an heauie Ennemy to such as [contemn thy power and] for thy sake are oʳ Ennemies, and afflict them [wᵗ repentance or correction] whoe seeke to afflict vs for oʳ trewe honoringe of thee and thy sonne Jesus Christ. And direct oʳ Armies yet [contynuyng] vppon the seas by thy prouidence.]
[17 noble Quene, and hir Realme.]
[18 wᵗʰ all the sayd Nauie.]
[19 and oʳ valiant Countriemen seruing them thearein, maie.]
[20 from all mortallitie by.]
[21 of such as did wᵗʰstand, and yᵗ of such only as did mightily inuade and wʰstand them with force both.]
[22 shippes, fortes, and Castles.]
[23 riches. All wᶜʰ.]

that did yield, or of any women or children, or Religious persons, to whom all favour was shewed that they did require. All which prosperous successes we do most justly acknowledge[1] (O Lord) to have proceeded only from thy special favour, to whom, with thy Son and Holy Ghost, be all honour[2] and praise. Amen.

Set foorth by authoritie.

Imprinted at London by the Deputies of Christopher Barker, Printer to the Queenes most excellent Maieſtie.

Anno Domini. 1596.

[[1] to haue proceaded from thy fauo^r.]
[[2] praise, glorie and dominion nowe and for euer.]

CERTAIN PRAYERS set forth by Authority, to be used for the prosperous success of her Majesty's Forces and Navy.

Imprinted at London by the Deputies of Christopher Barker, Printer to the Queen's most excellent Majesty. 1597.

Certain Prayers set forth by Authority.

O GOD[3] all-maker, keeper, and guider: Inurement[4] of thy rare-seen, unused, and seeld-heard-of goodness, poured in so plentiful sort upon us full oft, breeds now this boldness, to crave with bowed knees, and hearts of humility, thy large hand of helping power, to assist with wonder our just cause, not founded on Pride's-motion, nor begun on Malice-stock; But, as thou best knowest, to whom nought is hid, grounded on just defence from wrongs, hate, and bloody desire of conquest. For since means thou hast imparted to save that thou hast given, by enjoying such a people, as scorns their bloodshed, where surety[5] ours is one: Fortify (dear GOD) such hearts in such sort, as their best part may be worst, that to the truest part meant worst, with least loss to such a Nation, as despise their lives for their Country's good. That all Foreign lands may laud and admire the Omnipotency of thy work: a fact alone for thee only to perform. So shall thy Name be spread for wonders wrought, and the faithful encouraged to repose in thy unfellowed Grace: And we that minded nought but right, [be] in-chained in thy bonds for perpetual slavery, and live and

[[3] This obscure prayer, which occurs not in all the copies, and, when it does occur, is printed in a different character from the rest, was the composition of Elizabeth herself. The royal arms, however, are not prefixed, as Strype intimates (Annals, Vol. IV. p. 316), to point out that circumstance; they are merely on the reverse of the title-page, where we very commonly find them. Lingard (Vol. VIII. p. 334) considers it to have been the queen's private prayer for a fair wind to allow the fleet to set sail, 'before it was published for the use of her people.' Birch, Vol. II. p. 351. The same may also have been the case in 1596. See p. 666.]

[[4] Inurement: experience. See p. 31, note 3.]

[[5] Sorocold's reading (p. 275.) is 'safetie ours is none,' the last word of which will, at least, give a definite meaning to one sentence.]

die the sacrificers of our souls for such obtained favour. Warrant, dear Lord, all this with thy command. Amen.

Most[1] mighty God and merciful Father, as hitherto of thine infinite goodness thou hast very miraculously protected thy humble Servant, our Sovereign Lady and Queen, and all us her subjects the people of her Dominions, from many dangerous conspiracies, malicious attempts, and wicked designments of her and our very obstinate and implacable enemies: Forasmuch as, they still continuing their malice, and preparing their Forces to assail us both by Land and Sea, thou (O Lord), to withstand their fury, hast stirred up the heart of thine Anointed, our Sovereign, to send out some of her Forces for our defence: we thine unworthy servants do most humbly beseech thee, through the merits of our Saviour Christ, so to conduct them, encourage them, and defend them with thy strong and mighty arm, as that whatsoever they shall attempt and take in hand for defence of this Realm against her enemies, may prosper and have most happy success. Direct and lead them (O Lord) in safety, strengthen their Governors and Leaders with sound counsel and valiant resolution. Bless their conflicts with notable victories both by Sea and Land: preserve them from all contagion and mortality either by sword or sickness, and give unto them (O Lord), if it be thy blessed will, such an honourable and happy return, as may tend to our defence by confusion of our enemies, to the renown and comfort of our Sovereign, to the benefit of thy Church, to the good of this Kingdom, and to the praise and glory of thy most mighty Name, through Jesu Christ our Lord: To whom with thee and the Holy Ghost be ascribed all honour, power, and dominion, both now and for ever. Amen.

O MOST mighty GOD, and Lord of Hosts, which reignest over all the Kingdoms of the world, who hast power in thine hand to save thy chosen, and to judge thine Enemies, and in all ages hast given great and glorious Victories unto thy Church, with small handfuls overthrowing great multitudes and terrible Armies: Let thine ears be now attent unto our prayers, and thy merciful eye upon this Realm and kingdom. And as of thine unspeakable goodness thou hast blessed us

[[1] Compare this with the prayer on p. 668.]

with infinite and extraordinary blessings, all the years of her
Majesty's most happy reign over us, and of late hast also
miraculously delivered us from sundry the bloody practises of
our very implacable enemies: So now we humbly beseech thee
(O merciful Father) to aid us with thy mighty Arm in this
our present just cause, waging war not in pride or ambition of mind, or any other worldly respect, but only for the
necessary defence of Religion, our lives, and Country. Be
merciful therefore, O Lord, to our present Forces, and, passing
over both their transgressions and ours, prosper them both
by Sea and land. Give our Leaders and companies the
strength of Unicorns, the hearts of Lions, arms of steel, hands
of iron, and feet of flint, to beat and tread down all thine
enemies and ours. Let thine help from above at this time
strengthen our Navy and Army, thy mercy overshadow
them, thy power as a wall of fire environ them, thy wisdom
direct them, thy providence secure them, thine holy Angels
guard them, thy Son our Lord Jesus Christ stand up for
them, and thy Justice confound, and Majesty overwhelm, all
adversary power exalting itself against this land and thy
Gospel: that all the world may know, that it is thy favour
that prospereth, thy blessing that preserveth, and thine arm
that overcometh in the day of battle. So we that be thy
people and sheep of thy fold, shall sing unto thy glory the
songs of praise and thanksgiving, and magnify thy goodness
in the midst of thine holy Temple for ever, through Jesus
Christ our Lord, our only Saviour and Mediator. Amen.

O Almighty Lord God of Hosts, it is thine own gracious
promise, that when thy people shall go out to battle against
their enemies, by the way that thou shalt send them, and shall
call upon thee for thy holy help, that then thou (Lord) wilt
hear their prayers in heaven, and judge their cause: In
assured trust of this thy good promise, we present this our
supplication before thee. O Lord, judge thou our cause,
judge thou between us and our cruel enemies. Thou seest,
Lord, that they first invaded us, and so do still continue, and
not we them: that they first conspired to root us out, that
we might be no more a people of *English* birth; and that
then, though thou from heaven didst shew thyself, in scattering their proud forces, to be displeased with their attempt,

yet notwithstanding by mighty preparations at this present they seek our ruin still. That which armeth us, is neither desire[1] of enlarging our own borders, nor thirst of blood, nor ravin of spoil, but only our own just defence, only to break the power of our enemies, and to turn away the battle from our own gates; for that, if we sit still, and suffer them to gather strength, they will suddenly make a breach upon us, and destroy the mother with the children. This they seek, O Lord, and as thou seest, that the heart of thine Anointed in all her actions is upright before thee, so maintain thou our right, and be enemy to our enemies. Great is their malice (as thou, Lord, seest), and great is the mischief they intend against us. Let not the wicked have their desire: O Lord, let not their mischievous imaginations prosper, lest they be too proud. And albeit our many and grievous iniquities may testify against us, and justly deserve that thou shouldest make the enemies' sword the avenger of thy covenant which we have broken; yet deal thou with us according to thy mercy, O Lord. We have sinned, Lord, do thou unto us what seemeth good in thine eyes: only at this time we pray thee to succour us, and not make us a scorn and derision to our oppressors. The rather, O Lord, for that we put not our trust in any strength of our own, but our eyes look only to thee. We know, Lord, the battle is thine, and that with thee it is nothing to save with many, or with few: For that, except thou command the winds, we can not stir, and except thou bless with counsel and courage, we shall not prevail, and all these are in thine hands to give or to withhold. Help us, O Lord God, for we rest on thee, and in thy Name go we forth against these mighty preparations. O Lord, thou art our God, let not man prevail against thee: let thine arm rise up, and put on strength to preserve us now as of old, even the same arm that was mighty for us and against them in their former pride and fury.

Wherefore from thy holy Sanctuary, O Lord, open thine eyes and behold, incline thine ear and hear the prayer of thy servants. Go forth, O Lord, with our Hosts, by Sea and by land. Send forth the winds out of thy treasures to bring

[[1] Here, as well as elsewhere, the writer seems to have copied the sentiments, and even the expressions, of the prayer written by Elizabeth in the preceding year. See p. 666.]

them to the place appointed. Take all contagious sickness from the midst of them, O Lord, the strength of our salvation. Cover their heads in the day of battle. Send thy fear before thy servants, and make their enemies to flee and fall before them. Let thy faith (Lord) make them valiant in battle, and put to flight the Armies of Aliens. And by this shall we know, O Lord, that thou favourest us, in that our enemy doth not triumph over us, and shall always confess to the praise of thy Name, that it was thy hand, and that it was thou, Lord, the shield of our help and sword of our glory, that hast done these great things for us, and evermore say, Praised be the Lord, that hath pleasure in the prosperity of his servants. Hear us, O Lord, for the glory of thy Name, for thy loving Mercy, and for thy truth sake, even for the merits and intercession of our Lord Jesus Christ. Amen.

O ETERNAL God, in power most mighty, in strength most glorious, without whom the Horse and Chariot is in vain prepared against the day of battle: vouchsafe (we beseech thee) from thy high throne of Majesty to hear and receive the hearty and humble prayers, which on bended knees we, the people of thy pasture, and sheep of thy hands, do in an unfeigned acknowledgment of thy might and our own weakness pour out before thee on the behalf of our gracious Sovereign, and on the behalf of her Armies, her Nobles, her Valiants, and men of war: who by thee inspired have put their lives in their hands, and at this time do oppose themselves against the malice and violence of such, as bear a mortal hate at thy Sion, and do daily conspire and rise up against it, even against the Church, thine Anointed, and the people of this her Land. Arise then (O Lord) and stand up, we pray thee, to help and defend them: be thou their Captain to go in and out before them, and to lead them in this journey: teach their fingers to fight, and their hands to make battle. The General and Chieftains bless with the spirit of wisdom, counsel, and direction; the Soldiers with minds ready to perform and execute. Gird them all with strength, and pour out upon them the spirit of courage: give them in the day of battle hearts like the hearts of Lions, invincible and fearless against evil, but terrible to such as come out against them. Where the enemy doth rage, and danger approach, be thou (O Lord) a rock of salvation, and a tower of defence unto them. Break the enemies' weapons: As smoke vanisheth, so let their enemies be scattered, and such as hate them, fly before them. Thou seest (O Lord) the malice of our adversaries, how for thy Name, which is called on over us, and for the truth of thy Gospel wherein we rejoice, they bear a tyrannous hate against us, continually vexing and troubling us, that fain would live in peace. Stir up therefore (O Lord) thy strength, and avenge our just quarrel: turn the sword of our enemy upon his own head, and cause his delight in war to become his own destruction. As thou hast dealt with him heretofore, so now scatter his Forces, and spoil his mighty Ships, in which he trusteth; so shall we the people of thine inheritance, give praise unto thy Name, and for thy great mercy give thanks unto thee in the great Congregation: yea, the World shall know, and the Nations shall understand to the praise of thy glory, that thou alone defendest them that trust in thee, and givest victory unto Princes. Hear us (O Lord our strength) in these our prayers, for Jesus Christ his sake. Amen.

O ALMIGHTY God, which only doest great wonders, shew forth (we pray thee) at this time the power of thy might, and the glory of thy strength, by preserving our Armies at Sea and Land, from death and sickness, and all perils on the Sea, and by helping them in the day of battle against the rage and violence of the Adversary. Thou seest (O Lord) that not for any worldly respects, but for the defence of this Realm, and the peace of thy Church in it, this journey is undertaken, to abate and withstand the pride, and to daunt the insolencies, of our enemies, who conspire and bandy themselves against us, breathing out wrath and utter subversion. Arise therefore, we pray thee, (O Lord of Hosts), unto our help, and let our enemies feel that thou still defendest our just cause, and in the day of battle dost fight for us. Not in our own sword, nor in the arm of our own flesh, do we put our trust; but our trust is in the multitude of thy mercies, and in the strength of thy mighty Arm, who art God alone. Bless therefore the Chieftains and Leaders of our bands with the spirit of wisdom, counsel, and magnanimity, and the Soldiers with courage and fortitude, to stand undaunted and without fear in the day of battle. But as for their enemies, and such as come out against them, cast a fear and astonishment upon them, that they may fall, and cover their faces with shame and confusion: that all the world may know, that thou (O God) resistest the proud and wicked men, and that thou avengest the cause of such as put their trust in thee. Hear us, O God of Hosts, even for Christ his sake our only Saviour and Redeemer. Amen.

O GOD, most glorious, the shield of all that trust in thee, who alone dost send Peace to thy people, and causest War to cease in all the world, consider the daily troubles of thy servants, and behold the malice of our Adversaries, who for thy Name's sake, which is called on over us, and for the truth of thy Gospel wherein we rejoice, do conspire and band themselves against us, breathing out wrath and utter subversion. Many a time hath their wrath been kindled, so that they would have swallowed us up quick: but by thy power their purpose hath been frustrated, their counsels prevented, their preparations overthrown, and we delivered. Yet, O Lord, their heart is set against us, still to vex and trouble us that fain would live in peace. But for the quiet of thy Church, and that thine enemies may know thee to be a God of mercy, cause them to return at last, and not any longer to hate those whom thou hast loved: Make them to see that their plots and designments are against thee, who for us fightest against them, drowning their ships, and casting down their strong-holds in which they do trust; that thy Name may be glorified in the day of their conversion. But if they shall still harden their hearts, and will not understand either our defence, or their own calamity to come of thee: make void their devices, disclose their counsels, discover their secret complots, that in the snare, which they have laid for us, their own feet may be taken. Finally, O Lord, whensoever they prepare themselves to battle, take the defence of our just cause into thine hand: Break their Navies, disperse their Armies, and cast upon them a fear and astonishment, that they may tremble at thy presence, and fly before they be pursued: Grant this, O Lord our strength, even for Christ his sake. Amen.

O ETERNAL God, Lord of the whole World, and guide of Sea and Land, who by thy mighty power sortest to what effect thou wilt the Counsels and actions of all men: graciously vouchsafe to bless and order unto happy issue the late begun work of our gracious Sovereign, in the hand of her Nobles and men of war, now sent out by Seas, to withstand the Enemies of her life, her people, and thy Church. As Guide and General of the journey, let it please thee (mighty Lord of Hosts) to go in and out before them, with best fore-winds and straightest course to speed and prosper them in the way. And when thou hast brought them to the appointed place, in a pillar of fire give light to direct their steps, and in a pillar of a Cloud defend them. Put upon them thy spirit of counsel and fortitude, and under the banner of thy power and protection let the work be effected. Courage and embolden them in the day of conflict, to stand undaunted and without fear. Make way and opportunity for them to attempt with advantage, and for thy Name's sake grant (O glorious God) to their puissant attempts happy success in battle, to their battle a joyful victory, and to their victory a safe and triumphant return. So will we the people of thine inheritance, which now pray for the blessing of thy grace upon them, praise thy Name for ever, and together with them ascribe both cause and glory of the work, not to our own strength, but unto thy power, who alone givest victory in the day of battle; and for thy great mercies will give thanks unto thee in the midst of the Congregation. Hear us, O Father, even for Christ his sake. Amen.

Finis.

AN ORDER FOR PRAYER AND THANKSGIVING (necessary to be XLI
used in these dangerous times) for the safety and preservation of her Majesty and this Realm.

Set forth by Authority. Anno 1594. And renewed with
some alterations upon the present occasion.

¶ Imprinted at London by the deputies of Christopher Barker, printer to the Queen's most excellent Majesty.
Anno 1598.

¶ *An admonition to the Reader.*

THERE have been sundry, but heathen men (as *Plato* and others), being
no better instructed than the lame reach of reason could guide them, nor
any clearer enlightened than by the dimmed glimpse of nature, who
nevertheless arrived thus far, as to know and acknowledge that God, who
is above all, extendeth his careful providence over all, and especially in
preservation of kingdoms, and of other politic societies, and of their Governors and Rulers. *For that which may be known of God, is manifest* Rom. 1. 19, 20.
(saith Saint Paul) *among them: for God hath opened it unto them. For
his invisible things being understood by his works through the creation of the
world, are seen: that is, both his eternal power and Godhead, so that they are
without excuse.* Then how much more must all Christians, to whom the
Day-star hath in greater brightness and measure appeared, and the treasures of *God* the Father in his Son *Christ Jesu* been opened, acknowledge
this his providence, and reverently adore and magnify that good *God*,
which to the heap of all other his mercies towards them addeth this blessing and protection of *Magistracy* and government, whereby men live
peaceably with all honesty in this life!

But if ever any Nation, yea, if all the nations in the world besides, have
cause with thankfulness to acknowledge this kind of benefit, surely, we
the people of *England* have most just and abundant occasion of all others,
to perform this duty unto God. First, for placing over us our most gracious dread Sovereign Lady *Queen Elizabeth,* by whose happy government we have so long breathed from the burden of intolerable miseries of
scarcity, bloodshed, and spiritual *bondage,* under which afore we lay grovelling, and pitifully groaned. Then, for preserving these her Realms
and Dominions so long in the true profession of the Gospel, and in peace
and tranquillity, notwithstanding the sundry privy conspiracies and open
hostilities practised both inward and outward for the interruption of our
quiet repose and holy profession. Thirdly, for protecting so long and so
often her sacred Royal person from the cruel and bloody hands of such
and so many several detestable and treacherous Conspirators. And like-

wise for the Lord's provident and watchful eye over her and us, and for the wonderful happy discoveries of so manifold cruel designments so closely plotted against her innocent life, and so dangerously against her *Highness'* Realms and dominions. Which mischievous devices as they have all flowed from none other fountain, than from that City of seven hills, the *See* of *Rome*, and seat of the *Beast*, not in regard of any desert of ours, but because we have abandoned the cup of spiritual abominations, wherewith these have long intoxicated the Kings of the earth: So have they been continually projected, carried forward, and managed by idolatrous *Priests* and *Jesuits* his creatures, the very loathsome *Locusts* that crawl out of the bottomless pit. Howbeit they have been and are mightily seconded by certain *Potentates* of the earth, who do nothing else but serve themselves of that idolatrous *Romish religion*, as of a Mask and stalking-horse, therewith to cover the unsatiable ambition, wherewith they are possessed, of usurping other men's *kingdoms*. For if we will first particularly cast our eyes upon the variable conspiracies that have been entered into but against her Highness' Realms: shall we not find that treason of the two *Pooles*[1], of *Felton*, and of the late Duke of *Northfolk*, of *Throgmorton*, of *Englefield*, of *Paget*, of *Shelly*, and *Stanley*, and *Yorke*, and of all the Seminary *Priests* and *Jesuits*, to have been tickled up by Romish busses and practices, and to have been carried forward by their own gross dotage upon that absurd Religion?

Apoc.13.& 17.

As for those other attempts against her dominions, which have not stayed themselves in the bare terms of conspiracy only, but have also broken farther into open rebellion and hostility: they likewise have no less been blown up by that brood of *Massing Priests*, being unnatural subjects (for the most part) of these *kingdoms*. For was not *Moreton* a priest sent from the *Pope's* own side to stir up the two Earls and others unto the Northern rebellion? Did not *Sanders* second his bookish treasons even with banner displayed, and by commotion in *Ireland*? And doth not that *carnal arch-traitor Allen* proclaim to the world, unto his own everlasting reproach, that he and others excited the king of *Spain's* invincible *Navy* (vainly so surnamed) by invasion to have conquered his own native country, and to have swallowed us all up? And those unnatural and disloyal defections in *Ireland*, which turned eftsoons into violent commotions, and in the end brast out into open rebellion, and that cruel bloodshed wherewith that country is now so sorely afflicted and gored, arose they not from the irreption of those undermining vermin the *Priests* and *Jesuits* covertly sent in, first alienating the minds of true subjects from their *Prince*, and the faith of sound professors from religion, and then inciting and persuading them to this open hostility and cruelty? Yea, and in all those their latter hidden, hellish and damnable designs against her Majesty's own person and life, such *Priests* have also been the principal stirrers and agents under their unholy father. *Somerfield* and Arden, were they not drawn into that action by *Hall* the priest? *Parry* by Cardinal *Como*, and by certain English fugitive priests at *Milan*

[1 See pp. 655-658 for explanatory notes.]

and *Paris*, and also by *Allen's* traitorous writings? *Babington* and all the other bloody conspirators his complices by *Ballard* the priest? So *Lopez* his late purposed empoisoning is said to have been first plotted and set forward in *Spain* by *Parsons* the *Jesuit* Friar. And *Patrick o'Cullen, Laton, Kale, Poule Wheele,* and sundry others, very lately were animated by *Holt, Hart, Sherewood,* and other priests, the detestable instruments of the Bish. of *Rome,* and of the King of *Spain's* most dishonourable intended executions.

But that which passeth the rest, and may be an effectual motive to work in all Christian hearts a sounder devotion of thankfulness to our God, and a greater detestation of that blood-sucking *Romish Antichrist* with his whole swarm of shavelings, was that dreadful attempt of *Squire*[2], being appointed not only quite to extinguish one of the bright stars of our Nobility, the Earl of Essex, even in the time of that his great employment[3] for the Realm and State; but withal, which we her true subjects do tremble at to remember, utterly to quench the light of *Israel*, and by poison to make away our *Sovereign Prince;* both which he to his power executed, as well on her Majesty's Saddle, as the Earl his Chair, by a confection so strong, that the very smell thereof did presently strike dead a Dog, upon which he first had tried it. To which horrible practice the said *Squire* in his voluntary confession, without any torture at all, professed that he was first incited, and afterward at several times persuaded, and, appearing somewhat backward, at last encouraged by one *Walpoole,* a cursed *Jebusite* (*Jesuite,* I should say) both by a blasphemous application or rather detortion of that excellent Scripture, *Unum necessarium,* One thing is necessary, as if our Saviour by that *One* had meant the treasonable slaughter of his *Holy ones;* as also by a promise of a large Fee from D. *Bagshaw,* the Pope's *Judas* or purse-bearer (as it seemeth), and withal the hope of eternal merit from God, as if with such bloody sacrifices of Christian princes God were promerited[4], (to use their own word, *Heb.* xiii. 16,) and in the end armed with the confection itself from *Walpoole* to effect it throughly, and adjured, by receiving the Sacrament,

Octob. Anno 1598.

Rhem. Testa.

[2 '*Edward Squire* [of Greenwich] had been at first an ordinary Scrivener, afterward a Groom in the Queen's stable, and going as a Souldier in *Drake's* last expedition [in 1595, against the Spanish settlements in the West Indies] was taken prisoner, and carryed into Spaine [to Seville], there he became acquainted with one Wallpoole, an English Jesuite, who caused him to be put into the Inquisition for an Heretick, and the fellow, tasting of misery, was easily drawn to become a Papist, and afterward to attempt any thing for the Catholique cause.' Baker's Chronicle, Elizabeth, p. 101. Foulis, p. 465. Squire was arraigned at Westminster, November the 9th, 1598, and executed at Tyburn on the 13th. Stow, p. 1308. Lingard, Vol. VIII. p. 453.]

[3 In 1597, Essex had been promoted to the dignity of Earl Marshal of England. Hume, Vol. v. p. 384.]

[4 'And beneficence and communication do not forget, for with such hostes God is promerited.']

to perform it secretly. These and many other complots we see how desperately they have been attempted, yet (thanked be God) are not achieved: how perilously plotted, but are not perfected: how secretly devised, yet most happily hitherto discovered, and this last attempt most strangely revealed, their own consciences, like the *Midianites'* swords, mutually disbowelling their own secret conspiracies. For *Walpoole*, having received intelligence that *Squire*, being in the Earl's company, had fit opportunity to execute it, yet the purpose not effected; in an affrighted mind fearing that *Squire* had of himself revealed it, and yet with a mischievous device more devilishly to act it, addressed over one *Stanly* and others, to detect the plot and designment of *Squire;* by which mask of Discovery an easier entry being made for the said *Stanly* into the Earl's affection and company, he might more safely and with less suspicion execute and effect the intended villany. So that it may aptly be verified, that her Majesty's life hath all this while been sustained *in manu Altissimi*, and that under the shadow of his wings she hath not miscarried: and that the sacred oil, wherewith he hath anointed her royal majesty, is a sovereign Antidote and preservative against all the venomous infections, or empoisoning confections, whether *Romish* or *Spanish.*

All which whosoever he be that will attentively weigh and consider, and cannot see the very finger of God mightily working herein by his providence and mercy, no doubt he is insensibly blockish: who seeth and will not acknowledge it, is wilfully malicious: but who acknowledgeth and also tasteth of the sweet blessings that are enjoyed thereby, and is not most heartily thankful to God therefore, is extremely impious, and doth but add this ungratefulness unto the mass of all his other wickedness, even unto his own greater damnation. Let every one of us therefore, who have good will to Sion, turn from our wicked ways, and from the evil that is betwixt our hands, and incessantly with heart and voice yield most humble and hearty thanks to God our deliverer. But let it not be for a day or two only, whiles the intended wound doth (as it were) present itself fresh and green before the eyes of our minds; but continually, even so long as we may justly imagine the same devil in his imps still to rage and to be prest to devour us; so long as *our habitation is amongst the Tents of Mesech,* and our *souls amongst Lions who hunt after our lives,* and do greedily seek to *give our Dearling to the dog, and to lay our honour in the dust:* to the intent, that (if it be so God's good will) our joy may long and long be redoubled and trebled unto us, under the happy government of so gracious a *Sovereign.* Which our bounden duty that it may the more frequently and fruitfully be performed of us; it hath been thought meet to publish this form of prayer for the continuance of God's mercies towards us, and of thanksgiving for his unspeakable goodness in detecting so many conspiracies, and averting so great mischiefs intended against us. Which duty of praying and thanksgiving there is no doubt but every true hearted *Englishman* and faithful *Subject* will both privately and publicly from the bottom of his heart perform.

Psalm 20.   Psalm 21.   Psalm 27.   Psalm 31.   Psalm 33.
Psalm 91.

Prayers for the preservation of the Queen's Majesty.

ALMIGHTY and everlasting God, Creator and Governor of all the world, by whom *Kings* do bear rule, and under whose providence they are wonderfully and mightily oftentimes protected from many fearful dangers, by which the malice of Satan and his wicked imps do seek to entrap them : We give unto thy heavenly Majesty most humble and hearty thanks, for that it hath pleased thee of thine infinite mercy and goodness in Christ Jesu so wonderfully to uphold, deliver and preserve thine Handmaid, our most dread and Sovereign Queen *Elizabeth,* so many and sundry times from the cruel and bloody treacheries of desperate men, who address themselves to all wickedness ; and at this time especially, wherein her innocent life was not only attempted, but had it not been thy merciful power to prevent it, much endangered by wretched traitors appointed to that purpose, who had performed, as much as in them lay, their wicked designments of impoisoning her sacred Majesty, which notwithstanding it pleased thee most strangely to defeat, causing the authors thereof to be their own betrayers, and killing the force of that strong confection provided for her and applied. And what are we, that thou shouldest thus respect us ? or what may we do to requite these thy benefits, but still most humbly and from the bottom of our hearts pray and beseech thee in Christ Jesu, to continue this thine unspeakable goodness towards her and this Realm, and evermore to defend and protect them. O Lord, dissipate and confound all practices, conspiracies, and treasons against her, against this Realm of *England,* and against the truth of thine Holy word here taught and professed: so that the whole world and all posterity may see and know, how mightily with thy fatherly care and providence thou watchest over and defendest those which put their trust in thee, and that we, whom thou vouchsafest these thy favours more than ordinary, may the more devoutly give thanks unto thee, and hereafter more carefully labour to serve and please thee in newness of life and uprightness of heart. Grant this (O most loving and merciful Father) for thy dear Son's sake Jesus Christ, our Lord and only Saviour. Amen.

Another.

O ALMIGHTY and eternal God, Creator and Governor of the whole world, unto whom all power belongeth over all creatures both in heaven and earth, and by whom alone it is, that not only all Kings and Princes do rule and govern the people committed to their charge, but are likewise by thy divine providence and mighty protection defended and delivered, even in the midst of all their perils and dangers, out of the hands of all their enemies: We yield unto thee most humble and hearty thanks, for that it hath pleased thy gracious goodness, according to thine accustomed favour towards her, still to preserve and defend thy well-beloved Handmaid and our most gracious Queen *Elizabeth* from all the wicked conspiracies, traitorous attempts, and devilish devices, which either the foreign and professed enemies abroad, or else her most unloyal, desperate, and rebellious subjects at home, were able at any time to devise and practise against her. But especially (O Lord) at this time, as just occasion is offered unto us all, we all even from the bottom of our hearts praise thy holy name, and give thee most hearty and unfeigned thanks for this thy late and most happy delivery of her Majesty's most royal person from those desperate treasons, which were most wickedly invented, and cruelly attempted against her: most humbly beseeching thee, of thine infinite goodness and mercy, still to continue thy fatherly protection over her, daily to increase and multiply thy heavenly blessings and graces upon her. Be thou ever unto her (O Lord God of hosts) even a strong rock and tower of defence against the face of all her enemies, which either openly abroad, or secretly at home, go about to bring her life unto the grave, and lay her honour in the dust. Disclose their wicked counsels, and make frustrate all their devilish practices, in such sort, as that all the world may learn and know, that there is no counsel, no wisdom, no policy against the Lord. Let them fall into the ditch which they have digged for others, and be taken in their own nets: but let her Majesty (O Lord) ever escape them, that all the world may see how dear and precious in thy sight the life of this thine anointed is, who doth not so much as imagine this evil against them that thus continually thirst after her blood; and so behold her with thine eye of pity and compassion, daily with thy mighty power and stretched out arm so save and deliver her from all her enemies, preserve and keep her as the apple of thine own eye, and grant unto her (O most merciful Father) a long, prosperous, and happy reign over us, and so prolong her days as the days of heaven here upon earth, that she may be an old mother in Israel, and see her desire upon all thine and her enemies, though in number never so many, or in power never so mighty. And finally, after this life, give unto her everlasting life, through Jesus Christ thine only Son, and our only Saviour.

Another.

O MOST gracious God and our most loving and merciful Father, which hast not only created us and all things by thy power, but hast also continued our preservation by thy holy providence, therein working wonderfully, revealing things hidden and secret, as thou dost discover the bottoms and foundations of the deep: that though our foes have taken wicked counsels together, saying, None shall be able to espy it; yet thou hast opened them, and brought them out of darkness into light: for thou art God alone, which destroyest the wisdom of the wise, and castest away the understanding of the prudent, and defeatest the executions of the malignant: therefore do we worship thee, and praise thy holy name, rejoicing continually in thy strength and thy salvation; for thou art the glory of our power, and by thy favour and loving kindness are we preserved. Our shield and defence belongeth to thee (O Lord of hosts), and our gracious prince to thee, O thou Holy One of Israel. Thou (O Lord) hast preserved her honour from the ignominy, her life from the cruelty, and her crown from the tyranny of the wicked, her estate from ruin, her peace from disturbance, her kingdom and her people from being a prey to the malignant. The foot of pride hath come against us, but the hand of iniquity hath not cast us down: Therefore do we rejoice before thee, and be glad in thee, yea, our songs do we make of thy name, O thou most Highest, and will be ever setting forth thy praise and thy glory, thy might, and thy mercy from one generation to another. Only, O Lord, forsake us not in this time of our age, but give courage and constancy to our Sovereign to persevere in perils: prudence and wisdom to her Council, wisely to foresee and discover the subtile sleights and dangers of all enemies: faithfulness and fortitude to the Nobles of the land, duty and obedience to us all that are under her. Forgive also, we most humbly pray thee, through thy fatherly kindness in Jesus Christ, the multitude of our sins and transgressions against thy divine Majesty, and thy commandments, and according to the multitude of thy mercies do away all our offences, that the light and candle of thy servant *Elizabeth* our gracious Queen and Governor, which is our life in the light of thy countenance, and the breath of our nostrils, be not put out, but may still shine and burn bright, illumined by the beams of thy heavenly grace. Protect her (O Lord), we still beseech thee, in safety, save her in majesty, keep her in peace, guide her in counsel, and defend her in danger: bless her, Lord, in all temporal and celestial blessings in Christ, that she may still bless thee. Detect and reveal still the foundations and buildings of all treasons and conspiracies both at home and abroad; and herein (O Lord) either convert the wicked hearts and secret conceits from their wicked imaginations, or confound their devices, and make them as the untimely fruit, that they never see the Sun. Hear, Lord, and save us, O King of heaven, when we call upon thee; and so shall we all, both Prince and people, dwell still under the shadow of thy wings, protected by thy power, and preserved by thy providence, and ordered by thy governance, to thy everlasting praise, and our unspeakable comfort in Jesus Christ, to whom with thee, O Father and God of all consolation, and the Holy Spirit of sanctification, be all honour and glory both now and for ever. Amen.

Another.

MOST gracious God, which by thy word appointedst man to rule thy other creatures, but in wisdom hast lifted up Kings and Princes to command and rule men in their several places: We the people of thy choice, and the subjects of this land, heartily acknowledge thy especial providence in anointing over us so gracious a Princess, so careful of thy glory, so religious in thy fear, so tender of our good, and yet so maligned and shot at by the enemies of thy Gospel, both foreign professed rebels, and homeborn unloyal and discontented runagates, as, were not thy mercy her shield of defence, and thy power the sword of her revenge, long since they had brought her life to the grave, and laid our honour in the dust: Of late especially having prepared and applied very near the sacred body of her royal Majesty a most deadly poison, the purpose strangely thou didst reveal, and the practice mightily thou didst defeat: For which exceeding kindness, most loving Father, we on our knees and from our hearts do give thee thanks, and desire the assistance of thy grace for the amendment of our lives, and the repentance of our sins, which are more deadly than any poison to infect us, and more strong than any foe to overthrow us, and the only motives of thy wrath against us, which if thou canst not but execute upon us, our crying sins so calling for thy vengeance, yet, gracious Lord, enter not so far in just revenge as to quench the light of our land, our most Sovereign Queen, lest the enemies of thy Gospel, her prosperity, and our welfare, take occasion thereby to triumph and say, that thou hast forsaken us; but rather, we humbly beseech thee, prosper her days and prolong her life, and renew her years to the advancement of thy glory, the amazement of the foe, and the establishing of our peace by Jesus Christ thy only Son, and our only Saviour. To whom, &c.

Another.

ETERNAL God, which createdst all men after thy likeness, but hast advanced Kings more like thyself in places of government, and to that end hast both anointed them with thy *Holy oil* above others, and also laid a curse upon them which touch thine anointed: We render unto thee, in all dutiful service, most hearty thanks for thy continual protection of our sacred Prince, *Queen Elizabeth*, whom as thou hast many times heretofore preserved from dangerous attempts plotted against her by malignant wretches, either frustrating their counsels, or preventing their executions, or revealing their intentions; so of late most strangely thou hast kept her from a danger not only intended, but practised; from a poison not only confected, but applied very near her; wherein as thou didst manifest thy power in quelling the *Asp* and the *Basilisk*, qualifying the deadly force of that dreadful compound, so didst thou shew thy mercy unto us of this land, who, if the *Shepherd* of Israel had been stroken, might be either confusedly scattered, or cruelly massacred. Good Lord, strike a sense of this thy powerful mercy into our hearts, from thence to fetch a sorrowful sighing for our sins, an earnest desire of amendment, and most entire unfeigned thanks to thee our gracious Preserver: But those priests of *Baal*, the hellish Chaplains of *Antichrist*, accursed runagates from their God and Prince, the bellows and fuel of these flagrant conspiracies, confound them in thy wrath, since thy Grace will not convert them, and that which thy power cannot work on them in defeating their enterprizes, let thy fury perform in revenge upon their persons; the rather, O Lord, because that most blasphemously they abuse thy holy Word for the furtherance of their devilish complots: But let our gracious Queen still reign and rule in despite of *Rome*, and *Rheims*[1], and *Spain* and Hell; preserve her government over us, unite our hearts to her, continue both her and our thankfulness to thyself, which blessest us daily with so many benefits. Hear us, O Lord, for Jesus Christ his sake.

[[1] A Seminary had been sometime established in this city. See p. 656, note 5.]

Certain Prayers fit for the time. XLIV.
Set forth by authority.

Imprinted at London by ROBERT BARKER, Printer to the Queen's most excellent Majesty.
Anno Dom. 1600.

¶ *Certain Prayers fit for the time.*

ALMIGHTY God and most merciful Father, who of thy infinite goodness towards all Countries and Nations, for the avoiding of confusion, hast appointed Kings and Princes as thine Angels and Lieutenants, and the Seals of thy similitude, full of wisdom and beauty, to rule and govern in thy Name the people on the earth committed to their charge: commanding all their Subjects to honour, and in no sort to resist them, but to obey them in thy fear, even for conscience sake; and likewise to offer unto thee for them all Supplications, Prayers, Intercessions, and Thanksgiving, as being the Lights, the preservation, and the means under thy Divine Majesty of the Peace, the Health, Prosperity and Glory of all their Subjects and Kingdoms: We thy humble servants, bowing down the knees of our hearts, and prostrating ourselves before thy glorious Throne, do render unto thee all Praise, Power, Honour and Thanksgiving for thy most gracious favour and merciful deliverance of our most dread *Sovereign Lady* (thy Vicegerent in her Dominions) QUEEN ELIZABETH, as ever heretofore, so at this time, from the traitorous attempts and desperate designments of sundry most unkind and disloyal wicked persons; who, forgetting their duty both towards thee (O Lord) and towards thine Anointed, have in the height of their Pride, after a popular sort, with divers false pretences, and many slanderous calumniations, sought in open Rebellion not only the destruction and extinguishing of thy Servant, our Comfort, our Health, and our Glory; but the utter ruin also and tragical overthrow of this our native Country, her Majesty's (through thy manifold mercies) so worthy, so happy, and so renowned a Kingdom. This thy most mighty and Fatherly protection (O Lord God

[LITURG. QU. ELIZ.]

of hosts) we entirely beseech thee, with penitent hearts for our former offences, to continue over us from age to age, by defending still the sacred person of our *Sovereign Lady*, from all such dangerous designments; her Kingdoms and Countries from all treacherous practices; and us her Subjects from the deceitful baits and crafty allurements of all popular and ambitious dissembling *Absalons*: that so our hearts being still replenished with the joy of thy Salvation, we may daily present in all thankfulness before thy Fatherly goodness the freewill offerings and sacrifices of our lips, always praising and magnifying thy blessed Name, through Jesus Christ our Lord: to whom with thee and the Holy Ghost, three persons and one God, be all honour and glory from this time forth for evermore.

O ETERNAL and gracious GOD, Father of peace, and Protector of government; who with a special eye of providence watchest over the heads of Princes, upon whose safety the lives of many thousands do depend: We thy humble Servants do bow down the knees of our hearts, and pour forth our souls in thankfulness before thee, for thy so gracious and merciful deliverance of our dread Sovereign thy Handmaid from the traitorous intents and desperate Conspiracies of disloyal Subjects, who have risen up against thine Anointed, and like unnatural Children have rebelled against the Mother of their own lives, that took them up from their cradles, and cherished them in her own bosom, and laded them with honours and preferments; to the great dishonour of thy Name, to the slander of thy Gospel, to the danger of confusion to their own native Country. But thou, O Lord of Hosts, our deliverer, didst overthrow them in their own imaginations, and by thy judgments hast declared them enemies to thine own Majesty; Thou didst put thy obedience into the hearts of thy faithful people, and, without shedding of their innocent blood, didst miraculously beat down the swords of all that rose up against thine ordinance. For which thy unspeakable goodness towards us, vouchsafe, we beseech thee, to receive the freewill offerings of our hearts, and calves of our lips in praises to thy glorious Name; Who, notwithstanding our manifold sins and transgressions, hast not yet forgotten to be gracious, but heapest mercy upon mercy, and causest blessing to follow and overtake blessing, as the waves of the Sea. To thee therefore, our Saviour and Defender, our Watch-tower, and our Rock, we will sing the Songs of thankfulness, and call upon thy blessed Name for evermore; Beseeching thee so to continue the favour of thy countenance towards thine own anointed Magistrate, and us her faithful people; that our Light may never go out, and our Song may never cease in this land: but that thy glorious acts may sound in every Congregation, ever praise and honour and glory to thee, that sittest upon the Throne for ever and ever. Amen.

Most mighty God, which art the author of order, and the hater of confusion, to which purpose thou hast generally shewed thy wisdom in advancing Princes to rule, whom it hath pleased thee to dignify with thine own name; and more particularly, in thy exceeding love to this our land, hast placed over us a most renowned Queen, religious to thee her God, kind to her Subjects, merciful even to her enemies: As we magnify thy glorious name for that unspeakable benefit, so at this time principally we yield thee in all humble duty most hearty thanks for this thy late protection, both of her sacred Royal person, and of her faithful people, from this mutiny thus rebelliously complotted, this rebellion so outrageously attempted, this outrage so dangerously continued, by defeating their popular hopes upon which they trusted, by uniting true subjects' hearts unto their Prince anointed, by appeasing this sudden uproar without much bloodshed, and in the end by quelling the enraged spirits of the chief Conspirators: who, if either their Sovereign's countenance and continuance of her gracious favours, or her magnificence in their extraordinary advancements, or her clemency in pardoning their manifold contempts, could have moderated them, would never have shewed themselves either causelessly discontented, or discontentedly disobedient. Lord, how often hath thy power and mercy been manifested in revealing Conspiracies devised, in preventing treasons intended, in terrifying hearts outraged, in scattering forces assembled! All which we ascribe not to any merit of ours, whose sins do daily provoke thy favour to wrath, but only to that love which thou bearest unto thy chosen Anointed, and to thy Gospel professed. The prosperous continuance of them both we humbly crave of thee, most gracious God, with assistance of thy grace to make us more thankful than heretofore we have been, that walking worthy of our vocation, and loyally to her Majesty, we may perform that due obedience to them both, which in thy sight is better than sacrifice, and adorneth those which profess the name of thy Son Christ Jesus; to whom, with thee and the Holy Spirit, we acknowledge all praise and glory for this late, and all other thy mercies extended now and for evermore. Amen.

THE more thy providence (O Lord) doth even visibly from heaven still manifest itself by so many, so strange deliverances of thine Anointed our Queen, and in Her, of us all: the more and the more often are we bound to have our hearts bent to the considering, and our mouths opened to the magnifying, of thine unceasant goodness towards us, to no people of the earth ever the like. The more are we bound, and as we are bound (as is our duty), so is it our desire thus to do: and though we have no thankfulness, wherewith to come near it, yet it is our desire in some sort to seek to express it: and the more our desires, the less our deserts have been, ever to see such and so many mercies, so often shewed upon us. For what are we, Lord? or what is there in our unworthy profession of thy holy Truth, that thou shouldst respect us at all? Yet how many, how marvellous have been those demonstrations, which heretofore thou hast vouchsafed us, in preserving thy chosen servant our Sovereign from a number of plots and practices, some foreign, some domestical, some deep and secret, some sudden and violent, all of them to the hazard of her Sacred person and life; on whose life dependeth the life and life's-joy of so many thousands! And this was yet a small thing in thy sight (O Lord): but even now again, even at this very instant, thou hast renewed thy mercy, in discovering and disappointing this late dangerous and desperate resolution. And what can we say more unto thee? For thou, Lord, knowest thy servants. For thy truth's sake, and according to thine abundant lovingkindness and compassion over us, hast thou done all these great things. O Lord our God, as they should, and as we would they should; so cause these, all these thy mercies, first and last, to enter into our hearts, and keep them for ever in the minds and memories of this people, and prepare our hearts to be thankful unto thee. And, O Lord, (for it is thou that hast done this) let it please thee to confirm for ever thine own work: and as thou hast, by thus often delivering thine Handmaid our Queen, brought her hitherto, that she is now thy First-born, the most renowned and ancient[1] Prince of all that profess thy Name; so let her be blessed for ever with thy blessing, that she may long enjoy this honour. And now and ever shew thou thy marvellous lovingkindness, that she may long enjoy it, remaining ever happy, happy in the love and loyalty of her people, happy in the folly and fall of her enemies, and thrice happy in the continual comfortable experience of thy favour, power, and care, still upon every occasion thus mightily, mercifully, miraculously preserving her, to the continuance of thy truth still among us, of the comfort and contentment of thy people, and of the everlasting remembrance of thy goodness, and praise of thy holy Name, through Christ our Lord. Amen.

Most holy and everliving God, the inestimable riches of whose mercies toward us we are more willing to confess than able to comprehend, daily and hourly drawing from that infinite Treasury which we never can consume, from the deepest acknowledgement of our own wretchedness and highest admiration and adoration of thy glorious goodness, we bless thy sacred Majesty, and from the ground of our hearts ascribe honour to thy praiseworthy Name: that it hath pleased thee from time to time with the early and late showers of all sufficient blessings to water thine inheritance, this little Kingdom, and by infallible arguments of continual graces to make known to the whole world, that thou lovest the Gates of *England* more than all the Habitations of our neighbour Countries about us. Namely thou hast dwelt in the midst of us with the presence and protection of thy good will to keep us from the danger of those fires, which both abroad and at home men of unquiet spirits have kindled against us. Many mischiefs have the ungodly devised, which they were not able to bring to pass. The bottomless deep of

[1 Elizabeth at this time was in her sixty-eighth year.]

thy Counsel hath laid open their shallow and ungrounded policies. Thy faithfulness above the Clouds hath prevented their treacherous, unfaithful earthly conspiracies, and thy judgments as the great mountains have overwhelmed and dasht in pieces all the power of their malice.

Why did the ungodly of late so rage, and the children of this Land imagine a vain thing? The Princes banded themselves, and assembled together against thee (O Lord) and against thine Anointed, saying amongst themselves, Let us break their bonds, and cast their cords from us. But thou that sittest in heaven hast laughed them to scorn, thou hast had them all in derision, thou hast dissolved their knots, dissociated their bandings, defeated and frustrated their whole designments. They travailed with wind, and brought forth a whirlwind, which hath scattered their devices, and brought a woful recompence upon their own heads.

We are not worthy to entreat mercy at thy hands, worms of the earth, of thee who art the Former of our spirits, and Creator of all things, transgressors from our mothers' bellies, and laden with sin, of thee that hast pure eyes. The sacrifices we offer up, either of our praises or prayers, proceed but from hearts of ashes and polluted lips: but under the warrant and wings of thy dear Son, in whom thou art pleased and we hid, hoping that the sacrifice of his most precious blood shall answer all our defects, and cover our infirmities, we pour out our whole souls before thee, humbly beseeching thee for thy Christ's sake, that the line of thy mercies and the line of her life may be lengthened and run forth together: that thou wilt always quiet her Realms both from foreign invasions and intestine Rebellions, secure her person, keep her people in allegiance to her Highness, and amity amongst themselves, and meet with[1] the purposes and practices of all ambitious *Absalons*, blasphemous *Shemeis*, seditious *Shevas*[2], traitorous *Achitophels*, rebellious *Cores*, which strive against thine ordinance in her Heroical hands.

Finally, O our strongest Redeemer, make us mindful of all thy forepassed benefits, thankful for the present, fearful of nothing but thy plagues, careful of nothing but of thy service and worship; that with hands and hearts everlastingly lift up

[[1] Meet with: frustrate, defeat.]
[[2] Shebas. 2 Sam. xx. 1, &c.]

to heaven, Prince and people knit together as it were in one soul, we may glorify thy holy Name, and seek the advancement of thy kingdom through our blessed Redeemer and Intercessor, Jesus Christ.

[The prayer composed by Whitgift (Register, Lambeth, part III. fol. 148. b.) for Elizabeth the day before her death, will constitute a fitting termination to these public Forms. Sancroft also wrote it on one of the leaves of that volume in his collection, which is marked 3. 4. 30.]

O most heauenlie Father, and God of all mercie, we most humbly beseech thee to behoulde thy seruaunt our queen with the eies of pity and compassion: giue vnto her the comforts of thy holie spirit, worke in her a constant and liuelie faith, graunt hir true repentance, and restore vnto her (if it be thy will) hir former health and strength of bodie and soule. Let not the enemy, nor his wicked instruments have anie power ouer hir, to do her harme. O Lord, punish hir not for our offences, neither punish vs in hir. Deal not with vs, O Lord, as we haue deserued, but for thy mercies sake, and for thy Christ his sake, forgiue vs all our sinnes, and prolong hir daies, that we may still enioy hir to the glory of thy holy name, and ioy of all such as truelie fear thee, through Jesus Christ our Lord. Amen.

www.ingramcontent.com/pod-product-compliance
Lightning Source LLC
Chambersburg PA
CBHW052037290426
44111CB00011B/1538